murach's
Java
Servlets
and JSP

3RD EDITION

murach's Java Servlets and JSP

3RD EDITION

Joel Murach

Michael Urban

MIKE MURACH & ASSOCIATES, INC.

4340 N. Knoll Ave. • Fresno, CA 93722

www.murach.com • murachbooks@murach.com

Authors:	Joel Murach
	Michael Urban
Editor:	Ray Halliday
Production:	Maria Spera

Books for Java programmers

Murach's Beginning Java with Eclipse
Murach's Beginning Java with NetBeans
Murach's Java Programming (4th Edition)
Murach's Android Programming (2nd Edition)
Murach's Java Servlets and JSP (3rd Edition)

Books for web developers

Murach's HTML5 and CSS3 (3rd Edition)
Murach's Dreamweaver CC
Murach's JavaScript (2nd Edition)
Murach's jQuery (2nd Edition)
Murach's PHP and MySQL (2nd Edition)

Books for .NET programmers

Murach's C# 2015
Murach's ASP.NET 4.5 Web Programming with C# 2012

Books for database developers

Murach's MySQL (2nd Edition)
Murach's Oracle SQL and PL/SQL (2nd Edition)
Murach's SQL Server 2012 for Developers

Books for IBM mainframe programmers

Murach's OS/390 and z/OS JCL
Murach's Mainframe COBOL
Murach's CICS for the COBOL Programmer

Please check www.murach.com for the most up-to-date Murach books

10 9 8 7 6 5 4 3 2
ISBN-13: 978-1-890774-78-3

Content

Introduction

Expanded contents

Section 2 Essential servlet and JSP skills

Chapter 6   How to develop JavaServer Pages

Chapter 7   How to work with sessions and cookies

Section 3   Essential database skills

Section 4 Advanced servlet and JSP skills

Section 5   The Music Store website

Chapter 22   An introduction to the Music Store website

Introduction

Java servlets and JavaServer Pages (JSPs) came into widespread use in the late 1990s. For many years, servlets and JSPs were the dominant technology for building web applications, especially for large enterprises. Although servlets and JSPs are no longer the dominant approach to web programming, they have some advantages over other newer approaches. In addition, since there are still many legacy web applications powered by them, servlets and JSPs will continue to be relevant for many years to come.

A quick search on a typical job website shows that there is still plenty of demand for servlet and JSP developers. In addition, many of the skills for working with servlets and JSPs also apply to newer approaches to Java web development such as JavaServer Faces (JSF). As a result, learning servlets and JSPs is still a great way to get started with Java web programming.

Who this book is for

This book is for anyone who wants to learn how to develop web applications using servlets and JSP. The only prerequisite is a basic understanding of the Java programming language roughly equivalent to chapters 1 through 14 of our core Java book, *Murach's Java Programming*. Once you have the necessary Java skills, this book should work for you even if you have no experience developing web applications.

Why you'll learn faster and better with this book

When we started writing this book, we knew we had to take a new approach if we wanted to teach you everything you need to know in a way that's faster and better than the other books. Here, then, are a few of the ways in which our book differs from the others:

- Chapter 2 shows how to use the MVC pattern (or Model 2 architecture) to get the most from JSPs and servlets. This allows you to use servlets when they're appropriate and JSPs when they're appropriate. As a result, you won't waste your time learning how to use servlets for tasks that should be handled by JSPs, or vice versa.

- Chapter 3 shows how to use the NetBeans IDE with a Tomcat server to develop web applications on your own computer. By using this IDE, you'll learn faster and better than you would without one. In contrast, most competing books leave you to figure this out on your own.

- Chapter 4 of this book provides a crash course in HTML5 and CSS3. Since this is essential background for the use of JSPs, this means you won't have to use a second book to figure out how HTML and CSS work.

- This book includes dozens of examples that range from the simple to the complex. That way, you can quickly see how a feature works from the simple examples, but you'll also see how the feature is used in more complex, real-world examples, including the complete e-commerce application that's presented in section 5.

- At the end of most chapters, you'll find exercises that help you practice what you've learned. They also encourage you to experiment and challenge you to apply what you've learned in new ways. To help you get the most practice in the least time, you'll start these exercises from existing applications.

- If you page through this book, you'll see that all of the information is presented in "paired pages," with the essential syntax, guidelines, and examples on the right page and the perspective and extra explanation on the left page. This helps you learn faster by reading less...and this is the ideal reference format when you need to refresh your memory about how to do something.

What you'll learn in this book

- In section 1, you'll learn the concepts and terms that you need for web programming. You'll learn how to use the MVC pattern to structure your web applications. And you'll learn how to use the NetBeans IDE with a Tomcat server to develop servlets and JSPs for web applications. When you're done with this section, you'll be ready to learn how to code and run servlets and JSPs on your own computer.

- In section 2, you'll get a crash course in HTML and CSS, which is essential to the use of JSPs. Then, you'll learn the skills for creating servlets and JSPs that you'll need for almost every application. These chapters move from the simple to the complex as they show you how to work with servlets, JSPs, sessions, cookies, JavaBeans, Expression Language (EL), the JSP Standard Tag Library (JSTL), and custom JSP tags.

- In section 3, you'll learn how to use both JDBC (an older access method) and the newer Java Persistence API (JPA) to work with a database. Since MySQL is a popular open-source database that is commonly used for web applications, this section shows how to work with it, but these principles can be applied to the use of any database.

- In section 4, you'll learn the advanced servlet and JSP skills that you will need for certain types of web applications. This includes the use of JavaMail, SSL, authentication, encryption, HTTP, listeners, and filters. Then, it ends with an introduction to JavaServer Faces (JSF), an alternate approach to JSP. Since we designed the chapters in this section to work independently of each other, you can read them in any order you want. This makes it easy to learn new skills whenever you need them.

- To complete your Java web programming skills, section 5 presents an e-commerce website that puts the skills presented in the first four sections into context. This downloadable application illustrates best practices and provides code that you can use in your own applications. Once you understand how this website works, you will have all the skills you need for creating your own web applications.

What operating systems this book supports

The software you need for developing web applications with servlets and JSP is available for Windows, Mac OS X, and Linux. If you're using Windows, you can use appendix A to download and install this software. If you're using Mac OS X, appendix B shows how to download and install this software. If you're using another platform such as Linux, you probably already know how to install this software! If not, you can use appendix B as a general guide and search the Internet for more information if you need it.

How to get the software you need for this book

You can download all of the software that you need for this book for free from the Internet. To make that easier for you, appendix A (PC) and B (Mac) show how to download and install the software for this book. This software includes Java SE, NetBeans, Tomcat, MySQL, and MySQL Workbench.

How our downloadable files make learning easier

To make learning easier, you can download the source code, files, and databases for all the web applications presented in this book from our website (www.murach.com). This includes the Music Store e-commerce application. Then, you can view the complete code for these applications as you read each chapter; you can compile and run these applications to see how they work; and you can copy portions of code for use in your own web applications.

You can also download the starting points and solutions for the exercises in this book. That way, you don't have to start every exercise from scratch. This takes the busywork out of doing these exercises. As a result, you get more practice in less time. In addition, if you encounter a problem, you can easily check the solution. This helps you to keep moving forward with less chance that you'll get stuck on a minor issue. For more information about these downloads, please see appendix A (PC) or appendix B (Mac).

Support materials for trainers and instructors

If you're a corporate trainer or a college instructor who would like to use this book for a course, we offer an Instructor's CD that includes: (1) PowerPoint slides, (2) test banks, (3) objectives, (4) additional exercises that aren't in this book, (5) solutions to those exercises, (6) projects, and (7) solutions to those projects.

To learn more about this Instructor's CD and to find out how to get it, please go to our website at www.murach.com. Or, if you prefer, you can call Kelly at 1-800-221-5528 or send an email to kelly@murach.com.

Please let us know how this book works for you

When we started the first edition of this book, our goal was to teach you how to develop real-world web applications with servlets and JSPs as quickly and easily as possible. Now, with this third edition of this book, we hope we've taken that to a new level. So if you have any comments, please email us at murachbooks@murach.com.

Thanks for buying this book. Thanks for reading it. And good luck with your web programming.

Joel Murach
Joel Murach
Author

Section 1

Get started right

The three chapters in this section provide the background information that you need for developing web applications with servlets and JavaServer Pages (JSPs). In chapter 1, you'll learn what web programming is and how servlets and JSPs work. In chapter 2, you'll learn how to use the MVC pattern to structure a web application that uses servlets and JSPs.

Then, in chapter 3, you'll learn how to use the NetBeans IDE (Integrated Development Environment) to work with the HTML, servlet, JSP, and XML files that make up a servlet/JSP application. In addition, you'll learn how to use NetBeans to run a Java web application on a Tomcat server that's running on your computer.

1

An introduction to web programming with Java

This chapter introduces some concepts and terms that you should learn before you start web programming with servlets and JavaServer Pages (JSPs). In addition, it describes three approaches that you can use for developing Java web applications. Finally, it describes some software that you can use to develop and deploy servlet/JSP applications.

An introduction to web applications

A *web application* is a set of web pages that are generated in response to user requests. The Internet has many different types of web applications, such as search engines, online stores, auctions, news sites, discussion groups, and games.

A typical web application

Figure 1-1 shows the first two pages of the shopping cart application that's available from www.murach.com. Here, the first page presents some information about our Java book. This page contains an Add To Cart link. When you click on this link, the web application adds the book to your cart and displays the second page, which shows all of the items in your cart.

The second page lets you change the quantity for an item or remove an item from the cart. It also lets you continue shopping or begin the checkout process. In this book, you'll learn all the skills you need to create a shopping cart application like this one.

If you take a closer look at these web pages, you can learn a little bit about how this application works. For the first page, the Address box of the browser shows an address that has an htm extension. This means that the HTML code for this page is probably stored in a file with an htm extension.

In contrast, the Address box for the second page shows the address of a servlet that was mapped to the ordering/cart URL. This means that the HTML code for this page was generated by a servlet. After the servlet address, you can see a question mark and one parameter named productCode that has a value of "htm5". This is the parameter that was passed from the first page.

The first page of a shopping cart application

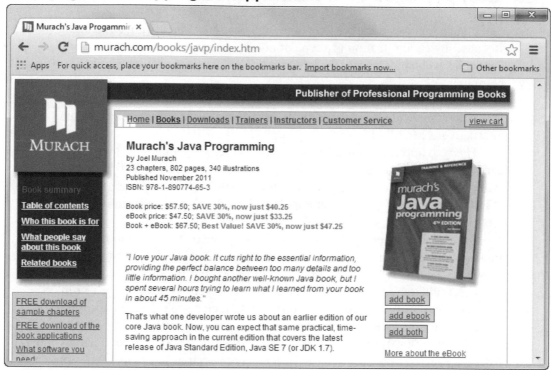

The second page of a shopping cart application

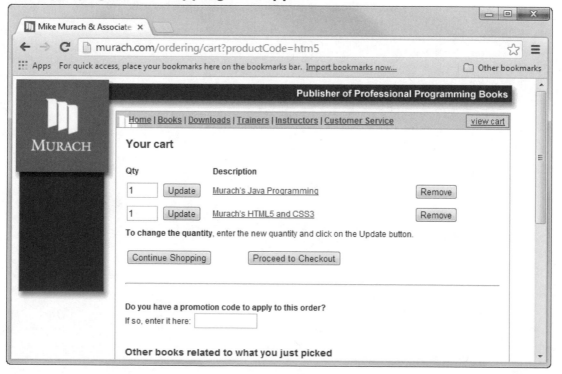

Figure 1-1   A typical web application

The components of a web application

Figure 1-2 shows the basic components that make up a web application. Because a web application is a type of *client/server application*, the components of a web application are stored on either the *client* computer or the *server* computer.

To access a web application, you use a *web browser* that runs on a client computer. One widely used web browser is Google Chrome, and a popular alternative is Mozilla Firefox.

The web application itself is stored on the server computer. This computer runs *web server* software that enables it to send web pages to web browsers. Although there are many web servers, the Apache Software Foundation's Apache HTTP Server is one of the most popular. Many developers refer to it just as Apache.

Because most web applications work with data that's stored in a database, most servers also run a *database management system* (*DBMS*), which is also known as a *database server*. Two of the most popular for Java development are MySQL and Oracle. When you use a database server, it doesn't have to run on the same server as the web server software. In fact, a separate database server is often used to improve an application's overall performance.

Although this figure shows the client and server computers connected via the Internet, this isn't the only way a client can connect to a server in a web application. If the client and the server are on the same *Local Area Network* (*LAN*), they function as an *intranet*. Since an intranet uses the same protocols as the Internet, a web application works the same on an intranet as it does on the Internet.

Components of a web application

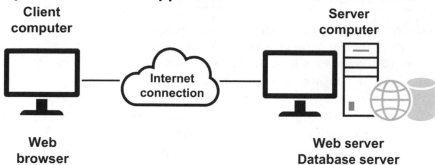

**Client
computer**

**Internet
connection**

**Server
computer**

**Web
browser**

**Web server
Database server**

Description

- Web applications are a type of *client/server application*. In a client/server application, a user at a *client* computer accesses an application at a *server* computer. For a web application, the client and server computers are connected via the Internet or an intranet.

- In a web application, the user works with a *web browser* at the client computer. The web browser provides the user interface for the application. One widely used web browser is Google Chrome, but other web browsers such as Mozilla Firefox and Internet Explorer are also widely used.

- A web application runs on the server computer under the control of *web server* software. The Apache server is one of the most widely used web servers.

- For most web applications, the server computer also runs a *database management system (DBMS)*, which is also known as a *database server*. For servlet and JSP applications, Oracle and MySQL are two of the most popular database management systems.

Figure 1-2   The components of a web application

How static web pages work

HTML (*Hypertext Markup Language*) is the language that the browser renders to the web pages that make up a web application's user interface. Some web pages are *static web pages*, which are the same each time they are viewed. In other words, they don't change in response to user input.

Figure 1-3 shows how a web server handles static web pages. The process begins when a user at a web browser requests a web page. This can occur when the user enters a web address into the browser's Address box or when the user clicks a link that leads to another page. In either case, the web browser uses a standard Internet protocol known as *Hypertext Transfer Protocol* (*HTTP*) to send a request known as an *HTTP request* to the website's server.

When the web server receives an HTTP request from a browser, the server gets the requested HTML file from disk and sends the file back to the browser in the form of an *HTTP response*. The HTTP response includes the HTML document that the user requested along with any other resources specified by the HTML code such as graphics files.

When the browser receives the HTTP response, it renders the HTML document into a web page that the user can view. Then, when the user requests another page, either by clicking a link or typing another web address in the browser's Address box, the process begins again.

How a web server processes static web pages

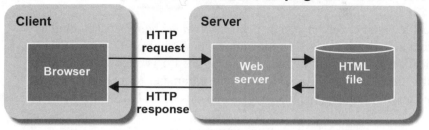

Description

- *Hypertext Markup Language* (*HTML*) is the language that the web browser converts into the web pages of a web application.

- A *static web page* is an HTML document that's stored in a file and does not change in response to user input. Static web pages have a filename with an extension of .htm or .html.

- *Hypertext Transfer Protocol* (*HTTP*) is the protocol that web browsers and web servers use to communicate.

- A web browser requests a page from a web server by sending the server a message known as an *HTTP request*. For a static web page, the HTTP request includes the name of the HTML file that's requested.

- A web server replies to an HTTP request by sending a message known as an *HTTP response* back to the browser. For a static web page, the HTTP response includes the HTML document that's stored in the HTML file.

Figure 1-3   How static web pages work

How dynamic web pages work

In contrast to a static web page, a *dynamic web page* changes based on the parameters that are sent to the web application from another page. For instance, when the Add To Cart button in the first page in figure 1-1 is clicked, the static web page calls the web application and sends one parameter to it. Then, the web application generates the dynamic web page and sends the HTML for it back to the browser.

Figure 1-4 shows how this works. When a user enters data into a web page and clicks the appropriate button, the browser sends an HTTP request to the server. This request contains the address of the next web page along with any data entered by the user. Then, when the web server receives this request and determines that it is a request for a dynamic web page, it passes the request back to the web application.

When the web application receives the request, it processes the data that the user entered and generates an HTML document. Next, it sends that document to the web server, which sends the document back to the browser in the form of an HTTP response. Then, the browser displays the HTML document that's included in the response so the process can start over again.

How a web server processes dynamic web pages

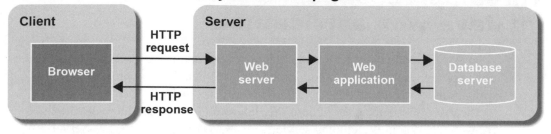

Description

- A *dynamic web page* is an HTML document that's generated by a web application. Often, the web page changes according to parameters that are sent to the web application by the web browser.

- When a web server receives a request for a dynamic web page, the server passes the request to the web application. Then, the application generates a response, such as an HTML document, and returns it to the web server. The web server, in turn, wraps the generated HTML document in an HTTP response and sends it back to the browser.

- Most modern web applications store and retrieve data from a database that runs on a database server.

- The browser doesn't know or care whether the HTML was retrieved from a static HTML file or was dynamically generated by the web application. Either way, the browser displays the HTML document that is returned.

Figure 1-4   How dynamic web pages work

Three approaches for Java web applications

There are many ways to develop Java web applications. Figure 1-5 describes three approaches that are commonly used today. When developing Java web applications, you typically use parts of the *Java Enterprise Edition* (*Java EE*) specification. This specification describes how web servers can interact with all Java web technologies including servlets, JavaServer Pages (JSP), JavaServer Faces (JSF), Java Persistence API (JPA), Enterprise JavaBeans (EJB), and more.

Servlet/JSP

In a well-structured servlet/JSP application, *servlets* store the Java code that does the server-side processing, and *JavaServer Pages* (*JSPs*) store the HTML that defines the user interface. This HTML typically contains links to CSS and JavaScript files. To run a web application that uses servlets and JSPs, you only need to work with the servlet/JSP part of the Java EE specification.

Since the servlet/JSP API is a relatively low-level API, it doesn't do as much work for the developer as the other two APIs. However, the servlet/JSP API gives the developer a high degree of control over the HTML, CSS, and JavaScript that's returned to the browser. In addition, the servlet/JSP API is the foundation for the other two approaches. As a result, it's a good place to get started with Java web programming. As you progress through this book, you'll learn how to develop servlet/JSP applications.

JSF

JavaServer Faces (*JSF*) is a newer technology that's designed to replace both servlets and JSPs. It provides a higher-level API that does more work for the programmer. When you use JSF, you typically use more Java EE features than you do with the servlet/JSP approach.

When you use JSF, you can also use *Enterprise JavaBeans* (*EJBs*) to define server-side components. Although there are some benefits to using EJBs, they're overkill for most websites. As a result, this book doesn't show how to use them.

Spring Framework

Like JSF, the Spring Framework is a higher-level API that does more work for the programmer than the servlet/JSP API. However, due to the way it's structured, the Spring Framework still gives the developer a high degree of control over the HTML/CSS/JavaScript that's returned to the browser. As a result, if control over HTML/CSS/JavaScript is a priority for your website, the Spring Framework might be the right approach for you.

Three approaches for developing Java web apps

Servlet/JSP

- Is a lower-level API that does less work for the programmer.
- Provides a high degree of control over the HTML/CSS/JavaScript that's returned to the browser.

JSF

- Is a higher-level API that does more work for the programmer.
- Makes it more difficult to control the HTML/CSS/JavaScript that's returned to the browser.

Spring Framework

- Is a higher-level API that does more work for the programmer.
- Provides a high degree of control over the HTML/CSS/JavaScript that's returned to the browser.

Description

- The *Java Enterprise Edition* (*Java EE*) specification describes how web servers can interact with all Java web technologies including servlets, JavaServer Pages (JSP), JavaServer Faces (JSF), Java Persistence API (JPA), and Enterprise JavaBeans (EJB).

- In a well-structured servlet/JSP application, *servlets* store the Java code that does the server-side processing, and *JavaServer Pages* (*JSPs*) store the HTML that defines the user interface. This typically includes links to the CSS and JavaScript for the user interface.

- *JavaServer Faces* (*JSF*) is a newer technology than servlet/JSP that provides a higher-level API that replaces both servlets and JSPs. For more on JSF, see chapter 21.

- *Java Persistence API* (*JPA*) is an API for working with databases. It can be used with servlet/JSP, JSF, or Spring. For more on JPA, see chapter 13.

- *Enterprise JavaBeans* (*EJB*) can be used to define server-side components. Since these components are overkill for most websites, they aren't described in this book.

Figure 1-5   Three approaches for developing Java web apps

An introduction to servlet/JSP web development

This topic introduces you to servlet/JSP development. In particular, it presents the software components, application architecture, and standard directories that you typically use when you develop Java web applications.

The software components

Figure 1-6 shows the primary software components for a servlet/JSP web application. By now, you should understand why the server must run web server software. In addition, to work with servlets and JSPs, the server must also run a *servlet/JSP engine*, which is also known as a *servlet/JSP container*. In this book, you'll learn how to use the Tomcat server. This server is one of the most popular servers for Java web applications, and it includes both a web server and a servlet/JSP engine.

For a servlet/JSP engine to work properly, the engine must be able to access the *Java Development Kit (JDK)* that comes as part of the *Java Standard Edition* (*Java SE*). The JDK contains the Java compiler and the core classes for working with Java. It also contains the *Java Runtime Environment* (*JRE*) that's necessary for running compiled Java classes. Since this book assumes that you already have some Java experience, you should already be familiar with the JDK and the JRE.

Since all servlet/JSP engines must implement the servlet/JSP part of the Java EE specification, all servlet/JSP engines should work similarly. In theory, this makes servlet/JSP code portable between servlet/JSP engines and application servers. In practice, though, there are minor differences between each servlet/JSP engine and web server. As a result, you may need to make some modifications to your code when switching servlet/JSP engines or web servers.

Since most servlet/JSP web applications store their data in a database, the server typically runs a database server too. In this book, you'll learn how to use MySQL as the database server. This software is open-source and commonly used with servlet/JSP applications.

The components of a servlet/JSP application

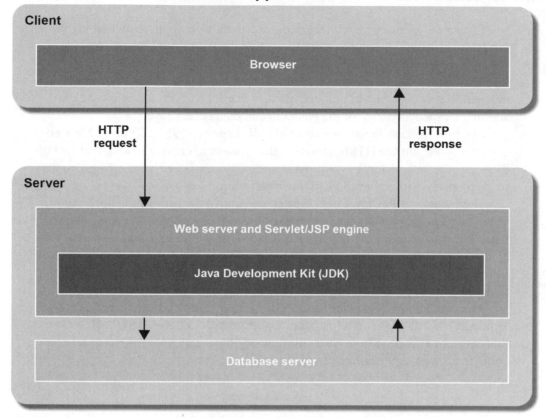

Description

- A servlet/JSP application must have a web server and a *servlet/JSP engine*, also known as a *servlet/JSP container*, to process the HTTP request and return an HTTP response, which is typically an HTML page. Most servlet/JSP applications use Tomcat as both the web server and the servlet/JSP engine.

- Most servlet/JSP applications use a database to store the data that's used by the application. Many servlet/JSP applications use MySQL as the database, though there are many other databases to use.

- For a servlet/JSP engine to work, it must have access to Java's *Java Development Kit* (*JDK*), which comes as part of the *Java Standard Edition* (*Java SE*). Among other things, the JDK contains the core Java class libraries, the Java compiler, and the *Java Runtime Environment* (*JRE*).

Figure 1-6   The components of a servlet/JSP application

The architecture

Figure 1-7 shows the architecture for a typical web application that uses servlets and JSPs. This architecture uses three layers: (1) the *presentation layer*, or *user interface layer*, (2) the *business rules layer*, and (3) the *data access layer*. In theory, the programmer tries to keep these layers as separate and independent as possible. In practice, though, these layers are often interrelated, and that's especially true for the business and data access layers.

The presentation layer consists of HTML pages and JSPs. Typically, a web designer works on the HTML stored in these pages to create the look and feel of the user interface. Later, a Java programmer may need to edit these pages so they work properly with the servlets of the application.

The business rules layer uses servlets to control the flow of the application. These servlets may call other Java classes to store or retrieve data from a database, and they may forward the results to a JSP or to another servlet. Within the business layer, Java programmers often use a special type of Java class known as a *JavaBean* to temporarily store and process data. A JavaBean is typically used to define a business object such as a User or Invoice object.

The data layer works with the data of the application on the server's disk. Typically, this data is stored in a relational database such as MySQL. However, this data can also be stored in text files, binary files, and XML files. Or, it can come from web services running on the other servers.

The architecture for a typical servlet/JSP application

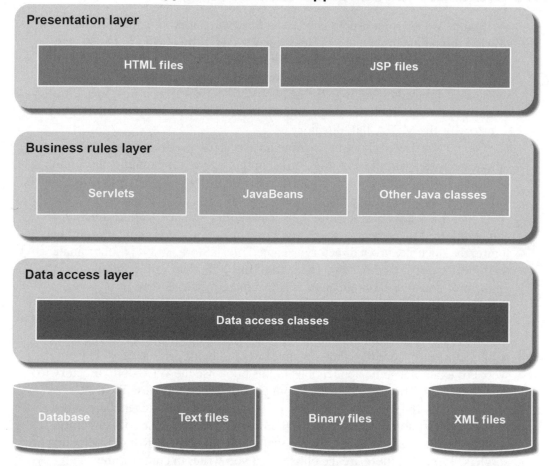

Description

- The *presentation layer* for a typical servlet/JSP web application consists of HTML pages and JSPs.

- The *business rules layer* for a typical servlet/JSP web application consists of servlets. These servlets may call other Java classes including a special type of Java class known as a *JavaBean*. As you progress though this book, you'll learn how to use several special types of tags within a JSP to work with JavaBeans.

- The *data access layer* for a typical Java web application consists of classes that read and write data that's stored on the server's disk drive.

- For most web applications, the data is stored in a relational database such as MySQL. However, it may also be stored in binary files, text files, or XML files.

Figure 1-7   The architecture for a servlet/JSP web application

The standard directories and files

Figure 1-8 shows a simplified version of the directory structure for the Music Store application that's presented at the end of this book. Some of these directories are part of the servlet and JSP specifications. As a result, they are standard for all web applications. For example, all web applications that use servlets must have the WEB-INF and WEB-INF\classes directories. In addition, you can optionally include other standard directories such as the WEB-INF\lib directory or the META-INF directory.

Of course, to organize and structure an application, a programmer can create other directories within these directories. In this figure, for example, the admin, cart, and download directories organize the Administration, Cart, and Download sections of the Music Store application.

To start, each web application must have a root directory. This directory can be referred to as the *document root directory*, or just *document root*. In this figure, the document root directory is named musicStore, and it is subordinate to Tomcat's webapps directory. Then, all of the other directories and files for the application must be subordinate to this document root directory.

The WEB-INF directory that's subordinate to the document root directory typically contains a web.xml file for the application. You'll learn more about this file in the next chapter. In addition, you can use this directory or any of its subdirectories to store files that you don't want to be directly accessible from the web. For example, some applications in this book use the WEB-INF directory to store data files. This prevents users from directly accessing these files.

The WEB-INF directory also has a few standard directories that are subordinate to it. In particular, the WEB-INF\classes directory is the root directory for all Java classes for the application that aren't stored in JAR files, including servlets. Typically, these are the classes that you write. In contrast, the WEB-INF\lib directory contains the JAR files that contain any Java class libraries for the application. Typically, you get these JAR files from a third party. Remember, though, that Tomcat's lib directory stores the JAR files for the class libraries that are available to all web applications running on the web server. As a result, if you want to use a JAR file that's in Tomcat's lib directory, you don't need to add it to the application's WEB-INF\lib directory.

To organize the classes that you create for the application, you can store them in *packages*. In that case, you need to create one subdirectory for each package. For example, this figure shows four packages. Three of these packages (music.admin, music.cart, and music.download) contain servlets that work with the Administration, Cart, and Download sections of the application while the other two contain the Java classes that provide the business objects (music.business) and data access objects (music.data) for the application.

As you progress through this book, you'll learn how to use some other standard directories and files to deploy web applications. For example, if you want to use the database connection pool that's available from Tomcat, you can modify the context.xml file that's stored in the META-INF directory as described in chapter 12. For now, though, this figure should give you a general idea of what it takes to deploy a web application. The music.controllers package contains the servlets for the application, while the other three packages contain regular Java classes that define business objects and provide for data access.

The directory structure for a web application named musicStore

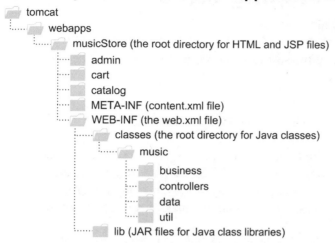

```
tomcat
    webapps
        musicStore (the root directory for HTML and JSP files)
            admin
            cart
            catalog
            META-INF (content.xml file)
            WEB-INF (the web.xml file)
                classes (the root directory for Java classes)
                    music
                        business
                        controllers
                        data
                        util
            lib (JAR files for Java class libraries)
```

A summary of the directories and files for a web application

Directory	Description
(root)	This directory and its subdirectories typically contain the HTML and JSP files for the application.
\WEB-INF	This directory typically contains a file named web.xml. You can use this file to configure the servlets and other components that make up the application. In addition, this directory is not directly accessible from the web.
\WEB-INF\classes	This directory and its subdirectories contain the servlets and other Java classes for your application. Each subdirectory must correspond with the package for the Java class.
\WEB-INF\lib	This directory contains any JAR files that contain Java class libraries that are used by the web application.
\META-INF	This directory contains the context.xml file. You can use this file to configure the web application context.

Description

- The top-level directory for a web application is known as its *root directory*.
- A Java web application is a hierarchy of directories and files in a standard layout defined by the Java EE specification. All Java web applications must use the first three directories that are summarized above.

Figure 1-8   The standard directories and files for a servlet/JSP web application

Software for developing Java web applications

This topic presents some of the software options that you have for developing Java web applications.

IDEs for developing Java web applications

In the early days of Java web programming, programmers commonly used text editors to enter, edit, compile, and test the HTML, JSP, Java, servlet, and XML files that make up a web application. Today, however, many *Integrated Development Environments* (*IDEs*) are available that make Java web programming more efficient.

Two of the most popular IDEs for developing Java web applications are NetBeans and Eclipse. Both are open-source, and both are available for free. Of the two, we think that NetBeans is easier to use, especially when you're getting started with web programming. That's why we recommend that you use NetBeans with this book.

In figure 1-9, for example, you can see the NetBeans IDE with the project for chapter 2 in the Projects window, the code for a servlet class in the editor window, and runtime messages in the Output window. This is similar to what you'll find in most IDEs. As a result, once you're done with this book, you can easily apply the skills that you learn with NetBeans to another IDE.

Although we recommend using NetBeans with this book, you should be able to use another IDE with this book if you prefer. To do that, though, you will need to figure out how to import the source code for this book into your IDE so you can compile and run the sample applications and complete the exercises. In addition, you will need to use your IDE to perform the tasks presented in chapter 3.

Since the JDK, NetBeans, Tomcat, and MySQL can be run by most operating systems, Java web developers aren't tied to a specific operating system. In fact, developers often use Windows or Mac OS X during development. However, when the applications are ready for release, they are often deployed to a Linux or Unix server.

The NetBeans IDE

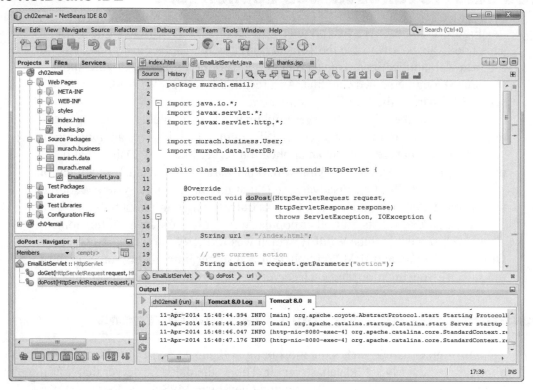

Popular IDEs for Java web development

- NetBeans
- Eclipse
- IntelliJ IDEA

Description

- An *Integrated Development Environment* (*IDE*) is a tool that provides all of the functionality that you need for developing web applications.

- *NetBeans* and *Eclipse* are popular IDEs for Java web development that are open-source and free.

- Chapter 3 shows how to use NetBeans for developing Java web applications. We recommend using this IDE with this book.

Figure 1-9   IDEs for developing Java web applications

Web servers for Java web applications

Figure 1-10 describes two popular web servers for Java web applications. This book shows how to use the Tomcat server, which is the most popular server for Java web applications. Tomcat includes a web server named Coyote and a servlet/JSP engine named Catalina. As a result, this server can work with the servlet/JSP part of the Java EE specification.

In contrast, the GlassFish server implements the complete Java EE specification. Since it's more than just a servlet/JSP engine, it's known as an *application server*. The advantage of using an application server like GlassFish is that it provides more features for working with other parts of the Java EE specification such as JSF and JPA. One disadvantage is that it requires more system resources than Tomcat. As a result, it may not run as quickly on your computer.

This figure also lists four other popular web servers for Java applications. These web servers include WildFly, which was formerly known as JBoss, Jetty, Oracle WebLogic, and IBM WebSphere. Each server implements some or all of the Java EE specification, and each server has its advantages and disadvantages.

Database servers for Java web applications

This figure also describes the most popular database server for Java web applications, the MySQL database server. This is the database server that you'll learn to use in this book. Like Tomcat and GlassFish, MySQL is open-source and runs on all modern operating systems. In addition, MySQL implements most of the SQL standard. As a result, database code developed for the MySQL server should be mostly portable between database servers.

Although many Java web applications use a MySQL database, some developers prefer other open-source databases, such as PostgreSQL. On the other hand, some large enterprises prefer using a proprietary database like Oracle to store mission-critical data.

Two popular web servers

Tomcat

- Is a servlet/JSP engine that includes a web server.
- Is free, open-source, and runs on all modern operating systems.
- Is a popular web server for Java web applications.

GlassFish

- Is a complete Java EE application server.
- Is free, open-source, and runs on all modern operating systems.
- Provides more features than Tomcat.
- Requires more system resources than Tomcat.

Other popular web servers

- WildFly (formerly JBoss)
- Jetty
- Oracle WebLogic
- IBM WebSphere

A popular database server

MySQL

- Is a relational database server that implements most of the SQL standard.
- Is free, open-source, and runs on all modern operating systems.
- Is the most popular database server for Java web applications.

Other popular database servers

- PostgreSQL
- Oracle

Description

- A servlet/JSP engine is the software that allows a web server to work with the servlet/JSP part of the Java EE specification.

- Tomcat is one of the most popular servlet/JSP engines. It includes a web server named Coyote and a servlet/JSP engine named Catalina.

- A Java EE *application server* is the software that allows the web server to work with the entire Java EE specification including servlets, JSP (JavaServer Pages), JSF (JavaServer Faces), JPA (Java Persistence API), EJB (Enterprise JavaBeans), and so on.

- GlassFish is one of the most popular application servers. It includes a web server, a servlet/JSP engine that's based on Tomcat's servlet/JSP engine, and more.

- MySQL is one of the most popular database servers.

Figure 1-10   Web and database servers for Java web applications

Tools for deploying Java web applications

Once you've tested your servlets and JSPs on your own computer or an intranet, you may want to deploy your web application on the Internet. To do that, you need to get a *web host*. One way to do that is to find an *Internet service provider* (*ISP*) that provides web hosting that supports servlets and JSPs. If you read the text for the ISP on the web page shown in figure 1-11, for example, you can see that this ISP supports servlets and JSPs.

If you search the web, you'll be able to find many other ISPs and web hosts. Just make sure that the one you choose not only supports servlet and JSP development, but also the database management system that your application requires.

When you select a web host, you get an *IP address* like 64.71.179.86 that uniquely identifies your website (IP stands for Internet Protocol). Then, you can get a *domain name* like www.murach.com and have it associated with your IP address. This allows you to use either the domain name or the IP address to access your website. To do that, you can use any number of companies that you can find on the Internet. Until you get your domain name, you can use the IP address to access your site.

After you get a web host, you need to transfer your files to the web server. To do that, you can use *File Transfer Protocol* (*FTP*). The easiest way to use FTP is to use an FTP client such as the FileZilla client shown in this figure. An FTP client like this one lets you upload files from your computer to your web server and download files from your web server to your computer.

An ISP that provides web hosting that supports servlets and JSPs

The FileZilla program

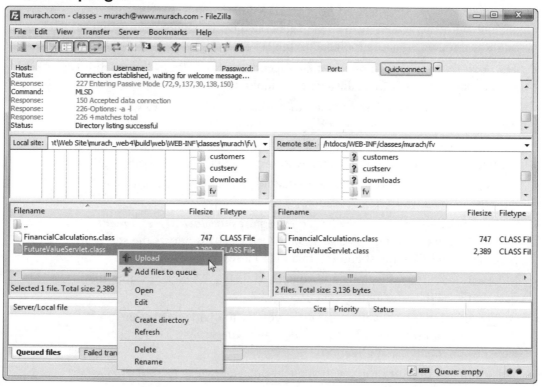

Figure 1-11   Tools for deploying Java web applications

Perspective

The goal of this chapter has been to provide the background that you need for developing servlets and JSPs. Now, if this chapter has succeeded, you should be ready to learn how to use the MVC pattern to structure a web application.

Summary

- A *web application* is a set of web pages that are generated in response to user requests.

- To run a web application, the client requires a web browser and the server requires *web server* software. The server may also require a *database management system* (*DBMS*).

- *Hypertext Markup Language* (*HTML*) is the language that the browser converts into the web pages of a web application, while *Hypertext Transfer Protocol* (*HTTP*) is the protocol that web browsers and web servers use to communicate.

- A web browser requests a page from a web server by sending an *HTTP request*. A web server replies by sending an *HTTP response* back to the browser.

- A *static web page* is generated from an HTML document that doesn't change, while a *dynamic web page* is generated by a web application based on the parameters that are included in the HTTP request.

- The *Java Enterprise Edition* (*Java EE*) specification describes how web servers can interact with all Java web technologies.

- A *servlet/JSP engine* is the software that allows a web server to work with the servlet/JSP part of the Java EE specification.

- Tomcat is one of the most popular servlet/JSP engines, and most servlet/JSP applications use Tomcat as both the web server and the servlet/JSP engine.

- An *application server* is the software that allows the web server to work with the entire Java EE specification.

- To run Java web applications, the server requires the *Java Development Kit* (*JDK*), a web server, and a servlet/JSP engine. This allows the server to process the HTTP request and return an HTTP response.

- Most servlet/JSP applications use a database such as MySQL to store the data that's used by the application.

- As you develop a Java web application, you try to divide its classes into three layers: *presentation*, *business rules*, and *data access*. This makes it easier to maintain the application.

- The top-level directory for a web application is known as its *root directory*.

- An *Integrated Development Environment* (*IDE*) is a tool that provides most of the functionality that you need for developing web applications.

- NetBeans and Eclipse are popular IDEs for Java web development. Both are open-source, free, and work on all modern operating systems.

- To deploy your web application on the Internet, you can get an *Internet service provider* (*ISP*) that provides *web hosting* that supports servlets and JSPs.

- When a web application runs on the Internet, it has an *IP* (*Internet Protocol*) *address* like 64.71.179.86 and a *domain name* like www.murach.com. These addresses provide two ways to uniquely identify the website.

- To transfer your web application files to a web server, you can use a *File Transfer Protocol* (*FTP*) client such as FileZilla.

2

How to structure a web application with the MVC pattern

This chapter begins by presenting two patterns that you can use for servlet/JSP web development. Then, it shows how to use the second pattern, which is known as the MVC pattern, to structure a web application. There are several advantages to this approach, and it's generally considered a best practice.

Two patterns
for servlet/JSP applications

A *pattern* is a standard approach that programmers use to solve common programming problems. This topic describes two patterns that you can use when you develop Java web applications. However, for a serious web application, most developers consider the second pattern to be a best practice and recommend avoiding the first pattern.

The Model 1 pattern

The *Model 1 pattern* that's shown in figure 2-1 uses a JSP to handle both the request and response of the application. In addition, the JSP does all of the processing for the application.

To do that, the JSP interacts with Java classes and objects that represent the data of the business objects in the application and provide the methods that do the business processing. In this figure, for example, the application stores the data for a user in a User object.

To save the data of the business classes, the application maps the data to a database or files that can be called the *data store* for the application. This is also known as *persistent data storage* because it exists after the application ends. Usually, *data access classes* like the UserDB class shown in this figure store the data of the business objects in a database. Later in this book, you'll learn two ways to create data access classes like this one.

Although the Model 1 pattern is sometimes adequate for applications that have limited processing requirements, this pattern is not recommended for most applications. As a result, it isn't presented in this book.

The Model 1 pattern

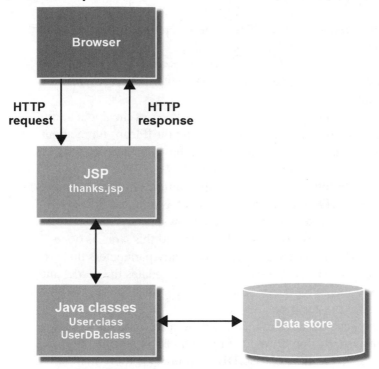

Description

- The *Model 1* pattern uses JSPs to handle all of the processing and presentation for the application. This pattern is sometimes adequate for web applications with limited processing requirements, but it is generally considered a bad practice.

- In the Model 1 pattern, the JSPs can use regular Java classes to store the data of the application and to do the business processing of the application. In addition, they can use *data classes* to work with the data store.

- The *data store* is typically a database, but it can include disk files. This is often referred to as *persistent data storage* because it exists after the application ends.

Figure 2-1   The Model 1 pattern

The Model 2 (MVC) pattern

Figure 2-2 shows the *Model 2 pattern*. This pattern separates the code for the application into three layers: the model, the view, and the controller. As a result, this pattern is also known as the *Model-View-Controller pattern* (*MVC pattern*). This pattern works better than the Model 1 pattern whenever the processing requirements are substantial.

In the MVC pattern, the *model* defines the business layer of the application. This layer is usually implemented by JavaBeans, which you'll learn more about in a moment. This type of class defines the data for the business objects and provides the methods that do the business processing.

The *view* defines the presentation layer of the application. Since it's cumbersome to use a servlet to send HTML to a browser, an MVC application uses HTML documents or JSPs to present the view to the browser.

The *controller* manages the flow of the application, and this work is done by one or more servlets. To start, a servlet usually reads any parameters that are available from the request. Then, if necessary, the servlet updates the model and saves it to the data store. Finally, the servlet forwards the updated model to one of several possible JSPs for presentation.

Here again, most applications need to map the data in the model to a data store. But the JavaBeans usually don't provide the methods for storing their own data. Instead, data access classes like the UserDB class provide those methods. That separates the business logic from the data access operations.

When you use the MVC pattern, you should try to keep the model, view, and controller as independent of each other as possible. That makes it easier to modify an application later on. If, for example, you decide to modify an application so it presents the view in a different way, you should be able to modify the view layer without making any changes to the controller or model layers. In practice, it's difficult to separate these layers completely, but complete independence is the goal.

The Model 2 (MVC) pattern

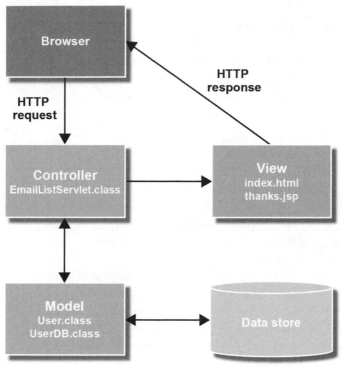

Description

- The *Model 2 pattern* separates the code into a model, a view, and a controller. As a result, it's also known as the *Model-View-Controller (MVC) pattern*.

- The MVC pattern is commonly used to structure web applications that have significant processing requirements. That makes them easier to code and maintain.

- In the MVC pattern, the *model* consists of business objects like the User object, the *view* consists of HTML pages and JSPs, and the *controller* consists of servlets.

- Usually, the methods of *data access classes* like the UserDB class are used to read and write business objects like the User object to and from the data store.

- When you use the MVC pattern, you try to construct each layer so it's as independent as possible. Then, if you need to make changes to one layer, any changes to the other layers are minimized.

Figure 2-2   The Model 2 (MVC) pattern

A servlet/JSP application that uses the MVC pattern

Now that you understand how the MVC pattern works, you're ready to see the code for a servlet/JSP application that uses this pattern. To start, you can view the user interface for this application. Then, you can see the code for the most important files of this application.

The user interface

Figure 2-3 shows the user interface for a web application that allows a user to join an email list. Here, the first page is a static HTML page that allows the user to enter his or her email address, first name, and last name. When the user enters his or her data and clicks on the Join Now button, the web browser sends an HTTP request to the server that contains this data.

On the server, a servlet gets the data that the user entered from the HTTP request, stores that data in a User object, uses the UserDB class to save the data, and returns an HTTP response to the browser. This HTTP response is a dynamic HTML page that includes the data that the user entered on the first page.

To display the first page of this app on a development computer, the browser calls this URL:

```
localhost:8080/ch02email/
```

The first part of this URL indicates that the server is running on the same server as the browser on port 8080, which is the default port for the version of Tomcat that's included with NetBeans. The second part of this URL indicates that the name of the app is ch02email. Since the URL doesn't specify a file name, Tomcat displays the default file for the directory, which is typically named index.html, index.htm, or index.jsp.

To display the second page of this app, the user can click on the Join Now button. This displays this URL:

```
localhost:8080/ch02email/emailList
```

The first two parts of this URL are the same as the first page. However, the third part of the URL is mapped to a servlet that processes the data that's entered on the first page. You'll see how this works in the next few figures.

The HTML page that gets data from the user

The JSP that displays the data

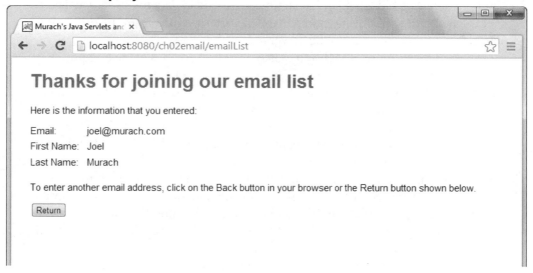

Description

- The first page of this application is an HTML page that gets data from the user and sends it to the server as an HTTP request.
- The second page of this application is a JSP that displays the data that the user has entered.

Figure 2-3   The user interface

The HTML for the first page

Figure 2-4 shows the HTML for the first page of the application. If you're already familiar with HTML, you shouldn't have any trouble understanding this code. If your HTML skills are a little rusty, chapter 4 presents a crash course in HTML that should get you up to speed for this book. For now, focus on the general concepts, and don't worry if you don't understand all of the details of this code.

Since there isn't any Java code in a static HTML page, these pages are often written by web designers, not web programmers. However, web programmers may need to modify the attributes of the form or input tags to get them to work correctly with the servlet that processes the data that's submitted by a static HTML page.

The HTML in this figure contains the tags that define the first page. In short, the h1 and p tags identify the text that's displayed above the form. Then, the form tags mark the beginning and end of the form. Within the form, the first input tag defines a hidden field that submits hard-coded data to the server. The next three input tags define the three text boxes that get data from the user and a button that submits the data to the server.

These input tags use HTML5 to create three text boxes that have required values. As a result, if the user doesn't enter a value for one of these text boxes, the browser displays an appropriate message that asks the user to enter a value.

All three text boxes use the name attribute to specify a name that the servlet can use to access the value that's stored in the text box. The first text box has a name of "email", the second text box has a name of "firstName", and the third text box has a name of "lastName".

The fifth input tag is for a button that submits an HTTP request to the server. Since the form tag specifies an action attribute of "emailList", this form submits this data to the servlet URL described in the previous figure. Similarly, since the form tag specifies a method attribute of "post", this form uses the POST method for its HTTP request.

When you're performing a request that modifies data on the server, you typically use the POST method. However, if you're not modifying data, you typically use a method attribute of "get" to use the GET method for the HTTP request. You'll learn more about how this works in chapter 5.

The index.html file

```html
<!DOCTYPE html>
<html>
<head>
    <meta charset="utf-8">
    <title>Murach's Java Servlets and JSP</title>
    <link rel="stylesheet" href="styles/main.css" type="text/css"/>
</head>
<body>
    <h1>Join our email list</h1>
    <p>To join our email list, enter your name and
       email address below.</p>

    <form action="emailList" method="post">
        <input type="hidden" name="action" value="add">

        <label>Email:</label>
        <input type="email" name="email" required><br>

        <label>First Name:</label>
        <input type="text" name="firstName" required><br>

        <label>Last Name:</label>
        <input type="text" name="lastName" required><br>

        <label> </label>
        <input type="submit" value="Join Now" id="submit">
    </form>
</body>
</html>
```

Description

- An HTML file contains the tags that define the content of the web page.
- The action and method attributes of the form tag set up a request for the URL that's executed when the user clicks on the submit button.
- The three text boxes represent *parameters* that are passed to the servlet when the user clicks the submit button.
- The parameter names are firstName, lastName, and email, and the parameter values are the strings that the user enters into the text boxes.

Figure 2-4   The HTML for the first page

The CSS for both web pages

Figure 2-5 shows the CSS for both web pages of the application. If you're already familiar with CSS, you shouldn't have any trouble understanding this code. If your CSS skills are a little rusty, chapter 4 presents a crash course in CSS that should get you up to speed for this book. For now, focus on the general concepts, and don't worry if you don't understand all of the details of this code.

The *CSS* (*Cascading Style Sheet*) contains the formatting for the web pages. In this figure, the web page uses the CSS that's stored in a file named main.css that is in the styles subdirectory of the current directory. Here, the CSS specifies the font and margins for most of the HTML elements. In addition, it specifies that the label tags should be floated to the left of the other tags until a br (break) tag is encountered.

CSS provides a way to separate the formatting of the pages from the content of the pages, which is generally considered a best practice. Since CSS controls the appearance and format of the page, it's typically created by a web designer, not a web programmer. Of course, it's always helpful for web programmers to understand the CSS too. In fact, the programmer and the designer often end up being the same person.

The main.css file in the styles subdirectory

```css
body {
    font-family: Arial, Helvetica, sans-serif;
    font-size: 11pt;
    margin-left: 2em;
    margin-right: 2em;
}
h1 {
    color: teal;
}
label {
    float: left;
    width: 6em;
    margin-bottom: 0.5em;
}
input[type="text"], input[type="email"] {
    width: 15em;
    margin-left: 0.5em;
    margin-bottom: 0.5em;
}
br {
    clear: both;
}
#submit {
    margin-left: 0.5em;
}
```

Description

- A *CSS* (*Cascading Style Sheet*) file contains the formatting for the web pages.

Figure 2-5   The CSS file for both pages

The servlet for the back-end processing

To give you a better idea of how servlets work, figure 2-6 shows the code for a servlet. In short, a *servlet* is a special type of Java class that runs on a server and does the processing for the dynamic web pages of a web application. That's why the servlets for a web application are written by web programmers, not web designers.

Each servlet is a Java class that extends the HttpServlet class. In this figure, for example, the servlet is a Java class named EmailListServlet that extends the HttpServlet class. This servlet begins by overriding the doPost method of the HttpServlet class. This method is executed when its URL receives an HTTP request that uses the POST method.

The doPost method accepts both a request and a response object from the web server. Within the body of this method, the first statement defines a string for a URL. Then, the second statement uses the getParameter method of the request object to get the parameter named "action" from the HTTP request. After that, this code checks whether the action is null. If so, this code sets the action string to a value of "join".

After setting up the URL and action variables, this code uses an if/else statement to check the action variable to determine what action to perform. If the action variable is equal to a value of "join", this code sets the URL string so it will display the first page of the application, the index.html page.

However, if the action variable is equal to a value of "add", this code processes the data that has been sent to the server. To do that, the first three statements within the else clause use the getParameter method of the request object to get the parameters from the HTTP request. Then, the servlet performs the required processing by using normal Java code. In this figure, for example, it stores the data in a User object, which is described in detail in the next figure, and uses the insert method of the UserDB class to save the User object in the database. After that, this code sets the User object as an attribute of the request object so it's available to a JSP, and it sets the URL string to the JSP for the second page of the application, which is stored in a file named thanks.jsp.

After the if/else statement finishes, the servlet can return HTML to the browser by forwarding the request and response objects to the specified URL. This URL is typically a JSP, but can also be an HTML page. In this figure, for example, the code can forward these objects to the HTML file for the first page of the application or the JSP for the second page of the application. Since this code *controls* the flow of the web application, this servlet is known as a *controller* in the MVC pattern.

The EmailListServlet class   **Page 1**

```java
package murach.email;

import java.io.*;
import javax.servlet.*;
import javax.servlet.http.*;

import murach.business.User;
import murach.data.UserDB;

public class EmailListServlet extends HttpServlet  {

    @Override
    protected void doPost(HttpServletRequest request,
                          HttpServletResponse response)
                          throws ServletException, IOException {

        String url = "/index.html";

        // get current action
        String action = request.getParameter("action");
        if (action == null) {
            action = "join";          // default action
        }

        // perform action and set URL to appropriate page
        if (action.equals("join")) {
            url = "/index.html";     // the "join" page
        }
        else if (action.equals("add")) {
            // get parameters from the request
            String firstName = request.getParameter("firstName");
            String lastName = request.getParameter("lastName");
            String email = request.getParameter("email");

            // store data in User object and save User object in database
            User user = new User(firstName, lastName, email);
            UserDB.insert(user);

            // set User object in request object and set URL
            request.setAttribute("user", user);
            url = "/thanks.jsp";     // the "thanks" page
        }

        // forward request and response objects to specified URL
        getServletContext()
            .getRequestDispatcher(url)
            .forward(request, response);
    }
```

Figure 2-6   The servlet and web.xml file for the back-end processing (part 1 of 2)

The servlet in this figure finishes by overriding the doGet method of the HttpServlet class. This method allows this servlet to handle HTTP requests that use the GET method.

Like the doPost method, the doGet method accepts both a request and a response object from the web server. The body of this method contains a single statement that calls the doPost method defined earlier in this servlet and passes it the request and response objects. As a result, the doGet method can be used to do the same processing as the doPost method. This is typical for many servlets. However, it's also a potential security risk. To learn how to control the types of processing that the doGet and doPost methods do, please see chapter 22.

In chapter 5, you'll learn the details for coding servlets. When you complete that chapter, you'll be able to write significant servlets of your own.

The web.xml file

Figure 2-6 also shows the web.xml file for this application. Since the web.xml file describes how the web application should be configured when it is deployed on a server, this file is known as the *deployment descriptor* (*DD*). If this file exists, it is always stored in the WEB-INF directory of the application.

At the minimum, this file must contain the shaded code. This code defines the XML version and the Java EE standards for the web.xml file. Typically, though, a web.xml file contains some additional code that's used to configure the web application.

In this figure, for example, the web.xml file uses the servlet element to provide a name for the servlet presented in this figure. Then, it uses the servlet-mapping element to map that name to a URL pattern that you can use to call the servlet.

In addition, the web.xml file defines two welcome files: index.html and index.jsp. Then, if a browser specifies a URL that only includes a directory, the web server attempts to display one of the welcome pages for the application. In this figure, for example, the web server starts by attempting to display the index.html page. If this page doesn't exist in the directory, it attempts to display the index.jsp page. These settings are typical for a Java web application.

As you progress through this book, you'll learn more about working with a web.xml file. In chapter 5, for example, you'll learn how to use the web.xml file to work with initialization parameters and error handling.

Before you go on, you should know that there's a new and easier way of mapping servlets that was introduced with the servlet 3.0 specification (Tomcat 7). You'll learn how to use it in chapter 5. Unfortunately, this technique doesn't work with earlier versions of the servlet specification. As a result, if you're using an older version of Tomcat, you'll still need to use the web.xml file to map your servlets to URLs.

The EmailListServlet class   **Page 2**

```
    @Override
    protected void doGet(HttpServletRequest request,
                         HttpServletResponse response)
                         throws ServletException, IOException {
        doPost(request, response);
    }
}
```

The web.xml file

```xml
<?xml version="1.0" encoding="UTF-8"?>
<web-app version="3.1"
         xmlns="http://xmlns.jcp.org/xml/ns/javaee"
         xmlns:xsi="http://www.w3.org/2001/XMLSchema-instance"
         xsi:schemaLocation="http://xmlns.jcp.org/xml/ns/javaee
                 http://xmlns.jcp.org/xml/ns/javaee/web-app_3_1.xsd">

    <servlet>
        <servlet-name>EmailListServlet</servlet-name>
        <servlet-class>murach.email.EmailListServlet</servlet-class>
    </servlet>
    <servlet-mapping>
        <servlet-name>EmailListServlet</servlet-name>
        <url-pattern>/emailList</url-pattern>
    </servlet-mapping>

    <session-config>
        <session-timeout>30</session-timeout>
    </session-config>

    <welcome-file-list>
        <welcome-file>index.html</welcome-file>
        <welcome-file>index.jsp</welcome-file>
    </welcome-file-list>

</web-app>
```

Description

- Servlets contain Java code for a web application. When a servlet controls the flow of the application, it's known as a *controller*.

- With the servlet 3.0 specification and later, you can use the @WebServlet annotation to map the servlet to a URL pattern. Prior to the servlet 3.0 specification, you must use the web.xml file to map a servlet to a URL pattern.

- A servlet provides a request object that you can use to get data from the HTTP request.

- A servlet provides a response object that you can use to return an HTTP response to the browser. Typically, you return an HTTP response for an HTML page by forwarding the request and response objects to a JSP page.

- Since the web.xml file describes how the web application should be configured when it is deployed on a server, this file is known as the *deployment descriptor* (*DD*). If this file exists, it is always stored in the WEB-INF directory of the application.

Figure 2-6   The servlet and web.xml file for the back-end processing (part 2 of 2)

The User class

Figure 2-7 shows the code for the User class. This class is a *JavaBean*, or *bean*, because it follows the three rules that all JavaBeans must follow.

First, a JavaBean must contain a zero-argument constructor, which is a constructor that doesn't accept any arguments. In this figure, the zero-argument constructor uses three statements to set all three instance variables equal to empty strings. As a result, a newly created User object stores empty strings for its instance variables instead of null values, which is usually what you want.

Second, a JavaBean must contain get and set methods for all of the properties that need to be accessed by JSPs. In this figure, for example, the methods provide access to all of the instance variables of the User class, so this class qualifies as a bean. Of course, you can also code get and set methods that provide access to other properties in a bean.

To provide access to a Boolean value, you code is and set methods instead of get and set methods. For example, you could code methods named isEmailUpdated and setEmailUpdated to provide access to a Boolean property named emailUpdated.

When you code the get, set, and is methods, you must follow the capitalization conventions used in this figure. In other words, each method name must start with a lowercase letter, followed by a property name that starts with an uppercase letter as in firstName.

Third, a JavaBean must implement the Serializable or Externalizable interface. The Serializable interface is a tagging interface in the java.io package that indicates that a class contains get, set, and is methods that another class can use to read and write an object's instance variables to and from a persistent data source. In this figure, for example, the User class implements the Serializable interface and contains all the necessary get and set methods. As a result, some servlet engines can save and restore this object if that's necessary. For example, the Tomcat container can save the User object's state before it shuts down, and it can restore the User object's state when it starts up the next time.

When coding a web application, it's common to use JavaBeans to define the business objects of an application. These beans can be called *invisible JavaBeans* because they don't define visible components. The focus of this book is on this type of JavaBean.

You should realize, though, that JavaBeans are capable of doing much more than defining business objects. For instance, JavaBeans can be used to define buttons and other user interface controls.

You should also realize that there's another type of JavaBean called an *Enterprise JavaBean* (*EJB*). Although EJBs are similar in some ways to JavaBeans, EJBs are more complex and difficult to code than JavaBeans. To learn more about them, you can get a book that covers the advanced features of the Java EE specification.

The User class

```
package murach.business;

import java.io.Serializable;

public class User implements Serializable {
    private String firstName;
    private String lastName;
    private String email;

    public User() {
        firstName = "";
        lastName = "";
        email = "";
    }

    public User(String firstName, String lastName, String email) {
        this.firstName = firstName;
        this.lastName = lastName;
        this.email = email;
    }

    public String getFirstName() {
        return firstName;
    }

    public void setFirstName(String firstName) {
        this.firstName = firstName;
    }

    public String getLastName() {
        return lastName;
    }

    public void setLastName(String lastName) {
        this.lastName = lastName;
    }

    public String getEmail() {
        return email;
    }

    public void setEmail(String email) {
        this.email = email;
    }
}
```

Description

- A JavaBean, or bean, is a Java class that (1) provides a zero-argument constructor, (2) provides get and set methods for all of its instance variables, and (3) implements the Serializable or Externalizable interface.

- Since JavaBeans are just Java classes, they are a type of *plain old Java object* (*POJO*).

Figure 2-7   The User class

The JSP for the second page

The main benefit that you get from coding your business classes so they qualify as JavaBeans is that you can then use special JSP tags for working with the beans. This is illustrated by the JSP in figure 2-8.

Most of this code is HTML code. In fact, the only other code in this page is the three special JSP tags that are shaded. This makes JSPs easy to write if you know HTML.

The three JSP tags shown in this figure are *Expression Language* (*EL*) tags, and they're easy to identify because they begin with a dollar sign ($) followed by an opening brace ({), and they end with a closing brace (}). These tags work because the servlet in figure 2-6 stored the User object as an attribute of the request object with a name of user. In addition, this works because the User object has getEmail, getFirstName, and getLastName methods that provide access to the data that's stored in the User object.

Although it's possible to embed Java code in a JSP, that's generally considered a bad practice. Instead, it's considered a good practice to restructure the app to move the Java code into a servlet that forwards the request and response objects to the JSP. That way, the servlet does the processing, and the JSP provides the HTML for the user interface. With this approach, the JSP doesn't require any embedded Java code, only special JSP tags like the ones shown in this figure. And that means that the web designer can develop the JSPs with minimal interaction with the Java programmer, and the Java programmer can develop the servlets without worrying about the HTML.

When a JSP is requested for the first time, the JSP engine (which is part of the servlet/JSP engine) converts the JSP code into a servlet and compiles the servlet. Then, the JSP engine loads that servlet into the servlet engine, which runs it. For subsequent requests, the JSP engine runs the servlet that corresponds to the JSP. In the old days, this sometimes led to a delay when the JSP was requested for the first time. Today, most servlet/JSP engines precompile JSPs to avoid that delay.

The thanks.jsp file

```
<!doctype html>
<html>
<head>
    <meta charset="utf-8">
    <title>Murach's Java Servlets and JSP</title>
    <link rel="stylesheet" href="styles/main.css" type="text/css"/>
</head>

<body>
    <h1>Thanks for joining our email list</h1>

    <p>Here is the information that you entered:</p>

    <label>Email:</label>
    <span>${user.email}</span><br>
    <label>First Name:</label>
    <span>${user.firstName}</span><br>
    <label>Last Name:</label>
    <span>${user.lastName}</span><br>

    <p>To enter another email address, click on the Back
    button in your browser or the Return button shown
    below.</p>

    <form action="" method="get">
        <input type="hidden" name="action" value="join">
        <input type="submit" value="Return">
    </form>

</body>
</html>
```

Description

- A *JavaServer Page* (*JSP*) consists of special Java tags such as *Expression Language* (*EL*) tags that are embedded within HTML code. An EL tag begins with a dollar sign ($).

- When a JSP is first requested, the JSP engine translates it into a servlet and compiles it. Then, the servlet is run by the servlet engine. In the old days, this often led to a delay the first time a JSP was requested after it was compiled. Today, most servlet/JSP engines precompile JSPs in order to avoid that delay.

Figure 2-8   The JSP for the second page

Perspective

The primary goal of this chapter has been to show you how to use the MVC pattern to structure a web application. In addition, this chapter has presented the different types of files that you need to work with in a servlet/JSP application. These files include HTML, JSP, CSS, servlet, Java, and XML files. In the next chapter, you'll learn how to use NetBeans to work with these types of files.

As you review this chapter, you may notice that it doesn't include the code for the UserDB class. For now, all you need to know is that the insert method of the UserDB class adds the data that's stored in a User object to the database for the application. Later, in section 3, you'll learn about two different approaches to working with databases.

Summary

- The *Model 1 pattern* uses JSPs to handle all of the processing and presentation for the application. It's generally considered a bad practice.

- The *Model 2* pattern, also known as the *Model-View-Controller* (*MVC*) *pattern*, uses business objects to define the *model*, HTML pages and JSPs to define the *view*, and servlets to act as the *controller*.

- The data for the business objects in a web application are stored in *data stores* like files and databases. This can be referred to as *persistent data storage*. To work with the data store, you typically use a *data access class*.

- An HTML file contains the tags that define the content of the web page and a *CSS* (*Cascading Style Sheet*) file contains the formatting for the web pages.

- A *servlet* is a special type of Java class that runs on a server and does the processing for the dynamic web pages of a web application.

- A web.xml file describes how a web application should be configured when it is deployed on a server. As a result, it's known as the *deployment descriptor* (*DD*).

- A *JavaBean*, or *bean*, is a Java class that (1) provides a zero-argument constructor, (2) provides get and set methods for all of its private instance variables, and (3) implements the Serializable or Externalizable interface.

- An *Enterprise JavaBean* (*EJB*) is similar in some ways to a regular JavaBean. However, EJBs are more complex and difficult to code than JavaBeans and aren't necessary for most websites.

- Since JavaBeans are just Java classes, they are a type of *plain old Java object* (*POJO*).

- A *JavaServer Page* (*JSP*) consists of special Java tags such as *Expression Language* (*EL*) tags that are embedded within HTML code. An EL tag begins with a dollar sign ($).

3

How to use NetBeans and Tomcat

This chapter shows how to use the NetBeans IDE for developing Java web applications with servlets and JavaServer Pages. We recommend that you use this IDE with this book because we think it's the easiest and most intuitive way to get started. If you prefer to use another IDE, you can do that. But our recommendation is that you use NetBeans with this book. Then, when you're done with this book, you can switch to whatever IDE you prefer.

Similarly, this chapter shows how to run Java web applications on the Tomcat server. We recommend that you use this server for this book because it's the most commonly used server for servlet/JSP applications. However, if you prefer to use another server such as GlassFish, you should be able to do that too.

How to get started with NetBeans

Appendixes A (PC) and B (Mac) show how to install and configure NetBeans. Once you've done that, you can use NetBeans to create new applications and to open old applications. Then, you can use NetBeans to build, deploy, and run those applications.

How to start NetBeans

When you start NetBeans for the first time, it may display a Start Page tab like the one in figure 3-1. Since you don't need this Start Page tab to work with NetBeans, you can close it if you like. To do that, click the X that's displayed on the right side of the tab.

If you're curious to see what version of Java NetBeans uses by default, you can select the Java Platforms command from the Tools menu to display the Java Platform Manager dialog box. By default, NetBeans uses the latest version of Java that's installed on your system, which is usually what you want. However, if you want to use another version of Java, you can install that version of Java on your system and use the Java Platform Manager to specify that version of Java.

The Start page

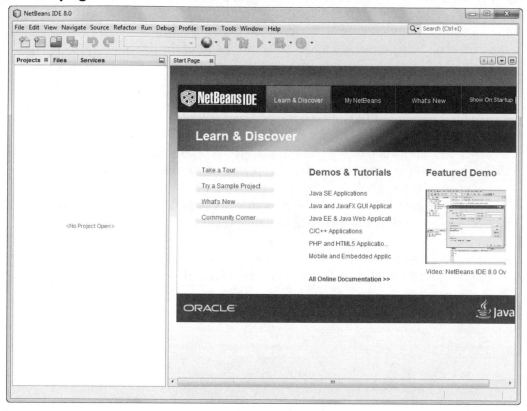

Description

- You can start NetBeans just as you would start any other program.
- When you start NetBeans for the first time, it displays a Start Page tab like the one shown above.
- You can use the Tools→Java Platforms command to find out what version of Java the NetBeans IDE is using.

Figure 3-1   How to start NetBeans

How to create a new web application

Figure 3-2 shows how to create a new NetBeans project for a web application. Essentially, a *project* is a folder that contains all of the files that make up an application. To create a new project, select the New Project command from the File menu. Then, NetBeans displays a New Project dialog box like the first one in this figure.

In the New Project box, you select the Java Web category and the Web Application option. Then, when you click on the Next button, NetBeans displays a New Web Application dialog box like the second one in this figure. In this dialog box, you can enter a name for the project. In this figure, for example, the project name is "testApp".

After you enter the name for the project, you can select the folder that the project should be stored in. In this figure, for example, the application is stored in this folder:

`\murach\servlet_and_jsp\netbeans\ex_starts`

If you install the source code for this book as described in appendix A (PC) or B (Mac), all of the applications for this book are stored in subfolders of the netbeans folder.

The first dialog box for creating a new web application

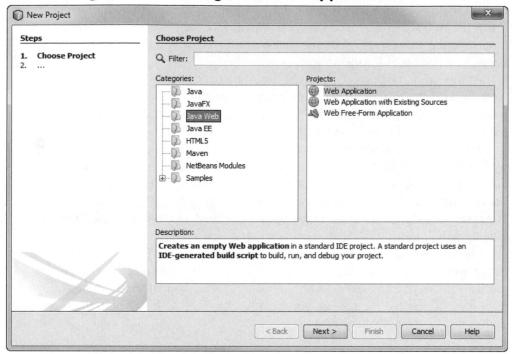

The second dialog box for creating a new web application

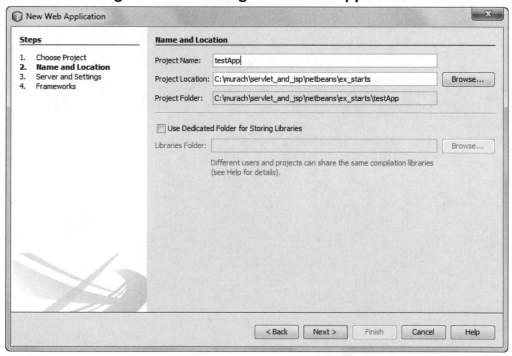

Figure 3-2   How to create a new web application (part 1 of 2)

When you click on the Next button, NetBeans displays a Server and Settings options dialog box like the third one in this figure. In this dialog box, you can select the web server and Java EE version to use for the project. If you want to change the web server for the project later on, you can do that by using the Properties command for the project.

At this point, you can click on the Finish button to create the project. Then, NetBeans creates a folder that corresponds to the project name. This folder contains the folders and files for a web application that contains a single HTML page. It also contains some other files that are used to configure the project.

These configuration files include a *build script* that's automatically generated by NetBeans. This build script is a standard Apache Ant script, and it specifies how NetBeans builds and deploys the application when you run it. Since this build script usually works the way you want it to, you'll rarely need to modify it. However, you should know that this script is required and that NetBeans uses it when you build, run, and debug your project.

Please note that if you click on the Next button instead of the Finish button in the third dialog box in this figure, a fourth dialog box for selecting frameworks is displayed. However, you won't need to select any of these frameworks as you use this book. As a result, you can click on the Finish button in the fourth dialog box to create the new project.

The third dialog box for creating a new web application

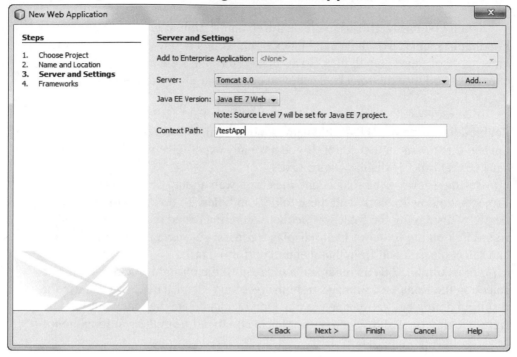

Description

- To create a new project, select the File→New Project command. When you complete the third dialog box, you can click on the Finish button. Or, you can click on the Next button to display a fourth dialog box, make no entries, and then click the Finish button.

Figure 3-2   How to create a new web application (part 2 of 2)

How to use the Projects window

When you use NetBeans to create a web application, it creates an application that has an HTML file named index.html. At this point, you may want to view some of these default files. To do that, you can use the Projects window to expand or collapse the folders. Then, you can open a file by double-clicking on it.

In figure 3-3, for example, I expanded the Web Pages folder and double-clicked on the HTML file named index.html. When I did, NetBeans opened this file in its text editor. If you have any experience with HTML, you can see that this file displays some text.

Besides viewing the folders and files for a web application, you can use the Projects window to work with these folders and files. To do that, you typically begin by displaying the folder or file that you're interested in. Then, you can right-click on the folder or file to display a context-sensitive menu. Finally, you can select a command from that menu to perform a task.

For example, you can rename the index.html file by right-clicking on it and selecting the Rename command from the resulting menu. Then, you can use the resulting dialog box to rename the file. Or, you can delete the index.html file by right-clicking on it and selecting the Delete command from the resulting menu.

The default web application

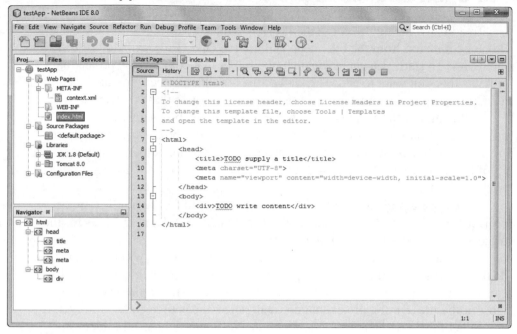

Description

- When you use NetBeans to create a web application, it creates a web application that includes an HTML file that displays some text.
- To view the files that are available for a web application, you can expand or collapse the folders that are available in the Projects window.
- To open a file in the appropriate editor, you can double-click on the file.
- To rename a file, you can right-click on it, select the Rename command or the Refactor→Rename command, and respond to the resulting dialog box.
- To delete a file, you can right-click on it, select the Delete command, and respond to the resulting dialog box.
- To display the Projects window if it isn't visible, use the Window→Projects command.

Figure 3-3   How to use the Projects window

How to open and close projects

To add an existing project to the Projects window, you can select the Open Project command from the File menu and use the Open Project dialog box in figure 3-4. To start, you can navigate to the folder that contains the project or projects that you want to add. Then, all of the possible projects are displayed in the Open Project dialog box so you can select the project that you want to add.

In this figure, for example, the Open Project dialog box shows all of the projects that you'll use as you do the exercises for this book. Note that they are stored in the ex_starts subfolder that's in the NetBeans folder. In contrast, all of the book applications are stored in the book_apps subfolder that's in the NetBeans folder.

To remove a project from the Projects window, you can right-click on the project and select the Close command. Since this doesn't delete the files for the project, you can easily re-open the project.

Alternately, you can remove the project from the Projects window and delete its files by right-clicking on the project and selecting the Delete command. Then, NetBeans prompts you to confirm the deletion. By default, NetBeans deletes most of the files for the project but does not delete the source code. However, if you select the "Also Delete Sources" option, NetBeans deletes all folders and files for the project. Of course, you'll only want to use this option if you want to permanently delete all of the files for the project.

The Open Project dialog box

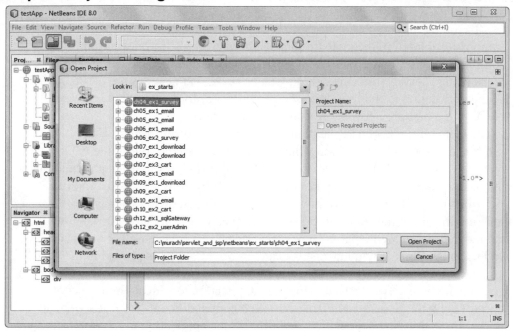

Description

- To open a project for a web application in the Projects window, select the File→Open Project command. Then, use the Open Project dialog box to locate the folder for the project and click on the Open Project button.

- To remove a project from the Projects window, right-click on the project in the Projects window and select the Close command.

Figure 3-4   How to open and close projects

How to build, deploy, and run a web application

To run the project that's currently selected, you can press F6 or click the Run Project button in the toolbar. Then, NetBeans builds the current project by compiling all files that need to be compiled, deploys the files for the project to the specified server, starts the default web browser, and displays the first page of the application in that web browser. In figure 3-5, for example, the browser displays the first page for the ch04email application.

When you run a web application, NetBeans displays information about the run process in the Output window that's displayed at the bottom of the main NetBeans window. For example, the "ch04email (run)" tab displays information that shows that this application has been successfully built, deployed, and run.

In addition, the Output window includes two Tomcat windows that display information about the status of the Tomcat server. One Tomcat window shows the messages that are displayed when the Tomcat server is started or stopped, and the other Tomcat window displays any information that's printed to the Tomcat log files.

When you use NetBeans to deploy an application to a local Tomcat server, it doesn't copy the folders and files for the web application into Tomcat's webapps folder. Instead, it maps the folders and files for the application to the root folder on the web server, which has the same effect as copying all of the folders and files for the web application into Tomcat's webapps folder.

When you test a web application, you may want to display another page besides the first page of the web application. Or, you may want to test a servlet without running a JSP first. To do that, you can run a specific file by right-clicking on the file and selecting the Run File command. This deploys the web application and displays the file in the default web browser.

In addition, you may want to make sure that your web application runs correctly with all types of web browsers. To do that, you can test the web application with multiple web browsers. In this figure, Google Chrome is the default browser. But you can change the default browser by selecting the Tools→Options command, selecting the General category, and selecting any browser that's installed on your computer.

The web browser that's displayed when you run a project

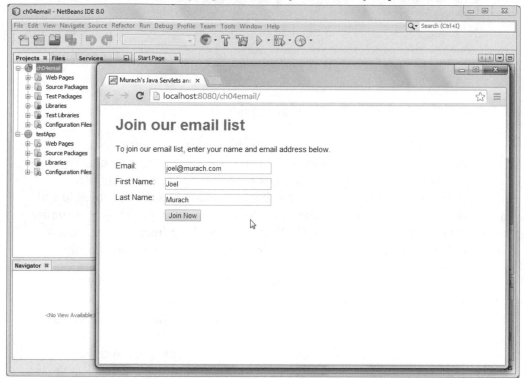

Description

- To run the current project, press F6 or select the Run Project command from the toolbar or the Run menu.

- When you run a web application, NetBeans automatically compiles all files that need to be compiled, deploys the files for the project to the specified server, starts the default web browser, and displays the first page of the application in that browser.

- To run a specific file, right-click on the file and select the Run File command. This deploys the web application and displays the file in the default web browser.

- To change the default browser, select the Tools→Options command, select the General category, and select the browser that you want to use.

- To view information about a test run, use the tabs in the Output window. To open this window, use the Window→Output command. To clear the data from one of the tabs, right-click in the window and select the Clear command.

- When NetBeans deploys an application to a local Tomcat server, it doesn't copy the folders and files for the application to the webapps folder on the web server. Instead, it maps the folders and files for the application to the webapps folder.

Figure 3-5   How to build, deploy, and run a web application

How to work with HTML and JSP files

Once you know how to run the default web application, you're ready to learn how to use NetBeans to create your own web application. To do that, you can start by adding HTML and JSP files to your web application.

How to add an HTML or JSP file

To add an HTML or JSP file to an application, you can right-click on the Web Pages folder or one of its subfolders and select the appropriate command. Then, you can use the resulting dialog box to specify the name of the file.

In figure 3-6, for example, the New JSP File dialog box is being used to add a JSP file named test.jsp to the Web Pages folder. However, you can use a similar technique to add an HTML file to the Web Pages folder. Either way, NetBeans automatically adds the extension to the file, so you don't need to include the extension in the filename.

The main difference between HTML and JSP files is that the dialog box for JSP files allows you to specify whether you want to use Standard Syntax or XML Syntax. For most JSP files, you can select the JSP File (Standard Syntax) option.

If you want to add an HTML or JSP file to a subfolder of the Web Pages folder, you can right-click on that folder in the Projects window and select the appropriate command. If, for example, you have a folder named cust_serv, you can right-click on that folder to add a file to it. Or, you can use the Folder text box to specify a location or to create a new subfolder. Either way, the Created File text box shows the complete path and filename for the file that will be created.

The New File dialog box

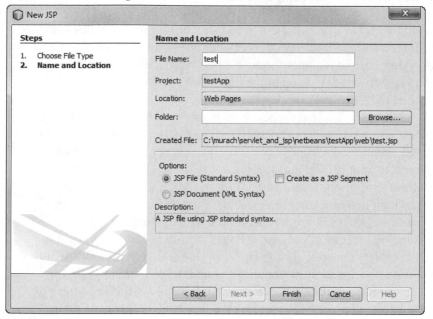

Description

- To add an HTML file, right-click on the Web Pages folder or one of its subfolders and select the New→HTML command. Then, use the resulting dialog box to specify the name and location of the file.

- To add a JSP file, right-click on the Web Pages folder or one of its subfolders and select the New→JSP command. Then, use the resulting dialog box to specify the name and location of the file.

- To enter a name for the HTML or JSP file, enter the name in the File Name text box. Note that you don't need to enter the extension for the file.

- To specify a location, you can use the Folder text box. To create a new subfolder, enter the name in the Folder text box. To select an existing folder, click the Browse button to the right of the Folder text box and use the resulting dialog box to select the folder where you want to store the file.

- The Created File text box shows the complete path and filename for the file that will be created.

- For most JSP files, you can use the JSP File (Standard Syntax) option.

Figure 3-6   How to add an HTML or JSP file

How to edit an HTML or JSP file

When you add an HTML or JSP file to a website, NetBeans generates some starting code. Before you can use these files in your application, you need to delete or modify this code so it's appropriate for your application. To do that, you can use the Projects window to open the file in a text editor that's designed for working with HTML and JSP files, as shown in figure 3-7.

In general, you can use the same types of techniques with this editor that you use with other text editors. However, since this editor is specifically designed to work with HTML and JSP files, it provides several features that can help you work more efficiently with HTML and JSP tags.

First, this editor displays different parts of the HTML and JSP syntax in different colors, which makes it easier to work with the code. In particular, this editor clearly identifies JSP tags so you can tell them apart from HTML tags.

Second, when you enter an HTML or JSP tag, the *code completion* feature often helps you complete the code for the tags. If it doesn't, you can activate this feature by pressing Ctrl+Spacebar as you make your entries. In this figure, for example, you can see the list of entries that are automatically displayed after you enter the starting bracket for a tag followed by the first letter of the tag's name.

Third, NetBeans displays red or yellow markers if you enter a tag incorrectly or if you attempt to use a tag or attribute that has been deprecated. Then, you can position the mouse pointer over a marker or click on a marker to get more information about an error. This helps you avoid some entry errors that can take a long time to fix without this kind of help. However, if you find these markers to be distracting, you can disable the error checking by clicking on the marker and selecting the appropriate option.

Fourth, if you don't want to enter a tag manually, you can use the Palette window to add HTML or JSP tags to the file. To do that, you can drag the tag you want to add from the Palette window and drop it into the appropriate location in the editor window. Then, NetBeans may prompt you with a dialog box that gets some information about the tag before it inserts the code for the tag into the window.

When you do the exercises for this chapter, you'll get a chance to experiment with these features. At this point, though, you don't need to understand this code. You just need to understand how to use this editor to edit the code. Then, as you progress through this book, you'll learn more about writing code like this.

The HTML and JSP editor

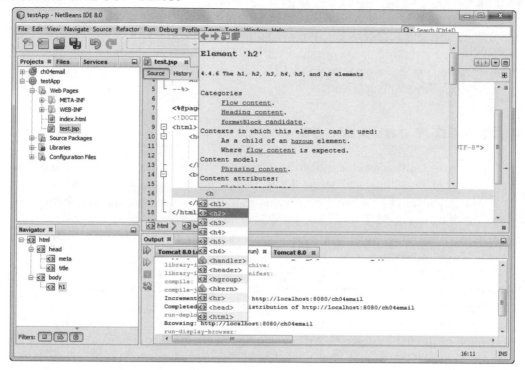

Description

- When you add a new HTML or JSP file to a web application, NetBeans includes some starting code. You can delete this code or modify it for use in your application.

- To edit source code, you can use the same techniques that you use with other text editors.

- After you enter the starting bracket for an HTML or JSP tag, the *code completion* feature provides a list of possible entries. Then, you can select an item and press the Tab or Enter key to insert the starting code for the tag.

- To insert the ending code for a tag right after the starting tag, press Ctrl+Spacebar. You can also press Ctrl+Spacebar to activate the code completion feature at other points in your entries.

- To open the Palette window, use the Window→IDE Tools→Palette command. Then, to add HTML or JSP tags, drag the tag you want to add from the Palette window into the code editor. Or, move the insertion point to where you want to insert the code and double-click on the tag in the Palette window. For most of these tags, NetBeans will prompt you with a dialog box that gets some information before it inserts the code into the code editor.

- To identify lines of code with entry errors, NetBeans displays yellow or red markers in the bar at the left of the editor window. Then, you can position the mouse pointer over a marker or click on a marker to get more information about an error.

Figure 3-7   How to edit an HTML or JSP file

How to work with Java files

Once you add HTML and JSP files to a web application, you typically need to add one or more regular Java classes. In addition, you typically need to add one or more *servlets*, which are special Java classes that you can use to control the flow of a Java web application.

How to add a Java class

For any significant web application, it's generally considered a best practice to use regular Java classes to define the business objects for the application. You may also want to use regular Java classes to handle data access and to help organize the Java code. If you have some Java programming experience or if you've read *Murach's Java Programming*, you should already know how to code regular Java classes.

To add a Java class to a web application, you can right-click on the folder in the Projects window in which you want to add the class. By default, that's the Source Packages folder or one of its subfolders. Then, you can select the New→Java Class command and use the New Java Class dialog box to specify the name of the file. In figure 3-8, for example, the dialog box creates a class named User.

If necessary, you can also specify a package for the file. A *package* is a special type of folder that's used to store and organize the classes within an application or library. In this figure, for example, the dialog box creates the User class in the murach.business package, which is stored in the Source Packages folder.

If you don't enter a package when you add a new class, the New Java Class dialog box displays a message that encourages you to enter a package for the class. Although you don't have to specify a package for every class, it's a good programming practice. That's why all of the classes presented in this book are stored in packages.

The New Java Class dialog box

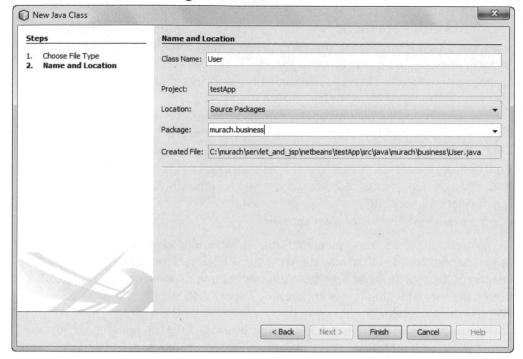

Description

- To add a Java class, right-click on one of the project folders and select the New→Java Class command. Then, use the resulting dialog box to specify the name and location of the file.
- To specify a package for the class, use the Package combo box to select an existing package or to enter the name for a new package.

Figure 3-8   How to add a Java class

How to add a servlet

Since a servlet is a special type of Java class, the procedure for adding a servlet to a web application is similar to the procedure for adding a Java class. In particular, the first dialog box in figure 3-9 is similar to the dialog box shown in the previous figure. Here, the first dialog box specifies that a class named TestServlet should be stored in the murach.test package.

However, a servlet requires some configuration information that isn't required for a regular Java class. In particular, you typically map a servlet to a URL or a URL pattern so it can be requested by a web browser. In this figure, for example, the servlet named TestServlet is mapped to the /test URL pattern. Since this servlet is being added to the testApp project, a browser can request this servlet with this URL:

`http://localhost:8080/testApp/test`

With the servlet 3.0 specification (Tomcat 7.0) and later, you can use the @WebServlet annotation to map the servlet to a URL pattern as shown in chapter 5. To do that, make sure the "Add information to deployment descriptor" box in the second dialog box is unchecked. Then, NetBeans generates the @WebServlet annotation for the servlet.

However, prior to the servlet 3.0 specification, the URL mapping must be stored in the web.xml file for the application. To do that, check the "Add information" check box. Then, NetBeans automatically adds this mapping to the web.xml file for the application, which is usually what you want.

If you want to change this mapping later, you can edit the web.xml file for the web application or the @WebServlet annotation for the servlet. In chapter 5, you'll learn more about the pros and cons of these servlet mapping techniques.

The first New Servlet dialog box

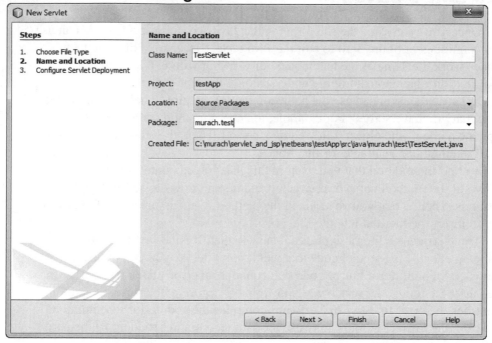

The second dialog box

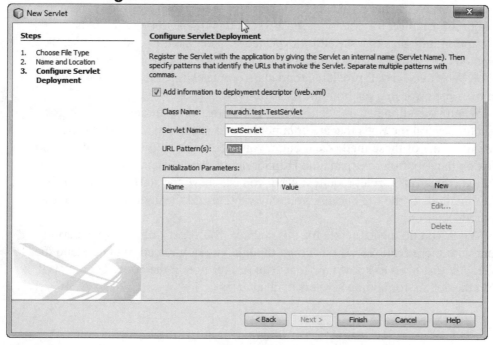

Description

- To add a servlet, right-click on the package, select the New→Servlet command, and use the resulting dialog boxes to specify a name and URL for the servlet.

Figure 3-9   How to add a servlet

How to edit a Java file

Once you've created the file for a regular Java class or a servlet, you can use the techniques in figure 3-10 to edit the Java code. Since some of these techniques work the same as the techniques for working with HTML and JSP files, you shouldn't have much trouble understanding them.

In particular, you can use the code completion feature to help you complete code that you have started. For example, to enter a method for an object, you can type the name of the object followed by a period. Then, the editor displays a list of all the methods available for that object.

To find the method that you want in this list, you can enter the first letter or two of the method name or use the up and down arrows to scroll through the methods. Then, when you've selected the method, you can press the Tab or Enter key to insert the method into the file.

The NetBeans editor also makes it easy to identify and fix errors. In this context, an *error* is a line of code that won't compile. As you enter code, the editor often identifies a line of code that contains an error with a red marker in the bar at the left of the window as shown in this figure. Otherwise, the editor identifies the error lines when NetBeans compiles the code prior to running it. In addition, the Project window may use the same red marker to identify the parts of the project that contain errors.

If you position the mouse pointer over an error marker in the editor or click on a marker, NetBeans displays a description of the error. This usually provides enough information for you to fix the error. In this figure, for example, the description indicates that the editor expected the statement to end with a semi-colon. When you fix this problem, the editor removes the error marker from the editor. When you fix all problems for a class or a package, the Project window removes the error marker from the class or the package.

When you edit a new servlet, you'll see that the file contains the starting code for several methods that are commonly used in servlets. To display the code for some of these methods, though, you need to scroll to the end of file and click on the + button to expand the HttpServlet methods. Then, you can edit the methods that your servlet requires. Also, you can leave the starting code for the other methods in the file because you may want to add the code for one of these methods later on.

When you do the exercises for this chapter, you'll get a chance to experiment with these features. At this point, though, you don't need to understand the code. You just need to know how to use this editor to edit the code. Then, you'll learn the details for coding servlets in chapter 5.

The Java editor with an error displayed

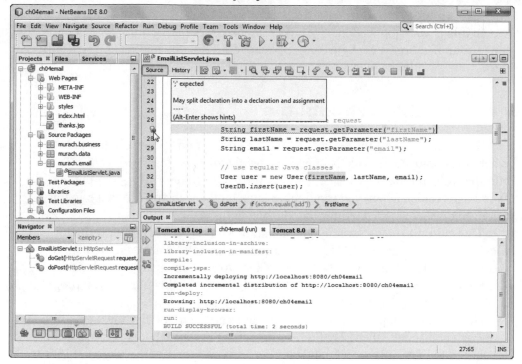

Description

- When you add a Java class or servlet to a web application, NetBeans includes some starting code. You can delete this code or modify it for use in your application.

- To enter and edit source code, you can use the same types of techniques that you use with most code editors.

- After you enter a class or object name and a period, the code completion feature provides a list of possible entries. Then, you can select an item and press the Tab or Enter key to insert the code into the file.

- To activate the code completion feature at other points in your entries, you can press Ctrl+Spacebar.

- To identify lines of code that contain errors, NetBeans displays red markers in the bar at the left of the code editor window. Then, you can position the mouse pointer over a marker or click on a marker to get more information about an error.

Figure 3-10   How to edit a Java file

How to work with XML files

In a Java web application, XML files are used to store information about how the application is configured. In particular, a Java web application typically has a web.xml file that contains some basic configuration information.

How to edit the web.xml file

Since the web.xml file describes how the application will be configured when it is deployed, this file is known as the *deployment descriptor* (*DD*). To edit the web.xml file, you can expand the WEB-INF folder that's stored in the Web Pages folder. Then, you can double-click on the web.xml file that's in this folder to display an XML editor like the one in figure 3-11.

This editor displays several tabs that allow you to work with the web.xml file. To manually edit the XML file, you can click on the Source tab to display the source code for the entire XML file. Then, you can manually edit this file. For now, don't worry if you don't understand the tags in this file. As you progress through this book, you'll learn more about them.

However, if you prefer to use a graphical interface to modify the web.xml file, you can use the other tabs. For example, the Servlets tab lets you map servlet classes to their URLs, and the Pages tab lets you specify the welcome files for the application. These tabs generate the required XML code.

After you edit a web.xml file, you can check to see if it is still valid by checking it against its *XML schema*, which is an XML file that specifies what elements are valid. To do that, you can right-click on the file and select the Validate XML command from the resulting menu. Then, NetBeans displays the results of the validation within the Output window, including any errors.

When you modify a web.xml file and use NetBeans to run the application, NetBeans automatically saves the file and forces Tomcat to read it again. However, if you notice that the changes to the web.xml file aren't taking effect, you may need to save the web.xml file and restart Tomcat. That's because Tomcat reads the web.xml file for an application when it starts. Later in this chapter, you'll learn one easy way to use NetBeans to restart Tomcat.

How to edit other XML files

To edit any XML file, you can double-click on it in the Projects window. Then, NetBeans opens the file in an XML editor that looks similar to the second screen in this figure. For example, when you use NetBeans to create a new web application, it automatically adds an XML file named context.xml to the META-INF folder. To view or edit this file, you can begin by double-clicking on it in the Projects window.

The XML editor with the Pages tab displayed

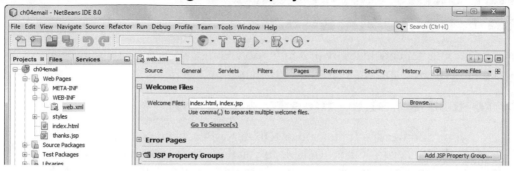

The XML editor with the Source tab displayed

Description

- The web.xml file is known as the *deployment descriptor* (*DD*).

- To edit an XML file, double-click on it to open it. Then, you can use the tabs across the top of the page to modify the web.xml file. Of these tabs, you can use the Source tab to manually edit the file in the XML editor.

- To validate an XML file against its schema, you can right-click on the file and select the Validate XML command from the resulting menu. Then, the results of the validation will be displayed in an XML Check window within the Output window.

- When you run an application after you modify its web.xml file, NetBeans saves the file and forces Tomcat to read it again so the changes will take effect. Then, if the elements in the web.xml file aren't in the correct order or if there is another problem with the file, the errors will be noted in the Tomcat and Tomcat Log windows within NetBeans.

Figure 3-11   How to work with XML files

Other skills for working with web applications

This chapter concludes by presenting some other skills that you may need as you develop web applications with NetBeans.

How to add existing files to a project

If you're converting from another IDE to NetBeans, you may have existing HTML, JSP, or Java files available to you that aren't stored in a NetBeans project. In that case, you may want to add those files to a NetBeans project. To do that, you can use the Windows Explorer (PC) or Finder (Mac) to copy the files into an appropriate folder in the Projects window.

For example, on a Windows system, you can copy a JSP file into a NetBeans project by using the Windows Explorer to locate the file, right-clicking on the file, and selecting the Copy command. That places the file on the clipboard. Then, you can switch to the NetBeans IDE, use the Projects window to display the Web Pages folder or one of its subfolders, right-click on the folder you want, and select the Paste command to paste the file from the clipboard into the NetBeans project.

To copy a Java file, you can use a similar technique. However, it usually makes sense to start by copying the folder that corresponds with the package for the Java class. Then, you can paste that folder into the Source Packages folder in the Projects window. That way, NetBeans stores the files in the correct packages.

When you work with the Projects window, you should realize that the folders in this window aren't the actual folders that are stored on your hard drive. Instead, NetBeans maps these folders to the actual folders that are stored on your hard drive. If you want to view the actual folders that are stored on your hard drive, you can use the Files window as shown in figure 3-12. Here, the Web Pages folder in the Projects window maps to the web folder in the Files window, and the Source Packages folder in the Projects window maps to the src folder in the Files window.

In addition, the build\web folder in the Files window contains the files for the web application after it has been built, and the dist folder contains the WAR file for the application. A *WAR (web archive) file* is a compressed file that contains all of the files in the build\web directory.

How to deploy a web application to a remote server

After you've tested a web application, you can deploy it to a remote server by copying its WAR file from the dist folder to the appropriate folder on the remote server. To do that, you may need to use an FTP application like the one described in chapter 1. Once the WAR file has been copied to the remote server, the server can run the web application. In most cases, the remote server extracts all the files from the WAR file before it begins running the application.

The Files window for the ch04email project

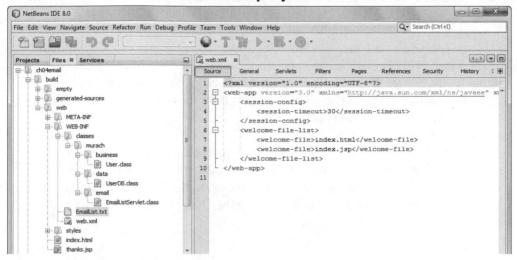

The folders that NetBeans uses

Folder	Description
build\web	Contains all necessary folders and files for the web application after it has been built.
dist	Contains the WAR file for the application.
nbproject	Contains the configuration files and build scripts for the NetBeans project.
src	Contains the source code for the Java files and servlets.
test	Contains the source code for any automated testing for the project.
web	Contains the HTML, JSP, and XML files for the application.

How to add existing files to a project

- Copy the files from the Windows Explorer or Mac Finder and paste them into an appropriate folder in the Projects window or the Files window.

How to deploy an application to a remote server

- Copy the WAR file for the application from the dist folder to the appropriate folder for web applications on the remote server.

Description

- The Files window shows the actual folder structure that's used for storing the files of an application. The Projects window shows the logical structure of these folders and files.

Figure 3-12   How to use the Files window

How to work with a web application server

As you develop a web application, you may need to use NetBeans to start and stop a server. To do that, you begin by displaying a Services window like the one in figure 3-13. Then, you can expand the Servers group to display a server. In this figure, for example, the Tomcat server is displayed. Next, you can right-click on the server and select a command from the resulting menu to start, stop, or restart the server. Of course, restarting a server has the same effect as stopping and starting a server.

In addition, you may want to start, stop, or undeploy any of the applications that are running on a Tomcat server. To do that, you can use the Services window shown in this figure. For example, you can undeploy an application by right-clicking on the application and selecting the Undeploy command from the resulting menu.

The Services window with the Servers group displayed

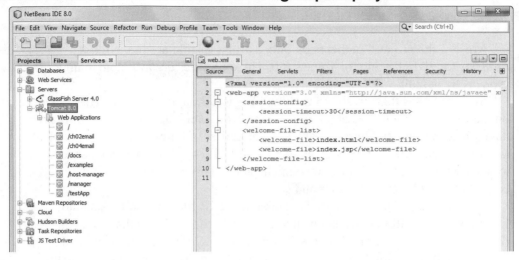

Description

- To open the Services window, use the Window→Services command. The Services window shows the services and other runtime resources that are available to NetBeans.

- To view a server, expand the Servers group. Then, you can start, stop, restart, or refresh the server by right-clicking on the server and selecting the appropriate command.

- To view the web applications that are running on the Tomcat server, expand the Web Applications folder for the server. Then, you can start, stop, or undeploy a web application by right-clicking on the application and selecting the appropriate command. For this to work, you may need to run NetBeans as an administrator.

Note

- You can also start, stop, restart, or refresh the Tomcat server, by clicking on one of the symbols to the left of the Tomcat tab in the Output window or by right-clicking in the Tomcat tab in the Output window and selecting a command from the resulting menu.

Figure 3-13   How to use the Services window

How to add a class library or a JAR file to a project

Most of the projects in this book only use classes that are in the *class libraries* for JDK 1.8 and for Tomcat 8.0. These libraries are available to all projects by default.

To use classes that are stored in other libraries, though, you can right-click on the Libraries folder, select the Add Library command, and use the resulting dialog box to select the library that you want to use. In figure 3-14, for example, the Add Library dialog box is about to add the JSTL 1.2.2 library that's needed to work with JSTL tags as described in chapter 9. This class library actually consists of two JAR files: jstl.jar and standard.jar.

If the classes you want to use are stored in a JAR file that isn't a standard library, you can still make them available to your project. To do that, you can right-click on the Libraries folder, select the Add JAR/Folder command, and use the resulting dialog box to select the JAR file. For example, you can use this technique to add a database driver to the project.

Once you add a JAR file to a project, the JAR file appears under the Libraries folder in the Projects window and your application can use any classes within that JAR file.

The Add Library dialog box for the JSTL 1.2.2 library

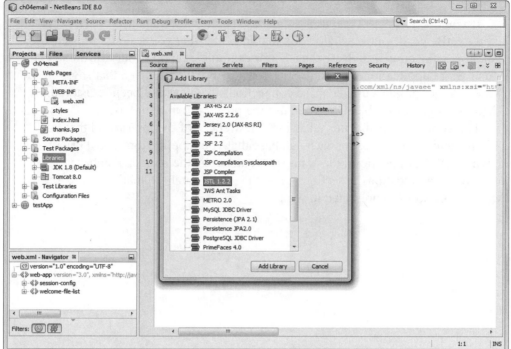

Description

- If you add a library or a JAR file to a project, the JRE will be able to find and run any of the classes within the JAR files that are added to the project. When the application is deployed, these JAR files will be stored in the application's WEB-INF\lib folder.

- To add a library file to the libraries for a project, right-click on the Libraries folder, select the Add Library command, and use the resulting dialog box to select the library. This may add one or more JAR files to the project.

- To add a JAR file to a project, right-click on the Libraries folder, select the Add JAR/Folder command and use the resulting dialog box to select the JAR file.

- To remove a JAR file from the libraries for a project, right-click on the JAR file and select the Remove command.

Figure 3-14   How to add a class library or a JAR file to a project

How to register a database connection

If you open a project that uses a database connection that hasn't been registered, NetBeans displays a dialog box that indicates that you need to register the database connection with NetBeans. If, for example, you open our downloadable Music Store application with NetBeans, a dialog box is displayed that says, "One or more projects use database connections that have not been registered." Then, to solve this problem, you can use the procedure in figure 3-15.

The good news is that this takes just a few clicks of the mouse and that you only have to do this once for each database that your applications use. For our downloadable applications, that's just two databases: the murach database that's used by the applications in section 3, and the music database that's used by the Music Store website presented in section 5.

The dialog box for resolving a database connection

The dialog box for registering the database connection

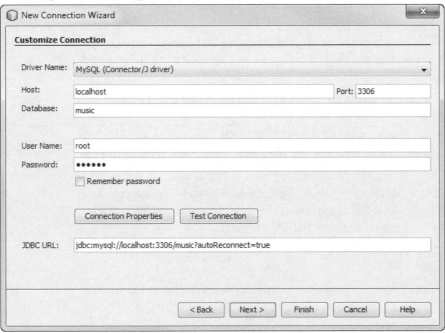

How to register a database connection for a project

1. Right-click on the project in the Project window and select the Resolve Data Source Problem command to display the Resolve Data Sources dialog box.

2. Select the data source that you want to resolve, and click the Add Connection button to display the New Database Connection dialog box.

3. If necessary, change any of the entries for the connection. Then, click on the OK button to register the database connection.

Figure 3-15   How to register a database connection

Perspective

The goal of this chapter has been to show you how to use the NetBeans IDE for developing Java web applications. We think that NetBeans will help you learn faster than you will with any other IDE. That's why we recommend that you use NetBeans as you do the exercises for this book. And that's why our downloadable source files have the directory and file structure that NetBeans requires.

If you prefer to use some other IDE, you will have to convert the NetBeans directory and file structure so it's appropriate for that IDE. If you're comfortable with doing that, you should be able to use this book with your IDE. If not, we recommend that you use NetBeans for doing the exercises for this book. Then, when you're done with this book, you can switch to the other IDE.

Summary

- The NetBeans IDE and the Tomcat web server are open-source, available for free, and run on all modern operating systems.

- A *project* is a folder that contains all of the folders and files that make up an application. You can use the Projects window to work with the folders and files of a project.

- You can run the project that's currently selected by pressing F6 or by clicking the Run Project button in the toolbar.

- You can use NetBeans to add and edit HTML, JSP, Java, servlet, and XML files. When you edit a file, you can use the *code completion* feature to help you enter code.

- Since the web.xml file describes how the application will be configured when it is deployed, this file is known as the *deployment descriptor* (*DD*). The web.xml file is stored in the WEB-INF folder.

- You can add existing folders and files to a project by copying them to the appropriate folders.

- You can use the Files window to view the physical locations of the folders and files for a project.

- You can deploy a web application to a remote server by copying its *WAR* (*web archive*) *file* from the dist folder for a project to the appropriate folder on the remote server.

- You can use the Services window to start or stop a server such as the Tomcat web server. In addition, you can use this window to undeploy a web application from a Tomcat server.

- You can add a library to a project by right-clicking on the Libraries folder, selecting the Add Library command, and using the resulting dialog box to select the library.

- If NetBeans displays a dialog box that indicates that you need to register the database connection, right-click on the project, select the Resolve Data Source Problem command, and use the resulting dialog boxes to register the database connection.

Before you do the exercises for this chapter

If you haven't already done so, you should install the software and source files for this book as described in appendix A (PC) or B (Mac). When you install the source code for this book, the starting points for the exercises are stored in the ex_starts directory:

`\murach\servlet_and_jsp\netbeans\ex_starts`

However, in this chapter, you'll run some of the applications presented in this book, and they are stored in the book_apps directory:

`\murach\servlet_and_jsp\netbeans\book_apps`

Exercise 3-1   Install and use the NetBeans IDE

This exercise makes sure that you can use NetBeans to run a web application on a Tomcat server.

Test NetBeans and Tomcat

1. Create a new project for a web application named testApp, and save it in the ex_starts directory.

2. Make sure this project uses the Tomcat server.

3. Use the Projects window to review the folders and files for the testApp project.

4. Run the testApp web application, and review the information that's in the NetBeans Output window.

Add a JSP file to the project

5. Add a JSP file named test.jsp to the project.

6. Edit the code for the test.jsp file so it includes this tag within its body tags:

   `<h2>Test JSP</h2>`

   To do that, type an opening bracket (<), select the h2 tag from the resulting list, and press the Enter key. Next, press the Enter key again to complete the tag, and type "Test JSP" within the tag.

7. Right-click on the test.jsp file in the Projects window, and select the Run File command to display this JSP in a browser.

8. Use the Window→IDE Tools→Palette command to open the Palette window, and click on the plus signs for HTML, HTML Forms, and JSP to expand these items. Then, drag the Text Input item to the test.jsp file right after the h2 tag that you just entered. In the dialog box that opens, type testName for the Name and click on the OK button. Note the HTML tags that are added to the JSP.

9. Right-click on the test.jsp file, and select the Run File command to display this JSP in a browser.

10. Press the F6 button to run the application. Note that the index.html file runs instead of the test.jsp file, which is usually what you want.

Add a servlet file to the project

11. Add a Java servlet named TestServlet to a package named murach.test, and map it to the /test URL.

12. In the editor window, scroll to the bottom of the TestServlet file and click on the + sign before the HttpServlet methods. That should expand the starting code for these methods. Then, note that the doGet and doPost methods call the processRequest method that's earlier in the servlet. You'll learn how to code the doGet and doPost methods of a servlet in chapter 5.

13. In the Projects window, right-click on the TestServlet file and select the Run File command. In the resulting dialog box, click OK. At this point, NetBeans should display a browser window with some text in it that indicates that this servlet has executed. Note that NetBeans uses the URL that you specified in step 11 to call the servlet.

14. Close the testApp project.

Exercise 3-2   Experiment with an existing application

This exercise gives you a chance to run and review one of the applications that has been downloaded from our website.

1. Open the ch02email project in the book_apps directory. Then, use the Project window to view the code that's stored in the HTML, JSP, Java, servlet, and XML files for this application.

2. Run this application to make sure that it runs correctly on your system. Then, enter a first name, last name, and email address into the application and click on the Join Now button. This should display the second page for the application.

3. Use the Files window to view the files for this application. Note that the web.xml file is stored in the web\WEB-INF folder.

4. Use the Services window to view the applications running on the Tomcat server.

5. Use the Services window to undeploy the ch02email application. To do that, you may need to run NetBeans as an administrator.

6. Close the ch02email project.

Exercise 3-3   Run web applications that use a database

This exercise has you run two of the web applications presented in this book that use a database. This forces you to register the connections for the two databases that are used by this book. For this to work, you must install and configure the MySQL database server as described in appendix A (PC) or B (Mac).

Use the murach database

1. Open the ch12email project that's in the book_apps directory.

2. If that displays a dialog box that says the database connection needs to be registered with NetBeans, click on the Close button for this dialog box. Then, right-click on the project, select the Resolve Data Sources Problem item, and use the resulting dialog boxes to resolve the data source problem and register the database connection for the murach database.

3. Run the application to see how it works. After you enter your name and email address and click on the Join Now button, your entries are saved to a MySQL database.

4. Close the project.

Use the music database

5. Open the musicStore application that's in the book_apps directory.

6. If necessary, resolve the data source problem and register the database connection for the music database.

7. Run the application to see how it works. When you browse through the catalog, the application is getting data from a MySQL database.

8. Close the project.

Were you able to do both parts of this exercise successfully?

If so, all of the software that you'll need for this book has been successfully installed and configured. Congratulations!

Section 2

Essential servlet and JSP skills

The best way to learn how to develop web applications is to start developing them. That's why the chapters in this section take a hands-on approach to application development. When you complete this section, you'll have the essential skills that you need for designing, coding, and testing servlet/JSP web applications.

To get you started right, chapter 4 shows you how to code HTML pages, which is a prerequisite for coding servlets or JavaServer Pages (JSPs). Then, chapter 5 shows you the basic skills for coding servlets. And chapter 6 shows you the basic skills for coding JSPs.

With that as background, you'll be ready to learn the other web programming essentials. To start, chapter 7 shows you how to work with sessions and cookies so your application can keep track of its users. Then, chapter 8 shows you more details for using JSP Expression Language (EL) in your JSPs. Chapter 9 shows you how to use the JSP Standard Tag Library (JSTL) in your JSPs. And chapter 10 shows you how to code custom JSP tags that you can use in your JSPs.

If you're familiar with previous editions of this book, you may notice that this section no longer includes a chapter on standard JSP tags for working with JavaBeans. That's because these tags have been replaced by EL. As a result, most programmers don't consider it a good practice to use these tags for new development. However, there is a brief description of these tags in chapter 6.

4

A crash course in HTML5 and CSS3

Chapter 2 presented the HTML and CSS for the Email List application. As a result, you should have a general idea of how the HTML and CSS works for this application.

Now, this chapter dives into the details of how HTML and CSS work for a modern web application. In general, the HTML should provide the content and structure for a web page, and the CSS should provide the formatting. That separates the concerns, and that's what you'll learn how to do in this chapter.

Of course, if you're already familiar with modern HTML and CSS techniques, you can skip or skim this chapter. On the other hand, if this chapter moves too quickly for you, or if you want to expand your HTML and CSS skills, we recommend *Murach's HTML5 and CSS3* as a companion to this book.

How to work with HTML

This chapter begins by reviewing the basic HTML elements that are necessary for most pages.

The starting HTML for a web page

When you use an IDE or other tool to create a new HTML page, it typically generates code like the first example in figure 4-1. Then, the second example shows how you can modify the generated code.

Here, the DOCTYPE declaration at the top of the page says that the web page uses HTML5. If you're familiar with the declarations for earlier versions of HTML, you know that they were far more complicated than that.

This declaration is followed by the html element that includes all of the other elements for the page. In the head element, you should code some text in the title element. The browser displays this text in its title bar or tab when the application is run. In this figure, for example, the browser shows the contents of the title element in the tab for the application.

When you use an external style sheet for the CSS, you also code a link element within the head element. This link element identifies the file that stores the external style sheet. You'll learn more about that in a moment.

Last, you can usually delete the generated div tags. Instead, you should use the HTML5 semantic elements shown later in this chapter to clearly identify the structure of a document.

The HTML that's generated for a new HTML page

```
<!DOCTYPE html>
<html>
    <head>
        <title>TODO supply a title</title>
        <meta charset="UTF-8">
        <meta name="viewport" content="width=device-width">
    </head>
    <body>
        <div>TODO write content</div>
    </body>
</html>
```

The HTML after it has been modified

```
<!DOCTYPE html>
<html>
    <head>
        <title>Murach's Java Servlets and JSP</title>
        <link rel="stylesheet" href="styles/main.css" type="text/css"/>
        <meta charset="UTF-8">
    </head>
    <body>
        <div>TODO write content</div>
    </body>
</html>
```

The title displayed in the browser's tab

Description

- The DOCTYPE element specifies that the document uses HTML5.
- The title element specifies the name that the browser shows in its title bar or tab.
- The link element references the external style sheet that contains the CSS for the page.

Figure 4-1   The starting HTML for a web page

How to code HTML elements

Figure 4-2 shows how to code *HTML elements* within an *HTML document*. To start, each HTML element is coded within a *tag* that starts with an opening bracket (<) and ends with a closing bracket (>). For example, <h1>, <p>, and <br> are all HTML tags.

Most HTML elements are made up of three parts. The *start tag* marks the start of the element. It consists of the element name (such as h1) plus one or more optional *attributes* (such as src or alt) that provide additional information for the tag. After the start tag is the *content*, which is the text or other data that makes up the element. After the content is the *end tag* that marks the end of the element. The end tag consists of a slash followed by the element's name.

Not all HTML elements have content and end tags, though. For instance, the br and img elements don't have closing tags. These can be referred to as *self-closing tags*.

Most attributes are coded with an attribute name, an equals sign, and a value in quotation marks, as shown in the second group of examples in this figure. Here, for example, the a element has an href attribute that provides the URL that the link should go to when it is clicked, as well as a title attribute that provides the text that's displayed for the link.

Boolean attributes, however, can be coded with just the name of the attribute. For instance, the checked attribute for the input element in the second group indicates that the checked attribute is "on", so the check box that this element represents is checked. If a Boolean attribute isn't coded, the attribute is considered to be "off".

You can also code *comments* within an HTML document as shown in the second to last example in this figure. That way, you can describe sections of code that might be confusing. You can also use comments to *comment out* a portion of HTML code. That way, the code is ignored when the web page is displayed in a browser. That can be useful when testing a web page.

If you want to code a space within a line that the web browser doesn't ignore, you can use   (for non-breaking space) as shown in the last example in this figure. This is just one of the many *character entities* that you can use to display special characters in HTML. Each character entity starts with an ampersand (&) and ends with a semicolon (;).

Some of the elements are *block elements* and some are *inline elements*. The difference is that by default block elements are displayed on their own lines. In contrast, inline elements flow to the right of preceding elements and don't start new lines. As a result, you need to use a br element after an inline element if you want to start a new line after it.

Common HTML elements

Element	Type	Defines
h1	Block	A level-1 heading with content in bold at 200% of the base font size.
h2	Block	A level-2 heading with content in bold at 150% of the base font size.
p	Block	A paragraph at 100% of the base font size.
img	Block	An image.
form	Block	A form that can be submitted to the web server for processing.
a	Inline	A link that goes to another page or a location on the current page when clicked.
input	Inline	A control on a form like a text box or button.
label	Inline	A label that identifies a control on a form.
br		A line break that starts a new line.

How to code HTML elements

Two block elements with opening and closing tags
```
<h1>Email List application</h1>
<p>Here is a list of links:</p>
```

Two self-closing tags
```
<br>
<img src="logo.gif" alt="Murach Logo">
```

How to code the attributes for HTML elements

How to code an opening tag with attributes
```
<a href="contact.html" title="Click to Contact Us">
```

How to code a Boolean attribute
```
<input type="checkbox" name="mailList" checked>
```

How to code an HTML comment
```
<!-- The text in a comment is ignored -->
```

How to code a character entity for a space
```
<td> </td>
```

Description

- An *HTML document* contains *HTML elements* that specify the content of a web page.
- By default, *block elements* are displayed on new lines, but *inline elements* flow to the right of the elements that precede it.
- An *attribute* consists of an attribute name, an equals sign, and a value in quotation marks. But to show that a Boolean attribute is on, you can code just the name of the attribute.
- *Comments* can be used to describe or *comment out* portions of HTML code.
- *Character entities* provide for special characters, like a non-breaking space ( )

Figure 4-2   Basic rules for coding HTML elements

When you use HTML5, you can use the syntax for either of its predecessors: HTML or XHTML. In this figure, the examples are for HTML, which has a less rigid syntax. For instance, these self-closing tags have the HTML syntax:

```
<br>
<img src="logo.gif" alt="Murach Logo">
```

And these have the XHTML syntax:

```
<br />
<img src="logo.gif" alt="Murach Logo"/>
```

The code should work equally well either way.

How to use the HTML5 semantic elements

Figure 4-3 presents the *HTML5 semantic elements* that improve the structure of an HTML page. By using them, you improve the *search engine optimization* (*SEO*) of your web pages, at least in some search engines. So, if you aren't already using them, you should start soon.

Besides SEO improvements, the semantic elements make it easier to apply CSS to these elements because you don't have to code id attributes that are used by the CSS. Instead, you can apply the CSS to the elements themselves. You'll learn more about this in a moment.

Be aware, however, that older browsers won't recognize the HTML5 semantic elements, which means that you won't be able to use CSS to apply formatting to them. So, if you want your CSS to work in older browsers, you need to code a script element in the head section of the HTML document that provides a *JavaScript shiv*. You also need to use CSS to identify the semantic elements as block elements. In a moment, you'll learn how to do both.

The primary HTML5 semantic elements

Element	Contents
header	The header for a page.
section	A generic section of a document that doesn't indicate the type of content.
article	A composition like an article in the paper.
nav	A section of a page that contains links to other pages or placeholders.
aside	A section of a page like a sidebar that is related to the content that's near it.
figure	An image, table, or other component that's treated as a figure.
footer	The footer for a page.

A page that's structured with header, section, and footer elements

```
<body>
    <header>
        <h1>San Joaquin Valley Town Hall</h1>
    </header>
    <section>
        <p>Welcome to San Joaquin Valley Town Hall. We have some
            fascinating speakers for you this season!</p>
    </section>
    <footer>
        <p>&copy; San Joaquin Valley Town Hall.</p>
    </footer>
</body>
```

The page displayed in a web browser

San Joaquin Valley Town Hall

Welcome to San Joaquin Valley Town Hall. We have some fascinating speakers for you this season!

© San Joaquin Valley Town Hall.

Description

- HTML5 provides new *semantic elements* that you should use to structure the contents of a web page. Using these elements can be referred to as *HTML5 semantics*.

- All of the HTML5 elements in this figure are supported by the modern browsers. They also work on older browsers if you use the workarounds in figure 4-5.

- Two benefits that you get from using the semantic elements are (1) simplified HTML and CSS, and (2) improved *search engine optimization* (*SEO*).

Figure 4-3   How to use the HTML5 semantic elements

How to use the div and span elements with HTML5

If you have experience with HTML, you are probably familiar with the div element. Traditionally, it was used to divide an HTML document into divisions that are identified by id attributes, as shown in the first example of figure 4-4. Then, CSS can use the ids to apply formatting to the divisions.

But now that HTML5 is available, div elements shouldn't be used to structure a document. Instead, they should only be used when the HTML5 semantic elements aren't appropriate and no structure is implied. If, for example, you want to group a series of elements so you can apply CSS to them, you can put them within a div element. But that doesn't affect the structure of the content that's implied by the HTML5 elements.

Note too that div elements are often used in JavaScript applications. If, for example, a section element contains three h2 elements with each followed by a div element, JavaScript can be used to display or hide a div element whenever the heading that precedes it is clicked. Here again, this doesn't affect the structure of the content that's implied by the HTML5 elements.

Similarly, span elements have historically been used to identify portions of text that can be formatted by CSS. By today's standards, though, it's better to use elements that indicate the contents of the elements, like the cite, code, and q elements.

But here again, span elements are often used in JavaScript applications. This is illustrated by the second example in this figure. Here, span elements are used to display the error messages for invalid entries.

The div and span elements

Element	Description
div	A block element that provides a container for other elements.
span	An inline element that lets you identify text that can be formatted with CSS.

The way div elements were used before HTML5

```
<div id="header">
    <h1>San Joaquin Valley Town Hall</h1>
</div>
<div id="contents">
    <p>Welcome to San Joaquin Valley Town Hall. We have some
        fascinating speakers for you this season!</p>
</div>
<div id="footer">
    <p>&copy; San Joaquin Valley Town Hall.</p>
</div>
```

Span elements in the HTML for a JavaScript application

```
<label>Email Address:</label>
<input type="text" name="email_address1">
<span id="email_address1_error">*</span><br>

<label>Re-enter Email Address:</label>
<input type="text" name="email_address2">
<span id="email_address2_error">*</span><br>
```

Description

- Before HTML5, div elements were used to organize the content within the body of a document. Then, the ids for these div elements were used to apply CSS formatting to the elements.

- Today, HTML5 semantic elements should replace most div elements. That makes the structure of a page more apparent.

- Before HTML5, span elements were used to identify portions of text that you could apply formatting to. Today, a better practice is to use elements that identify the contents.

Figure 4-4   How to use the div and span elements with HTML5

How to ensure cross-browser compatibility

If you want your website to be used by as many visitors as possible, you need to make sure that your web pages are compatible with as many browsers as possible. That's known as *cross-browser compatibility*. That means you should test your applications on as many browsers as possible, including the five browsers summarized in figure 4-5.

The table in this figure shows the current release numbers of these browsers and their rating for HTML5 support. To get an updated version of this information, you can go to the URL shown in this figure. This website also rates the browser that you're using when you access it.

In general, Internet Explorer (IE) gives web developers the most problems because it's the least standard. In contrast, the other four browsers generally support the same features so if a web page runs on one of them, it also runs on the others. The other four browsers also provide for automatic updates, but IE typically hasn't done that.

To provide for old browsers that don't support the HTML5 semantic elements, you need to use the two workarounds shown in this figure. The first one is to include a script element that runs a *JavaScript shiv* that tells the browser that the semantic elements are being used. The script element in this example gets the shiv from a Google website, but it is also available from other sites. It consists of just one line of code for each of the semantic elements, so it loads fast and runs quickly.

However, before you can start using CSS to format the semantic elements in older browsers, you also need to code the CSS rule set that's shown as the second workaround. This rule set tells older browsers that the semantic elements are block elements. Otherwise, the browsers might treat them as inline elements.

For this book, you should test all of your applications on Chrome as well as one other browser, like Firefox or Internet Explorer. That's an adequate test of browser compatibility. In contrast, you should test production applications on all five of the browsers, including the older versions of these browsers that are still in use.

The current browsers and their HTML5 ratings (perfect score is 555)

Browser	Release	HTML5 Test Rating
Google Chrome	33	505
Opera	20	496
Mozilla Firefox	29	467
Apple Safari	7	397
Internet Explorer	11	376

The website for these ratings

http://www.html5test.com

Guidelines for cross-browser compatibility

* Test your web pages on all of the major browsers, including all of the older versions of these browsers that are still commonly used.

* Use the HTML5 features that are supported by all of the modern browsers, especially the HTML5 semantic elements. In addition, use the two workarounds that follow so these applications run on the older browsers too.

The two workarounds for using the HTML5 semantic elements

The JavaScript shiv that lets older browsers know about the elements

```
<script src="http://html5shiv.googlecode.com/svn/trunk/html5.js"></script>
```

The CSS rule set that sets the eight semantic elements to block elements

```
article, aside, figure, figcaption, footer, header, nav, section {
    display: block;
}
```

Description

* Today, there are still differences in the way that different browsers handle HTML and CSS, and especially HTML5 and CSS3.

* As a developer, though, you want your web pages to work on as many different web browsers as possible. This is referred to as *cross-browser compatibility*.

* To provide for cross-browser compatibility, you need to test your applications on all of the browsers that your users might use.

* In general, Internet Explorer gives web developers the most problems because it is the least standard and hasn't provided for automatic updates.

* Eventually, all browsers will support HTML5 and CSS3 so the workarounds won't be necessary.

Figure 4-5   How to ensure cross-browser compatibility

How to code links

Most websites and web applications use *links* to connect a series of web pages. To code a link, you can use the a (anchor) element as shown in figure 4-6. With this element, you use the href attribute to specify the URL for the link. Between the opening and closing tags, you code the text that describes the link. By default, the web browser underlines the text for a link. Then, the user can click on the link to jump to the specified URL.

The first group of examples in this figure shows how to code a *relative link*. Here, the first link specifies a web page named join.html that's in the same directory as the current web page. Then, the second link specifies the join.html page that's stored in the email subdirectory of the current directory. If necessary, you can code a link that navigates down several directories like this:

```
books/java/ch01/toc.html
```

The second group of examples shows how to navigate up the directory hierarchy. To do that, you can start your link with a slash or two periods (..). Here, the first example navigates up one directory, and the second example navigates up two directory levels.

Since these examples and the ones that follow don't include the name of a web page, they select the index page for that directory. By default, Tomcat looks for index pages with these names: index.html, index.htm, and index.jsp. However, you can change this behavior for each application by modifying the web.xml file for the application as shown in the next chapter.

The third group of examples shows how to use a slash to navigate to the directory that's defined as the web applications directory by your web server. For Tomcat, this directory is the webapps directory, and the first example goes to this directory. In contrast, the second example specifies the musicStore directory that's in the web applications directory of the web server.

The fourth group of examples shows how to use an *absolute link* to specify a web page. Here, the first link shows how to specify a web page that's stored in the email subdirectory of the root HTML directory for the www.murach.com website. The second link specifies the same web page, but it uses an IP address instead of a URL. Although you rarely need to use IP addresses, you may need to use them for sites that are under development and haven't yet been assigned their domain names.

Two links viewed in a browser

The Email List application 1
The Email List application 2

Examples of links

Relative to the current directory

```
<a href="join.html">The Email List application 1</a><br>
<a href="email/join.html">The Email List application 2</a><br>
<a href="../">Go back one directory level</a><br>
<a href="../../">Go back two directory levels</a><br>
```

Relative to the webapps directory

```
<a href="/">Go to the default root directory for the web server</a><br>
<a href="/musicStore">Go to the root directory of the musicStore app</a>
```

Absolute URLs

```
<a href="http://www.murach.com/email">An Internet address</a>
<a href="http://64.71.179.86/email">An IP address</a>
```

The a (anchor) element

Element	Description
a	Defines a link to another URL. When the user clicks on the text that's displayed by the tag, the browser requests the page that is identified by the href attribute of the tag.

One attribute of the anchor element

Attribute	Description
href	Specifies the URL for the link.

Description

- When you code a *relative URL* in the href attribute, the URL can be relative to the current directory, which is the one for the current HTML page, or the URL can be relative to the web server's directory for web applications.

- When you code an *absolute URL*, you code the complete URL. To do that, you can code the name of the host or the IP address for the host.

Figure 4-6   How to code links

How to include images

Although text and links are an important part of any website, most web pages include one or more images. Figure 4-7 shows how to use the img (image) element to display an image. Unlike most of the elements presented so far, the img element doesn't have a closing tag. As a result, you just need to code the opening tag and its attributes.

The example in this figure shows how to code an img element and its three required attributes. Here, you must code the src (source) attribute to specify the image that you want to include. In this case, the src attribute specifies the filename of an image that's stored in the images directory. If you have any trouble specifying the file for the image, please refer to figure 4-6 because many of the skills that apply to the href attribute of the a element also apply to the src attribute of the img element.

After the src attribute, you can code the alt attribute. This attribute specifies the text that's displayed if an image can't be loaded. A web browser may display this text if it's taking a long time to load all of the images on a page, but it can also be displayed for text-only browsers.

After the alt attribute, you can code the width or the height attribute so the browser can display the image correctly. When you specify these values, you typically want to specify the height and width of the image in *pixels*, which is the number of dots that are used to draw the image. If necessary, you can open the image in an image editor to determine the number of pixels for the width or height.

When you include images in a web page, you can use a *Graphic Interchange Format* (*GIF*) file, a *Portable Network Graphic* (*PNG*) file, or a *Joint Photographic Experts Group* (*JPEG*) file. Typically, a web designer uses imaging software such as Adobe Photoshop to create and maintain these files for a website and saves these files in a directory named images or graphics. In this book, for example, all images used by the applications are stored in an images subdirectory of the applications root directory. GIF files are stored with a GIF extension, PNG files are stored with a PNG extension, and JPEG files can be stored with either a JPEG or JPG extension.

HTML code that includes an image

```
<img src="images/murachlogo.jpg" alt="Murach Logo" width="100">
```

The image displayed in a browser

The image element

Element	Description
img	Specifies how to place a PNG, GIF, or JPEG image.

Common attributes of the Image tag

Attribute	Description
src	Specifies the relative or absolute URL for the GIF or JPEG file.
alt	Specifies the text that's displayed when the image can't be displayed.
height	Specifies the height of the image in pixels.
width	Specifies the width of the image in pixels.

Other examples

```
<img src="java.png" alt="Java Logo" width="175">

<img src="../../images/murachlogo.jpg" width="100">

<img src="http://www.murach.com/images/murachlogo.jpg"
    alt="Murach Logo" width="100">
```

Description

- The three types of image formats that are supported by most web browsers are *Portable Network Graphics* (*PNG*), *Graphic Interchange Format* (*GIF*), and *Joint Photographic Experts Group* (*JPEG*).

- JPEG files, which have a JPEG or JPG extension, are typically used for photographs and scans, while PNG and GIF files are typically used for other types of images.

Figure 4-7   How to include images

How to code tables

As you work with HTML, you may need to use one or more *tables* to present data in *rows* and *columns* as shown in figure 4-8. To start, you use the table element to identify the start and end of the table. Within the table element, you use the tr (table row) tag to specify a new row, and you use the th (table head) and td (table data) tags to specify a new column. In this figure, for example, the table contains three columns and three rows.

The intersection of a row and column is known as a *cell*. Typically, each cell of a table stores text as shown in this figure. However, cells can store any type of data including links, images, or controls.

In the early days of web programming, it was common to use tables to control the layout of a website. Today, that's considered a bad practice. Still, tables are useful for presenting tabular data such as data that's stored in a database.

Once you define a table, you can use CSS to format it. In this figure, for example, I used CSS to add borders to the cells, to add padding to the cells, and to align the text within the cells. You'll learn more about how that works later in this chapter.

When you code a table, you may sometimes want to join two or more cells into a single cell. To do that, you can use the colspan attribute to join two or more cells horizontally. Or, you can use the rowspan attribute to join two or more cells vertically.

The HTML code for a table

```
<table>
    <tr>
        <th>Code</th>
        <th>Description</th>
        <th class="align_right">Price</th>
    </tr>
    <tr>
        <td>pf01</td>
        <td>Paddlefoot - The first CD</td>
        <td class="align_right">12.95</td>
    </tr>
    <tr>
        <td>jr01</td>
        <td>Joe Rut - Genuine Wood Grained Finish</td>
        <td class="align_right">14.95</td>
    </tr>
</table>
```

The table displayed in a browser

Code	Description	Price
pf01	Paddlefoot - The first CD	12.95
jr01	Joe Rut - Genuine Wood Grained Finish	14.95

The elements for working with tables

Element	Description
table	Defines a table.
tr	Defines a row.
th	Defines a header cell within a row.
td	Defines a data cell within a row.

Attributes of the td element

Attribute	Description
colspan	Specifies the number of columns that the cell spans.
rowspan	Specifies the number of rows that the cell spans.

Description

- A *table* consists of *rows* and *columns*. The intersection of a row and column creates a *cell* that can hold data.

Figure 4-8   How to code tables

How to work with CSS

Now that you know how to use some of the basic HTML tags to define the content and structure of a web page, you're ready to learn the basic skills for using CSS to format that page.

How to provide CSS styles for an HTML page

Figure 4-9 shows the three ways you can provide CSS styles for an HTML page. The first way is to code a link element in the head section of an HTML document that specifies a file that contains the CSS for the page. This file is referred to as an *external style sheet*. Since this separates the HTML from the CSS, it's generally considered a best practice to provide styles in this way. As a result, that's the approach that the applications in this book use.

The second way is to code a style element in the head section that contains the CSS for the page. This can be referred to as *embedded styles*. The benefit of using embedded styles is that you don't have to switch back and forth between HTML and CSS files as you develop a page. Overall, though, it's better to use external style sheets because that makes it easier to use them for more than one web page.

The third way to provide styles is to code style attributes within HTML elements. This can be referred to as *inline styles*. But then, there's no separation between the HTML and the CSS.

If you maintain old web pages, you may encounter both embedded and inline styles. However, whenever possible, you should move all of the styles for a page to an external style sheet. For some web pages, it also makes sense to use two or more external style sheets for a single page, as illustrated by the last example in this figure.

When you provide external styles, embedded styles, and inline styles, the inline styles override the embedded styles, which override the external styles. If, for example, all three types of styles set the font color for h1 elements, the inline style is used. Similarly, if two external style sheets are used for a page, the styles in the second style sheet override the ones in the first sheet.

When you provide the styles for a web page in an external style sheet, you need to *attach* the style sheet to the page. To do that, you code a link element in the head section of the HTML that points to the style sheet, as shown by the examples in this figure.

Three ways to provide styles

Use an external style sheet by coding a link element in the head section

```
<link rel="stylesheet" href="styles/main.css">
```

Embed the styles in the head section

```
<style>
    body {
        font-family: Arial, Helvetica, sans-serif;
        font-size: 87.5%; }
    h1 { font-size: 250%; }
</style>
```

Use the style attribute of an element to provide inline styles

```
<span style="color: red; font-size: 14pt;">Warning!</span>
```

The sequence in which styles are applied

- Styles from an external style sheet
- Embedded styles
- Inline styles

A head element that includes two external style sheets

```
<head>
    <title>Fresh Corn Records</title>
    <link rel="stylesheet" href="main.css">
    <link rel="stylesheet" href="order.css">
</head>
```

The sequence in which styles are applied

- From the first external style sheet to the last

Description

- It's a best practice to use *external style sheets* because that leads to better separation of concerns. Specifically, you separate the content for a page (HTML) from its formatting (CSS).

- Using external style sheets also makes it easy to use the same styles for two or more pages. In contrast, if you use *embedded styles* or *inline styles*, you have to copy the styles to other documents before you can use them again.

- If more than one rule for the same property is applied to the same element, the last rule overrides the earlier rules.

Figure 4-9   Three ways to provide CSS styles for an HTML page

How to code the basic CSS selectors

Figure 4-10 shows how to code the basic CSS *selectors* for applying styles to HTML elements. To start, this figure shows the body of an HTML document that contains a section element and a footer element. Here, the h1 element is assigned an id of "first_heading", and the two p elements in this section have class attributes with the value "blue". Also, the p element in the footer has a class attribute with two values: "blue" and "right". This means that this element is assigned to two classes.

The three rule sets in the first group of examples are *type* (or *element*) *selectors*. To code a type selector, you just code the name of the element. As a result, the first rule set in this group selects the body element. The second rule set selects the section element. And the third rule set selects all p elements.

In these examples, the first rule set changes the font for the body element, and all of the elements within the body inherit this change. This rule set also sets the width of the body and centers it in the browser. Then, the second rule set puts a border around the section element and puts some padding inside the section. Last, the rule set for the paragraphs sets the margins for the sides of the paragraphs in this sequence: top, right, bottom, and left. That's why the paragraphs in the section are indented.

The two rule sets in the second group of examples use *class selectors* to select HTML elements by class. To do that, the selector is a period (.) followed by the class name. As a result, the first rule set selects all elements that have been assigned to the "blue" class, which are all three p elements. The second rule set selects any elements that have been assigned to the "right" class. That is the paragraph in the footer division. Here, the first rule set sets the color of the font to blue and the second rule set aligns the paragraph on the right.

The rule set in the last example uses an *id selector* to select an element by its id. To do that, the selector is a pound sign (#) followed by the id value that uniquely identifies an element. As a result, this rule set selects the h1 element that has an id of "first_heading". Then, its rule set sets the margins for the heading.

One of the key points here is that a class attribute can have the same value for more than one element on a page. Then, if you code a selector for that class, it's used to format all the elements in that class. In contrast, since the id for an element must be unique, an id selector can only be used to format a single element.

Another key point is that a more specific style overrides a less specific style. For instance, an id selector is more specific than a class selector, and a class selector is more specific than a type selector. That means that a style for an id selector overrides the same style for a class selector, which overrides the same style for a type selector. Beyond that, the rules in a rule set flow from top to bottom. So, if you've set multiple rules for a property of an element, the last one overrides the previous ones.

As you may know, there are many other types of selectors that you can use with CSS. But the ones in this figure should get you started with CSS. They are also the only ones that are used by the applications in this book.

HTML that can be selected by element type, class, or id

```
<body>
    <section>
        <h1 id="first_heading">The Speaker Lineup</h1>
        <p class="blue">October 19: Jeffrey Toobin</p>
        <p class="blue">November 16: Andrew Ross Sorkin</p>
    </section>
    <footer>
        <p class="blue right">Copyright SJV Town Hall</p>
    </footer>
</body>
```

CSS rule sets that select by element type, class, and id

Three rule sets with type selectors

```
body {
    font-family: Arial, Helvetica, sans-serif;
    width: 400px;
    margin: 1em auto; }
section {
    border: 2px solid black;
    padding: 1em; }
p { margin: .25em 0 .25em 3em; }
```

Two rule sets with class selectors

```
.blue { color: blue; }
.right { text-align: right; }
```

One rule set with an id selector

```
#first_heading { margin: 0 1em .25em; }
```

The elements displayed in a browser

Description

- You code a selector for all elements of a specific type by naming the element. This is referred to as a *type* or *element selector*.
- You code a selector for an element with a class attribute by coding a period followed by the class name. Then, the rule set applies to all elements with that class name. This is known as a *class selector*.
- You code an id selector for an element with an id attribute by coding a pound sign (#) followed by the id value. This is known as an *id selector*.

Figure 4-10   How to code the basic CSS selectors

How to code CSS rule sets and comments

CSS code consists of *rule sets* that are applied to HTML elements by their selectors. This is illustrated by the rule sets in figure 4-11. Here, each rule set consists of a selector, a set of braces { }, and one or more *rules* within the braces. Within each rule, there's the name for a *property*, a colon, the value or values for the property, and an ending semicolon.

Now, to give you a better idea of how CSS works, here's a quick description of the rule sets in this figure. Remember, though, that this book is about servlet and JSP programming, not CSS, so it isn't going to try to teach you how to use the dozens of properties that CSS provides.

The first rule set consists of five rules. The first rule specifies the font to be used for the body of the document, and all the elements within the body inherit that font. The second rule specifies that the base font for the application should be 85% of the default font size for the user's browser. Remember, from earlier in this chapter, that a p element is 100% of that base font size, and an h1 element is 200% of that size. The third and fourth rules for the body of the document sets its left and right margins to 2em. Since an *em* is a unit of measure that's roughly equal to the width of a capital M in the font that's being used, it varies based on the font size that's used for an element. In this case, that 2 em margin provides the space that separates the body from the left and right edges of the browser window. Finally, the fifth rule sets the width of the body to 400 pixels (px). As a result, the body is 400 pixels wide.

The second rule set is for all h1 elements. It sets the font size to 140% of the base font, the color to teal, and the bottom margin to half of an em.

The third rule set applies to all of the label elements on the page. Here, the first rule floats the labels to the left. As a result, the element that follows each label flows to the right of it. The second rule sets the width of each label to 7 ems. That provides the alignment for the four labels and controls without using a table. The third rule sets the bottom margin to half of an em. That provides vertical space between labels. And the fourth rule specifies that the label should use a bold font.

The fourth rule set applies to input elements that have their type attribute set to "text" or "email". That includes all three of the text boxes used by the application presented in chapter 2. The first rule sets the width of these text boxes to 15 ems. Then, the next two rules set a left and bottom margin for those text boxes.

The fifth rule set applies to span elements. Within this set, the rules provide for left and bottom margins that are the same as the previous rule set.

The sixth rule set applies to br elements. The lone rule in this set clears the float specified by the CSS for the label element and causes the next element to display on the left side of the page.

The seventh and eighth rule sets are for classes named pad_top and margin_left. You can use the pad_top class to add some padding to the top of an element. Similarly, you can use the margin_left class to add some margin to the left of an element. In the Email List application, for example, the first page uses the pad_top class to align the label elements, and it uses the margin_left class to align the submit button.

The external style sheet for the Email List application

```css
/* The styles for the elements */
body {
    font-family: Arial, Helvetica, sans-serif;
    font-size: 85%;
    margin-left: 2em;
    margin-right: 2em;
    width: 400px;
}
h1 {
    font-size: 140%;
    color: teal;
    margin-bottom: .5em;
}
label {
    float: left;
    width: 7em;
    margin-bottom: 0.5em;
    font-weight: bold;
}
input[type="text"], input[type="email"] {   /* An attribute selector */
    width: 15em;
    margin-left: 0.5em;
    margin-bottom: 0.5em;
}
span {
    margin-left: 0.5em;
    margin-bottom: 0.5em;
}
br {
    clear: both;
}

/* The styles for the classes */
.pad_top {
    padding-top: 0.25em;
}
.margin_left {
    margin-left: 0.5em;
}
```

Description

- A CSS *rule set* consists of a selector and one or more rules within braces.

- A CSS *selector* consists of the identifiers that are coded at the beginning of the rule set. If more than one selector is coded for a rule set, the selectors are separated by commas.

- A CSS *rule* consists of a *property*, a colon, a *value*, and a semicolon. Although the semicolon for the last declaration in a block is optional, it's a best practice to code it.

- To make your code easier to read, you can use spaces, indentation, and blank lines within a rule set.

- CSS *comments* begin with /* and end with */. A CSS comment can be coded on a single line, or it can span multiple lines.

Figure 4-11   How to code CSS rule sets and comments

How to use CSS to format a table

Figure 4-12 presents some of the CSS properties for formatting tables. However, you can also use many of the other properties that you've already learned about to format a table.

By default, a table doesn't include borders. In many cases, though, you'll want to add a border around the table to make it stand out on the page. You may also want to add borders around the cells or rows in a table to help identify the columns and rows. To do that, you can add a border property to the appropriate element. In this figure, for example, the border property adds a solid black border around the table and around each cell in the table.

By default, a small amount of space is included between the cells of a table. To remove that space, you can set the border-collapse property to a value of "collapse". Then, the browser collapses the borders between adjacent cells to a single border as shown in the first table in the figure.

When you use the padding property with table elements, it works similarly to the way it works for other elements. In this figure, the padding property adds half an em of padding to all four sides of the cell.

To complete the formatting, the CSS right aligns those elements that are in the "align_right" class. That includes all three cells in the third column (the Price column).

Common properties for formatting table, tr, th, and td elements

Property	Description
border-collapse	A keyword that determines whether space exists between the borders of adjacent cells. Possible values are "separate" and "collapse". The default is "separate".
padding	The space between the cell contents and the outer edge of the cell.
text-align	The horizontal alignment of text.
vertical-align	The vertical alignment of text.

The CSS for the table presented earlier in this chapter

```
table {
    border: 1px solid black;
    border-collapse: collapse;
}
th, td {
    border: 1px solid black;
    text-align: left;
    padding: .5em;
}
.align_right {
    text-align: right;
}
```

The table with collapsed borders

Code	Description	Price
pf01	Paddlefoot - The first CD	12.95
jr01	Joe Rut - Genuine Wood Grained Finish	14.95

The table without collapsed borders

Code	Description	Price
pf01	Paddlefoot - The first CD	12.95
jr01	Joe Rut - Genuine Wood Grained Finish	14.95

Description

- With HTML5, you should use CSS, not HTML, to format tables.

Figure 4-12   How to use CSS to format a table

How to code HTML forms

This topic shows how to code an HTML *form* that contains one or more *controls* such as text boxes and buttons. In this topic, you'll learn how to code some of the most common types of controls to gather data. In the next chapter, you'll learn how to process the data that's gathered by these controls.

How to code a form

Figure 4-13 shows how to code a form that contains three controls: two text boxes and a button. To code a form, you begin by coding the opening and closing form tags. Within the opening form tag, you must code an action attribute that specifies the servlet or JSP that's called when the user clicks on the submit button. In addition, you can code a method attribute that specifies the method that's used for the HTTP request. Within the opening and closing form tags, you code the controls for the form.

This example shows a form that contains two text boxes and a submit button. When the user clicks on the submit button, the data that's in the text boxes is passed to the servlet that's mapped to a URL that ends with contactList. This URL is specified by the action attribute of the form. Although a form can have many controls, it should always contain at least one control that executes the action attribute of the form. Typically, this control is a submit button like the one shown in this figure.

When you code the action attribute, you typically specify a servlet as shown in this figure. However, you can also specify a JSP by specifying a URL for its file name like this:

```
action="contact_list.jsp"
```

Within a form element, you typically use the input element to code one or more controls. This figure shows how to use the input element to code a text box and a button. In a moment, you'll learn more about coding these controls.

When coding controls, you can use the name attribute to specify a name that you can use in your Java code to access the parameter that's passed from the HTML form to a servlet or JSP. To access the data in the two text boxes in this figure, for example, you can use firstName to access the data that's been entered in the first text box, and you can use lastName to access the data in the second text box.

In addition, you can use the value attribute to specify a value for a control. This works differently depending on the control. If, for example, you're working with a button, the value attribute specifies the text that's displayed on a button. However, if you're working with a text box, the value attribute specifies the default text that's displayed in the box.

The HTML code for a form

```
<form action="contactList" method="post">
    <label>First Name:</label>
    <input type="text" name="firstName"><br>
    <label>Last Name:</label>
    <input type="text" name="lastName">
    <input type="submit" value="Submit">
</form>
```

The form displayed in a browser before the user enters data

Elements for working with a simple form

Element	Description
form	Defines the start and end of the form.
input	Defines the input type. You'll learn more about this tag in the following figures.

Attributes of the form element

Attribute	Description
action	Specifies the URL of the servlet or JSP that's called when the user clicks on the submit button.
method	Specifies the HTTP method that the browser uses for the HTTP request. The default method is the GET method, but the POST method is also commonly used, especially when the request includes data that's saved on the server.

Common control attributes

Attribute	Description
name	Specifies the name of the control. When writing Java code, you can use this attribute to refer to the control.
value	The default value of the control. This varies depending on the type of control. For a text box, this attribute sets the default text that's displayed in the box. For a button, this attribute sets the text that's displayed on the button.

Description

- A *form* contains one or more *controls* such as text boxes, buttons, check boxes, and list boxes.

Figure 4-13   How to code a form

How to code text boxes

Figure 4-14 shows how to use the input element to code three types of *text boxes*. You can use a *standard text box* to accept text input from a user. You can use a special type of standard text box to let a user enter an email address. You can use a *password box* to let a user enter a password that's displayed as one asterisk or dot for each character that's entered. And you can use a *hidden field* to store text that you want to send to the server, but don't want to display on the HTML page.

To create a text box, you set the type attribute to "text", "email", "password", or "hidden". Then, you code the name attribute so you'll be able to access the text that's stored in the text box from your Java code.

If you want the text box to contain a default value, you can code the value attribute. When you code visible text boxes, you often don't need to code a value attribute since you want the user to enter the value for these text boxes. In contrast, when you use a hidden field, you typically need to code a value attribute.

When coding text boxes, you can use the maxlength attribute to specify the maximum number of characters that the user can enter into a text box. This can be helpful if you create a database that can only store a fixed number of characters for certain fields. If, for example, the FirstName column in the database accepts a maximum of 20 characters, you can set the maxlength attribute of its text box to 20. That way, the user won't be able to enter more than 20 characters for this column.

One of the features of HTML5 is that it provides an easy way to validate some of the data that the user enters into a form without having to use JavaScript. In particular, if you include a required attribute for a text box, the browser checks to make sure the user has entered a value before it submits the form to the server. If the text box is empty, the browser displays a message like the one shown in the second screen in this figure.

Similarly, if you use a type attribute of "email" for an input element, some browsers will check the validity of the email entry. For example, a browser might check to make sure the user enters an at sign (@) with text on both sides of it. Normally, though, this checking is limited so the servlet needs to do a thorough job of validity checking when the data is submitted to it.

Beyond that, how the validation works and how the validation messages are displayed varies from one browser to another. For that reason, most validation on the client is still done with JavaScript and jQuery.

The code for four types of text controls

```
Email:      <input type="email" name="email" required><br>
Username:   <input type="text" name="username" required><br>
Password:   <input type="password" name="password" required>
            <input type="hidden" name="action" value="register">
```

The text controls displayed in a browser

The text controls when a required field hasn't been entered

Attributes of these text controls

Attribute	Description
type	Specifies the type of input control. Traditional values are "text", "password", and "hidden". But HTML5 introduced some new types like "email" for a text box that should receive an email entry.
name	Specifies the name of the control. This is the name that is used to refer to the data in the control from a servlet or JSP.
value	Specifies the value of data in the control.
maxlength	Specifies the maximum number of characters that can be entered into the text box.
required	Specifies that the user must enter a value for a text box. If the user submits the form and the field is empty, the browser displays its default error message.

Description

- You can use the type attribute to specify the type of *text box*.
- A value of "text" creates a *standard text box*.
- A value of "email" creates a special type of text box that's designed for working with email addresses. This type of text box was introduced with HTML5.
- A value of "password" creates a *password box* that displays asterisks instead of text.
- A value of "hidden" creates a *hidden field* that stores a name and value that's sent to the server but isn't shown by the browser.

Figure 4-14   How to code text boxes

How to code buttons

Figure 4-15 shows how to use the input element to code three types of buttons. A submit button executes the action attribute that's specified in the form element. A reset button resets all controls on the current form to the default values that are set by their value attributes. And a generic button can be used to trigger JavaScript actions like data validation.

To create a button, you set the type attribute of the input element to "submit", "reset", or "button". Then, you typically code a value attribute that contains the text that's displayed on the button.

When coding a web page, you often need to have two or more submit buttons that link to different servlets. One way to do that is to code more than one form per page. For instance, the second example in this figure shows two forms where the first form contains only the Continue Shopping button and the second form contains only the Checkout button.

The code for three types of buttons

```
<input type="submit" value="Submit">
<input type="reset" value="Reset">
<input type="button" value="Validate">
```

The buttons displayed in a browser

The code for two submit buttons on the same page

```
<form action="quickOrder" method="get">
    <input type="submit" name="continue" value="Continue Shopping">
</form>
<form action="cart" method="get">
    <input type="submit" name="checkout" value="Checkout">
</form>
```

The buttons displayed in a browser

Description

- The type attribute identifies the type of *button* to be used.
- A type attribute of "submit" creates a *submit button* that activates the action attribute of the form when it's clicked.
- A type attribute of "reset" creates a *reset button* that resets all controls on the form to their default values when it's clicked.
- A type attribute of "button" creates a generic button that can be used to trigger JavaScript actions.

Figure 4-15   How to code buttons

How to code check boxes and radio buttons

Figure 4-16 shows how to use the input element to code *check boxes* and *radio buttons*. Although check boxes work independently of other check boxes, radio buttons can be set up so the user can select only one radio button from a group of radio buttons. In this figure, for example, you can select only one of the three radio buttons. However, you can select or deselect any combination of check boxes.

To create a check box, you set the type attribute of the input element to "checkbox". Then, you can set the name attribute for the check box so you can access the value from your Java code. If you want the check box to be checked by default, you can also code the checked attribute. Unlike the type and name attributes, you don't need to supply a value for the checked attribute.

To create a radio button, you can set the type attribute of the input element to "radio". Then, you can set the name attribute just as you do for other controls. However, you should specify the same name for all of the radio buttons in a group. In this figure, for example, all three radio buttons are named contactVia. That way, the user can only select one of these radio buttons at a time. When coding radio buttons, you typically supply a value for each radio button. Later, when you write your Java code, you can access the value that's coded for the selected radio button.

The code for four check boxes and three radio buttons

```
<p><input type="checkbox" name="addEmail" checked>
Yes, add me to your mailing list.</p>

<p>Contact me by:
<input type="radio" name="contactVia" value="Email">Email
<input type="radio" name="contactVia" value="Postal Mail">Postal mail
<input type="radio" name="contactVia" value="Both" checked>Both</p>

<p>I'm interested in these types of music:<br>
<input type="checkbox" name="rock">Rock<br>
<input type="checkbox" name="country">Country<br>
<input type="checkbox" name="bluegrass">Bluegrass</p>
```

The check boxes and radio buttons when displayed in a browser

Attributes of these controls

Attribute	Description
type	Specifies the type of control. A value of "checkbox" creates a check box while a value of "radio" creates a radio button.
checked	Selects the control. When several radio buttons share the same name, only one radio button can be selected at a time.

Description

- You can use *check boxes* to allow the user to supply a true/false value.
- You can use *radio buttons* to allow a user to select one option from a group of options. To create a group of radio buttons, use the same name for all of the radio buttons.
- If you don't group radio buttons, more than one can be on at the same time.

Figure 4-16   How to code check boxes and radio buttons

How to code combo boxes and list boxes

Figure 4-17 shows how to code *combo boxes* and *list boxes*. You can use a combo box to allow the user to select one option from a drop-down list, and you can use a list box to allow the user to select one or more options. In this figure, for example, the combo box lets you select one country, and the list box lets you select more than one country.

To code a combo or list box, you must use the select element and two or more option elements. To start, you code the opening and closing tags for the select element. Within the opening select tag, you must code the name attribute. Within the select element, you can code two or more option elements. These elements supply the options that are available for the box. In the opening tag for the option element, you code a value attribute that you can access from your Java code.

Within the option element, you can supply the text that's displayed to the user. This text is sometimes the same as the text for the value attribute, but it can also be different. In this figure, for example, the value attribute uses a standard three-letter code for each country, but the complete name of the country is displayed to the user.

The size attribute of the select element determines whether the control is a combo box or a list box. If the value of this attribute is 1, which is the default, the control is a combo box. If it is greater than 1, the control is a list box with that many options displayed.

With a list box, you can also code the multiple attribute. Then, the user can select more than one option from the box.

If you want to select a default option for a combo or list box, you can code the selected attribute within an option element. Since a combo box only allows one option to be selected, you should only code one selected attribute. However, for a list box, you can code the selected attribute for one or more options.

The code for a combo box

```
Select a country:<br>
<select name="country">
    <option value="USA" selected>United States</option>
    <option value="CAN">Canada</option>
    <option value="MEX">Mexico</option>
</select>
```

The combo box displayed in a browser

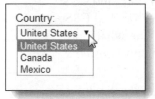

The code for a list box with 3 options displayed

```
<select name="country" size=3 multiple>
```

The list box displayed in a browser

Attributes of the select element

Attribute	Description
size	The number of items to display in the control. If the value is 1, the control will be a combo box. If more than 1, the control will be a list box.
multiple	If coded, the user can select more than one option. This is only valid with a list box.

Attributes of the option element

Attribute	Description
selected	Selects the option.

Description

- A combo box provides a drop-down list that lets the user select a single option.
- A list box provides a list of options lets the user select more than one option if the multiple attribute is coded.
- To select more than one option from a list box, the user can hold down the Ctrl key on a Windows system or the Command key on a Mac and then click on the options.

Figure 4-17   How to code combo boxes and list boxes

Perspective

Now that you've completed this chapter, you know the right way to use HTML and CSS in a servlet/JSP application. That means using HTML for the content and structure of a page and using CSS in an external style sheet for all of the formatting. That separates the content and structure of each page from its formatting, which makes it easier to create and maintain a web page.

Because this book is about servlet/JSP programming, not HTML and CSS, this chapter has presented only what you need to know about HTML and CSS for this book. Of course, there's a lot more to HTML and CSS than what's presented in this chapter. So if you want to learn more, we recommend *Murach's HTML5 and CSS3*.

Similarly, this chapter hasn't presented any JavaScript or jQuery, which is often used to do processing such as data validation on the client. So, if you want to learn more about that, we recommend *Murach's JavaScript and jQuery*. Of course, you should always validate the data on the server too as described in the next chapter.

Summary

- A best practice today is to use HTML for the content and structure of a web page and CSS for formatting the page. It's also considered a best practice to use *external style sheets* to provide the CSS for your pages.

- To *attach* an external style sheet to a web page, you code a link element in the head section of the *HTML document* that points to the location of the style sheet.

- By default, *block elements* in HTML are displayed on their own lines in browsers. In contrast, *inline elements* don't start new lines.

- The *HTML5 semantic elements* include the header, section, nav, aside, and footer elements. Using them makes it easier to apply CSS and also improves *SEO* (*search engine optimization*) in some search engines.

- Now that the HTML5 semantic elements are available, a div element should only be used when there isn't an appropriate semantic element for the purpose.

- To move from one URL to another, you can code *links* within HTML. These can be *relative links* that are relative to the current directory or *absolute links*.

- An HTML page can include images in Graphic Interchange Format (GIF), Portable Network Graphic (PNG), or Joint Photographic Experts Group (JPEG) format.

- You can use *tables* to organize data in *rows* and *columns*. The *cells* within the table can store links, images, and controls.

- *Embedded styles* are coded in a style element in the head section of an HTML document, which provides some separation between HTML elements and their styles. But *inline styles* are coded as attributes in the HTML elements themselves.

- The basic *CSS selectors* are *type* (or *element*) *selectors*, *class selectors*, and *id selectors*. Those are the ones that are used in the applications for this book.

- When you use CSS, you need to understand the order in which styles override other styles. For instance, more specific styles override less specific styles, and the last style that's applied overrides previous styles.

- A CSS *rule set* consists of one or more *rules*, and each rule consists of a *property* name and values.

- To assure *cross-browser compatibility*, you need to test your web applications in all of the browsers that are likely to access your application.

- To make sure the HTML5 semantic elements work in older browsers, you need to add a *JavaScript shiv* to your HTML document. You also need to provide a CSS rule set that sets the semantic elements to block elements.

- An *HTML form* contains one or more controls like text boxes, check boxes, radio buttons, combo boxes, and list boxes. It should also contain a submit button that calls a JSP or servlet when the user clicks it. If necessary, one HTML document can contain two or more forms.

Exercise 4-1   Modify a web page

In this exercise, you'll view and modify a web page for a survey. This should give you some hands-on experience with working with HTML and CSS.

Review the HTML and CSS

1. Start your IDE and open the ch04_ex1_survey project in the ex_starts directory.

2. Open the index.html page and review its HTML.

3. Open the survey.css page in the styles subdirectory and review its CSS.

Test the page

4. Run the project. This should display the web page in your web browser. In the browser's address bar, the URL for the page should use the Tomcat server.

5. Open the Windows Explorer (PC) or Finder (Mac) and double-click on the index.html file that's in the ch04survey/web folder to display the page in your web browser. This time, the URL for the page should use the file system, not the Tomcat server.

6. Run the project again. When Tomcat displays the web page, click the Submit button. Since you didn't enter the required fields, this should cause the browser to display an error.

7. Fill out all required fields and click the Submit button again. This should request this URL:

   `http://localhost:8080/ch04_ex1_survey/survey`

   For now, this should display an error that indicates that no resource exists at this URL. In the next chapter, you'll learn how to map a servlet to this URL.

Modify the page

After each step that follows, run the page to make sure the changes are correct. If necessary, click the browser's Refresh button to refresh the page.

8. Edit the index.html page so it displays the image for the Murach logo at the top of the page. This image is in the images directory of your web application.

9. After the label and text box that let the user enter an email address, add another label and text box that let the user enter a date of birth. This data should be optional, not required.

10. Turn the Search engine button on as the default button for the group of radio buttons.

11. Add a Social Media radio button before the Other radio button.

12. After the check box, add another check box with a name of emailOK and text that says, "YES, please send me email announcements." Then, modify both check boxes so that neither one is checked by default.

13. When you've got everything working right, close the project.

5

How to develop servlets

Chapter 2 showed how to use the MVC pattern to structure a web application that uses servlets and JSPs. Now, this chapter presents the skills that you need to develop servlets within the MVC pattern. When you complete this chapter, you should be able to code the servlets for web applications of your own.

Before you start this chapter, though, take a few minutes to review the figures in chapter 2 that present the Email List application. That will refresh your memory about how the HTML, JSP, servlet, and web.xml files are related and how servlets fit into the MVC pattern.

How to create and map a servlet

There are two steps to creating a servlet. You must code the class for the servlet, and you must map that class to a URL. Prior to the servlet 3.0 specification (Tomcat 7.0), you had to use the web.xml to map a servlet to a URL. With the servlet 3.0 specification and later, you can use the @WebServlet annotation to map a servlet to one or more URL patterns.

How to create a servlet

Figure 5-1 shows the basic structure for a servlet that handles both HTTP GET and POST requests. For now, you can use this basic structure to get started with servlets. As you progress through this chapter, you'll learn more about working with servlets.

The first statement for this servlet specifies the package for the servlet's class. This package must correspond to the directory that contains the servlet. Then, the next six statements import the classes that are required by this servlet. Most of these classes are required by all servlets. The only class that isn't required by all servlets is the PrintWriter class, which is only necessary for a servlet that needs to send text like HTML or XML to the client.

After the first four statements, the class declaration provides the name for the class and indicates that it extends the HttpServlet class. In theory, a servlet can extend the GenericServlet class. In practice, however, all servlets extend the HttpServlet class.

The doGet and doPost methods in this figure accept the same arguments and throw the same exceptions. Within these methods, you can use the methods of the request object to get incoming data, and you can use the methods of the response object to set outgoing data.

In this example, the doGet method calls the doPost method. As a result, an HTTP GET request executes the doPost method of the servlet. This allows a servlet to use the same code to handle both the GET and POST methods of an HTTP request. Although this is a common practice, it's better to use the doGet and doPost methods only to execute code that's appropriate for the corresponding method of the HTTP request.

The second statement in the doPost method calls the getWriter method of the response object to get a PrintWriter object named out. Once you get this object, you can use one println statement or a series of print and println statements to return HTML or other text to the browser as shown by the third statement. Since this statement can throw an IOException, it's enclosed in a try block.

The last statement closes and flushes the output stream and releases any resources that are being used by the PrintWriter object. Since you always want to execute this statement, even if an exception is encountered, it's enclosed in a finally block.

A simple servlet that returns HTML

```
package murach.email;

import java.io.IOException;
import java.io.PrintWriter;
import javax.servlet.ServletException;
import javax.servlet.http.HttpServlet;
import javax.servlet.http.HttpServletRequest;
import javax.servlet.http.HttpServletResponse;

public class TestServlet extends HttpServlet {

    @Override
    protected void doPost(HttpServletRequest request,
            HttpServletResponse response)
            throws ServletException, IOException {

        response.setContentType("text/html");
        PrintWriter out = response.getWriter();
        try {
            out.println("<h1>HTML from servlet</h1>");
        }
        finally {
            out.close();
        }
    }

    @Override
    protected void doGet(HttpServletRequest request,
            HttpServletResponse response)
            throws ServletException, IOException {

        doPost(request, response);
    }
}
```

Description

- In practice, all servlets extend the HttpServlet class. To extend this class, the servlet must import some of the classes in the java.io, javax.servlet, and javax.servlet.http packages.

- The doGet method overrides the doGet method of the HttpServlet class and processes all HTTP requests that use the GET method, and the doPost method overrides the doPost method of the HttpServlet class and processes all HTTP requests that use the POST method.

- The doGet and doPost methods use two objects that are passed to it by the web server: (1) the HttpServletRequest object, or the *request object*, and (2) the HttpServletResponse object, or the *response object*.

- The setContentType method of the response object sets the *content type* of the response that's returned to the browser. Then, the getWriter method of the response object returns a PrintWriter object that can be used to send HTML to the browser.

- Before you can create a PrintWriter object, you must set the content type. This allows the getWriter method to return a PrintWriter object that uses the proper content type.

Figure 5-1   How to code a servlet

How to map a servlet with the web.xml file

Before you can request a servlet, you need to map the servlet to a URL. One way to do that is to use the web.xml file for the application as shown in this figure. The advantage of this approach is that it works with all versions of Tomcat, new and old. However, if you're using the 3.0 servlet specification (Tomcat 7.0) or later, you may find it easier to use annotations to map servlets as shown in the next figure.

In figure 5-2, the web.xml file contains XML elements that map two servlets. The first servlet element in this figure declares a name that refers to the EmailListServlet class that's stored in the murach.email class. Here, the servlet-name element provides a unique name for the class. This name is used internally by the web.xml file. Then, the servlet-class element uses a fully-qualified name to identify the class for the servlet. In this example, the servlet-name entry is the same as the name for the class, but it isn't qualified by the package name. This is a common convention for naming a servlet. However, if the same servlet name is used in two or more packages, you can use servlet elements to specify a unique name for each servlet.

The second servlet element uses the same naming convention as the first servlet element. It declares an internal name of TestServlet for a servlet named TestServlet that's stored in the murach.email package.

The first servlet-mapping element maps the EmailListServlet to a single URL that's available from the root directory of the application. As a result, the user is able to request this servlet by specifying a URL pattern like this one:

`http://localhost:8080/ch05email/emailList`

Note that this URL removes the word *Servlet* from the end of the servlet name. I have used this convention throughout this book because it shortens the URL and hides the fact that this application uses servlets from the user.

The second servlet-mapping element uses a wildcard character (*) to map the EmailListServlet to any URL that resides within the email directory. This allows this servlet to be requested by multiple URLs. For example, you could request this servlet with this URL:

`http://localhost:8080/ch05email/email/add`

Or, you could request this servlet with this URL:

`http://localhost:8080/ch05email/email/addToList`

It's important to note that this servlet mapping works even if the email directory is a virtual directory that doesn't actually exist on the server.

The third servlet-mapping element maps the TestServlet to a single URL. This element uses the same naming convention as the first servlet-mapping element.

If you have any trouble working with the web.xml file, you can review the skills for working with the web.xml file that are presented later in this chapter. Or, if necessary, you can get more information about working with XML from our Java book, *Murach's Java Programming*.

XML tags that add servlet mapping to the web.xml file

```
<!-- the definitions for the servlets -->
<servlet>
    <servlet-name>EmailListServlet</servlet-name>
    <servlet-class>murach.email.EmailListServlet</servlet-class>
</servlet>
<servlet>
    <servlet-name>TestServlet</servlet-name>
    <servlet-class>murach.email.TestServlet</servlet-class>
</servlet>

<!-- the mapping for the servlets -->
<servlet-mapping>
    <servlet-name>EmailListServlet</servlet-name>
    <url-pattern>/emailList</url-pattern>
</servlet-mapping>
<servlet-mapping>
    <servlet-name>EmailListServlet</servlet-name>
    <url-pattern>/email/*</url-pattern>
</servlet-mapping>
<servlet-mapping>
    <servlet-name>TestServlet</servlet-name>
    <url-pattern>/test</url-pattern>
</servlet-mapping>
```

XML elements for working with servlet mapping

Element	Description
`<servlet-class>`	Specifies the class for the servlet. Note that this element includes the package and name for the class but not the .class extension.
`<servlet-name>`	Specifies a unique name for the servlet that's used to identify the servlet within the web.xml file. This element is required for both the servlet element and the servlet-mapping element and maps each servlet-mapping element to a servlet element.
`<url-pattern>`	Specifies the URL or URLs that are mapped to the specified servlet. This pattern must begin with a front slash, but the URL pattern can specify a virtual directory or file that doesn't actually exist.

Some URL pattern examples

URL pattern	Description
`/emailList`	Specifies the emailList URL in the root directory of the application.
`/email/*`	Specifies any URL in the email directory.
`/email/add`	Specifies the add URL in the email directory.

Description

- Before you can request a servlet, you should use the application's web.xml file to map a servlet to a URL pattern.

Figure 5-2   How to map a servlet with the web.xml file

How to map a servlet with an annotation

As mentioned earlier, if you're using the 3.0 servlet specification (Tomcat 7.0) or later, you can use annotations to map servlets as shown in figure 5-3. The advantage of this approach is that it requires less code. Also, some developers find it easier to maintain the servlet mapping when it's stored in the same file as the source code for the servlet.

If you want to use annotations to map your servlets, you can begin by adding an import statement for the WebServlet class. Then, you can code the @WebServlet annotation just before the class declaration for the servlet. To map a servlet to a single URL, you can code the URL within the parentheses that follow the @WebServlet annotation as shown in the first example.

However, if you want to map a servlet to multiple URLs, you can use the urlPatterns attribute of the @WebServlet annotation as shown in the second example. Here, you code an equals sign (=) followed by a set of braces ({}). Then, within the braces, you code two or more URLs, separating each URL with a comma. If you want, you can use the wildcard character (*) to map a servlet to any URL that resides within a directory. This works as described in the previous figure.

By default, the internal name that's used for the servlet is the same as the class name of the servlet, which usually works fine. However, if this leads to a naming conflict, you can use the name attribute of the @WebServlet annotation to specify a unique internal name for the servlet. For instance, if you have a servlet class named TestServlet that's in two different packages, you can use the name attribute to specify a unique internal name for each servlet. In the third example, for instance, the annotation specifies a name of MurachTestServlet for the TestServlet class.

Typically, you use either the web.xml file or @WebServlet annotations to map the servlets in an application. As a result, you don't usually need to worry about which technique takes precedence. However, if you use both techniques to map a servlet name to the same URL, the mapping in the web.xml file overrides the mapping in the annotation.

A servlet that uses an annotation to map itself to a URL

```
package murach.email;

import java.io.IOException;
import java.io.PrintWriter;
import javax.servlet.ServletException;
import javax.servlet.annotation.WebServlet;
import javax.servlet.http.HttpServlet;
import javax.servlet.http.HttpServletRequest;
import javax.servlet.http.HttpServletResponse;

@WebServlet("/test")
public class TestServlet extends HttpServlet {
...
...
```

How to map a servlet to multiple URLs

```
@WebServlet(urlPatterns={"/emailList", "/email/*"})
```

How to specify a name for the servlet

```
@WebServlet(name="MurachTestServlet", urlPatterns={"/test"})
```

Description

- With the servlet 3.0 specification (Tomcat 7.0) and later, you can use the @WebServlet annotation to map a servlet to one or more URL patterns.

- To map a servlet to a single URL pattern, code the URL pattern in the parentheses that follow the @WebServlet annotation.

- To map a servlet to multiple URL patterns, code the urlPatterns attribute within the parentheses that follow the @WebServlet annotation. Then, code an equals sign followed by a set of braces ({}). Within the braces, you can code multiple URL patterns, separating each pattern with a comma.

- If you encounter a naming conflict, you can use the name attribute of the @WebServlet annotation to specify a unique mapping name for the servlet.

- If you use both the web.xml and the @WebServlet annotation to map the same servlet name to one or more URLs, the mapping in the web.xml file overrides the mapping in the annotation.

Figure 5-3   How to map a servlet with an annotation

How to request a servlet

After you create and map a servlet, you can request the servlet to test it. When you do that, you can use an HTTP GET or POST request.

How to use the HTTP GET method

Figure 5-4 shows several ways to request a servlet. To do that, you typically code a form tag or an anchor (a) tag that requests the servlet as shown by the examples in this figure. However, if the web server and servlet engine are running, you can also enter a URL directly into the browser.

When you test a servlet, you often need to pass parameters to it. To do that, you can append the parameters to the end of the URL as shown by the first example. Here, the question mark after the servlet's URL indicates that one or more parameters will follow. Then, you code the parameter name, the equals sign, and the parameter value for each parameter that is passed, and you separate multiple parameters with ampersands (&).

The browser shown in this figure contains a URL that calls a servlet and passes three parameters named action, firstName, and lastName. Since this request doesn't include a parameter for the email address, the email address isn't shown on the resulting web page.

There are three ways you can request a servlet. First, you can enter its URL into a browser as shown by the second set of examples. Here, the first URL requests a servlet that's mapped to the emailList directory that's running on a local server using port 8080 in an app named ch05email. Then, the second URL requests a servlet that's mapped to the email/list directory that's running on the web server for www.murach.com using the default port, port 80.

Second, you can use a form tag to request a servlet. When you use this technique, you code the action attribute of the form to provide a path and file-name to the servlet's URL. In this figure, the first form tag requests a servlet that's mapped to the emailList subdirectory of the current directory. However, if the servlet is stored in a different directory, you can specify a relative or absolute path for the action attribute.

When you use a form tag to request a URL, you can use the method attribute to specify the HTTP method that's used for the request. By default, the form tag uses the GET method. However, you can explicitly specify the GET method if you want. In this figure, both of the form tags use the GET method. In the next figure, you'll learn when and how to specify the POST method.

When you use the GET method to request a servlet, any parameters that are passed to the servlet are displayed in the browser's URL address. In this figure, for example, the browser's URL includes three parameters. In the next figure, you'll learn that the POST method doesn't display the parameters in the URL for the browser.

Third, you can use an anchor tag to call a servlet. When you use an anchor tag, it always uses the HTTP GET method, and you can append parameters to the end of the URL. In this figure, the anchor tag appends one parameter to the URL.

A URL that's requested with the HTTP GET method

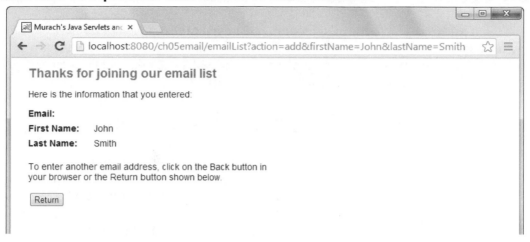

How to append parameters to a URL

```
emailList?action=add
emailList?firstName=John&lastName=Smith
```

Three ways to append parameters to a GET request

Enter the URL into the browser's address bar

```
http://localhost:8080/ch05email/emailList?action=add&firstName=John
http://www.murach.com/email/list?action=add&firstName=John
```

Code a form that uses the GET method

```
<form action="emailList">
<form action="emailList" method="get">
```

Code an anchor tag

```
<a href="emailList?action=join">Display Email Entry Test</a>
```

Description

- To append a parameter to a URL, code a question mark at the end of the URL followed by the name of the parameter, an equals sign, and the value of the parameter.

- To append multiple parameters to a URL, use ampersands (&) to separate the parameters.

- If you enter a URL into the browser's address bar, the browser uses the HTTP GET method.

- When you code a form, it uses the HTTP GET method by default, but you can specify this method for clarity if you want. When you use the HTTP GET method with a form, any parameters within the form are automatically appended to the URL displayed by the browser.

- When you code an anchor tag, you can append parameters to it. This tag always uses the HTTP GET method.

- To process an HTTP GET request, a servlet must implement the doGet method.

Figure 5-4   How to request a URL with the HTTP GET method

How to use the HTTP POST method

When you use a form tag to request a URL, you can use the HTTP POST method. To do that, you use the method attribute to specify the POST method as shown in figure 5-5. Then, the request uses the POST method, and browser doesn't display the parameters for the request in its URL.

When to use the HTTP GET and POST methods

So, when should you use the HTTP GET method and when should you use the POST method? In general, you should use the GET method when you want to *get* (read) data from the server. Similarly, you should use the POST method when you want to *post* (write) data to the server.

When you use the GET method, you need to make sure that the page can be executed multiple times without causing any problems. If, for example, the servlet just reads data from the server and displays it to the user, there's no harm in executing the servlet multiple times. If, for example, the user clicks the Refresh button, the browser requests the URL again, and this doesn't cause any problems.

However, if the servlet writes or sends data to the server, you typically don't want the user to execute the servlet multiple times. As a result, it makes more sense to use the POST method. Then, if the user clicks the Refresh button, the browser displays a dialog box like the one shown in this figure that warns the user that the data is about to be submitted again. At that point, the user can click on the Cancel button to cancel the request.

There are also a few other reasons to use the POST method. First, since the POST method doesn't append parameters to the end of the URL, it is more appropriate for working with sensitive data. Second, since the POST method prevents the web browser from including parameters in a bookmark for a page, you'll want to use it if you don't want the parameters to be included in the bookmark. Third, if your parameters contain more than 4 KB of data, the GET method won't work so you'll need to use the POST method.

For all other uses, the GET method is preferred. It runs slightly faster than the POST method, and it lets the user bookmark the page along with the parameters that are sent to the page.

When you request a servlet by using an anchor tag or by entering a URL into a browser, remember that these techniques automatically use the HTTP GET method. As a result, a servlet can process these requests only if it has implemented the doGet method. If you attempt to use one of these methods with a servlet that doesn't implement the doGet method, the server returns an error message that indicates that the HTTP GET method is not supported by the specified URL. Conversely, if you use the HTTP POST method to request a servlet that doesn't implement the doPost method, the server returns an error message that indicates that the HTTP POST method is not supported by the specified URL.

A URL that's requested with the HTTP POST method

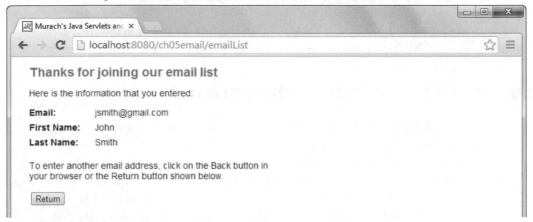

A Form tag that uses the POST method

```
<form action="emailList" method="post">
```

Use the GET method when...

- The request reads data from the server.
- The request can be executed multiple times without causing any problems.

Use the POST method when...

- The request writes data to the server.
- Executing the request multiple times may cause problems.
- You don't want to include the parameters in the URL for security reasons.
- You don't want users to be able to include parameters when they bookmark a page.
- You need to transfer more than 4 KB of data.

A typical browser dialog that's displayed if the user tries to refresh a post

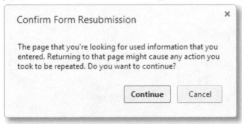

Figure 5-5   How to request a URL with the HTTP POST method

Skills for working with servlets

In the previous figures, you learned how to create a servlet, map it to a URL, and request it. Now, you'll learn some skills for processing the request.

How to get the values of the parameters

Figure 5-6 summarizes two of the methods available from the HttpServletRequest object, which is typically named request. This object is available to both the doGet and doPost methods of a servlet, and you can use the methods of this object to get the values of the parameters of the request.

To get the text that a user has entered into a text box, you can call the getParameter method from the request object and specify the name of the text box. In this figure, for instance, the first example gets the text that's stored in the text box that has a name attribute of "firstName". You can use a similar technique to work with other controls. For example, you can use this technique to get the selected value from a combo box or a group of radio buttons.

For checkboxes that have a value attribute, the getParameter method returns that value if the checkbox is selected and a null value if it isn't. However, if the checkbox doesn't have a value attribute, the getParameter method returns an "on" value if the checkbox is selected and a null value if it isn't. As a result, you can determine whether the user has selected a check box by checking whether its value is null as shown in the second example.

To retrieve multiple values for one parameter name, you can use the getParameterValues method as illustrated by the third example. This is useful for controls like list boxes that allow multiple selections. After you use the getParameterValues method to return an array of String objects, you can use a loop to get the values from the array as shown in the third example.

Two methods available from the HttpServletRequest object

Method	Description
getParameter(String param)	Returns the value of the specified parameter as a string if it exists or null if it doesn't. Often, this is the value defined in the value attribute of the control in the HTML or JSP file.
getParameterValues(String param)	Returns an array of String objects containing all of the values that the given request parameter has or null if the parameter doesn't have any values.

Servlet code that gets text from a text box

```
String firstName = request.getParameter("firstName");
```

Servlet code that determines if a check box is checked

```
// returns the value or "on" if checked, null otherwise.
String rockCheckBox = request.getParameter("rock");
if (rockCheckBox != null)
{
    // rock music was checked
}
```

Servlet code that reads and processes multiple values from a list box

```
// returns the values of the items selected in a list box.
String[] selectedCountries = request.getParameterValues("country");
for (String country : selectedCountries)
{
    // code that processes each country
}
```

Description

- Within a servlet, the doGet and doPost methods both provide an HttpServletRequest object. This object is typically named request.

- You can use the methods of the request object to get the values of the parameters that are stored in the request.

Figure 5-6   How to get the values of the parameters

How to get the real path for a file

When you work with servlets, you typically use relative paths to refer to files that are available within the web application. Sometimes, though, you need to get the real path for one of these files.

To do that, you can use the technique shown in figure 5-7. First, you call the getServletContext method to get a ServletContext object. Then, you call the getRealPath method of the ServletContext object to return the real path for the specified file. When you use the getRealPath method, a front slash navigates to the root directory for the current application, so

```
getRealPath("/EmailList.txt")
```

specifies the EmailList.txt file in the current application's root directory.

In this figure, the first example gets the real path for a file named EmailList. txt that's stored in the WEB-INF subdirectory of the application. Here, the getRealPath method returns a string for an absolute path to this file. If, for example, this method is used in the ch05email application that's in the NetBeans directory that's used for our downloadable applications, the getRealPath method returns the path shown in this figure.

The second example shows a more concise way to code the first example. Here, the code doesn't supply a name for the ServletContext object. Instead, it calls the getRealPath method directly from the getServletContext method. Since this technique calls one method from another method, it's known as *method chaining*. Often, this technique results in code that is shorter and easier to read. The only disadvantage is that it doesn't create a variable name for the ServletContext object that you can use multiple times in your code. But, if your code only uses the ServletContext object once, it usually makes sense to use method chaining.

If you store a file in a directory that's web accessible, such as the root directory for a web application, any user who enters the correct URL can access the file. However, the WEB-INF directory and its subdirectories aren't directly web-accessible. As a result, if you want to keep a file private, you can store it in the WEB-INF directory or one of its subdirectories. Or, you can restrict access to the file or directory as described in chapter 16.

If you use the getRealPath method, you should be aware that it may work differently on different systems. For example, with Tomcat 8, you must start the path parameter with a front slash. However, with Tomcat 7, this front slash isn't required. Similarly, the getRealPath method fails and returns a null value if you are attempting to get a path to a resource that's inside a WAR file, or if you are trying to get a path to a resource that's located in or on a virtual file system.

A method of the GenericServlet class

Method	Description
getServletContext()	Returns a ServletContext object that contains information about the application's context.

A method of the ServletContext class for working with paths

Method	Description
getRealPath(String path)	Returns a String object for the absolute path of the specified relative path.

Code that gets the absolute path for a file

```
ServletContext sc = this.getServletContext();
String path = sc.getRealPath("/WEB-INF/EmailList.txt");
```

A more concise way to get the absolute path for a file

```
String path = this.getServletContext()
        .getRealPath("/WEB-INF/EmailList.txt");
```

A possible value for the real path variable

```
C:\murach\servlet_and_jsp\netbeans\book_apps\ch05email\build\web\WEB-INF\
EmailList.txt
```

Description

- All servlets inherit the GenericServlet class. As a result, the getServletContext method is available to all servlets.

- In addition to working with relative paths as described here, you can use the ServletContext object to read global initialization parameters, to work with global variables, and to write data to log files. You'll learn more about these skills as you progress through this book.

Figure 5-7   How to get the real path for a file

How to get and set request attributes

To store any object in the request object, you can use the setAttribute method as shown in figure 5-8. Here, the first example creates a User object named user and stores it in the request object with a name of "user".

Once you store an object in the request object, you can use the getAttribute method to retrieve the object. In this figure, the second example gets the User object stored in the first example. Since the getAttribute method returns a value of the Object type, this type must be cast to the User type.

When you work with request attributes, you should realize that the attributes are reset between requests. As a result, if you store a User object as a request attribute and forward that request to a JSP, that User object is only available to that JSP and isn't available later in the session. In chapter 7, you'll learn how to store an object so it's available to any servlet or JSP in the current session.

Two methods available from the HttpServletRequest object

Method	Description
setAttribute(String name, Object o)	Stores any object in the request as an attribute and specifies a name for the attribute. Attributes are reset between requests.
getAttribute(String name)	Returns the value of the specified attribute as an Object type. If no attribute exists for the specified name, this method returns a null value.

How to set a request attribute

```
User user = new User(firstName, lastName, email);
request.setAttribute("user", user);
```

How to get a request attribute

```
User user = (User) request.getAttribute("user");
```

How to set a request attribute for a primitive type

```
int id = 1;
request.setAttribute("id", new Integer(id));
```

How to get a request attribute for a primitive type

```
int id = (Integer) request.getAttribute("id");
```

Description

* These methods are most often used in conjunction with a RequestDispatcher object that's used to forward a request as described in the next figure.

Figure 5-8   How to get and set request attributes

How to forward requests

Figure 5-9 shows how to *forward* a request from a servlet to an HTML page, a JSP, or another servlet. To do that, you begin by calling the getServletContext method from the HttpServlet class to return a ServletContext object. Then, you call the getRequestDispatcher method of the ServletContext object to return a RequestDispatcher object. Within this method, you must code a URL that starts with a slash so it is relative to the root directory of the current web application. Then, you use the forward method to forward the request and response objects to the HTML page, JSP, or servlet specified by the URL.

In the examples in this figure, the first statement sets the string for the URL. Then, the second statement gets the ServletContext object, gets the RequestDispatcher object for the URL, and forwards the request. In these examples, the second statement uses method chaining as described earlier in this chapter.

How to redirect responses

This figure also shows how to *redirect* a response. To do that, you use the sendRedirect method of the response object. You typically use this technique when you want to transfer control to a URL outside of your application. To use this method, you often supply an absolute URL. However, you can also supply a relative URL because the servlet engine can convert it to an absolute URL. If you begin the pathname with a slash, the servlet engine interprets the path as relative to the root directory for the servlet engine.

When you call the sendRedirect method, the server sends an absolute URL to the browser. Then, the browser sends a request for that URL. Since this processing occurs on the client side rather than the server side, this isn't as efficient as forwarding a request as shown earlier in this figure. In addition, the sendRedirect method doesn't transfer the request and response objects. As a result, you should only use the sendRedirect method when you want to redirect to a URL that's available from another web application.

A method of the ServletContext object for working with paths

Method	Description
getRequestDispatcher(String path**)**	Returns a RequestDispatcher object for the specified path.

A method of the RequestDispatcher object

Method	Description
forward(ServletRequest request, ServletResponse response**)**	Forwards the request and response objects to another resource on the server (usually a JSP or servlet).

How to forward the request to an HTML page

```
String url = "/index.html";
getServletContext().getRequestDispatcher(url)
    .forward(request, response);
```

How to forward the request to a JSP

```
String url = "/thanks.jsp";
getServletContext().getRequestDispatcher(url)
    .forward(request, response);
```

How to forward the request to a servlet

```
String url = "/cart/displayInvoice";
getServletContext().getRequestDispatcher(url)
    .forward(request, response);
```

A method of the HttpServletResponse class

Method	Description
sendRedirect(String path**)**	Sends a temporary redirect response to the client using the specified redirect location URL.

How to redirect a response relative to the current directory

```
response.sendRedirect("email");
```

How to redirect a response relative to the servlet engine

```
response.sendRedirect("/musicStore/email/");
```

How to redirect a response to a different web server

```
response.sendRedirect("http://www.murach.com/email/");
```

Figure 5-9   How to forward requests and redirect responses

How to validate data

When a user enters data into an application, the application often needs to check the data to make sure that the data is valid. This is referred to as data validation. Then, if the user enters data that isn't valid, the application can display an error message and give the user another chance to enter the data.

How to validate data on the client

In a typical web application, the data that's entered by the user is validated by JavaScript in the browser. That way, some invalid entries are caught and fixed before they're sent to the server for processing. That makes the application more responsive to the user and reduces the workload on the server. To learn how to perform data validation on the client, we recommend that you refer to *Murach's JavaScript and jQuery*.

How to validate data on the server

Whether or not the user data is validated on the client, though, it is always validated on the server. One reason for that is that JavaScript on the client can't always do all of the validation that's required. For instance, checking whether an email address is already in the database can only be done on the server. Another reason is that client validation doesn't work if JavaScript is disabled in a user's browser.

To illustrate data validation on the server, figure 5-10 presents an enhanced version of the Email List application. To start, the code for the first page of the application is now stored in a JSP file, not an HTML file. This allows the first page to use EL to display a validation message like the one shown in this figure, and it allows the first page to use EL to retain any valid values that the user has entered.

When a user requests this JSP for the first time, the page doesn't display a validation message, and it does display empty strings in the three text boxes of the form. Then, if the user submits the data with invalid strings in any of its text boxes, this JSP displays a validation message in italics before the form, and it displays any values that the user has already entered within the text boxes. That way, the user doesn't have to re-enter any valid values that he or she has already entered.

When the user clicks the Join Now button, this page sends the values in the text boxes to the servlet. Then, if a value is still missing, this servlet forwards the request to this JSP again. In other words, this request and response cycle continues until the user enters valid data or ends the application.

In chapter 4, you learned how to use HTML5 to do some rudimentary validation on the client. For example, you learned how to use the required attribute to require the user to enter a value for a text box. In this chapter, the Email List application doesn't include that client-side validation. This allows the developer to test the server-side validation. However, once the developer finishes testing the server-side validation, he or she should restore the client-side validation.

The JSP that's displayed when an entry isn't made

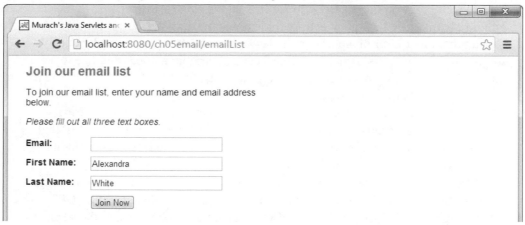

The code for the JSP (index.jsp)

```
<!DOCTYPE html>
<html>
<head>
    <meta charset="utf-8">
    <title>Murach's Java Servlets and JSP</title>
    <link rel="stylesheet" href="styles/main.css" type="text/css"/>
</head>
<body>
    <h1>Join our email list</h1>
    <p>To join our email list, enter your name and
       email address below.</p>
    <p><i>${message}</i></p>
    <form action="emailList" method="post">
        <input type="hidden" name="action" value="add">
        <label class="pad_top">Email:</label>
        <input type="email" name="email" value="${user.email}"><br>
        <label class="pad_top">First Name:</label>
        <input type="text" name="firstName" value="${user.firstName}"><br>
        <label class="pad_top">Last Name:</label>
        <input type="text" name="lastName" value="${user.lastName}"><br>
        <label> </label>
        <input type="submit" value="Join Now" class="margin_left">
    </form>
</body>
</html>
```

Figure 5-10   How to validate data on the server (part 1 of 2)

Part 2 of this figure shows the code in the doPost method of the servlet that validates the data on the server. If the user is attempting to add a name to the email list, this code begins by getting three request parameters from the form and storing them in a User object. Then, it checks that the user has entered values for all three parameters. If not, this code sets the variable named message to an appropriate validation message, and it sets the variable named url to the JSP that displays the validation message (index.jsp).

Otherwise, this code sets the variable named message to an empty string so no validation message is displayed, it sets the variable named url to the JSP that displays the data to the user (thanks.jsp), and it uses the UserDB class to write the data in the User object to the database.

After the if/else statement, the servlet stores the User object and the message string in the request object. Then, it forwards the request to the specified URL. If, for example, the user hasn't entered valid data, this code forwards the request to the JSP shown in part 1 of this figure.

If you study this servlet, it should give you a better idea of how a servlet can function as a controller in the MVC pattern. In particular, this shows how a servlet can get data from the request, update the model based on that data, and forward the request to the appropriate part of the view.

Keep in mind, though, that checking to make sure an entry has been made in a field is minimal data validation. In practice, the data validation code would also check that the email entry is a valid email address with an at sign (@), a period, and more.

Since this servlet works with strings, it doesn't need any code that converts the data. But what if you want to make sure that the user enters an integer? To do that, you can attempt to convert the string to an int value within a try/catch statement. Then, if the parsing fails and an exception is thrown, the servlet can supply code in the catch statement that displays an appropriate validation message and forwards the request to an appropriate JSP.

A doPost method that validates the data

```java
@Override
protected void doPost(HttpServletRequest request,
        HttpServletResponse response)
        throws ServletException, IOException {

    String url = "/index.jsp";

    // get current action
    String action = request.getParameter("action");
    if (action == null) {
        action = "join";  // default action
    }

    // perform action and set URL to appropriate page
    if (action.equals("join")) {
        url = "/index.jsp";     // the "join" page
    }
    else if (action.equals("add")) {
        // get parameters from the request
        String firstName = request.getParameter("firstName");
        String lastName = request.getParameter("lastName");
        String email = request.getParameter("email");

        // store data in User object
        User user = new User(firstName, lastName, email);

        // validate the parameters
        String message;
        if (firstName == null || lastName == null || email == null ||
            firstName.isEmpty() || lastName.isEmpty() || email.isEmpty()) {
            message = "Please fill out all three text boxes.";
            url = "/index.jsp";
        }
        else {
            message = "";
            url = "/thanks.jsp";
            UserDB.insert(user);
        }
        request.setAttribute("user", user);
        request.setAttribute("message", message);
    }
    getServletContext()
            .getRequestDispatcher(url)
            .forward(request, response);
}
```

Figure 5-10   How to validate data on the server (part 2 of 2)

How to work with the web.xml file

In chapter 2, you learned that most applications have one web.xml file that contains information about the configuration of the application. Then, earlier in this chapter, you learned how to use the web.xml file to map servlets to URLs. Now, you'll learn more about working with the web.xml file for an application.

The code in this topic has been tested against the Tomcat server. If you're using a different servlet engine, you may need to modify the code presented in this topic so it works with your servlet engine. In general, though, the code presented here should work on all servlet engines.

A complete web.xml file

Figure 5-11 shows the web.xml file that works with the application presented in this chapter. This web.xml file begins with two tags that define the type of XML document that's being used. For now, you don't need to understand this code. However, these tags must be included at the start of each web.xml file. Fortunately, most IDEs create them automatically. Otherwise, you can copy these tags from another web.xml file.

After this code, the web.xml file contains *XML tags* that define *elements*. For example, the opening and closing web-app tags define the web-app element. Since all other elements are coded within this element, the web-app element is known as the *root element*. Any element coded within this element or a lower-level element is known as a *child element*.

To modify a web.xml file, you should be able to use your IDE. As you're making the modifications, if you want to leave code in the XML file but you don't want the servlet engine to use it, you can use XML *comments* to comment out those portions of code. These comments work the same way HTML comments do.

When you're done modifying the file, you must redeploy the application to Tomcat so the changes take effect. With most IDEs, this happens automatically when you run the application. If not, you can always restart Tomcat to make sure that it reads the changes to the web.xml file.

When you modify a web.xml file, you should make sure to nest the XML elements correctly as shown in this figure. Otherwise, when you start Tomcat or attempt to deploy your application, Tomcat won't be able to read the web.xml file. In that case, Tomcat displays an error message. To solve this problem, you can edit the web.xml file and redeploy the application. Or, you can restart Tomcat to read the file again.

A complete web.xml file

```xml
<?xml version="1.0" encoding="UTF-8"?>
<web-app version="3.0" xmlns="http://java.sun.com/xml/ns/javaee"
         xmlns:xsi="http://www.w3.org/2001/XMLSchema-instance"
         xsi:schemaLocation="http://java.sun.com/xml/ns/javaee
             http://java.sun.com/xml/ns/javaee/web-app_3_0.xsd">

    <context-param>
        <param-name>custServEmail</param-name>
        <param-value>custserv@murach.com</param-value>
    </context-param>

    <servlet>
        <servlet-name>EmailListServlet</servlet-name>
        <servlet-class>murach.email.EmailListServlet</servlet-class>
        <init-param>
            <param-name>relativePathToFile</param-name>
            <param-value>/WEB-INF/EmailList.txt</param-value>
        </init-param>
    </servlet>

    <servlet-mapping>
        <servlet-name>EmailListServlet</servlet-name>
        <url-pattern>/emailList</url-pattern>
    </servlet-mapping>

    <!-- you can comment out these tags when the app is in development -->
    <error-page>
        <error-code>404</error-code>
        <location>/error_404.jsp</location>
    </error-page>
    <error-page>
        <exception-type>java.lang.Throwable</exception-type>
        <location>/error_java.jsp</location>
    </error-page>

    <session-config>
        <session-timeout>30</session-timeout>
    </session-config>

    <welcome-file-list>
        <welcome-file>index.html</welcome-file>
        <welcome-file>index.jsp</welcome-file>
    </welcome-file-list>
</web-app>
```

Description

- The web.xml file is stored in the WEB-INF directory for an application. When Tomcat starts, it reads the web.xml file.

- If the elements in the web.xml aren't nested correctly, Tomcat displays an error message when it reads the web.xml file.

- After you modify the web.xml file, you must redeploy the application so the changes take effect. Or, you can restart Tomcat.

Figure 5-11   A complete web.xml file

How to work with initialization parameters

If you want to store some *initialization parameters* for an application in a central location, you can add them to the web.xml file as shown in part 1 of figure 5-12. Then, your servlets can read these parameters as shown in part 2 of this figure.

To define a *context initialization parameter* that's available to all servlets in the web application, you code a context-param element. Then, you code two child elements: the param-name element and the param-value element. To define multiple context parameters, you can code additional context-param elements after the first one. In this figure, the context-param element defines a parameter named custServEmail that has a value that provides an email address.

To define a *servlet initialization parameter* that's available to a specific servlet, you can code an init-param element within a servlet element. This element follows the servlet-name and servlet-class elements that you learned about earlier in this chapter.

Within the init-param element, you must code the param-name and param-value elements to define the name and value of the parameter. To define multiple initialization parameters for a servlet, you can code additional init-param elements after the first one. In this figure, the init-param element defines a parameter named relativePathToFile that has a relative path as its value.

With the servlet 3.0 specification (Tomcat 7.0) and later, you can use the @WebServlet and @InitParam annotations to specify servlet initialization parameters. To do that, you can code the @WebServlet annotation as described earlier in this chapter. However, you use the urlPatterns attribute to specify the URL mapping for the servlet. Then, you use the initParams attribute to specify the initialization parameters for the servlet. To do that, you can code one or more @WebInitParam annotations. Each of these annotations includes name and value attributes that specify the name and value of the parameter.

XML tags that set initialization parameters in a web.xml file

```
<context-param>
    <param-name>custServEmail</param-name>
    <param-value>custserv@murach.com</param-value>
</context-param>

<servlet>
    <servlet-name>AddToEmailListServlet</servlet-name>
    <servlet-class>email.AddToEmailListServlet</servlet-class>
    <init-param>
        <param-name>relativePathToFile</param-name>
        <param-value>/WEB-INF/EmailList.txt</param-value>
    </init-param>
</servlet>
```

XML elements for working with initialization parameters

Element	Description
`<context-param>`	Defines a parameter that's available to all servlets within an application.
`<servlet>`	Identifies a specific servlet within the application.
`<servlet-name>`	Defines the name for the servlet that's used in the rest of the web.xml file.
`<servlet-class>`	Identifies the servlet by specifying the servlet's package and class name.
`<init-param>`	Defines a name/value pair for an initialization parameter for a servlet.
`<param-name>`	Defines the name of a parameter.
`<param-value>`	Defines the value of a parameter.

An annotation that sets initialization parameters for a servlet

```
@WebServlet(urlPatterns={"/emailList"},
            initParams={@WebInitParam(name="relativePathToFile",
                                      value="/WEB-INF/EmailList.txt")})
```

Description

- To create an *initialization parameter* that's available to all servlets (called a *context initialization parameter*), you code the param-name and param-value elements within the context-param element.

- To create an initialization parameter that's available to a specific servlet (called a *servlet initialization parameter*), you code the param-name and param-value elements within the init-param element. But first, you must identify the servlet by coding the servlet, servlet-name, and servlet-class elements.

Figure 5-12   How to work with initialization parameters (part 1 of 2)

Part 2 of this figure shows you how to read initialization parameters like those in part 1. To retrieve an initialization parameter that's available to all servlets, you begin by calling the getServletContext method from anywhere in the servlet to get a ServletContext object. Then, you call the getInitParameter method from the ServletContext object.

To retrieve an initialization parameter that's available only to the current servlet, you begin by calling the getServletConfig method from anywhere in the servlet to get a ServletConfig object. Then, you call the getInitParameter method from the ServletConfig object.

Note that the getInitParameter method works the same whether you call it from the ServletContext object or the ServletConfig object. The only difference is that the ServletContext object returns parameters that are available to all servlets while the ServletConfig object returns parameters that are only available to the current servlet.

When you call the getInitParameter method, you must specify the name of the parameter. If the parameter exists, the getInitParameter method returns the value of the parameter as a string. Otherwise, this method returns a null value.

Two methods of the GenericServlet class

Method	Description
getServletContext()	Returns a ServletContext object that contains information about the entire web application's context.
getServletConfig()	Returns a ServletConfig object that contains information about a single servlet's configuration.

A method of the ServletContext and ServletConfig interfaces

Method	Description
getInitParameter(String name)	Returns a String object that contains the value of the specified initialization parameter. If the parameter doesn't exist, this method returns a null value.

Code that gets an initialization parameter that's available to all servlets

```
String custServEmail = this.getServletContext()
                       .getInitParameter("custServEmail");
```

Code that gets an initialization parameter that's available to the current servlet only

```
String relativePath = this.getServletConfig()
                      .getInitParameter("relativePathToFile");
```

Description

- To get an initialization parameter that's available to all servlets, you use the getInitParameter method of the ServletContext object.

- To get an initialization parameter for a specific servlet, you use the getInitParameter method of the ServletConfig object.

Figure 5-12   How to work with initialization parameters (part 2 of 2)

How to implement custom error handling

Figure 5-13 shows how to use the web.xml file to specify custom error pages that apply to the entire application. When you're developing an application, you probably won't want to implement custom error pages. That way, when an error occurs, Tomcat displays an error page that you can use to debug the error. Before you deploy an application, though, you may want to implement custom error pages that present errors in a user-friendly way that's consistent with the rest of your application.

To specify a custom error page for a specific *HTTP status code*, you begin by coding an error-page element. Within this element, you code two child elements: the error-code element and the location element. The error-code element specifies the HTTP status code for the error. The location element specifies the location of the custom error page.

The first example in this figure shows how to code the error-page element for the HTTP 404 status code. Here, the error-code element specifies the number for the HTTP status code. Then, the location element specifies a URL that points to an error page named error_404.jsp that's stored in the application's root directory. Note that this element must begin with a slash.

The second example shows some of the code for a custom error page for the 404 status code. This page is a JSP that displays a user-friendly message that describes the HTTP 404 status code.

The 404 status code indicates that the server wasn't able to find a file at the requested URL. As you gain more experience with web programming, you'll become familiar with other HTTP status codes. Also, some of the more common ones are summarized in chapter 18.

To specify a custom error page that's displayed when an uncaught exception is thrown, you begin by coding an error-page element. Within this element, you code two child elements: the exception-type element and the location element. The exception-type element specifies the type of exception by identifying the package name and the class name for the exception. The location element specifies the location of the custom error page.

The third example shows how to code an error-page element that handles all Java exceptions. Here, the exception-type element specifies the Throwable class in the java.lang package. Since all exceptions inherit this class, this causes a custom error page to be displayed for all uncaught exceptions. However, if you want to display different error pages for different types of exceptions, you can code multiple error-page elements. For example, you can display one error page for exceptions of the NullPointerException type and another error page for exceptions of the ServletException type.

The fourth example shows some of the code for a custom error page that handles all Java exceptions. This error page uses EL to display the name of the exception's class and its message. For more information about EL, see chapter 8.

XML elements for working with error handling

Element	Description
`<error-page>`	Specifies an HTML page or JSP that's displayed when the application encounters an uncaught exception or a certain type of HTTP status code.
`<error-code>`	Specifies the number of a valid HTTP status code.
`<exception-type>`	Uses the fully qualified class name to specify a Java exception.
`<location>`	Specifies the location of the HTML page or JSP that's displayed.

The XML tags that provide error-handling for an HTTP 404 status code

```
<error-page>
    <error-code>404</error-code>
    <location>/error_404.jsp</location>
</error-page>
```

The code for a file named error_404.jsp

```
<h1>404 Error</h1>
<p>The server was not able to find the file you requested.</p>
<p>To continue, click the Back button.</p>
```

The XML tags that provide error-handling for all Java exceptions

```
<error-page>
    <exception-type>java.lang.Throwable</exception-type>
    <location>/error_java.jsp</location>
</error-page>
```

The code for a file named error_java.jsp

```
<h1>Java Error</h1>
<p>Sorry, Java has thrown an exception.</p>
<p>To continue, click the Back button.</p>

<h2>Details</h2>
<p>Type: {pageContext.exception["class"]}</p>
<p>Message: {pageContext.exception.message}</p>
```

Figure 5-13   How to implement custom error handling (part 1 of 2)

When you code a custom error page, you can use an HTML document or a JSP. If you use a JSP, you can use the exception object to customize the error page. In addition, you can use any other techniques that are available to a JSP.

Part 2 of figure 5-13 shows how the error pages appear when displayed in a browser. Here, the first screen shows the error page that's displayed for an HTTP 404 status code. By default, however, Microsoft Internet Explorer uses its own error pages for HTTP status codes. So if you want to use this browser to view a custom page, you must select the Tools→Internet Options command and use the Advanced tab of the dialog box to deselect the "Show friendly HTTP error messages" option. That's why I used Chrome to display this error page.

The second screen shows the error page that's displayed when a servlet throws an exception. Here, the details at the bottom of the page show that one of the paths used by the application threw an IllegalArgumentException. In addition, the message indicates that exception was thrown because a front slash wasn't coded at the start of the path for the thanks.jsp file.

In this case, this is all the information you need to debug the error. However, this error page doesn't give as much information as the error pages that are provided by Tomcat. As a result, it's easier to debug errors when you're using Tomcat's error pages. That's why you should only use an error page like this when you're ready to put your web application into a production environment. Until then, you can comment out the error-page element in the web.xml file.

The JSP page for the 404 error

The JSP page that's displayed when a Java exception is thrown

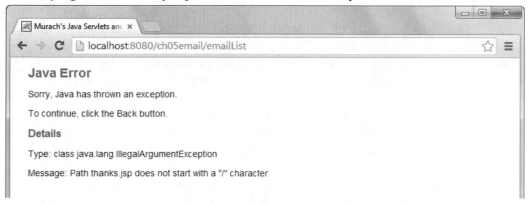

Description

- In the web.xml file, you can use the error-page element to specify the error pages that should be displayed when the application encounters (1) specific HTTP status codes or (2) uncaught exceptions.

- By default, Internet Explorer uses its own error pages for HTTP status codes. As a result, if you want to use this browser to view a custom page, you must select the Tools→Internet Options command and use the Advanced tab of the dialog box to deselect the "Show friendly HTTP error messages" option.

Figure 5-13   How to implement custom error handling (part 2 of 2)

More skills for working with servlets

Now that you have a basic understanding of how to code a servlet, you're ready to learn some other background concepts for working with servlets. Understanding these concepts can help you avoid some common pitfalls. First, it's generally considered a bad practice to override a servlet's service method. Second, it's generally considered a bad practice to code instance variables for a servlet.

How the methods of a servlet work

Figure 5-14 presents some common methods of the HttpServlet class. When you code these methods, you need to understand that the servlet engine only creates one instance of a servlet. This usually occurs when the servlet engine starts or when the servlet is first requested. Then, each request for the servlet starts (or "spawns") a thread that can access that one instance of the servlet.

When the servlet engine creates the instance of the servlet, it calls the init method. Since this method is only called once, you can override it in your servlet to supply any initialization code that's required as shown in the next figure.

After the servlet engine has created the one instance of the servlet, each request for that servlet spawns a thread that calls the service method of the servlet. This method checks the method that's specified in the HTTP request and calls the appropriate doGet or doPost method.

When you code servlets, you shouldn't override the service method. Instead, you should override the appropriate doGet or doPost methods. To handle a request that uses the GET method, for example, you can override the doGet method. If, on the other hand, you want to handle a request that uses the POST method, you can override the doPost method. To use the same code to handle both types of requests, you can override both of them and have one call the other as shown in figure 5-1.

If a servlet has been idle for some time or if the servlet engine is shut down, the servlet engine unloads the instances of the servlets that it has created. Before unloading a servlet, though, it calls the destroy method of the servlet. If you want to provide some cleanup code, such as writing a variable to a file, you can override this method. However, the destroy method can't be called if the server crashes. As a result, you shouldn't rely on it to execute any code that's critical to your application.

Five common methods of a servlet

```
protected void init() throws ServletException

protected void service(HttpServletRequest request,
        HttpServletResponse response) throws IOException, ServletException

protected void doGet(HttpServletRequest request,
        HttpServletResponse response) throws IOException, ServletException

protected void doPost(HttpServletRequest request,
        HttpServletResponse response) throws IOException, ServletException

protected void destroy()
```

The lifecycle of a servlet

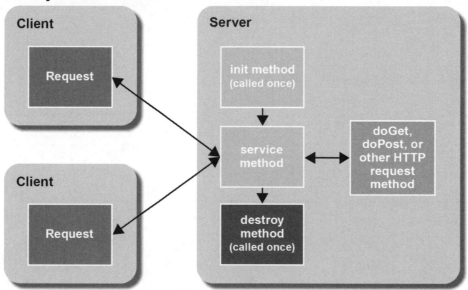

Description

- A server loads and initializes the servlet by calling the init method.
- The servlet handles each browser request by calling the service method. This method then calls another method to handle the specific HTTP request type.
- The server removes the servlet by calling the destroy method. This occurs either when the servlet has been idle for some time or when the server is shut down.

Notes

- All the methods shown above are located in the abstract HttpServlet class. As a result, you can override these methods in your own servlets.
- It's generally considered a bad practice to override the service method. Instead, you should override a method like doGet or doPost to handle a specific type of HTTP request.

Figure 5-14   How the methods of a servlet work

Why you shouldn't use instance variables in servlets

Figure 5-15 shows an example of how instance variables were sometimes used with servlets. But using instance variables is not an acceptable practice.

The problem with instance variables is that they aren't thread-safe and they can lead to lost updates and other serious problems. Worse, there's no easy way to make instance variables thread-safe. As a result, you should never code instance variables for a servlet. As you progress through this book, though, you'll learn several thread-safe techniques for working with global variables so you won't have to use instance variables.

Code that adds an instance variable to the EmailServlet class

```
package murach.email;

import java.io.*;
import javax.servlet.*;
import javax.servlet.http.*;

public class EmailListServlet extends HttpServlet
{
    // declare an instance variable for the page
    private int globalCount; // instance variables are not thread-safe

    @Override
    public void init() throws ServletException
    {
        globalCount = 0;         // initialize the instance variable
    }

    @Override
    protected void doPost(
        HttpServletRequest request,
        HttpServletResponse response)
        throws ServletException, IOException
    {
        // update global count variable
        globalCount++;            // this is not thread-safe

        // the rest of the code goes here
    }
}
```

Description

- An *instance variable* of a servlet belongs to the one instance of the servlet and is shared by any threads that request the servlet.

- Instance variables are not *thread-safe*. In other words, two threads may conflict when they try to read, modify, and update the same instance variable at the same time, which can result in lost updates or other problems.

- That's why you should never use instance variables in servlets.

Figure 5-15   Why you shouldn't use instance variables in servlets

How to work with servlet errors

When you develop servlets, you will inevitably encounter errors. That's why this topic gives you some ideas on how to solve common problems and how to print debugging data to the console or to a log file.

How to solve common servlet problems

Figure 5-16 lists four common problems that can occur when you're working with servlets. Then, it lists some possible solutions for each of these problems. Unfortunately, the solutions to these problems vary depending on the IDE you're using. As a result, the solutions presented here are only described in general terms.

If your servlet won't compile, the error message that's displayed should give you an idea of why the servlet won't compile. If the compiler can't find a class that's in one of the Java APIs, for example, you may need to make the API available to your application. To do that, you can usually use the IDE to add the appropriate library or JAR file to the application.

If the servlet compiles but won't run, it may be because the servlet engine isn't running. To solve this problem, of course, you can start the servlet engine. However, if the servlet engine is already running, you should double-check the URL to make sure that it's correctly mapped to the servlet. A common mistake, for example, is to change the name of the servlet and forget to update the mapping for the servlet in the web.xml file.

If you make changes to a servlet and the changes don't show up when you run the servlet, it may be because the servlet engine hasn't reloaded the modified class. In this case, you can enable servlet reloading. That way, the servlet engine automatically detects changes to servlets and reloads them. Or, you can redeploy the application, and many IDEs do this automatically when you run the web application. Finally, if all else fails, you can shut down Tomcat and restart it so Tomcat has to reload all of the applications that are running on it.

If the HTML page that's returned by a servlet doesn't look right when it's rendered by the browser, the servlet is probably sending bad HTML to the browser. To troubleshoot this problem, you can use your browser to view the source HTML that's sent to it. The procedure for doing this varies from browser to browser, but you can typically find a command in the menu system that allows you to view the HTML for the page. Then, you can identify the problem and modify the servlet or JSP to fix it.

Common servlet problems

Problem	Possible solutions
The servlet won't compile	Make sure the compiler has access to the JAR files for all necessary APIs.
The servlet won't run	Make sure the web server is running.
	Make sure you're using the correct URL.
Changes to the servlet aren't showing up	Make sure servlet reloading is on.
	Redeploy the application.
	Restart the server so it reloads all applications.
The page doesn't display correctly	Use your browser to view the HTML code for the page. Then, you can go through the HTML code to identify the problem, and you can fix the problem in the servlet.

Note

- Chapter 3 shows how to make JAR files available to the NetBeans IDE. You can use a similar technique to make a JAR file available to most other modern IDEs.

Figure 5-16   How to solve common servlet problems

How to print debugging data to the console

You can print debugging messages to the console for the servlet engine as shown in figure 5-17. To do that, you can use the println method of the System. out and System.err objects. You can use these messages to help track the methods that are executed or to view the value of a variable.

When you use println statements to check the value of a variable, you'll often want to include the name of the class and the name of the variable. That way, your messages are easier to understand. This also makes it easier to find and remove the println statements once the error is debugged.

When you use println statements to print debugging data to the console, this data may be printed to different locations depending on your development environment. If, for example, you're using the NetBeans IDE, the data is printed to the Tomcat tab of the Output window. However, if you're using Tomcat in a stand-alone environment, the data is printed to a Tomcat console.

Code that prints debugging data to the console

```
public void doPost(HttpServletRequest request,
                   HttpServletResponse response)
                   throws IOException, ServletException
{
    // code

    String email = request.getParameter("email");
    System.out.println("EmailListServlet email: " + email);

    // more code
}
```

The output that's printed to the Tomcat console

```
EmailListServlet email: jsmith@gmail.com
```

Description

- When you're testing an application on your local system, you can use the println method of the System.out or System.err objects to display debugging messages on the console for the servlet engine.

- When you use debugging messages to display variable values, it's a good practice to include the servlet name and the variable name so the messages are easy to interpret.

- When you use NetBeans, it displays a tab for the Tomcat console within its Output window.

Figure 5-17   How to print debugging data to the console

How to print debugging data to a log file

If you want to keep a permanent history of some key debugging data, you can print debugging data to a *log file* as shown in figure 5-18. Although each servlet engine uses log files a little differently, you should be able to use these log methods with any servlet engine. However, you may need to check the documentation for your servlet engine to see how these methods work.

To write data to a log file, you can use the two log methods of the HttpServlet class. If you just want to write a message to a log file, you can use the first log method. However, if you want to write a message to the log file along with the stack trace for an exception, you can use the second log method. A *stack trace* is a series of messages that presents the chain of method calls that precede the current method.

The first example in this figure uses the first log method to write the value for the emailAddress variable to the log file. Here, Tomcat automatically writes some additional information before the message. First, it writes a timestamp that shows the date and time that this data was written to the log file. Then, it writes the word INFO followed by the name of the servlet class. Note, however, that this information may vary from one servlet engine to another.

The second example in this figure uses the second log method to write a message and a stack trace for an IOException. In this case, Tomcat ignores the message and doesn't write it to the log file. Instead, Tomcat writes some other information to the log file. First, it writes a timestamp that shows the date and time that this stack trace was written to the log file. Then, it writes the word WARNING followed by the name of the method that threw the exception and the name of the servlet class. Finally, it writes the stack trace. Note that the stack trace indicates that the exception was thrown by the 11th line of the UserIO class. As a result, this helps you locate the code that's causing the bug.

Tomcat stores its log files in its logs directory. Within this directory, Tomcat stores several types of log files with one file of each type for each date. To view a log file, you can navigate to this directory and open the log file with a text editor. For example, to view the data that's written by the examples in this figure, I opened the log file that's specified at the bottom of this figure. This log file contains the data for any log methods that were executed on the localhost server for June 29th, 2014.

When you use the NetBeans IDE with Tomcat, the server's log file is shown in the Tomcat Log tab of the Output window. As a result, you can view the current log file by displaying that tab.

Two methods of the HttpServlet class used to log errors

Method	Description
log(String message)	Writes the specified message to the server's log file.
log(String message, Throwable t)	Writes the specified message to the server's log file, followed by the stack trace for the exception.

Servlet code that prints the value of a variable to a log file

```
log("email=" + email);
```

The data that's written to the log file

```
Jun 29, 2014 6:26:04 PM org.apache.catalina.core.ApplicationContext log
INFO: EmailListServlet: email=jsmith@gmail.com
```

Servlet code that prints a stack trace to a log file

```
try {
    UserIO.add(user, path);
}
catch(IOException e) {
    log("An IOException occurred.", e);
}
```

The data that's written to the log file

```
Jun 29, 2014 6:30:38 PM org.apache.catalina.core.StandardWrapperValve invoke
WARNING: Servlet.service() for servlet EmailListServlet threw exception
java.io.FileNotFoundException: C:\murach\servlet_and_jsp\netbeans\ch05email\
build\web\WEB-INF\EmailList.txt (Access is denied)
        at java.io.FileOutputStream.openAppend(Native Method)
        at java.io.FileOutputStream.<init>(FileOutputStream.java:177)
        at java.io.FileWriter.<init>(FileWriter.java:90)
        at murach.data.UserIO.add(UserIO.java:11)
        at murach.email.EmailListServlet.doPost(EmailListServlet.java:38)
...
...
```

The location of a typical Tomcat log file

```
C:\tomcat\logs\localhost.2014-06-29.log
```

Description

- You can use the log methods of the HttpServlet class to write debugging data to a web server's *log file*.
- A *stack trace* is the chain of method calls for any statement that calls a method.
- The data that's written by the log methods varies from one server to another. In fact, Tomcat doesn't include the specified message when you use the second method above. The name and location of the log files may also vary from one server to another.
- When you use NetBeans, it displays a tab for the server log within its Output window.

Figure 5-18   How to print debugging data to a log file

Perspective

The goal of this chapter has been to teach you the basics of coding servlets that work within the MVC pattern. Now, you should be able to develop servlets of your own that act as the controllers of an application. Then, you should be able to forward the HTTP request and response to a JSP that sends the appropriate HTML back to the browser. In the next chapter, you'll learn the details for coding a JSP.

Before you go on to the next chapter, though, you should know that some of the skills described in this chapter also apply to JSPs. For example, you can use the log method within a JSP to write data to a log file. However, if you use the MVC pattern, you typically won't need to add any log statements to your JSPs.

Summary

- A *servlet* is a Java class that extends the HttpServlet class and runs within a servlet container such as Tomcat.

- When you write servlets, you typically override the doGet and doPost methods to provide the processing that's required. These methods receive the *request object* and the *response object* that are passed to them by the server.

- After you use the setContentType method of the response object to set the *content type* of the response that's returned to the browser, you use the getWriter method to create a PrintWriter object. Then, you can use the println and print methods of that object to send HTML back to the browser.

- To request a servlet, you request a URL that has been mapped to the servlet. This mapping is specified in the web.xml file by the servlet and servlet-mapping elements. Or, with the servlet 3.0 specification (Tomcat 7.0) or later, you can use the @WebServlet annotation to map a servlet to a URL.

- When you use the HTTP GET method to pass parameters to a JSP, the browser displays the parameters in its URL. When you use the HTTP POST method, the browser doesn't display these parameters. If executing a request multiple times may cause problems, you should use the POST method.

- Within a servlet's doGet or doPost method, you can use the getParameter and getParameterValues methods of the request object to get the parameter values from the request.

- You can use the getRealPath method of the ServletContext object to get a relative path to refer to a file that's used by your web application.

- The web.xml file consists of *XML tags* that define *XML elements*. The *root element* for this file is the web-app element. When one element is coded within another element, it can be called a *child element*.

- You can use the web.xml file or @WebServlet annotations to provide *initialization parameters* that apply to the entire web application or to specific servlets.

- You can use the web.xml file to provide custom error pages for specific Java exceptions or for HTTP errors represented by specific *HTTP status codes*.

- You can use JavaScript or jQuery to perform *data validation* on the client. You can use a servlet to perform data validation on the server. It's considered a best practice to perform data validation on both the client and the server.

- It's generally considered a bad practice to override the service method of a servlet.

- Since instance variables in a servlet are not thread-safe and can result in serious problems, you should never use instance variables in a servlet.

- To print debugging data to the server console, you can use the println method of the System.out or System.err object. Or, you can use the log methods of the HttpServlet class to write debugging data to a *log file*.

Exercise 5-1   Modify the servlet for the Email List application

In this exercise, you'll modify the servlet that's used by the email application that's presented in this chapter.

1. Open the ch05_ex1_email project in the ex_starts directory, and review its files. This should include an EmailListServlet class. Note that the EmailListServlet class validates the data entered by the user and that this class does not contain a doGet method.

2. Run the application. Then, enter some valid values on the first web page and click on the Join Now button to run the EmailListServlet class. This should use the HTTP POST method to request the /emailList URL, and the browser should not show any parameters in its URL.

3. Click on the Return button. This should use the HTTP POST method to request the /emailList URL, it should display the first page of the application, and the browser should not show any parameters in its URL.

4. Click the Join Now button without entering any values. This should display the same page again, but with a validation message that indicates that all three values are required.

5. Append two parameters to the /emailList URL that's displayed by your browser like this:

    `/emailList?action=add&email=jsmith@gmail.com`

    This uses the HTTP GET method. Since the EmailListServlet doesn't have a doGet method, this should display an error page that indicates that the HTTP GET method isn't supported by the URL.

6. Open the code for the servlet and add a doGet method that calls the doPost method of the servlet. Then, run the application again and enter the /emailList URL with the same parameters. It should display the first page of the web application with a validation message.

    This tests whether your development environment automatically reloads servlets after they have been changed. If the change you made to the servlet isn't working, you may need to manually reload the servlet class. One way to do that is to stop and restart Tomcat.

7. Open the code for the servlet and add a statement that prints a debugging message to the Tomcat console. This message should show the value of the action parameter that's passed to the servlet.

8. Run the application and click the Join Now button to display the message in the console. If you're using NetBeans, it should display a tab for the Tomcat console within the Output window. If it doesn't, you can usually display this tab by using the Services tab to restart the Tomcat server.

9. Repeat the previous two steps, but use a log file this time. If you're using NetBeans, it should display a tab for the Tomcat log file within its Output window.

Exercise 5-2   Create a new servlet

In this exercise, you'll modify the HTML document for the Email List application, and you'll create a new servlet that responds to the HTML document. This is comparable to what you did for exercise 5-1, but the details are repeated here.

1. Open the ch05_ex2_email project that's in the ex_starts directory.

2. Add a servlet named TestServlet to the murach.email package and map that servlet to the /test URL.

3. Modify the code for the servlet so it implements the doPost method and the doGet method, but not the service method.

4. Modify the doGet method so it displays a message that says "TestServlet Get".

5. Modify the doPost method so it displays a message that says "TestServlet Post".

6. Run the project and enter the /test URL into the browser to run the test servlet. This should show that the test servlet works for the HTTP GET method.

7. Open the index.jsp file and modify it so it calls the /test URL instead of the /emailList URL.

8. Run the project and click the Join Now button to run the test servlet. This should show that the test servlet works for the HTTP POST method.

9. If the project uses the web.xml file to map the servlet, delete the mapping from the web.xml file and use the @WebServlet annotation to map the servlet instead.

10. Run the project and test the servlet to make sure that the new mapping works.

6

How to develop JavaServer Pages

Chapter 2 showed how to use the MVC pattern to structure a web application that uses servlets and JSPs, and chapter 5 showed you how to develop the servlets for those applications. Now, this chapter presents the skills you need to develop JSPs within the MVC pattern. When you complete this chapter, you should be able to code the JSPs for web applications of your own. In addition, you should be able to maintain existing JSPs for older web applications.

A crash course in EL and JSTL

EL (Expression Language) and JSTL (JSP Standard Tag Library) were introduced with the JSP 2.0 specification. These tags have several advantages over the older JSP tags that were used prior to the JSP 2.0 specification. As a result, if you're developing new Java web applications, you will probably want to use EL and JSTL.

This topic presents enough EL and JSTL to get you started. However, the next chapter presents another example that uses EL and JSTL. Then, chapter 8 provides in-depth coverage of EL, and chapter 9 provides in-depth coverage of JSTL. Since you often use EL with JavaBeans, this topic begins by showing how to code a JavaBean.

How to code a JavaBean

Chapter 2 presented the rules for coding a JavaBean. Now, figure 6-1 reviews these rules. Here, the User class is a *JavaBean*, or *bean*, because it follows the three rules that all JavaBeans must follow.

First, a JavaBean must contain a constructor that doesn't accept any arguments. In this figure, for example, the zero-argument constructor uses three statements to set all three instance variables equal to empty strings. As a result, a newly created User object stores empty strings for its instance variables instead of null values, which is usually what you want.

Second, a JavaBean must contain get and set methods for all of the properties that need to be accessed by JSPs. In this figure, for example, the methods provide access to all of the instance variables of the User class, so this class qualifies as a bean. Of course, you can also code get and set methods that provide access to other properties in a bean.

To provide access to a Boolean value, you code is and set methods instead of get and set methods. For example, you could code methods named isEmailUpdated and setEmailUpdated to provide access to a Boolean property named emailUpdated.

When you code the get, set, and is methods, you must follow the capitalization conventions used in this figure for the method names. In other words, each method name must start with a lowercase letter and each property name must start with an uppercase letter. In this figure, for example, the setFirstName method uses a lowercase s to start the method name and an uppercase f to start the property name.

The third rule is that a JavaBean must implement the Serializable or Externalizable interface. The Serializable interface is a tagging interface in the java.io package that indicates that a class contains get, set, and is methods that another class can use to read and write an object's instance variables to and from a persistent data source. In this figure, for example, the User class implements the Serializable interface and contains all the necessary get and set methods. As a result, some servlet engines can save and restore this object if that's necessary. For example, the Tomcat container can save the User object's state before it shuts down, and it can restore the User object's state when it starts up the next time.

The code for the User bean class

```
package murach.business;

import java.io.Serializable;

public class User implements Serializable {

    private String firstName;
    private String lastName;
    private String email;

    public User() {
        firstName = "";
        lastName = "";
        email = "";
    }

    public User(String firstName, String lastName, String email) {
        this.firstName = firstName;
        this.lastName = lastName;
        this.email = email;
    }

    public String getFirstName() {
        return firstName;
    }

    public void setFirstName(String firstName) {
        this.firstName = firstName;
    }

    public String getLastName() {
        return lastName;
    }

    public void setLastName(String lastName) {
        this.lastName = lastName;
    }

    public String getEmail() {
        return email;
    }

    public void setEmail(String email) {
        this.email = email;
    }
}
```

Description

- A *JavaBean*, or *bean*, is a Java class that (1) provides a zero-argument constructor, (2) provides get and set methods for all of its private instance variables that follow standard Java naming conventions, and (3) implements the Serializable or Externalizable interface.

- Since JavaBeans are just Java classes, they are a type of *plain old Java object* (*POJO*).

Figure 6-1   How to code a JavaBean

How to use EL to get attributes and JavaBean properties

The JSP *Expression Language* (*EL*) provides a compact syntax that lets you access attributes and JavaBean properties from a request object. This is illustrated in figure 6-2.

Whenever you use EL, you begin by coding a dollar sign ($) followed by an opening brace ({) and a closing brace (}). Then, you code the expression within the braces.

The first example in this figure shows how to retrieve an attribute for a simple object like a String or Date object. Here, the servlet code uses a GregorianCalendar object to create an int variable named currentYear that stores the current year. Then, the servlet code stores this int value as an attribute of the request object. Last, the JSP code uses EL to access this attribute, convert it to a string, and display it.

The second example shows how to display a property of an attribute for a JavaBean. Here, the servlet code creates a JavaBean for the user and stores this bean as an attribute of the request. Then, the JSP code uses EL to access this attribute, and it uses the dot operator to specify the property of the JavaBean that it's going to display.

When you store an attribute in the HttpServletRequest object, that attribute is available only for the current request. This is known as request scope. However, if you want the attribute to be available to all servlets, you can set the attribute in the ServletContext object. This is known as application scope. Or, if you want the attribute to be available to all servlets for the user's current session, you can set the attribute in the HttpSession object. This is known as session scope. You'll learn how to do that in the next chapter. Note, however, that application scope isn't thread-safe.

When you use EL, you don't have to specify the scope. Instead, EL automatically searches through all scopes starting with the smallest scope (page scope) and moving towards the largest scope (application scope).

How to display an attribute

Syntax
```
${attribute}
```

Servlet code
```
GregorianCalendar currentDate = new GregorianCalendar();
int currentYear = currentDate.get(Calendar.YEAR);
request.setAttribute("currentYear", currentYear);
```

JSP code
```
<p>The current year is ${currentYear}</p>
```

How to display the property of an attribute

Syntax
```
${attribute.property}
```

Servlet code
```
User user = new User(firstName, lastName, email);
request.setAttribute("user", user);
```

JSP code
```
<p>Hello ${user.firstName}</p>
```

The sequence of scopes that Java searches to find the attribute

Scope	Description
page	The bean is stored in the implicit PageContext object.
request	The bean is stored in the HttpServletRequest object.
session	The bean is stored in the HttpSession object.
application	The bean is stored in the ServletContext object.

Description
- The JSP *Expression Language* (*EL*) makes it easy to access attributes and JavaBean properties from a request object.
- When you use the dot operator with a JavaBean, the code to the left of the operator specifies the JavaBean, and the code to the right of the operator specifies a property of the JavaBean.
- When you use this syntax, EL looks up the attribute starting with the smallest scope (page scope) and moving towards the largest scope (application scope).
- Attributes that have application scope are not thread-safe.

Figure 6-2   How to use EL to get attributes and JavaBean properties

How to enable the core JSTL library

Before you can use JSTL tags within an application, you must make the JSTL library available to the application. With the NetBeans IDE, for example, you can add the JSTL 1.2 library to the application by right-clicking on the project's Library folder, selecting the Add Library command, and selecting the library. In figure 6-3, for example the JSTL 1.2 library has been added to the project, and the jstl-impl.jar and jstl-api.jar files are shown beneath the Libraries folder.

JSTL is divided into several libraries. Of these libraries, the JSTL core library is the most commonly used library. Before you can use JSTL tags from this library, you must code a taglib directive to specify the URI and prefix for this library. In this figure, the taglib directive specifies the URI for the JSTL core library with a prefix of c, which is the prefix that's typically used for this library. In fact, all of the examples in this chapter assume that the page includes a taglib directive like this one before the JSTL tags. Although you can use a different prefix, we recommend using c as the prefix for the core library.

How to use the JSTL if tag

When coding a JSP, you may need to perform conditional processing to change the appearance of the page depending on the values of the attributes that are available to the page. To do that, you can use the if tag as shown in this figure.

To start, you code an opening if tag that includes the test attribute. In this figure, for instance, the first if tag has a test attribute that uses EL to get the value of the message attribute. If this message is not equal to a null value, the code within the opening and closing if tags returns HTML to the browser to display a validation message. Otherwise, this code doesn't return any HTML to the browser.

Sometimes you need to use EL to test whether the value of an attribute is equal to a specified string. To do that, you can use an if tag like the second one shown in this figure. Here, the test attribute checks whether the wantsUpdates property of the User bean is equal to a string value of "Yes". If so, this example returns HTML to the browser that indicates that the current user wants updates. Otherwise, this code doesn't return any HTML to the browser.

The NetBeans IDE after the JSTL 1.2 library has been added

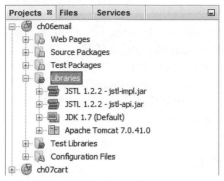

The taglib directive that specifies the JSTL core library

```
<%@ taglib prefix="c" uri="http://java.sun.com/jsp/jstl/core" %>
```

A JSTL if tag that displays or hides a validation message

```
<c:if test="${message != null}">
    <p><i>${message}</i></p>
</c:if>
```

A JSTL if tag that tests for a string value

```
<c:if test="${user.wantsUpdates == 'Yes'}">
    <p>This user wants updates!</p>
</c:if>
```

Description

- The *JSP Standard Tag Library* (*JSTL*) provides tags for common JSP tasks.

- Before you can use JSTL tags within an application, you must make the jstl-impl.jar and jstl-api.jar files available to the application.

- To add the JSTL library to a NetBeans project, switch to the Projects tab, right-click on the Libraries folder, select the Add Library command, and select the JSTL library.

- Before you can use JSTL tags within a JSP, you must code a taglib directive that identifies the JSTL library and its prefix.

- You can use the if tag to perform conditional processing that's similar to an if statement in Java. Within the if tag, you can use the test attribute to specify the Boolean condition for the if statement.

- JSTL provides many other tags that you'll learn about as you progress through this book.

Figure 6-3   How to enable the core JSTL library and use the if tag

How to use JSP tags

The JSP tags described in this topic have been part of JSP since its beginning. These tags allow you to embed Java statements directly into a JSP. Unfortunately, when you use these tags in a JSP, they typically result in an unwieldy mix of Java and HTML. As a result, it's generally considered a best practice to avoid these tags unless you're maintaining an old web application and you want to continue using them for the sake of consistency.

How to code directives, scriptlets, and expressions

The top of figure 6-4 summarizes five types of JSP tags. Of these tags, the first three (directives, scriptlets, and expressions) are the most commonly used. Since it's not a good practice to use the fifth tag (declaration), this book doesn't show how to use it.

You can use a *directive* to import classes in a JSP. In the previous figure, you learned how to use a *taglib directive* to import the JSTL core library. In this figure, the first example shows how to use a *page directive* to import classes. To do that, you can code a page directive like the one shown on the first line of this example.

To start, you code the starting tag and the word *page* followed by the import attribute. Then, you code an equals sign and a pair of quotes. Within the quotes, you code the names of the Java classes that you want to import, separating each class with a comma. In this figure, the page directive imports two classes in the java.util package. Alternately, you could use a wildcard to import both of these classes like this:

```
<%@ page import="java.util.*" %>
```

Once this page directive imports the classes, the JSP can access the GregorianCalendar and Calendar classes without fully qualifying them.

To code a *scriptlet*, you code Java statements that end with semicolons within the scriptlet tags. In the first example, for instance, the scriptlet contains two statements that use the GregorianCalendar and Calendar classes to get an int value for the currentYear.

To code an *expression*, you code any Java expression that evaluates to a primitive data type such as an int value or an object such as a String object. If an expression evaluates to a primitive type like an int value, JSP automatically converts the primitive type to a string that represents the value. In the first example, for instance, the last line works because the JSP automatically converts the int value to a string. If, on the other hand, the expression evaluates to an object, the JSP calls the object's toString method to get a string for the object.

The second example shows how to use a scriptlet and an expression to display or hide a validation message. This performs the same task as the JSTL if tag shown in the previous figure. However, the JSTL shown in the previous figure requires less code and looks more like HTML.

The five types of JSP tags

Tag	Name	Purpose
`<%@ %>`	JSP directive	To set conditions that apply to the entire JSP.
`<% %>`	JSP scriptlet	To insert a block of Java statements.
`<%= %>`	JSP expression	To display the string value of an expression.
`<%-- --%>`	JSP comment	To tell the JSP engine to ignore code.
`<%! %>`	JSP declaration	To declare instance variables and methods for a JSP.

Code that uses a directive, scriptlet, and expression

```
<%@ page import="java.util.GregorianCalendar, java.util.Calendar" %>
<%
    GregorianCalendar currentDate = new GregorianCalendar();
    int currentYear = currentDate.get(Calendar.YEAR);
%>
<p>&copy; Copyright <%= currentYear %> Mike Murach &amp; Associates</p>
```

JSP tags that display or hide a validation message

```
<%
    String message = (String) request.getAttribute("message");
    if (message != null) {
%>
    <p><i><%= message %></i></p>
<% } %>
```

Description

- To import classes in a JSP, you use the import attribute of the *page directive*.

- To get the values of attributes or parameters that are passed to a JSP, you can use the getAttribute or getParameter method of the *implicit request object* named request. These methods work the same as the methods that are available from the request object that's available to the doGet and doPost methods of a servlet.

Figure 6-4   How to use JSP tags

When you're coding a scriptlet or an expression, an HttpServletRequest object named request is automatically available to your code. This object is known as the *implicit request object*, and you can use any of its methods. In figure 6-4, the second example uses the getAttribute method of the implicit request object to get the message. However, figure 6-5 shows how to use the getParameter method of the request object to get parameters from the request object.

How to code comments in a JSP

Figure 6-5 shows how to code comments in a JSP. To start, the first example uses an HTML comment to comment out a line that includes a JSP expression that displays a date. Then, the second example uses a *JSP comment* to comment out the same line.

When you code HTML and JSP comments, any Java code within an HTML comment is compiled and executed, but the browser doesn't display it. For instance, the first example creates a new Date object even though it doesn't display the date in the browser. In fact, the value for the date object is returned to the browser as an HTML comment. To check this, you can view the HTML for the page that's returned to the browser.

In contrast, any Java code within a JSP comment isn't compiled or executed or returned to the browser in any way. For instance, the second example doesn't create a Date object and it doesn't return it to the browser as a comment. As a result, if you want to comment out code that contains HTML and JSP tags, you typically use a JSP comment. This is critical if the code you're commenting out performs tasks that you no longer want to perform. If, for example, the code updates a variable that you no longer want to update, you need to make sure to use a JSP comment.

The third example shows how you can code Java comments within a scriptlet. Here, a single-line comment is coded before the three statements that get the request parameters. Then, this code uses a multi-line comment to comment out the two statements that create the User object and write it to a database. Since these types of comments work the same as they do with normal Java code, you shouldn't have any trouble using them.

An HTML comment in a JSP

```
<!--
<p>This email address was added to our list on <%= new Date() %></p>
-->
```

A JSP comment

```
<%--
<p>This email address was added to our list on <%= new Date() %></p>
--%>
```

Java comments in a JSP scriptlet

```
<%
    // get parameters from the request
    String firstName = request.getParameter("firstName");
    String lastName = request.getParameter("lastName");
    String emailAddress = request.getParameter("emailAddress");

    /*
    User user = new User(firstName, lastName, emailAddress);
    UserDB.insert(user);
    */
%>
```

Description

- When you code HTML comments, the comments are compiled and executed, but the browser doesn't display them.
- When you code *JSP comments*, the comments aren't compiled or executed.
- When you code Java comments within a scriptlet, the comments aren't compiled or executed.

Figure 6-5   How to code comments in a JSP

How to use standard JSP tags with JavaBeans

Standard JSP tags for working with JavaBeans were widely used before the JSP 2.0 specification. As a result, if you need to maintain the code for an older Java web application, you may need to know how to use these tags.

An introduction to standard JSP tags

The main benefit that you get from coding your business classes so they qualify as JavaBeans is that you can then use EL or standard JSP tags to work with the beans. This is illustrated by the JSP code in figure 6-6.

The first example shows how to use a directive, a scriptlet, and three expressions to display the data for the User bean. Here, the directive imports the User class. Then, the scriptlet, gets the User object that's stored in the request object. Or, if the request object doesn't contain a User object, this code creates a new User object. Next, the three expression tags display the data that's stored in the User object. Although this code works, it's an unwieldy mixture of Java code and HTML.

The second example uses standard JSP tags to perform the same task. Here, the useBean tag accesses the User object that's stored in the request object. Or, if the User object doesn't exist in the request object, this tag creates the object by calling the zero-argument constructor of the User class. Next, the three getProperty tags display the values of the properties that have been set in the User object.

If you compare the second example with the first example, it's easy to see how using standard JSP tags can make your JSPs easier to code and maintain. In fact, the second example doesn't require any Java code at all. This makes it easier for web designers and other non-programmers to work on JSPs.

However, the EL shown in the third example also doesn't require any Java code. In addition, the EL is even shorter and simpler than the standard JSP tags. As a result, it's even easier for web designers and other programmers to work on JSPs that use EL.

Standard JSP tags do have a couple of advantages when compared with EL. First, the useBean tag creates the JavaBean even if it doesn't already exist. Second, you can also use the setProperty tag to set the properties of a JavaBean. However, when you use the MVC pattern, the servlet typically creates the JavaBean and sets its properties. In other words, when you use the MVC pattern, there's not much advantage to using standard JSP tags.

Code that uses JSP tags to access the User bean

```
<%@ page import="murach.business.User" %>
<%
    User user = (User) request.getAttribute("user");
    if (user == null) {
        user = new User();
    }
%>
<label>Email:</label>
<span><%= user.getEmail() %></span><br>
<label>First Name:</label>
<span><%= user.getFirstName() %></span><br>
<label>Last Name:</label>
<span><%= user.getLastName() %></span><br>
```

The same code using standard JSP tags

```
<jsp:useBean id="user" scope="request" class="murach.business.User"/>
<label>Email:</label>
<span><jsp:getProperty name="user" property="email"/></span><br>
<label>First Name:</label>
<span><jsp:getProperty name="user" property="firstName"/></span><br>
<label>Last Name:</label>
<span><jsp:getProperty name="user" property="lastName"/></span><br>
```

The same code using EL

```
<label>Email:</label>
<span>${user.email}</span><br>
<label>First Name:</label>
<span>${user.firstName}</span><br>
<label>Last Name:</label>
<span>${user.lastName}</span><br>
```

Advantages of standard JSP tags

- Standard JSP tags create a JavaBean if it doesn't already exist.
- Standard JSP tags provide a way to set properties.

Advantages of EL

- EL has a more elegant and compact syntax.
- El allows you to access nested properties.
- EL does a better job of handling null values.
- El provides more functionality.

Description

- Standard JSP tags make it easier for non-programmers to use beans because they look more like HTML tags and don't require Java code.
- EL makes it even easier for non-programmers to use beans because they are shorter and easier to code than standard JSP tags.

Figure 6-6   An introduction to standard JSP tags

How to code the useBean tag

Figure 6-7 shows how to code the useBean tag to access a bean. Although this tag looks and works much like an HTML tag, all of the JSP tags for working with JavaBeans use XML syntax. As a result, when you code these tags, you must use lowercase and uppercase characters as shown in this figure; you must code a front slash to mark the end of the opening tag or the start of a closing tag; and you must code single or double quotation marks around all attributes of a tag.

To code a simple useBean tag, you code the name of the tag followed by the attributes of the tag. In this example, the id attribute specifies the name that's used to access the bean, the class attribute specifies the package and class of the bean, and the scope attribute specifies the *scope* of the bean.

When you code the scope attribute, you can specify one of four values: page, request, session, and application. The value of the scope attribute specifies the object that stores the bean and that determines how long the bean is available to the rest of the application. For instance, the example sets the scope attribute to request, which stores the bean in the request object. As a result, any JSP or servlet that has access to the request object has access to this bean. If you don't specify the Scope attribute, the scope is set to "page" by default, which means that the bean is only available to the current JSP.

If a bean that matches the attributes specified in the useBean tag exists, this tag creates a reference to that object. Otherwise, the useBean tag creates a new object by calling the zero-argument constructor of the specified class.

For now, don't worry if you don't understand how session scope works. You'll learn more about it in the next chapter.

The useBean tag

Syntax
```
<jsp:useBean id="beanName" class="package.Class" scope="scopeValue" />
```

Example
```
<jsp:useBean id="user" class="murach.business.User" scope="request" />
```

Scope values

Value	Description
page	The bean is stored in the implicit pageContext object for the JSP and is only available to the current page. This is the default setting.
request	The bean is stored in the HttpServletRequest object and is available to all JSPs and servlets that have access to the current request object.
session	The bean is stored in the HttpSession object and is available to all JSPs and servlets that have access to this object. For more information about session objects, see chapter 7.
application	The bean is stored in the ServletContext object and is available to all JSPs and servlets that have access to this object.

Description

- The useBean tag is used to access a bean and, if necessary, create a bean from the JavaBean class.

- The *scope* of a bean refers to the object that stores the bean. This controls how long the bean is available to the rest of the application.

- The JSP tags for working with beans use XML syntax. As a result, these tags are case-sensitive, a front slash indicates the end of the opening tag or the start of a closing tag, and all attributes must be enclosed by single or double quotes.

Figure 6-7   How to code the useBean tag

How to code the getProperty and setProperty tags

Once you code a useBean tag to access or create a bean, you can use the getProperty tag to get the values stored in the bean, and you can use the setProperty tag to set the values stored in the bean. Figure 6-8 shows how.

To get the value of a property that's stored in a bean, you code a getProperty tag. Here, the name attribute specifies the name of the bean, so it should match the id attribute of the useBean tag. If, for example, you set the name attribute to "user," this attribute accesses the User bean specified by the useBean tag in the previous figure. Then, the property attribute specifies the name of the property that you want to access. For example, a value of "firstName" accesses the firstName property of the User bean.

To set a property of a bean, you code a setProperty tag. In this tag, you code the name attribute and the property attribute to specify the name of the bean and the property that you want to set. Then, you code the value attribute to specify the value that you want the property set to.

If you need to code one of the special characters shown in this figure as part of a value attribute, you can use the escape sequences shown here. If, for example, you're using single quotes to identify your attributes, you can use an escape sequence like the one in the first escape sequence example to set the lastName property of the User bean to O'Neil. However, you can often avoid using escape sequences by switching the type of quotation mark that you use to identify an attribute. This is illustrated by the second escape sequence example.

When you work with the getProperty tag, you should be aware that it won't get the value of a property if the value is null or an empty string. Similarly, you can't use the setProperty tag to set the value of a property to null or an empty string. If you need to do that, though, you can do it in the constructor of the bean or in a servlet that accesses the bean.

The getProperty tag

Syntax
```
<jsp:getProperty name="beanName" property="propertyName" />
```

Example
```
<jsp:getProperty name="user" property="firstName" />
```

The setProperty tag

Syntax
```
<jsp:setProperty name="beanName" property="propertyName" value="value" />
```

Example
```
<jsp:setProperty name="user" property="firstName" value="John" />
```

Escape sequences within attributes

Character	Escape sequence
'	\'
"	\"
\	\\
<%	<\%
%>	%\>

How to use an escape sequence
```
<jsp:setProperty name='user' property='lastName' value='O\'Neil' />
```

How to avoid an escape sequence
```
<jsp:setProperty name="user" property="lastName" value="O'Neil" />
```

Description

- The name attribute for the getProperty and setProperty tags must match the ID attribute in the useBean tag.

- To code special characters within an attribute, you can use escape sequences. However, if you enclose an attribute in double quotes, you don't need to use escape sequences for single quotes. Conversely, if you enclose an attribute in single quotes, you don't need to use the escape sequence for double quotes.

- The getProperty tag can't be used to get a null value or an empty string, and the setProperty tag can't be used to set a property to a null value or an empty string. However, you can use the constructor of a bean or the code in a servlet to set a property to a null value or an empty string.

Figure 6-8   How to code the getProperty and setProperty tags

How to include a file in a JSP

When you're coding a web application, you may want to include the same block of code in several JSPs. For example, you may want to use the same header and footer for several JSPs. Or, you may want to use the same menus or the same combo box for several JSPs. If so, you can store this code in a separate file. Then, you can include the code in that file in a JSP. Files like this are often referred to as *includes*, and using includes can reduce code duplication and simplify the coding and maintenance of an application.

A JSP that includes a header and footer file

Figure 6-9 begins by showing an HTML file that contains the tags that define the beginning of an HTML document. These tags include the opening DOCTYPE tag, the opening HTML tag, the head tag, the tags within the head tag, and the opening body tag. Since this file only contains HTML tags, not any JSP tags, it is stored in an HTML file named header.html. Here, the title tag sets the title of the web page that's displayed in the browser's to "Murach's Java Servlets and JSP".

This figure also shows the footer.jsp file that contains the HTML and JSP tags that define a footer for a document. This footer begins by using a JSP directive to import the GregorianDate and Calendar classes from the java.util package. Then, a JSP scriptlet uses these classes to get an int value for the current year. After the scriptlet, the footer uses an expression within HTML code to display a copyright notice that uses the int value for the current year. Within this HTML code, "©" and "&" are HTML entities that represent the copyright symbol (©) and the ampersand (&). Finally, the footer provides the closing body and html tags.

After the header and footer files, this figure shows a JSP file that uses the shaded statements to include the header.html and footer.jsp files. Here, the first line in the JSP file imports the core JSTL library as described earlier in this chapter, and the second line uses the JSTL import tag to include all the code needed to start the web page. Then, the last line in the file includes the code that displays the copyright notice and all code that's needed to finish the web page.

In this figure, the header and footer files are stored in a directory named includes. When working with include files, it's a common practice to store them in a separate directory like this.

In this example, the included files are so small that they don't illustrate the power of this technique. Imagine, though, that the included files contain larger blocks of code and that this code is appropriate for dozens or hundreds of JSPs. Then, this coding technique can reduce the total amount of code in the application and make the application easier to maintain. If, for example, you want to change the header for all the JSPs that include the header file, you just have to change one file.

A header file named header.html

```
<!DOCTYPE html>
<html>
<head>
    <meta charset="utf-8">
    <title>Murach's Java Servlets and JSP</title>
    <link rel="stylesheet" href="styles/main.css" type="text/css"/>
</head>
<body>
```

A footer file named footer.jsp

```
<%@ page import="java.util.GregorianCalendar, java.util.Calendar" %>
<%
    GregorianCalendar currentDate = new GregorianCalendar();
    int currentYear = currentDate.get(Calendar.YEAR);
%>
<p>&copy; Copyright <%= currentYear %> Mike Murach &amp; Associates</p>
</body>
</html>
```

A JSP file that uses both include files

```
<%@ taglib prefix="c" uri="http://java.sun.com/jsp/jstl/core" %>
<c:import url="/includes/header.html" />

<h1>Join our email list</h1>
<p>To join our email list, enter your name and
    email address below.</p>

<c:if test="${message != null}">
    <p><i>${message}</i></p>
</c:if>

<form action="emailList" method="post">
    <input type="hidden" name="action" value="add">
    <label class="pad_top">Email:</label>
    <input type="email" name="email" value="${user.email}"><br>
    <label class="pad_top">First Name:</label>
    <input type="text" name="firstName" value="${user.firstName}"><br>
    <label class="pad_top">Last Name:</label>
    <input type="text" name="lastName" value="${user.lastName}"><br>
    <label> </label>
    <input type="submit" value="Join Now" class="margin_left">
</form>

<c:import url="/includes/footer.jsp" />
```

Description

- You can use a JSTL import tag to include HTML or JSP files within a JSP.
- In this example, the header and footer files are both stored in a directory named includes.

Figure 6-9   A JSP that includes a header and a footer file (part 1 of 2)

Part 2 of figure 6-9 starts by showing the page that's displayed by the JSP in part 1. As you can see, this page includes the header.html and footer.jsp files. Here, the title in the browser is from the header file, and the copyright notice at the bottom of the page is from the footer file.

Part 2 also shows another page that includes the header and footer files. As a result, it displays the same title in the browser, and the same copyright notice at the bottom of the page.

The web page displayed in a browser

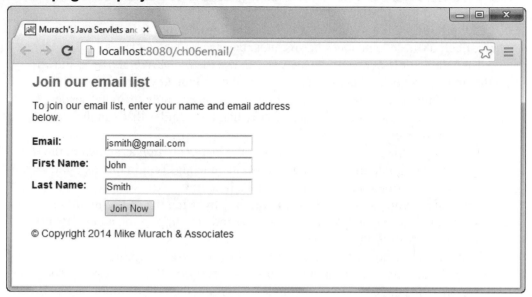

Another web page that uses the same header and footer

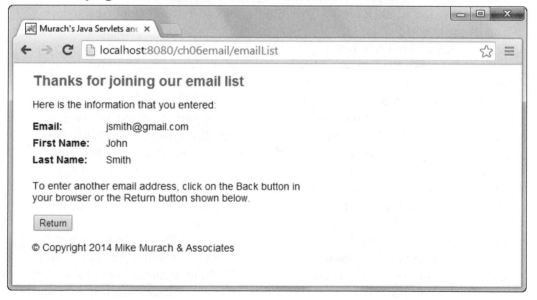

Figure 6-9   A JSP that includes a header and a footer file (part 2 of 2)

Three techniques for including files in a JSP

JSP provides three techniques for including files. Figure 6-10 shows all three. Each of these techniques has its advantages and disadvantages.

To include a file at *compile-time*, you can use the *include directive* as shown in the first example. Within this tag, you type the include keyword followed by the file attribute and the relative path of the file. This example includes header and footer files that are located in a directory named includes that's in the root directory of the web application.

To include a file at *runtime*, you can use the *include action* as shown in the second example. To do that, you code the jsp:include tag. Within this tag, you set the page attribute to the relative path of the include file.

Alternately, you can include a file at runtime by using the JSTL import tag as shown in the third example. To do that, you code the import tag and set its url attribute to the path of the include file.

Neither the include action or the JSTL import tag uses scripting. As a result, it usually doesn't matter which tag you use. However, the JSTL import tag does provide one advantage: it lets you include files from other applications and web servers. For instance, the last line of code shows how to include a footer.jsp file that's available from the server for the www.murach.com website.

When you include a file at compile-time, the code within the file becomes part of the generated servlet. The advantage of this approach is that it allows the servlet engine to return a response to the browser more quickly. However, if you make a change to the included file, the server might not display the change until the JSP is modified and recompiled.

When you include a file at runtime, the included file never becomes part of the generated servlet, so the servlet makes a runtime call to get the included file each time the page is requested. The advantage of this approach is that the server always uses the most current version of the included file. However, since this approach makes the generated servlet do extra work with each request, it doesn't run as efficiently as the first approach.

In the end, the approach that you choose depends on the requirements of your application. If you are fairly certain that the include files won't change often, you should use the first approach since it's more efficient. For example, since the header and footer files presented in the previous figure probably won't change once the web application is put into production, it makes sense to include them at compile-time. In addition, many servlet engines, including Tomcat 5 and later, automatically detect changes to included files. As a result, if you're using a newer servlet engine, you can usually include files at compile-time.

However, if you want to use include files to display information that may change regularly, and you need to guarantee that these changes will be displayed immediately, you should use the second or third approach. That way, the servlet for the JSP doesn't need to be regenerated and recompiled to display the updated include file.

How to include a file at compile-time with an include directive

Syntax
```
<%@ include file="fileLocationAndName" %>
```

Examples
```
<%@ include file="/includes/header.html" %>
<%@ include file="/includes/footer.jsp" %>
```

How to include a file at runtime with include action

Syntax
```
<jsp:include page="fileLocationAndName" />
```

Examples
```
<jsp:include page="/includes/header.html" />
<jsp:include page="/includes/footer.jsp" />
```

How to include a file at runtime with the JSTL import tag

Syntax
```
<c:import url="fileLocationAndName" />
```

Examples
```
<c:import url="/includes/header.html" />
<c:import url="/includes/footer.jsp" />

<c:import url="http://localhost:8080/musicStore/includes/footer.jsp" />
<c:import url="www.murach.com/includes/footer.jsp" />
```

Description

- To include a file in a JSP at *compile-time*, you can use the *include directive*.

- When you use the include directive, the code in the included file becomes part of the generated servlet. As a result, any changes to the included file won't appear in the JSP until the JSP is regenerated and recompiled. However, some of the newer web servers automatically detect changes to included files and automatically regenerate and recompile the servlets for the JSPs that need to be updated.

- To include a file in a JSP at *runtime*, you use the *include action* or the JSTL import tag.

- When you include a file at runtime, any changes to the included file appear in the JSP the next time it is requested.

- One advantage of the import tag is that it lets you include files from other applications and web servers.

Figure 6-10   Three techniques for including files in a JSP

How to fix common JSP errors

Figure 6-11 presents the two most common errors that you will encounter when working with JSPs. HTTP Status 404 means that Tomcat received the HTTP request but couldn't find the requested resource. To fix this type of problem, make sure that you have entered the correct path and filename for the request, and that the requested file is in the correct location.

In contrast, HTTP Status 500 means that the server received the request and found the resource but couldn't fill the request. This usually means that the JSP engine wasn't able to compile the JSP due to a coding error in the JSP. To fix this type of error, you can review the information provided by the error page.

In this figure, for example, the message displayed by the error page shows that the EL for the page specifies the emailAddress property of the User bean. However, the JSP can't find this property. In this case, that's because the User bean only provides a property named email, not emailAddress. To correct this type of error, you should fix the JSP so it compiles correctly.

An error page for a common JSP error

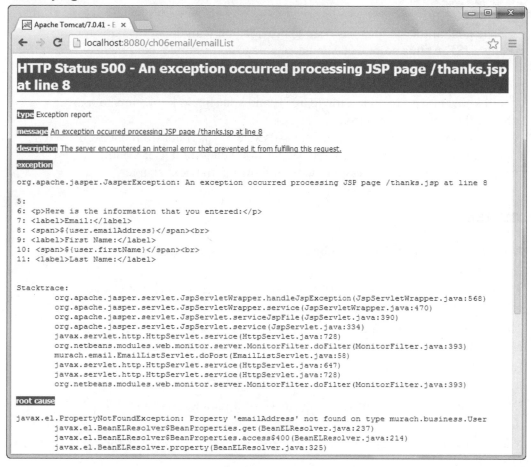

Common JSP errors

- HTTP Status 404 – File Not Found Error
- HTTP Status 500 – Internal Server Error

Tips for fixing JSP errors

- Make sure that the URL is valid and that it points to the right location for the requested page.
- Make sure all of the HTML, JSP, and Java class files are in the correct locations.
- Read the error page carefully to get all available information about the error.

Figure 6-11   How to fix common JSP errors

Perspective

The goal of this chapter has been to provide you with the basic skills for coding a JSP. At this point, you should be able to code simple, but practical, JSPs of your own that use simple EL and JSTL tags. In addition, you should understand why you typically use EL and JSTL instead of older JSP tags, you should know how to include a file in a JSP, and you should know how to fix some of the common JSP errors.

So far, this book has only used request scope to pass data from one web page to another. However, when you need to store data for a user's entire session, you typically use session scope as shown in the next chapter.

Summary

- A *JavaBean* is a special type of object that provides a standard way to access its *properties*.
- The JSP *Expression Language* (*EL*) provides a compact syntax that lets you get attributes and JavaBean properties from a request object.
- The *JSP Standard Tag Library* (*JSTL*) provides tags for common tasks that need to be performed in JSPs.
- Before you can use JSTL tags, you must import the JSTL library, which makes the jstl-impl.jar and jstl-api.jar files available to the application.
- Before you can use the core JSTL tags in a JSP, you must code a *taglib directive* for the core JSTL library.
- You use a *JSP directive* known as a *page directive* to import classes for use in a JSP.
- Within a JSP, you can include *scriptlets* and *expressions* that include Java code.
- Within the scriptlets and expressions, you can use the methods of the *implicit request object* to work with the HTTP request that's passed to the JSP.
- You can use standard JSP tags to work with JavaBeans that have been stored as an attribute of the web application.
- The JSP useBean tag lets you access or create a bean object, and the JSP getProperty and setProperty tags let you get and set the properties of the object.
- When you use *JSP comments*, the comments aren't compiled or executed or returned to the browser. In contrast, HTML comments are compiled and executed and returned to the browser, but the browser doesn't display them.
- You can include files such as header and footer files in a JSP at *compile-time* or *runtime*. This is known as working with *includes*.
- When working with JSPs, an HTTP Status 500 error often indicates that the JSP engine wasn't able to compile the servlet class for the JSP.

Exercise 6-1   Modify the JSPs for the Email List application

In this exercise, you'll modify the JSPs that are used by the email application that's presented in this chapter.

1. Open the ch06_ex1_email project in the ex_starts directory, and review its files. This should include JSP files named index.jsp and thanks.jsp.

2. Open the index.jsp and thanks.jsp files and review their code. Note that these files use the JSTL import tag to include files from the includes directory.

3. Open the footer.jsp file and review its code. Note that this file uses JSP tags to display a copyright message that includes the current year.

4. Run the application. The first page should display a copyright notice that includes the current year.

5. Enter some valid values on the first web page and click on the Join Now button. The second page should display a copyright notice that includes the current year.

6. Open the source code for the EmailListServlet class and modify it so it gets an int value for the current year and sets that int value as an attribute of the request object. To do that, you can start by copying the scriptlet from the footer.jsp file into the servlet.

7. Modify the footer.jsp file so it uses EL to display the current year instead of using a directive, a scriptlet, and an expression.

8. Run the application again. The first page should display a copyright notice, but this notice shouldn't include the date since the date hasn't been set yet by the servlet.

9. Enter some valid values on the first web page and click on the Join Now button. The second page should display a copyright notice that includes a valid date.

10. Modify the index.jsp and thanks.jsp files so they use the header.html and footer.jsp files at compile-time instead of at runtime.

11. Run the application again to make sure that the compile-time includes work correctly. They should.

Exercise 6-2   Create a new JSP

In this exercise, you'll modify the HTML document for the Email List application, and you'll create a new servlet that responds to the HTML document. This is comparable to what you did for exercise 6-1, but the details are repeated here.

1. Open the ch06_ex2_survey project that's in the ex_starts directory.

2. Open the index.html file and review its code. Note that it calls the servlet that's mapped to the /survey URL.

3. Open the source code for the User class and review it. Note that it provides for six properties that correspond with the six parameters of the index.html file.

4. Open the source code for the SurveyServlet class and review it. Note that it gets six parameters from the request object, processes them, stores them in a User object, and forwards them to a JSP named survey.jsp.

5. Run the application, enter some valid values, and click on the Submit button. This should display an HTTP Status 404 error since the survey.jsp file doesn't exist.

6. Create a survey.jsp file that displays the data in the User object like this:

    Thanks for taking our survey!

    Here is the information that you entered:

Email:	jsmith@gmail.com
First Name:	John
Last Name:	Smith
Heard From:	Search Engine
Updates:	Yes
Contact Via:	Email

7. Run the project and test it to make sure it displays this data correctly.

8. Modify the code for the survey.jsp file so it does not return HTML for the Contact Via row when the user does not want updates. To do that, you can use a JSTL if tag.

9. Run the project and test it to make sure that the JSTL if tag works correctly.

7

How to work with sessions and cookies

In all but the simplest of web applications, you need to keep track of the user as the user moves through the web application. Fortunately, the servlet API makes it relatively easy to do this. In this chapter, you'll learn how to use the servlet API to keep track of sessions, and you'll learn how to use the servlet API to work with cookies.

An introduction to session tracking

Keeping track of users as they move around a website is known as *session tracking*. To start, you'll learn how the servlet API tracks sessions, and you'll be introduced to a web application that needs session tracking.

Why session tracking is difficult with HTTP

Figure 7-1 shows why session tracking is more difficult for web applications that use HTTP than it is for other types of applications. To start, a browser on a client requests a page from a web server. After the web server returns the page, it drops the connection. Then, if the browser makes additional requests the web server has no way to associate the browser with its previous requests. Since HTTP doesn't maintain *state*, it is known as a *stateless protocol*. In contrast, FTP maintains state between requests so it is known as a *stateful protocol*.

How session tracking works in Java

Figure 7-1 also shows how the servlet API keeps track of sessions. To start, a browser on a client requests a JSP or servlet from the web server, which passes the request to the servlet engine. Then, the servlet engine checks if the request includes an ID for the Java session. If it doesn't, the servlet engine creates a unique ID for the session plus a *session object* that can be used to store the data for the session. From that point on, the web server uses the session ID to relate each browser request to the session object, even though the server still drops the HTTP connection after returning each page.

By default, the servlet API uses a *cookie* to store the session ID within the client's browser. This is an extension of the HTTP protocol. Then, when the next request is made, this cookie is added to the request. However, if cookies have been disabled within a browser, this type of session tracking won't work.

To get around this problem, the servlet API provides a way to rewrite the URL so it includes the session ID. This is known as *URL encoding*, and it works even if cookies have been disabled within a browser. However, there are several problems with this approach. First, URL encoding presents a security hole that can allow session hijacking. Second, URL encoding can cause a site to malfunction if the user bookmarks a page that includes a session ID.

Fortunately, cookies have become such an integral part of the web experience that it's extremely rare for someone to use the web with cookies disabled. As a result, you can usually handle this issue by displaying a message that notifies the user that the website requires cookies to be enabled.

Before you continue, you should know that there are two types of cookies. A *per-session cookie* is stored on the browser until the user closes the browser and a *persistent cookie* can be stored on the user's hard disk for up to 3 years. The session tracking code presented in this chapter relies on per-session cookies. As a result, per-session cookies must be enabled in the user's browser for this to work.

Why session tracking is difficult with HTTP

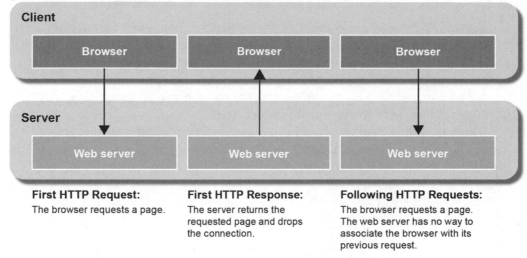

First HTTP Request:
The browser requests a page.

First HTTP Response:
The server returns the requested page and drops the connection.

Following HTTP Requests:
The browser requests a page. The web server has no way to associate the browser with its previous request.

How Java keeps track of sessions

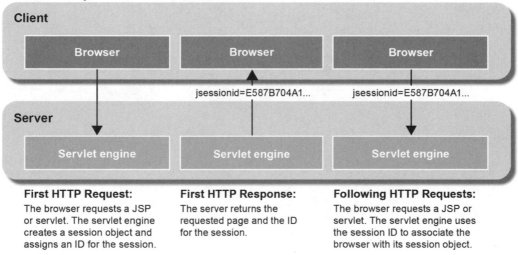

First HTTP Request:
The browser requests a JSP or servlet. The servlet engine creates a session object and assigns an ID for the session.

First HTTP Response:
The server returns the requested page and the ID for the session.

Following HTTP Requests:
The browser requests a JSP or servlet. The servlet engine uses the session ID to associate the browser with its session object.

Description

- HTTP is a *stateless protocol*. Once a browser makes a request, it drops the connection to the server. So to maintain *state*, a web application must use *session tracking*.

- By default, the servlet API uses a *cookie* to store a session ID in each browser. Then, the browser passes the cookie to the server with each request.

- To store the data for each session, the server creates a *session object*.

- To provide session tracking when cookies are disabled in the browser, you can use *URL encoding* to store the session ID in the URL for each page of an application. However, there are several problems with this technique, and it is *not* considered a best practice.

- There are two types of cookies: *persistent cookies* are stored on the user's PC, and *per-session cookies* are deleted when the session ends.

Figure 7-1   An introduction to session tracking

An application that needs session tracking

Figure 7-2 shows the user interface for the first two pages of a Cart application. Here, the first page allows the user to add an item to the Cart, and the second page displays the items in the cart and allows the user to update the quantity or remove an item. Without session tracking, this application wouldn't be able to associate the second request with the first request. As a result, the cart would never be able to display more than one item.

Throughout this chapter, you'll be introduced to snippets of code that are used in this Cart application. If necessary, you can refer back to this figure to view the user interface.

The Index page

The Cart page

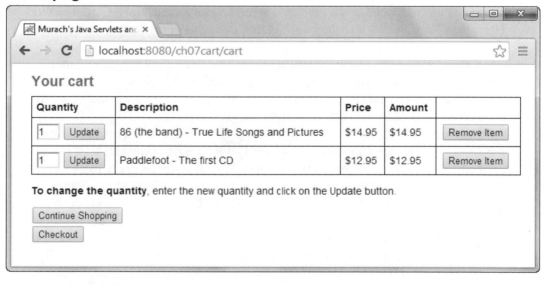

Figure 7-2   An application that needs session tracking

How to work with sessions

This topic shows how to use the servlet API to track sessions. As mentioned earlier, for this to work, the user must have per-session cookies enabled in his or her browser. Fortunately, these days, virtually all users have per-session cookies enabled in their browsers.

How to set and get session attributes

Figure 7-3 shows how to get a session object and how to get and set the attributes of that object. Since the session object is a built-in JSP object, you only need to get a session object when you're working with servlets. To do that, you can call the getSession method of the request object as shown in the first example. Then, if the session object doesn't exist, this method creates a new one. Usually, though, it just accesses the one that already exists.

From the session object, you can call the setAttribute method to set any object as an attribute of the current session. To do that, you specify a name for the attribute and the name of the object that you want to store. For instance, the second and third examples show how to store a String object and a Cart object. Here, the Cart object is a business object that stores all of the items for the user's cart.

Similarly, you can use the getAttribute method to return any attribute that you've set. To do that, you specify the name of the attribute. Since this method returns an object of the Object type, you need to cast each object to the appropriate type as shown by the fourth and fifth examples.

In chapter 5, you learned how to use the getAttribute and setAttribute methods of the request object. Now, you can see that the getAttribute and setAttribute methods of the session object work similarly. The main difference is the scope of the attributes. When you set an attribute in the request object, the attributes are removed after the request has been completed. However, when you set an attribute in the session object, the attributes are available until the user closes the browser, until the session times out, or until you use the removeAttribute method to remove an attribute from the session object.

If you work with an older web application, you may find that it uses the putValue, getValue, and removeValue methods instead of the setAttribute, getAttribute, and removeAttribute methods. That's because the Attribute methods were introduced in version 2.2 of the servlet API. However, the Value methods have been deprecated in the later releases. As a result, all new web applications should use the Attribute methods.

A method of the request object

Method	Description
getSession()	Returns the HttpSession object associated with this request. If the request is not associated with a session, this method creates a new HttpSession object and returns it.

Three methods of the session object

Method	Description
setAttribute(String name, Object o)	Stores any object in the session as an attribute and specifies a name for the attribute.
getAttribute(String name)	Returns the value of the specified attribute as an Object type. If no attribute exists for the specified name, this method returns a null value.
removeAttribute(String name)	Removes the specified attribute from this session.

Examples

Code that gets a session object
```
HttpSession session = request.getSession();
```

Code that sets a String object as an attribute
```
session.setAttribute("productCode", productCode);
```

Code that sets a user-defined object as an attribute
```
Cart cart = new Cart(productCode);
session.setAttribute("cart", cart);
```

Code that gets a String object
```
String productCode = (String) session.getAttribute("productCode");
```

Code that gets a user-defined object
```
Cart cart = (Cart) session.getAttribute("cart");
if (cart == null) {
    cart = new Cart();
}
```

Code that removes an object
```
session.removeAttribute("productCode");
```

Description

- A session object is created when a browser makes the first request to a site. It is destroyed when the session ends.
- A session ends when a specified amount of time elapses without another request or when the user exits the browser.

Figure 7-3   How to set and get session attributes

More methods of the session object

Most of the time, you can use the methods presented in the previous figure to work with the session object. However, figure 7-4 presents some other methods of the session object that you may want to use.

You can use the getAttributeNames method of the session object to return the names of all attributes stored in the session object. To do that, you use the getAttributeNames method to return an Enumeration object. Then, you can use the hasMoreElements and nextElement methods of the Enumeration object to loop through the names as shown in the first code example. This can be useful for debugging.

You can use the getId method to return the ID that the servlet engine is using for the current session. This ID is a long string that uniquely identifies each Java session. This can also be useful for debugging or for making the session object thread-safe as described in the next figure.

You can use the isNew method to check if the client is new or if the client chooses to not join the session. This method returns a true value if the client is accessing the site for the first time in a new session or if cookies have been disabled on the browser.

You can use the last two methods to control when a session is invalidated. When this happens, all objects that have been stored in the session object are released from the session object. By default, the session is invalidated if a user is inactive for half an hour, but you can use the setMaxInactiveInterval method to change this default. If, for example, you supply an argument of –1, the session object won't be invalidated until the user exits the browser. If necessary, though, you can call the invalidate method whenever you want to invalidate the session. If you call a method from the session object after it has been invalidated, that method throws an IllegalStateException.

More methods of the session object

Method	Description
getAttributeNames()	Returns a java.util.Enumeration object that contains the names of all attributes in the HttpSession object.
getId()	Returns a string for the unique Java session identifier that the servlet engine generates for each session.
isNew()	Returns a true value if the client does not yet know about the session or if the client chooses not to join the session. This can happen if the session relies upon cookies and the browser doesn't accept cookies.
setMaxInactiveInterval(int seconds)	By default, the maximum inactive interval for the session is set to 1800 seconds (30 minutes). As a result, if the user is inactive for 30 minutes, the session is invalidated. To increase or decrease this interval, supply a positive integer value. To create a session that won't end until the user closes the browser, supply a negative integer such as −1.
invalidate()	Invalidates the session and unbinds any objects that are bound to it.

Examples

A method that gets all the names of the attributes for a session

```
Enumeration names = session.getAttributeNames();
while (names.hasMoreElements()) {
    System.out.println((String) names.nextElement());
}
```

A method that gets the ID for a session

```
String jSessionId = session.getId();
```

A method that sets the inactive interval for a session

```
session.setMaxInactiveInterval(60*60*24);   // one day
session.setMaxInactiveInterval(-1);          // until the browser is closed
```

A method that invalidates the session and unbinds any objects

```
session.invalidate();
```

Description

- If the session object has been explicitly or implicitly invalidated, all methods of the session object throw an IllegalStateException.

- For more information about these and other methods of the session object, you can look up the HttpSession interface in the javax.servlet.http package in the documentation for the Servlet and JavaServer Pages API.

Figure 7-4   More methods of the session object

How to provide thread-safe access to the session object

In chapter 5, you learned that the servlet container only creates and loads one instance of a servlet. Then, it uses one thread for each request that's made by a client. Most of the time, that means that there's only one thread for each client that can access the session object. As a result, it's almost always thread-safe to access the session object with the getAttribute and setAttribute methods.

However, it's possible that the user may access the same servlet from multiple tabs within a browser as shown in figure 7-5. In that case, all tabs within the browser run in different threads that have access to the same session object. As a result, it's possible (though unlikely) that two threads might try to get or set an attribute in the session object at the same time, which might result in a lost update or another type of problem.

In addition, HTML5 allows a single web page to have multiple worker threads that make independent HTTP requests. As a result, it's possible that even a single browser tab could attempt to concurrently modify the session through sloppy front-end programming.

For many applications, you may not need to make access to the session object thread-safe. Unfortunately, if you do need to make access to the session object thread-safe, you can't synchronize on the session object like this:

```
synchronized(session) {
    session.setAttribute("cart", cart);
}
```

The problem with this code is that the servlet specification doesn't guarantee that it will always return the same session object. As a result, this code is *not* thread-safe. Instead, you must use the code shown in this figure.

The code in the figure works because the servlet specification *does* guarantee that the session ID will always be the same, even if the session object is different. As a result, you can create a lock object based on the session ID and synchronize on that object.

The intern method is a little known method of the String class that allows you to store a string in a pool of strings. The purpose is to save memory and reduce garbage collection by only storing one object of identical strings in the pool, rather than creating separate objects for each string, even if the strings have identical content. As a result, the first time this code accesses a session ID and calls the intern method on it, the string is stored the string pool. After that, every time this code requests the session ID, it gets the shared string object from the pool instead of a new string object. Because of that, it's safe to synchronize on the session ID string that's stored in the pool.

Unfortunately, this solution is not thread-safe in an environment where multiple application servers are running behind a load balancer. In that case, each server has its own string pool. Fortunately, this type of environment is typically only necessary for websites with large amounts of traffic. As a result, this isn't an issue for most websites.

An example that synchronizes access to the session object

```
Cart cart;
final Object lock = request.getSession().getId().intern();
synchronized(lock) {
    cart = (Cart) session.getAttribute("cart");
}
```

Another example that synchronizes access to the session object

```
final Object lock = request.getSession().getId().intern();
synchronized(lock) {
    session.setAttribute("cart", cart);
}
```

A web browser with three tabs accessing the same session object

Description

- Each servlet creates one session object that exists for multiple requests that come from a single client.

- If the client has one browser window open, access to the session object is thread-safe.

- If the client has multiple browser windows open, it's possible (though unlikely) that two threads from the same client could access the session object at the same time. As a result, the session object isn't thread-safe.

- Since the servlet specification doesn't guarantee that it will always return the same session object, you can't make the session object thread-safe by synchronizing on it. Instead, you can synchronize on the session ID string for the session object.

Figure 7-5   How to provide thread-safe access to the session object

How to work with cookies

In the last topic, you learned that the servlet API uses per-session cookies. Now, you'll learn more about working with cookies including how to create a persistent cookie that can be stored on the user's computer for up to three years.

An introduction to cookies

Figure 7-6 introduces you to some basic facts about cookies. To start, it shows some examples of cookies. These examples show that a cookie is essentially a name/value pair. For example, the name of the first cookie is jsessionid, and its value is

`D1F15245171203E8670487F020544490`

This is a typical value for the cookie that's generated by the servlet API to keep track of sessions. However, you can create your own cookies to store any type of string data.

Once you create a cookie, you include it in the server's response to the browser. Then, the browser stores the cookie on the client machine, and sends it back to the server with all subsequent requests. Remember, though, that some browsers may have disabled cookies, especially persistent cookies. As a result, you can't always rely on using them.

Once you have stored a cookie on a browser's PC, you can use it to make your web application work better for the user. For instance, you can use cookies to verify that users have registered before so they don't have to register again. You can use them to customize pages that display information that's specific to the users. And you can use them to focus advertising that is likely to appeal to the users.

Examples of cookies

```
jsessionid=D1F15245171203E8670487F020544490
user_id=87
email=jsmith@hotmail.com
```

How cookies work

- A cookie is a name/value pair that is stored in a browser.

- On the server, a web application creates a cookie and sends it to the browser. On the client, the browser saves the cookie and sends it back to the server every time it accesses a page from that server.

- Cookies can be set to persist within the user's browser for up to 3 years.

- Some users disable cookies in their browsers. As a result, you can't always count on all users having their cookies enabled.

- Browsers generally accept only 20 cookies from each site and 300 cookies total. In addition, they can limit each cookie to 4 kilobytes.

- A cookie can be associated with one or more subdomain names.

Typical uses for cookies

- **To allow users to skip login and registration forms** that gather data like user name, password, address, or credit card data.

- **To customize pages** that display information like weather reports, sports scores, and stock quotations.

- **To focus advertising** like banner ads that target the user's interests.

Description

- A per-session cookie that holds the session ID is automatically created for each session. That cookie is used to relate the browser to the session object.

- You can also create and send other cookies to a user's browser. You can use these cookies to access user-specific data that's stored in a file or database.

Figure 7-6   An introduction to cookies

How to create and use cookies

To create and use cookies, you use the constructors and methods shown in figure 7-7. After you create a Cookie object, you can use its methods to set its parameters and to get its name and value. Then, you can use the addCookie method of the response object to add that cookie to a browser's PC. And you can use the getCookies method of the request object to get an array of all the cookies on the browser's PC. These methods are illustrated by the two examples.

The first example uses four statements to create a cookie and add it to the response object. The first statement creates the Cookie object. The second statement calls the setMaxAge method to set the life of the cookie on the browser's PC to two years (60 seconds times 60 minutes times 24 hours times 365 days times 2 years). The third statement sets the path for the cookie so it's available to the entire web application. And the fourth statement adds the cookie to the response object so it is returned to the browser and added to the browser's PC.

The second example retrieves a cookie from the request object that's been sent from a browser. Here, the first statement returns an array of Cookie objects from the request object. Then, the following statements loop through the array to return the cookie with a name of "userIdCookie". To do that, these statements use the getName and getValue methods of the Cookie object.

Constructor of the Cookie class

Constructor	Description
Cookie(String name, String value)	Creates a cookie with the specified name and value.

The methods of the Cookie class

Method	Description
setMaxAge(int maxAgeInSeconds)	To create a persistent cookie, set the cookie's maximum age to a positive number.
	To create a per-session cookie, set the cookie's maximum age to –1. Then, the cookie is deleted when the user exits the browser.
setPath(String path)	To allow the entire application to access the cookie, set the cookie's path to "/".
getName()	Returns a string for the name of the cookie.
getValue()	Returns a string that contains the value of the cookie.

A method of the response object

Method	Description
addCookie(Cookie c)	Adds the specified cookie to the response.

A method of the request object

Method	Description
getCookies()	Returns an array of Cookie objects that the client sent with this request. If no cookies were sent, this method returns a null value.

Code that creates a cookie and sets it in a response

```
Cookie c = new Cookie("userIdCookie", userId);
c.setMaxAge(60*60*24*365*2);      // set age to 2 years
c.setPath("/");                   // allow access by entire app
response.addCookie(c);
```

Code that gets a cookie value from a request

```
Cookie[] cookies = request.getCookies();
String cookieName = "userIdCookie";
String cookieValue = "";
for (Cookie cookie: cookies) {
    if (cookieName.equals(cookie.getName()))
        cookieValue = cookie.getValue();
}
```

Figure 7-7   How to create and use cookies

How to view and delete cookies

When you're testing or debugging an application, you may want to view all of the cookies for a browser to make sure the right ones are being stored. Similarly, you may want to delete all the cookies from the browser so you can add new cookies to it. Or, if you know the name of a cookie, you may want to display its value. Figure 7-8 shows how to perform all three of these tasks.

The first example shows how to display all the cookies that the browser is sending to the current page. To do that, you can write a JSP that uses EL to access the *implicit cookie object*. This object stores a map of all cookies that the browser is sending to the server. Then, you can use JSTL to loop through each item in the map. Here, the JSTL loop assigns a variable named c for each item. Then, the first value property returns the Cookie object. After that, the name property gets the name of the cookie and the second value property gets its value.

Don't worry if you don't completely understand the EL and JSTL code shown here. For now, you can use this code in a JSP anytime you need to view cookies. Then, in the next two chapters, you'll learn more about EL and JSTL, which should help clarify how this code works.

The second example shows how to delete all the cookies for a browser. To do that, you can write servlet code that uses the getCookies method to get an array of cookies. Then, this code loops through this array and uses the setMaxAge method to set the age of each cookie to zero, which deletes the cookie. To complete the deletion, this code sets each cookie in the response object.

The third example shows how to display the value of the cookie with the specified name. To do that, you can code EL within a JSP that accesses the implicit cookie object that stores all cookies. Then, you get the cookie you want by specifying its name as the first property, and you get the value that's stored in the cookie by specifying the value as the second property. In this figure, for instance, the example gets the value of the cookie named emailCookie.

A JSP that shows all cookies for the current server

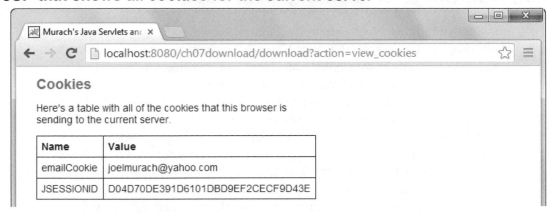

JSP code that displays the names and values for all cookies

```
<%@ taglib prefix="c" uri="http://java.sun.com/jsp/jstl/core" %>
<table>
  <tr>
    <th>Name</th>
    <th>Value</th>
  </tr>
  <c:forEach var="c" items="${cookie}">
  <tr>
    <td>${c.value.name}</td>
    <td>${c.value.value}</td>
  </tr>
  </c:forEach>
</table>
```

Servlet code that deletes all persistent cookies

```
Cookie[] cookies = request.getCookies();
for (Cookie cookie : cookies) {
    cookie.setMaxAge(0); //delete the cookie
    cookie.setPath("/");  //allow the download application to access it
    response.addCookie(cookie);
}
```

JSP code that displays the value for a cookie named emailCookie

```
<p>Email cookie value: ${cookie.emailCookie.value}</p>
```

Description

- To display all the cookies for a user's browser, use JSTL to loop through all cookies stored in the built-in map named cookie. Then, code the key property to get the name of each cookie and code the value property to get the value of each cookie.
- To delete a persistent cookie from a browser, set the age of a cookie to 0.

Figure 7-8   How to view and delete cookies

Four methods for working with cookies

Most of the time, you'll use the techniques shown in the last two figures to work with Cookie objects. However, figure 7-9 presents more information about four of the methods of the Cookie object that you may find useful.

As you've already seen, you can use the setPath method to set the path for a cookie. By default, when a browser returns a cookie, it returns it to the directory that originally sent the cookie to the browser and to all subdirectories of that directory. But that's often not what you want. If, for example, a servlet that's mapped to the email directory sends a cookie to the browser, then a servlet or JSP that's available from the download directory won't be able to access the cookie. As a result, it's common to use the setPath method to set the path for the cookie to a slash (/) so that the entire web application can access the cookie.

You can use the setDomain method to set the domain for a cookie. By default, when a browser returns a cookie, it returns it only to the exact domain name that originally sent the cookie to the browser. Since that's usually what you want, you usually don't need to use this method. But if you have a website that uses server subdomains, you can use this method to return the cookie to all of the subdomains.

To illustrate, assume that you have a website named www.murach.com that has two subdomains www.java.murach.com and www.cobol.murach.com. Then, if you set the domain to

`.murach.com`

all three of these domains can access the cookie. In other words, when the browser sends the cookie to one subdomain, it's possible for the other subdomains to retrieve the cookie.

You can use the setSecure method to create a secure cookie. By default, a browser returns a cookie across a regular HTTP connection or across a secure, encrypted connection. But if you're sending sensitive data, you can use this method to specify that the cookie should only be sent across a secure connection.

You can use the setVersion method to set the version of the cookie protocol that you want to use. By default, a cookie uses version 0 of the cookie protocol. Since this protocol has been around the longest and is the most widely supported, that's usually what you want. But if there's a compelling reason to use version 1 of the cookie protocol, you can use this protocol by specifying an integer value of 1 for this method.

Four methods of the Cookie class

Method	Description
setPath(String path**)**	By default, when you send a cookie to a browser, the browser returns the cookie to all servlets and JSPs within the directory that sent the cookie and all subdirectories of that directory. To make a cookie available to the entire application, you can set the path to a slash (/).
	To make a cookie available to a directory and its subdirectories, you can specify a path like /cart. Then, the browser returns the cookie to the cart directory and all subdirectories. However, the directory that originally sent the cookie must be within this directory or one of its subdirectories.
setDomain(String domainPattern**)**	By default, the browser only returns a cookie to the host that sent the cookie. To return a cookie to other hosts within the same domain, you can set a domain pattern like .ads.com. Then, the browser returns the cookie to any subdomain of www.ads.com like www.travel.ads.com or www.camera.ads.com.
setSecure(boolean flag**)**	By default, the browser sends a cookie over a regular connection or an encrypted connection. To protect cookies that store sensitive data, you can supply a true value for this method. Then, the cookie is only sent over a secure connection.
setVersion(int version**)**	By default, Java creates cookies that use version 0 of the cookie protocol that was developed by Netscape. Since this is the cookie protocol that has been around the longest, it is the most widely supported. However, you can specify an int value of 1 for this method to use the new version of the cookie protocol, which is version 1.

Description

- All of these set methods have corresponding get methods.
- For more information about these methods and other methods for working with cookies, use your web browser to look up the Cookie class in the javax.servlet.http package that's in the documentation for the Servlet and JavaServer Pages API.

Figure 7-9   Four methods for working with cookies

A utility class for working with cookies

As you've already seen, you must loop through an array of cookies whenever you want to get the value for one cookie. Since this can be tedious, it's common to place the code that loops through the array of cookies in a utility class like the one shown in figure 7-10. Then, you can easily retrieve the value of a cookie by calling the utility class.

The CookieUtil class in this figure contains one static method named getCookieValue. This method accepts an array of cookies and the name of the cookie that you want to get. Then, it loops through the array of cookies and returns the value that matches the name of the cookie. If it doesn't find the name of the cookie in the array, this method returns an empty string.

Since you might want to access this class from more than one servlet or JSP, you should store this class in a central location. For instance, this class is stored in the murach.util package. As a result, you need to import this class before you can use it. Once you do that, you can use Java statements like the two at the bottom of this figure to get the value of any cookie.

A utility class that gets the value of a cookie

```
package murach.util;

import javax.servlet.http.*;

public class CookieUtil {

    public static String getCookieValue(
            Cookie[] cookies, String cookieName) {

        String cookieValue = "";
        if (cookies != null) {
            for (Cookie cookie: cookies) {
                if (cookieName.equals(cookie.getName())) {
                    cookieValue = cookie.getValue();
                }
            }
        }
        return cookieValue;
    }
}
```

Code that uses the CookieUtil class to get the value of a cookie

```
Cookie[] cookies = request.getCookies();
String emailAddress = CookieUtil.getCookieValue(cookies, "emailCookie");
```

Description

- To make it easier to get the value of a cookie, you can create a utility class that contains a method that accepts an array of Cookie objects and the name of the cookie and then returns the value of the cookie.

Figure 7-10   A utility class for working with cookies

How to work with URL rewriting and hidden fields

In the early days of web programming, programmers used URL rewriting and hidden fields to track sessions. Today, you can use the servlet API to track sessions. However, you can still use URL rewriting and hidden fields to pass parameters between the browser and the server.

In particular, URL rewriting and hidden fields are handy if you need to pass data for a single request. Rather than storing that type of data in the session object, which takes up memory, you can use URL rewriting and hidden fields to pass data from page to page.

How to use URL rewriting to pass parameters

Figure 7-11 shows how to use *URL rewriting* to pass parameters from the browser to the server. This should already be familiar to you because that's how parameters are passed from HTML documents to a servlet when the HTTP GET method is used.

For instance, the first example shows how to code a link that specifies a URL that adds a product to a cart. Here, the URL calls the servlet that's mapped to the /cart URL and passes a parameter named productCode with a value of 8601. Since a link always uses the HTTP GET method, this causes the productCode parameter to be displayed in the browser as shown in this figure.

The second example shows that you can also use URL rewriting within a form tag. Here, the method attribute of the form tag specifies the HTTP POST method. As a result, the productCode parameter isn't appended to the end of the URL that's displayed in the browser.

The third example shows that you can use EL to pass a value to a URL. Here, EL supplies a product code that's evaluated at runtime.

The fourth example shows how to append multiple parameters to a URL. Here, the code uses the HTML entity for the ampersand (&) to separate the parameters. Although a plain ampersand (&) works in most cases, you need to use the HTML entity if you want to write valid HTML5.

URL rewriting has a couple of limitations. To get around these limitations, you can use hidden fields as shown in the next figure. But, as you will see, hidden fields have some limitations too.

Since URL rewriting stores parameters values in the URL, it also has a couple of security risks. First, parameter values can leak to third-party sites such as Google Analytics or Facebook. Second, these values are stored in the browser history. As a result, you shouldn't use URL rewriting for any values that store sensitive information.

Another issue is that search engines call these URLs when crawling your site. In this figure, that would create and fill one or possibly more shopping carts. This creates unnecessary work for your server.

The syntax for URL rewriting

```
url?paramName1=paramValue1&amp;paramName2=paramValue2&amp;...
```

A link that adds a product code to a URL

```
<a href="cart?productCode=8601">Add To Cart</a>
```

The link displayed in a browser

86 (the band) - True Life Songs and Pictures	$14.95	Add To Cart

The URL that's displayed when you click on the link

More examples

A form tag that calls a JSP

```
<form action="cart?productCode=jr01" method="post">
```

A link that uses EL for the product code value

```
<a href="cart?productCode=${productCode}">Add To Cart</a>
```

A link that includes two parameters

```
<a href="download?action=checkUser&amp;productCode=8601">Download</a>
```

Two limitations of URL rewriting

- Most browsers limit the number of characters that can be passed by a URL to 2,000 characters.
- It's difficult to include spaces and special characters such as the ? and & characters in parameter values.

Two security risks with URL rewriting

- Parameter values can leak to third-party sites such as Google Analytics or Facebook.
- Parameter values are stored in the browser history.

Description

- You can use *URL rewriting* to pass parameters to a servlet or JSP. To do that, you add the parameters to the end of the URL.

Figure 7-11   How to use URL rewriting to pass parameters

How to use hidden fields to pass parameters

In chapter 4, you learned how to code *hidden fields* within an HTML form. Now, figure 7-12 shows how to use hidden fields to pass a parameter from a browser to the server. In particular, it shows how to pass a parameter named productCode to the servlet that's mapped to the /cart URL.

The first example uses hidden fields to accomplish the same task as the first URL rewriting example in the previous figure. However, there are a couple advantages to using hidden fields. First, a hidden field can contain spaces and other special characters that are difficult to work with when using URL rewriting. Second, there is no limit on the number of characters that can be stored in a hidden field. Third, since this example uses the HTTP POST method, it doesn't display the parameter values in the URL, which removes the security risks mentioned in the previous figure.

The second example in this figure shows that you can use a JSP expression to assign a value to a hidden field. Here, the form contains a hidden field that contains the product code, a text box for the quantity, and an Update button. However, the value for the hidden field isn't hard-coded. Instead, a JSP expression retrieves the value for the hidden field. That way, when the user clicks on the Update button, the servlet can tell which product the user wants to update.

A form tag that uses a hidden text field and a button

```
<form action="cart" method="post">
    <input type="submit" value="Add To Cart">
    <input type="hidden" name="productCode" value="8601">
</form>
```

The form displayed in a browser

The URL that's displayed when you click on the button

A form tag that uses EL to set hidden field values

```
<form action="cart" method="post">
    <input type="hidden" name="productCode" value="${product.code}">
    <input type=text size=2 name="quantity" value="${lineItem.quantity}">
    <input type="submit" name="updateButton" value="Update">
</form>
```

One limitation of hidden fields

• Because hidden fields are displayed in the source code for the page that's returned to the browser, anyone can view the parameters. As a result, hidden fields aren't appropriate for secure data like passwords.

Description

• You can use *hidden fields* to pass parameters to a servlet or JSP. To do that, you code hidden fields within a form tag.

Figure 7-12   How to use hidden fields to pass parameters

The Download application

At this point, you should have the basic skills for working with sessions, cookies, URL rewriting, and hidden fields. But it's hard to understand how to use these skills without seeing them in a complete application. That's why figure 7-13 presents an application that lets registered users download sound files from a website. Although this application is eight pages long, you can learn a lot from studying it.

The user interface

The user interface for the Download application consists of three pages. The Index page lets a user select an album. Then, if the user hasn't already registered with the site, the Register page registers the user by gathering the user's email address, first name, and last name. Once the user is registered, the Downloads page lets the user select a song to download. If, for example, the user clicks on the MP3 link to the right of a song, that song is downloaded and played.

The Index page

The Register page

The Downloads page

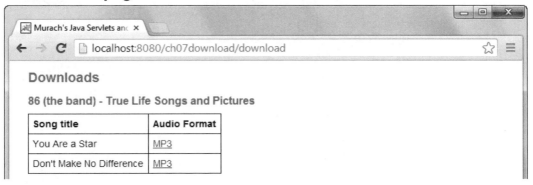

Figure 7-13   The Download application (part 1 of 8)

The file structure

Part 2 begins by showing the files that make up the Download application. To start, this application uses six JSP files: one for the Index page, one for the Register page, and one for the Download page for each of the four albums. Here, the Download pages follow a rigid naming convention. All of these pages begin with a four-character product code that identifies the album, followed by an underscore character, followed by "download.jsp".

The MP3 files that are used by the album follow a similar naming convention. These files are all stored in a subdirectory of the sound directory that's available from another application named musicStore. Here, each subdirectory uses the four-character product code for the album. When a modern browser goes to the URL for one of these MP3 files, it downloads and plays it.

The web.xml file

Part 2 also shows the web.xml file for the application. This file maps the DownloadServlet class to the /download URL. In addition, it sets the default session timeout to 30 minutes. As a result, the session is invalidated if a client doesn't access the session object within 30 minutes. To change this, you can modify the web.xml file or write Java code that uses the setMaxInactiveInterval method to change the maximum inactive interval for the session. Finally, the web.xml file sets the welcome file list for the application to index.jsp. As a result, if a user requests the root directory of the application, the index.jsp file is displayed.

The names of the jsp files

```
index.jsp
register.jsp
8601_download.jsp
pf01_download.jsp
pf02_download.jsp
jr01_download.jsp
```

The name of the controller servlet class

```
murach.download.DownloadServlet
```

The file structure for the mp3 files

```
musicStore/sound/8601/*.mp3
musicStore/sound/pf01/*.mp3
musicStore/sound/pf02/*.mp3
musicStore/sound/jr01/*.mp3
```

The web.xml file

```xml
<?xml version="1.0" encoding="UTF-8"?>
<web-app version="3.0" xmlns="http://java.sun.com/xml/ns/javaee"
    xmlns:xsi="http://www.w3.org/2001/XMLSchema-instance"
    xsi:schemaLocation="http://java.sun.com/xml/ns/javaee
                        http://java.sun.com/xml/ns/javaee/web-app_3_0.xsd">
    <servlet>
        <servlet-name>DownloadServlet</servlet-name>
        <servlet-class>murach.download.DownloadServlet</servlet-class>
    </servlet>

    <servlet-mapping>
        <servlet-name>DownloadServlet</servlet-name>
        <url-pattern>/download</url-pattern>
    </servlet-mapping>

    <session-config>
        <session-timeout>30</session-timeout>
    </session-config>

    <welcome-file-list>
        <welcome-file>index.jsp</welcome-file>
    </welcome-file-list>
</web-app>
```

Figure 7-13   The Download application (part 2 of 8)

The code for the JSPs

Part 3 shows the code for the Index page. Here, the links for each album pass two parameters to the DownloadServlet class. The first parameter has a name of action and a value of checkUser. The second parameter has a name of product and a value that specifies the product code for the album.

Part 4 shows the code for the Register page. Since this code works similarly to the Email List application of the previous chapters, it should be easy to follow. Here, the form passes a hidden field to the DownloadServlet class. This hidden field has a name of action and a value of registerUser.

Part 5 shows the code for the Download page. This code uses the product code that's stored in the session object to locate the MP3 sound files for the album. On most systems, clicking on one of these links causes the MP3 file to download and automatically begin playing.

The code for the index.jsp file

```
<!DOCTYPE html>
<html>
<head>
    <meta charset="utf-8">
    <title>Murach's Java Servlets and JSP</title>
    <link rel="stylesheet" href="styles/main.css" type="text/css"/>
</head>
<body>

<h1>List of albums</h1>

<p>
<a href="download?action=checkUser&amp;productCode=8601">
    86 (the band) - True Life Songs and Pictures
</a><br>

<a href="download?action=checkUser&amp;productCode=pf01">
    Paddlefoot - The First CD
</a><br>

<a href="download?action=checkUser&amp;productCode=pf02">
    Paddlefoot - The Second CD
</a><br>

<a href="download?action=checkUser&amp;productCode=jr01">
    Joe Rut - Genuine Wood Grained Finish
</a>
</p>

</body>
</html>
```

Figure 7-13   The Download application (part 3 of 8)

The code for the register.jsp file

```
<!DOCTYPE html>
<html>
<head>
    <meta charset="utf-8">
    <title>Murach's Java Servlets and JSP</title>
    <link rel="stylesheet" href="styles/main.css" type="text/css"/>
</head>
<body>

<h1>Download registration</h1>

<p>To register for our downloads, enter your name and email
    address below. Then, click on the Submit button.</p>

<form action="download" method="post">
    <input type="hidden" name="action" value="registerUser">
    <label class="pad_top">Email:</label>
    <input type="email" name="email" value="${user.email}"><br>
    <label class="pad_top">First Name:</label>
    <input type="text" name="firstName" value="${user.firstName}"><br>
    <label class="pad_top">Last Name:</label>
    <input type="text" name="lastName" value="${user.lastName}"><br>
    <label> </label>
    <input type="submit" value="Register" class="margin_left">
</form>

</body>

</html>
```

Figure 7-13   The Download application (part 4 of 8)

The code for the 8601_download.jsp file

```
<!DOCTYPE html>
<html>
<head>
    <meta charset="utf-8">
    <title>Murach's Java Servlets and JSP</title>
    <link rel="stylesheet" href="styles/main.css" type="text/css"/>
</head>
<body>

<h1>Downloads</h1>

<h2>86 (the band) - True Life Songs and Pictures</h2>

<table>
<tr>
    <th>Song title</th>
    <th>Audio Format</th>
</tr>
<tr>
    <td>You Are a Star</td>
    <td>
        <a href="/musicStore/sound/${productCode}/star.mp3">MP3</a>
    </td>
</tr>
<tr>
    <td>Don't Make No Difference</td>
    <td>
        <a href="/musicStore/sound/${productCode}/no_difference.mp3">MP3</a>
    </td>
</tr>
</table>

</body>
</html>
```

Description

- This is one of the four JSPs for downloading songs. The others are similar.

- When a browser receives the URL for a sound file, it downloads and plays it. That's one of the capabilities of a modern browser.

- This JSP gets the product code from the session object and uses it in the URLs for the sound files. This isn't necessary, though, because the URLs could be hard-coded.

- Another way to handle the downloads is to write one JSP that works for all of the albums. To implement that, you can store the data for the downloadable songs in one file for each album. Then, the download JSP can get the product code from the session object, read the related file, and load its data into the table.

Figure 7-13   The Download application (part 5 of 8)

The code for the servlet

Part 6 shows the code for the DownloadServlet class, which acts as the controller for the Download application. This code starts by declaring a doGet method that handles requests that use the HTTP GET method.

Within the doGet method, the code begins by getting the action parameter. If the action parameter hasn't been set, this code sets it to a default value of viewAlbums.

After setting the action variable, this code uses an if/else statement to perform the appropriate action and forward to the appropriate JSP. To view albums, this code just sets the variable named url to the Index page. To check the user, this code calls the checkUser method that's shown in part 7 of this figure and passes the request and response objects to it. This method checks whether the user has already registered and returns an appropriate URL. If the user has not registered, for example, this method returns the URL for the Register page. Otherwise, this method returns the URL for the appropriate Download page. Either way, the last statement in the method forwards the request and response to the specified URL.

The doPost method works like the doGet method. However, it only handles the action for registering users. To register the user, this code calls the registerUser method that's shown in part 8 of this figure and passes it the request and response objects. This method registers the user and returns a URL for the appropriate Download page. Since the doPost method doesn't handle the other actions, you can't use the HTTP POST method to view albums or to check the user. Conversely, since the doGet method doesn't handle the registerUser action, you must use the HTTP POST method to register the user. Since registering the user writes data to the server, this is usually what you want.

The code for the DownloadServlet class   Page 1

```java
package murach.download;

import java.io.*;
import javax.servlet.*;
import javax.servlet.http.*;

import murach.business.User;
import murach.data.UserIO;
import murach.util.CookieUtil;

public class DownloadServlet extends HttpServlet {

    @Override
    public void doGet(HttpServletRequest request,
            HttpServletResponse response)
            throws IOException, ServletException {

        // get current action
        String action = request.getParameter("action");
        if (action == null) {
            action = "viewAlbums";  // default action
        }

        // perform action and set URL to appropriate page
        String url = "/index.jsp";
        if (action.equals("viewAlbums")) {
            url = "/index.jsp";
        } else if (action.equals("checkUser")) {
            url = checkUser(request, response);
        }

        // forward to the view
        getServletContext()
                .getRequestDispatcher(url)
                .forward(request, response);
    }

    @Override
    public void doPost(HttpServletRequest request,
            HttpServletResponse response)
            throws IOException, ServletException {

        String action = request.getParameter("action");

        // perform action and set URL to appropriate page
        String url = "/index.jsp";
        if (action.equals("registerUser")) {
            url = registerUser(request, response);
        }

        // forward to the view
        getServletContext()
                .getRequestDispatcher(url)
                .forward(request, response);
    }
```

Figure 7-13   The Download application (part 6 of 8)

In part 7, the checkUser method begins by getting the product code from the request object that was passed from the Index page. Then, it creates a session object by calling the getSession method of the request object, and it sets the product code as an attribute of the session object. From this point on, this product code can be retrieved from the session object.

After that, the code creates a new User object and attempts to get the data for this object from the User attribute of the session object. If the session object contains a User object, the new User object gets the data from the session object. This indicates that the user has called this servlet at least once before in this session. Otherwise, the getAttribute method returns a null value and the User object is set to null. This indicates that the user is calling this servlet for the first time.

The nested if statements that follow provide for three possibilities. First, if the User object is null and a cookie named emailCookie isn't available from previous sessions, the user hasn't registered before. As a result, the code sets the variable named url to a URL that points to the Register page. Second, if the User object is null but the cookie exists, the user has registered before. As a result, the code (1) uses the getUser method of the UserIO class to get the data for the User object from a file, (2) sets the User object as an attribute of the session object, and (3) sets the url variable to the appropriate Download JSP. Third, if the User object exists, the user has registered before. As a result, the code sets the url variable to the appropriate Download JSP. Finally, after the nested if statements, the last statement returns the url variable.

If you study this code, you should be able to follow it. It may help to understand, though, that the checkUser method creates a User object from the user entries and adds this object to the session object. It also creates an emailCookie and adds it to the response object. As a result, if your browser has cookies enabled, you don't have to register the next time you use this application. Otherwise, you would have to register each time you use this application.

The code for the DownloadServlet class   **Page 2**

```java
    private String checkUser(HttpServletRequest request,
        HttpServletResponse response) {

        String productCode = request.getParameter("productCode");
        HttpSession session = request.getSession();
        session.setAttribute("productCode", productCode);
        User user = (User) session.getAttribute("user");

        String url;
        // if User object doesn't exist, check email cookie
        if (user == null) {
            Cookie[] cookies = request.getCookies();
            String emailAddress =
                CookieUtil.getCookieValue(cookies, "emailCookie");

            // if cookie doesn't exist, go to Registration page
            if (emailAddress == null || emailAddress.equals("")) {
                url = "/register.jsp";
            }
            // if cookie exists, create User object and go to Downloads page
            else {
                ServletContext sc = getServletContext();
                String path = sc.getRealPath("/WEB-INF/EmailList.txt");
                user = UserIO.getUser(emailAddress, path);
                session.setAttribute("user", user);
                url = "/" + productCode + "_download.jsp";
            }
        }
        // if User object exists, go to Downloads page
        else {
            url = "/" + productCode + "_download.jsp";
        }
        return url;
    }
```

Figure 7-13   The Download application (part 7 of 8)

In part 8, the registerUser method starts by getting the parameters that the user entered on the Register page. Then, this method creates a User object from these parameters and uses the UserIO class to write the User object to a file that's stored in the WEB-INF directory. After writing the file, this method stores the User object in the session object, and creates a persistent cookie that stores the user's email address for two years. Next, this method gets the productCode attribute that has already been stored in the session object and uses it to create a variable named url that points to the appropriate Download page. Finally, the last statement in this method returns the url variable.

The code for the DownloadServlet class

```
private String registerUser(HttpServletRequest request,
        HttpServletResponse response) {

    // get the user data
    String email = request.getParameter("email");
    String firstName = request.getParameter("firstName");
    String lastName = request.getParameter("lastName");

    // store the data in a User object
    User user = new User();
    user.setEmail(email);
    user.setFirstName(firstName);
    user.setLastName(lastName);

    // write the User object to a file
    ServletContext sc = getServletContext();
    String path = sc.getRealPath("/WEB-INF/EmailList.txt");
    UserIO.add(user, path);

    // store the User object as a session attribute
    HttpSession session = request.getSession();
    session.setAttribute("user", user);

    // add a cookie that stores the user's email to browser
    Cookie c = new Cookie("emailCookie", email);
    c.setMaxAge(60 * 60 * 24 * 365 * 2); // set age to 2 years
    c.setPath("/");                      // allow entire app to access it
    response.addCookie(c);

    // create an return a URL for the appropriate Download page
    String productCode = (String) session.getAttribute("productCode");
    String url = "/" + productCode + "_download.jsp";
    return url;
    }
}
```

Figure 7-13   The Download application (part 8 of 8)

Perspective

The goal of this chapter has been to show you how to use the servlet API to track sessions and work with cookies. If you understand the code in the Download application that's presented at the end of this chapter, this chapter has achieved its goal. As a result, you should now be able to develop web applications that require session tracking.

In the previous chapter, you learned how to work with a special type of Java class known as a JavaBean. In that chapter, you stored a JavaBean as an attribute of the request object. However, it's also common to store a JavaBean as an attribute of the session object as shown in this chapter.

In the early days of servlet/JSP programming, it was more common for web browsers to have per-session cookies disabled, and the security flaws with URL encoding weren't widely known. As a result, it was more common to use URL encoding to provide for session tracking.

Today, it's less common for web browsers to have per-session cookies disabled, and the security flaws with URL encoding are widely known. As a result, it isn't considered a good practice to use URL encoding.

Summary

- Because HTTP is a *stateless protocol*, web applications must provide for *session tracking*. That way, an application is able to relate each request to a specific browser and to the data for that session.

- To provide for session tracking, Java creates one *session object* for each browser. Then, you can add attributes like variables and objects to this session object, and you can retrieve the values of these attributes in any of the servlets and JSPs that are run during the session.

- In general, it's considered a best practice to implement session tracking by using *cookies*. Then, the session ID is stored in a cookie on the user's browser. This type of session tracking is done automatically by the servlet API, but it doesn't work unless the browser enables cookies.

- *Persistent cookies* are stored on the user's PC, while *per-session cookies* are deleted when the session ends.

- It's also possible to implement session tracking by using *URL encoding*. This works even when the browser doesn't enable cookies. However, it can lead to session hijacking. As a result, it's considered a bad practice.

- To create cookies, use the methods of the Cookie class. To store a cookie on the user's browser, use the addCookie method of the response object. To get the cookies from a browser, use the getCookies method of the request object.

- To pass parameters to a servlet, you can use *URL rewriting* or *hidden fields*. When you use hidden fields, you can easily include spaces and special characters in your parameter values. In addition, you can pass parameters more securely than you can with URL rewriting.

Exercise 7-1   Use a cookie

1. Open the ch07_ex1_download project in the ex_starts directory.

2. Run the project. This should display a list of album links.

3. Click on the link for an album. This should display the Register page.

4. User the Register page to register. This should take you to a Downloads page where you can listen to an MP3 file.

    When you click on an MP3 link on the Downloads page, your browser should play the corresponding sound file. For this to work, *the Music Store application must be deployed*. If it isn't, you'll get a 404 error when you click on the MP3 link. To fix this, you can open the musicStore project in the book_apps directory and run it.

5. From a Downloads page, click the View All Cookies link. This should display all of the cookies that this application has sent to your browser. This should include the cookie named emailCookie and a cookie named JSESSIONID.

6. Click the Delete All Persistent Cookies link to delete all persistent cookies.

7. Close your browser and run the application again. Then, click on a link for an album. This should display the Register page again.

8. Use the Register page to register again.

9. Open the source code for the DownloadServlet. Then, modify the code that adds the cookie so it stores the cookie with a name of "userEmail". Also, modify this code so it stores the cookie for 3 years.

10. Open the index.jsp file and add code to the top of the page that displays the name and value of the cookie. For an email address of jsmith@gmail.com, this code should display this output:

    ```
    User Email: jsmith@gmail.com
    ```

    To do this, you can add a p tag to the page with EL that uses the implicit cookie object to get the value of the cookie that stores the user's email address.

11. Run the project again. Then, test to make sure it works correctly. To do that, you can register, use the View All Cookies link to view the name and value of this cookie, and use the Index page to view the value of the email cookie.

Exercise 7-2   Use a session attribute

1. Open the ch07_ex2_download project in the ex_starts directory.

2. Open the source code for the DownloadServlet class. Then, in the checkUser method, modify the code so it sets the Product object as a session attribute instead of setting the product code as a session attribute. To do that, you can create a Product object that holds the data for the current product by using the getProduct method of the murach.data.ProductIO class like this:

```
ServletContext sc = this.getServletContext();
String productPath = sc.getRealPath("WEB-INF/products.txt");
Product product = ProductIO.getProduct(productCode, productPath);
```

3. In the registerUser method, modify the code so it uses the Product object that's stored in the session to build the URL for the appropriate Download page.

4. For each product's Download page, get the Product object from the session object and use it to get the product code for the album as well as the description for the album.

5. Run the Download application and test it to make sure it works correctly. To get the MP3 links to work correctly, you may need to open the musicStore project in the book_apps directory and run it.

6. View the cookies for this application. Then, click the Delete All Persistent Cookies link to delete all persistent cookies.

7. Close the browser and run the Download application again to make sure the DownloadServlet class still works correctly.

Exercise 7-3   Use URL rewriting instead of hidden fields

1. Open the ch07_ex3_cart project in the ex_starts directory.

2. Open the source code for the CartServlet class. Note that this servlet only supports the HTTP POST method.

3. Open the cart.jsp file. Then, convert the Remove button to a Remove link that uses URL rewriting.

4. Run the application and test the Remove link. This link shouldn't work since it uses the HTTP GET method.

5. Modify the CartServlet class so it includes a doGet method that includes a single statement that calls the doPost method. That way, the CartServlet uses the same code to handle the HTTP POST and GET methods.

6. Run the application again and test the Remove link. Now, this link should work correctly, and it should display the parameter names and values in the browser's URL.

7. Test the Update button too. Since this button uses the HTTP POST method, it should not display the parameter names and values in the browser's URL.

8

How to use EL

In chapter 6, you learned how to code a JavaBean. In addition, you learned how to use the Expression Language (EL) that was introduced with JSP 2.0 to get properties from that JavaBean. Now, you'll learn more about using EL. In addition, you'll see that EL is a significant improvement over the standard JSP tags that were typically used prior to JSP 2.0.

If you skipped chapter 6, you should still be able to understand this chapter, as long as you know how to code a JavaBean. If you don't, you should go back to chapter 6 and read about JavaBeans at the start of that chapter. Then, you'll be ready for this chapter.

An introduction to JSP Expression Language

The JSP *Expression Language* (*EL*) provides a compact syntax that lets you get data from JavaBeans, maps, arrays, and lists that have been stored as attributes of a web application. To illustrate, figure 8-1 presents two examples that get data from a User object named user that has been stored as an attribute of the session object.

Both of these examples assume that the User class follows all the rules for creating a JavaBean that are shown in figure 6-1 of chapter 6. Then, the first example uses EL to get the properties of the User bean, and the second example uses standard JSP tags to get those properties. This should give you a quick idea of how EL can improve your JSPs.

Advantages of EL

EL has several advantages over standard JSP tags. First, EL is more compact and elegant. This makes it easier to code and read.

Second, although it isn't shown in this figure, EL makes it easy to access nested properties. For example, you can access a property named code from a JavaBean named product that's in a JavaBean named item like this:

`${item.product.code}`

Third, although standard JSP tags only let you access JavaBeans, EL lets you access collections such as arrays, maps, and lists. A *map* is a collection that implements the Map interface, such as a HashMap collection. A *list* is a collection that implements the List interface, such as the ArrayList<> collection. For more information about arrays and collections, you can refer to *Murach's Java Programming*.

Fourth, EL usually handles null values better than standard JSP tags. For example, instead of returning a null value for a string variable, EL returns an empty string, which is usually what you want.

Fifth, EL provides functionality that isn't available from the standard JSP tags. For example, it lets you work with HTTP headers, cookies, and context initialization parameters. It also lets you perform calculations and comparisons.

Disadvantages of EL

Unlike the standard JSP tags, EL doesn't create a JavaBean if the JavaBean hasn't already been stored as an attribute. In addition, EL doesn't provide a way to set the properties of a JavaBean. However, when you use the MVC pattern, you typically use a servlet to create a JavaBean, set its properties, and store it as an attribute. As a result, these disadvantages aren't an issue. In fact, many developers would say that having the view directly create JavaBeans and set their properties, violates good MVC practices.

Code in a JSP that accesses a User object that's stored in the session object

EL

```
<label>Email:</label>
<span>${user.email}</span><br>
<label>First Name:</label>
<span>${user.firstName}</span><br>
<label>Last Name:</label>
<span>${user.lastName}</span><br>
```

Standard JSP tags

```
<jsp:useBean id="user" scope="session" class="murach.business.User"/>
<label>Email:</label>
<span><jsp:getProperty name="user" property="email"/></span><br>
<label>First Name:</label>
<span><jsp:getProperty name="user" property="firstName"/></span><br>
<label>Last Name:</label>
<span><jsp:getProperty name="user" property="lastName"/></span><br>
```

Advantages of EL

- EL has a more elegant and compact syntax than standard JSP tags.
- EL lets you access nested properties.
- EL lets you access collections such as maps, arrays, and lists.
- EL does a better job of handling null values.
- EL provides more functionality.

Disadvantages of EL

- EL doesn't create a JavaBean if it doesn't already exist.
- EL doesn't provide a way to set properties.

Description

- The JSP *Expression Language* (*EL*) provides a compact syntax that lets you get data from JavaBeans, maps, arrays, and lists that have been stored as attributes of a web application.

Figure 8-1 An introduction to EL

Essential skills for working with EL

Now that you have a general idea of how EL can simplify and improve your JSP code, you're ready to learn the details of working with it.

How to use the dot operator to work with JavaBeans and maps

As you learned in chapters 5 and 7, you can use the setAttribute method of the HttpServletRequest and HttpSession objects to store an object with request or session scope. If you need a larger scope, you can use the setAttribute method of the ServletContext object to store an object with application scope. Or, if you need a smaller scope, you can use the setAttribute method of the implicit PageContext object to store an object with page scope. Then, you can use the getAttribute method of the appropriate object to retrieve the attribute.

Figure 8-2 shows how to use EL to access an attribute of a web application. Whenever you use EL, you begin by coding a dollar sign ($) followed by an opening brace ({) and a closing brace (}). Then, you code the expression within the braces.

The first example in this figure shows how to retrieve an attribute for a simple object like a String or Date object. Here, the servlet code creates a Date object named currentDate that stores the current date. Then, the servlet code stores this object as an attribute of the request object. Last, the JSP code uses EL to access this attribute, convert it to a string, and display it.

Note here that you don't have to specify the scope when you use EL. Instead, EL automatically searches through all scopes starting with the smallest scope (page scope) and moving towards the largest scope (application scope).

The second example shows how to display a property of an attribute for a more complex object like a JavaBean or a map. Here, the servlet code creates a JavaBean for the user and stores this bean as an attribute of the session. Then, the JSP code uses EL to access this attribute, and it uses the dot operator to specify the property of the JavaBean that it's going to display.

You can use the same technique to work with a map. In that case, though, you code the name of the key after the dot operator to get the associated object that's stored in the map. You'll see this used in the next figure.

An example that accesses the currentDate attribute

Syntax
```
${attribute}
```

Servlet code
```
Date currentDate = new Date();
request.setAttribute("currentDate", currentDate);
```

JSP code
```
<p>The current date is ${currentDate}</p>
```

An example that accesses the firstName property of the user attribute

Syntax
```
${attribute.property}
```

Servlet code
```
User user = new User(firstName, lastName, email);
session.setAttribute("user", user);
```

JSP code
```
<p>Hello ${user.firstName}</p>
```

The sequence of scopes that Java searches to find the attribute

Scope	Description
page	The bean is stored in the implicit PageContext object.
request	The bean is stored in the HttpServletRequest object.
session	The bean is stored in the HttpSession object.
application	The bean is stored in the ServletContext object.

Description

- A JavaBean is a special type of object that provides a standard way to access its *properties*.

- A *map* is a special type of collection that's used to store key/value pairs. For example, a HashMap collection is a map.

- When you use the dot operator, the code to the left of the operator must specify a JavaBean or a map, and the code to the right of the operator must specify a JavaBean property or a map key.

- When you use this syntax, EL looks up the attribute starting with the smallest scope (page scope) and moving towards the largest scope (application scope).

Figure 8-2   How to use the dot operator to work with JavaBeans and maps

How to use EL to specify scope

Since Java automatically searches through the scope objects when you use EL, you typically don't need to use the implicit EL objects shown in figure 8-3 for specifying scope. However, if you have a naming conflict, you may need to use them. When you work with these objects, you should be aware that they are all maps. As a result, you can use the dot operator to specify a key when you want to return the object for that key.

To illustrate the use of these EL objects, this figure presents the same examples as in figure 8-3. However, they work even if there is an attribute with the same name stored in a larger scope. Here, the first example uses request scope to identify the user object. The second example uses session scope.

The implicit EL objects for specifying scope

Scope	Implicit EL object
page	pageScope
request	requestScope
session	sessionScope
application	applicationScope

An example that specifies request scope

Syntax
```
${scope.attribute}
```

Servlet code
```
Date currentDate = new Date();
request.setAttribute("currentDate", currentDate);
```

JSP code
```
<p>The current date is ${requestScope.currentDate}</p>
```

An example that specifies session scope

Syntax
```
${scope.attribute.property}
```

Servlet code
```
User user = new User(firstName, lastName, email);
session.setAttribute("user", user);
```

JSP code
```
<p>Hello ${sessionScope.user.firstName}</p>
```

Description
- If you have a naming conflict, you can use the *implicit EL objects* to specify scope.
- All of the implicit EL objects for specifying scope are maps. As a result, you can use the dot operator to specify a key when you want to return the object for that key.

Figure 8-3   How to use EL to specify scope

How to use the [ ] operator to work with arrays and lists

Figure 8-4 shows how to use the [ ] operator. Although this operator can be used to work with JavaBeans and maps, it is commonly used to work with arrays and lists.

The first example in this figure shows how to use the [ ] operator to access the firstName property of an attribute named user. This has the same effect as the second example in figure 8-2. However, the second example in that figure is easier to code and read. That's why you'll typically use the dot operator to access the properties of JavaBeans and the values of maps.

The primary exception to this is if you use a dot in a name. If, for example, you use a map key named "murach.address", you can't use the dot operator to access that value. However, you can use the [ ] operator. If necessary, you can use an implicit EL object to specify the scope so you can use the [ ] operator to access an attribute that uses a dot in its name.

The second example shows how to use the [ ] operator to access an array of strings. Here, the servlet code creates an array of strings that stores three colors. Then, it gets a ServletContext object so it can store the array in this object, which makes it available to the entire application. Finally, the JSP code uses EL to retrieve the first two strings that are stored in the array.

Note that this code is similar to the Java syntax for accessing strings that are stored in an array, and that the index values can be enclosed in quotation marks. Although quotation marks are required for using the [ ] operator to access a property of a JavaBean or a key of a map, they are optional for specifying the index of an array or a list.

The third example shows how to use the [ ] operator to access a list of User objects. Here, the servlet code uses the getUsers method of the UserIO class to retrieve a list of User objects. Then, the servlet code stores the list in the session object. Finally, the JSP code uses the [ ] operator to access the first two User objects, and it uses the dot operator to display the emailAddress property of these objects. This shows that you can mix the [ ] and dot operators if that's required.

The syntax for the [ ] operator

```
${attribute["propertyKeyOrIndex"]}
```

An example that works with a JavaBean property

Servlet code

```
User user = new User("John", "Smith", "jsmith@gmail.com");
session.setAttribute("user", user);
```

JSP code

```
<p>Hello ${user["firstName"]}</p>
```

An example that works with an array

Servlet code

```
String[] colors = {"Red", "Green", "Blue"};
ServletContext application = this.getServletContext();
application.setAttribute("colors", colors);
```

JSP code

```
<p>The first color is ${colors[0]}<br>
   The second color is ${colors[1]}
</p>
```

Another way to write the JSP code

```
<p>The first color is ${colors["0"]}<br>
   The second color is ${colors["1"]}
</p>
```

An example that works with a list

Servlet code

```
ArrayList<User> users = UserIO.getUsers(path);
session.setAttribute("users", users);
```

JSP code

```
<p>The first address on our list is ${users[0].email}<br>
   The second address on our list is ${users[1].email}
</p>
```

Another way to write the JSP code

```
<p>The first address on our list is ${users["0"].email}<br>
   The second address on our list is ${users["1"].email}
</p>
```

Description

- A *list* is a special type of collection such as an ArrayList<> that uses an index to retrieve an object that's stored in the collection.
- Although the [ ] operator can be used to work with JavaBeans and maps, it is commonly used to work with arrays and lists.
- With EL, the quotation marks are required for specifying a property in a JavaBean or a key in a map, but the quotation marks are optional when specifying an index of an array or a list.

Figure 8-4   How to use the [ ] operator to access arrays and lists

How to use the dot operator to access nested properties

The first example in figure 8-5 illustrates the most commonly used syntax for accessing nested properties. Here, the servlet code creates a Product object that has a property named code. Then, the servlet code stores this Product object in a LineItem object, and stores the LineItem object as a session attribute named item.

Since both the LineItem and Product classes follow the rules for JavaBeans, the JSP code can then use EL to retrieve the code property for the Product object that's stored in the item attribute. Although this figure only shows how to work with one nested property, there is no limit to the number of nested properties that you can access with the dot operator.

The second example shows that you can use the dot operator after the [ ] operator. Here, the only catch is that the object that's returned by the [ ] operator must be a JavaBean or a map. In this example, this works because the [ ] operator returns the same Product bean as the first example.

An example that accesses a nested property

Syntax

```
${attribute.property1.property2}
```

Servlet code

```
Product p = new Product();
p.setCode("pf01");
LineItem lineItem = new LineItem(p, 10);
session.setAttribute("item", lineItem);
```

JSP code

```
<p>Product code: ${item.product.code}</p>
```

Another way to access the same property

Syntax

```
${attribute["property1"].property2}
```

Servlet code

```
Product p = new Product();
p.setCode("pf01");
LineItem lineItem = new LineItem(p, 10);
session.setAttribute("item", lineItem);
```

JSP code

```
<p>Product code: ${item["product"].code}</p>
```

Description

- If a JavaBean has a property that returns another JavaBean, you can use the dot operator to access nested properties.
- There is no limit to the number of nested properties that you can access with the dot operator.

Figure 8-5   How to use the dot operator to access nested properties

Other skills for working with EL

Most of the time, the EL skills that you've learned so far are the ones that you use when you develop your JSPs. However, there are times when you may need some of the skills presented in the rest of this chapter.

How to use the [ ] operator to access attributes

The first example in figure 8-6 shows how you can use the [ ] operator to access an attribute. To start, the servlet code creates a map named usersMap that contains User objects, and it sets this map as an attribute. Although it isn't shown by this code, this map uses the email address as a key that can be used to get the associated User object. Then, the servlet code gets an email address from the request object, and it sets this string as an attribute named email.

Next, the JSP code retrieves the User object associated with the email attribute by coding the attribute within the [ ] operator. Since no quotation marks are coded around the attribute, EL attempts to evaluate the attribute. Here, it uses the value stored in the email attribute in the expression. In other words, if the email variable is "jsmith@gmail.com", the expression evaluates to:

```
${usersMap["jsmith@gmail.com"].firstName}
```

As a result, the User object that's mapped to "jsmith@gmail.com" is returned, and the first name for this user is displayed.

Note, however, that EL doesn't evaluate the variable within the [ ] operator if you code quotation marks around the emailAddress like this:

```
${usersMap["email"].firstName}
```

As a result, this expression returns an empty string.

The second example shows how you can use nested [ ] operators to access attributes. Here, the servlet code stores a map of User objects and an array of email addresses. Then, the JSP code uses nested [ ] operators to get the User object that's mapped to the first email address in the array of email addresses.

This works because the expression within the [ ] operator isn't enclosed in quotes. As a result, EL evaluates the expression as

```
${usersMap["jsmith@gmail.com"].firstName}
```

This means that the User object that's mapped to "jsmith@gmail.com" is returned, and the first name for this user is displayed. Here again, this example won't work if you enclose the expression within quotes.

An example that uses an attribute within the [ ] operator

Syntax
```
${attribute[attribute].property}
```

Servlet code
```
HashMap<String, User> usersMap = UserIO.getUsersMap(path);
session.setAttribute("usersMap", usersMap);

String email = request.getParameter("email");
session.setAttribute("email", email);
```

JSP code
```
<p>First name: ${usersMap[email].firstName}</p>
```

JSP code that returns an empty string
```
<!-- this doesn't work because the attribute is enclosed in quotes -->
<p>First name: ${usersMap["email"].firstName}</p>
```

Another example

Syntax
```
${attribute[attribute[index]].property}
```

Servlet code
```
HashMap<String, User> usersMap = UserIO.getUsersMap(path);
session.setAttribute("usersMap", usersMap);

String[] emails = {"jsmith@gmail.com", "joel@murach.com"};
session.setAttribute("emails", emails);
```

JSP code
```
<p>First name: ${usersMap[emails[0]].firstName}</p>
```

JSP code that returns an empty string
```
<!-- this doesn't work because the attribute is enclosed in quotes -->
<p>First name: ${usersMap["emails[0]"].firstName}</p>
```

Description

- If the expression within the [ ] operator isn't enclosed within quotes, EL evaluates the expression. To start, EL checks to see if the expression is an attribute. Then, it attempts to evaluate the expression.

- If multiple [ ] operators exist, the expression is evaluated from the innermost [ ] operator to the outermost [ ] operator. As a result, you can nest as many [ ] operators as necessary.

Figure 8-6   How to use the [ ] operator to access attributes

How to work with the other implicit EL objects

In figure 8-3, you learned how to use the implicit EL objects to specify scope. Now, figure 8-7 presents some other implicit EL objects that you can use to perform other tasks in a JSP. If you use the MVC pattern, though, you typically won't need to use these implicit objects.

The first example in this figure shows how to use the implicit objects for working with request parameters. Here, the HTML form has a parameter named firstName for the first name text box and a parameter named emailAddress for the next two text boxes. In other words, this form lets you enter one first name and two email addresses. Then, the JSP code shows how you can use the param object to get the value of the firstName parameter. In addition, this JSP code shows how you can use the paramValues parameter to get an array of strings that contains the values for the emailAddress parameter.

The second example shows how you can use the header object to get data from the HTTP header. Here, you can use the dot operator to get the value for any request headers that have a single word name. For instance, you can use the dot operator to get the value of the Accept header.

If a request header has more than one word in its name, you can use the [ ] operator to get its value. For instance, you can use this operator to get the value of the Accept-Encoding header. For now, don't worry if you don't understand how HTTP request headers work because you'll learn more about them in chapter 18.

When you learn more about HTTP request headers, you'll find that some HTTP request headers return a list of values. For example, the Accept header returns a list of MIME types that the browser can accept. If you want to return this list as an array, you can use the implicit headerValues object. Then, you can use the array that's returned to process these values.

The third example shows how to use the implicit cookie object to get the value of a cookie. Here, the servlet code creates a Cookie object with a name of emailCookie that stores an email address. Then, the JSP code uses the implicit cookie object to get the Cookie object, and it uses the value property of the cookie to get the email address that's stored within the cookie.

This works because the Cookie class follows all of the rules for a JavaBean, and it includes a method named getValue that can be used to get the value that's stored within the cookie. If necessary, you can use similar code to retrieve other properties of the cookie. For example, you can use the maxAge property to get the maximum age for the cookie.

Other implicit objects that you can use

EL implicit object	Description
`param`	A map that returns a value for the specified request parameter name.
`paramValues`	A map that returns an array of values for the specified request parameter name.
`header`	A map that returns the value for the specified HTTP request header. For a list of HTTP request headers, see chapter 18.
`headerValues`	A map that returns an array of values for the specified HTTP request header.
`cookie`	A map that returns the Cookie object for the specified cookie.
`initParam`	A map that returns the value for the specified parameter name in the context-param element of the web.xml file.
`pageContext`	A reference to the implicit pageContext object that's available from any JSP.

How to get parameter values from the request

An HTML form that has two parameters with the same name

```
<form action="emailList" method="post">
    <p>First name: <input type="text" name="firstName"></p>
    <p>Email address 1: <input type="text" name="email"></p>
    <p>Email address 2: <input type="text" name="email"></p>
</form>
```

JSP code

```
<p>First name: ${param.firstName}<br>
    Email address 1: ${paramValues.email[0]}<br>
    Email address 2: ${paramValues.email[1]}
</p>
```

How to get an HTTP header

JSP code

```
<p>MIME types: ${header.accept}<br>
    Compression types: ${header["accept-encoding"]}
</p>
```

The text that a browser might display

```
MIME types: text/html,application/xml;q=0.9,image/webp,*/*;q=0.8
Compression types: gzip,deflate,sdch
```

How to work with cookies

Servlet code

```
Cookie c = new Cookie("emailCookie", email);
c.setMaxAge(60*60);   //set its age to 1 hour
c.setPath("/");        //allow the entire application to access it
response.addCookie(c);
```

JSP code

```
<p>The email cookie: ${cookie.emailCookie.value}</p>
```

Figure 8-7   How to work with the implicit EL objects (part 1 of 2)

The fourth example in figure 8-7 shows how to use the initParam object to get a context initialization parameter. Here, the web.xml file uses the context-param element to store a context initialization parameter named custServEmail with a value of "custserv@murach.com". Then, the JSP code uses the initParam object to retrieve the value for this parameter. Note that this parameter is a context initialization parameter that's available to the entire web application, not a servlet initialization parameter that's only available to the current servlet.

The fifth example shows how to use the implicit pageContext object that's available from any JSP. Since the pageContext object follows the rules for a JavaBean, you can easily access any of its properties. In addition, the properties of the pageContext object allow you to access the objects for request, response, session, and application scope.

For example, you can use the request property to return an HttpRequest object that lets you get information about the current request. You can use the response property to return an HttpResponse object that lets you get information about the current response. You can use the session property to return an HttpSession object that lets you get information about the current session. And you can use the servletContext property to return a ServletContext object that lets you get information about the context for the application.

How to get a context initialization parameter

XML in the web.xml file

```
<context-param>
    <param-name>custServEmail</param-name>
    <param-value>custserv@murach.com</param-value>
</context-param>
```

JSP code

```
<p>The context init param: ${initParam.custServEmail}</p>
```

How to use the pageContext object

JSP code

```
<p>HTTP request method: ${pageContext.request.method}<br>
   HTTP response type: ${pageContext.response.contentType}<br>
   HTTP session ID: ${pageContext.session.id}<br>
   HTTP contextPath: ${pageContext.servletContext.contextPath}<br>
</p>
```

The text that a browser might display

```
HTTP request method: POST
HTTP response type: text/html
HTTP session ID: 4C1CFDB54B0339B53BE3AC8E9BADC0F5
HTTP servletContext path: /ch8email
```

Description

- The four implicit EL objects for specifying scope are presented in figure 8-3.
- All of the implicit objects used by EL are maps, except for the pageContext object, which is a JavaBean.

Figure 8-7   How to work with the implicit EL objects (part 2 of 2)

How to work with other EL operators

Earlier in this chapter, you learned how to use the dot operator and the [ ] operator that are available from EL. Now, figure 8-8 shows how to use some of the other operators that are available from EL. If necessary, you can use these operators to perform calculations and comparisons.

If you know how to code arithmetic, relational, and logical expressions in Java as described in *Murach's Java Programming*, you shouldn't have any trouble using these operators since they work similarly to the Java operators. Although you usually won't need to use these operators, they may come in handy from time to time.

You can use the arithmetic operators to perform mathematical calculations. The examples in this figure show that you can use scientific notation for extremely large or small numbers and that you can use parentheses to control or clarify the order of precedence.

These examples also show that EL treats any null values as zero. To illustrate, let's assume that you have an attribute named userID that can store an int value. Then, if the attribute stores an int value, EL uses the int value in the calculation. However, if the attribute stores a null value, EL uses zero in the calculation.

You can use the relational operators to compare two operands and return a true or false value. Although these operators work like the standard Java operators, you can use an alternate syntax that uses two letter combinations instead of symbols. For example, you can use eq instead of ==.

When you create relational expressions, you can use the null keyword to specify a null value, the true keyword to specify a true value, and the false keyword to specify a false value. In addition, when you create relational expressions, EL treats a null value as a false value. To illustrate, let's assume that you have an attribute named isDirty that stores a Boolean value. Then, if the attribute stores a true or false value, EL uses that value in the expression. However, if the attribute stores a null value, EL uses a false value for the isDirty attribute.

Arithmetic EL operators

Operator	Alternative	Description
+		Addition
–		Subtraction
*		Multiplication
/	div	Division
%	mod	Modulus (remainder)

Example / Result

Example	Result
${1+1}	2
${17.5+10}	27.5
${2.5E3}	2500.0
${2.5E3+10.4}	2510.4
${2-1}	1
${7*3}	21
${1 / 4}	0.25
${1 div 4}	0.25
${10 % 8}	2
${10 mod 8}	2
${1 + 2 * 4}	9
${(1 + 2) * 4}	12
${userID + 1}	9 if userID equals 8; 1 if userID equals 0

Relational operators

Operator	Alternative	Description
==	eq	Equal to
!=	ne	Not equal to
<	lt	Less than
>	gt	Greater than
<=	le	Less than or equal to
>=	ge	Greater than or equal to

Example / Result

Example	Result
${"s1" == "s1"}	true
${"s1" eq "s1"}	true
${1 == 1}	true
${1 != 1}	false
${1 ne 1}	false
${3 < 4}	true
${3 lt 4}	true
${3 > 4}	false
${3 gt 4}	false
${3 <= 4}	true
${3 >= 4}	false
${user.firstName == null}	true if firstName returns a null value
${user.firstName == ""}	true if firstName returns an empty string
${isDirty == true}	true if isDirty is true, false if isDirty is false, false if isDirty is null

Figure 8-8   How to work with the other EL operators (part 1 of 2)

You can use logical operators to combine multiple relational expressions and return a true or false value. The examples in this figure show how to use all three types of logical operators. You can use the And operator to specify that both relational expressions must be true for the entire expression to evaluate to true. You can use the Or operator to specify that at least one of the relational expressions must be true. And you can use the Not operator to reverse the value of the relational expression.

In addition, you may occasionally want to use the last two operators described in this figure. First, you may want to use the empty operator to check if a variable contains a null value or an empty string. If so, this operator returns a true value.

Second, you may want to use the ? and : operators to create a simple if statement. Here, you can code the condition for the if statement, followed by the ? operator, followed by the value that's returned for a true value, followed by the : operator, followed by the value that's returned for a false value. In the examples for these operators, the true and false keywords are used for the condition because this clearly shows how the ? and : operators work. However, you can substitute any relational or logical expression for the condition.

Logical operators

Operator	Alternative	Description
&&	and	And
||	or	Or
!	not	Not

Example

Example	Result
`${"s1" == "s1" && 4 > 3}`	true
`${"s1" == "s1" and 4 > 3}`	true
`${"s1" == "s1" && 4 < 3}`	false
`${"s1" == "s1" || 4 < 3} true`	
`${"s1" != "s1" || 4 < 3} false`	
`${"s1" != "s1" or 4 < 3}`	false
`${!true}`	false
`${not true}`	false

Other operators

Syntax	Description
`empty x`	Returns true if the value of x is null or equal to an empty string.
`x ? y : z`	If x evaluates to true, returns y. Otherwise, returns z.

Example

Example	Result
`${empty firstName}`	true if firstName returns a null value or an empty string
`${true ? "s1" : "s2"}`	s1
`${false ? "s1" : "s2"}`	s2

Keywords you can use in expressions

Keyword	Description
null	A null value
true	A true value
false	A false value

Description

- For arithmetic expressions, you can use parentheses to control or clarify the order of precedence.
- In arithmetic expressions, EL treats a null value as a zero.
- In logical expressions, EL treats a null value as a false value.

Figure 8-8   How to work with the other EL operators (part 2 of 2)

How to disable EL

For JSP 2.0 and later, the servlet container evaluates any code within the ${ and } characters as an EL expression. Most of the time, this is what you want. However, there's an outside chance that you may have one or more old JSPs that use the EL syntax for another purpose. In that case, you can disable EL as shown in figure 8-9.

To disable EL for a single JSP, you add a page directive to the JSP, and you set the isELIgnored attribute to true. Then, the servlet container won't evaluate any expressions that use the EL syntax. Instead, the servlet container passes this syntax on to the web browser, which typically causes the web browser to display the expression.

To disable EL for multiple pages, you can edit the jsp-config tag in the web.xml file for the application. This figure, for example, shows how to disable EL for all of the JSPs in the application. If necessary, though, you can modify the url-pattern element to disable EL only for selected JSPs within the application.

How to disable scripting

One of the benefits of EL is that it lets you remove JSP scripts from your JSPs, which makes it easier for web designers to work with them. In fact, once you learn how to use EL with JSTL as described in the next chapter, you can usually remove all scripting from your application.

When you're replacing old JSP scripts with EL and JSTL, it is sometimes hard to tell whether you've removed all scripting from your JSPs. Then, to check if you've done that, you can disable scripting for the entire application as described in this figure. After that, when you request a JSP that contains scripting, the servlet container displays an error page. In that case, you can edit the JSP to replace the scripting with EL, JSTL, or a combination of the two.

When you are developing new web applications, you may want to disable scripting from the start. This forces you (and any other programmers working on the application) to always use standard JSP tags, EL, and JSTL instead of scripting. Although this may require you to do more work up front to get the web application structured correctly with the MVC pattern, it should pay off in the long run by making your code easier to read and maintain.

How to disable EL

For a single page (a page directive)

```
<%@ page isELIgnored ="true" %>
```

For the entire application (the web.xml file)

```
<jsp-config>
    <jsp-property-group>
        <url-pattern>*.jsp</url-pattern>
        <el-ignored>true</el-ignored>
    </jsp-property-group>
</jsp-config>
```

How to disable scripting

For the entire application (the web.xml file)

```
<jsp-config>
    <jsp-property-group>
        <url-pattern>*.jsp</url-pattern>
        <scripting-invalid>true</scripting-invalid>
    </jsp-property-group>
</jsp-config>
```

Description

- For JSP 2.0 and later, the servlet container evaluates any text that starts with ${ and ends with } as an EL expression. Most of the time, this is what you want. If it isn't, you can ignore EL for a single JSP or for all JSPs in the entire application.

- If you want to remove all scripting from all JSPs in your application, you can modify the web.xml file so it doesn't allow scripting. Then, if you request a JSP that contains scripting, the servlet container displays an error page.

Figure 8-9   How to disable EL or scripting

Perspective

The goal of this chapter has been to show you how to use EL to get data from JavaBeans, maps, arrays, and lists that have been stored as an attribute in one of the four scopes of a web application. Along the way, you learned how to use some of the implicit EL objects and operators to perform some other useful tasks. Although there's more to learn about EL, this is probably all you need to know if you use the MVC pattern in your web applications.

When you use EL, you can remove much of the Java scripting and expressions from your JSPs, and that makes your code easier to read and maintain. That also makes it easier for web designers to work with these pages. To take this a step further, though, the next chapter shows you how to use the JSP Standard Tag Library (JSTL) to remove the rest of the scripting from your JSPs. As you'll see, JSTL tags work well with EL, and the two are often mixed in a JSP.

Summary

- The JSP *Expression Language* (*EL*) provides a compact syntax that lets you get data from JavaBeans, maps, arrays, and lists that have been stored as an attribute of a web application.

- A *JavaBean* is a special type of object that provides a standard way to access its *properties*.

- A *map* is a special type of collection that's used to store *key/value pairs*.

- A *list* is a type of collection that uses an *index* to retrieve an object that's stored in the collection.

- You can use the dot operator to work with JavaBeans and maps.

- You can use the [ ] operator to work with arrays and lists.

- If the expression within an [ ] operator isn't enclosed within quotes, EL evaluates the expression.

- If necessary, you can use the implicit EL objects to explicitly specify scope.

- You can use EL to get nested properties.

- You can use the implicit EL objects to work with request parameters, HTTP headers, cookies, context initialization parameters, and the implicit pageContext object that's available to all JSPs.

- You can use other EL operators to perform calculations and make comparisons.

- If necessary, you can disable EL or scripting for one or more pages in a web application.

Exercise 8-1   Modify the Email List application

In this exercise, you'll enhance the Email List application so it uses EL to display attributes.

Convert standard JSP bean tags to EL

1. Open the ch08_ex1_email project in the ex_starts directory.

2. Run the application. Then, enter data for a user, click the Join button, and click the Return button. Note how the user's data is displayed on both pages.

3. Open the index.jsp and thanks.jsp files. Then, convert the standard JSP tags to EL. Note how the EL is shorter and easier to read than the standard JSP tags.

4. Run the application. It should work the same as it did before.

Use EL to work with a collection and an initialization parameter

5. Open the EmailListServlet class. Note that it stores the current date as a request attribute. Note also that it stores an ArrayList of User objects as a session attribute.

6. Open the web.xml file. Note that it doesn't allow scripting for the current application. Note also that the custserv@murach.com email address is stored as a context initialization parameter named custServEmail.

7. Open the thanks.jsp file. Then, complete the code at the end of the page so it displays the current date, the first two users in the ArrayList of User objects, and the customer service email.

8. Run the application. Then, enter data for a user, click on the Return button, and note how the user's data is displayed on the first page.

Use EL to specify scope

9. Open the thanks.jsp file and explicitly specify the scope for the user attribute and the currentDate attribute.

10. Test the application to make sure that it still works correctly.

9

How to use JSTL

Chapter 6 introduced you to the JSP Standard Tag Library (JSTL) and its if and import tags. Then, chapter 7 introduced you to the forEach tag. Now, in this chapter, you'll review those tags, and you'll learn how to use other JSTL tags. These tags provide a way to reduce the amount of scripting in your applications. For most applications, you can use JSTL and EL to remove all scripting.

An introduction to JSTL

The *JSP Standard Tag Library* (*JSTL*) provides tags for common tasks that need to be performed in JSPs.

The JSTL libraries

Figure 9-1 shows the five tag libraries that are included with JSTL 1.2. In this chapter, you'll learn the details for working with the common tags in the core library. This library contains tags that you can use to encode URLs, loop through collections, and code if/else statements. If you use the MVC pattern, the tags in the core library are often the only JSTL tags you'll need as you develop your JSPs. If necessary, though, you can use the other four libraries to work with internationalization, databases, XML, or strings.

How to make the JSTL JAR files available to your application

Before you can use JSTL tags within an application, you must make the jstl-impl.jar and jstl-api.jar files available to the application. With the NetBeans IDE, for example, you can add the JSTL 1.2 library to the application as shown in figure 3-14 in chapter 3. Then, the jstl-impl.jar and jstl-api.jar files are shown beneath the Libraries folder in the Projects window.

How to code the taglib directive

Before you can use JSTL tags within a JSP, you must code a taglib directive to specify the URI and prefix for the JSTL library. In this figure, for example, the taglib directive specifies the URI for the JSTL core library with a prefix of c, which is the prefix that's typically used for this library. In fact, all of the examples in this chapter assume that the page includes a taglib directive like this one before the JSTL tags are used. Although you can use different prefixes than the ones in this figure, we recommend using the standard prefixes.

How to code a JSTL tag

Once you've added the appropriate JAR files to your application and used the taglib directive to identify a library, you can code a JSTL tag. In this figure, for example, the out tag is used to escape output that's returned to the browser. In this example, the prefix for this tag is c. As you'll learn later in this chapter, most developers consider it a good practice to use this tag for most kinds of output.

JSTL tags use a syntax that's similar to HTML. As a result, these tags are easy to code and read, especially for web designers and other nonprogrammers who are already familiar with HTML syntax.

The primary JSTL libraries

Name	Prefix	URI	Description
Core	**c**	http://java.sun.com/jsp/jstl/core	Contains the core tags for common tasks such as looping and if/else statements.
Formatting	**fmt**	http://java.sun.com/jsp/jstl/fmt	Provides tags for formatting numbers, times, and dates so they work correctly with internationalization (i18n).
SQL	**sql**	http://java.sun.com/jsp/jstl/sql	Provides tags for working with SQL queries and data sources.
XML	**x**	http://java.sun.com/jsp/jstl/xml	Provides tags for manipulating XML documents.
Functions	**fn**	http://java.sun.com/jsp/jstl/functions	Provides functions that can be used to manipulate strings.

The NetBeans IDE after the JSTL 1.2 library has been added

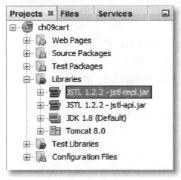

The taglib directive that specifies the JSTL core library

```
<%@ taglib prefix="c" uri="http://java.sun.com/jsp/jstl/core" %>
```

An example that uses JSTL to escape output

```
<td><c:out value="${item.product.description}" /></td>
```

Description

- The *JSP Standard Tag Library* (*JSTL*) provides tags for common JSP tasks.
- Before you can use JSTL tags within an application, you must make the jstl-impl.jar and jstl-api.jar files available to the application. To do that for NetBeans, you can add the JSTL 1.2 class library to your project as in figure 3-14 in chapter 3. Otherwise, you can consult the documentation for your IDE.
- Before you can use JSTL tags within a JSP, you must code a taglib directive that identifies the JSTL library and its prefix.

Figure 9-1   An introduction to JSTL

How to view the documentation for a library

As you progress through this chapter, you'll learn how to code the tags in the JSTL core library that you'll use most of the time. If necessary, though, you can view the documentation for any of the tags in this library as shown in figure 9-2.

If, for example, you want to learn more about the out tag in the core library, you can click on the "JSTL core" link in the upper left window. Then, you can click on the "c:out" link in the lower left window to display the documentation for this tag in the window on the right. This documentation provides a general description of the tag, a list of all available attributes for the tag, and detailed information about each of these attributes.

You can also use this documentation to learn more about the JSTL libraries that aren't covered in this chapter. If, for example, you want to learn more about the formatting library for working with internationalization, you can click on the "JSTL fmt" link in the upper left window. Then, you can click on the tags in the lower left window to display information in the window on the right. Incidentally, *i18n* is sometimes used as an abbreviation for *internationalization* because *internationalization* begins with an *i*, followed by *18* letters, followed by an *n*.

Note that this figure shows how to view the documentation for the JSTL 1.1 library even though the previous figure shows how to add the JSTL 1.2 library to a project. That's because there isn't an easy way to view the documentation for the JSTL 1.2 library. Fortunately, most of the documentation for the JSTL 1.1 library also applies to the JSTL 1.2 library. As a result, you don't usually need to view the documentation for the JSTL 1.2 library.

The URL for the JSTL 1.1 documentation

`http://docs.oracle.com/javaee/5/jstl/1.1/docs/tlddocs`

A browser that displays the JSTL documentation

Description

- The easiest way to view the JSTL documentation is to use your browser to visit the URL for version 1.1 of the library as shown above. Most of the tags in this library work the same for the version 1.2. As a result, you typically don't need to view the documentation for JSTL 1.2.

Figure 9-2   How to view the documentation for a library

How to work
with the JSTL core library

Now that you have a general idea of how JSTL works, you're ready to learn the details for coding the most commonly used JSTL tags. All of these tags are available from the JSTL core library.

How to use the out tag

So far in this book, the code has used EL to output data to the browser. Unfortunately, this approach is vulnerable to a type of attach known as a cross-site scripting (XSS) attach. In a *cross-site scripting (XSS) attack*, an attacker attempts to inject Javascript into your page to trick your users into sending them personal data such as usernames and passwords.

To prevent an XSS attack, you can use the out tag to escape the output for your application. This replaces characters such as the left angle bracket (<) and right angle bracket (>) with their corresponding HTML entities. As a result, if an attacker attempts to insert HTML tags, the browser displays them instead of executing them, which is usually what you want. Because of that, it's generally considered a best practice to escape all output that's sent to the browser. For instance, the first example in figure 9-3 shows how to use the out tag to escape the output for the second page of the Email List application.

Although it's especially important to escape output that's been entered by a user, it's also considered a good practice to escape output when it comes from other parts of the HTTP request such as cookies and other headers. That's why the second example in this figure uses the out tag to escape the names and values of the cookies. If you read the previous chapter, you should understand how you can use EL to access the implicit cookie object. In the next figure, you'll learn more about using the forEach tag to code a loop.

The third example shows two techniques for displaying a default value. The first way uses the default attribute to specify the default message, and the second way uses the tag's body. Either way, if the message attribute is equal to a null value, the out tag outputs a default message of "No Message".

When you code JSTL tags, you need to be aware that they use XML syntax, not HTML syntax. As a result, you must use the exact capitalization shown in this example for the name of the tag and its attributes. In addition, you must enclose attributes in either double quotes or single quotes. Typically, you can use double quotes. However, if the entire out tag is coded within double quotes, you can use single quotes to differentiate between the nested attribute values as shown in the fourth example.

An example that escapes output entered by the user

```
<label>Email:</label>
<span><c:out value="${user.email}" /></span><br>
<label>First Name:</label>
<span><c:out value="${user.firstName}" /></span><br>
<label>Last Name:</label>
<span><c:out value="${user.lastName}" /></span><br>
```

The output for an XSS attack

Thanks for joining our email list

Here is the information that you entered:

Email:	jsmith@gmail.com
First Name:	John
Last Name:	<script>This JavaScript is displayed, not executed</script>

An example that escapes output that displays cookie names and values

```
<table>
  <tr>
    <th>Name</th>
    <th>Value</th>
  </tr>
  <c:forEach var="cook" items="${cookie}">
  <tr>
    <td><c:out value="${cook.value.name}" /></td>
    <td><c:out value="${cook.value.value}" /></td>
  </tr>
  </c:forEach>
</table>
```

An example that displays a default value

Using the default attribute

```
<p><c:out value="${message}" default="No message" /></p>
```

Using the tag's body

```
<p><c:out value="${message}">No message</c:out></p>
```

An example that uses single quotes

```
<input type="hidden" name="productCode"
       value="<c:out value='${item.product.code}' />">
```

Description

- In a *cross-site scripting (XSS) attack*, an attacker attempts to inject Javascript into your page to trick your users into sending them personal data.
- To prevent an XSS attack, you can use the out tag to escape the output for your application. This replaces characters such as the left angle bracket (<) and right angle bracket (>) with their corresponding HTML entitles.
- It's generally considered a best practice to escape all output that's sent to the browser, including other parts of the HTTP request such as cookies and other headers.

Figure 9-3   How to use the out tag

How to use the forEach tag

You can use the forEach tag to loop through items that are stored in most collections, including arrays. For example, figure 9-4 shows how to use the forEach tag to loop through the LineItem objects that are available from the items property of the cart attribute. Here, the var attribute specifies a variable name of item to access each item within the collection. Then, the items attribute uses EL to specify the collection that stores the data. In this case, the collection is the ArrayList<LineItem> object that's returned by the getItems method of the Cart object for the current session. This Cart object has been stored as an attribute with a name of cart.

Within the forEach loop, the JSP code creates one row with four columns for each item in the cart. Here, each column uses EL to display the data that's available from the LineItem object. In particular, the first column displays the quantity, the second column displays the product description, the third column displays the price per item, and the fourth column displays the total amount (quantity multiplied by price). Note that the LineItem object includes code that applies currency formatting to the price and amount.

If you have trouble understanding the examples in this figure, you may want to study the code for the Cart, LineItem, and Product objects that are presented in figure 9-12. In particular, note how a Cart object can contain multiple LineItem objects and how a LineItem object must contain one Product object. Also, note how the appropriate get methods are provided for all of the properties that are accessed by EL. For example, the Cart class provides a method named getItems that returns an ArrayList of LineItem objects. As a result, with EL, you can use the items property of the cart attribute to get this ArrayList object.

If necessary, you can nest one forEach tag within another. For example, if you wanted to display several Invoice objects on a single web page, you could use an outer forEach tag to loop through the Invoice objects. Then, you could use an inner forEach tag to loop through the LineItem objects within each invoice. However, for most JSPs, you won't need to nest forEach statements.

An example that uses JSTL to loop through a collection

```
<c:forEach var="item" items="${cart.items}">
<tr>
    <td>${item.quantity}</td>
    <td>${item.product.description}</td>
    <td>${item.product.priceCurrencyFormat}</td>
    <td>${item.totalCurrencyFormat}</td>
</tr>
</c:forEach>
```

The result that's displayed in the browser for a cart that has two items

Your cart

Quantity	Description	Price	Amount
1	86 (the band) - True Life Songs and Pictures	$14.95	$14.95
1	Paddlefoot - The first CD	$12.95	$12.95

To change the quantity, enter the new quantity and click on the Update button.

[Continue Shopping]
[Checkout]

Description

- You can use the forEach tag to loop through most types of collections, including arrays.
- You can use the var attribute to specify the variable name that is used to access each item within the collection.
- You can use the items attribute to specify the collection that stores the data.
- If necessary, you can nest one forEach tag within another.

Figure 9-4   How to use the forEach tag

How to use the forTokens tag

You can use the forTokens tag to loop through items that are stored in a string as long as the items in the string are separated by one or more delimiters, which are characters that are used to separate the items. For instance, the string in the first example in figure 9-5 uses a comma as the delimiter. As a result, this string can be referred to as a *comma-delimited string*.

The first example in this figure also shows how to use the forTokens tag to loop through the four product codes that are stored in the string. Here, the var attribute specifies a variable name of productCode to identify each product code in the list. Then, the items attribute uses EL to specify the productCodes attribute as the string that stores the items. Finally, the delims attribute specifies the comma as the delimiter.

To keep this example simple, the servlet code creates the productCodes attribute by storing a hard-coded list of four product codes that are separated by commas. In a more realistic example, of course, the servlet code would dynamically generate this list.

The second example works similarly to the first example, but it uses two delimiters instead of one. In particular, the delims attribute specifies the at symbol (@) as the first delimiter and the period (.) as the second delimiter. As a result, the loop processes three items, one for each part of the email address.

If necessary, you can nest one forTokens tag within another. Or, you can nest a forTokens tag within a forEach tag. However, since you'll rarely need to nest forTokens tags, this technique isn't illustrated in this figure.

An example that uses JSTL to loop through a comma-delimited string

Servlet code

```
session.setAttribute("productCodes", "8601,pf01,pf02,jr01");
```

JSP code

```
<p>Product codes</p>
<ul>
<c:forTokens var="productCode" items="${productCodes}" delims="," >
    <li>${productCode}</li>
</c:forTokens>
</ul>
```

The result that's displayed in the browser

Product codes

- 8601
- pf01
- pf02
- jr01

An example that uses JSTL to parse a string

Servlet code

```
session.setAttribute("emailAddress", "jsmith@gmail.com");
```

JSP code

```
<p>Email parts</p>
<ul>
<c:forTokens var="part" items="${emailAddress}" delims="@.">
    <li>${part}</li>
</c:forTokens>
</ul>
```

The result that's displayed in the browser

Email parts

- jsmith
- gmail
- com

Description

- You can use the forTokens tag to loop through delimited values that are stored in a string.
- You can use the var attribute to specify the variable name that is used to access each delimited string.
- You can use the items attribute to specify the string that stores the data.
- You can use the delims attribute to specify the character or characters that are used as the delimiters for the string.
- If necessary, you can nest one forTokens tag within another.

Figure 9-5   How to use the forTokens tag

Four more attributes for looping

When working with collections, the servlet code typically creates a collection and passes it to the JSP so the collection can be displayed to the user. Then, the JSP uses the forEach tag to loop through the collection and display it to the user as shown in figure 9-4.

However, there may be times when the JSP needs to do some additional processing. For example, the JSP may need to know whether the item is the first or last item, so it can apply special formatting to that item. Or, the JSP may need to know the item number, so it can apply shading to alternating items. In that case, you can use the attributes described in figure 9-6. These attributes work the same for the forEach and the forTokens tags.

The example in this figure shows how to work with the begin, end, and step attributes that are available for the forEach and forTokens tags. Here, the begin attribute specifies the starting index for the loop; the end attribute specifies the last index for the loop; and the step attribute specifies the amount to increment the index each time through the loop. If you understand how a for loop works in Java, you shouldn't have much trouble understanding these attributes. In this example, these attributes are used to print the first 10 numbers that are stored in an array of 30 int values.

This example also shows how to use the varStatus attribute. This attribute specifies the name of a variable that can be used to get information about the status of the loop. In particular, this variable provides four properties named first, last, index, and count that you can use within the body of a loop. For example, you can use the first and last properties to return a Boolean value that indicates whether the item is the first or last item in the collection. Or, you can use the index and count properties to return an integer value for the item. Note, however, that the index property returns an integer value that's one less than the count value. That's because the index property starts at 0 while the count property starts at 1.

Attributes that you can use for advanced loops

Attribute	Description
begin	Specifies the first index for the loop.
end	Specifies the last index for the loop.
step	Specifies the amount to increment the index each time through the loop.
varStatus	Specifies the name of a variable that can be used to get information about the status of the loop. This variable provides the first, last, index, and count properties.

An example that uses all four attributes

Servlet code

```
int[] numbers = new int[30];
for (int i = 0; i < 30; i++) {
    numbers[i] = i+1;
}
session.setAttribute("numbers", numbers);
```

JSP code

```
<p>Numbers</p>
<ul>
<c:forEach items="${numbers}" var="number"
           begin="0" end="9" step="1"
           varStatus="status">
    <li>${number} | First: ${status.first} | Last: ${status.last} |
        Index: ${status.index} | Count: ${status.count} </li>
</c:forEach>
</ul>
```

The result that's displayed in the browser

Numbers

- 1 | First: true | Last: false | Index: 0 | Count: 1
- 2 | First: false | Last: false | Index: 1 | Count: 2
- 3 | First: false | Last: false | Index: 2 | Count: 3
- 4 | First: false | Last: false | Index: 3 | Count: 4
- 5 | First: false | Last: false | Index: 4 | Count: 5
- 6 | First: false | Last: false | Index: 5 | Count: 6
- 7 | First: false | Last: false | Index: 6 | Count: 7
- 8 | First: false | Last: false | Index: 7 | Count: 8
- 9 | First: false | Last: false | Index: 8 | Count: 9
- 10 | First: false | Last: true | Index: 9 | Count: 10

Description

- The begin, end, step, and varStatus attributes work for both the forEach and forTokens tags.

Figure 9-6   Four more attributes for looping

How to use the if tag

When coding a JSP, you may need to perform conditional processing to change the appearance of the page depending on the values of the attributes that are available to the page. To do that, you can use the if tag as shown in figure 9-7.

To start, you code an opening if tag that includes the test attribute. In the example in this figure, this test attribute uses EL to get the count property of the cart attribute, which indicates the number of items that are in the cart. Then, the code within the opening and closing if tags displays a message that's appropriate for the number of items in the cart. In particular, the first if tag displays a message if the cart contains 1 item, and the second if tag displays a message if the cart contains more than one item. The main difference between the two messages is that the second message uses the plural (items) while the first uses the singular (item).

If necessary, you can use the var and scope attributes to expose the Boolean condition in the test attribute as a variable with the specified scope. Then, you can reuse the Boolean condition in other if statements. This works similarly to the set tag that's briefly described later in this chapter. However, since you'll rarely need to use these attributes, they aren't illustrated in this figure.

As with the forEach and forTokens tags, you can nest one if tag within another. Or, you can nest an if tag within a forEach or forTokens tag. In short, as you might expect by now, you can usually nest JSTL tags within one another whenever that's necessary.

An example that uses JSTL to code an if statement

```
<c:if test="${cart.count == 1}">
    <p>You have 1 item in your cart.</p>
</c:if>
<c:if test="${cart.count > 1}">
    <p>You have ${cart.count} items in your cart.</p>
</c:if>
```

The result that's displayed in the browser for a cart that has two items

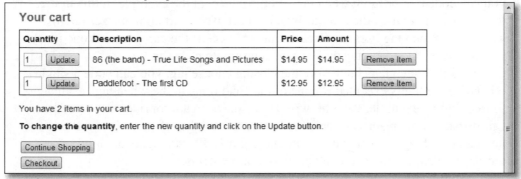

Description

- You can use the if tag to perform conditional processing that's similar to an if statement in Java.

- You can use the test attribute to specify the Boolean condition for the if statement.

- If necessary, you can nest one if tag within another.

Figure 9-7   How to use the if tag

How to use the choose tag

In the last figure, you learned how to code multiple if tags. This is the equivalent of coding multiple if statements in Java. However, there are times when you need to code the equivalent of an if/else statement. Then, you can use the choose tag as described in figure 9-8.

To start, you code the opening and closing choose tags. Within those tags, you can code one or more when tags. For instance, in the example in this figure, the first when tag uses the test attribute to check if the cart contains zero items. Then, the second tag uses the test attribute to check if the cart contains one item. In either case, the when tag displays an appropriate message.

After the when tags but before the closing choose tag, you can code a single otherwise tag that's executed if none of the conditions in the when tags evaluate to true. In this example, the otherwise tag displays an appropriate message if the cart doesn't contain zero or one items. Since the number of items in a cart can't be negative, this means that the otherwise tag uses EL to display an appropriate message whenever the cart contains two or more items.

An example that uses JSTL to code an if/else statement

```
<c:choose>
    <c:when test="${cart.count == 0}">
        <p>Your cart is empty.</p>
    </c:when>
    <c:when test="${cart.count == 1}">
        <p>You have 1 item in your cart.</p>
    </c:when>
    <c:otherwise>
        <p>You have ${cart.count} items in your cart.</p>
    </c:otherwise>
</c:choose>
```

The result that's displayed in the browser for a cart that has two items

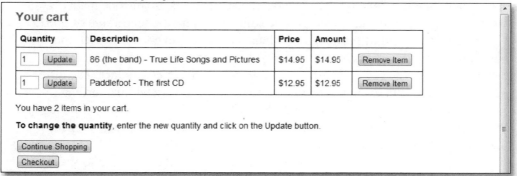

Description

- You can use the choose tag to perform conditional processing similar to an if/else statement in Java. To do that, you can code multiple when tags and a single otherwise tag within the choose tag.

- You can use the test attribute to specify the Boolean condition for a when tag.

- If necessary, you can nest one choose tag within another.

Figure 9-8   How to use the choose tag

How to use the url tag

Figure 9-9 shows how to use the url tag. Here, the first example shows an href attribute that does not use the url tag. Instead, it uses regular HTML to specify a cart directory that's relative to the current directory. The second example uses the url tag to specify a URL relative to the root directory for the web application. As a result, this calls the /cart URL that's relative to the root directory regardless of where this code is stored. Conversely, the code in the first example only calls the /cart URL that's relative to the root directory if it's stored in the root directory.

The next three examples show how to use a url tag that includes a parameter. Here, the third example shows how to use the url tag to encode a URL that includes a parameter named productCode with a hard-coded value of 8601. Then, the fourth and fifth examples both use the url tag to encode a URL that uses an EL expression to supply the value for the parameter. Here, the EL expression gets the code property of a Product object named product. The difference is that the fifth example shows how to use a param tag within a url tag to specify the name and value for a parameter. The benefit of using the param tag is that it automatically encodes any unsafe characters in the URL, such as spaces, with special characters, such as plus signs.

In general, the advantage of using the url tag is that it allows you to specify URLs relative to the application context. As a result, if the context changes later, it doesn't break your code. The main disadvantage is that they require a little more time and effort to code and the nested tags make the code more difficult to read.

One issue to be aware of when using the url tag is that it encodes the session ID in URLs that are returned to the client. This feature was designed to allow your application to track sessions even if the client doesn't support cookies. Unfortunately, this isn't secure as it can lead to session hijacking. To prevent the session ID from being encoded in the URL, you can add a tracking-mode element to the web.xml file like the one shown in the last example. This tracking-mode element is set to a value of COOKIE to specify that the application should only use cookies for session tracking.

An example that doesn't use the url tag

```
<a href="cart">Continue Shopping</a>
```

An example that uses the url tag

```
<a href="<c:url value='/cart' />">Continue Shopping</a>
```

An example that adds a parameter

```
<a href="<c:url value='/cart?productCode=8601' />">
    Add To Cart
</a>
```

An example that uses EL to specify the value of a parameter

```
<a href="<c:url value='/cart?productCode=${product.code}' />">
    Add To Cart
</a>
```

Another way to code the previous example

```
<a href="<c:url value='/cart'>
            <c:param name='productCode' value='${product.code}' />
         </c:url>">
    Add To Cart
</a>
```

A web browser with the session ID encoded in its URL

A web.xml file fragment that turns off URL encoding

```
<session-config>
    <session-timeout>30</session-timeout>
    <tracking-mode>COOKIE</tracking-mode>
</session-config>
```

Description

- You can use the JSTL url tag to encode URLs within your web application that are relative to the application's root directory. As a result, it can prevent your code from breaking if the application context changes.

- By default, the url tag automatically rewrites the URL to include the session ID whenever necessary. This isn't secure as it can lead to session hijacking. To prevent this, you can add a tracking-mode element to the web.xml file to specify that the application should only use cookies (not URL encoding) for tracking.

- You can use the JSTL param tag if you want to automatically encode unsafe characters such as spaces with special characters such as plus signs.

Figure 9-9   How to use the url tag

Other tags in the JSTL core library

Figure 9-10 shows five more tags in the JSTL core library. However, if you use the MVC pattern, you probably won't need to use these tags. As a result, I've only provided brief examples to give you an idea of how these tags work. If you do need to use them, though, you can look them up in the documentation for the JSTL core library as described in figure 9-2.

If you need to set the value of an attribute in a scope, you can use the set tag. For instance, the first example in this figure shows how to set an attribute named message with a value of "Test message" in session scope.

You can also use the set tag if you need to set the value of a property of an attribute within a specified scope. However, instead of using the var attribute to specify the name of the attribute, you use the target attribute to specify the attribute that contains the property. To do that, you use EL within the target attribute to specify a reference to the attribute. This is illustrated by the second example.

The third example shows how to use the remove tag to remove an attribute from a scope. When you use this tag, you use the var attribute to specify the name of the attribute that you want to remove, and you use the scope attribute to specify the scope that contains the attribute.

If your JSP includes code that may cause an exception to be thrown, you can use the catch tag to catch the exceptions. This is illustrated by the fourth example. Here, the opening and closing catch tags are coded around a Java scriptlet that causes an ArithmeticException to be thrown due to a divide by zero error. Then, when the exception is thrown, execution jumps over the Java expression that displays the result of the calculation. However, the catch tag also exposes the exception as a variable named e. As a result, the if tag that follows the catch tag is able to display an appropriate error message.

Of course, if you edit the Java scriptlet that's in the catch tag so it performs a legal calculation, no exception is thrown. In that case, the result of the calculation is displayed and the error message won't be displayed.

The fifth example shows how to use the redirect tag to redirect a client to a new URL. In this case, the redirect tag is coded within an if tag so the client isn't redirected unless the condition in the if statement is true.

Other tags in the JSTL core library

Tag name	Description
set	Sets the value of an attribute in a scope.
remove	Removes an attribute from a scope.
catch	Catches any exception that occurs in its body and optionally creates an EL variable that refers to the Throwable object for the exception.
redirect	Redirects the client browser to a new URL.
param	Adds a parameter to the parent tag.

A set tag that sets a value in an attribute

```
<c:set var="message" scope="session" value="Test message" />
```

A set tag that sets a value in a JavaBean

```
<c:set target="${user}" property="firstName" value="John" />
```

A remove tag that removes an attribute

```
<c:remove var="message" scope="session" />
```

A catch tag that catches an exception

```
<c:catch var="e">
    <%  // this scriptlet statement throws an exception
        int i = 1/0;
    %>
    <p>Result: <c:out value="${i}" /></p>
</c:catch>
<c:if test="${e != null}">
    <p>An exception occurred. Message: ${e.message}</p>
</c:if>
```

A redirect tag that redirects to another page

```
<c:if test="${e != null}">
    <c:redirect url="/error_java.jsp" />
</c:if>
```

Figure 9-10   Other tags in the JSTL core library

The Cart application

Now that you've learned the details for coding JSTL tags, you're ready to see how they're used within the context of an application. To show that, this chapter finishes by showing a Cart application that maintains a simple shopping cart for a user. Since this application uses the MVC pattern, the JSPs don't require extensive use of JSTL tags. However, the url tag is needed to encode URLs, and the forEach tag is needed to display the items in the user's cart.

The user interface

Figure 9-11 shows the user interface for the Cart application. From the Index page, you can click on the Add To Cart button for any of the four CDs to add the CD to your cart. Then, the Cart page displays all of the items that have been added to your cart.

On the Cart page, you can update the quantity for an item by entering a new quantity in the Quantity column and clicking on the Update button. Or, you can remove an item from the cart by clicking on its Remove Item button. Finally, you can return to the Index page by clicking on the Continue Shopping button, or you can begin the checkout process by clicking on the Checkout button.

The Index page

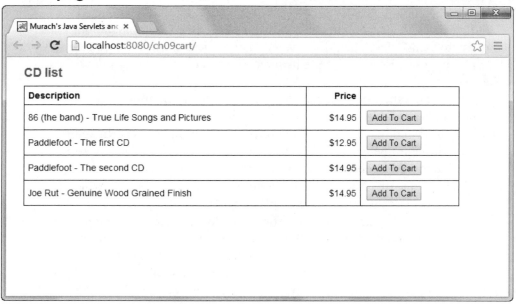

The Cart page

Figure 9-11   The user interface for the Cart application

The code for the business classes

Figure 9-12 shows the three business classes for the Cart application. These classes are the Model in the MVC pattern. All of these classes follow the rules for creating a JavaBean and implement the Serializable interface as described in chapter 6.

Part 1 shows the Product class. This class stores information about each product that's available from the website. In particular, it provides get and set methods for the code, description, and price fields for the product. In addition, this class provides the getPriceCurrencyFormat method, which gets a string for the price after the currency format has been applied to the price. For example, for a double value of 11.5, this method returns a string of "$11.50", which is usually the format that you want to display on a JSP.

Part 2 shows the LineItem class. This class stores information about each line item that's stored in the cart. To do that, this class uses a Product object as one of its instance variables to store the product information for the line item. In addition, this class always calculates the value of the total field by multiplying the product price by the quantity. As a result, there's no need to provide a set method for this field. Finally, this class provides a getTotalCurrencyFormat method that applies currency formatting to the double value that's returned by the getTotal method.

Part 3 shows the Cart class. This class stores each line item that has been added to the cart. To do that, the Cart class uses an ArrayList to store zero or more LineItem objects. When you use the constructor to create a Cart object, the constructor initializes the ArrayList object. Then, you can use the addItem method to add an item, or you can use the removeItem method to remove an item. In addition, you can use the getItems method to return the ArrayList object, or you can use the getCount method to get the number of items that are stored in the cart.

The code for the Product class

```
package murach.business;

import java.io.Serializable;
import java.text.NumberFormat;

public class Product implements Serializable {

    private String code;
    private String description;
    private double price;

    public Product() {
        code = "";
        description = "";
        price = 0;
    }

    public void setCode(String code) {
        this.code = code;
    }

    public String getCode() {
        return code;
    }

    public void setDescription(String description) {
        this.description = description;
    }

    public String getDescription() {
        return description;
    }

    public void setPrice(double price) {
        this.price = price;
    }

    public double getPrice() {
        return price;
    }

    public String getPriceCurrencyFormat() {
        NumberFormat currency = NumberFormat.getCurrencyInstance();
        return currency.format(price);
    }
}
```

Figure 9-12   The code for the business classes (part 1 of 3)

The code for the LineItem class

```
package murach.business;

import java.io.Serializable;
import java.text.NumberFormat;

public class LineItem implements Serializable {

    private Product product;
    private int quantity;

    public LineItem() {}

    public void setProduct(Product p) {
        product = p;
    }

    public Product getProduct() {
        return product;
    }

    public void setQuantity(int quantity) {
        this.quantity = quantity;
    }

    public int getQuantity() {
        return quantity;
    }

    public double getTotal() {
        double total = product.getPrice() * quantity;
        return total;
    }

    public String getTotalCurrencyFormat() {
        NumberFormat currency = NumberFormat.getCurrencyInstance();
        return currency.format(this.getTotal());
    }
}
```

Figure 9-12   The code for the business classes (part 2 of 3)

The code for the Cart class

```
package murach.business;

import java.io.Serializable;
import java.util.ArrayList;

public class Cart implements Serializable {

    private ArrayList<LineItem> items;

    public Cart() {
        items = new ArrayList<LineItem>();
    }

    public ArrayList<LineItem> getItems() {
        return items;
    }

    public int getCount() {
        return items.size();
    }

    public void addItem(LineItem item) {
        String code = item.getProduct().getCode();
        int quantity = item.getQuantity();
        for (int i = 0; i < items.size(); i++) {
            LineItem lineItem = items.get(i);
            if (lineItem.getProduct().getCode().equals(code)) {
                lineItem.setQuantity(quantity);
                return;
            }
        }
        items.add(item);
    }

    public void removeItem(LineItem item) {
        String code = item.getProduct().getCode();
        for (int i = 0; i < items.size(); i++) {
            LineItem lineItem = items.get(i);
            if (lineItem.getProduct().getCode().equals(code)) {
                items.remove(i);
                return;
            }
        }
    }
}
```

Figure 9-12   The code for the business classes (part 3 of 3)

The code for the servlets and JSPs

Figure 9-13 shows the one servlet and two JSPs for the Cart application. Here, the servlet is the Controller and the two JSPs are the View in the MVC pattern.

Part 1 shows the JSP code for the Index page that's displayed when the Cart application first starts. This displays a table that contains one row for each product. Here, each product row includes an Add To Cart button that you can use to add each product to the cart. This code works because the CartServlet shown in part 2 of this figure has been mapped to the "/cart" URL.

Although these four rows are hard-coded for this page, the product data could also be read from a database and stored in an ArrayList. Then, you could use a forEach tag to display each product in the ArrayList. The technique for doing this is similar to the technique for displaying each line item in the cart as shown in figure 9-4.

The code for the index.jsp file

```
<!DOCTYPE html>
<html>
<head>
    <meta charset="utf-8">
    <title>Murach's Java Servlets and JSP</title>
    <link rel="stylesheet" href="styles/main.css" type="text/css"/>
</head>
<body>

<h1>CD list</h1>
<table>
    <tr>
        <th>Description</th>
        <th class="right">Price</th>
        <th> </th>
    </tr>
    <tr>
        <td>86 (the band) - True Life Songs and Pictures</td>
        <td class="right">$14.95</td>
        <td><form action="cart" method="post">
                <input type="hidden" name="productCode" value="8601">
                <input type="submit" value="Add To Cart">
            </form></td>
    </tr>
    <tr>
        <td>Paddlefoot - The first CD</td>
        <td class="right">$12.95</td>
        <td><form action="cart" method="post">
                <input type="hidden" name="productCode" value="pf01">
                <input type="submit" value="Add To Cart">
            </form></td>
    </tr>
    <tr>
        <td>Paddlefoot - The second CD</td>
        <td class="right">$14.95</td>
        <td><form action="cart" method="post">
                <input type="hidden" name="productCode" value="pf02">
                <input type="submit" value="Add To Cart">
            </form></td>
    </tr>
    <tr>
        <td>Joe Rut - Genuine Wood Grained Finish</td>
        <td class="right">$14.95</td>
        <td><form action="cart" method="post">
                <input type="hidden" name="productCode" value="jr01">
                <input type="submit" value="Add To Cart">
            </form></td>
    </tr>
</table>

</body>
</html>
```

Figure 9-13   The code for the servlets and JSPs (page 1 of 4)

Parts 2 and 3 show the servlet code for the CartServlet. To start, this code gets the current action. If the current action hasn't been passed to the servlet, this code sets the current action to a default value of "cart".

After setting the default action, this code checks the action variables and performs an appropriate action. For an action of "shop", the code sets the URL to the index page, which allows the user to add items to the cart.

For an action of "cart", this code begins by getting the value of the productCode parameter from the request object. This parameter uniquely identifies the Product object. Then, this code gets the value of the quantity parameter if there is one. However, unless the user clicked on the Update button from the Cart page, this parameter is equal to a null value.

After getting the parameter values from the request, this code uses the getAttribute method to get the Cart object from a session attribute named cart. If this method returns a null value, this servlet creates a new Cart object.

After the Cart object has been retrieved or created, this servlet sets the value of the quantity variable. To do that, it starts by setting the quantity variable to a default value of 1. Then, if the quantityString variable contains an invalid integer value, such as a null value, the parseInt method of the Integer class throws an exception. This also causes the quantity to be set to 1. However, if the user enters a valid integer such as 0 or 2, the quantity is set to that value. Finally, if the quantity is a negative number, the quantity is set to 1.

After the quantity variable has been set, this servlet uses the getProduct method of the ProductIO class to read the Product object that corresponds with the productCode variable from a text file named products.txt that's stored in the application's WEB-INF directory. To do that, this code specifies the productCode variable as the first argument of the getProduct method. Although this application stores data in a text file to keep things simple, a more realistic application would typically read this data from a database as described in section 3 of this book.

The code for the CartServlet class   Page 1

```java
package murach.cart;

import java.io.*;
import javax.servlet.*;
import javax.servlet.http.*;

import murach.data.*;
import murach.business.*;

public class CartServlet extends HttpServlet {

    @Override
    protected void doPost(HttpServletRequest request,
            HttpServletResponse response)
            throws ServletException, IOException {

        ServletContext sc = getServletContext();

        // get current action
        String action = request.getParameter("action");
        if (action == null) {
            action = "cart";        // default action
        }

        // perform action and set URL to appropriate page
        String url = "/index.jsp";
        if (action.equals("shop")) {
            url = "/index.jsp";     // the "index" page
        }
        else if (action.equals("cart")) {
            String productCode = request.getParameter("productCode");
            String quantityString = request.getParameter("quantity");

            HttpSession session = request.getSession();
            Cart cart = (Cart) session.getAttribute("cart");
            if (cart == null) {
                cart = new Cart();
            }

            //if the user enters a negative or invalid quantity,
            //the quantity is automatically reset to 1.
            int quantity;
            try {
                quantity = Integer.parseInt(quantityString);
                if (quantity < 0) {
                    quantity = 1;
                }
            } catch (NumberFormatException nfe) {
                quantity = 1;
            }

            String path = sc.getRealPath("/WEB-INF/products.txt");
            Product product = ProductIO.getProduct(productCode, path);
```

Figure 9-13   The code for the servlets and JSPs (page 2 of 4)

After the Product object has been read from the text file, this servlet creates a LineItem object and sets its Product object and quantity. Then, if the quantity is greater than 0, this code adds the LineItem object to the Cart object. However, if the quantity is 0, this code removes the item from the Cart object.

After the line item has been added or removed from the cart, this code sets the Cart object as a session attribute named cart. Then it sets the URL to the cart page.

For an action of "checkout", the code sets the URL to the checkout page. This chapter doesn't show this page, but it allows the user to check out.

As you review this code, you may notice that the CartServlet only supports an HTTP POST method. As a result, you can't use the HTTP GET method to call this servlet. That's because you typically don't want a user to call this servlet multiple times in a row. As a result, you don't need to implement the HTTP GET method for this servlet.

Part 3 shows the start of the JSP code for the Cart page. This code starts like any other HTML page.

The code for the CartServlet class   Page 2

```
            LineItem lineItem = new LineItem();
            lineItem.setProduct(product);
            lineItem.setQuantity(quantity);
            if (quantity > 0) {
                cart.addItem(lineItem);
            } else if (quantity == 0) {
                cart.removeItem(lineItem);
            }

            session.setAttribute("cart", cart);
            url = "/cart.jsp";
        }
        else if (action.equals("checkout")) {
            url = "/checkout.jsp";
        }

        sc.getRequestDispatcher(url)
                .forward(request, response);
    }
}
```

The code for the cart.jsp file   Page 1

```
<!DOCTYPE html>
<html>
<head>
    <meta charset="utf-8">
    <title>Murach's Java Servlets and JSP</title>
    <link rel="stylesheet" href="styles/main.css" type="text/css"/>
</head>
<body>

<h1>Your cart</h1>
```

Figure 9-13   The code for the servlets and JSPs (page 3 of 4)

Part 4 shows the rest of the JSP code for the Cart page. This page uses the taglib directive to import the JSTL core library. Then, it uses a table to display one row for each item in the cart. To do that, it uses a forEach tag to loop through each LineItem object in the ArrayList that's returned by the items property of the cart attribute, and it uses EL to display the data for each line item.

At first glance, the code for this row seems complicated because the first and last columns contain HTML forms that include text boxes, hidden text boxes, and buttons. For example, the first column contains a form that includes a hidden text box that sets the productCode parameter for the form, a text box that allows the user to enter a quantity for the form, and a button that submits the form to the CartServlet.

Similarly, the last column contains a hidden text box that sets the product-Code parameter for the form, another hidden text box that sets the quantity parameter to 0 (which causes the item to be removed from the cart), and a button that submits the form to the CartServlet. However, if you study this code, you shouldn't have much trouble understanding how it works.

After the table, this code contains two forms where each form contains a single button. The button on the first form displays the Index page, and the button on the second form displays the Checkout page (which isn't shown or described in this chapter).

If you review the use of the JSTL and EL code in the Cart page, you'll see that the out tag is used to escape output for the values that are susceptible to an XSS attack. Here, the code doesn't escape the formatted values since they can't return a string that contains valid JavaScript code. However, it does escape all other output values. As a result, the Cart application is relatively secure against XSS attacks.

The only other JSTL tag that's used is the forEach tag. However, EL is used to display the nested properties that are available from the Product, LineItem, and Cart objects. This is typical JSTL and EL usage for applications that use the MVC pattern.

The code for the cart.jsp file   **Page 2**

```
<table>
  <tr>
    <th>Quantity</th>
    <th>Description</th>
    <th>Price</th>
    <th>Amount</th>
    <th></th>
  </tr>

<%@ taglib prefix="c" uri="http://java.sun.com/jsp/jstl/core" %>
<c:forEach var="item" items="${cart.items}">
    <tr>
      <td>
        <form action="" method="post">
          <input type="hidden" name="productCode"
                 value="<c:out value='${item.product.code}'/>">
          <input type=text name="quantity"
                 value="<c:out value='${item.quantity}'/>" id="quantity">
          <input type="submit" value="Update">
        </form>
      </td>
      <td><c:out value='${item.product.description}'/></td>
      <td>${item.product.priceCurrencyFormat}</td>
      <td>${item.totalCurrencyFormat}</td>
      <td>
        <form action="" method="post">
          <input type="hidden" name="productCode"
                 value="<c:out value='${item.product.code}'/>">
          <input type="hidden" name="quantity"
                 value="0">
          <input type="submit" value="Remove Item">
        </form>
      </td>
    </tr>
</c:forEach>
</table>

<p><b>To change the quantity</b>, enter the new quantity
      and click on the Update button.</p>

<form action="" method="post">
  <input type="hidden" name="action" value="shop">
  <input type="submit" value="Continue Shopping">
</form>

<form action="" method="post">
  <input type="hidden" name="action" value="checkout">
  <input type="submit" value="Checkout">
</form>

</body>
</html>
```

Note

- In the web.xml file, the CartServlet class is mapped to the "/cart" URL.

Figure 9-13   The code for the servlets and JSPs (page 4 of 4)

Perspective

The goal of this chapter has been to show you how to use JSTL with EL to eliminate or reduce scripting from your JSPs. However, it isn't always possible to remove all scripting from your applications by using JSTL. In that case, you may occasionally want to use scripting. Another option, though, is to create and use custom tags that are stored in a custom tag library as described in the next chapter.

Summary

- The *JSP Standard Tag Library* (*JSTL*) provides tags for common tasks that need to be performed in JSPs.

- Before you can use JSTL tags, you must make the jstl-impl.jar and jstl-api.jar files available to the application.

- Before you can use JSTL tags in a JSP, you must code a taglib directive for the library that you want to use.

- You can use a web browser to view the documentation for JSTL.

- It's generally considered a good practice to use the out tag to escape values that are output to a browser. This prevents most types of *cross-site scripting* (*XSS*) *attacks*, in which an attacker attempts to insert JavaScript into your HTML pages.

- You can use the forEach tag to loop through most types of collections, including regular arrays.

- You can use the forTokens tag to loop through items in a delimited string.

- You can use the if tag to code the equivalent of a Java if statement.

- You can use the choose tag to code the equivalent of a Java if/else statement.

Exercise 9-1   Use JSTL in the Download application

In this exercise, you'll use JSTL in the Download application that you were introduced to in the last chapter.

1. Open the ch09_ex1_download project in the ex_starts directory.

2. Make sure the JSTL library is available to this application.

3. Run the application to refresh your memory about how it works. Note that the first page displays a welcome message.

4. Open the register.jsp and view_cookies.jsp files. Then, add the taglib directive for the core JSTL library to the beginning of these files. Finally, use the out tag to escape all the values in this application that are output to the browser.

5. Test the application to make sure it works like it did before.

6. Open the index.jsp file. Then, modify it so it uses the if tag to only display the welcome message if the cookie for the first name doesn't contain a null value.

7. Test the application to make sure it works correctly.

Exercise 9-2   Use JSTL in the Cart application

In this exercise, you'll use JSTL to loop through an array list of Product objects.

1. Open the ch09_ex2_cart project in the ex_starts directory.

2. Open the web.xml file. Note that the ProductsServlet class is mapped to the /loadProducts URL and that this URL is set as the only welcome page. As a result, when this app starts, the browser issues an HTTP GET request for the ProductsServlet class.

3. Open the ProductsServlet.java file. Note how this servlet uses the doGet method to read an ArrayList of Product objects from the projects.txt file and store them as an attribute of the session object.

4. Make sure the JSTL library is available to this application.

5. Test the application to make sure it works correctly.

6. Open the index.jsp file and add the taglib directive that imports the core JSTL library. Then, add a forEach tag that loops through the ArrayList of Product objects and displays one row for each product. To do that, you can use EL to display the properties of each Product object. (Be sure to delete any old code that you no longer need.)

7. Test the application to make sure that it works correctly.

8. To prevent against XSS attacks, add the out tag to any EL values that should be escaped before they are returned to the browser.

9. Test the application to make sure that it still works correctly.

10

How to use custom JSP tags

For most applications, you can use the EL and JSTL tags that you learned about in the last two chapters to eliminate scripting from your JSPs. Sometimes, however, these tags don't provide all the functionality that you need.

In that case, you can use the skills presented in this chapter to create and use custom JSP tags. Because it's difficult to understand how these tags work without seeing examples, this chapter starts with a simple example and works toward more complex examples.

How to code a custom tag that doesn't have a body

This chapter begins by showing how to code the three components of a custom JSP tag that doesn't have a body. This is the simplest type of tag.

The tag

Part 1 of figure 10-1 shows how to code a *custom tag* that inserts the current date into a JSP. Before you can use a custom tag in a JSP, though, you must code a *taglib directive* in the JSP. Within this directive, the URI attribute must specify the location of the Tag Library Descriptor (or TLD), which you'll learn more about in the next part of this figure. In addition, the prefix attribute must specify a prefix that you can use for the custom tags that are defined by the TLD.

Once you code the taglib directive, you can use any of the custom tags in the TLD. To do that, you code an opening bracket (<), the prefix that's specified in the taglib directive, a colon, the name of the tag, and a slash followed by a closing bracket (/>).

In the example in this figure, you could get the same result by using a JSP scriptlet and expression. However, using a custom tag has a couple of advantages. First, custom tags reduce the amount of Java scripting that's required in your JSP pages. Second, custom tags can help you organize the code of an application so you can reduce code duplication, which can make the code for your application easier to maintain.

As you progress through this chapter, don't forget that all of the custom tag examples assume that a taglib directive like the one in this figure has been coded before the custom tags are used. That's why all of the custom tags in this chapter use a prefix of mma (an abbreviation for Mike Murach & Associates). And that's why all of the custom tags in this chapter use a TLD file named murach.tld that's stored in the application's WEB-INF directory.

A taglib directive that specifies a custom tag library

```
<%@ taglib prefix="mma" uri="/WEB-INF/murach.tld" %>
```

JSP code that uses the custom currentDate tag to display the date

```
<p>The current date is <mma:currentDate />.</p>
```

A JSP that displays the custom tag

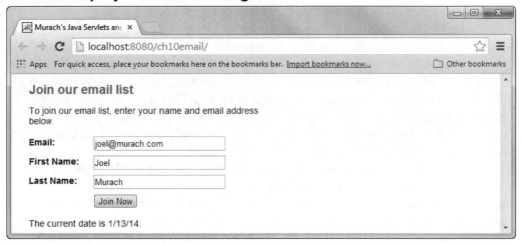

Description

- Before you can code a *custom tag* in a JSP, you must code a *taglib directive*. This directive must specify the location of the Tag Library Descriptor (TLD), and it must specify a prefix that can be used for the custom tags that are defined by this TLD.

- All of the custom tag examples in this chapter assume that the taglib directive shown above has been coded before the custom tags are used.

Figure 10-1   How to code a custom tag that doesn't have a body (part 1 of 3)

The tag element

Before you can use a custom tag in a JSP, you must create a *Tag Library Descriptor* (*TLD*) file that describes the tag. To illustrate, part 2 of this figure shows a TLD that contains two custom tags. As you progress through this chapter, you'll learn how to add other types of tags to this TLD. Although you can code as many TLDs as you like for an application, it's typical to code a single TLD that contains all of the custom tags for an application.

Since TLDs are XML documents, you must start a TLD with the standard XML header information. Since you don't need to understand this header information, you can just copy the header from an old TLD to the start of a new one. After the header information, the rest of the tags are XML tags that define the elements of the TLD. Since these tags are similar to HTML tags, you shouldn't have any trouble coding them. However, unlike HTML tags, XML tags are case-sensitive. As a result, when you work with the XML tags in a TLD, you must use the exact capitalization shown in these figures.

After the header information, the taglib element defines the *tag library*. Within this element, you can code the tag library version, a short name for the library, and a URI for the library. For Tomcat 7.0, the tag library version is the only one of these tags that's required. However, this may vary depending on the JSP engine.

After these elements, you code one tag element for each custom tag in the tag library. When you create a tag element, you're required to code a name element that defines the name of the tag as well as a tag-class element that defines the class that carries out the actions of the tag. This class is sometimes referred to as the *tag class*, or *tag handler class*, and you'll learn more about it in part 3 of this figure.

After the tag-class element, you can code an info element that provides a description of the custom tag. This information should describe the function of the tag so other programmers and web designers can decide whether they want to use it.

When you create a TLD file, you must save the file with a TLD extension. You must also save it in the WEB-INF directory or one of its subdirectories. In the applications that come with this book, for example, the TLD is saved in the murach.tld file of the WEB-INF directory.

A TLD file that contains two tag elements

```xml
<?xml version="1.0" encoding="UTF-8"?>
<taglib version="2.0" xmlns="http://java.sun.com/xml/ns/j2ee"
    xmlns:xsi="http://www.w3.org/2001/XMLSchema-instance"
    xsi:schemaLocation="http://java.sun.com/xml/ns/j2ee
        web-jsptaglibrary_2_0.xsd">

    <tlib-version>1.0</tlib-version>
    <short-name>murach</short-name>
    <uri>/WEB-INF/murach.tld</uri>

    <tag>
        <name>currentDate</name>
        <tag-class>murach.tags.CurrentDateTag</tag-class>
        <body-content>empty</body-content>
    </tag>

    <tag>
        <name>currentTime</name>
        <tag-class>murach.tags.CurrentTimeTag</tag-class>
        <body-content>empty</body-content>
    </tag>

</taglib>
```

Description

- The *Tag Library Descriptor (TLD)* is an XML document that describes a *tag library* that contains custom tags that can be used in an application. Although an application typically uses a single TLD to define all of its custom tags, there's no limit to the number of TLDs an application can have.

- The file for a TLD must be saved in the WEB-INF directory or one of its subdirectories, and it must be saved with an extension of TLD.

- If your application doesn't have an existing TLD, you can create one by copying one that's included with the source code for this book. Then, you can add your custom tag elements to this file.

- Within a tag element, you must use the name element to specify the name of the custom tag and the tag-class element to specify the *tag class* for the tag. The tag class is the Java class that does the actions of the tag.

- Within a tag element, you can use the info element to specify descriptive information about the tag, but this element is optional.

- The elements that are required by a TLD may vary depending on the JSP engine. As a result, if a TLD like the one in this figure doesn't work for you, you may need to consult the documentation for your JSP engine.

- Since Tomcat loads the TLD for an application at startup, you must restart your application whenever you modify this file. Otherwise, your changes won't take effect.

Figure 10-1   How to code a custom tag that doesn't have a body (part 2 of 3)

The tag class

Part 3 of this figure presents the tag class for the currentDate tag shown in part 1. This class displays the current date with the MM/DD/YY format.

To define a tag class for a custom tag, you must implement the Tag interface. Since you probably don't want to define every method in the Tag interface, though, it's easier to extend the TagSupport class instead. This class is a convenience class that implements the Tag interface. As a result, when you extend this class, you only need to define the methods that you want to use.

To define the actions of a custom tag, you can override the doStartTag method of the TagSupport class. This method is called when the custom tag is read. In this figure, for example, the first three statements in this method use the Date and DateFormat classes to get and format the current date. Then, a try/catch statement uses the built-in pageContext object to return a JspWriter object that's used to return the formatted date to the JSP. Last, the doStartTag method returns the SKIP_BODY constant that's defined in the TagSupport class. Whenever a tag doesn't have a body, you return the SKIP_BODY constant after you use the JspWriter to write the tag's data to the JSP.

When you code tag classes, you can save them in the same location as your other Java classes. However, it's common to store tag classes in a separate package. That's why all the tag classes shown in this chapter are saved in a package named tags.

At this point, you should have a pretty good idea of how custom tags work. When the JSP engine encounters a custom tag, it uses the tag prefix to relate the tag to the taglib directive, which points to the TLD for the tag. Then, the JSP engine uses the TLD to find the tag class that implements the custom tag. Once that's done, the JSP engine can translate the JSP into a servlet that calls the tag class.

A tag class for a tag that doesn't include a body

```java
package murach.tags;

import javax.servlet.jsp.*;
import javax.servlet.jsp.tagext.*;
import java.io.*;
import java.util.*;
import java.text.DateFormat;

public class CurrentDateTag extends TagSupport {

    @Override
    public int doStartTag() throws JspException {
        Date currentDate = new Date();
        DateFormat shortDate = DateFormat.getDateInstance(DateFormat.SHORT);
        String currentDateFormatted = shortDate.format(currentDate);

        try {
            JspWriter out = pageContext.getOut();
            out.print(currentDateFormatted);
        } catch (IOException ioe) {
            System.out.println(ioe);
        }
        return SKIP_BODY;
    }
}
```

Description

- The *tag class*, or *tag handler class,* is the Java class that defines the actions of the tag. A tag class must implement the Tag interface.

- For a tag that doesn't have a body, you can implement the Tag interface by extending the TagSupport class of the javax.servlet.jsp.tagext package. Then, you can override the doStartTag method.

- To display text on the JSP, you use the print method of the JspWriter object that's stored in the javax.servlet.jsp package. Since this print method throws an IOException, you must use a try/catch statement to handle the exception.

- To get a JspWriter object, you use the getOut method of the pageContext object that's defined in the TagSupport class.

- For a tag that doesn't have a body, the doStartTag method must return the SKIP_BODY constant.

- Although you can store tag classes wherever you store your other Java classes, it's common to create a separate package for the tag classes of a tag library.

Figure 10-1   How to code a custom tag that doesn't have a body (part 3 of 3)

How to code a custom tag that has a body

Now that you know how to create a custom tag that doesn't have a body, you're ready to learn how to create a custom tag that has a body.

The tag

Part 1 of figure 10-2 shows you how to use a custom tag with a body in a JSP. As with all custom tags, you must code a taglib directive before you can use the custom tag. In this figure, for example, you must code a taglib directive like the one shown in part 1 of figure 10-1 before you code the ifWeekday tag. Then, when you use the ifWeekday tag, you code the opening tag, followed by the body of the tag, followed by the closing tag.

In this figure, the custom tag determines if the body of the tag is displayed. In part 2 of this figure, you see that the class for this tag displays the body of the tag on Monday through Friday, but doesn't display it on Saturday or Sunday.

JSP code that uses a custom tag with a body

```
<mma:ifWeekday>
    <p>Live support available at 1-800-555-2222</p>
</mma:ifWeekday>
```

A JSP that displays the tag Monday through Friday

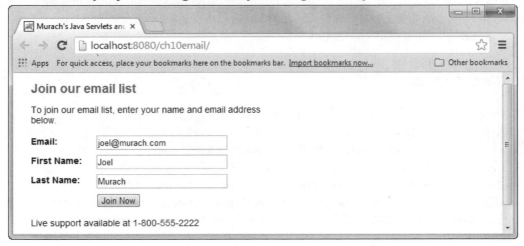

Description

- A tag that has a body must have an opening tag, a body, and a closing tag.
- The body of the tag can contain any HTML or JSP elements.
- The tag class for a custom tag can control whether the body of the tag is displayed in the JSP.

Figure 10-2   How to code a custom tag that has a body (part 1 of 2)

The tag element

Part 2 of this figure shows how to code the tag element for a tag that contains a body. In general, this tag follows the same rules as a tag that doesn't have a body. However, to inform the JSP engine that the tag has a body, you must code a bodycontent element that specifies a value of "JSP". In contrast, when you code a tag that doesn't have a body, you can omit the bodycontent element or you can specify a value of "empty".

The tag class

Part 2 of this figure also shows the tag class for the ifWeekday tag. This class displays the body of the tag if the current day is a weekday.

To start, this class extends the TagSupport class and overrides the doStart-Tag method. Within the doStartTag method, this class uses an if statement to check if the current day is Saturday or Sunday. If so, this method returns the SKIP_BODY field so the body of the tag is skipped. If not, this method returns the EVAL_BODY_INCLUDE field so the body of the tag is evaluated and displayed.

The tag element in the TLD file

```
<tag>
    <name>ifWeekday</name>
    <tag-class>murach.tags.IfWeekdayTag</tag-class>
    <body-content>JSP</body-content>
</tag>
```

A tag class that conditionally displays the body of the tag

```
package murach.tags;

import javax.servlet.jsp.*;
import javax.servlet.jsp.tagext.*;
import java.util.*;

public class IfWeekdayTag extends TagSupport {

    @Override
    public int doStartTag() throws JspException {
        Calendar currentDate = new GregorianCalendar();
        int day = currentDate.get(Calendar.DAY_OF_WEEK);
        if (day == Calendar.SATURDAY || day == Calendar.SUNDAY) {
            return SKIP_BODY;
        } else {
            return EVAL_BODY_INCLUDE;
        }
    }
}
```

Description

- When you add a tag that has a body to a TLD, you must specify a value of "JSP" for the bodycontent element. When you add a tag that doesn't have a body to a TLD, you can omit the bodycontent element or specify a value of "empty".

- To create a tag class for a tag that has a body, you can extend the TagSupport class and override the doStartTag method.

- To display the body of the tag in the JSP, the tag class should return the EVAL_BODY_INCLUDE constant. Otherwise, the tag class should return the SKIP_BODY constant.

Figure 10-2   How to code a custom tag that has a body (part 2 of 2)

How to code a custom tag that has attributes

In this topic, you'll learn how to add attributes to a custom tag. Although the example in this topic shows how to add attributes to a tag that doesn't have a body, you can also use attributes with a tag that has a body.

The tag

Part 1 of figure 10-3 shows a JSP that uses a custom tag named ifEmptyMark to display an asterisk after a text box that doesn't contain text. In the JSP, this tag is coded after each of the three text boxes. The two attributes for this tag are color and field, which are used to determine the color of the asterisk and the field that should be checked to see if its empty.

The first example in this figure shows how to use the ifEmptyMark tag to display a blue asterisk. Here, the color attribute is set to blue and the field attribute is set to an empty string. As a result, the asterisk is always displayed.

The second example shows how to use a JSP expression as the value of the field attribute. Here, the field attribute is set to the value that's returned by the getLastName method of the user object. Then, if that method returns a null value or an empty string, this tag displays an asterisk to the right of the text box for that field. If not, the tag handler doesn't do anything. In effect, then, the tag handler provides a type of data validation.

The third example works like the second example except that it uses EL instead of a JSP expression as the value of the field attribute. If you compare the second and third examples, you can see that using EL makes the code easier to read.

So, why would you ever want to use a JSP expression instead of EL? In general, you would only do that if you're working on a legacy application that was developed prior to JSP 2.0. In that case, the web server may not support EL, or you may prefer to use JSP expressions to keep your code consistent with the old code. If you're developing new applications, though, you'll want to use EL in your custom tags.

A JSP that marks required fields with asterisks if the field is empty

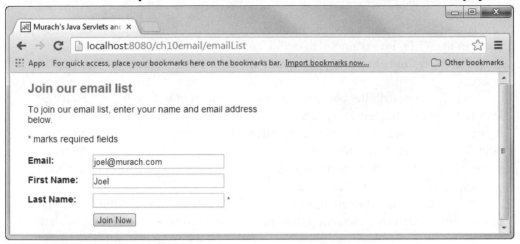

JSP code that uses a custom tag that has attributes

To display the asterisk

```
<p><mma:ifEmptyMark color="blue" field=""/> marks required fields</p>
```

To display the asterisk only if a field is empty (using a JSP expression)

```
<label class="pad_top">Last Name:</label>
<input type="text" name="lastName"
       value="<%= user.getLastName() %>">
<mma:ifEmptyMark color="blue" field="<%= user.getLastName() %>"/><br>
```

To display the asterisk only if a field is empty (using EL)

```
<label class="pad_top">Last Name:</label>
<input type="text" name="lastName" value="${user.lastName}">
<mma:ifEmptyMark color="blue" field="${user.lastName}"/><br>
```

Description

- The custom tags in this figure use attributes named color and field to send arguments from the JSP to the tag class.

Figure 10-3   How to code a custom tag that has attributes (part 1 of 3)

The tag element

To use attributes in a custom tag, you must add information about the attributes to the TLD. For example, to define an ifEmptyMark tag that has a color attribute and a field attribute, you can add the tag element shown in part 2 of this figure.

To define an attribute, you code an attribute element within the tag element. Within the attribute element, you can code the four elements shown in this figure. To start, you must code a name element to specify the name of the attribute. Then, you can code the required element to specify whether the attribute is required. In the first example in this figure, the color attribute is optional while the field attribute is required.

If an attribute is set to an expression that's determined at runtime, you must also set the rtexprvalue element to true or yes. This informs the JSP engine that the value of the attribute won't be determined until the page is requested. In the first example, this element is set to true for the field attribute.

By default, an attribute that's determined by a runtime expression is returned as a string, but you can use the type element to automatically convert a string attribute to a primitive data type or to an object of a wrapper class of a primitive data type. For instance, the second example in this figure shows the definition for the count attribute of a tag that automatically converts an expression to an int value. Otherwise, you can use the tag class to manually convert the data type.

The syntax for the attribute element in a tag element

```
<attribute>
    <name>attributeName</name>
    <required>true|false|yes|no</required>
    <rtexprvalue>true|false|yes|no</rtexprvalue>
    <type>data_type</type>
</attribute>
```

The tag element with two attributes

```
<tag>
    <name>ifEmptyMark</name>
    <tag-class>murach.tags.IfEmptyMarkTag</tag-class>
    <body-content>empty</body-content>
    <attribute>
        <name>color</name>
        <required>false</required>
    </attribute>
    <attribute>
        <name>field</name>
        <required>true</required>
        <rtexprvalue>true</rtexprvalue>
    </attribute>
</tag>
```

An attribute element that uses the integer data type

```
<attribute>
    <name>count</name>
    <required>true</required>
    <rtexprvalue>true</rtexprvalue>
    <type>int</type>
</attribute>
```

The attribute child elements

Element	Description
`<name>`	The name of the attribute.
`<required>`	A true/false value that specifies whether this attribute is required. If it isn't required, the tag class should provide a default value.
`<rtexprvalue>`	A true/false value that specifies whether the value of the attribute is determined from a runtime expression. If so, the type element can be any data type. Otherwise, the type element is a string.
`<type>`	The data type of the attribute value. You only need to code this element when the value of the attribute is determined from a runtime expression and the data type isn't a string.

Description

- The tag element for a tag can include the definitions for one or more attributes.
- For each attribute, you should include at least the name and required elements.

Figure 10-3   How to code a custom tag that has attributes (part 2 of 3)

The tag class

Part 3 of this figure shows how to code a tag class that works with attributes. To start, the class must define each attribute as a private instance variable and provide a set method for each attribute.

When you code the set method, you must follow the standard Java naming conventions. For example, if you have an attribute named field, you must code a set method named setField. Similarly, if you have an attribute named height, you must code a set method named setHeight.

When this tag class is executed, it begins by declaring the instance variables named field and color, and it sets the color field to its default value of "red". Then, this class calls the setField method to set the field instance variable. Since this attribute is required, this method is always called. This sets the value of the field instance variable equal to the value of the Field attribute in the custom JSP tag.

If a color attribute has been coded in the custom JSP tag, this class also calls the setColor method to set the color attribute. Otherwise, the color variable is equal to its default value of "red".

Once the instance variables have been set, the doStartTag method is called. Within this method, the code checks the value of the field variable. If the field is an empty string, this tag sends an asterisk with the specified color to the JSP. Otherwise, this tag doesn't send any output to the JSP.

A tag class that uses two attributes

```
package murach.tags;

import javax.servlet.jsp.*;
import javax.servlet.jsp.tagext.*;
import java.io.*;

public class IfEmptyMarkTag extends TagSupport {

    private String field;
    private String color = "red";

    public void setField(String field) {
        this.field = field;
    }

    public void setColor(String color) {
        this.color = color;
    }

    @Override
    public int doStartTag() throws JspException {
        try {
            JspWriter out = pageContext.getOut();
            if (field == null || field.length() == 0) {
                out.print("<font color=" + color + "> *</font>");
            }
        } catch (IOException ioe) {
            System.out.println(ioe);
        }
        return SKIP_BODY;
    }
}
```

How to code a tag handler that uses attributes

- Declare a private instance variable for each attribute.
- Define a set method for each attribute with the standard naming conventions.

Description

- This tag class causes the custom JSP tag to display an asterisk if the field attribute is an empty string.
- If the custom tag includes the color attribute, the asterisk that's displayed is that color. Otherwise, the asterisk is red.

Figure 10-3   How to code a custom tag that has attributes (part 3 of 3)

How to code a custom tag that reiterates its body

In this topic, you'll learn how to code a tag class that can repeat the body of a tag multiple times.

The tag

Part 1 of figure 10-4 presents a JSP that uses a custom tag to display all of the items contained in the user's cart. Here, the servlet code starts by getting a Cart object that's stored as an attribute of the session object. Then, this servlet code can add a LineItem object to the cart, or remove a LineItem object from the cart. Finally, this servlet code stores the cart as an attribute of the session. That way, the tag class is able to access the Cart object.

Once the servlet has set the Cart object as an attribute of the session, the cart tag can display one row of a table for each LineItem object in the Cart object. To do that, the body of the cart tag contains some HTML tags and some JSP expressions or EL. This returns the quantity, product description, product price, and total amount for each line item by calling the getAttribute method of the pageContext object. Although you only need to code this row once, you'll see that the tag handler repeats it once for each line item in the cart.

Here again, if you compare the use of JSP expressions with the use of EL, you can see how much easier it is to code and read EL. As a result, you should only use JSP expressions if you're working with an older version of JSP that doesn't support EL.

A page that displays all line items in the user's cart

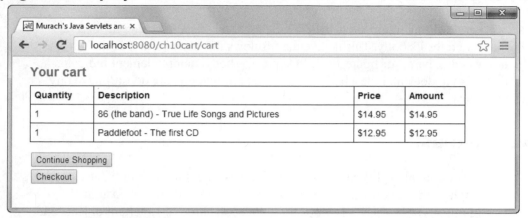

Servlet code that sets the cart attribute

```
Cart cart = (Cart) session.getAttribute("cart");
// code that adds or removes LineItem objects
session.setAttribute("cart", cart);
```

JSP code that displays all items in the cart (using JSP expressions)

```
<mma:cart>
    <tr>
        <td><%= pageContext.getAttribute("quantity") %></td>
        <td><%= pageContext.getAttribute("productDescription") %></td>
        <td><%= pageContext.getAttribute("productPrice") %></td>
        <td><%= pageContext.getAttribute("total") %></td>
    </tr>
</mma:cart>
```

JSP code that displays all items in the cart (using EL)

```
<mma:cart>
  <tr>
    <td>${quantity}</td>
    <td>${productDescription}</td>
    <td>${productPrice}</td>
    <td>${total}</td>
  </tr>
</mma:cart>
```

Description

- To pass data to the tag class, you can store that data as a session attribute.
- To use a JSP expression to get an attribute that has been set in the tag class, you can call the getAttribute method of the pageContext object.

Figure 10-4   How to code a custom tag that reiterates its body (part 1 of 3)

The tag element

Part 2 of this figure starts by showing how to code a tag element for a tag that reiterates its body. This tag element follows the same format as the tag described in part 2 of figure 10-2. In short, the bodycontent element indicates that this tag does include a body. Note, however, that this tag doesn't have any attributes.

The tag class

This figure also presents a tag class that gets each line item in the user's cart and displays the data for each LineItem object in the body of the custom JSP tag. In other words, this class loops through a collection of LineItem objects and returns the body of the tag with different attributes for each LineItem object.

To code a tag class that interacts with the body of the tag, the tag class must implement the BodyTag interface rather than the Tag interface. To do that, the tag class usually extends the BodyTagSupport class. Since this convenience class implements all methods of the BodyTag interface, you only need to override the methods that you want to use. Similarly, since the BodyTagSupport class extends the TagSupport class, all methods and fields that you've used so far are available to any tag class that extends the BodyTagSupport class.

The tag class in this figure contains three instance variables. The first instance variable is an ArrayList object that stores the LineItem objects. The second instance variable is an Iterator object that's used to loop through the LineItem objects stored in the ArrayList object. And the third instance variable is the LineItem object that's used to display data in the tag.

To determine if the tag body should be skipped or evaluated, the doStartTag method retrieves the ArrayList of LineItem objects from the session and checks if it's empty. To do that, this method calls the findAttribute method of the page-Context object. This method returns any attribute stored in the page, request, session, or application scope.

If the array list of line items is empty, the doStartTag method returns the SKIP_BODY constant. As a result, the body of the tag isn't displayed, and the rest of the class is skipped. Otherwise, the doStartTag method returns the EVAL_BODY_BUFFERED constant that's defined in the BodyTagSupport class. As a result, the tag class evaluates the body of the tag by calling the doInitBody and doAfterBody methods.

The doInitBody method initializes the body by preparing the first row of the tag. To do that, this method gets an Iterator object for the collection of LineItem objects. Then, it uses the next method of the Iterator object to get the first LineItem object in the collection and to move the cursor to the second LineItem object in the ArrayList object. After retrieving the first LineItem object, this method calls the setItemAttributes method on the next page, which is a helper method that uses the setAttribute method of the pageContext object to set the five attributes of the LineItem object.

The tag element for the TLD

```
<tag>
    <name>cart</name>
    <tag-class>murach.tags.CartTag</tag-class>
    <body-content>JSP</body-content>
</tag>
```

A tag class that reiterates the body of the tag   Page 1

```
package murach.tags;

import javax.servlet.jsp.*;
import javax.servlet.jsp.tagext.*;
import java.util.*;
import java.io.IOException;

import murach.business.*;

public class CartTag extends BodyTagSupport {

    private ArrayList<LineItem> lineItems;
    private Iterator iterator;
    private LineItem item;

    @Override
    public int doStartTag() {
        Cart cart = (Cart) pageContext.findAttribute("cart");
        lineItems = cart.getItems();
        if (lineItems.size() <= 0) {
            return SKIP_BODY;
        } else {
            return EVAL_BODY_BUFFERED;
        }
    }

    @Override
    public void doInitBody() throws JspException {
        iterator = lineItems.iterator();
        if (iterator.hasNext()) {
            item = (LineItem) iterator.next();
            this.setItemAttributes(item);
        }
    }
}
```

Description

- To access a tag that has a body, the tag class must implement the BodyTag interface. The easiest way to do this is to extend the BodyTagSupport class. Since the BodyTagSupport class extends the TagSupport class, this provides access to all of the methods and fields of the TagSupport class.
- If the doStartTag method returns the EVAL_BODY_BUFFERED constant, the body of the tag is evaluated by calling the doInitBody method and the doAfterBody method.
- The doInitBody method sets the initial values for the first row of the body.

Figure 10-4   How to code a custom tag that reiterates its body (part 2 of 3)

In this example, the custom cart tag doesn't use the productCode attribute. However, the setItemAttributes method of the CartTag class sets the productCode attribute along with the other four attributes. As a result, if you need to access the productCode attribute from within the custom cart tag, you can do that.

After the doInitBody method finishes executing, the body is stored in the bodyContent object that's provided by the BodyTagSupport class. However, the body hasn't yet been displayed. To display the body, you must write the body to the JSP as shown in the doAfterBody method.

The doAfterBody method starts by checking if another element exists in the array list of line items. If so, this method retrieves the LineItem object, and sets the pageContext attributes to the values for that line item. Then, it returns the EVAL_BODY_AGAIN constant. This adds the body to the existing body-Content object, and it calls the doAfterBody method to evaluate the body again. However, the body still hasn't been displayed.

Eventually, the doAfterBody method finishes looping through all of the line items in the array list. Then, it displays the body. To do that, this method calls the getEnclosingWriter method of the bodyContent object to obtain a JspWriter object. Then, it calls the writeOut method of the bodyContent object and provides the JspWriter object as an argument. This writes the body to the JSP. Last, this method returns the SKIP_BODY constant to indicate that the tag has finished.

Since the writeOut method throws an IOException, you need to catch this exception. That's why all of the code for the doAfterBody method is enclosed in a try/catch statement.

The tag class that reiterates the tag body

```java
        private void setItemAttributes(LineItem item) {
            Product p = item.getProduct();
            pageContext.setAttribute(
                    "productCode", p.getCode());
            pageContext.setAttribute(
                    "productDescription", p.getDescription());
            pageContext.setAttribute(
                    "productPrice", p.getPriceCurrencyFormat());
            pageContext.setAttribute(
                    "quantity", new Integer(item.getQuantity()));
            pageContext.setAttribute(
                    "total", item.getTotalCurrencyFormat());
        }

        @Override
        public int doAfterBody() throws JspException {
            try {
                if (iterator.hasNext()) {
                    item = (LineItem) iterator.next();
                    this.setItemAttributes(item);
                    return EVAL_BODY_AGAIN;
                } else {
                    JspWriter out = bodyContent.getEnclosingWriter();
                    bodyContent.writeOut(out);
                    return SKIP_BODY;
                }
            } catch (IOException ioe) {
                System.err.println("error in doAfterBody " + ioe.getMessage());
                return SKIP_BODY;
            }
        }
    }
```

Description

- If the doAfterBody method returns the EVAL_BODY_AGAIN constant, the doAfterBody method is called again.

- You can use the setAttribute method of the PageContext object to set any attributes that you need to access from the JSP tag.

- You can use the getEnclosingWriter and writeOut methods of the bodyContent object to write the body to the JSP.

Figure 10-4   How to code a custom tag that reiterates its body (part 3 of 3)

How to work with scripting variables

If you're using version 2.0 or later of JSP, you can use EL with your custom tags to display attributes that were stored by the tag class. In that case, you don't need to use scripting variables. However, if you're using an older version of JSP, you need to use JSP expressions to display attributes that were stored by the tag class. In that case, you can create *scripting variables* to make it easier to display these attributes.

An introduction to scripting variables

Figure 10-5 shows how scripting variables can be used to access variables that have been stored as attributes of the pageContext object. Here, the first example shows a custom JSP tag that doesn't use scripting variables. As a result, this tag must use the getAttribute method of the pageContext object to get the three variables that have been stored in the pageContext object by the tag class.

In contrast, the second example uses scripting variables. As a result, you only need to code the name of a scripting variable in an expression when you want to get the related attribute from the pageContext object.

To make this work, you have to do three tasks. First, the tag class must add the scripting variables to the pageContext object as shown in the third example in this figure. Second, you must code a TEI class that defines the scripting variables as shown in the next figure. And third, you must add a tei-class element to the tag element in the TLD as shown in the last example in this figure.

A custom JSP tag without scripting variables

```
<mma:cart>
    <tr valign="top">
        <td><%= pageContext.getAttribute("quantity") %></td>
        <td><%= pageContext.getAttribute("productDescription") %></td>
        <td><%= pageContext.getAttribute("productPrice") %></td>
        <td><%= pageContext.getAttribute("total") %></td>
    </tr>
</mma:cart>
```

A custom JSP tag with scripting variables

```
<mma:cart>
  <tr valign="top">
    <td><%= quantity %></td>
    <td><%= productDescription %></td>
    <td><%= productPrice %></td>
    <td><%= total %></td>
  </tr>
</mma:cart>
```

The code in the tag class that adds the scripting variables to the pageContext object

```
pageContext.setAttribute("productDescription", p.getDescription());
pageContext.setAttribute("productPrice", p.getPriceCurrencyFormat());
pageContext.setAttribute("quantity", new Integer(item.getQuantity()));
pageContext.setAttribute("total", item.getTotalCurrencyFormat());
```

The tag element in the TLD

```
<tag>
    <name>cart</name>
    <tag-class>tags.CartTag</tag-class>
    <tei-class>tags.CartTEI</tei-class>
    <body-content>JSP</body-content>
</tag>
```

How to create a scripting variable

- The tag class must add the scripting variables to the pageContext object.
- The TEI class must define the scripting variables as shown in the next figure.
- The tag element in the TLD must specify both the tag class and the TEI class for the custom tag.

Description

- To make attributes easier to access, you can use *scripting variables*. Then, you can code just the name of a scripting variable in a JSP expression when you want to get the value of an attribute from the pageContext object.

Figure 10-5   An introduction to scripting variables

The TEI class for four scripting variables

Figure 10-6 shows how to code a *TEI class (tag extra information class)* that defines the scripting variables for a tag handler. To code a TEI class, you extend the TagExtraInfo class and override its getVariableInfo method. When you override that method, you must return an array of VariableInfo objects. These objects define the scripting variables.

For each scripting variable, you create a VariableInfo object using the constructor shown in this figure. When you code this constructor, you must provide a string that specifies the name of the variable and you must specify the data type of the variable. For the data type, you can specify a String object, a primitive data type, or a wrapper class for a primitive data type.

After coding the data type, you must code a boolean value that specifies whether the variable is a new scripting variable. If the variable hasn't been declared anywhere else, which is usually the case, you code a true value. Otherwise, you code a false value.

Last, you must define the scope of the scripting variable. Most of the time, you'll want to use the NESTED field. That way, the scripting variables are available between the opening and closing tags.

The constructor of the VariableInfo class

```
VariableInfo(String varName, String dataType, boolean declare, int scope)
```

A TEI class that creates four scripting variables

```
package tags;

import javax.servlet.jsp.tagext.*;

public class CartTEI extends TagExtraInfo
{
    public VariableInfo[] getVariableInfo(TagData data)
    {
        return new VariableInfo[]
        {
            new VariableInfo(
                "productDescription", "String", true, VariableInfo.NESTED),
            new VariableInfo(
                "productPrice", "String", true, VariableInfo.NESTED),
            new VariableInfo(
                "quantity", "Integer", true, VariableInfo.NESTED),
            new VariableInfo(
                "total", "String", true, VariableInfo.NESTED),
        };
    }
}
```

The VariableInfo constants that define the scope of a scripting variable

Constant	Scope
AT_BEGIN	From the start of the tag to the end of the JSP.
AT_END	From the end of the tag to the end of the JSP.
NESTED	From the start of the tag to the end of the tag.

Description

- To define scripting variables for a tag class, you create a *tag extra information (TEI) class*. You can store this class in the same location as the tag classes.

- To code a TEI class, you extend the TagExtraInfo class in the javax.servlet.jsp.tagext package. Then, you override the getVariableInfo method to return an array of VariableInfo objects that define the scripting variables.

- For each scripting variable, you create a VariableInfo object that provides this data: the name and data type of the variable, a true/false value that tells whether the variable needs to be declared, and the scope of the variable.

- For the data type of a scripting variable, you can specify a String object, any primitive data type, or any wrapper class for a primitive type.

- To specify whether the scripting variable needs to be declared, you can usually specify a true value to indicate that the variable is new and should be declared.

Figure 10-6   The TEI class for four scripting variables

Classes, methods, and fields for working with custom tags

This topic summarizes the common classes, methods, and fields for working with custom tags. Since this chapter has already presented examples that use these classes, this topic should help you review the skills that you've already learned. In addition, it should give you some ideas for how to use other capabilities of custom tags.

Methods and fields of the TagSupport class

Figure 10-7 presents the common methods of the TagSupport class and shows the fields that these methods can return. When a tag is processed, the doStartTag method is called first, followed by the doEndTag method, followed by the release method. When you extend this class, you only need to override the methods that you want to code.

For many types of tags, you need to override the doStartTag method. If a tag doesn't have a body, you can return the SKIP_BODY field after the statements that process the tag. Then, the body of the tag won't be evaluated. However, if a tag does have a body, you can return the EVAL_BODY_INCLUDE field. Then, the body of the tag is evaluated.

After the doStartTag method finishes executing, the doEndTag method is called. By default, this method returns the EVAL_PAGE field, which causes the rest of the JSP to be evaluated. Since that's usually what you want, you usually don't need to override this method. However, if you don't want to continue evaluating the JSP below the custom tag, you can override this method and return the SKIP_PAGE field. Then, any part of the JSP below the custom tag won't be displayed.

After the doEndTag method finishes executing, the release method is called. You can use this method to clean up any system resources that are in use. For example, you can use this method to close streams that you have used in the tag class.

Common methods and fields of the TagSupport class

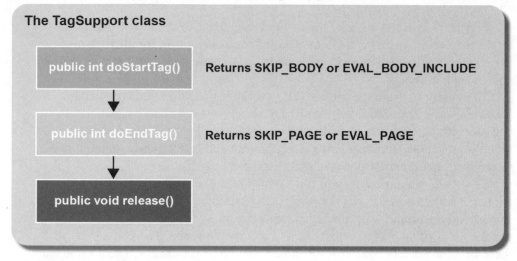

Description

- The doStartTag method is the first method that's called for a custom tag. Typically, this method contains the statements that perform the processing for the tag.
- If a tag doesn't have a body, the doStartTag method should return the SKIP_BODY field. That way, the body of the tag won't be displayed.
- If a tag has a body, the doStartTag method should return the EVAL_BODY_INCLUDE field. That way, the body of the tag is displayed.
- If you need to execute any statements at the end of the tag, you can override the doEndTag method.
- To display the rest of the JSP after the custom tag, the doEndTag method should return the EVAL_PAGE field.
- To not display the rest of the JSP after the custom tag, the doEndTag method should return the SKIP_PAGE field.
- If you need to execute any statements that release any system resources that the tag is using, you can code a release method.

Figure 10-7   Methods and fields of the TagSupport class

Methods and fields of the PageContext class

Figure 10-8 shows some of the methods and fields of the PageContext class. Since an instance of this class named pageContext is built-in for all JSPs and tag classes, it allows JSPs and tag classes to communicate by getting and setting objects and attributes.

To get objects from the calling JSP, you can use the first three methods shown in this figure. Since you've already seen how a tag class can use the getOut method to get the JspWriter object for the calling JSP, you shouldn't have much trouble understanding how the getRequest and getResponse methods can return the request and response objects for the calling JSP.

To set and get attributes, you can call any of the set and get methods of the pageContext class. If you don't explicitly specify a scope when setting an attribute, the attribute is only available within page scope. However, you can use the fields of the PageContext class to specify the scope. Then, you can use these fields to specify the scope when you attempt to get the attribute, or you can use the findAttribute method to search through all four scopes from smallest to largest.

The pageContext object defined in the TagSupport class

```
protected PageContext pageContext
```

Common methods of the PageContext class

Method	Description
getOut()	Returns the JspWriter object from the JSP.
getRequest()	Returns the request object from the JSP.
getResponse()	Returns the response object from the JSP.
setAttribute(String name, Object o)	Sets the named attribute with page scope to the value.
setAttribute(String name, Object o, int scope)	Sets the named attribute with the specified scope to the value. To set the scope, you can use the fields shown below.
getAttribute(String name)	Searches the page scope for an attribute with the specified name. If this method finds the attribute, it returns an object of the Object type. Otherwise, it returns a null value.
getAttribute(String name, int scope)	Searches the specified scope for an attribute with the specified name. If this method finds the attribute, it returns an object of the Object type. Otherwise, it returns a null value. To set the scope, you can use the fields shown below.
findAttribute(String name)	Searches the page, request, session, and application scopes in that sequence for the specified attribute. If this method finds the specified attribute, it returns an object of the Object type. Otherwise, it returns a null value.

The fields of the PageContext class for setting scope

```
PAGE_SCOPE
REQUEST_SCOPE
SESSION_SCOPE
APPLICATION_SCOPE
```

Description

- You can use the pageContext object to set and get JSP objects and attributes.
- For more information about the PageContext class, you can look in the javax.servlet.jsp package of the Java EE API documentation.

Figure 10-8   Methods and fields of the PageContext class

Methods and fields of the BodyTagSupport class

Figure 10-9 shows some of the methods and fields of the BodyTagSupport class. Since this class extends the TagSupport class, you can access the pageContext object and its methods directly from the BodyTagSupport class. In addition, the doEndTag and release methods work much as they do in the TagSupport class.

By default, the doStartTag method of the BodyTagSupport class returns the EVAL_BODY_BUFFERED field. This field indicates that the tag has a body and it causes the doInitBody and doAfterBody methods to be called. As a result, you only need to override this method if you want to add code that writes data to the JSP before the body is evaluated, or if you want to skip the body under certain conditions. To skip the body, the doStartTag method can return the SKIP_BODY field. In that case, the doEndTag and release methods are called.

If the doStartTag method returns EVAL_BODY_BUFFERED, the doInitBody method is called. Then, you can override this method to initialize any values before the body is evaluated for the first time. After the doInitBody method is executed, the body is evaluated. In other words, the body is read and placed in the built-in bodyContent object, which stores the body. In the next figure, you'll learn more about working with the bodyContent object.

After the doInitBody method finishes executing, the doAfterBody method is called. You can override this method to code statements that need to be executed each time the body is evaluated. If you want to evaluate the body again and add it to the bodyContent object, you return the EVAL_BODY_AGAIN field. Then, when you finish evaluating the body, you return the SKIP_BODY field. But first, you'll probably want to use the bodyContent object to write the body that's stored in the bodyContent object to the JSP.

Once the doAfterBody method returns the SKIP_BODY field, the doEndTag and release methods are called. Since the default values for these methods are usually adequate, you usually don't need to override these methods.

Common methods and fields of the BodyTagSupport class

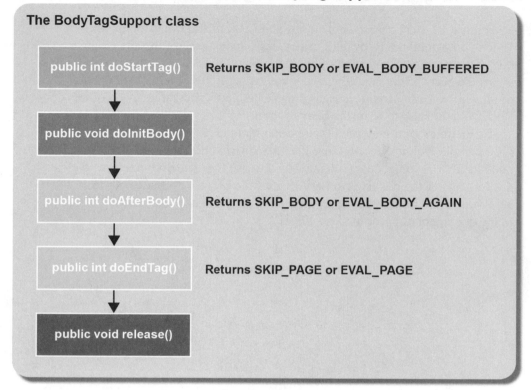

The BodyTagSupport class

public int doStartTag()	**Returns SKIP_BODY or EVAL_BODY_BUFFERED**
public void doInitBody()	
public int doAfterBody()	**Returns SKIP_BODY or EVAL_BODY_AGAIN**
public int doEndTag()	**Returns SKIP_PAGE or EVAL_PAGE**
public void release()	

Description

- The BodyTagSupport class extends the TagSupport class. As a result, the methods and fields that are available in the TagSupport class are also available to the BodyTagSupport class.

- If you want to perform some initial processing for a tag, you can override the doStartTag method of the BodyTagSupport class.

- If the doStartTag method returns the EVAL_BODY_BUFFERED field, the doInitBody and doAfterBody methods are called to display the body of the tag.

- The doInitBody method should contain all of the initialization statements that are needed for the first evaluation of the body.

- The doAfterBody method should contain all of the statements that are needed for additional evaluations of the body.

- If the doAfterBody method returns the EVAL_BODY_AGAIN field, the body is added to the bodyContent object and the doAfterBody method is called again.

- If the doAfterBody method returns the SKIP_BODY field, the processing for the tag is finished and the body is skipped.

Figure 10-9   Methods and fields of the BodyTagSupport class

Methods and fields of the BodyContent class

Figure 10-10 shows some methods and fields of the BodyContent class. When you extend the BodyTagSupport class, an instance of this class named bodyContent is automatically available to your tag class and it automatically stores the body of the tag. When the tag class is through evaluating the body of the tag, you can use the getEnclosingWriter and writeOut methods of the BodyContent class to write the body to the JSP.

Sometimes, you may need to use other methods of the BodyContent class. For example, you may need to use the getString method to return the text of the body as a String object. Or, you may need to use the clearBody method to clear the contents of the bodyContent object after the body is evaluated. To learn more about these and other methods of the BodyContent class, you can look them up in the documentation for the Java EE API.

The bodyContent object defined in the BodyTagSupport class

```
protected BodyContent bodyContent
```

Common methods of the BodyContent class

Method	Description
clearBody()	Clears the body.
getEnclosingWriter()	Returns the JspWriter object for the body.
getString()	Returns the body as a String object.
writeOut(Writer out)	Writes the body to the specified out stream.

Description

- The bodyContent object stores the body of the tag before it is written to the JSP.
- To display the body in the JSP, you can use the getEnclosingWriter and writeOut methods of the BodyContent class.
- For more information about the BodyContent class, you can look in the javax.servlet.jsp.tagext package in the Java EE API documentation.

Figure 10-10 Methods and fields of the BodyContent class

Perspective

The goal of this chapter has been to show you how to create and use custom JSP tags. These tags are useful when you need to go beyond the functionality that's available from the standard JSP tags or the JSTL tags. You also need to understand custom tags if you're maintaining legacy code that uses them.

Although it requires a significant amount of effort to create custom tags, there are a couple of advantages to using them. First, custom tags reduce the amount of Java scripting that's required in your JSP pages, which makes it easier for web designers to work with the JSPs. Second, custom tags help organize the code of an application and reduce code duplication, which makes the application easier to maintain.

Summary

- To create a *custom tag* that can be used in a JSP, you must create an XML file called the *Tag Library Descriptor* (*TLD*). This TLD defines the *tag library* that contains the custom tags for an application.

- To implement a custom tag that's defined in the TLD, you code a *tag class*, which can also be referred to as a *tag handler class*. This is a class that implements the Tag interface, usually by extending the TagSupport class.

- Before you can use a custom tag in a JSP, you must code a *taglib directive* that specifies the location of the TLD and a prefix. Then, to use a custom tag, you code the prefix followed by the name of the custom tag.

- You can use custom tags with a body, without a body, with attributes, and with a repeating body.

- Since JSP 2.0, you can use EL with custom tags to get the value of an attribute. Prior to JSP 2.0, you had to use a JSP expression to get the value of an attribute.

- Prior to JSP 2.0, it was a common practice to use *scripting variables* to make it easier to get the value of an attribute. To provide for these variables, you need to code a *tag extra information* (*TEI*) *class* that is related to a tag class by the TLD.

- As you code the tag classes, you can use the methods and fields of the TagSupport, PageContext, BodyTagSupport, and BodyContent classes of the Java EE API.

Exercise 10-1 Create and use a custom tag

In this exercise, you'll enhance the custom tags for the Email List application.

Use the currentDate tag

1. Open the ch10_ex1_email application that's in the ex_starts folder.

2. Open the murach.tld file that's in the WEB-INF folder. Then, review the information for the custom tag named currentDate.

3. Open the index.jsp file. Note how it uses the custom currentDate tag to display the current date below the form that gets data from the user.

4. Open the thanks.jsp file. Then, modify it so uses the custom currentDate tag to display the current date below the table that displays data about the user. To do this, you'll need to add a taglib directive before the currentDate tag.

5. Run the application to make sure it works correctly.

Modify the ifEmptyMark tag

6. Open the index.jsp file and modify the ifEmptyMark tags so they use the default color, which is defined as red by the class for the tag.

7. Run the application to make sure it works correctly.

Create and use a currentTime tag

8. Create a custom tag for the current time. To do that, you can create a tag class that works much like the CurrentDateTag class. Then, you can add a tag element for this class to the murach.tld file in the WEB-INF folder.

9. Modify the index.jsp file so it displays the current date and the current time.

10. Modify the thanks.jsp file so it displays the current time after the current date.

11. Run the application to make sure it works correctly.

Modify tag classes

12. Modify the CurrentDateTag and CurrentTimeTag classes so they use the LONG format instead of the SHORT format.

13. Run the application to make sure it works correctly. Note how this changes the tags on both of the JSPs.

14. Modify the IfEmptyMarkTag class so the default color is green.

15. Run the application to make sure it works correctly. This should change the color for all of the tags on the first page.

Exercise 10-2   Create and use a reiterating tag

In this exercise, you'll create a custom tag that reiterates through an array list of Product objects.

Create a custom tag that displays a table of products

1. Open the ch10_ex2_cart project that's in the ex_starts folder.

2. Open the ProductsServlet class and the web.xml file. Note that the ProductsServlet class is called when this application starts. Note also that this servlet reads an ArrayList of Product objects from the projects.txt file and stores them as an attribute of the session object.

3. Create a tag class named ProductsTag that's like the CartTag class. However, the new tag class should display all Product objects that are in the ArrayList that has been stored in the session object by the ProductsServlet class.

4. Open the murach.tld file that's stored in the WEB-INF directory and add a tag element for a custom tag named products that uses the ProductsTag class.

5. Open the index.jsp file and modify it so it uses the custom products tag. To do that, you'll need to delete all of the hard-coded rows except one. Then, you can use the attributes that are available from the tag in place of hard-coded values for the row.

6. Run the application to make sure that it works correctly.

Section 3

Essential database skills

For most web applications, the critical data is stored in a database. That's why the three chapters in this section present the essential database skills that you need for developing web applications.

In chapter 11, you'll learn how to use MySQL as the database management system for your databases because MySQL is one of the most popular systems for Java web applications. It is also free. That makes it a great product for learning how to develop web applications that use databases.

In chapter 12, you'll learn how to use JDBC to work with a database. JDBC is an approach that many developers used in the early days of web programming. As a result, you may need to use JDBC to work with legacy web applications.

In chapter 13, you'll learn how to use JPA to work with a database. JPA is a newer approach that makes it easier to write the database layer for an object-oriented web application. As a result, if you're developing a new web application, you may want to use JPA.

JDBC and JPA both work for any database that has a JDBC driver. Since there is a JDBC driver for most databases, the skills presented in chapters 12 and 13 should apply to most databases including MySQL, Oracle, SQL Server, and DB2.

11

How to use a MySQL database

Although there are several database management systems that work well with web applications, MySQL is one of the most popular systems for Java web applications. It's also free for the purposes of this book. That's why we used it as the database management system for the applications in this book. In this chapter, you'll learn how to create a MySQL database and how to use SQL statements to work with the data in that database.

Before you start this chapter, you should know that it assumes that you already have some database knowledge or experience. It assumes, for example, that you know that a relational database is made up of tables that consist of columns and rows, that the tables are related by keys, and that you use SQL statements to access and update the data in a database. Although this chapter does review some of these terms, its focus is on the specific skills that you need for using MySQL.

An introduction to MySQL

Figure 11-1 presents an introduction to MySQL, which is an open-source database management system (DBMS) that you can download for free from the MySQL website (www.mysql.com) as described in appendix A (PC) or B (Mac). It is also available as part of a hosting package from many Internet Service Providers (ISPs).

What MySQL provides

Figure 11-1 begins by listing some of the reasons that MySQL enjoys such popularity among web developers. To start, it's inexpensive and easy to use when compared with products like Oracle Database or Microsoft SQL Server. It runs fast when compared to those products, especially when you consider the costs. And it runs on most modern operating systems, while Microsoft SQL Server runs only on Windows.

Even though it's free for most uses, MySQL provides most of the features that you would expect from a modern *relational database management system* (*RDBMS*). In particular, it provides support for *Structured Query Language* (*SQL*), which is the industry standard. It provides support for multiple clients. And it provides for connectivity and security.

In terms of web applications, that means you can write Java applications that use SQL statements to access and update the data in a MySQL database. You can connect a Java web application to a MySQL database that's running on an intranet or the Internet. And you can secure your data by restricting access to it.

As of release 5.5, MySQL provides referential integrity and transaction processing by default. As a result, these features can be handled on the back-end, which reduces the chance that your data becomes corrupted. This works similarly to commercial databases such as Oracle Database and Microsoft SQL Server.

Prior to MySQL 5.0, MySQL didn't provide referential integrity or transaction processing. As a result, each application that was using MySQL had to provide for these features. In the early days of web programming, this was adequate for many types of web applications. These days, it usually makes sense to have MySQL implement these features.

MySQL is...

- **Inexpensive.** MySQL is free for most uses and relatively inexpensive for other uses.

- **Fast.** By many accounts, MySQL is one of the fastest relational databases that's currently available.

- **Easy to use.** Compared to other database management systems, MySQL is easy to install and use.

- **Portable.** MySQL runs on most modern operating systems including Windows, OS X, and Linux.

MySQL provides...

- **Support for SQL.** Like any modern database product, MySQL supports SQL, which is the standard language for working with data that's stored in relational databases.

- **Support for multiple clients.** MySQL supports access from multiple clients from a variety of interfaces and programming languages including Java, PHP, Python, Perl, and C.

- **Connectivity.** MySQL can provide access to data via an intranet or the Internet.

- **Security.** MySQL can protect access to your data so only authorized users can view the data.

- **Referential integrity.** With MySQL 5.5 and later, InnoDB tables are used by default. These tables support referential integrity, just like commercial databases such as Oracle Database or Microsoft SQL Server.

- **Transaction processing.** With version 5.5, MySQL uses InnoDB tables by default. These tables provide support for transaction processing, just like commercial databases such as Oracle Database or Microsoft SQL Server.

Figure 11-1   An introduction to MySQL

Two ways to interact with MySQL

Figure 11-2 shows two ways that you can interact with MySQL. When you install MySQL as described in appendix A or B, it includes a command-line tool like the one at the top of this figure. Although this shows the command-line for the Windows operating system, MySQL's command-line tool works similarly on all operating systems. In this example, the user has started the command-line tool, logged into a database named murach, and displayed three rows from the User table in that database.

If you install MySQL Workbench as described in appendix A or B, you can use it to work with a database as shown in this chapter. To do that, you can enter a SQL statement in the SQL tab at the top of the tool and click on the Execute button to run the SQL statement. Then, the results for the statement are displayed in the Output window. You can also use the Schemas section of the Navigator window to view and work with the databases that are running on the current server. In this figure, for example, the Schemas section shows the columns for the User table of the murach database.

When you work with MySQL, you may notice that the terms *database* and *schema* are often used interchangeably. For example, the murach database is sometimes referred to as the murach schema.

In general, it's easier to use MySQL Workbench than a command-line tool to work with databases. That's why this chapter shows you how to use MySQL Workbench.

A command-line tool

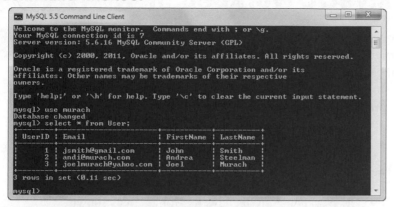

MySQL Workbench

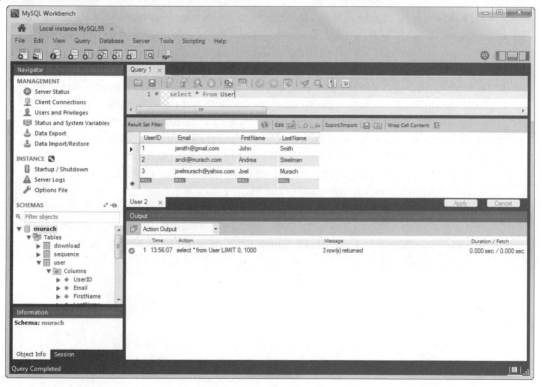

Figure 11-2   Two ways to interact with MySQL

How to use MySQL Workbench

MySQL Workbench is a free graphical tool that makes it easy to work with MySQL. We recommend using this tool as you work through this book. As of press time for this book, the current version of MySQL Workbench is version 6.0, so that's the version presented in this chapter. However, with some minor variations, the skills presented in this chapter should work for earlier and later versions as well.

The Home tab of MySQL Workbench

When you start MySQL Workbench, it displays its Home tab as shown in figure 11-3. This tab is divided into three sections: MySQL Connections, Models, and Shortcuts.

The MySQL Connections section contains links that you can use to open a connection to a MySQL server. Then, you can use that connection to run SQL statements. By default, this tab contains one connection that allows you to connect to a MySQL server that's running on the local computer as the root user. In this book, this is the only connection you'll need. However, you can use the + icon to the right of MySQL Connections to create other connections.

The Models section contains links that let you create a database diagram from a type of data model known as an EER model. Since this book doesn't show how to work with EER models, you can ignore this section.

The Shortcuts section contains links to MySQL documentation, utilities, bug reporting, and other links. You can ignore this section too.

You can return to the Home tab by clicking the tab with the house icon near the top left corner of the Workbench window. In this figure, the Home tab is the only tab that's shown, but you'll see some other tabs in the next few figures.

The Home tab of MySQL Workbench

Description

- The Home tab of MySQL Workbench is divided into three main sections: MySQL Connections, Models, and Shortcuts.

- You can use the MySQL Connections section to stop and start the database server and to code and run SQL statements.

- You can use the Models section to design databases.

- You can use the Shortcuts section to connect to MySQL documentation, utilities, bug reporting, and other links.

- You can return to the Home tab by clicking the tab with the house icon. This tab is always displayed in the top left corner of the Workbench window.

Figure 11-3   The Home tab of MySQL Workbench

How to open a database connection

Before you can work with a database, you need to connect to the database server. When you start MySQL Workbench, the MySQL Connections section displays a list of saved connections.

By default, MySQL Workbench has one saved connection in this list. This connection is named "Local instance MySQL55", and it connects as the root user to a MySQL server that's running on port 3306 of the local host computer. (This assumes that you're using MySQL version 5.5. If you're using another version, the number at the end of the connection name will be different.) Since this is what you want when you're first getting started, you typically use this connection to connect to the server. To do that, you double-click on the connection and enter the password for the root user if you're prompted for it.

If you installed MySQL following the directions in appendix A (PC) or B (Mac), the password for the root user is "sesame." This is necessary for the applications presented in this book to work properly.

Figure 11-4 shows the dialog box that MySQL Workbench displays to prompt for a password. This dialog box shows that it's attempting to use the root user to connect to a MySQL server running on port 3306 of the local host. In addition to entering a password in this dialog box, you can select the "Save password in vault" option to save the password so you don't have to enter it every time you connect to this server. Then, if you ever want to clear the password from the vault, you can select the Manage Connections item from the Database menu, select the connection, and click the Clear button.

If you need to connect as another user, or if you need to connect to a MySQL server running on a different computer, you can use MySQL Workbench to specify custom connection parameters. To do that, select the Manage Connections item from the Database menu. This displays a dialog box that lets you specify the connection parameters, such as the username, the host address, and the port number.

If you want to save a custom connection, you can click the + icon to the right of MySQL Connections in the Home tab and enter the parameters for the connection. Then, this connection appears in the list of connections, and you can double-click it to use it.

The dialog box for opening database connections

Description

- To connect as the root user to an instance of MySQL that's running on the local host computer, double-click on the stored connection named "Local instance MySQL", and enter the password for the root user if prompted.

- To save the password for a connection so you don't have to enter it every time, check the "Save password in vault" option when you're prompted for your password.

- To clear the password from the vault so you are prompted for your password, select the Manage Connections item from the Database menu, select the connection, and click the Clear button.

- To specify your own connection parameters, select the Manage Connections item in the Database menu, enter the connection parameters, click the Close or Test Connection button, and enter the password for the specified user if prompted. This lets you specify the username, the host address, the port number, and other connection parameters.

- To save a connection and add it to the Home tab, click the + icon to the right of MySQL Connections and enter the connection parameters. Then, the connection appears in the list of connections.

Figure 11-4   How to open a database connection

How to start and stop the MySQL server

If you installed MySQL on your computer as described in appendix A (PC) or B (Mac), the *database server* starts automatically when you start your computer. This piece of software is sometimes referred to as the *database service* or *database engine*. It receives SQL statements that are passed to it, processes them, and returns the results.

Before you can work with a MySQL database, the database server must be started. To check whether the MySQL database server is running on your computer, you can use the Startup/Shutdown option of MySQL Workbench as shown in figure 11-5. Then, if the server isn't already running, you can start it by clicking on the Start Server button. When you do that, MySQL Workbench displays a message that indicates the status of the MySQL server, and it displays the Stop Server button.

You may also want to stop the database server from time to time. For example, you can stop the server if you aren't going to be using it and you want to free the resources on your computer. Or, you can stop the server if the port that is being used by the MySQL database server conflicts with another program. Then, when you want to work with the database server again, you can start it.

The easiest way to stop the database server is to use the Stop Server button that's available from the Startup/Shutdown option of the Navigator window of MySQL Workbench as described in this figure. When you click this button, MySQL Workbench displays a message when the MySQL server has successfully stopped, and it displays the Start Server button.

When you're running the MySQL database server on your own computer for training purposes, you can stop the database server whenever you want. However, if a database server is running in a production environment, you should make sure that all users are logged off and that no applications are using the database server before you stop it.

The Startup/Shutdown option of MySQL Workbench

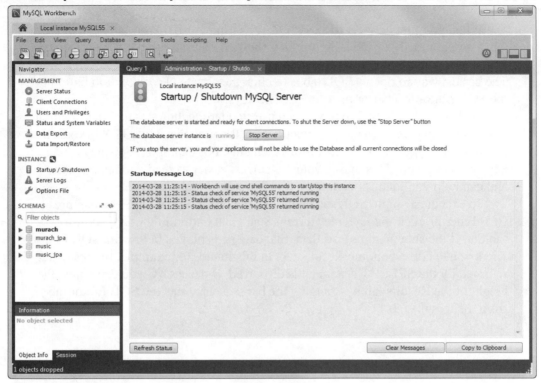

How to stop and start the database server

1. Display the Home tab of MySQL Workbench.

2. In the MySQL Connections section, double-click on the connection to the local server. This should connect you to the local MySQL server as the root user. If necessary, enter the password for the root user. This displays a SQL tab where you can run SQL statements.

3. In the Navigator window, select the Startup/Shutdown option.

4. Click the Stop Server button to stop the database server, or click the Start Server button to start it.

Description

- After you install MySQL, the *database server* usually starts automatically each time you start your computer.

- The database server can also be referred to as the *database service* or the *database engine*.

Figure 11-5   How to start and stop the database server

How to enter and execute a SQL statement

When you first connect to a MySQL server in MySQL Workbench, a SQL tab is automatically opened. Figure 11-6 shows how to use the SQL tab to enter and execute a SQL statement. Note that you can open several SQL tabs at a time. The easiest way to open a SQL tab is to click the Create New SQL Tab button in the SQL Editor toolbar or press the Ctrl+T keys.

Once you open a SQL tab, you can use standard techniques to enter or edit a SQL statement. As you enter statements, you'll notice that MySQL Workbench automatically applies colors to various elements. For example, it displays keywords in green. This makes your statements easier to read and understand and can help you identify coding errors.

To execute a single SQL statement like the one in this figure, you can press Ctrl+Enter or click the Execute Current Statement button in the SQL Editor toolbar. If the statement returns data, that data is displayed below the SQL Editor window in a corresponding Results tab. In this figure, for example, the result set returned by the SELECT statement is displayed. If necessary, you can adjust the height of the Results tab by dragging the bar that separates the SQL Editor tab from the Results tab.

A SELECT statement and its results

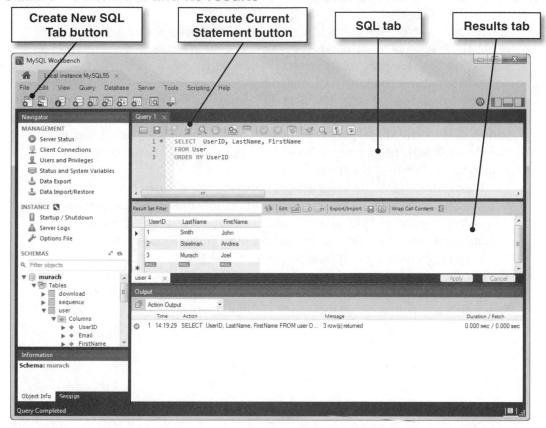

Description

- To open a new SQL tab, press Ctrl+T or click the Create New SQL Tab button (🗔) in the SQL editor toolbar.

- To select the current database, double-click it in the Schemas section of the Navigator window. This displays the selected database in bold.

- To enter a SQL statement, type it into the SQL tab.

- As you enter the text for a statement, the SQL tab applies color to various elements, such as SQL keywords, to make them easy to identify.

- To execute a SQL statement, press Ctrl+Enter, or click the Execute Current Statement button (🗲)in the SQL editor toolbar. If the statement retrieves data, the data is displayed in a Results tab below the SQL tab.

Figure 11-6   How to enter and execute a SQL statement

How to enter and execute a SQL script

In the last topic, you saw a *SQL script* that contained a single SQL statement. However, a SQL script typically contains multiple statements. Figure 11-7 shows how to enter and execute scripts like that.

When you code multiple SQL statements within a script, you must code a semicolon at the end of each statement. For example, this figure shows a script that contains two SELECT statements. To execute both of these statements, you can press the Ctrl+Shift+Enter keys, or you can click the Execute SQL Script button in the SQL editor toolbar. When you do, the results of each script are displayed in a separate Results tab.

If you want to execute a single SQL statement that's stored within a script, you can do that by moving the insertion point into the statement and pressing the Ctrl+Enter keys or clicking the Execute Current Statement button. Then, if the statement retrieves data, the data is displayed in a single Results tab.

If you need to, you can also execute two or more statements in a script. To do that, you select the statements and then press the Ctrl+Shift+Enter keys or click the Execute SQL Script button. This is useful if a script contains many statements and you just want to execute some of them.

A SQL script and its results

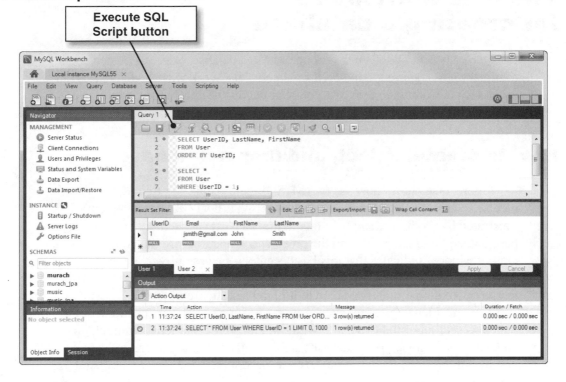

Description

- When you code a script that contains more than one statement, you must code a semicolon at the end of each statement.

- To run an entire SQL script, press the Ctrl+Shift+Enter keys or click the Execute SQL Script button ( ) that's located just to the left of the Execute Current Statement button in the SQL editor toolbar.

- When you run a SQL script, the results of each statement that returns data are displayed in a separate Results tab.

- To execute one SQL statement within a script, move the insertion point into that statement and press Ctrl+Enter or click the Execute Current Statement button ( ). If the statement retrieves data, the data is displayed in a Results tab.

- To execute two or more statements within a script, select them in the editor and then press Ctrl+Shift+Enter or click the Execute SQL Script button.

Figure 11-7   How to enter and execute a SQL script

The SQL statements for creating a database

Once MySQL Workbench is connected to a database server, you can use it to run *MySQL commands* and *SQL statements* that work with the databases that are available from that server. As you read the rest of this chapter, you'll see examples of each.

How to create, select, and drop a database

Figure 11-8 shows how use two MySQL commands and two SQL statements. To create a database, you use the CREATE DATABASE statement as illustrated by the first example in this figure. Here, this statement creates a database named "murach_test", and the green check mark before the command in the Output window indicates that this has been done successfully. Note, however, that this database hasn't been defined yet and it doesn't contain any data. You'll learn how to define it and add data to it in the next figures.

To view the names of the databases stored on a server, you can look at the Schemas section of the Navigator window. Here, the "murach", "murach_jpa", "music", and "music_jpa" databases are the databases that are created when you install our downloadable databases as described in the appendices. And the "murach_test" database is the one created by the first example.

To select the database that you want to work with, you use the USE command as illustrated by the second example. This selects the "murach_test" database, and the "murach_test" database appears in bold in the Schemas window to indicate that the statement was successful. After you select a database, the commands and statements that you enter work with that database. You can also select a database by double clicking on it in the Schemas window in MySQL Workbench. The selected database will appear in bold in the Schemas window.

To delete a database from the server, you use the DROP DATABASE statement as illustrated by the third example. Here, the "murach_test" database is deleted. When you successfully delete a database, MySQL Workbench displays a message in the Output window with a green check mark along with the number of rows that were deleted from the tables in the database.

MySQL Workbench after a statement has been executed

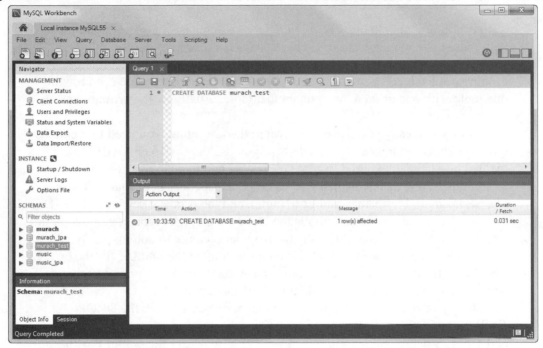

How to create a database

```
CREATE DATABASE murach_test
```

How to select a database for use

```
USE murach_test
```

How to drop a database

```
DROP DATABASE murach_test
```

Description

- You can use the CREATE DATABASE statement to create a database and the DROP DATABASE statement to delete a database. These are *SQL statements*.

- You can use the USE command to select the database that you want to work with. This is a *MySQL command*.

- You can also select a database by double-clicking on it in the Schemas section in MySQL Workbench.

- The selected database will appear in bold in the Schemas section.

Figure 11-8   How to create, select, and drop a database

How to create and drop a table

As you probably know, a *relational database* consists of one or more *tables* that consist of *rows* and *columns*. These tables are related by the *keys* in the rows. The *primary key* is a column that provides a unique value that identifies each row in a table. A *foreign key* is a column that is used to relate each row in one table with one or more rows in another table, usually by the primary keys in those rows.

After you create a database as shown in the last figure, you need to create its tables as shown in figure 11-9. To do that, you use the CREATE TABLE statement. This statement is used to name each table and to define its columns.

In this figure, a table named User is created that consists of four columns (UserID, Email, FirstName, and LastName), and the primary key is the UserID column. Here, the UserID column is the INT (integer) data type, it can't contain a null value, and it uses MySQL's auto-increment feature to automatically generate a unique integer for each new row by incrementing the number for the last row. In contrast, the other three columns have the VARCHAR (variable character) data type and can hold a maximum of 50 characters.

Once you've created the tables for a database, you can use the DROP TABLE statement to delete one of them. This deletes the structure of the table and all of its data. That's useful when you want to modify the definitions for the columns in a table. An efficient way to do that is to delete the table you want to change, modify the script for the table, and rerun the script to recreate the table.

If the specified table doesn't exist, this statement generates an error. To prevent this, you can add the IF EXISTS keywords to the statement as shown in the third example.

Please note, however, that the purpose of this figure is *not* to teach you how to create the tables for a database. Instead, the purpose of this figure is to introduce you to the statements for creating and deleting the tables in a database.

How to create a table

```
CREATE TABLE User (
    UserID INT NOT NULL AUTO_INCREMENT,
    Email VARCHAR(50),
    FirstName VARCHAR(50),
    LastName VARCHAR(50),
    PRIMARY KEY(UserID)
)
```

How to drop a table

```
DROP TABLE User
```

How to drop a table only if it exists

```
DROP TABLE IF EXISTS User
```

Description

- A *relational database* consists of one or more *tables* that consist of *rows* (*records*) and *columns* (*fields*). These tables are related by *keys*. The *primary key* in a table is the one that uniquely identifies each of the rows in the table. A *foreign key* is used to relate the rows in one table to the rows in another table.

- When you create a table, you define each of its columns and you identify its primary key. To define a column, you must supply the name and the data type, whether it's automatically generated for new rows, and so on.

- If a specified table does not exist, the DROP TABLE statement will generate an error. You can avoid this by using the DROP TABLE IF EXISTS statement.

- On Unix systems, the table and column names are case-sensitive.

Figure 11-9   How to create and drop a table

How to insert multiple rows into a table

After you've created a table, you can fill the table with data. Figure 11-10 shows how to do that. You can use the INSERT statement to insert one or more rows into a table.

This figure starts by showing how to execute an INSERT statement that inserts three rows into the User table that you learned how to create in the last figure. You can store the statement in an SQL script and execute the script.

To begin an INSERT statement, you code the INSERT INTO keywords. Then, you code the table name followed by a set of parentheses. Within the parentheses, you code a list of the column names for the table. Although the SQL keywords aren't case-sensitive, the table and column names are case-sensitive on Unix systems. As a result, it's a good programming practice to code these names using the correct case.

After the list of column names, you code the VALUES keyword followed by a set of parentheses. Within these parentheses, you can code the values that should be inserted into each row. If you want to code more than one row of values, you can separate each row with a comma. In this figure, for example, the INSERT statement inserts three rows. Note that you don't need to include values for columns that use MySQL's auto increment feature or are defined with default values. In this case, since the value for the UserID column is automatically generated, you don't need to include it.

How to use the INSERT statement

```
INSERT INTO User
   (FirstName, LastName, Email)
VALUES
   ('John', 'Smith', 'jsmith@gmail.com'),
   ('Andrea', 'Steelman', 'andi@murach.com'),
   ('Joel', 'Murach', 'joelmurach@yahoo.com')
```

Description

- The INSERT statement lets you insert one or more rows into one table of a database. When you code it, you need to include data for all columns that aren't defined with default values or aren't automatically generated.

- On a Unix system, table and column names are case-sensitive.

Figure 11-10   How to insert multiple rows into a table

The SQL statements for data manipulation

With the exception of the INSERT statement, the SQL statements that you've seen thus far have been part of SQL's *Data Definition Language (DDL)*. These statements let you create databases, create tables, drop tables, and so on, but they don't work with the data in the tables.

In contrast, the statements that you'll learn about next make up SQL's *Data Manipulation Language (DML)*. These statements work with the data in a database, and they include the SELECT, INSERT, UPDATE, and DELETE statements. As a result, these are the statements that you typically use in your Java applications.

How to select data from a single table

The SELECT statement is the most commonly used SQL statement. It can be used to retrieve data from one or more tables in a database. When you run a SELECT statement, it is commonly referred to as a *query* (although the execution of any SQL statement can also be referred to as a query). The result of this query is always a table known as a *result set*, or a *result table*.

In figure 11-11, the first example shows how to use this statement to retrieve all rows and columns from the User table. Here, the SELECT clause uses the asterisk wildcard to indicate that all of the columns in the table should be retrieved. Then, the FROM clause identifies the User table. In the result table, three rows and four columns are returned by this query.

The second example shows how to use this statement to retrieve two columns and two rows from the User table. Here, the SELECT clause identifies the two columns, and the FROM clause identifies the table. Then, the WHERE clause limits the number of rows that are retrieved by specifying that the statement should only retrieve rows where the value in the UserID column is less than 3. Last, the ORDER BY clause indicates that the retrieved rows should be sorted in ascending order (from A to Z) by the LastName column.

The result set is a logical table that's created temporarily within the database. Then, the *current row pointer*, or *cursor*, keeps track of the current row. You can use this pointer from your web applications.

As you might guess, queries can have a significant effect on the performance of a database application. In general, the more columns and rows that a query returns, the more traffic the network has to bear. As a result, when you design queries, you should try to keep the number of columns and rows to a minimum.

The syntax for a SELECT statement that gets all columns

```
SELECT *
FROM table-1
[WHERE selection-criteria]
[ORDER BY column-1 [ASC|DESC] [, column-2 [ASC|DESC] ...]]
```

Example

```
SELECT * FROM User
```

Result set

	UserID	Email	FirstName	LastName
▶	1	jsmith@gmail.com	John	Smith
	2	andi@murach.com	Andrea	Steelman
	3	joelmurach@yahoo.com	Joel	Murach
✻	NULL	NULL	NULL	NULL

The syntax for a SELECT statement that gets selected columns

```
SELECT column-1 [,column-2] ...
FROM table-1
[WHERE selection-criteria]
[ORDER BY column-1 [ASC|DESC] [,column-2 [ASC|DESC] ...]]
```

Example

```
SELECT FirstName, LastName
FROM User
WHERE UserID < 3
ORDER BY LastName ASC
```

Result set

	FirstName	LastName
▶	John	Smith
	Andrea	Steelman

Description

- A SELECT statement is a SQL DML statement that returns a *result set* (or *result table*) that consists of the specified rows and columns.
- To specify the columns, you use the SELECT clause.
- To specify the rows, you use the WHERE clause.
- To specify the table that the data should be retrieved from, you use the FROM clause.
- To specify how the result set should be sorted, you use the ORDER BY clause.

Figure 11-11   How to select data from a single table

How to select data from multiple tables

Figure 11-12 shows how to use the SELECT statement to retrieve data from two tables. This is commonly known as a *join*. The result of any join is a single result table.

An *inner join* is the most common type of join. When you use one, the data from the rows in the two tables are included in the result set only if their related columns match. In this figure, the SELECT statement joins the data from the rows in the User and Download tables only if the value of the UserID column in the User table is equal to the UserID column in the Download table. In other words, if there isn't any data in the Download table for a user, that user won't be added to the result set.

Another type of join is an *outer join*. With this type of join, all of the records in one of the tables are included in the result set whether or not there are matching records in the other table. In a *left outer join*, all of the records in the first table (the one on the left) are included in the result set. In a *right outer join*, all of the records in the second table are included. To illustrate, assume that the SELECT statement in this figure had used a left outer join. In that case, all of the records in the User table would have been included in the result set…even if no matching record was found in the Download table.

To code a join, you use the JOIN clause to specify the second table and the ON clause to specify the columns to be used for the join. If a column in one table has the same name as a column in the other table, you code the table name, a dot, and the column name to specify the column that you want to use. You can see this in the ON clause of the example in this figure.

Although this figure only shows how to join data from two tables, you can extend this syntax to join data from additional tables. If, for example, you want to create a result set that includes data from three tables named User, Download, and Product, you can code the FROM clause of the SELECT statement like this:

```
FROM User
    INNER JOIN Download
        ON User.UserID = Download.UserID
    INNER JOIN Product
        ON Download.ProductCode = Product.ProductCode
```

Then, you can include any of the columns from the three tables in the column list of the SELECT statement.

The syntax for a SELECT statement that joins two tables

```
SELECT column-1 [,column-2] ...
FROM table-1
    {INNER | LEFT OUTER | RIGHT OUTER} JOIN table-2
    ON table-1. column-1 {=|<|>|<=|>=|<>} table-2.column-2
[WHERE selection-criteria]
[ORDER BY column-1 [ASC|DESC] [,column-2 [ASC|DESC] ...]]
```

A statement that gets data from related User and Download tables

```
SELECT Email, DownloadFilename, DownloadDate
FROM User
    INNER JOIN Download
    ON User.UserID = Download.UserID
WHERE DownloadDate > '2014-01-01'
ORDER BY Email ASC
```

Result set

Email	DownloadFilename	DownloadDate
andi@murach.com	jr01_filter.mp3	2014-03-27 13:05:39
joelmurach@yahoo.com	jr01_so_long.mp3	2014-03-27 13:05:39
jsmith@gmail.com	jr01_so_long.mp3	2014-02-01 00:00:00
jsmith@gmail.com	jr01_filter.mp3	2014-03-27 13:05:39

Description

- To return a result set that contains data from two tables, you *join* the tables. To do that, you can use a JOIN clause. Most of the time, you'll want to code an *inner join* so that rows are only included when the key of a row in the first table matches the key of a row in the second table.

- In a *left outer join*, the data for all of the rows in the first table (the one on the left) are included in the table, but only the data for matching rows in the second table are included. In a *right outer join*, the reverse is true.

- An inner join is the default type of join. As a result, it's common to omit the INNER keyword from a SELECT statement for an inner join.

Figure 11-12   How to select data from multiple tables

How to insert, update, and delete data

Figure 11-13 shows how to use the INSERT, UPDATE, and DELETE statements to add, update, or delete one or more records in a database.

The syntax and examples for the INSERT statement show how to use this statement to add one record to a database. To do that, the statement supplies the names of the columns that are going to receive values in the new record, followed by the values for those columns. Here, the first example inserts one row into the Download table. The second example also inserts one row into the Download table, but it uses the NOW function provided by MySQL to automatically insert the current date and time into the DownloadDate column.

Similarly, the syntax and examples for the UPDATE statement show how to update records. In the first example, the UPDATE statement updates the FirstName column in the record where the Email is equal to jsmith@gmail.com. In the second example, the ProductPrice column is updated to 36.95 in all of the records where the ProductPrice is equal to 36.50.

Last, the syntax and examples for the DELETE statement show how to delete records. Here, the first example deletes the record from the User table where the Email column equals jsmith@gmail.com. Since each record contains a unique value in the Email column, this only deletes a single record. However, in the second example, multiple records in the Download table may have a DownloadDate column that's less than June 1, 2014. As a result, this statement deletes all records that satisfy this condition.

When you issue an INSERT, UPDATE, or DELETE statement from a Java application, you usually work with one record at a time. You'll see this illustrated by the Email List application in the next chapter. SQL statements that affect more than one record are typically issued by database administrators.

The syntax for the INSERT statement

```
INSERT INTO table-name [(column-list)]
VALUES (value-list)
```

A statement that adds one row to the Download table

```
INSERT INTO Download (UserID, DownloadDate, DownloadFilename, ProductCode)
VALUES (1, '2014-05-01', 'jr01_so_long.mp3', 'jr01')
```

A statement that uses the MySQL Now function to get the current date

```
INSERT INTO Download (UserID, DownloadDate, DownloadFilename, ProductCode)
VALUES (1, NOW(), 'jr01_filter.mp3', 'jr01')
```

The syntax for the UPDATE statement

```
UPDATE table-name
SET expression-1 [, expression-2] ...
WHERE selection-criteria
```

A statement that updates the FirstName column in one row

```
UPDATE User
SET FirstName = 'Jack'
WHERE Email = 'jsmith@gmail.com'
```

A statement that updates the ProductPrice column in selected rows

```
UPDATE Product
SET ProductPrice = 36.95
WHERE ProductPrice = 36.50
```

The syntax for the DELETE statement

```
DELETE FROM table-name
WHERE selection-criteria
```

A statement that deletes one row from the User table

```
DELETE FROM User WHERE Email = 'jsmith@gmail.com'
```

A statement that deletes selected rows from the Downloads table

```
DELETE FROM Download WHERE DownloadDate < '2014-06-01'
```

Description

- Since the INSERT, UPDATE, and DELETE statements modify the data that's stored in a database, they're sometimes referred to as *action queries*. These statements don't return a result set. Instead, they return the number of rows that were affected by the query.

Figure 11-13   How to insert, update, and delete data

Perspective

The primary goal of this chapter is to present the basic skills that you need for using MySQL. A secondary goal is to introduce you to the SELECT, INSERT, UPDATE, and DELETE statements that you'll use as you develop database applications with Java. If this chapter has succeeded, you should now be able to use the MySQL Workbench to run MySQL commands, SQL statements, and SQL scripts.

In the next chapter, you'll learn how to use a servlet to connect to a MySQL database. You'll also learn how to use the SELECT, INSERT, UPDATE, and DELETE statements in your web applications.

Keep in mind, though, that this chapter has presented just a small subset of SQL skills. In particular, it has presented the least you need to know about SQL statements for understanding the Java code that is presented in the next chapter. For a complete mastery of SQL, you'll probably want to get a book about SQL for the database that you're using. If, for example, you're using MySQL for your applications, *Murach's MySQL* presents all of the SQL statements that you'll need for your applications.

Summary

- MySQL is a *relational database management system* (*RDBMS*) that can manage one or more *databases*. To retrieve and modify the data in one of its databases, MySQL provides support for *Structured Query Language* (*SQL)*, which is the standard language for working with databases.

- Whenever you use MySQL, its *database server* must be running. Usually, this server starts automatically whenever you start your system.

- To work with a MySQL database, you can use a graphical tool called MySQL Workbench. It makes it easy to enter and run *MySQL commands* and *SQL statements*.

- A *SQL script* is a file that stores SQL statements.

- The SQL statements that you use for creating and deleting databases and tables are part of the *Data Definition Language* (*DDL*).

- The SQL statements that you use for retrieving and modifying the data in a database make up the *Data Manipulation Language* (*DML*). These are the SELECT, INSERT, UPDATE, and DELETE statements.

- The SELECT statement is used to get data from one or more tables and put it in a *result set*, or *result table*. This is commonly referred to as a *query*.

- The INSERT, UPDATE, and DELETE statements are used to add one or more rows to a table, update the data in one or more rows, and delete one or more rows.

Before you do the exercises for this chapter

If you haven't already done so, you should install MySQL, MySQL Workbench, and the source files for this book as described in appendix A or B.

Exercise 11-1   Review a SQL script

1. Start MySQL Workbench.

2. In the MySQL Connections section, double-click on the "Local instance MySQL" item. If prompted, enter the password for the root user. This should connect you to the local MySQL server as the root user.

3. Use MySQL Workbench to open the create_databases.sql file that's in the servlets_and_jsp\db directory.

4. Note that this script contains the statements that create the murach and music databases, create their tables, and insert rows into some tables.

5. Note that this script also contains the statements that create the murach_jpa and music_jpa databases. However, for the murach_jpa database, it lets JPA create the tables as described in chapter 13.

6. Note that this script uses the DROP DATABASE command to delete the databases before it builds them.

7. Run this script. It should execute without displaying any errors. If it displays any errors, read the error message and troubleshoot the problem.

Exercise 11-2   Use MySQL Workbench

1. Start MySQL Workbench.

2. In the MySQL Connections section, double-click on the "Local instance MySQL" item. If prompted, enter the password for the root user. This should connect you to the local MySQL server as the root user.

3. View the Schemas section of the Navigator window and note which databases are installed on your system.

4. View the tables for the music database by expanding it and its Tables node.

5. View the tables for the murach database by expanding it and its Tables node.

6. Select the music database by double clicking on it in the Schemas section. This should display the database name in bold.

7. Select the murach database by running the USE command. This should display the database name in bold.

8. Run the first SELECT statement in figure 11-11 to view the data stored in the User table of the murach database.

9. Run the first UPDATE statement in figure 11-13. Then, run the SELECT statement in figure 1-11 again to view the updated data.

12

How to use JDBC to work with a database

This chapter shows how to use the JDBC API to work with a database. This API requires the developer to write a significant amount of low-level data access code. Many legacy applications use JDBC. As a result, you may need to use it when working on old applications.

For new development, you might prefer to use JPA, which doesn't require the developer to write as much code. In that case, you can skip to the next chapter. However, since JPA uses a JDBC driver, you should read the first two figures of this chapter to learn how to use a JDBC driver to connect to a database.

The basic skills for using JDBC are the same for web applications as they are for other types of applications. As a result, if you've used JDBC before, you're probably already familiar with most of the skills presented in this chapter.

How to work with JDBC

To write Java code that works with a database, you can use *JDBC*, which is sometimes referred to as *Java Database Connectivity*. The core JDBC API is stored in the java.sql package, which comes as part of the Standard Edition of Java. In this topic, you'll learn how to use JDBC to connect to a database, and you'll learn how to retrieve and modify the data that's stored in a database.

An introduction to database drivers

Before you can connect to a database, you must make a *database driver* available to your application. Figure 12-1 lists the four types of JDBC database drivers that you can use. Then, it shows how to download a database driver and make it available to your web applications. Since type-1 and type-2 database drivers require installation on the client side, they aren't ideal for allowing an application that's running on the client to directly access a database that's running on the server. As a result, you'll typically want to use a type-3 or type-4 driver for this type of application.

With a web application, of course, all of the data access code runs on the server side. As a result, you can use any type of driver to connect to the database. However, you'll typically want to use a type-4 driver whenever one is available for the database that you're using.

If you want to connect to a MySQL database, you can use the type-4 driver named Connector/J that's available for free from the MySQL website. However, this driver is typically included in Tomcat's lib directory. As a result, you don't usually need to download this driver from the MySQL site.

For other types of databases, you can usually download a type-4 driver from the website for that database. The documentation for these drivers typically shows how to install and configure the driver.

To use the database driver in an application, you must add the JAR file that contains the database driver to the application's classpath. The easiest way to do that is to use your IDE to add the JAR file for the database driver to your application. To add a MySQL driver to NetBeans, you can right-click on the project's Library folder, select the Add Library command, and use the resulting dialog box to select the library named MySQL JDBC Driver.

The four types of JDBC database drivers

Type 1	A *JDBC-ODBC bridge driver* converts JDBC calls into ODBC calls that access the DBMS protocol. For this data access method, the ODBC driver must be installed on the client machine.
Type 2	A *native protocol partly Java driver* converts JDBC calls into calls in the native DBMS protocol. Since this conversion takes place on the client, some binary code must be installed on the client machine.
Type 3	A *net protocol all Java driver* converts JDBC calls into a net protocol that's independent of any native DBMS protocol. Then, middleware software running on a server converts the net protocol to the native DBMS protocol. Since this conversion takes place on the server side, no installation is required on the client machine.
Type 4	A *native protocol all Java driver* converts JDBC calls into a native DBMS protocol. Since this conversion takes place on the server side, no installation is required on the client machine.

How to download a database driver

- For MySQL databases, you can download a JDBC driver named Connector/J from the MySQL website. This driver is an open-source, type-4 driver that's available for free. However, you don't usually need to do this since Tomcat includes this driver in its lib directory.

- For other databases, you can usually download a type-4 JDBC driver from the database's website.

How to make a database driver available to an application

- Before you can use a database driver, you must make it available to your application. The easiest way to do this is to use your IDE to add the JAR file for the driver to your application.

- To add the MySQL JDBC driver to a NetBeans project, right-click on the Libraries folder, select the Add Library command, and use the resulting dialog box to select the MySQL JDBC Driver library.

- To add any JDBC driver to a NetBeans project, right-click on the Libraries folder, select the Add JAR/Folder command, and use the resulting dialog box to select the JAR file for the driver.

Figure 12-1   An introduction to database drivers

How to connect to a database

Before you can access or modify the data in a database, you must connect to the database as shown in figure 12-2. To start, this figure shows the syntax for a database URL. You can use this syntax within the code that gets the connection.

The first example shows how to use a type-4 MySQL driver to get a connection to a database. To start, you use the getConnection method of the DriverManager class to return a Connection object. This method requires three arguments: the URL for the database, a username, and a password. In the first example, the URL consists of the API (jdbc), the subprotocol for MySQL drivers (mysql), the host machine (localhost), the port for the database service (3306), and the name of the database (murach).

Since this code supplies a username of root, this connection has all privileges for all databases on the server. For security reasons, it's considered a best practice to only give a connection the database privileges that the connection needs. That's why the script that creates the murach database creates a user named murach_user that only has limited privileges for working with the murach database. As a result, the user named murach_user is appropriate for most of the sample applications presented in this chapter.

The second example shows how to connect to an Oracle database. Here again, you provide the URL for the database, a user name, and a password. This is true no matter what type of database you're using with JDBC.

In practice, connecting to the database is often frustrating because it's hard to figure out what the URL, username, and password need to be. So if your colleagues have already made a connection to the database that you need to use, you can start by asking them for this information.

Since the getConnection method of the DriverManager class throws an SQLException, you need to handle this exception whenever you connect to a database. With JDBC 4.0 (Java SE 6) and later, you can use an enhanced for statement to loop through any exceptions that are nested within the SQLException object. In this figure, the catch block in the first example loops through all the exceptions that are nested in the SQLException object.

To do that, this loop retrieves a Throwable object named t for each nested exception. Then, it prints the stack trace for this exception. This works because the Throwable class is the superclass for all exceptions, and a Throwable object is returned by the iterator for the SQLException class.

The first two examples present a new feature of JDBC 4.0 called *automatic driver loading*. This feature loads the database driver automatically based on the URL for the database.

If you're working with an older version of Java, though, you need to use the forName method of the Class class to explicitly load the driver before you call the getConnection method as shown by the third example. Since this method throws a ClassNotFoundException, you also have to handle this exception.

Even with JDBC 4.0, you sometimes get a message that says, "No suitable driver found." In that case, you can use the forName method of the Class class to explicitly load the driver. However, if automatic driver loading works, it usually makes sense to remove this method call from your code. That way, you can

Database URL syntax

```
jdbc:subprotocolName:databaseURL
```

How to connect to a MySQL database with automatic driver loading

```
try {
    String dbURL = "jdbc:mysql://localhost:3306/murach";
    String username = "root";
    String password = "sesame";
    Connection connection = DriverManager.getConnection(
        dbURL, username, password);
} catch(SQLException e) {
    for (Throwable t : e)
        t.printStackTrace();
}
```

How to connect to an Oracle database with automatic driver loading

```
Connection connection = DriverManager.getConnection(
    "jdbc:oracle:thin@localhost/murach", "scott", "tiger");
```

How to load a MySQL database driver prior to JDBC 4.0

```
try {
    Class.forName("com.mysql.jdbc.Driver");
} catch(ClassNotFoundException e) {
    e.printStackTrace();
}
```

Description

- Before you can get or modify the data in a database, you need to connect to it. To do that, you use the getConnection method of the DriverManager class to return a Connection object.

- When you use the getConnection method of the DriverManager class, you must supply a URL for the database, a username, and a password. This method throws an SQLException.

- With JDBC 4.0, the SQLException class implements the Iterable interface. As a result, you can use an enhanced for statement to loop through any nested exceptions.

- With JDBC 4.0, the database driver is loaded automatically. This new feature is known as *automatic driver loading*. Prior to JDBC 4.0, you needed to use the forName method of the Class class to load the driver. This method throws a ClassNotFoundException.

- Although the connection string for each driver is different, the documentation for the driver should explain how to write a connection string for that driver.

- Typically, you only need to connect to one database for an application. However, it's possible to load multiple database drivers and establish connections to multiple types of databases.

Figure 12-2   How to connect to a database

connect to the database with less code, and you don't have to hard code the name of the database driver.

How to return a result set and move the cursor through it

Once you connect to a database, you're ready to retrieve data from it as shown in figure 12-3. Here, the first two examples show how to use Statement objects to create a *result set*, or *result table*. Then, the next two examples show how to move the *row pointer*, or *cursor*, through the result set.

Both of the result sets in this figure are read-only, forward-only result sets. This means that you can only move the cursor forward through the result set, and that you can read but not write rows in the result set. Although JDBC 4.0 supports other types of scrollable, updateable result sets, these features require some additional overhead, and they aren't necessary for most web applications.

In the first example, the createStatement method is called from a Connection object to return a Statement object. Then, the executeQuery method is called from the Statement object to execute an SQL SELECT statement that's coded as a string. This returns a ResultSet object that contains the result set for the SELECT statement. In this case, the SELECT statement only retrieves a single column from a single row (the user ID for a specific email address) so that's what the ResultSet object contains. This object can be checked to see whether a row exists.

The second example works like the first example. However, it returns all of the rows and columns for the Product table and puts this result set in a ResultSet object named products. This object can be used to display all products.

The third example shows how to use the next method of the ResultSet object to move the cursor to the first row of the result set that's created by the first example. When you create a result set, the cursor is positioned before the first row in the result set so the first use of the next method attempts to move the cursor to the first row in the result set. If the row exists, the cursor is moved to that row and the next method returns a true value. Otherwise, the next method returns a false value. In the next figure, you'll learn how to retrieve values from the row that the cursor is on.

The fourth example shows how to use the next method to loop through all of the rows in the result set that's created in the second example. Here, the while loop calls the next method. Then, if the next row is a valid row, the next method moves the cursor to the row and returns a true value. As a result, the code within the while loop is executed. Otherwise, the next method returns a false value and the code within the while loop isn't executed.

Since all of the methods described in this figure throw an SQLException, you either need to throw or catch this exception when you're working with these methods. The applications presented later in this chapter show how this works.

Although there are other ResultSet methods, the one you'll use the most with a forward-only, read-only result set is the next method. In this figure, though, three other methods are summarized that you may occasionally want to use for this type of result set.

How to create a result set that contains 1 row and 1 column

```
Statement statement = connection.createStatement();
ResultSet userIDResult = statement.executeQuery(
    "SELECT UserID FROM User " +
    "WHERE Email = 'jsmith@gmail.com'");
```

How to create a result set that contains multiple columns and rows

```
Statement statement = connection.createStatement();
ResultSet products = statement.executeQuery(
    "SELECT * FROM Product ");
```

How to move the cursor to the first row in the result set

```
boolean userIDExists = userIDResult.next();
```

How to loop through a result set

```
while (products.next()) {
    // statements that process each row
}
```

ResultSet methods for forward-only, read-only result sets

Method	Description
next()	Moves the cursor to the next row in the result set.
last()	Moves the cursor to the last row in the result set.
close()	Releases the result set's resources.
getRow()	Returns an int value that identifies the current row of the result set.

Description

- To return a *result set*, you use the createStatement method of a Connection object to create a Statement object. Then, you use the executeQuery method of the Statement object to execute a SELECT statement that returns a ResultSet object.

- By default, the createStatement method creates a forward-only, read-only result set. This means that you can only move the *cursor* through it from the first row to the last and that you can't update it. Although you can pass arguments to the createStatement method that create other types of result sets, the default is appropriate for most web applications.

- When a result set is created, the cursor is positioned before the first row. Then, you can use the methods of the ResultSet object to move the cursor. To move the cursor to the next row, for example, you call the next method. If the row is valid, this method moves the cursor to the next row and returns a true value. Otherwise, it returns a false value.

- The createStatement, executeQuery, and next methods throw an SQLException. As a result, any code that uses these methods needs to catch or throw this exception.

Figure 12-3   How to return a result set and move the cursor through it

How to retrieve data from a result set

When the cursor is positioned on the row that you want to get data from, you can use the methods in figure 12-4 to get that data. Although the examples show how to use the getString and getDouble methods of the ResultSet object to return String values and double values, you can use similar get methods to return other types of data.

The methods in this figure show the two types of arguments accepted by the get methods. The first method accepts an int value that specifies the index number of the column in the result set, where 1 is the first column, 2 is the second column, and so on. The second method accepts a string value that specifies the name of the column in the result set. Although the get methods with column indexes run slightly faster and require less typing, the get methods with column names lead to code that's easier to read and understand.

The first example shows how to use column indexes to return data from a result set named products. Here, the first two statements use the getString method to return the code and description for the current product while the third statement uses the getDouble method to return the price of the product. Since these methods use the column index, the first column in the result set must contain the product code, the second column must contain the product description, and so on.

The second example shows how to use column names to return data from the products result set. Since this code uses the column names, the order of the columns in the result set doesn't matter. However, the column names must exist in the result set or an SQLException is thrown that indicates that a column wasn't found.

The third example shows how you can use the get methods to create a Product object. Here, the constructor for the Product object uses three values that are returned by the get methods to create a new product. Since objects are often created from data that's stored in a database, code like this is commonly used.

If you look up the ResultSet interface in the java.sql package of the documentation for the Java API, you'll see that get methods are available for all of the primitive types and for other types of data too. For example, get methods are available for the Date, Time, and Timestamp classes that are a part of the java.sql package. For many purposes, though, like displaying numbers and dates, you can use the getString method to return a string representation of the data type.

Methods of a ResultSet object that return data from a result set

Method	Description
getXXX(int columnIndex)	Returns data from the specified column number.
getXXX(String columnName)	Returns data from the specified column name.

Code that uses indexes to return columns from the products result set

```
String code = products.getString(1);
String description = products.getString(2);
double price = products.getDouble(3);
```

Code that uses names to return the same columns

```
String code = products.getString("ProductCode");
String description = products.getString("ProductDescription");
double price = products.getDouble("ProductPrice");
```

Code that creates a Product object from the products result set

```
Product product = new Product(products.getString(1),
                              products.getString(2),
                              products.getDouble(3));
```

Description

- The getXXX methods can be used to return all eight primitive types. For example, the getInt method returns the int type and the getLong method returns the long type.

- The getXXX methods can also be used to return strings, dates, and times. For example, the getString method returns any object of the String class, and the getDate, getTime, and getTimestamp methods return objects of the Date, Time, and Timestamp classes of the java.sql package.

Figure 12-4   How to retrieve data from a result set

How to insert, update, and delete data

Figure 12-5 shows how to use JDBC to modify the data in a database. To do that, you use the executeUpdate method of a Statement object to execute SQL statements that add, update, and delete data. Since this method has been a part of Java since version 1.0 of JDBC, it should work for all JDBC drivers.

When you work with the executeUpdate method, you just pass an SQL statement to the database. In these examples, the code adds, updates, and deletes a product in the Product table. To do that, the code combines data from a Product object with the appropriate SQL statement. For the UPDATE and DELETE statements, the SQL statement uses the product's code in the WHERE clause to select a single product.

Unfortunately, if you build an SQL statement from user input and use a method of the Statement object to execute that SQL statement, you may be susceptible to a security vulnerability known as a SQL injection attack. An *SQL injection attack* allows a hacker to execute SQL statements against your database to read sensitive data or to delete or modify data. For the Email List application, for instance, the user might be able to execute a DROP TABLE statement by entering the following code for the email address:

```
jsmith@gmail.com'); DROP TABLE Users; --
```

Here, the first semicolon ends the first SQL statement. Then, the database might execute the second SQL statement. To prevent most types of SQL injection attacks, you can use a prepared statement as described in the next figure.

How to use the executeUpdate method to modify data

How to add a row

```
String query =
    "INSERT INTO Product (ProductCode, ProductDescription, ProductPrice) " +
    "VALUES ('" + product.getCode() + "', " +
            "'" + product.getDescription() + "', " +
            "'" + product.getPrice() + "')";
Statement statement = connection.createStatement();
int rowCount = statement.executeUpdate(query);
```

How to update a row

```
String query = "UPDATE Product SET " +
    "ProductCode = '" + product.getCode() + "', " +
    "ProductDescription = '" + product.getDescription() + "', " +
    "ProductPrice = '" + product.getPrice() + "' " +
    "WHERE ProductCode = '" + product.getCode() + "'";
Statement statement = connection.createStatement();
int rowCount = statement.executeUpdate(query);
```

How to delete a row

```
String query = "DELETE FROM Product " +
                "WHERE ProductCode = '" + productCode + "'";
Statement statement = connection.createStatement();
int rowCount = statement.executeUpdate(query);
```

Description

- The executeUpdate method is an older method that works with most JDBC drivers. Although there are some newer methods that require less SQL code, they may not work properly with all JDBC drivers.

- The executeUpdate method returns an int value that identifies the number of rows that were affected by the SQL statement.

Warning

- If you build an SQL statement from user input and use a method of the Statement object to execute that SQL statement, you may be susceptible to a security vulnerability known as an SQL injection attack.

- An *SQL injection attack* allows a hacker to bypass authentication or to execute SQL statements against your database that can read sensitive data, modify data, or delete data.

- To prevent most types of SQL injection attacks, you can use prepared statements as described in the next figure.

Figure 12-5   How to insert, update, and delete data

How to work with prepared statements

Each time a Java application sends a new SQL statement to the database server, the server checks the statement for syntax errors, prepares a plan for executing the statement, and executes the statement. If the same statement is sent again, though, the database server checks to see whether it has already received one exactly like it. If so, the server doesn't have to check its syntax and prepare an execution plan for it so the server just executes it. This improves the performance of the database operations.

To take advantage of this database feature, Java provides for the use of *prepared statements* as shown in figure 12-6. This feature lets you send statements to the database server that get executed repeatedly by accepting the parameter values that are sent to it. That improves the database performance because the database server only has to check the syntax and prepare the execution plan once for each statement.

In addition, prepared statements automatically check their parameter values to prevent most types of SQL injection attacks. As a result, it's generally considered a best practice to use prepared statements whenever possible.

The first example uses a prepared statement to create a result set that contains a single product. Here, the first statement uses a question mark (?) to identify the parameter for the SELECT statement, which is the product code for the book, and the second statement uses the prepareStatement method of the Connection object to return a PreparedStatement object. Then, the third statement uses a set method (the setString method) of the PreparedStatement object to set a value for the parameter, and the fourth statement uses the executeQuery method of the PreparedStatement object to return a ResultSet object.

The second example shows how to use a prepared statement to execute an UPDATE query that requires four parameters. Here, the first statement uses four question marks to identify the four parameters of the UPDATE statement, and the second statement creates the PreparedStatement object. Then, the next four statements use set methods to set the four parameters in the order that they appear in the UPDATE statement. The last statement uses the executeUpdate method of the PreparedStatement object to execute the UPDATE statement.

The third and fourth examples show how to insert and delete rows with prepared statements. Here, the type of SQL statement that you're using determines whether you use the executeQuery method or the executeUpdate method. If you're using a SELECT statement to return a result set, you use the executeQuery method. But if you're using an INSERT, UPDATE, or DELETE statement, you use the executeUpdate method. This holds true whether you're using a Statement object or a PreparedStatement object.

How to use a prepared statement

To return a result set

```
String preparedSQL = "SELECT ProductCode, ProductDescription, ProductPrice "
                   + "FROM Product WHERE ProductCode = ?";
PreparedStatement ps = connection.prepareStatement(preparedSQL);
ps.setString(1, productCode);
ResultSet product = ps.executeQuery();
```

To modify a row

```
String preparedSQL = "UPDATE Product SET "
                   + "    ProductCode = ?, "
                   + "    ProductDescription = ?, "
                   + "    ProductPrice = ?"
                   + "WHERE ProductCode = ?";
PreparedStatement ps = connection.prepareStatement(preparedSQL);
ps.setString(1, product.getCode());
ps.setString(2, product.getDescription());
ps.setDouble(3, product.getPrice());
ps.setString(4, product.getCode());
ps.executeUpdate();
```

To insert a row

```
String preparedQuery =
     "INSERT INTO Product (ProductCode, ProductDescription, ProductPrice) "
   + "VALUES (?, ?, ?)";
PreparedStatement ps = connection.prepareStatement(preparedQuery);
ps.setString(1, product.getCode());
ps.setString(2, product.getDescription());
ps.setDouble(3, product.getPrice());
ps.executeUpdate();
```

To delete a row

```
String preparedQuery = "DELETE FROM Product "
                     + "WHERE ProductCode = ?";
PreparedStatement ps = connection.prepareStatement(preparedQuery);
ps.setString(1, productCode);
ps.executeUpdate();
```

Description

- When you use *prepared statements* in your Java programs, the database server only has to check the syntax and prepare an execution plan once for each SQL statement. This improves the efficiency of the database operations. In addition, it prevents most types of SQL injection attacks.

- To specify a parameter for a prepared statement, type a question mark (?) in the SQL statement.

- To supply values for the parameters in a prepared statement, use the set methods of the PreparedStatement interface. For a complete list of set methods, look up the PreparedStatement interface of the java.sql package in the documentation for the Java API.

- To execute a SELECT statement, use the executeQuery method. To execute an INSERT , UPDATE, or DELETE statement, use the executeUpdate method.

Figure 12-6   How to work with prepared statements

The SQL Gateway application

This topic presents the SQL Gateway application that allows you to use a web-based interface to execute any type of SQL statement. An application like this makes it easy to view and modify the data in a database. For example, you can cut and paste SQL scripts into this application and execute them. In addition, if you enter an SQL statement with incorrect syntax, this application displays an error message when you try to execute it. Then, you can edit the SQL statement and attempt to execute it again.

When working with a database, you'll usually want to use an application like this one instead of a command-line interface. If you're working with a database that's hosted by an ISP, the ISP usually includes a web-based way to work with the database. If not, you can upload this application to work with the database. However, before you do that, you need to make sure that this application is only available to its intended users. Otherwise, deploying this application to an ISP opens a potentially disastrous security hole.

The user interface

Figure 12-7 shows the user interface for the SQL Gateway application. To use this application, you enter an SQL statement in the SQL Statement text area. Then, you click on the Execute button to run the SQL statement. When you do that, the result is displayed at the bottom of the page.

If the SQL statement is a SELECT statement that runs successfully, the result set is displayed within an HTML table as in the second page in this figure. For other types of statements, the result is a message that indicates the number of rows that were affected by the statement as in the first page in this figure. In addition, if the SQL statement doesn't execute successfully, the result is a message that displays information about the SQLException that was thrown.

The SQL Gateway application after executing an INSERT statement

The SQL Gateway application after executing a SELECT statement

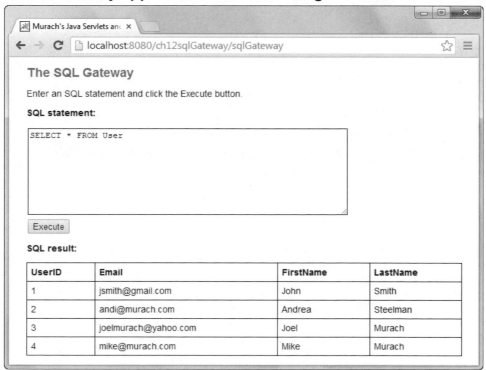

Figure 12-7   The user interface for the SQL Gateway application

The code for the JSP

Figure 12-8 shows the code for the single JSP for the SQL Gateway application. Here, the JSTL if tag at the start of the page checks if the sqlStatement attribute contains a null value. If so, this code uses a JSTL set tag to set the value of this attribute to "select * from User". That way, this SQL statement is displayed when a user requests this page for the first time in a session.

The form for this JSP contains a text area and a submit button. Here, the text area allows the user to enter the SQL statement. This code creates a text area that's approximately 60 characters wide and 8 lines tall. Within this area, the browser displays the text that's stored in the attribute named sqlStatement. Then, when the user clicks the submit button, this JSP calls the sqlGateway URL, which is mapped to the SQLGatewayServlet that's shown in the next figure.

The end of this JSP displays the string that contains the result of the SQL statement. If the SQL statement returns a result set, this string contains all the HTML tags needed to display the result set within an HTML table. Otherwise, this string contains an HTML tag that displays some text that indicates the success or failure of the SQL statement.

The code for the JSP

```
<!DOCTYPE html>
<html>
<head>
    <meta charset="utf-8">
    <title>Murach's Java Servlets and JSP</title>
    <link rel="stylesheet" href="styles/main.css" type="text/css"/>
</head>
<body>

<%@ taglib prefix="c" uri="http://java.sun.com/jsp/jstl/core" %>
<c:if test="${sqlStatement == null}">
    <c:set var="sqlStatement" value="select * from User" />
</c:if>

<h1>The SQL Gateway</h1>
<p>Enter an SQL statement and click the Execute button.</p>

<p><b>SQL statement:</b></p>
<form action="sqlGateway" method="post">
    <textarea name="sqlStatement" cols="60" rows="8">${sqlStatement}</textarea>
    <input type="submit" value="Execute">
</form>

<p><b>SQL result:</b></p>
${sqlResult}

</body>
</html>
```

Figure 12-8   The code for the JSP

The code for the servlet

Figure 12-9 shows the code for the SQLGatewayServlet. To start, this servlet imports the java.sql package so it can use the JDBC classes.

Within the doPost method of this servlet, the first statement gets the SQL statement that the user entered in the JSP, and the second statement declares the sqlResult variable.

Within the try block, the first statement explicitly loads the MySQL database driver. This statement isn't necessary on all systems, but it solves the "No suitable driver found" problem that occurs on some systems. The next four statements create a Connection object for the murach database that's running on the local MySQL service. These statements connect as the user named murach_user. This user only has privileges to execute certain types of SQL statements against the database named murach. As a result, if an unauthorized user was able to gain access to this application, at least he or she wouldn't be able to gain access to other databases running on the server.

After creating the Connection object, the fifth statement uses the Connection object to create a Statement object.

After getting the Statement object, a series of if statements parse the SQL string. To start, the first statement uses the trim method to remove any leading or trailing spaces from the SQL string. Then, an if statement checks to makes sure that the SQL string contains 6 or more characters, which is the minimum amount of characters needed to prevent a NullPointerException from being thrown by the following substring method. If the SQL string contains more than 6 characters, the substring method returns the first six letters of the SQL statement.

If the first six letters of the SQL statement are "select", the executeQuery method of the Statement object returns a ResultSet object. Then, this object is passed to the getHtmlTable method of the SQLUtil class that's shown in the next figure, and it returns the result set formatted with all the HTML tags needed to display all rows and columns of the result set in an HTML table.

However, if the first six letters of the SQL statement aren't "select", the executeUpdate method of the Statement object is called, which returns the number of rows that were affected. If the number of rows is 0, the SQL statement was a DDL statement like a DROP TABLE or CREATE TABLE statement. Otherwise, the SQL statement was an INSERT, UPDATE, or DELETE statement. Either way, the code sets the sqlResult variable to an appropriate message.

The SQLGatewayServlet class   Page 1

```java
package murach.sql;

import java.io.*;
import javax.servlet.*;
import javax.servlet.http.*;

import java.sql.*;

public class SqlGatewayServlet extends HttpServlet {

    @Override
    protected void doPost(HttpServletRequest request,
            HttpServletResponse response)
            throws ServletException, IOException {

        String sqlStatement = request.getParameter("sqlStatement");
        String sqlResult = "";
        try {
            // load the driver
            Class.forName("com.mysql.jdbc.Driver");

            // get a connection
            String dbURL = "jdbc:mysql://localhost:3306/murach";
            String username = "murach_user";
            String password = "sesame";
            Connection connection = DriverManager.getConnection(
                    dbURL, username, password);

            // create a statement
            Statement statement = connection.createStatement();

            // parse the SQL string
            sqlStatement = sqlStatement.trim();
            if (sqlStatement.length() >= 6) {
                String sqlType = sqlStatement.substring(0, 6);
                if (sqlType.equalsIgnoreCase("select")) {
                    // create the HTML for the result set
                    ResultSet resultSet
                            = statement.executeQuery(sqlStatement);
                    sqlResult = SQLUtil.getHtmlTable(resultSet);
                    resultSet.close();
                } else {
                    int i = statement.executeUpdate(sqlStatement);
                    if (i == 0) { // a DDL statement
                        sqlResult =
                                "<p>The statement executed successfully.</p>";
                    } else {        // an INSERT, UPDATE, or DELETE statement
                        sqlResult =
                                "<p>The statement executed successfully.<br>"
                                + i + " row(s) affected.</p>";
                    }
                }
            }
            statement.close();
            connection.close();
```

Figure 12-9   The SQLGatewayServlet class (part 1 of 2)

If any of the statements within the try block throw an exception, the catch blocks set the sqlResult variable to display information about the exception. If, for example, you enter an SQL statement that contains incorrect syntax, this message helps you troubleshoot your syntax problem.

After the catch blocks, the next three statements get the session object and set the sqlStatement and sqlResult variables as attributes of that object. Then, the last statement gets a RequestDispatcher object and uses it to forward the request and response objects to the JSP shown in the previous figure.

The SQLGatewayServlet class   **Page 2**

```
        } catch (ClassNotFoundException e) {
            sqlResult = "<p>Error loading the database driver: <br>"
                    + e.getMessage() + "</p>";
        } catch (SQLException e) {
            sqlResult = "<p>Error executing the SQL statement: <br>"
                    + e.getMessage() + "</p>";
        }

        HttpSession session = request.getSession();
        session.setAttribute("sqlResult", sqlResult);
        session.setAttribute("sqlStatement", sqlStatement);

        String url = "/index.jsp";
        getServletContext()
                .getRequestDispatcher(url)
                .forward(request, response);
    }
}
```

Note

* The web.xml file for this application maps the SQLGatewayServlet class to the /sqlGateway URL.

Figure 12-9   The SQLGatewayServlet class (part 2 of 2)

The code for the utility class

Figure 12-10 shows the code for the utility class named SQLUtil. This class contains a static method named getHtmlTable that's called by the servlet in the previous figure. Since this utility class works with SQL statements, it's stored in the murach.sql package.

The getHtmlTable method accepts a ResultSet object and returns a String object that contains the HTML tags that are needed to display the columns and rows in the result set within an HTML table. To build the information for that String object, the getHtmlTable method declares a StringBuilder object named htmlTable and appends data to it as the method is executed. At the end of the method, the toString method is used to convert the StringBuilder object to the String object that is returned to the servlet.

To get the column headings that are returned, the getHtmlTable method uses the getMetaData method of the ResultSet object to create a ResultSetMetaData object. This type of object contains information about the result set including the number of columns and the names of the columns. To get that information, the getHtmlTable method uses the getColumnCount and getColumnName methods of the ResultSetMetaData object.

To get the data from the result set, the getHtmlTable method uses a for loop within a while loop to get the data for each column in each row. Within these loops, the code uses the getString method of the result set to get the data for each column. That converts the data to a string no matter what data type the column is.

The SQLUtil class

```
package murach.sql;

import java.sql.*;

public class SQLUtil {

    public static String getHtmlTable(ResultSet results)
            throws SQLException {

        StringBuilder htmlTable = new StringBuilder();
        ResultSetMetaData metaData = results.getMetaData();
        int columnCount = metaData.getColumnCount();

        htmlTable.append("<table>");

        // add header row
        htmlTable.append("<tr>");
        for (int i = 1; i <= columnCount; i++) {
            htmlTable.append("<th>");
            htmlTable.append(metaData.getColumnName(i));
            htmlTable.append("</th>");
        }
        htmlTable.append("</tr>");

        // add all other rows
        while (results.next()) {
            htmlTable.append("<tr>");
            for (int i = 1; i <= columnCount; i++) {
                htmlTable.append("<td>");
                htmlTable.append(results.getString(i));
                htmlTable.append("</td>");
            }
            htmlTable.append("</tr>");
        }

        htmlTable.append("</table>");
        return htmlTable.toString();
    }
}
```

Description

- The getHtmlTable method in this class accepts a ResultSet object and returns a String object that contains the HTML code for the result set so it can be displayed by a browser.

- The getMetaData method of a ResultSet object returns a ResultSetMetaData object.

- The getColumnCount method of a ResultSetMetaData object returns the number of columns in the result set.

- The getColumnName method of a ResultSetMetaData object returns the name of a column in the result set.

Figure 12-10   The SQLUtil class

How to work with connection pooling

Opening a connection to a database is a time-consuming process that can degrade an application's performance. As a result, it's a common programming practice to create a collection of Connection objects and store them in another object that's commonly known as a *database connection pool* (*DBCP*). Then, the Connection objects in the pool are shared by all the users of a web application. This limits the number of times that connections are opened as well as the total number of Connection objects.

How connection pooling works

Figure 12-11 shows how connection pooling works. To start, when the connection pool is created for the first time, a ConnectionPool object that contains multiple Connection objects is created. Then, when a user accesses a servlet, the servlet spawns a thread. This thread gets a Connection object from the ConnectionPool object, uses that Connection object to access the database, and returns the Connection object to the connection pool.

Typically, you create a single connection pool for a web application. Then, all of the servlets in the application use the same connection pool to access the database. In the next two figures, you'll learn how to install, customize, and share a connection pool among all of the servlets in an application.

How to make a connection pool available

Although you can write the Java code for your own connection pool, this code is already available from third-party sources. As a result, you'll almost always want to use a connection pool that has already been developed and tested by someone else. Then, you can install and customize that connection pool so it works with your database.

For instance, Tomcat 7 includes the database connection pool that's available from the Jakarta-Commons project. The files for this database connection pool are stored in the JAR file named tomcat-dbcp.jar that's in Tomcat's lib directory.

The easiest way to make this connection pool available to your project is to use your IDE to add this JAR file to your application. To add this JAR file to a NetBeans project, for example, you can right-click on the Libraries folder, select the Add JAR/Folder command, and use the resulting dialog box to select the JAR file for the connection pool.

Before you add the JAR file to your project, though, you might want to copy the JAR file for the connection pool to the WEB-INF/lib directory for your application. That way, the connection pool is stored with the other files for the project.

How connection pooling works

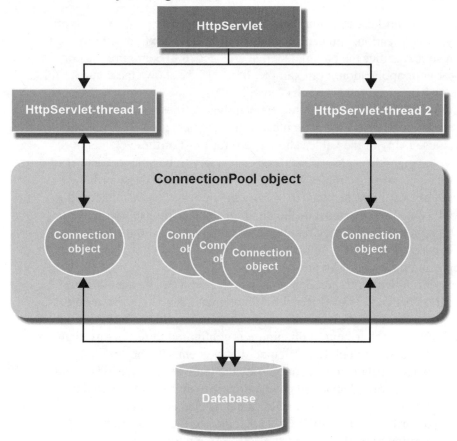

Description

- When *database connection pooling* (*DBCP*) is used, a limited number of connections are opened for a database and these connections are shared by the users who connect to the database. This improves the performance of the database operations.

- When one of the threads of a servlet needs to perform a database operation, the thread gets a Connection object from the ConnectionPool object and uses that Connection object to do the operation. When it is finished, it returns the Connection object to the pool.

- Tomcat 6 and later includes the database connection pool that's available from the Jakarta-Commons project. The files for this database connection pool are stored in Tomcat's lib directory in a JAR file named tomcat-dbcp.jar.

- Before you can use the connection pool, you must make it available to your application. The easiest way to do this is to use your IDE to add the JAR file for the connection pool to your application.

- To add a JAR file to a NetBeans project, right-click on the Libraries folder, select the Add JAR/Folder command, and use the resulting dialog box to select the JAR file for the connection pool.

Figure 12-11   How connection pooling works

How to implement a connection pool

To customize the Jakarta-Commons database connection pool so it's appropriate for your application, you can start by editing the context.xml file for your application so it specifies the parameters that are needed to configure the connection pool for your application. For example, figure 12-12 shows the context.xml file for the web application named ch12email.

This XML file contains a Resource element that defines a connection pool for the application. Many of the attributes for this element are self-explanatory, and you can use many of the values shown here for most of these elements. However, you can modify these attributes as necessary to be able to connect to the correct database. For example, you can use the username, password, driverClassName, and url attributes to specify the information that's needed to connect to the database. For most of the other attributes, you can use the values shown in this figure because they're adequate for most small- to medium-sized websites. If necessary, though, you can modify these attributes so the connection pool is appropriate for your website.

When working with a connection pool, a connection can be abandoned if the web application doesn't close its ResultSet, Statement, and Connection objects. This can cause a "leak" that eventually results in no connections being available. However, the Resource element in this figure is configured to return any abandoned connections to the pool. In particular, this element sets the removeAbandoned attribute to true, and it sets the removeAbandonedTimeout attribute to 60. That way, abandoned connections are returned to the pool after they have been idle for 60 seconds. In addition, this element sets the logAbandoned attribute to true so the code that caused the connection to be abandoned is written to the log file for the connection pool.

Once you've configured the context.xml file correctly, you can create a class to make it easy to get a connection to the database. In this figure, for example, the ConnectionPool class makes it easy for any class in the application to get a connection from the connection pool for the murach database that's running on the MySQL server.

To start, the ConnectionPool class imports the interfaces and classes that it needs to be able to get a connection from the connection pool. This includes the DataSource interface that the Jakarta-Commons connection pool uses to store the connections, and it includes the InitialContext class that's used to get a DataSource object.

After the class declaration, this class declares a private static instance variable that holds the ConnectionPool object, and it declares a private static instance variable that holds the DataSource object.

After these declarations, the ConnectionPool class uses a private constructor to create an instance of the connection pool. To do that, it uses the InitialContext object to return a DataSource object. Note that this code works because the end of the string that's passed to the lookup method (jdbc/murach) matches the name attribute that's specified in the context.xml file.

After the constructor, the static getInstance method returns a reference to the ConnectionPool object. To start, this method checks to see if the ConnectionPool

A context.xml file that configures a connection pool

```
<?xml version="1.0" encoding="UTF-8"?>
<Context path="/ch12email">

    <Resource name="jdbc/murach" auth="Container"
        driverClassName="com.mysql.jdbc.Driver"
        url="jdbc:mysql://localhost:3306/murach?autoReconnect=true"
        username="murach_user" password="sesame"
        maxActive="100" maxIdle="30" maxWait="10000"
        logAbandoned="true" removeAbandoned="true"
        removeAbandonedTimeout="60" type="javax.sql.DataSource" />

</Context>
```

A class that defines a connection pool   Page 1

```
package murach.data;

import java.sql.*;
import javax.sql.DataSource;
import javax.naming.InitialContext;
import javax.naming.NamingException;

public class ConnectionPool {

    private static ConnectionPool pool = null;
    private static DataSource dataSource = null;

    private ConnectionPool() {
        try {
            InitialContext ic = new InitialContext();
            dataSource = (DataSource) ic.lookup("java:/comp/env/jdbc/murach");
        } catch (NamingException e) {
            System.out.println(e);
        }
    }

    public static synchronized ConnectionPool getInstance() {
        if (pool == null) {
            pool = new ConnectionPool();
        }
        return pool;
    }
```

Figure 12-12   How to implement and use a connection pool (part 1 of 2)

object exists. Most of the time, the object exists so this method just returns a reference to the ConnectionPool object. However, if the ConnectionPool object hasn't been created, this method creates the ConnectionPool object and returns a reference to this object.

Please note that the private constructor and getInstance method of the ConnectionPool class allow only a single instance of the ConnectionPool class to be created. This is known as the *singleton pattern*, and it's commonly used by programmers when they want to make sure that only a single instance of an object is created.

Once the connection pool has been created, the application can use the getConnection method in this figure to return a Connection object that can be used to access the database. To get a connection object, this method calls the getConnection method of the DataSource object. If this method throws an SQLException, this code prints the exception and returns a null value.

Finally, the application can use the freeConnection method to close the specified Connection object. This returns the connection to the connection pool. If the close method of the Connection object throws an SQLException, this method prints the exception.

How to use a connection pool

Figure 12-12 also shows the code that you can use to get a Connection object from a ConnectionPool object. This should give you a clearer idea of how you can use this ConnectionPool object in your own code.

To start, you can call the static getInstance method of the ConnectionPool class to return a ConnectionPool object. Then, you can call the getConnection method of the ConnectionPool object to return a Connection object that can be used to access the database. Finally, after all the code that uses the Connection object has been executed, you can call the freeConnection method of the connection pool to return the Connection object to the pool. Since a typical database operation takes only a fraction of a second, a relatively low number of Connection objects can handle a high volume of user requests.

A class that defines a connection pool   Page 2

```java
    public Connection getConnection() {
        try {
            return dataSource.getConnection();
        } catch (SQLException e) {
            System.out.println(e);
            return null;
        }
    }

    public void freeConnection(Connection c) {
        try {
            c.close();
        } catch (SQLException e) {
            System.out.println(e);
        }
    }
}
```

Code that uses the connection pool

```java
ConnectionPool pool = ConnectionPool.getInstance();
Connection connection = pool.getConnection();

// code that uses the connection to work with the database

pool.freeConnection(connection);
```

Description

- With Tomcat 6 and later, you can use the context.xml file to configure connection pooling for an application.
- The ConnectionPool class provides the getConnection and freeConnection methods that make it easy for programmers to get connections and to return connections to the connection pool.

Figure 12-12   How to implement and use a connection pool (part 2 of 2)

The Email List application

Now that you know how to work with connection pooling and JDBC, you're ready to learn how to code an Email List application that uses a class named UserDB to write the user data to a database. This application also uses the connection pool described in the previous topic so it quickly connects its threads to the database.

The user interface

Figure 12-13 shows the user interface for the new Email List application. This is similar to the interface that you've seen in earlier versions of this application, but it displays an error message if a user enters an email address that already exists in the database.

The code for the JSP

This figure also shows the code for the JSP that displays the user interface for the Email List application. Since this code is similar to JSPs that have been presented in earlier chapters, you shouldn't have any trouble understanding how this code works. Here, three text boxes use the HTML5 required attribute to require the user to enter values. In addition, the shaded line of code displays an error message if the servlet sets this message as a request attribute.

The Email List application as it displays an error message

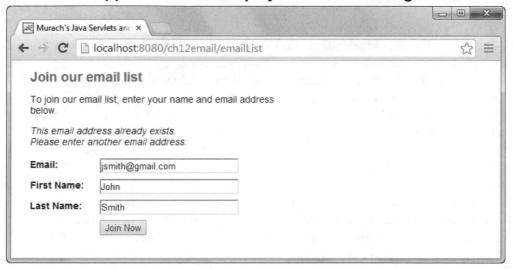

The code for this JSP

```
<!DOCTYPE html>
<html>
<head>
    <meta charset="utf-8">
    <title>Murach's Java Servlets and JSP</title>
    <link rel="stylesheet" href="styles/main.css" type="text/css"/>
</head>
<body>
    <h1>Join our email list</h1>
    <p>To join our email list, enter your name and
        email address below.</p>
    <p><i>${message}</i></p>
    <form action="emailList" method="post">
        <input type="hidden" name="action" value="add">
        <label class="pad_top">Email:</label>
        <input type="email" name="email" value="${user.email}"
                required><br>
        <label class="pad_top">First Name:</label>
        <input type="text" name="firstName" value="${user.firstName}"
                required><br>
        <label class="pad_top">Last Name:</label>
        <input type="text" name="lastName" value="${user.lastName}"
                required><br>
        <label> </label>
        <input type="submit" value="Join Now" class="margin_left">
    </form>
</body>
</html>
```

Figure 12-13   The user interface and JSP for the Email List application

The code for the servlet

Figure 12-14 shows the code for the doPost method of the EmailListServlet class. By now, most of the code in this doPost method should be review, with the exception of the statements that call methods from the UserDB class.

In particular, the nested if statement uses the emailExists method of the UserDB class to check if the email address already exists in the database. If so, the message variable is set to an appropriate message, and the url variable is set to the JSP that's shown in the previous figure. If not, the insert method of the UserDB class is used to write the data that's stored in the User object to the database, and the url variable is set to a JSP that displays the data that has been entered.

Since the methods of the UserDB class don't throw any exceptions, the servlet class doesn't need to handle any of these exceptions. If necessary, though, it can use the values that are returned by the methods of the UserDB class to determine if the action succeeded or failed and to display an appropriate message. For example, if the insert method of the UserDB class is successful, it returns an int value that indicates the number of rows that it added to the database. If this method returns a value of 0, no rows were added to the database. Although the code in this figure doesn't check this value, you could easily add code that does.

If you review this code, I think you'll agree that the methods of the UserDB class are easy to use. That's because these methods handle all of the details for working with the database. For example, these methods handle all the details for getting a connection to the database from the connection pool, and they handle all the details for executing the appropriate SQL statements. To see how this works, you can view the code shown in the next figure. For now, though, note how separating the database layer from the rest of the application lets the servlet focus on its job as the controller in the MVC pattern.

The code for the servlet

```java
package murach.email;

import java.io.*;
import javax.servlet.*;
import javax.servlet.http.*;

import murach.business.User;
import murach.data.UserDB;

public class EmailListServlet extends HttpServlet {

    @Override
    protected void doPost(HttpServletRequest request,
            HttpServletResponse response)
            throws ServletException, IOException {
        String url = "/index.html";

        // get current action
        String action = request.getParameter("action");
        if (action == null) {
            action = "join";        // default action
        }

        // perform action and set URL to appropriate page
        if (action.equals("join")) {
            url = "/index.jsp";     // the "join" page
        }
        else if (action.equals("add")) {
            // get parameters from the request
            String firstName = request.getParameter("firstName");
            String lastName = request.getParameter("lastName");
            String email = request.getParameter("email");

            // store data in User object
            User user = new User(firstName, lastName, email);

            // validate the parameters
            if (UserDB.emailExists(user.getEmail())) {
                message = "This email address already exists.<br>" +
                          "Please enter another email address.";
                url = "/index.jsp";
            }
            else {
                message = "";
                url = "/thanks.jsp";
                UserDB.insert(user);
            }
            request.setAttribute("user", user);
            request.setAttribute("message", message);
        }
        getServletContext()
                .getRequestDispatcher(url)
                .forward(request, response);
    }
}
```

Figure 12-14   The servlet for the Email List application

The code for the database class

Figure 12-15 shows the code for the UserDB class. This class contains the emailExists and insert methods that are used by the servlet in the previous figure. In addition, this class contains three more methods (update, delete, and selectUser) that can be used to modify and retrieve user data.

The methods in this class map the User object to the User table in the murach database. In particular, the insert method stores a User object in a new row in the User table. Conversely, the selectUser method creates a User object from the data that's stored in a row in the User table. This is known as *object-relational mapping, O/R mapping*, or *ORM*.

Although using JDBC to write all of the object-relational mapping for an application gives you low-level control over how it works, this can also be tedious and time-consuming. As a result, you may want to try using a higher-level API such as JPA as described in the next chapter.

In the UserDB class, the methods begin by getting a Connection object from the ConnectionPool object that allows them to connect to the database. Then, these methods declare the PreparedStatement object, the ResultSet object (if necessary), and a string that contains the SQL statement. Within the try block for these methods, the statements create the PreparedStatement object, set its parameters, execute the PreparedStatement statement, and return an appropriate value. If an exception occurs, the catch block prints the exception to the standard output stream and returns an appropriate value. Either way, the finally block closes any PreparedStatement, ResultSet, or Connection objects that have been opened. To do that, it uses the DBUtil class that's described in the next figure.

The insert method adds a new row to the User table. To do that, it executes an INSERT statement that includes the data from the User object that was passed to the method. If this method executes successfully, it returns an integer value of 1 to the calling method. Otherwise, it prints the exception and returns an integer value of 0 to indicate that the row was not inserted.

The update method works like the insert method, but it uses an UPDATE statement instead of an INSERT statement. Within the UPDATE statement, the WHERE clause uses the email address to find the row to be updated.

The UserDB class   Page 1

```java
package murach.data;

import java.sql.*;

import murach.business.User;

public class UserDB {

    public static int insert(User user) {
        ConnectionPool pool = ConnectionPool.getInstance();
        Connection connection = pool.getConnection();
        PreparedStatement ps = null;

        String query
                = "INSERT INTO User (Email, FirstName, LastName) "
                + "VALUES (?, ?, ?)";
        try {
            ps = connection.prepareStatement(query);
            ps.setString(1, user.getEmail());
            ps.setString(2, user.getFirstName());
            ps.setString(3, user.getLastName());
            return ps.executeUpdate();
        } catch (SQLException e) {
            System.out.println(e);
            return 0;
        } finally {
            DBUtil.closePreparedStatement(ps);
            pool.freeConnection(connection);
        }
    }

    public static int update(User user) {
        ConnectionPool pool = ConnectionPool.getInstance();
        Connection connection = pool.getConnection();
        PreparedStatement ps = null;

        String query = "UPDATE User SET "
                + "FirstName = ?, "
                + "LastName = ? "
                + "WHERE Email = ?";
        try {
            ps = connection.prepareStatement(query);
            ps.setString(1, user.getFirstName());
            ps.setString(2, user.getLastName());
            ps.setString(3, user.getEmail());

            return ps.executeUpdate();
        } catch (SQLException e) {
            System.out.println(e);
            return 0;
        } finally {
            DBUtil.closePreparedStatement(ps);
            pool.freeConnection(connection);
        }
    }
```

Figure 12-15   The database class for the Email List application (part 1 of 3)

The delete method works like the update method, but it uses the DELETE statement instead of the UPDATE statement.

The emailExists method checks if the specified email address already exists in the User table. To do that, this method executes a SELECT statement that searches for the specified email address. If this method finds the address, it returns a true value. Otherwise, it returns a false value.

The UserDB class   **Page 2**

```java
public static int delete(User user) {
    ConnectionPool pool = ConnectionPool.getInstance();
    Connection connection = pool.getConnection();
    PreparedStatement ps = null;

    String query = "DELETE FROM User "
            + "WHERE Email = ?";
    try {
        ps = connection.prepareStatement(query);
        ps.setString(1, user.getEmail());

        return ps.executeUpdate();
    } catch (SQLException e) {
        System.out.println(e);
        return 0;
    } finally {
        DBUtil.closePreparedStatement(ps);
        pool.freeConnection(connection);
    }
}

public static boolean emailExists(String email) {
    ConnectionPool pool = ConnectionPool.getInstance();
    Connection connection = pool.getConnection();
    PreparedStatement ps = null;
    ResultSet rs = null;

    String query = "SELECT Email FROM User "
            + "WHERE Email = ?";
    try {
        ps = connection.prepareStatement(query);
        ps.setString(1, email);
        rs = ps.executeQuery();
        return rs.next();
    } catch (SQLException e) {
        System.out.println(e);
        return false;
    } finally {
        DBUtil.closeResultSet(rs);
        DBUtil.closePreparedStatement(ps);
        pool.freeConnection(connection);
    }
}
```

Figure 12-15   The database class for the Email List application (part 2 of 3)

The selectUser method creates a User object that gets the data from the row in the User table that corresponds with the email address that's passed to the method. If the email address is found in the User table, this method uses the set methods of the User class to fill the User object with values from the database. Then, this method returns the User object to the calling method. Otherwise, this method prints the exception and returns a null value.

So far in this book, the User and UserDB classes have only worked with three columns: email, first name, and last name. In the real world, though, a single business class or database table may contain dozens of columns. To give you some idea of this complexity, section 5 presents a more realistic application. When you code an application like that, the good news is that all the skills you've just learned still apply. The bad news is that you have to write many more lines of code as you develop typical business and database classes.

If you configure your connection pool as described earlier in this chapter, the connection pool automatically returns abandoned connections to the pool. However, it's still a good programming practice to close all database resources when you're done with them as illustrated by the methods in this figure. This helps your database code run more efficiently, and it reduces the likelihood of running into resource usage problems.

The UserDB class   **Page 3**

```java
public static User selectUser(String email) {
    ConnectionPool pool = ConnectionPool.getInstance();
    Connection connection = pool.getConnection();
    PreparedStatement ps = null;
    ResultSet rs = null;

    String query = "SELECT * FROM User "
            + "WHERE Email = ?";
    try {
        ps = connection.prepareStatement(query);
        ps.setString(1, email);
        rs = ps.executeQuery();
        User user = null;
        if (rs.next()) {
            user = new User();
            user.setFirstName(rs.getString("FirstName"));
            user.setLastName(rs.getString("LastName"));
            user.setEmail(rs.getString("Email"));
        }
        return user;
    } catch (SQLException e) {
        System.out.println(e);
        return null;
    } finally {
        DBUtil.closeResultSet(rs);
        DBUtil.closePreparedStatement(ps);
        pool.freeConnection(connection);
    }
}
}
```

Figure 12-15   The database class for the Email List application (part 3 of 3)

The code for the utility class

Before you close a Statement, PreparedStatement, or ResultSet object, it's a good practice to check if the object is null. Then, if the object is null, you can avoid a NullPointerException by not calling the close method. On the other hand, if the object isn't null, you can safely call the close method to close it. However, you still need to catch the SQLException that's thrown by the close method.

Since this requires a significant amount of code, and since you often need to close these objects, it often makes sense to create a utility class like the DBUtil class shown in figure 12-16. A class like this can make it easier to close database objects. Note, for example, how this class makes it easier to code the UserDB class shown in the previous figure.

The DBUtil class

```
package murach.data;

import java.sql.*;

public class DBUtil {

    public static void closeStatement(Statement s) {
        try {
            if (s != null) {
                s.close();
            }
        } catch (SQLException e) {
            System.out.println(e);
        }
    }

    public static void closePreparedStatement(Statement ps) {
        try {
            if (ps != null) {
                ps.close();
            }
        } catch (SQLException e) {
            System.out.println(e);
        }
    }

    public static void closeResultSet(ResultSet rs) {
        try {
            if (rs != null) {
                rs.close();
            }
        } catch (SQLException e) {
            System.out.println(e);
        }
    }
}
```

Description

- To make it easier to close statements and result sets, you can use a utility class like the one shown in this figure.

Figure 12-16   The utility class for the Email List application

Perspective

The goal of this chapter has been to show you how to use JDBC and connection pooling within the context of a web application. Although there's a lot more to database programming than that, this should get you off to a good start. In fact, the skills in this chapter are adequate for most small- to medium-sized websites.

For large websites, though, the skills presented in this chapter may not be adequate. In that case, you may want to use other third-party tools to design and create a database, to map objects to a database, and to manage a connection pool. For example, you may want to use JPA (Java Persistence API) to map your objects to a relational database as described in the next chapter. Or, you may need to use EJBs (Enterprise JavaBeans). To learn more about EJBs, you can start by reading more about them on the Internet.

Summary

- To write Java code that works with a database, you use *Java Database Connectivity* (*JDBC*). To do that, you use the classes in the JDBC API.

- Before you can access a database, you must install a database driver on the database server. Then, before you can work with the database, you must load the driver and create a Connection object that connects to the database.

- With JDBC 4.0, the database driver is loaded automatically. This new feature is known as *automatic driver loading*.

- You use the createStatement method of the Connection object to create a Statement object that contains the SQL statement that you want to run. Then, you use the executeQuery or executeUpdate method to run the SQL statement.

- When you run a SELECT statement, it returns a result set to your program. Then, you can use the methods of the ResultSet object to move the *cursor* through the rows of the result set and to get the data from the rows.

- An *SQL injection attack* allows a hacker to execute SQL statements against your database that read sensitive data, modify data, or delete data.

- Prepared statements can improve the performance of database operations and prevent most types of SQL injection attacks. To use them, you can use a PreparedStatement object instead of a Statement object to run SQL statements.

- A ResultSetMetaData object contains information about a result set like the number of columns in the table and the names of the columns.

- *Database connection pooling* (*DBCP*) can improve the performance of a web application by sharing the connections to a database between all of the users of the application.

Before you do the exercises for this chapter

The exercises for this chapter assume that you've already installed Tomcat and MySQL as described in appendix A (PC) or B (Mac). As a result, the JAR files for the JDBC driver for MySQL and the connection pool should be available to this project through the Tomcat libraries. If they aren't, you can add these JAR files to your project as described in this chapter.

If you're using NetBeans, you may need to register the connection to the murach database when you open the projects for these exercises. To do that, you can use the procedure in figure 3-15.

Exercise 12-1   Implement connection pooling

In this exercise, you'll enhance the SQL Gateway application shown in this chapter so that it uses connection pooling.

1. Open the ch12_ex1_sqlGateway project in the ex_starts directory.

2. Run the application and execute the default SELECT statement to see how this application works. If you get an error message that says, "No suitable driver found," you may need to make the JAR file for the MySQL driver available to your project.

3. Add the library for the connection pool to the project. To do that, right-click on the Libraries folder, select the Add JAR/Folder command, and use the resulting dialog box to select the tomcat-dbcp.jar file.

4. Open the context.xml file in the META-INF folder. Then, modify it so it includes a Resource element that configures a connection pool. The easiest way to do this is to copy the Resource element from the ch12email application's context.xml file.

5. Create a ConnectionPool class in a package named data that you can use to get or free a connection. The easiest way to do this is to copy the ConnectionPool class from the ch12email application.

6. Open the SQLGatewayServlet.java file that's stored in the murach.sql package. Then, modify this servlet so it uses the ConnectionPool class to get a connection. Make sure to free this connection after you're done using it. To do that, you can add a finally clause to the try/catch statement.

7. Run the application and make sure it works as before.

Exercise 12-2   Create a User Admin application

In this exercise, you'll create an application that allows you to view all users, update existing users, and delete users in the User table of the murach database.

Review the code
1. Open the project named ch12_ex2_userAdmin in the ex_starts directory.

2. Review the Java code for this application. Note that the UsersServlet and UserDB classes aren't finished.

3. Review the configuration files for this application. Note that the context.xml file configures connection pooling and that the web.xml file maps the servlet to a URL.

Add code to display the users

4. Open the UserDB class that's located in the murach.data package. Then, add code to the selectUsers method to return an ArrayList of User objects that corresponds with the rows in the User table.

5. Open the UsersServlet class and add code to the display_users action that gets an ArrayList of User objects from the User table, sets that list as a request attribute, and forwards the request to the index.jsp file.

6. Run the application to make sure it works correctly for the display_users action.

Add code to update a user

7. Open the index.jsp file. Note that the Update and Delete links request the UsersServlet and pass an action parameter to it to specify the action and an email address to specify the user.

8. Open the UsersServlet class and add code for the display_user action that gets the User object for the specified email, stores this object in the request, and forwards the request to the user.jsp file. This should display the user.

9. Open the user.jsp file. Note that it displays user data and submits it to the UsersServlet class with an action that specifies that the user should be updated.

10. Open the UsersServlet class and add code to the update_user action that updates the first and last name of the user in the User table. This servlet should forward the request to the UsersServlet so it displays the current users.

11. Run the application to make sure it works correctly for the update_user action.

Add code that deletes a user

12. Open the UsersServlet class and add code to the delete_user action that deletes the specified user. This servlet should forward the request to the UsersServlet so it displays the current users.

13. Run the application to make sure it works correctly. You shouldn't be able to delete any users that have related rows in the Download table. This includes the three users added as part of the database creation script. However, you should be able to delete any users that you add with the ch12email application in the book_apps directory.

13

How to use JPA to work with a database

JPA (Java Persistence API) is a relatively new way to work with databases in Java that has many advantages over the older JDBC API described in the previous chapter. As you will see in this chapter, JPA makes it easier to work with object-oriented data and relationships between objects. As a result, you may want to use it for developing new applications. Although this chapter presents JPA in the context of web applications, you can also use JPA in other types of Java applications such as desktop applications.

An introduction to JPA

JPA (Java Persistence API) is an *object-relational mapping* specification that makes it easier to convert between the business objects and the relational database of an application. This is also known as *O/R mapping* or *ORM*.

JPA offers several features that make it easier to use than JDBC. First, JPA can automatically create database tables based on relationships between business objects. Second, JPA can automatically convert between objects and rows in a relational database. Third, JPA can automatically perform joins to satisfy relationships between objects.

JPA runs on top of JDBC. As a result, it's compatible with any database that has a JDBC driver.

A summary of JPA implementations

There are several implementations of JPA. All of them follow the JPA specification. As a result, you can use the skills presented in this chapter with any of these implementations.

Figure 13-1 lists three of the most popular implementations. Full Java EE servers typically provide their own implementation of JPA. For example, Glassfish uses TopLink, and WildFly uses Hibernate.

When you use Tomcat, you can choose the JPA implementation. This chapter shows how to use EclipseLink. If you want to use another implementation, such as Hibernate, you should be able to do that too. However, some of the configuration details may be different. As a result, you may need to consult the documentation for your JPA implementation to configure JPA.

Entities and the entity manager

When working with JPA, business objects are known as *entities* and are managed by an *entity manager*. In a full Java EE server such as Glassfish, the server provides a built-in entity manager that includes advanced features such as automatic transaction rollback. However, this chapter shows you how to use entity managers outside of a full Java EE server. That way, you can use them in Tomcat or in a desktop application.

To turn a normal business class into an entity, you code annotations in the class. These annotations specify how the class should be stored in a database, and they specify how one class relates to another. Because these classes are just plain old Java objects (POJOs) with annotations, you can still use these classes without JPA. In that case, the annotations are ignored.

JPA...

- is an object-relational mapping specification.
- makes it easier to map objects to rows in a relational database.
- shields the developer from having to write JDBC and SQL code.
- runs on top of JDBC.
- is compatible with any database that has a JDBC driver.

Three popular JPA implementations

- Hibernate
- EclipseLink
- TopLink

Entities and the entity manager

- Business classes intended to be used with JPA are called *entities*. You can convert a business class to an entity by adding JPA annotations to the class.
- Entities are managed by an *entity manager*.
- Full Java EE application servers such as Glassfish have a built-in entity manager that includes advanced features such as automatic transaction management.
- If you want to use JPA outside of a full Java EE application server, such as in Tomcat or a desktop application, you can create your own entity managers.

Description

- The examples in this book use the EclipseLink library. However, you should be able to use similar skills to work with other JPA implementations.

Figure 13-1   An introduction to JPA

How to configure NetBeans to work with JPA

Before you can work with JPA, you need to configure your IDE. In particular, you need to add a JDBC driver for the database, the JPA library that you want to use, and a persistence unit. Figure 13-2 shows how to add these components to NetBeans.

To add a MySQL JDBC driver, you can use the skills presented in the previous chapter. To review, you can right-click on the project's Libraries folder, select the Add Library command, and select the library for the driver. In this figure, the project includes the MySQL JDBC Driver library.

To add a JPA library to a project, you can right-click on the project's Libraries folder, select the Add Library command, and select the library. NetBeans includes libraries for both EclipseLink and Hibernate. In this figure, the project includes the library for EclipseLink. However, you can use the same skills to add the Hibernate library to a project.

Before you can use JPA, you need to configure a persistence unit that tells JPA how to connect to a database. If you use the EclipseLink library, you use a file named persistence.xml to configure a persistence unit.

To add a persistence.xml file to a project, you can select the File→New File command from the menus. Then, you can select the Persistence category, the Persistence Unit file type, and use the resulting dialog box to configure the persistence unit.

To modify the persistence unit, you can open its persistence.xml file and edit it. To do that, you can expand your project's Configuration Files folder and double-click the persistence.xml file. This usually opens the file in Design view, which provides a graphical user interface for modifying this file. However, it's easier to follow along with this chapter if you click the Source button to view the source code for this file as shown in this figure.

NetBeans with a JDBC driver, JPA library, and persistence.xml file

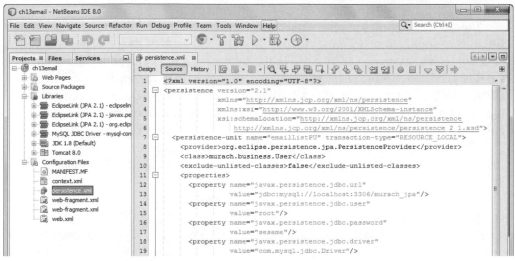

How to add a JDBC driver and the JPA library

- To add a JDBC driver to a project, right-click on its Libraries folder, select the Add Library command, and use the resulting dialog box to select the library.

- To add a JPA library to a project, right-click on its Libraries folder, select the Add Library command, and use the resulting dialog box to select the library.

How to work with a persistence unit

- To add a persistence.xml file to a project, select the File→New File command from the menus. Then, select the Persistence category, the Persistence Unit file type, and use the resulting dialog box to configure the persistence unit.

- To view the source code for a persistence unit, expand the Configuration Files folder, double-click the persistence.xml file, and click the Source button.

Description

- NetBeans includes libraries for both EclipseLink and Hibernate.

- If you forget to add a persistence.xml file, NetBeans may prompt you to create one when you add JPA annotations to your business classes. In that case, you can use the resulting dialog box to create the persistence.xml file.

Figure 13-2   How to use NetBeans to work with JPA

How to configure a persistence unit

Figure 13-3 shows a simple persistence.xml file for a JPA version of the Email List application. To start, you use the name attribute of the persistence-unit element to specify the name you use in the source code to get an entity manager for this persistence unit. Then, you can set the transaction-type attribute to RESOURCE_LOCAL. This tells JPA that you intend to write code that creates the entity managers and handles transactions. Other options require a full Java EE server to do this automatically. As a result, this book doesn't cover them.

The provider element specifies the fully qualified path for the PersistenceProvider class. In this case, it specifies the class for the EclipseLink implementation of JPA.

The exclude-unlisted-classes element determines whether you want this persistence unit to manage all classes you have annotated as entities, or only specific classes that you list here. This application only uses a single database and a single persistence unit. Because of that, you want to set this to false. If you were writing a complex application that used multiple databases and multiple persistence units, you might want to set this to true so you could explicitly list the entity classes you want this persistence unit to manage.

The shared-cache-mode element specifies the caching strategy you want this persistence unit to use. Caching allows the results of recent database queries to be stored in memory. Then, when the application requests those results again, the application gets them from the memory cache rather than performing a more expensive database lookup. This can improve application performance significantly, but at the cost of increased memory usage.

The first four property elements specify the JDBC connection information. If you read the first two figures of the previous chapter, you should understand how these elements work.

The fifth property element, tells JPA what it should do when the application starts and encounters entities that don't already have corresponding tables in the database. In this case, a value of "create" tells JPA to automatically create tables for the entities, as well as any tables necessary to create relationships between tables. Although this is convenient, it causes the application to pause for a very long time after each start up as JPA examines the entities and database schemas to determine whether it needs to make any changes. Because of that, you typically want to turn off automatic schema generation after JPA creates the tables. To do that, you can set this property to a value of "none".

The JPA specification does not require that providers support automatic schema generation. However, all common providers, including EclipseLink and Hibernate, do.

The persistence.xml file

```
<?xml version="1.0" encoding="UTF-8"?>
<persistence version="2.1"
             xmlns="http://xmlns.jcp.org/xml/ns/persistence"
             xmlns:xsi="http://www.w3.org/2001/XMLSchema-instance"
             xsi:schemaLocation="http://xmlns.jcp.org/xml/ns/persistence
                 http://xmlns.jcp.org/xml/ns/persistence/persistence_2_1.xsd">
    <persistence-unit name="emailListPU" transaction-type="RESOURCE_LOCAL">
      <provider>org.eclipse.persistence.jpa.PersistenceProvider</provider>
      <exclude-unlisted-classes>false</exclude-unlisted-classes>
      <properties>
        <property name="javax.persistence.jdbc.url"
                  value="jdbc:mysql://localhost:3306/murach_jpa"/>
        <property name="javax.persistence.jdbc.user"
                  value="root"/>
        <property name="javax.persistence.jdbc.password"
                  value="sesame"/>
        <property name="javax.persistence.jdbc.driver"
                  value="com.mysql.jdbc.Driver"/>
        <property name="javax.persistence.schema-generation.database.action"
                  value="create"/>
      </properties>
    </persistence-unit>
</persistence>
```

A summary of the elements

Element	Description
persistence-unit	The name attribute specifies the name you use in your code to get a reference to the database.
	The transaction-type attribute specifies how the application works with entity managers. RESOURCE_LOCAL specifies that you will create and manage the entity managers yourself. This is necessary if you're using Tomcat.
provider	Specifies the full class name of the JPA PersistenceProvider class.
exclude-unlisted-classes	A false value specifies that JPA uses all classes annotated as entities. Otherwise, you have to list each class you want JPA to use as an entity.
shared-cache-mode	Determines the caching strategy used by JPA. Caching can improve performance. This is covered later in this chapter.

Description

- The first four property elements configure the various JDBC connection parameters described in the previous chapter.

- The property element with a name of schema-generation.database.action specifies what JPA should do when it encounters missing tables or tables that already exist. This is covered later in this chapter.

Figure 13-3   How to configure a persistence unit

How to code JPA entities

A JPA entity is a business class with annotations added to it. JPA uses these annotations to determine how to use the data in the class within the application.

How to code the class for an entity

Figure 13-4 shows the class for a simple JPA entity that's suitable for use with the Email List application. In fact, it's similar to the User class for the Email List application from previous chapters. The main difference is that this class includes annotations. To convert a business class into an entity, you only need to add a few annotations.

First, you add the @Entity annotation immediately before the class declaration itself. This annotation tells JPA that this class defines an entity that should be stored in a database.

Second, you add the @Id annotation. This annotation tells JPA that the following field is the primary key for the entity.

Third, if you want JPA to automatically generate values for the primary key, you add the @GeneratedValue annotation as shown in this figure. This annotation includes a strategy attribute that tells JPA how to generate the primary key. In this figure, the example uses the AUTO strategy, which allows the JPA implementation to determine which strategy to use. EclipseLink uses a sequence table to do this. The AUTO strategy is the safest one to use because it should work with any database.

A simple JPA entity

```
import java.io.Serializable;
import javax.persistence.Entity;
import javax.persistence.GeneratedValue;
import javax.persistence.GenerationType;
import javax.persistence.Id;

@Entity
public class User implements Serializable {

    @Id
    @GeneratedValue(strategy = GenerationType.AUTO)
    private Long userId;
    private String firstName;
    private String lastName;
    private String email;

    public Long getUserId() {
        return userId;
    }

    public void setUserId(Long userId) {
        this.userId = userId;
    }

    // the rest of the get and set methods for the fields
}
```

Description

- The @Entity annotation specifies that this class is a managed bean that's part of a persistence unit.

- The @Id annotation specifies which field in the class is the primary key.

- The @GeneratedValue annotation specifies how the primary key should be generated. The AUTO strategy lets JPA determine how to generate the primary key. Since it doesn't rely on the database having any built-in method to automatically generate primary keys, it works with any database.

- By default, JPA uses the same name for the table in the database as the name of the class.

- To override the default table name, code the @Table annotation on the line immediately following the @Entity annotation. For example, to map the entity in this figure to a table named Customer, you could include this annotation:

    ```
    @Table(name = "Customer")
    ```

- By default, JPA uses the same names for the columns in the database as the names of the fields in the class.

- If you want to override the default column name, you can code the @Column annotation immediately above the field. For example, if you want to map the lastName field to a column named LAST_NAME, you could add this annotation:

    ```
    @Column(name = "LAST_NAME")
    ```

Figure 13-4   How to code the class for a JPA entity

How to use getter and field annotations

In the previous figure, the example places the @Id annotation directly above the userId field. This is called a *field annotation*. Another option is to place the annotation directly above the getUserId method instead. This is called a *getter annotation*. Figure 13-5 shows examples of both getter and field annotations. In addition, it describes an important difference between how these two types of annotations work.

When you use getter annotations, JPA uses the get and set methods of your class to get and set the fields. This works as if you were to write code that used the get and set methods to access these fields.

When you use field annotations, JPA uses reflection to get and set the field values. Reflection is an advanced topic that isn't covered in this book. For now, all you need to know is that reflection allows JPA to access the fields directly, even if they are private. That means that even if you have get and set methods in your class, JPA doesn't call them when you use field annotation. As a result, any code you have inside the get and set methods doesn't run when you use field annotations. Because of that, if you need to run code in your get or set methods, you should use getter annotations, not field annotations.

Code that uses getter annotations

```
private Long userId;

@Id
@GeneratedValue(strategy = GenerationType.AUTO)
public Long getUserId() {
    return userId;
}

public void setUserId(Long userId) {
    this.userId = userId;
}
```

Code that uses field annotations

```
@Id
@GeneratedValue(strategy = GenerationType.AUTO)
private Long userId;

public Long getUserId() {
    return userId;
}

public void setUserId(Long userId) {
    this.userId = userId;
}
```

Description

- *Getter annotations* use the get and set methods of the class to access the fields.
- *Field annotations* use reflection to access the fields in your class directly, even if they are declared as private. It does not call the get and set methods. As a result, any code in your get and set methods does not run when JPA accesses the fields.
- You cannot mix field and getter annotations in the same class.

Figure 13-5   How to use getter and field annotations

How to code relationships between entities

When you define an entity, it can have a relationship to other entities. For example, the entity for an invoice may contain one or more line item entities that are dependent on the invoice entity.

When you code a query in JPA, it automatically performs any joins necessary to satisfy the relationships between entities. Also, when you save an entity, JPA automatically saves any dependent entities. To make these automatic relationships work, you code annotations in your entity classes that define the relationships. Figure 13-6 shows how to code the annotations for an invoice class.

One customer can have many invoices. However, each invoice can only belong to one customer. To show this relationship in JPA, you code a @ManyToOne annotation directly before the field for the user or directly before the getUser method, depending on whether you are using field or getter annotations.

Similarly, one invoice can have many line items. However, each line item can only belong to one invoice. To show this relationship, you code a @OneToMany annotation above the line items field, or above the getLineItems method.

The @OneToMany annotation typically includes some additional elements. The fetch element determines when JPA loads the line items for the invoice. By default, JPA uses lazy loading. That means that when JPA first gets the invoice from the database, its line items are empty. Then, JPA fetches these items the first time you attempt to access the line items in this invoice.

If you don't want to use lazy loading, you can set the fetch element to a value of FetchType.EAGER. This tells JPA that it should load all of the invoice's line items when it loads the invoice. For an invoice, that's usually what you want.

If you want to use lazy loading, you can set the fetch attribute to a value of FetchType.LAZY. However, this is only a request to JPA, not a guarantee. If JPA determines that it can use eager loading with minimal performance overhead, it may choose to use eager loading instead.

So how do you decide whether to use lazy or eager loading? As a general rule, lazy loading gets the initial entity faster, but may run more slowly later. Conversely, eager loading may take longer to get the initial entity, but should run fast after that. If the list contained by the entity is likely to be small, or the entity is not useful without the list, you should probably use eager fetching. However, if the list isn't likely to be accessed often, or if it is likely to contain a large number of items, you should probably use lazy fetching.

The cascade element of the @OneToMany annotation tells JPA how to handle the line items when it updates an invoice. In this figure, the cascade element has been set to a value of CascadeType.ALL. This tells JPA to apply any updates to the invoice to the line items too. For example, when JPA inserts the invoice, it should also insert its line items. When JPA updates the invoice, it should also update its line items. And when JPA deletes an invoice, it should also delete its line items.

A JPA entity with relationships

```
import java.io.Serializable;
import javax.persistence.CascadeType;
import javax.persistence.Entity;
import javax.persistence.FetchType;
import javax.persistence.GeneratedValue;
import javax.persistence.GenerationType;
import javax.persistence.ManyToOne;
import javax.persistence.OneToMany;
import javax.persistence.Temporal;

@Entity
public class Invoice implements Serializable {

    @ManyToOne
    private User user;

    @OneToMany(fetch=FetchType.EAGER, cascade=CascadeType.ALL)
    private List<LineItem> lineItems;

    @Temporal(javax.persistence.TemporalType.DATE)
    private Date invoiceDate;

    @Id
    @GeneratedValue(strategy = GenerationType.AUTO)
    private Long invoiceNumber;

    private boolean isProcessed;

    // getters and setters for fields
}
```

Two elements of the @OneToMany annotation

Element	Description
fetch	A value of FetchType.EAGER specifies that all of the line items for the invoice should be loaded when the invoice is loaded from the database.
	A value of FetchType.LAZY requests, but does not guarantee, that line items for the invoice only be loaded when the application actually accesses them.
cascade	A value of CascadeType.ALL specifies that all operations that change the invoice should also update all of the line items.
	A value of CascardType.PERSIST specifies that any time a new invoice is inserted into the database, any line items it has should also be inserted.
	A value of CascadeType.MERGE specifies that any time an invoice is updated, any changes to its line items should also be updated.
	A value of CascadeType.REMOVE specifies that any time an invoice is removed from the database, all of its line items should also be removed.

Description

- The @ManyToOne annotation specifies that many invoices can belong to one user.
- The @OneToMany annotation specifies that an invoice can have many line items.

Figure 13-6   How to code relationships in a JPA entity

The table in figure 13-6 also shows some other values you can use with the cascade element. If you want to combine values, you can use the standard way of combining an element's values. For example, if you want to combine the PERSIST and the MERGE values of the cascade element, you can code them like this:

```
cascade={CascadeType.PERSIST, CascadeType.MERGE}
```

Here, you code the values within a set of braces ({ }). Then, you separate values with a comma.

How to work with dates and times

In the java.util package, the Date and Calendar types can map to multiple possible SQL data types. As a result, when you use either a Date or Calendar type in an entity, you need to use the @Temporal annotation to specify its SQL data type. To do that, you can use the skills shown in figure 13-7.

Within the @Temporal annotation, you can code one of the three values shown in this figure. The TemporalType.DATE value specifies that JPA should only store the date, not the time. The TemporalType.TIME value specifies that JPA should only store the time, not the date. And the TemporalType. TIMESTAMP value specifies that JPA should store both the date and time.

In most cases, it makes sense to use the TemporalType.TIMESTAMP value to store both the date and the time. That way, both the date and time are stored in the database. Then, when you write the code for your application, you can ignore any part of the value that you don't need.

The annotation for a temporal type

```
@Temporal(TemporalType.TIMESTAMP)
private Date invoiceDate;
```

SQL mappings for temporal annotations

Annotation value	SQL type
TemporalType.DATE	java.sql.Date
TemporalType.TIME	java.sql.Time
TemporalType.TIMESTAMP	java.sql.TimeStamp

Description

- The @Temporal annotation specifies the SQL type for the java.util.Date and java.util.Calendar types.

Figure 13-7   How to work with dates and times

How to retrieve data

Retrieving data using JPA is significantly easier than retrieving data with JDBC. Unlike JDBC, JPA automatically converts between objects and SQL. As a result, you don't have to write your own methods to do this. Furthermore, JPA automatically performs any joins necessary to satisfy the relationships between entities.

How to get an entity manager factory

When you are using a full Java EE server such as Glassfish or JBoss, the server provides built-in entity managers for you. When you aren't using a full Java EE server, JPA provides a class named EntityManagerFactory that you can use to get entity managers.

Entity manager factories are thread safe. However, entity managers are not. Because of that, you need to request a new entity manager for each method where you need access to one.

The easiest way to do this is to code a class like the one shown in figure 13-8. This class begins by creating a static entity manager factory. To do that, it begins by calling the static createEntityManagerFactory method of the Persistence class. This method takes the persistence unit name as a parameter. This must match the name that you defined in the persistence.xml file for this persistence unit.

After creating a static entity manager factory, this class provides a static method named getEmFactory that gets the entity manager factory. This method makes it easy to get an entity manager factory whenever you need one. Then, you can get an entity manager from the factory as shown in the next figure.

A utility class that gets an entity manager factory

```
import javax.persistence.EntityManagerFactory;
import javax.persistence.Persistence;

public class DBUtil {
    private static final EntityManagerFactory emf =
            Persistence.createEntityManagerFactory("emailListPU");

    public static EntityManagerFactory getEmFactory() {
        return emf;
    }
}
```

A static method of the Persistence class

Method	Description
`createEntityManagerFactory()`	Returns an EntityManagerFactory object for the specified persistence unit. The persistence unit name must match the unit name defined in the persistence.xml file.

Description

- You can use a utility class to make it easy to get an EntityManagerFactory object for the specified persistence unit.

Figure 13-8   How to get an entity manager factory

How to retrieve an entity by primary key

Figure 13-9 shows how to retrieve an entity by primary key. First, you need to get an entity manager from the entity manager factory. To do this, you can use the DBUtil class shown in the previous figure to get an entity manager factory. Then, you can call the factory's createEntityManager method to get an entity manager.

Once you have an entity manager, you can retrieve an object by its primary key. To do that, you can call its find method. The find method takes two parameters. The first parameter specifies the class type of the entity you want to find. This allows the entity manager to know where in the database to look for the entity, what its primary key is, and what type of object it should return. The second parameter specifies a value for the primary key. This parameter can be any valid object type but is typically the long type.

If the find method finds an entity with that primary key, it returns the entity as the specified type. Otherwise, it returns null. Here, JPA automatically converts the result set to the correct type of object. With JDBC, you would have to write code to do that.

When you are done with the entity manager, you need to close it. If you don't, you may end up with a resource leak. That's why this code calls the close method of the entity manager in the finally clause. That way, this code closes the entity manager, even if the find method throws an exception.

It's important to remember that entity manager factories are thread safe, but entity managers are not. As a result, you can't share entity managers between methods. If you do, multiple threads may attempt to use the entity manager at the same time, which can cause data corruption.

How to retrieve an entity by primary key

```
import javax.persistence.EntityManager;
import murach.business.User;

public class UserDB {
    public static User getUserById(long userId) {
        EntityManager em = DBUtil.getEmFactory().createEntityManager();
        try {
            User user = em.find(User.class, userId);
            return user;
        } finally {
            em.close();
        }
    }
}
```

A method of the EntityManagerFactory class

Method	Description
createEntityManager()	Returns an EntityManager object.

Two methods of the EntityManager class

Method	Description
find(entityClass, primaryKey)	Returns an object of the specified entity class that has the specified primary key. If the specified primary key doesn't exist, this method returns a null value.
close()	Closes the entity manager object and releases its resources. This prevents resource leaks.

Description

- Entity managers are not thread safe, so you need to create local entity managers for each method that needs one.
- The find method throws an IllegalArgumentException at runtime if the first parameter is not an entity, or if the second parameter doesn't specify the correct type for the primary key.

Figure 13-9   How to retrieve an entity by primary key

How to retrieve multiple entities

To retrieve multiple entities, you need to code a *JPQL (Java Persistence Query Language)* statement as shown in 13-10. In addition, you need to use JPQL to retrieve entities based on a column other than the primary key. Although JPQL may look like SQL, it is actually an object-oriented query language defined as part of the JPA specification.

The method shown in this figure fetches all invoices that have not yet been processed. To do that, the second statement in this method defines a JPQL statement. Here, the variable named i refers to the Invoice object, not the Invoice table in the database. Similarly, i.isProcessed refers to the isProcessed field of the Invoice object. This is known as a *path expression*.

To create a JPQL query object from the query string, you call the entity manager's createQuery method. This method returns a Query object or a TypedQuery object, depending on the arguments that you supply. If you supply a query string and a result class, this method returns a TypedQuery object that's type safe. In general, typed queries are more robust than untyped queries. As a result, you should use typed queries whenever possible.

To retrieve the list of invoices, you call the query's getResultList method. This method returns a List object that contains the Invoice objects. As a result, you can use any of the methods of the List class to work with these Invoice objects. Note that JPA automatically converts the result set to this List object. With JDBC, you have to write the code that performs this conversion. That's why it's usually easier to use JPA than JDBC.

Unfortunately, the JPA specification doesn't define whether a query should return a null value or an empty list if there are no results. Because of that, some implementations of JPA return null, and others return an empty list. To make sure your methods work consistently, you can use an if statement to check for both conditions. When you do that, you can avoid a NullPointerException by checking for the null value before you check for the empty list. Then, if either condition is true, you can return a null value.

When you use JPA, you don't have to code any joins in your JPQL query to get the line items for the invoice. That's because JPA knows how the line items relate to the invoice based on the annotations in your business classes. This allows JPA to perform the necessary joins to get the line items automatically. With JDBC, you have to write SQL code to perform the joins and Java code to get the line items. Once again, this makes JPA easier use than JDBC.

This figure also shows an example of how you can use a path expression in JPQL to select only part of an entity instead of the entire entity. This expression only selects the date of the invoice. When you use path expressions like this, the query returns a list of the specified type. In this case, it returns a List object that contains multiple Date objects, since the invoiceDate field is declared with the Date type in the Invoice class.

How to retrieve multiple entities

```java
import java.util.List;
import javax.persistence.EntityManager;
import javax.persistence.TypedQuery;

import music.business.Invoice;

public class InvoiceDB {
    public static List<Invoice> selectUnprocessedInvoices() {
        EntityManager em = DBUtil.getEmFactory().createEntityManager();
        String qString = "SELECT i from Invoice i" +
                            "WHERE i.isProcessed = 'n'";
        TypedQuery<Invoice> q = em.createQuery(qString, Invoice.class);

        List<Invoice> invoices;
        try {
            invoices = q.getResultList();
            if (invoices == null || invoices.isEmpty())
                invoices = null;
        } finally {
            em.close();
        }
        return invoices;
    }
}
```

A JPQL statement that selects only one field of an entity

```
SELECT i.invoiceDate FROM Invoice i WHERE i.isProcessed = 'n'
```

Two methods of the EntityManager class

Method	Description
createQuery(queryString)	Returns a Query object that returns the result as an Object or list of Object types. This version is not type safe.
createQuery(queryString, resultClass)	Returns a TypedQuery object that returns the result as an object of the specified result class or a list of objects of the specified result class.

Description

- *JPQL* (*Java Persistence Query Language*) is an object-oriented query language defined as part of the JPA specification. It works similarly to SQL, but it isn't SQL.

- JPQL uses *path expressions* to refer to the fields of an entity. These expressions don't refer to the columns of a table.

- In some JPA implementations, the getResult list method returns a null value if the query doesn't return any results. In others, this method returns an empty list.

- The getResultList method may automatically perform joins or additional queries to satisfy the relationships between entities.

Figure 13-10   How to retrieve multiple entities

How to retrieve a single entity

Figure 13-11 shows how to retrieve a single entity. This code is similar to the code for retrieving multiple entities. However, to get a single entity, you call the getSingleResult method from the query instead of the getResultList method.

The getSingleResult method returns an Object type if you call it from a Query object. If you call it from a TypedQuery object, it returns the type of object specified by the second parameter of the createQuery method.

Unlike the getResultList method, the getSingleResult method can throw two exceptions. First, it can throw the NoResultException. As its name implies, this exception is thrown if the query doesn't return any results. Second, this method can throw the NonUniqueResultException. This exception is thrown if the query returns more than one result.

This example also introduces *parameterized queries*, which work much like prepared statements in JDBC. To create a parameterized query, you code a placeholder that begins with a colon (:) like this:

```
:email
```

Then, you call the setParameter method on the query. Within this method, the first argument specifies the name of the parameter, and the second argument specifies the value of the parameter.

It's possible to build a query string that includes the parameters directly in the string. For example, you could build the query string shown in this figure like this:

```
"SELECT u FROM User u " +
"WHERE u.email = " + email;
```

However, this code is subject to SQL injection attacks, which are a common security hole in web applications. As a result, it's generally considered a best practice to use parameterized queries as shown in this figure, especially when working with data supplied by the user. Since parameterized queries are precompiled, they aren't subject to SQL injection attacks.

How to retrieve a single entity

```java
import javax.persistence.EntityManager;
import javax.persistence.NoResultException;
import javax.persistence.TypedQuery;

import murach.business.User;

public class UserDB {
    public static User selectUser(String email) {
        EntityManager em = DBUtil.getEmFactory().createEntityManager();
        String qString = "SELECT u FROM User u " +
                         "WHERE u.email = :email";
        TypedQuery<User> q = em.createQuery(qString, User.class);
        q.setParameter("email", email);

        User user = null;
        try {
            user = q.getSingleResult();
        } catch (NoResultException e) {
            System.out.println(e);
        } finally {
            em.close();
        }
        return user;
    }
}
```

Some exceptions thrown by getSingleResult

Exception	Description
NoResultException	The query returned no results.
NonUniqueResultException	The query returned more than one result.

Description

- To specify a *named parameter* in a query string, code a colon (:) followed by the name of the parameter.

- To set a parameter, code the setParameter method and specify the name of the parameter as the first argument and the value of the parameter as the second argument.

Figure 13-11   How to retrieve a single entity

How to modify data

This topic shows how to use JPA to insert, modify, and delete entities from the database. Once again, thanks to the fact that JPA understands the relationships between your entities, these operations are much simpler to perform in JPA than JDBC.

How to insert, update, or delete a single entity

Figure 13-12 shows how to use JPA to insert, modify, and delete a single entity from the database. When you do that, you need to use a *transaction* to *commit* all operations to the database. Or if any operations fail, you can use the transaction to *roll back* any changes. This ensures data integrity. In other words, it ensures that your data isn't left in an inconsistent state.

The first example shows how to wrap an operation in a transaction. To start, you can call the getTransaction method from the entity manager. This returns an EntityTransaction object. Then, you code a try block. Within that try block, you can start the transaction by calling the begin method from the transaction object. Then, you perform any database operations you want to include in this transaction.

When you're done with the database operations, you can call the commit method of the transaction to save the changes to the database. Or, if an exception is thrown, you can call the rollback method of the transaction object to roll back the changes.

The next three examples show how to insert, update, or delete data in the database. In particular, the second example shows how to use the persist method to insert an entity, the third example shows how to use the merge method to update an entity, and the fourth example shows how to use the merge and remove methods to delete an entity.

The fourth example assumes that the code is running outside of a full Java EE server. As a result, the user entity is detached, and you can't use the remove method directly on it. To solve this issue, this code calls the merge method to update the user entity and attach it to the database. Then, it uses the remove method to delete that entity.

It's important to note that the changes are also saved when you call the flush method or if JPA chooses to flush automatically. JPA may flush changes to the database at any time, even before a transaction has finished. However, your code can roll back these changes. As a result, if the transaction fails, you need to make sure to roll it back. Otherwise, you could end up with inconsistent data.

It's also important to note that until you call the commit method on the transaction, there is no guarantee that your data has been saved to the database. The commit method saves all changes since the beginning of the transaction to the database.

Once again, because JPA understands the relationships between your entities, you only have to save the main entity in your transaction. When you do, JPA automatically saves any dependent entities. For example, when you call the persist method for an Invoice object, JPA also inserts any dependent LineItem objects.

How to wrap an operation in a transaction

```
EntityTransaction trans = em.getTransaction();
try {
    trans.begin();
    em.persist(user);
    trans.commit();
} catch (Exception ex) {
    trans.rollback();
} finally {
    em.close();
}
```

How to insert a single entity

```
em.persist(user);
```

How to update a single entity

```
em.merge(user);
```

How to delete a single entity

```
em.remove(em.merge(user));
```

Methods of the EntityManager object

Method	Description
persist(entity)	Inserts an entity into the database.
merge(entity)	Updates an entity in the database and returns an attached entity.
remove(entity)	Deletes an entity from the database.
flush()	Force any unsaved changes to synchronize to the database.

Description

- If you aren't using a Java EE server, you need to code database operations within a *transaction*. Then, if the transaction is successful, you can *commit* the changes to the database. Conversely, if the transaction isn't successful, you can *roll back* any changes. This ensures data integrity.

- JPA may flush unsaved changes before you finish a transaction. However, if the rollback method of that transaction is called, JPA can still roll back those changes.

- A transaction can be rolled back any time before the commit method is called, or if the commit method is called but fails.

- The methods in this figure may trigger additional inserts, updates, or deletions to satisfy the relationships between entities.

Figure 13-12   How to insert, update, or delete a single entity

How to update or delete multiple entities

Figure 13-13 shows how you can update or delete multiple entities. The first example sets the isProcessed field for all entities to 'y' as long as the invoice ID is below 200. To perform this update, this code uses a try/catch statement. Within the try block, the code begins a transaction, calls the executeUpdate method on the query, and commits the transaction. Here, the executeUpdate method returns a count of the number of rows updated by the query.

The second example deletes the same records instead of updating them. Here, the only statement that's different is the second statement that defines the query string.

As with other queries in JPA, these queries may trigger additional automatic updates and deletions. For instance, deleting invoices as shown in the second example automatically deletes any line items that belong to those invoices.

How to modify multiple entities

To update multiple entities

```
EntityTransaction trans = em.getTransaction();
String qString = "UPDATE Invoice i SET i.isProcessed = 'y' " +
                 "WHERE i.id < :id";
Query q = em.createQuery(qString);
q.setParameter(id, 200);
int count = 0;
try {
    trans.begin();
    count = q.executeUpdate();
    trans.commit();
} catch (Exception ex) {
    trans.rollback();
} finally {
    em.close();
}
```

To delete multiple entities

```
EntityTransaction trans = em.getTransaction();
String qString = "DELETE FROM Invoice i WHERE i.id < :id";
Query q = em.createQuery(qString);
q.setParameter(id, 200);
int count = 0;
try {
    trans.begin();
    count = q.executeUpdate();
    trans.commit();
} catch (Exception ex) {
    trans.rollback();
} finally {
    em.close();
}
```

Description

- The executeUpdate method returns a count of the number of entities affected by the query.
- These queries may trigger additional automatic updates or deletions. For example, deleting an invoice will automatically delete all of its line items.

Figure 13-13   How to update or delete multiple entities

A complete JPA class

Figure 13-14 shows the code for a JPA version of the UserDB class. This class contains the emailExists and insert methods that are used by the Email List application presented in the previous chapter. In addition, this class contains three more methods (update, delete, and selectUser) that can be used to modify and retrieve user data.

If you compare the JPA version of the UserDB class to the JDBC version, you can see that the JPA version is shorter and simpler. That's because JPA automatically converts between the User object and the User table in the database.

In the JPA version of the UserDB class, the methods begin by using the DBUtil class shown earlier in this chapter to get an EntityManagerFactory object. Then, each method uses that factory object to get an EntityManager object.

The methods that modify data

The insert, update, and delete methods get an EntityTransaction object from the EntityManager object. Then, they use this object within a try/catch statement to commit or roll back the transaction. If the database operation succeeds, the try block commits the transaction. Otherwise, if an exception occurs, the catch block prints the exception to the standard output stream and rolls back the transaction.

The UserDB class

```java
package murach.data;

import javax.persistence.EntityManager;
import javax.persistence.EntityTransaction;
import javax.persistence.NoResultException;
import javax.persistence.TypedQuery;

import murach.business.User;

public class UserDB {

    public static void insert(User user) {
        EntityManager em = DBUtil.getEmFactory().createEntityManager();
        EntityTransaction trans = em.getTransaction();
        trans.begin();
        try {
            em.persist(user);
            trans.commit();
        } catch (Exception e) {
            System.out.println(e);
            trans.rollback();
        } finally {
            em.close();
        }
    }

    public static void update(User user) {
        EntityManager em = DBUtil.getEmFactory().createEntityManager();
        EntityTransaction trans = em.getTransaction();
        trans.begin();
        try {
            em.merge(user);
            trans.commit();
        } catch (Exception e) {
            System.out.println(e);
            trans.rollback();
        } finally {
            em.close();
        }
    }

    public static void delete(User user) {
        EntityManager em = DBUtil.getEmFactory().createEntityManager();
        EntityTransaction trans = em.getTransaction();
        trans.begin();
        try {
            em.remove(em.merge(user));
            trans.commit();
        } catch (Exception e) {
            System.out.println(e);
            trans.rollback();
        } finally {
            em.close();
        }
    }
```

Figure 13-14   The database class for the Email List application (part 1 of 2)

The methods that retrieve data

The selectUser method gets a User object that corresponds with the email address that's passed to the method. If the email address is found in the database, JPA automatically fills the User object with values from the database. Then, this method returns the User object to the calling method.

The emailExists method checks if the specified email address already exists in the database. To do that, this method calls the selectUser method to get the User object for the specified email address. If the User object is not equal to null, this method returns true. Otherwise, it returns false.

The UserDB class   **Page 2**

```java
    public static User selectUser(String email) {
        EntityManager em = DBUtil.getEmFactory().createEntityManager();
        String qString = "SELECT u FROM User u " +
                "WHERE u.email = :email";
        TypedQuery<User> q = em.createQuery(qString, User.class);
        q.setParameter("email", email);
        try {
            User user = q.getSingleResult();
            return user;
        } catch (NoResultException e) {
            return null;
        } finally {
            em.close();
        }
    }

    public static boolean emailExists(String email) {
        User u = selectUser(email);
        return u != null;
    }
}
```

Figure 13-14   The database class for the Email List application (part 2 of 2)

Perspective

The goal of this chapter has been to show you how to use JPA to work with databases in Java in a way that is easier than using JDBC. Although there are more features to JPA than what we have presented in this chapter, the skills you have learned here are the essential ones you will need for most small- to medium-sized web applications.

For large websites, you may want to take advantage of some of the additional features offered by a full Java EE server such as automatic transaction commits and rollbacks, and automatic management of entity managers. You can learn more about these features from several sources, including the Java EE tutorial available online from Oracle.

JPA 2 introduced another way to perform queries called the Criteria API. We don't cover the Criteria API in this book because none of the applications presented in this book needed to use it. This API is designed to make dynamic queries easier and safer. Dynamic queries can allow search-engine-like behavior on your website. However, with JDBC and JPQL, it is difficult to write dynamic queries that aren't vulnerable to SQL injection attacks. The Criteria API makes this easier. As a result, if you need to write dynamic queries, the Criteria API is worth looking into.

Summary

- *JPA* (*Java Persistence API*) is a standard API for working with databases in Java that makes object-oriented data easier and more natural to work with than JDBC.

- There are several JPA implementations. Three of the most popular are Hibernate, EclipseLink, and TopLink.

- A business class that's used with JPA is called an *entity*. Entities are managed by an *entity manager*.

- You can convert a business class to an entity by adding JPA annotations to the class.

- To use JPA in an application, you need to add a library for a JPA implementation and configure a persistence unit.

- To use JPA outside of a full Java EE server, you use an EntityManagerFactory object to obtain EntityManager objects.

- You use the @Entity annotation to specify that a business class is an entity.

- You use the @Id annotation to specify which field in your class is the primary key, and you can use the @GeneratedValue annotation to specify how to generate this value.

- *Field annotations* don't use the get and set methods of the class to get and set the values of the fields. Instead, they access the fields directly.

- *Getter annotations* use the get and set methods of the class to get and set the values of the fields.

- You can use the @OneToMany, @ManyToOne, and @OneToOne annotations to specify the relationships between your business classes.

- You can use the @Temporal annotation to specify the SQL type for the java.util.Date and java.util.Calendar types.

- *JPQL* (*Java Persistence Query Language*) is an object-oriented query language defined as part of the JPA specification. It works similarly to SQL, but it isn't SQL.

- JPQL uses *path expressions* to refer to the fields of an entity.

- To specify a *named parameter* in a JPQL query string, code a colon (:) followed by the name of the parameter.

- You can use the persist, merge, and remove methods of the entity manager to insert, update, and delete data.

- When modifying data, you can maintain data integrity by coding database operations within a *transaction*. Then, if the transaction is successful, you can *commit* the changes to the database. Conversely, if the transaction isn't successful, you can *roll back* any changes.

Before you do the exercises for this chapter

The exercises for this chapter assume that you've already installed Tomcat and MySQL as described in appendix A (PC) or B (Mac). As a result, the JAR file for the JDBC driver for MySQL should be available to this project through the Tomcat libraries. If it isn't, you can add this file to your project as described in this chapter.

Exercise 13-1   Test and modify the Email List application

In this exercise, you'll test and experiment with a version of the Email List application that uses JPA.

1. Open the project named ch13_ex1_email that's in the ex_starts directory.

2. Open the persistence.xml file and review its code. Note that it connects to the database named murach_jpa as the user named root and that it can create the database tables if they don't already exist.

3. Open the User class and review its code. Note that it includes an annotation that identifies it as an entity. In addition, it includes an annotation that identifies its userID field as the primary key.

4. Open the DBUtil and UserDB classes. Note that these classes use JPA to retrieve and modify user data.

5.   Run the application and use it to add a user to the email list.

6.   Use MySQL Workbench to view the tables of the murach_jpa database. It should include a table named user that has columns that correspond with the fields of the User class. In addition, it should include a table named sequence that keeps track of the numbers that are automatically generated for the user ID column.

7.   Open the User class and modify it so it uses getter annotations instead of field annotations.

8.   Run the application again and make sure it still works correctly.

Exercise 13-2   Create a User Admin application

In this exercise, you'll create an application that allows you to view all users, update existing users, and delete users in the User table of the murach_jpa database.

Add some users to the database

1.   Open the project named ch13_ex1_email that's in the ex_starts directory.

2.   Run this application and use it to add at least two email addresses to the database.

Review the code for the User Admin application

3.   Open the project named ch13_ex2_userAdmin in the ex_starts directory.

4.   Review the Java code for this application. Note that the UsersServlet and UserDB classes aren't finished.

5.   Review the configuration files for this application. Note that the web.xml file maps the servlet to a URL.

Add a persistence unit

6.   Add a new persistence.xml file named userAdminPU that connects to the database named murach_jpa as the root user.

7.   Open the DBUtil class that's located in the murach.data package. Make sure the name of the persistence unit matches the name in the persistence.xml file.

Add code to display the users

8.   Open the UserDB class that's located in the murach.data package. Then, add code to the selectUsers method to return a List of User objects that corresponds with the rows in the User table.

9.   Open the UsersServlet class and add code to the display_users action that gets a List of User objects from the User table, sets that list as a request attribute, and forwards the request to the index.jsp file.

10. Run the application to make sure it works correctly for the display_users action.

Add code to update a user

11. Open the index.jsp file. Note that the Update and Delete links request the UsersServlet and pass an action parameter to it to specify the action and an email address to specify the user.

12. Open the UsersServlet class and add code for the display_user action that gets the User object for the specified email, stores this object in the request, and forwards the request to the user.jsp file. This should display the user.

13. Open the user.jsp file. Note that it displays user data and submits it to the UsersServlet class with an action that specifies that the user should be updated.

14. Open the UsersServlet class and add code to the update_user action that updates the user in the User table. This servlet should forward the request to the UsersServlet so it displays the current users.

15. Run the application to make sure it works correctly for the update_user action.

Add code to delete a user

16. Open the UsersServlet class and add code to the delete_user action that deletes the specified user. This servlet should forward the request to the UsersServlet so it displays the current users.

17. Run the application to make sure it works correctly.

Section 4

Advanced servlet and JSP skills

This section contains seven chapters that present other servlet and JSP skills that you may need for some of your web applications. In addition, it includes a one-chapter introduction to JSF. Because each of these chapters is written as an independent module, you can read these chapters in whatever sequence you prefer. If, for example, you want to learn how to use listeners to respond to events that occur during a web application's lifecycle, you can skip to chapter 19. Or, if want to learn how to work with a secure connection, you can skip to chapter 15. Eventually, though, you should read all of the chapters in this section because they all provide useful capabilities.

14

How to use JavaMail to send email

When you create a web application, you sometimes need to send email to the users of the application. For example, when a user makes a purchase from an e-commerce site, the web application usually sends a confirmation email that contains information about the order. In this chapter, you'll learn how to use the JavaMail API to send an email from a servlet.

An introduction to the JavaMail API

The JavaMail API is a programming interface that makes it easy for Java developers to write code that automatically sends an email. This API depends on another API known as the JavaBeans Activation Framework (JAF) API. Figure 14-1 introduces you to these APIs and several of the protocols that these APIs use.

How email works

You're probably familiar with *mail client* software that allows you to send and receive messages. For example, the email app on your mobile device, the Microsoft Outlook application on your computer, or the Gmail application in your web browser. This type of software communicates with the *mail server* software that actually sends and retrieves your email. Most likely, your mail server software is provided by your Internet Service Provider (ISP) or through your company.

The diagram in figure 14-1 shows how this works. The protocol that's most commonly used to send email messages is *SMTP*. When you send an email message, the message is first sent from the mail client software on your computer to your mail server using the SMTP protocol. Then, your mail server uses SMTP to send the mail to the recipient's mail server. Finally, the recipient's mail client uses the *POP* protocol or the *IMAP* protocol to retrieve the mail from the recipient's mail server.

A fourth protocol you should know about is *MIME*. Unlike the other protocols described in this figure, MIME isn't used to transfer email messages. Instead, it defines how the content of an email message and its attachments are formatted. In this chapter, you'll learn how to send messages that consist of plain text messages as well as messages that use HTML format.

How email works

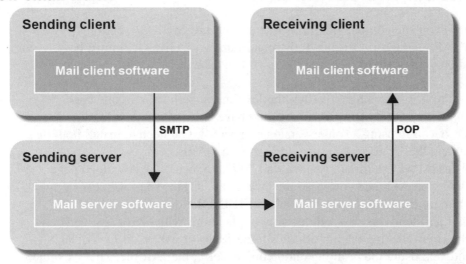

Three protocols for sending and retrieving email messages

Protocol	Description
SMTP	*Simple Mail Transfer Protocol* is used to send a message from one mail server to another.
POP	*Post Office Protocol* is used to retrieve messages from a mail server. This protocol transfers all messages from the mail server to the mail client. Currently, POP is in version 3 and is known as POP3.
IMAP	*Internet Message Access Protocol* is used by web-based mail services such as Gmail and Yahoo. This protocol allows a web browser to read messages that are stored on the mail server. Currently, IMAP is in version 4 and is known as IMAP4.

Another protocol that's used with email

Protocol	Description
MIME	The *Multipurpose Internet Mail Extension* type specifies the type of content that can be sent as a message or attachment.

The JAR files for the JavaMail API

File	Description
javax.mail.jar	Contains the Java classes for the JavaMail API.
activation.jar	Contains the Java classes for the JavaBean Activation Framework. These classes are necessary for the JavaMail API to run.

Description

- The JavaMail API is a high level API that allows you to use a mail protocol to communicate with a mail server. It depends upon another API known as the JavaBeans Activation Framework (JAF) API.

Figure 14-1   An introduction to the JavaMail API

How to install the JavaMail API

Before you can compile programs that use the JavaMail API, both the JavaMail API and the JavaBeans Activation Framework (JAF) API must be installed on your system. To install them, you can use the procedures shown in figure 14-2.

If you're using Java SE 6 or later, the JavaBeans Activation Framework API is installed with it. As a result, you only have to install the JavaMail API. However, if you're using an older version of Java SE, you need to install both the JavaMail and the JavaBeans Activation Framework APIs.

The easiest way to install the JavaMail API is to locate the download page for the JavaMail API, and download the javax.mail.jar file. Then, you can copy the javax.mail.jar file to the application's WEB-INF\lib directory, and add the javax.mail.jar file to the classpath for your application. With NetBeans, you can do that by right-clicking on the Libraries folder, selecting the Add Jar/Folder command, and using the resulting dialog box to select the JAR file. That way, the classes needed by the JavaMail API are available to your system.

To view the documentation for the JavaMail API, you can search the Internet for "javax.mail documentation". Then, you can follow the links to view the documentation for the JavaMail API. This documentation works similarly to the documentation for the Java SE API.

To install the JavaBeans Activation Framework API, you download a ZIP file that contains the JAR file for the library as well as the documentation for the library. As a result, you can view the documentation for the JAF API by navigating to the docs folder of the jaf-1.1 folder that's created on your system when you extract the files from the ZIP file.

How to install the JavaMail API

1. Locate the download page for the JavaMail API.
2. Download the javax.mail.jar file.
3. Copy the javax.mail.jar file to the application's WEB-INF\lib directory. If necessary, you can create this directory.
4. Add the javax.mail.jar file to the classpath for your application. With NetBeans, you can do that by right-clicking on the Libraries folder, selecting the Add Jar/Folder command, and using the resulting dialog box to select the JAR file.

How to install the JavaBeans Activation Framework API

1. Locate the download page for the JavaBeans Activation Framework API.
2. Click on the Download button and follow the instructions.
3. Save the ZIP file for the JavaBeans Activation Framework API to your hard disk. This file is typically named something like jaf-1_1.zip.
4. Extract the files from the ZIP file.
5. Copy the activation.jar file to the application's WEB-INF\lib directory. If necessary, you can create this directory.
6. Add the activation.jar file to the classpath for your application. With NetBeans, you can do that by right-clicking on the Libraries folder, selecting the Add Jar/Folder command, and using the resulting dialog box to select the JAR file.

Description

- Both the JavaMail and JavaBeans Activation Framework (JAF) APIs need to be installed to send email from a servlet.
- The JavaBeans Activation Framework API is included with Java SE 6. As a result, if you're using Java SE 6 or later, you don't need to install this API.
- To view the documentation for the JavaMail API, you can search the Internet for "javax.mail documentation" and follow the links.
- To view the documentation for the JAF API, you can navigate to the docs folder of the jaf-1.1 folder that's created on your system when you install the JAF API.
- If you want to use different versions of these APIs, you should be able to use a similar procedure to the ones shown above to download and install the version you want.

Figure 14-2 How to install the JavaMail API

Code that uses the JavaMail API to send an email message

Figure 14-3 shows the packages that you need to import to be able to send an email, and it shows some Java code that creates and sends an email message that contains plain text. Although you may not understand every line in this example, you can see how the Java API makes it easy to create and send an email. In the next four figures, you'll learn the details for writing code like this.

Three packages for sending email

Package	Description
java.util	Contains the Properties class that's used to set the properties for the email session.
javax.mail	Contains the Session, Message, Address, Transport, and MessagingException classes needed to send a message.
javax.mail.internet	Contains the MimeMessage and InternetAddress classes needed to send an email message across the Internet.

Code that uses the JavaMail API to send an email

```
try {
    // 1 - get a mail session
    Properties props = new Properties();
    props.put("mail.smtp.host", "localhost");
    Session session = Session.getDefaultInstance(props);

    // 2 - create a message
    Message message = new MimeMessage(session);
    message.setSubject(subject);
    message.setText(body);

    // 3 - address the message
    Address fromAddress = new InternetAddress(from);
    Address toAddress = new InternetAddress(to);
    message.setFrom(fromAddress);
    message.setRecipient(Message.RecipientType.TO, toAddress);

    // 4 - send the message
    Transport.send(message);

} catch (MessagingException e) {
    log(e.toString());
}
```

Description

- This code uses the classes that are available from the JavaMail API to send a simple email message that displays plain text.

Figure 14-3   Code that uses the JavaMail API to send an email message

How to create and send an email message

Now that you have a general idea of how to use the JavaMail API to create and send an email message, you'll learn the coding details.

How to create a mail session

Figure 14-4 shows how to create a *mail session* so you can create and send an email message. Before you create a mail session, you need to create a Properties object that contains any properties that the session needs to send or receive mail. A Properties object stores a list of properties where each property has a name, which is often referred to as a key, and a value. To specify properties for a mail session, you can use the put method of the Properties class to define any of the standard properties available from the JavaMail API.

To create a mail session, you can call the static getDefaultInstance method of the Session class to get a Session object that has all of the default settings for a mail session. Before you do that, though, you at the least need to use the Properties class to specify the property for the SMTP host as shown in the first example. Here, the localhost keyword is used to specify that the SMTP server is running on the same computer as the web application. This is often the case when you deploy a web application to a production server.

Like the first example, the second example uses the localhost keyword to specify that the SMTP server is running on the same server as the web application. However, this example explicitly sets two other properties. First, it sets the protocol to SMTP. Then, it sets the port to 25. Since these are the default values, this isn't necessary, but it does show how to set the protocol and port for a server.

After it creates the session object, the second example uses the setDebug method of the Session object to turn on debugging for the session. As a result, the Session object prints debugging information to the Tomcat console. This can be helpful when you're troubleshooting a connection to a new SMTP server.

The third example shows how to use an SMTP server that's running on a remote server. In particular, it shows how to use an SMTP server that's running on a Gmail server. Like many remote SMTP servers, this one uses the SMTPS protocol. Unlike SMTP, SMTPS always uses a secure connection and allows for authentication. For more information about secure connections and authentication, see chapters 15 and 16.

This third example starts by setting the protocol to SMTPS. Then, it sets the host, port, auth, and quitwait properties for the SMTPS protocol. Here, the auth property indicates that the user must be authenticated before the session can connect to the SMTP server, and the quitwait property prevents an SSLException that sometimes occurs when you use a Gmail SMTP server.

If you're running Tomcat on your computer, it can be difficult to find the right settings for testing the JavaMail API. One option is to install an SMTP server on your computer. Then, you can use the localhost keyword to connect to

Common properties that can be set for a Session object

Property	Description
`mail.transport.protocol`	Specifies the protocol that's used for the session. For sending email, the protocol is usually smtp or smtps.
`mail.smtp.host`	Specifies the host computer for the SMTP server.
`mail.smtp.port`	Specifies the port that the SMTP server is using.
`mail.smtp.auth`	Specifies whether authentication is required to log in to the SMTP server.
`mail.smtp.quitwait`	This property can be set to false to prevent an SSLException from occurring when you attempt to connect to a Gmail SMTP server.

How to get a mail session for a local SMTP server

```
Properties props = new Properties();
props.put("mail.smtp.host", "localhost");
Session session = Session.getDefaultInstance(props);
```

Another way to get a mail session for a local SMTP server

```
Properties props = new Properties();
props.put("mail.transport.protocol", "smtp");
props.put("mail.smtp.host", "localhost");
props.put("mail.smtp.port", 25);
Session session = Session.getDefaultInstance(props);
session.setDebug(true);
```

How to get a mail session for a remote SMTP server

```
Properties props = new Properties();
props.put("mail.transport.protocol", "smtps");
props.put("mail.smtps.host", "smtp.gmail.com");
props.put("mail.smtps.port", 465);
props.put("mail.smtps.auth", "true");
props.put("mail.smtps.quitwait", "false");
Session session = Session.getDefaultInstance(props);
session.setDebug(true);
```

Description

- A Session object contains information about the *mail session* such as the procotol, the host, the port, and so on. (This isn't the same as the HttpSession object.)
- To set the properties of a Properties object, you can use the put method to specify a property name and value for each property.
- The static getDefaultInstance method of the Session class returns the default Session object for the application.
- The setDebug method of the Session object can be used to print debugging information about the session to a log file.
- If you change the properties for a Session object, you must restart Tomcat before the changes take effect.
- If the Java application is running on the same computer as the SMTP server, you can usually use the localhost keyword to specify the SMTP host.

Figure 14-4   How to create a mail session

that server. Another option is to work with your network administrator or your ISP to get the details that you need for connecting to a remote SMTP server.

When you work with a mail session, keep in mind that there are many other mail session properties that aren't shown in this figure. If necessary, you can set these properties using the techniques that you've just learned.

However, when you change the properties that are stored in the Session object, you need to restart Tomcat to put them in force. That's because the static getDefaultInstance method of the Session object returns the existing Session object if one already exists. So if you want to create a new Session object that uses the new properties, you must get rid of the old Session object. The easiest way to do that is to restart Tomcat.

How to create a message

Once you've created the Session object, you can create an object that defines an email message as shown in figure 14-5. To do that, you pass a Session object to the constructor of the MimeMessage class to create a MimeMessage object. Then, you can set the subject, body, and addresses for the message. To set the subject, you use the setSubject method. To set the message body as plain text, you use the setText method. Then, you use the methods shown in the next figure to set the addresses for the message.

When you use the setText method to set the body of the message, the MIME type for the message is automatically set to text/plain. For many text messages, this is adequate. However, since most modern mail clients can display text that's formatted with HTML tags, it's also common to use the setContent method to change the MIME type for a message to text/html. Then, the body of the message can include HTML tags that format the text, display images, and provide links to web resources.

How to create a message
```
Message message = new MimeMessage(session);
```

How to set the subject line of a message
```
message.setSubject("Order Confirmation");
```

How to set the body of a plain text message
```
message.setText("Thanks for your order!");
```

How to set the body of an HTML message
```
message.setContent("<h1>Thanks for your order!</h1>", "text/html");
```

Description

- You can use the MimeMessage class that's stored in the javax.mail.internet package to create a message. This message extends the Message class that's stored in the javax.mail package.

- To create a MimeMessage object, you supply a valid Session object to the MimeMessage constructor.

- Once you've created a MimeMessage object, you can use the setSubject and setText methods to set the subject line and body of the email message. This automatically sets the MIME type to text/plain.

- You can use the setContent method to include an HTML document as the body of the message. To do that, the first argument specifies a string for the HTML document, and the second argument specifies text/html as the MIME type.

- All of the methods in this figure throw a javax.mail.MessagingException. As a result, you must handle this exception when you use these methods.

Figure 14-5   How to create a message

How to address a message

Figure 14-6 shows how to address a MimeMessage object like the one in the last figure. This allows you to specify the From address as well as the To, CC (*carbon copy*), and BCC (*blind carbon copy*) addresses. When you send a carbon copy, the CC addresses appear in the message, but when you send a blind carbon copy, the BCC addresses don't appear in the message.

Before you can set an address within a MimeMessage object, though, you must create an Address object that defines at least an email address. To do that, you create an object from the InternetAddress subclass of the Address class. When you create this object, the first argument specifies the email address.

If you want to associate a name with the email address, you can include a second argument. Then, the name is displayed next to the email address like this: andi@yahoo.com (Andrea Steelman). However, this constructor throws an exception of the java.io.UnsupportedEncodingException type. As a result, you must handle this exception if you associate a name with the email address.

To set the From address, you can use the setFrom method of the MimeMessage object. When you use this method, you must supply an Address object that defines the email address you wish to be displayed in the From attribute of the email message.

To set the To, CC, and BCC addresses, you can use the setRecipient method of the MimeMessage object. With this method, the first argument specifies the type of recipient for the address. Then, the second argument specifies an Address object. To specify the recipient type, you use one of the fields defined in the Message.RecipientType class.

If you want to send your message to multiple recipients, you can use the setRecipients method of the MimeMessage class. This method allows you to send a message to an array of Address objects. When you use this method, it replaces any recipients that were already set in the message. However, if you want to add recipients to an existing message, you can use the addRecipient or addRecipients methods. These methods work like the setRecipient and setRecipients methods, but they add recipients to an existing list.

Since the methods of the MimeMessage class throw a MessagingException, you must handle this exception in any code that uses these methods. In addition, the InternetAddress constructor throws an AddressException when an illegally formatted address is found. However, since the AddressException class extends the MessagingException class, you can catch both exceptions by catching the MessagingException.

How to set the From address

```
Address fromAddress = new InternetAddress("cds@murach.com");
message.setFrom(fromAddress);
```

How to set the To address

```
Address toAddress = new InternetAddress("andi@yahoo.com");
message.setRecipient(Message.RecipientType.TO, toAddress);
```

How to set the CC address

```
Address ccAddress = new InternetAddress("ted@yahoo.com");
message.setRecipient(Message.RecipientType.CC, ccAddress);
```

How to set the BCC address

```
Address bccAddress = new InternetAddress("jsmith@gmail.com");
message.setRecipient(Message.RecipientType.BCC, bccAddress);
```

How to include an email address and a name

```
Address toAddress =
    new InternetAddress("andi@yahoo.com", "Andrea Steelman");
```

How to send a message to multiple recipients

```
Address[] mailList = { new InternetAddress("andi@hotmail.com"),
                       new InternetAddress("joelmurach@yahoo.com"),
                       new InternetAddress("jsmith@gmail.com") };
message.setRecipients(Message.RecipientType.TO, mailList);
```

How to add recipients to a message

```
Address toAddress = new InternetAddress("joelmurach@yahoo.com");
message.addRecipient(Message.RecipientType.TO, toAddress);
```

Description

- To define an email address, use the InternetAddress class that's stored in the javax.mail.internet package. This class is a subclass of the Address class that's stored in the javax.mail package.

- To set the From address, use the setFrom method of the MimeMessage object.

- To set the To, CC (*carbon copy*), and BCC (*blind carbon copy*) addresses, use the setRecipient and setRecipients methods of the MimeMessage object.

- To include a name that's associated with an email address, you can add a second argument to the InternetAddress constructor. However, this constructor throws an exception of the java.io.UnsupportedEncodingException type.

- To send an email message to multiple recipients, you can pass an array of Address objects to the setRecipients method. This replaces any existing addresses.

- To add email addresses to any existing addresses for a message, use the addRecipient and addRecipients methods.

- All of the methods in this figure throw a javax.mail.MessagingException. As a result, you must handle this exception when using these methods.

Figure 14-6   How to address a message

How to send a message

Once you've created and addressed a MimeMessage object as shown in the last two figures, you can send the message as shown in figure 14-7. For an SMTP server that doesn't require authentication, you can call the static send method of the Transport class with the MimeMessage object as the argument.

However, if the SMTP server requires authentication, you use the getTransport method of the session object to return a Transport object. Then, you can use the connect method to specify a username and password that can be used to connect to the server. In this figure, for example, the connect method specifies a username of "johnsmith@gmail.com" and a password of "sesame".

Once you've connected to the SMTP server, you can use the sendMessage method to send the message. When you use this method, you can specify the MimeMessage object as the first argument, and you can specify the second argument by calling the getAllRecipients method of the MimeMessage object. Finally, you can use the close method to close the connection.

If the message can't be sent, the send or sendMessage method throws an exception of the SendFailedException type. This exception contains a list of (1) invalid addresses to which the message could not be sent, (2) valid addresses to which the message wasn't sent, and (3) valid addresses to which the message was sent. If necessary, you can use this exception to perform some processing such as writing these addresses to a log file.

How to send a message when no authentication is required

```
Transport.send(message);
```

How to send a message when authentication is required

```
Transport transport = session.getTransport();
transport.connect("johnsmith@gmail.com", "sesame");
transport.sendMessage(message, message.getAllRecipients());
transport.close();
```

Description

- If the SMTP server doesn't require authentication, you can use the static send method of the Transport class to send a message to the specified SMTP server.
- If the SMTP server requires authentication, you can use the getTransport method of the session object to return a Transport object. Then, you can use the connect method to specify a username and password that can be used to connect to the server; the sendMessage method to send the message; and the close method to close the connection.
- If the SMTP host is incorrect in the session object, the send method throws a SendFailedException object.
- The send method also throws a SendFailedException object when a message can't be sent. You can use this object to return the invalid addresses, the valid addresses that have been sent, and the valid addresses that haven't been sent.
- Since the SendFailedException class inherits the MessagingException class, you can catch both types of exceptions by catching the MessagingException.

Figure 14-7   How to send a message

Example classes
that send an email message

Now that you know the coding details for creating and sending an email message, here are three classes that put that code into use. The first is a helper class that can be used to send a message to a local SMTP server. The second is a servlet that uses the helper class to send a message. The third is a helper class that can be used to send a message to a remote SMTP server.

A helper class for sending an email
with a local SMTP server

Figure 14-8 shows a helper class named MailUtilLocal that you can use to send an email. This class contains a static method named sendMail that creates and sends a message from a single email address to a single email address. Since this method throws an exception of the MessagingException type, any class that calls this method must catch this exception.

The fifth parameter of the sendMail method is a Boolean value that specifies whether the body of the message contains HTML formatting. As a result, if this parameter is set to true, this method uses the setContent method to set the body of the message and to indicate that the body contains HTML formatting. Otherwise, this method uses the setText method to set the body of the message as plain text.

Although this MailUtilLocal class is simple, it is useful. To enhance it, you can add sendMail methods that provide for CC and BCC addresses. Or, you can add sendMail methods that provide for multiple TO, CC, and BCC addresses.

A helper class for sending an email with a local SMTP server

```java
package murach.util;

import java.util.Properties;
import javax.mail.*;
import javax.mail.internet.*;

public class MailUtilLocal {

    public static void sendMail(String to, String from,
            String subject, String body, boolean bodyIsHTML)
            throws MessagingException {

        // 1 - get a mail session
        Properties props = new Properties();
        props.put("mail.transport.protocol", "smtp");
        props.put("mail.smtp.host", "localhost");
        props.put("mail.smtp.port", 25);
        Session session = Session.getDefaultInstance(props);
        session.setDebug(true);

        // 2 - create a message
        Message message = new MimeMessage(session);
        message.setSubject(subject);
        if (bodyIsHTML)
            message.setContent(body, "text/html");
        else
            message.setText(body);

        // 3 - address the message
        Address fromAddress = new InternetAddress(from);
        Address toAddress = new InternetAddress(to);
        message.setFrom(fromAddress);
        message.setRecipient(Message.RecipientType.TO, toAddress);

        // 4 - send the message
        Transport.send(message);
    }
}
```

Description

- You can use the static sendMail method of this MailUtilLocal class to send an email message with a From address and a To address.

- Since the sendMail method throws the MessagingException, any class that uses this method must handle this exception.

Figure 14-8   A helper class for sending an email with a local SMTP server

A servlet that uses a helper class to send an email message

Figure 14-9 presents the code for the EmailListServlet class. Since you've seen variations of this class throughout this book, you shouldn't have any trouble understanding how it works. This time, though, the servlet uses the MailUtilLocal class presented in the last figure to send an email message to the email address that the user entered.

After the servlet writes the User object to the database, the servlet creates four strings that contain the information for the email message. First, it sets the To address to the email address that was passed with the request. Then, it sets the From address, the subject line, and the text for the body of the message.

In addition, this servlet creates a Boolean variable that specifies whether the body of the email contains HTML formatting. In this case, this variable is set to false. As a result, the email uses plain text formatting.

A servlet that sends an email

```
package murach.email;

import java.io.*;
import javax.mail.MessagingException;
import javax.servlet.*;
import javax.servlet.http.*;

import murach.business.User;
import murach.data.UserDB;
import murach.util.*;

public class EmailListServlet extends HttpServlet {

    @Override
    protected void doPost(HttpServletRequest request,
            HttpServletResponse response)
            throws ServletException, IOException {

        // get current action
        String action = request.getParameter("action");
        if (action == null) {
            action = "join";   // default action
        }

        // perform action and set URL to appropriate page
        String url = "/index.jsp";
        if (action.equals("join")) {
            url = "/index.jsp";      // the "join" page
        } else if (action.equals("add")) {
            // get parameters from the request
            String firstName = request.getParameter("firstName");
            String lastName = request.getParameter("lastName");
            String email = request.getParameter("email");

            // store data in User object
            User user = new User(firstName, lastName, email);
            UserDB.insert(user);
            request.setAttribute("user", user);

            // send email to user
            String to = email;
            String from = "email_list@murach.com";
            String subject = "Welcome to our email list";
            String body = "Dear " + firstName + ",\n\n"
                + "Thanks for joining our email list. We'll make sure to send "
                + "you announcements about new products and promotions.\n"
                + "Have a great day and thanks again!\n\n"
                + "Kelly Slivkoff\n"
                + "Mike Murach & Associates";
            boolean isBodyHTML = false;
```

Figure 14-9   A servlet that uses a helper class to send an email message (part 1 of 2)

To create and send the message, the servlet calls the sendMail method of the MailUtilLocal class. Since this method throws a MessagingException, the servlet catches that exception. Then, it stores a custom error message in a String variable named errorMessage, and it sets that message as an attribute of the request object. That way, the next JSP can display the error message.

Finally, this code uses the log method of the servlet to write the email that you were trying to send to a log file. That way, you can view the email even if the sendMail method isn't able to successfully send the email.

If you can't send an email message with a servlet, there are several possible causes. First, you might not be able to connect to your SMTP server. To solve this problem, you may need to make sure that you are connected to the Internet. Second, you might not have the correct name for the SMTP server or you might not have the proper security clearance for accessing the server. To solve this problem, you might need to contact your network administrator or ISP.

A servlet that sends an email   **Page 2**

```
        try {
            MailUtilLocal.sendMail(to, from, subject, body, isBodyHTML);
        } catch (MessagingException e) {
            String errorMessage
                = "ERROR: Unable to send email. "
                + "Check Tomcat logs for details.<br>"
                + "NOTE: You may need to configure your system "
                + "as described in chapter 14.<br>"
                + "ERROR MESSAGE: " + e.getMessage();
            request.setAttribute("errorMessage", errorMessage);
            this.log(
                "Unable to send email. \n"
                + "Here is the email you tried to send: \n"
                + "=====================================\n"
                + "TO: " + email + "\n"
                + "FROM: " + from + "\n"
                + "SUBJECT: " + subject + "\n"
                + "\n"
                + body + "\n\n");
        }
        url = "/thanks.jsp";
    }
    getServletContext()
            .getRequestDispatcher(url)
            .forward(request, response);
    }
}
```

Figure 14-9   A servlet that uses a helper class to send an email message (part 2 of 2)

A helper class for sending an email with a remote SMTP server

Figure 14-10 shows a helper class named MailUtilGmail that you can use to send an email with a remote SMTP server. In particular, you can use this class to send an email with an SMTP server that's available from Gmail. Of course, this only works if you have a Gmail account with a valid username and password.

If you compare this class with the MailUtilLocal class shown in figure 14-8, you'll see that it works similarly. The primary differences are that the properties for the Session object specify that the session should use the SMTPS protocol, an SMTP server from Gmail, and port 465. In addition, the auth property requires authentication for the SMTP server. As a result, the connect method of the Transport object must specify a valid username and password for a Gmail account.

A helper class for sending an email with a remote SMTP server

```
package murach.util;

import java.util.Properties;
import javax.mail.*;
import javax.mail.internet.*;

public class MailUtilGmail {

    public static void sendMail(String to, String from,
            String subject, String body, boolean bodyIsHTML)
            throws MessagingException {

        // 1 - get a mail session
        Properties props = new Properties();
        props.put("mail.transport.protocol", "smtps");
        props.put("mail.smtps.host", "smtp.gmail.com");
        props.put("mail.smtps.port", 465);
        props.put("mail.smtps.auth", "true");
        props.put("mail.smtps.quitwait", "false");
        Session session = Session.getDefaultInstance(props);
        session.setDebug(true);

        // 2 - create a message
        Message message = new MimeMessage(session);
        message.setSubject(subject);
        if (bodyIsHTML) {
            message.setContent(body, "text/html");
        } else {
            message.setText(body);
        }

        // 3 - address the message
        Address fromAddress = new InternetAddress(from);
        Address toAddress = new InternetAddress(to);
        message.setFrom(fromAddress);
        message.setRecipient(Message.RecipientType.TO, toAddress);

        // 4 - send the message
        Transport transport = session.getTransport();
        transport.connect("johnsmith@gmail.com", "sesame");
        transport.sendMessage(message, message.getAllRecipients());
        transport.close();
    }
}
```

Figure 14-10   A helper class for sending an email with a remote SMTP server

Perspective

In this chapter, you learned how to use the JavaMail API to send email from your servlets. Keep in mind, though, that you can use the JavaMail API to do more than that. For instance, you can use that API to send messages that have attachments and to retrieve messages. If you need to do tasks like that, you should be able to use the documentation for the JavaMail API to build on the skills you've learned in this chapter.

Summary

- When an email message is sent it goes from the *mail client* software to that client's *mail server* software to the receiving client's mail server and then to the receiving mail client.

- To send email messages from server to server, the *Simple Mail Transfer Protocol* (*SMTP*) is commonly used. Then, to retrieve messages from a server, *Post Office Protocol* (*POP*) and *Internet Message Access Protocol* (*IMAP*) are commonly used.

- To send email messages from your Java programs, you use the classes of the JavaMail API. In particular, you create a Session object that contains information about the *mail session* including an address for the SMTP server.

Exercise 14-1   Send an email from a servlet

1. Open the ch14_ex1_email project in the ex_starts directory. If NetBeans displays error markers next to the classes in the murach.email and murach.util packages, install the JavaMail API on your system as described in figure 14-2. If that doesn't fix the problem, install the Java Activation Framework too.

2. Review the helper classes in the murach.util package, including the one for Yahoo email users and the one for Gmail users. Then, choose the class that's closest to what you're going to need for sending email on your system, and modify it so it works on your system.

    If possible, get help from someone who knows what the properties for the mail session need to be. But if that isn't possible and you don't know what the properties should be, continue with this exercise anyway.

3. Review the servlet named EmailListServlet that's in the murach.email package. Note that it sends a message to the person who joins the email list. Then, modify this servlet so it uses the sendMail method of the helper class that you modified in step 2. In addition, modify the From address so it uses your email address.

4. Test the application by entering your name and email address and clicking on the Submit button. If the application works, you should receive an email message. Otherwise, you should see error messages at the bottom of the JSP that's displayed. Then, you can look at the Tomcat log file to see what the email message would have looked like if it had worked.

15

How to use SSL to work with a secure connection

If your application requires users to enter sensitive data such as credit card numbers and passwords, you should use a secure connection when you send data between the client and the server. Otherwise, a hacker might be able to intercept and view this data. In this chapter, you'll learn how to transfer data over a secure connection.

An introduction to SSL

To prevent others from reading data that is transmitted over the Internet, you can use the *Secure Sockets Layer* (*SSL*). This is the protocol that lets you transfer data between the server and the client over a secure connection.

How SSL works

Figure 15-1 shows a web page that uses SSL to transfer data between the server and the client over a *secure connection*. To determine if you're transmitting data over a secure connection, you can read the URL. If it starts with https rather than http, then you're transmitting data over a secure connection. In addition, a small lock icon typically appears to the left of the URL.

With a regular HTTP connection, all data is sent as unencrypted plain text. As a result, if a hacker intercepts this data, it is easy to read. With a secure connection, though, all data is encrypted before it's transferred between the client and server. Although hackers can still intercept this data, they won't be able to read it unless they can crack the encryption code.

How TLS works

Transport Layer Security (*TLS*) is another protocol that's used for working with secure connections. This protocol is more advanced than SSL, but it works similarly. As a user, it's hard to tell whether you're using an SSL connection or a TLS connection. Although TLS is only supported by newer browsers, any server that implements TLS also implements SSL. That way, the newer browsers can use TLS, and the older browsers can still use SSL.

When you're working with secure connections, you'll find that SSL is often used to describe the connection instead of TLS. That's because SSL is the older, more established protocol for working with secure connections. In this chapter, the term SSL is used even though the connection could also be a TLS connection.

When to use a secure connection

Due to the time it takes to encrypt and decrypt the data that's sent across a secure connection, secure connections are slower than regular HTTP connections. As a result, you usually use secure connections only when your application passes sensitive data between the client and the server.

A request made with a secure connection

Description

- *Transport Layer Security* (*TLS*) and *Secure Sockets Layer* (*SSL*) are the two protocols used by the Internet that allow clients and servers to communicate over a *secure connection*.

- TLS is the successor to SSL. Although there are slight differences between SSL and TLS, the protocol remains substantially the same. As a result, they are sometimes referred to as the TLS/SSL protocol or these terms are used interchangeably.

- With SSL, the browser encrypts all data that's sent to the server and decrypts all data that's received from the server. Conversely, the server encrypts all data that's sent to the browser and decrypts all data that's received from the browser.

- SSL is able to determine if data has been tampered with during transit.

- SSL is also able to verify that a server or a client is who it claims to be.

- The URL for a secure connection starts with HTTPS instead of HTTP.

- A web browser that is using a secure connection typically displays a lock icon to the left of the URL for the web page.

Figure 15-1   An introduction to SSL

How SSL authentication works

To use SSL to transmit data, the client and the server must provide *authentication* as shown in figure 15-2. That way, both the client and the server can accept or reject the secure connection. Before a secure connection is established, the server uses *SSL server authentication* to authenticate itself. It does this by providing a *digital secure certificate* to the browser.

By default, browsers accept digital secure certificates that come from trusted sources. However, if the browser doesn't recognize the certificate as coming from a trusted source, it displays a warning page like the one shown later in this chapter. Then, the user can decide whether to proceed anyway. To help decide, the user can view the certificate. Although the technique for doing this is different for each browser, the user can typically do this by clicking on the lock icon and using the resulting menu to view the certificate. If the user chooses to proceed, the secure connection is established.

In some rare cases, a server may want the client to authenticate itself with *SSL client authentication*. For example, a bank might want to use SSL client authentication to make sure it's sending sensitive information such as account numbers and balances to the correct person. To implement this type of authentication, a digital certificate must be installed on the client, which is usually a browser.

A digital secure certificate

Types of digital secure certificates

Certificate	Description
Server certificate	Issued to trusted servers so client computers can connect to them using secure connections.
Client certificate	Issued to trusted clients so server computers can confirm their identity.

How authentication works

- *Authentication* is the process of determining whether a server or client is who and what it claims to be.

- When a browser makes an initial attempt to communicate with a server over a secure connection, the server authenticates itself by providing a *digital secure certificate*.

- If the digital secure certificate is registered with the browser, the browser doesn't display the certificate by default. However, the user can typically view the certificate by clicking on the lock icon that's displayed by the browser and using the resulting menu.

- In some rare cases, the server may request that a browser authenticate itself by presenting its own digital secure certificate.

Figure 15-2   How SSL authentication works

How to get a digital secure certificate

If you want to establish a secure connection with your clients, you must get a *digital secure certificate* from a trusted source such as those listed in figure 15-3. These *certification authorities* (*CAs*) verify that the person or company requesting the certificate is a valid person or company by checking with a *registration authority* (*RA*). To obtain a digital secure certificate, you'll need to provide an RA with information about yourself or your company. Once the RA approves the request, the CA can issue the digital secure certificate.

A digital secure certificate from a trusted source is typically not free, and the cost of the certificate depends on a variety of factors such as the level of security. As a result, when you purchase a digital certificate, you want one that fits the needs of your web site. In particular, you'll need to decide what *SSL strength* you want the connection to support. SSL strength refers to the level of encryption that the secure connection uses when it transmits data.

In the early days of web programming, many web servers used certificates with 40-bit or 56-bit SSL strength. Since it's possible for a determined hacker to crack the encryption code for these strengths, these strengths are rarely used any more.

Today, most web servers use 128-bit or 256-bit SSL strength. Although these certificates are more expensive than 56-bit certificates, it's extremely hard for a hacker to crack the encryption code. Since most modern web browsers support 256-bit encryption, they are able to use this SSL strength. Meanwhile, older browsers that don't support this strength can use whatever lesser strength they support.

Once you purchase a secure certificate, you typically send it to your web host who installs it for your site. Once the certificate is installed, you can use SSL to transmit data over a secure connection.

Some certificate authorities that issue digital secure certificates

```
www.symantec.com/ssl-sem-page
www.godaddy.com/ssl
www.globalsign.com
www.startcom.org
www.comodo.com/
```

SSL strengths

Strength	Pros and Cons
40-bit	Most browsers support it, but it's relatively easy to crack the encryption code.
56-bit	It's thousands of times stronger than 40-bit strength and most browsers support it, but it's still possible to crack the encryption code.
128-bit	It's over a trillion times a trillion times stronger than 40-bit strength, which makes it extremely difficult to crack the encryption code, but it's more expensive.
256-bit	It's virtually impossible to crack the encryption code, but it's more expensive and not all browsers support it.

Description

- To use SSL in your web applications, you must first purchase a digital secure certificate from a trusted *certificate authority* (*CA*). Once you obtain the certificate, you send it to the people who host your web site so they can install it on the server.

- A CA is a company that issues and manages security credentials. To verify information provided by the requestor of the secure certificate, a CA must check with a *registration authority* (*RA*). Once the RA verifies the requestor's information, the CA can issue a digital secure certificate.

- Since SSL is built into all major browsers and web servers, installing a digital secure certificate enables SSL.

- *SSL strength* refers to the length of the generated key that is created during the encryption process. The longer the key, the more difficult to crack the encryption code.

- The SSL strength that's used depends on the strength provided by the certificate, the strength supported by the web server, and the strength supported by the browser. If a web server or browser isn't able to support the strength provided by the certificate, a lesser strength is used.

Figure 15-3　How to get a digital secure certificate

How to configure a testing environment for SSL

If you're using a commercial web server, you probably won't need to configure the server for SSL. To implement SSL, you just purchase a secure certificate and provide it to the web hosting company. Then, your web hosting company should configure SSL for you.

However, if you want to be able to test secure connections before you deploy them to your web server, you'll need to configure your testing environment. To do that, you can create and install a self-signed digital secure certificate for free.

Since a self-signed certificate doesn't come from a trusted source, it causes the browser to display a warning when you use it. However, it allows you to configure a secure connection for your local testing environment as described in this topic. Although this topic shows how to work with Tomcat 8.0, similar skills apply to other web servers.

The *Java Secure Socket Extension (JSSE)* API is a collection of Java classes that let you use secure connections within your Java programs. Without it, your application won't be able to connect to the server that transmits data over a secure connection. Fortunately, the JSSE API has been included as part of the Java SE library since version 1.4 of the JDK. As a result, if you're using a modern version of the JDK, the JSSE API should already be installed on your system.

How to create a certificate for testing

Figure 15-4 shows how to create a self-signed digital secure certificate for your system. To start, you must create a *keystore file*. To do that, you can open a Command Prompt (PC) or Terminal (Mac) window and use the cd command to change the current directory to the bin directory of your JDK. Next, you enter the keytool command with the parameters shown in this figure. Then, the keytool program prompts you to enter some passwords and other information.

When you're asked for the keystore password, you must enter "changeit". If you don't, the certificate won't work properly. Later, when the keytool program asks for the key password for Tomcat, you should press Enter to use the same password as the keystore password.

For the rest of the prompts, you can enter any information about yourself and your company that you want. The secure certificate for testing purposes displays this information.

When you finish responding to the prompts, the keytool program creates a keystore file named

`.keystore`

and it stores this file in your home directory. This directory varies depending on your operating system, but you should be able to find the keystore file by searching for it.

A command prompt after creating a secure certificate for testing

```
Command Prompt

C:\>cd \Program Files\Java\jdk1.7.0\bin

C:\Program Files\Java\jdk1.7.0\bin>keytool -genkey -alias tomcat -keyalg RSA
Enter keystore password:
What is your first and last name?
  [Unknown]:  Joel Murach
What is the name of your organizational unit?
  [Unknown]:  MMA Web
What is the name of your organization?
  [Unknown]:  MMA
What is the name of your City or Locality?
  [Unknown]:  Fresno
What is the name of your State or Province?
  [Unknown]:  CA
What is the two-letter country code for this unit?
  [Unknown]:  US
Is CN=Joel Murach, OU=MMA Web, O=MMA, L=Fresno, ST=CA, C=US correct?
  [no]:  y

Enter key password for <tomcat>
        (RETURN if same as keystore password):

C:\Program Files\Java\jdk1.7.0\bin>
```

Tomcat's server.xml file

The Connector element for an SSL connection

```
<!-- Define a SSL HTTP/1.1 Connector on port 8443 -->
<Connector port="8443" protocol="org.apache.coyote.http11.Http11NioProtocol"
           SSLEnabled="true" maxThreads="150" scheme="https" secure="true"
           clientAuth="false" sslProtocol="TLS"
           keystoreFile="${user.home}/.keystore" keystorePass="changeit"/>
```

The procedure for configuring SSL on a local system

1. Use the Command Prompt (Windows) or Terminal (Mac) to create a keystore file. To do that, open the command prompt, and use the cd command to navigate to the bin directory of your JDK. Then, run the keytool command shown above and respond to the prompts. Be sure to use "changeit" as the keystore password, and to press Enter to use the same password for the key password.

2. Edit the server.xml file in Tomcat's conf directory. Then, remove the comments from the Connector element for the SSL connector and edit its attributes as shown above.

3. Restart Tomcat.

Description

- The *Java Secure Socket Extension* (JSSE) API is a collection of Java classes that enable secure connections within Java programs by implementing a version of the SSL and TLS protocols. The JSSE API is included with JDK 1.4 and later.

- To test SSL connections in a local environment, you can create a self-signed certificate. To do that, you create a *keystore file* as shown above.

- By default, Tomcat's server.xml file defines the protocol as TLS, not SSL. As a result, newer browsers use TLS, and older browsers use SSL.

Figure 15-4   How to configure SSL on a local system

How to enable SSL in Tomcat

After you create the keystore file, you need to enable SSL in Tomcat by editing the server.xml file located in Tomcat's conf directory. To do that, you open this file in a text editor. Then, you can remove the comments from the Connector element that's shown in the figure 15-4. This Connector element defines a secure connection on port 8443, and it specifies the TLS as the SSL protocol. As a result, newer browsers use the TLS protocol, and older browsers use the SSL protocol.

After you remove the comments from this Connector element, you must add the two highlighted attributes in this figure. First, you must add a keystoreFile attribute that points to the .keystore file. Then, you must add a keystorePass attribute that specifies the password that's used for the keystore file.

How to test a local SSL connection

Once you've configured your testing environment as described in the last figure, you can test your local SSL connection by starting or restarting Tomcat and entering this URL:

`https://localhost:8443`

Note that this URL begins with https and includes the port number for the SSL connection. Although it's possible to change the SSL port to another value when you're using a testing environment, you must specify the number of a valid SSL port.

If the SSL connection works and you're using a temporary testing certificate, most browsers typically display a warning page like the one shown in the next figure. This page indicates that the certificate does not come from a trusted source. At this point, you can usually ignore the warning page and proceed to the requested page. In that case, you should be able to view a page like the one shown in figure 15-5. If this doesn't work, you'll need to troubleshoot your connection. To do that, you can check the problems described in this figure, and you can review the previous figure. If there's a problem with the keystore file, you may need to find the keystore file, delete it, and create a new one.

The URL you can use to test the local SSL connection

`https://localhost:8443`

A warning page for the security certificate

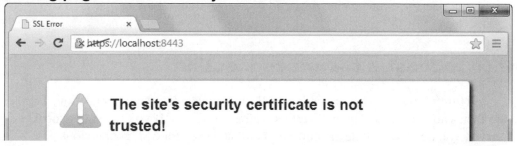

The page that's displayed if SSL is set up correctly on the local system

Common problems when configuring the local SSL connection

Problem 1

Problem: Tomcat can't find the keystore file. When you start Tomcat, it throws a java.io.FileNotFoundException.

Solution: Make sure the .keystore file is located in your home directory, which varies from system to system. For Windows, the home directory is C:\Users*user.name*.

Problem 2

Problem: The keystore password and key passwords that you used to create the keystore file don't match. When you start Tomcat, it displays a java.io.FileNotFoundException that says, "keystore was tampered with" or "password was incorrect."

Solution: Delete the old keystore file and create a new keystore file.

Notes

- The keystore file is named .keystore and it's stored in your operating system's home directory. For Windows, the home directory is C:\Users*user.name*.
- After you enter the URL, your web browser prompts you with dialog boxes like those in the next figure.

Figure 15-5   How to test a local SSL connection

How to work with a secure connection

Once a remote or local server has been configured to work with SSL, it's easy to request a secure connection, and it's easy to return to a regular HTTP connection.

How to request a secure connection

Figure 15-6 shows how to code a URL that requests a secure connection. To do that, you code an absolute URL that begins with https. If you're using a local server, you need to include the port number that's used for SSL connections. Although the two examples show how to request a JSP, you can use the same technique to request secure connections for any URL.

When a secure connection is requested, the server authenticates itself by sending its secure certificate to the browser. Then, if the certificate doesn't come from a certification authority that's registered with the browser, the browser should display a warning page like the one in this figure. Since a self-signed certificate doesn't come from a trusted source, your browser should display a dialog box like this when you request a secure connection in your local testing environment.

A URL that requests a secure connection over the Internet

```
https://www.murach.com/email/join.jsp
```

A URL that requests a secure connection from a local system

```
https://localhost:8443/ch15email/join.jsp
```

A warning page for the security certificate

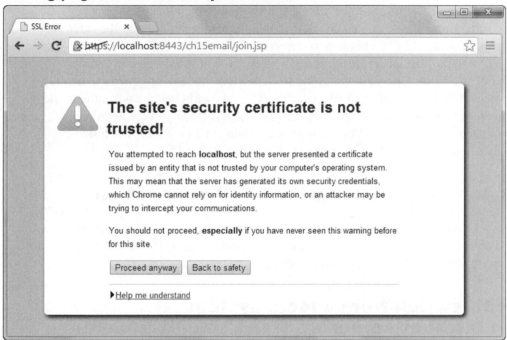

Description

- To request a secure connection, you use an absolute URL that starts with https. If you're requesting a resource from a local system, you also need to specify the port that's used for secure connections. For Tomcat, that port is usually 8443.

- Once you establish a secure connection, you can use relative URLs to continue using the secure connection.

Figure 15-6   How to request a secure connection

A JSP that uses a secure connection

Once the authentication process is complete, the server sends the response to the browser. For example, figure 15-7 shows the join.jsp page when it's displayed over a secure connection. This means that when the user submits data in this page, the data is encrypted before it's sent to the server.

You can tell that this page uses a secure connection since the URL starts with https. In addition, since this page is running on the local server, it uses port 8443 for the secure connection. If this page were running on the Internet, though, it wouldn't need the port number.

To view the secure certificate for a secure connection, you can usually click the lock icon to the left of the URL and use the resulting menu to display the certificate. When you view a certificate for a local testing environment, the browser displays the information that you entered when you created the self-signed certificate. When you view a certificate on the web, the browser should display a certificate similar to the one in figure 15-2.

How to return to a regular HTTP connection

Once you establish a secure connection, you can use relative paths to request web resources. In fact, the only way to return to a regular HTTP connection is to use an absolute URL that begins with http.

How to switch from a local system to an Internet server

When you transfer a web site from a local testing environment to a web server on the Internet, you need to modify the absolute URLs used in the application so they refer to the web site. If, for example, your web site is named www.trout.com, then you need to change all URLs that begin with

```
https://localhost:8443
```

to

```
https://www.trout.com
```

You also need to change all URLs that begin with

```
http://localhost:8080
```

to

```
http://www.trout.com
```

To make this switch easier, you can store variables that refer to the secure connection and the regular HTTP connection in a central location. Then, you only need to make two changes before you deploy your web application to a web server that's running on the Internet.

A JSP that uses a secure connection

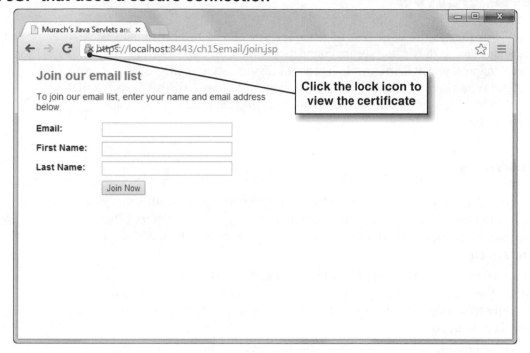

A URL that returns to a regular connection over the Internet

```
http://www.murach.com/email/join.jsp
```

A URL that returns to a regular connection from a local system

```
http://localhost:8080/ch15email/join.jsp
```

Description

- Once you establish a secure connection, the application continues using that connection as long as you use relative URLs.
- To return to a regular HTTP connection after using a secure connection, you code an absolute URL that starts with http.

Figure 15-7   How to return to a connection that isn't secure

Perspective

Now that you're done with this chapter, you should be able to modify your applications so they use a secure connection whenever that's needed. In the next chapter, you'll learn how to restrict access to certain portions of your web site by requiring the user to supply a username and a password. This is another form of security known as authentication that is often used with a secure connection.

Summary

- *Secure Sockets Layer* (*SSL*) is an older protocol that's used by the Internet to allow clients and servers to communicate over a *secure connection*. When a secure connection is used, the data that's passed between client and server is encrypted.

- *Transport Layer Security* (*TLS*) is the successor to SSL, and it works similarly. Since SSL is the older and more established protocol, it is often used to refer to a secure connection even when the connection is most likely using the TLS protocol.

- When a browser attempts to communicate with a server using a secure connection, the server *authenticates* itself by providing a *digital secure certificate*. This is referred to as *SSL server authentication*.

- To get a *digital secure certificate*, you contact a *certificate authority* that uses a *registration authority* to authorize your certificate. This certificate specifies the *SSL strength* of the encryption that's used. When you get the certificate, you install it on your web site.

- The *Java Secure Socket Extension* (*JSSE*) API makes it possible for a Java application to use a secure connection. This API is included with most modern versions of the JDK.

- To use a secure connection, you need to install a digital secure certificate on your web server, and you need to configure your web server so it defines a secure connection.

- To request a secure connection from a web application, you use an absolute URL that starts with https. Then, you use relative URLs to continue using the secure connection. To return to a regular connection, you use an absolute URL that starts with http.

Exercise 15-1   Configure and test a secure connection

Configure a secure connection

1. Use a Command Prompt (PC) or Terminal (Mac) window to create a self-signed certificate.

2. Edit Tomcat's server.xml file so it includes a Connector element for the secure connection.

3. Restart Tomcat.

Test the secure connection

4. Enter the URL shown in figure 15-5 into your browser. This should display a warning page.

5. Read the warning page, but proceed anyway. This should use a secure connection to display the page you requested, the default Tomcat page. If this doesn't work, you need to troubleshoot the problem, and test it again.

Experiment with a secure version of the Email List application

6. Open the ch15_ex1_email application in the ex_starts directory.

7. Open the index.jsp file and view the code for the links. Note how these links use absolute URLs to specify a secure HTTP connection and a regular HTTP connection.

8. Run this application.

9. Click on the "Use secure connection" link. This tests your secure connection and displays the warning page.

10. Read the warning page, but continue anyway. This should display the "Join our email list" page.

11. Click the lock icon and use the resulting menu to display the secure certificate. Then, return to the application.

12. Use the application to join the email list. Note how this uses a secure connection to send the user data to the server.

13. Click the Return button to return to the index.jsp page. Note how this page still uses a secure HTTP connection.

14. Click on the "Don't use secure connection" link. Note how this uses a regular HTTP connection to display the "Join our email list" page.

16

How to restrict access to a web resource

In this chapter, you'll learn how to restrict access to parts of a website. Then, you'll learn how to allow authorized users to access the restricted parts of the website. For example, many websites have an administrative section that can only be accessed by a user who logs in to the site with an authorized username and password.

An introduction to authentication

Although you can restrict access to certain parts of a web application by writing custom servlets and JSPs to work directly with HTTP requests and responses, doing that can be time-consuming and error-prone. That's why most modern servlet containers such as Tomcat provide a built-in way to restrict access to certain parts of a web application. This is known as *container-managed security*, or *container-managed authentication*.

How container-managed authentication works

Figure 16-1 shows what happens when a user requests a resource that has been restricted. Here, the user has run an application and clicked a link to access a web page within the admin subdirectory of this application. Since this resource has been restricted, a dialog box appears that requests a username and password. Then, if the user enters an authorized username and password, the user can access the resource. Otherwise, the user can't access that resource.

To restrict access to a resource, a *security constraint* must be coded in the web.xml file for the application. In this figure, for example, the security constraint restricts access to all files in the admin subdirectory of the application. As a result, when a browser requests any URL in this directory, the server notifies the browser that the user must identify himself or herself. This is known as *authentication*.

When the user sends the username and password to the server, the server attempts to authenticate the user. If the user provides a valid username and password, the server checks to see if that username is associated with a *role* that has the right to access the resource. In this figure, for example, users with the programmer and service roles can access the resource. This is known as *authorization*.

To authorize the username and password, the server uses a *security realm*. A security realm is an interface that provides a flexible way to store the usernames and passwords for the roles that are authorized. This makes it possible for the web developer to store the usernames and passwords for the authorized roles in an XML file, a database, or another type of data store.

In the example in this figure, the browser has requested a page in the admin subdirectory. Since this subdirectory is restricted, Tomcat has displayed a dialog box that requests a username and password. Then, if Tomcat authorizes the user to view the requested page, that authorization remains in effect for subsequent requests for any of the pages in the admin directory.

An authentication dialog box for a restricted web resource

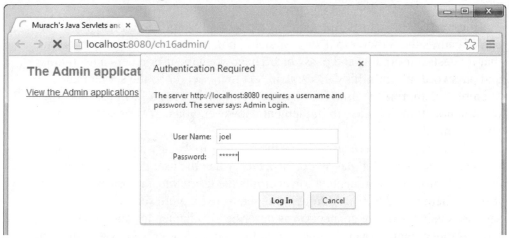

The security-constraint and login-config elements in the web.xml file

```
<security-constraint>
    <!-- Restrict access to all files in the /admin folder -->
    <web-resource-collection>
        <web-resource-name>Protected Area</web-resource-name>
        <url-pattern>/admin/*</url-pattern>
    </web-resource-collection>
    <!-- Authorize the programmer and service roles -->
    <auth-constraint>
        <role-name>programmer</role-name>
        <role-name>service</role-name>
    </auth-constraint>
</security-constraint>

<!-- Use basic authentication -->
<login-config>
    <auth-method>BASIC</auth-method>
    <realm-name>Admin Login</realm-name>
</login-config>
```

How to implement container-managed authentication with Tomcat

- To restrict access to a web resource, you code a security-constraint element in the application's web.xml file that specifies the URL patterns that you want to restrict and the *roles* that are authorized to access these URLs.

- To allow access to the restricted resources, you code a login-config element in the application's web.xml file that specifies the *authentication* method.

- You also need to implement a *security realm* that provides the usernames, passwords, and roles for the authorized users as in figures 16-4 through 16-6.

Figure 16-1   An introduction to container-managed authentication

Three types of authentication

Figure 16-2 presents three common types of authentication. *Basic authentication* causes the browser to display a dialog box like the one in the last figure that requests a username and password. Then, when the user enters a username and password, it sends this data as plain text to the server so the server can attempt to authorize the user. Since you don't have to code a form for this type of authentication, it is easy to implement. However, you can't control the appearance of this dialog box.

Digest authentication also causes the browser to display a dialog box that requests a username and password. However, when the user enters a username and password, digest authentication encrypts the username and password before it sends them to the server. Although this seems to be more secure, it isn't as secure as using a secure connection as described in chapter 15, and you don't have as much control over the encryption that's used. As a result, digest authentication isn't used as often as the other types of authentication.

Form-based authentication uses a web form instead of a login dialog box to request the username and password. This type of authentication allows a developer to control the look and feel of the web page. As a result, it's the most common type of authentication for production websites.

Since basic authentication and form-based authentication send the username and password as plain text, a hacker can possibly intercept an unencrypted username and password and gain access to a restricted web resource. As a result, it's common to use a secure connection as described in chapter 15 with these types of authentication. That way, the username and password are encrypted before they are sent to the server.

Basic authentication

- Causes the browser to display a dialog box like the one shown in the previous figure.
- Doesn't encrypt the username and password before sending them to the server.

Digest authentication

- Causes the browser to display a dialog box like the one shown in the previous figure.
- Encrypts the username and password before sending them to the server.

Form-based authentication

- Allows the developer to code a login form that gets the username and password.
- Doesn't encrypt the username and password before sending them to the server.

Description

- Since *basic authentication* and *form-based authentication* don't automatically encrypt the username and password before sending them to the server, these types of authentication are typically used over a secure connection as described in chapter 15.
- Since *digest authentication* isn't as secure as using a secure connection, it isn't used as often as basic authentication or form-based authentication over a secure connection.

Figure 16-2   Three types of authentication

How to restrict access to web resources

Now that you understand the general concept of how container-managed authentication works, you're ready to learn how to use Tomcat to create a constraint that restricts access to web resources. Although this topic uses Tomcat to create a constraint, these concepts also apply to other servlet containers.

How to add a security role

Before you restrict access to a web resource, you often want to add one or more security-role elements to the web.xml file for the application as shown in figure 16-3. These elements define the security roles that are allowed to access restricted web resources. In this figure, two security roles have been added: service and programmer.

How to add a security constraint

To restrict access to a web resource, you add a security-constraint element to the web.xml file for the application. This element specifies the web resources that are restricted and the roles that can access them.

When you code the url-pattern element, you can code a URL that specifies a single file. Or, you can use the asterisk character to restrict access to multiple files. In this figure, the asterisk restricts access to all URLs in the admin directory. This includes all HTML and JSP files as well as any servlets or other resources that are mapped to this directory.

When you code the auth-constraint element, you define the user roles that are authorized to access the restricted resource. In this figure, any user associated with the programmer or service role is authorized to access the resources available from the admin directory.

To restrict access to multiple files or directories, you can define several url-pattern elements within a single security-constraint element. Or, if you want to specify different roles for different URL patterns, you can create multiple security-constraint elements.

If you want to restrict access to a resource, but only for specified HTTP methods, you can use the http-method element to do that. For example, you could use this element to restrict access from the HTTP GET and POST methods. However, if you did that, other HTTP methods, such as the HEAD method, don't require authentication and can be used to access a resource, which isn't usually what you want. Fortunately, you can easily restrict access to all HTTP methods by omitting the http-method element, which is usually what you want.

In most cases, the data that's stored within a restricted resource should be transported between the client and the server over a secure connection. The easiest way to guarantee this is to include a transport-guarantee element that's set to a value of CONFIDENTIAL. For this to work, you need to have a secure connection set up as described in the previous chapter.

How to set a security constraint in a web.xml file

```
<security-role>
    <description>customer service employees</description>
    <role-name>service</role-name>
</security-role>

<security-role>
    <description>programmers</description>
    <role-name>programmer</role-name>
</security-role>

<security-constraint>
    <web-resource-collection>
        <web-resource-name>Protected Area</web-resource-name>
        <url-pattern>/admin/*</url-pattern>
        <!-- NOT SECURE - Don't include these elements
        <http-method>GET</http-method>
        <http-method>POST</http-method>
        -->
    </web-resource-collection>

    <auth-constraint>
        <role-name>programmer</role-name>
        <role-name>service</role-name>
    </auth-constraint>

    <user-data-constraint>
        <transport-guarantee>CONFIDENTIAL</transport-guarantee>
    </user-data-constraint>
</security-constraint>
```

Some elements used to create a security roles and constraints

Element	Description
`<security-role>`	Creates a security role for one or more web resources.
`<role-name>`	Specifies the name for a security role.
`<security-constraint>`	Creates a security constraint for one or more web resources.
`<web-resource-collection>`	Specifies a collection of restricted web resources.
`<url-pattern>`	Specifies the URL pattern for the web resources that you wish to restrict. You can use the asterisk character (*) to specify several files at once. By default, this restricts access to all HTTP methods, which is usually what you want.
`<http-method>`	Specifies the HTTP methods that require authentication. If you include this element, all other HTTP methods don't require authentication, which is not usually what you want.
`<auth-constraint>`	Specifies the security roles that are permitted to access a restricted web resource.
`<user-data-constraint>`	Specifies constraints that apply to the data that's stored within the restricted resources.
`<transport-guarantee>`	Guarantees a secure connection when set to a value of CONFIDENTIAL.

Figure 16-3   How to add security roles and constraints to the web.xml file

How to implement a security realm

When you use Tomcat to manage security, you need to determine what type of *security realm* (or just *realm*) you want to implement. A realm is the mechanism that identifies authorized users. In this topic, you'll learn how to use three of the most common types of security realms that are available with Tomcat.

How to implement the UserDatabaseRealm

By default, Tomcat stores usernames, passwords, and roles in the tomcat-users.xml file that's in its conf directory. To do that, the server.xml file that's stored in Tomcat's conf directory uses the Realm element shown in figure 16-4 to specify a UserDatabaseRealm named UserDatabase. Then, the server.xml file uses a Resource element to specify the tomcat-users.xml file as the user database. Since these elements are configured by default when you install Tomcat, you don't need to change them or understand how they work.

To add a user to the tomcat-users.xml file, you can open this file in a text editor. Then, you can add role elements that specify new roles. Or, you can add user elements that specify the username, password, and roles for each new user. When you do this, you can specify multiple roles for a user by separating them with commas.

In this figure, for example, the tomcat-users.xml file specifies three roles (manager, programmer, and service) and three users (admin, joel, and andrea). Of these users, andrea belongs to two roles (programmer and server). Then, to put these users into effect, you need to restart Tomcat.

When you edit the tomcat-users.xml file, the changes apply to all applications running on the current server. As a result, you don't want to remove any roles or users unless you're sure they're not being used by other applications. For example, the Tomcat Web Application Manager application that's included with Tomcat uses the admin username and the manager role.

The default Realm element in Tomcat's server.xml file

```
<Realm className="org.apache.catalina.realm.UserDatabaseRealm"
       resourceName="UserDatabase"/>
```

The default Resource element in Tomcat's server.xml file

```
<Resource name="UserDatabase" auth="Container"
          type="org.apache.catalina.UserDatabase"
          description="User database that can be updated and saved"
          factory="org.apache.catalina.users.MemoryUserDatabaseFactory"
          pathname="conf/tomcat-users.xml" />
```

A tomcat-users.xml file that specifies three roles and three users

```
<?xml version='1.0' encoding='utf-8'?>
<tomcat-users>
    <role rolename="manager"/>
    <role rolename="programmer"/>
    <role rolename="service"/>
    <user username="admin" password="sesame" roles="manager"/>
    <user username="joel" password="sesame" roles="programmer"/>
    <user username="andrea" password="sesame" roles="programmer,service"/>
</tomcat-users>
```

Description

- A *realm* is an interface that's used to authenticate users so they can access web resources that have been restricted.

- By default, the server.xml file in Tomcat's conf directory uses the UserDatabaseRealm to use the usernames, passwords, and roles that are defined in the tomcat-users.xml file that's stored in Tomcat's conf directory. However, you can change this default to one of the other realms.

- If you use the UserDatabaseRealm for authentication, you can edit the tomcat-users.xml file so it contains the role and user elements that you need.

Figure 16-4   How to implement the UserDatabaseRealm

How to implement the JDBCRealm

For simple applications, the UserDatabaseRealm provides a quick and easy way to implement a realm. However, for more serious web applications, you'll often want to use the JDBCRealm to store usernames, passwords, and roles in a relational database. In addition, you'll often want to implement a security realm for a specific application rather than for all applications on the current server.

To implement security for a specific application, you can add a Realm element to the application's context.xml file. In figure 16-5, for example, the context.xml file for the ch16admin application implements the JDBCRealm. Here, the JDBCRealm uses the Connector/J MySQL driver to connect to a MySQL database named murach with a username of root and a password of sesame.

The rest of the attributes in the Realm element for the JDBCRealm define the names of the tables and columns that are used to store the usernames, passwords, and roles for the application. These tables can be created and filled by using a SQL script like the one in part 2 of this figure.

A context.xml file that implements the JDBCRealm

```xml
<?xml version="1.0" encoding="UTF-8"?>
<Context path="/ch16admin">

    <Realm className="org.apache.catalina.realm.JDBCRealm" debug="99"
        driverName="com.mysql.jdbc.Driver"
        connectionURL="jdbc:mysql://localhost:3306/murach"
        connectionName="root" connectionPassword="sesame"
        userTable="UserPass" userNameCol="Username" userCredCol="Password"
        userRoleTable="UserRole" roleNameCol="Rolename" />

</Context>
```

The attributes of the Realm element for a JDBCRealm

Attribute	Description
className	The fully qualified name for the JDBCRealm class.
driverName	The fully qualified class name for the JDBC driver.
connectionURL	The database URL for the connection.
connectionName	The username for the connection.
connectionPassword	The password for the connection.
userTable	The name of the table that contains the usernames and passwords. This table must include at least the columns named by the userNameCol and userCredCol attributes.
userNameCol	The name of the column that contains usernames.
userCredCol	The name of the column that contains passwords.
userRoleTable	The name of the table that contains the usernames and their associated roles. This table must include the columns named by the userNameCol and roleNameCol attributes.
roleNameCol	The name of the column that contains the roles.

Description

- To specify a realm for a single application, you can code a Realm element within the context.xml file in the application's META-INF folder. This overrides the default Realm element that's specified in the server.xml file in Tomcat's conf folder.

- Tomcat's JDBCRealm uses a database to check a username and password against a table of valid usernames and passwords. In addition, the JDBCRealm uses a second table to associate a username with a role.

- For the JDBCRealm to work, the application must have access to a database driver for the database. To learn more about database drivers, databases, and connecting to databases, please see chapter 12.

Figure 16-5   How to implement the JDBCRealm (part 1 of 2)

If the tables for the JDBC realm don't already exist, you can create a table of users that contains a username and password for each user, and you can create a table of roles that can be associated with each user. To do that, you can use a SQL script like the one in part 2 of figure 16-5. Note how the table and column names in this script match the table and column names specified in the Realm element shown in part 1 of this figure.

After it creates the UserPass table, this script creates the UserRole table. Here, the user named "joel" is associated with the programmer role, and the user named "andrea" is associated with both the service and programmer roles. Note, however, that the user named "anne" isn't associated with any role, so she isn't authorized to access restricted portions of the application.

A SQL script that creates the tables used by the JDBCRealm

```sql
CREATE TABLE UserPass (
    Username varchar(15) NOT NULL PRIMARY KEY,
    Password varchar(15) NOT NULL
);

INSERT INTO UserPass VALUES ('andrea', 'sesame'),
                            ('joel', 'sesame'),
                            ('anne', 'sesame');

CREATE TABLE UserRole (
    Username VARCHAR(15) NOT NULL,
    Rolename VARCHAR(15) NOT NULL,

    PRIMARY KEY (Username, Rolename)
);

INSERT INTO UserRole VALUES ('andrea', 'service'),
                            ('andrea', 'programmer'),
                            ('joel', 'programmer');
```

Description

- The table and column names must match the table and column names specified by the Realm element for the JDBCRealm.

- A user can be associated with zero roles, one role, or multiple roles.

- The table that stores the username and password can contain other columns.

Figure 16-5   How to implement the JDBCRealm (part 2 of 2)

How to implement the DataSourceRealm

If your application is using connection pooling as described in chapter 12, you probably want to implement the DataSourceRealm as shown in figure 16-6. This realm is similar to the JDBCRealm.

Compared to the JDBCRealm, though, there are two advantages to using the DataSourceRealm. First, this realm can take advantage of connection pooling, which can allow your application to authenticate and authorize users more quickly.

Second, if you've already specified the database connection information for your application in a Resource element, you don't need to duplicate this information in the Realm element. Instead, you can code a Realm element that uses the dataSourceName and localDataSource attributes to use the same connection information as the Resource element. In this figure, for example, the Resource element specifies all the connection information that's needed to connect to the music database that's used by the Music Store application presented in section 5.

After you code the Realm attributes to connect to a data source, you code the rest of the attributes just as you would for a JDBCRealm. In this figure, for example, the Realm element uses the same tables and columns as the JDBCRealm shown in the previous figure.

A context.xml file that implements the DataSourceRealm

```xml
<?xml version="1.0" encoding="UTF-8"?>
<Context path="/musicStore">

    <Resource name="jdbc/musicDB" auth="Container"
        maxActive="100" maxIdle="30" maxWait="10000"
        username="root" password="sesame"
        driverClassName="com.mysql.jdbc.Driver"
        url="jdbc:mysql://localhost:3306/music?autoReconnect=true"
        logAbandoned="true" removeAbandoned="true"
        removeAbandonedTimeout="60" type="javax.sql.DataSource" />

    <Realm className="org.apache.catalina.realm.DataSourceRealm" debug="99"
        dataSourceName="jdbc/musicDB" localDataSource="true"
        userTable="UserPass" userNameCol="Username" userCredCol="Password"
        userRoleTable="UserRole" roleNameCol="Rolename" />

</Context>
```

The attributes of the Realm element for a DataSourceRealm

Attribute	Description
className	The fully qualified name for the DataSourceRealm class.
dataSourceName	The name that specifies the data source. If the Realm element is coded in the same context.xml file as the Resource element that's used to connect to the database, you can specify the same name that's specified by the Resource element.
localDataSource	By default, this attribute is set to false, which allows you to use the dataSourceName attribute to specify a global data source. However, if the Realm element is coded in the same context.xml file as the Resource element, you can set this attribute to true to specify a local data source.

Description

- Tomcat's DataSourceRealm works similarly to the JDBCRealm but it uses a data source that's specified by a Resource element. It can also take advantage of connection pooling.

- The userTable, userNameCol, userCredCol, userRoleTable, and roleNameCol attributes work the same for a DataSourceRealm as they do for a JDBCRealm.

Figure 16-6   How to implement the DataSourceRealm

How to allow access to authorized users

Once you've restricted access to web resources and implemented a security realm, you're ready to allow access to authorized users.

How to use basic authentication

Figure 16-7 shows how to use basic authentication to provide access to a restricted resource. In particular, it shows how to use basic authentication to provide access to the sample application for this chapter.

If you request a restricted web resource that uses basic authentication, your browser displays an authentication dialog box like the one in this figure. This box requests a username and password. Then, when the user selects the Log In button, the username and password are sent to the server.

When the server gets the username and password, it checks the security realm to see whether the username and password are valid, and it checks whether the user is associated with a role that is authorized to access the resource. If so, the user is allowed to access the resource.

Since basic authentication is the simplest type of authentication, the web.xml file only requires a few XML elements. To start, you code the login-config element. Within this element, you specify that you want to use basic authentication. Then, you specify a name for the realm. This name is displayed in the dialog box. When you add the XML tags for the login-config element to the web.xml file, they must immediately follow the security-constraint element that they relate to as shown in figure 16-1.

How to use digest authentication

If you have basic authentication working, you can easily switch to digest authentication by specifying DIGEST instead of BASIC in the auth-method element. Then, the username and password are encrypted even if the request isn't being sent over a secure connection. However, as mentioned earlier, it's more common to use basic authentication or form-based authentication over a secure connection.

Basic authentication

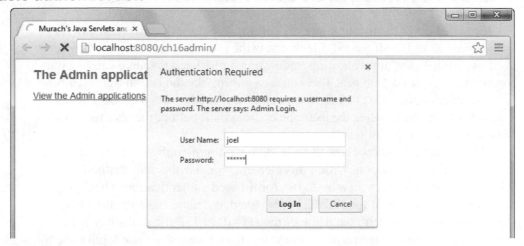

The web.xml elements that specify basic authentication

```
<login-config>
    <auth-method>BASIC</auth-method>
    <realm-name>Admin Login</realm-name>
</login-config>
```

The elements for basic authentication

Element	Description
`<login-config>`	Creates the authentication type to use.
`<auth-method>`	Specifies the authentication method. Valid entries include BASIC, DIGEST, FORM, and CLIENT-CERT. BASIC and DIGEST authentication display a dialog box like the one shown in this figure. FORM authentication displays a form as described in the next figure. And CLIENT-CERT uses SSL client authentication as described in chapter 15.
`<realm-name>`	Specifies the name that's displayed in the dialog box, but this is optional.

Figure 16-7   How to use basic authentication

How to use form-based authentication

Form-based authentication works similarly to basic authentication, but it lets you code an HTML or JSP file that gets the username and password. When you use form-based authentication, requesting a restricted resource causes your browser to display a web page that contains a form like the one in figure 16-8. This form contains a text box for a username, a text box for a password, and a submit button. Then, when the user clicks the submit button, the username and password are sent to the server.

This figure also shows how to code the form-login-config element for form-based authentication. Within this element, you use the auth-method element to specify that you want to use form-based authentication. Then, you can specify the name of the HTML or JSP file that defines the authentication form, and you can specify the name of the HTML or JSP file to display if the user enters an invalid username or password. If you want the same login page to be displayed again when a user enters an invalid username or password, you can specify the same name for both pages.

Form-based authentication

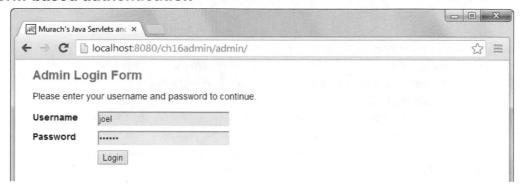

The web.xml elements that specify form-based authentication

```
<login-config>
    <auth-method>FORM</auth-method>
    <form-login-config>
        <form-login-page>/admin/login.html</form-login-page>
        <form-error-page>/admin/login_error.html</form-error-page>
    </form-login-config>
</login-config>
```

The additional web.xml elements for form-based authentication

Element	Description
`<form-login-config>`	Specifies the login and error pages that should be used for form-based authentication. If form-based authentication isn't used, these elements are ignored.
`<form-login-page>`	Specifies the location of the login page that should be displayed when a restricted resource that's set in the security constraint is accessed. This page can be an HTML page, JSP, or servlet.
`<form-error-page>`	Specifies the location of the page that should be displayed when an invalid username or password is entered in the login form.

Description

- When you use form-based authentication, you can use HTML to code the login form that's displayed when someone attempts to access a restricted resource. This form can be coded within an HTML document or a JSP.

Figure 16-8   How to use form-based authentication (part 1 of 2)

Part 2 of figure 16-8 shows the code for the login page that's shown in part 1. Although you can place any HTML or JSP tags in a login page, this page must at least provide an HTML form that contains a submit button and two text boxes, and this form must use the three highlighted attributes shown in this figure. Here, the action attribute for the form must be j_security_check. The name of the text box that gets the username must be j_username. And the name of the text box that gets the password must be j_password.

In this example, the text box that requests the password uses the password type. As a result, the password isn't displayed on the screen when the user types it. Instead, this text box displays a special character such as a bullet or an asterisk for each character. You can see how this works by looking at part 1 of this figure.

The code for a login web page

```
<!DOCTYPE html>
<html>
    <head>
        <meta charset="utf-8">
        <title>Murach's Java Servlets and JSP</title>
        <link rel="stylesheet" href="../styles/main.css" type="text/css"/>
    </head>
    <body>
        <h1>Admin Login Form</h1>
        <p>Please enter your username and password to continue.</p>
        <form action="j_security_check" method="post">
            <label class="pad_top">Username</label>
            <input type="text" name="j_username"><br>
            <label class="pad_top">Password</label>
            <input type="password" name="j_password"><br>
            <label> </label>
            <input type="submit" value="Login" class="margin_left">
        </form>
    </body>
</html>
```

Description

- The login form for form-based authentication must contain the three attributes highlighted above.

- The login form can be stored in any directory where HTML and JSP files can be stored.

Figure 16-8   How to use form-based authentication (part 2 of 2)

Perspective

Now that you've finished this chapter, you should be able to use Tomcat to implement container-managed security in your applications. However, you should keep in mind that this chapter doesn't cover all aspects of using Tomcat for authentication.

In particular, Tomcat provides several other security realms that aren't presented in this chapter. For example, the JNDIRealm allows you to look up users in an LDAP directory server that's accessed by a JNDI provider. So, if the security realms presented in this chapter aren't adequate for your applications, you can consult the documentation that's available from the Tomcat website.

Summary

- To restrict access to web resources such as HTML documents, JSPs, and servlets, you can use *container-managed security*, which is also known as *container-managed authentication*.

- You can use the web.xml file to specify the type of *authentication* for an application.

- *Basic authentication* displays a pre-defined dialog box to get the username and password. *Digest authentication* works similarly to basic authentication, but it encrypts the username and password. And *form-based authentication* lets the application use a custom web form to get the username and password.

- You can use the web.xml file to specify a *security constraint* that identifies the URL patterns that should have restricted access, and also to specify the *roles* that have the proper *authorization* to access the restricted pages.

- You can use Tomcat's server.xml file or an application's context.xml file to specify a *security realm* that uses an interface to provide the usernames, passwords, and roles for the authorized users.

- Three of the realms that are commonly used with Tomcat are the UserDatabaseRealm, the JDBCRealm, and the DataSourceRealm. You can use any of these realms with any of the authentication methods.

- When you use form-based authentication, the HTML code for the login page must include a form and two text boxes that use the required names for specific attributes.

Exercise 16-1 Work with authentication types

Review the application

1. Open the ch16_ex1_admin project in the ex_starts folder.

2. Open the web.xml file for the application. Note that it restricts access to all URLs in the admin folder, that it authorizes the programmer and service roles, and that it uses form-based authentication.

3. Open the context.xml file for the application. Note that the Realm element specifies the JDBCRealm. Note also that this element specifies the murach database and columns from the UserPass and UserRole tables.

4. If you're interested, use MySQL Workbench to review the data in the UserPass and UserRole tables of the murach database.

5. Open the admin/login.html file that's specified by the web.xml file for form-based authentication. Then, review the attributes that this form uses.

Use form-based authentication

6. Run the application and click on the link to access the admin subdirectory. That should display the login form. Then, test the application by entering an invalid username and password, and note that the login_error.html page is displayed.

7. Test the application by entering a valid username and password for the programmer role such as "joel" and "sesame". This should give you access to the restricted pages.

8. Modify the web.xml file so the programmer role is no longer authorized.

9. Test the application with a valid username and password for the programmer role such as "joel" and "sesame". You should not be able to view the restricted page.

10. Test the application with a valid username and password for the service role such as "andrea" and "sesame". You should be able to view the restricted page.

Use basic authentication

11. Modify the web.xml file so the application uses basic authentication instead of form-based authentication.

12. Restart Tomcat.

13. Test the application with a valid username and password for the service role such as "andrea" and "sesame". You should be able to view the restricted page.

17

More security skills

Identity theft as a result of IT security flaws is a serious problem, as many high-profile news stories have shown. So protecting the identity and confidentiality of your users is one of the most important parts of web application development. Although you've learned several skills already for securing your web application, this chapter will teach you additional important skills that didn't fit well in other sections of this book.

An introduction to website security

Before you can secure a website, it's helpful to understand some basic concepts and terms about website security.

Common website attacks

Figure 17-1 presents several techniques that attackers commonly use to gain unauthorized access to your users' personal information. So far in this book, you've already learned some techniques to prevent the first two types of attacks. In chapter 9, you learned how to prevent *cross-site scripting* (*XSS*) *attacks*. Then, in chapters 12 and 13, you learned how to prevent *SQL injection attacks*. In this chapter, you'll learn additional techniques to secure your web application, including how to prevent social engineering attacks and protect passwords.

How to prevent social engineering attacks

In a *social engineering* attack, an attacker attempts to gain unauthorized access to your user data by learning information about a user that allows them to access the user's account.

One common technique, often used to target employees of a business, is for an attacker to pose as an employee of the company's IT department. Then, the attacker calls the employee on the phone, claims to be troubleshooting an issue, and asks for the employee's username and password. To prevent this type of attack, make sure that your employees know that your IT department will never ask for their password.

Another technique that attackers sometimes use is to stand outside a company's offices to collect information. Often, these attackers will claim they are conducting a school project. Then, they interview your employees, asking them for information that they might be able to use to gain access to your IT systems. This type of attack is particularly dangerous and effective if your employees are using passwords made of information that is easily discovered about them such as the names of their children, the names of pets, their favorite foods, and so on.

To prevent this type of attack, you should train your employees to be wary of giving out information to persons who claim to be conducting research, school projects, and so on. Likewise, you should make sure your employees don't use passwords that are made of information about them that is easily discovered. The names of pets, children, favorite foods, and so on, can be easily discovered by social engineering attacks or by searching social networks on the Internet.

Finally, old or unpatched software running on your server can allow an attacker to exploit security vulnerabilities. To prevent this type of attack, you should make sure the server for your website is running software that includes the latest security patches.

Common website security attacks

- *Cross-site scripting (XSS) attacks* allow an attacker to inject Javascript into your page in an attempt to trick your users into sending them personal data such as usernames and passwords.

- *SQL injection attacks* allow an attacker to run malicious SQL code on your database. This can allow them to perform various actions including gaining access to user credentials and personal information, bypassing authentication mechanisms, and modifying or destroying data.

- In a *social engineering attack*, an attacker tricks someone into revealing their username and password, often by posing as an IT employee of the company.

- Out of date or unpatched software running on your server can allow an attacker to exploit security vulnerabilities to gain unauthorized access to your data.

How to prevent social engineering attacks

- Make sure your employees, customers, and users are aware that no one from your website will ever contact them and ask for their password.

- Be wary of unknown individuals talking to your employees who claim to be conducting surveys, research, and so on. They may be attempting to gather information that will help them access your IT systems.

- Make sure your employees, customers, and users are aware of the danger of using passwords made of information that attackers can easily discover about them. For example, an attacker can mine social networks for information about the names of pets, children, favorite foods, and so on.

- When seeking help with technical issues online, such as programming questions, don't reveal details regarding your internal network configuration, IT security, and other types of information that would be useful to an attacker.

Figure 17-1   An introduction to website security issues

An introduction to cryptography

Cryptography is the process of taking readable data and changing it in some way so it is no longer readable as the original text. One of the simplest forms of cryptography is a simple substitution cypher, which you are probably familiar with from games that children often play. In this type of system, you simply substitute different symbols for the characters in your text to produce a coded message. Then, someone who has the substitution key showing which symbol corresponds to which letter can decode the coded message.

Computer cryptography is significantly more complex than these simple substitution cyphers. However, the basic goal is the same: To take readable data and change it so that it is no longer readable. There are two types of cryptography commonly used in IT security.

The first is *one-way hashing*. In this type of cryptography, you pass a message through an algorithm that produces a scrambled version of it. With this type of encryption, it isn't possible to recover the original message from the scrambled version. In other words, you can't reverse the encryption. As a result, one-way hashing is useful for things like storing passwords in a database. In this case, you never need to reverse the encrypted password as long as the users know their passwords. When a user logs in you hash the password and make sure it matches the hash of the password in the database. If it does, the password is correct.

Because it isn't possible to reverse a one-way hash, it isn't possible to find out what a user's password is. If a user forgets his password, you can reset it to a new one. Also, because the hash cannot be reversed, this type of cryptography is not useful for tasks such as emailing a document to someone that they need to read. For those types of tasks, you need to use a second type of encryption, reversible encryption.

Reversible encryption, as the name implies, is encryption that can be reversed. To make this possible, the data is encrypted using a key. In the simplest forms of this encryption, you use one key to encrypt the data, and anyone who also has that key can decrypt the data. This type of encryption is useful for tasks such as storing secure data in a database and transferring secure data over the Internet.

Figure 17-2 summaries five algorithms that can be used for hashing and encrypting data. Some of these algorithms are more secure than others. For example, the SHA-2 algorithm is more secure than the SHA-1 or md5 algorithms. Similarly, the AES-256 algorithm is more secure than the AES-128 algorithm.

Common cryptographic algorithms

Algorithm	Description
md5	An older 128-bit one-way hash algorithm. Although common, it is known to be vulnerable to collisions and should not be used.
SHA-1	A 160-bit one-way hash algorithm. It is theoretically vulnerable to collisions, but none have been found.
SHA-2	SHA-2 supports hash sizes from 224 to 512 bits. A 256-bit key is generally considered to be uncrackable by today's standards of computing power.
AES-128	A reversible encryption standard with a 128-bit key. Generally considered suitable for most encryption needs.
AES-256	A 256-bit version of AES. This is generally the minimum level of encryption required by the U.S. government for top secret data.

Description

- A *one-way hash algorithm* takes a given input string, and hashes it to a string of a certain length. It cannot be reversed. As a result, it is useful for encrypting things such as passwords, where there is no need for anyone to read the original value of the password.

- *Reversible encryption* encrypts data against a key. The key can be used to decrypt the data at a later date when it needs to be read by a user. Without the key used to encrypt the data, it cannot be read.

Figure 17-2   An introduction to cryptography

Common password attacks

Figure 17-3 summarizes three types of attacks that are commonly used to discover passwords. To start, an attacker may use a social engineering attack. In addition, an attacker may use a *dictionary attack*. In a dictionary attack, the attacker uses an automated program to try every word in the dictionary as the password.

If an attacker gains access to a website's database, the attacker can easily read passwords that aren't encrypted. These types of passwords are known as *clear-text passwords* or *unhashed passwords*. That's why it's a good practice to hash passwords before you store them in the database.

Unfortunately, even hashed passwords are vulnerable to a type of attack known as a *rainbow table attack*. A rainbow table attack uses a pre-computed database of dictionary words and their hash values to speed up the process of password cracking significantly. If any of your users have passwords that can be found in a dictionary, cracking the password is as simple as looking up the stored hash value and revealing the word that generated it.

Passwords that are vulnerable to these types of attacks are known as *weak passwords*. Weak passwords include passwords that can be easily guessed, and passwords that can be easily cracked with an automated program. A weak password can be a password that's a word from the dictionary, a password that's too short, or a password that consists of all lowercase letters with no numbers, special characters, or uppercase characters mixed in.

To prevent password attacks, you should hash your passwords so they aren't stored in the database as clear-text passwords. In addition, you should educate your users on the danger of using weak passwords.

Common password attacks

Method	Description
Social engineering	An attacker tricks a user into revealing his login credentials, or learns everything he can about the user to determine likely passwords.
Dictionary attacks	An attacker simply tries different passwords until they find one that works. Typically, this is done using an automated program and an electronic dictionary. As a result, words found in the dictionary are particularly vulnerable to this type of attack.
Rainbow table attacks	Similar to a dictionary attack, except a pre-computed lookup table is used that contains the hashes for the words. This allows an attacker who has access to the hashed passwords to crack them much more efficiently and quickly.

A password is weak if it...

* Is made from information that can be easily discovered about the user.
* Is made only from words that are in the dictionary.
* Is too short.
* Is made of all lowercase letters.
* Doesn't include numbers or special characters.

Description

* *Weak passwords* are passwords that an attacker can easily guess or crack.
* *Clear-text passwords*, or *unhashed passwords*, aren't encrypted. As a result, if an attacker gains access to your database, these passwords are easy to read.

Figure 17-3   Common problems with passwords

How to protect passwords

Now that you understand some basic concepts and terms for securing a website, you're ready to learn how to write code that protects passwords.

How to hash passwords

To hash passwords in your web application, you can code a utility class like the PasswordUtil class shown in figure 17-4. This class uses the MessageDigest class from the Java security API to take a clear-text password and create a hashed version using the specified algorithm.

Because hash algorithms generate a fixed-length array of bytes, you can't pass a string directly to them. In this figure, for example, the update method of the MessageDigest object accepts an array of bytes. As a result, this code calls the getBytes method of the password string to convert it to an array of bytes. Then, this code calls the digest method of the MessageDigest object to generate an array of bytes for the hashed password.

Conversely, you can't get a string directly from an array of bytes. To work around that, you can use a for loop to convert the array of bytes to a string. In this figure, for example, the loop converts the array of bytes for the hashed password to a string.

When a user creates an account on your website, you can use this class to hash the password. To do that, you can pass the password entered by the user to the hashPassword method. Then, you can store the hashed version of the password that's returned by this method in your site's database. Later, when the user wants to login and enters his password, you pass it to the hashPassword method again and compare the value that's returned with the value that's stored in the database.

The hashPassword method shown in this figure uses the SHA-256 hashing algorithm. This is an extremely secure algorithm, but may not be available in all implementations of Java or in all regions of the world. If this class throws a NoSuchAlgorithmException, you may need to fall back on a weaker form of encryption such as SHA-128. However, weaker forms of encryption may be subject to collisions.

A *collision* occurs when two different input values generate the same hash. Because hash values are a fixed length, there are a finite number of different hash sequences that can be generated. As a result, collisions are inevitable, especially with hash algorithms that use smaller hash sizes. However, the possibility of them happening is small enough to be considered insignificant.

This code uses the Base64 class that was introduced in Java 8. As a result, it won't work on earlier versions of Java. If you need to run this code on an earlier version of Java, you can use the Base64 class from Tomcat. Note that this will only work if the Tomcat libraries are available in your classpath, such as when building a web application with Tomcat. If you aren't using Tomcat or Java 8, you can use the Base64 class from the Apache Commons Codec library. (commons.apache.org)

A utility class for hashing passwords

```java
import java.security.MessageDigest;
import java.security.NoSuchAlgorithmException;

public class PasswordUtil {

    /*  This code uses SHA-256. If this algorithm isn't available to you,
        you can try a weaker level of encryption such as SHA-128.
    */
    public static String hashPassword(String password)
            throws NoSuchAlgorithmException {
        MessageDigest md = MessageDigest.getInstance("SHA-256");
        md.update(password.getBytes());
        byte[] mdArray = md.digest();
        StringBuilder sb = new StringBuilder(mdArray.length * 2);
        for (byte b : mdArray) {
            int v = b & 0xff;
            if (v < 16) {
                sb.append('0');
            }
            sb.append(Integer.toHexString(v));
        }
        return sb.toString();
    }
}
```

Code that uses this class

```java
try {
    String hashedPassword = PasswordUtil.hashPassword("sesame");
} catch (NoSuchAlgorithmException e) {
    System.out.println(e);
}
```

Description

- You can use the MessageDigest class to compute a fixed-length hash value for an array of bytes.

- You can use the getBytes method of the String class to convert a string such as a password to an array of bytes.

- You can call the update method of the MessageDigest class to specify the array of bytes that you want to hash.

- You can call the digest method of the MessageDigest class to hash the input and return a fixed-length array of bytes for the hashed input.

- You can code a for loop to convert the array of bytes (which are 8 bits) to a string of characters (which are 16 bits in Java).

- Some versions of Java may not have certain hash algorithms available. If you attempt to use an algorithm that isn't available, the MessageDigest object throws a NoSuchAlgorithmException.

- A *collision* occurs when two input strings hash to the same value.

Figure 17-4   How to hash passwords

How to salt passwords

Hashing the passwords in your database is a good first step to preventing attackers from being able to use them should they gain access to the passwords. However, it doesn't always go far enough because even hashed passwords are vulnerable to a rainbow table attack. Furthermore, if two users are using the same password, they will hash to the same value. As a result, if an attacker can crack one user password, he can access more than one user account.

To prevent rainbow attacks, you can use a technique called *salting*. To salt a password, you generate a random string of characters when the password is created. Then, you append that to the end of the password before hashing it. The hash of the password plus the salt is what you store as the password in the database. You also store the salt value in the database because you will need it later when the user attempts to login to their account. When they do, you take the password the user entered, and append the salt from the database row for that user account. Then, you hash the password plus the salt value, and compare the hash to the hash stored in the database.

This technique makes sure that rainbow table attacks won't work because even weak passwords will hash to an entirely different value thanks to the salt. Furthermore, because the password is combined with the salt value before creating the hash, two users that have the same password will not have the same hash value because their salts will be different. This prevents attackers from discovering that two or more users are using the same password.

Figure 17-5 shows a method named getSalt that you can use to generate a random salt. This method uses the SecureRandom class, which is a subclass of the Random class. This class uses the SecureRandom class because random values generated by the Random class might be predictable. The problem is that the Random class often uses the current time to seed its number generator. As a result, an attacker might be able to predict the random number. By contrast, the SecureRandom class typically uses something like device driver noise to seed its random number generator. As a result, it is virtually impossible to know the seed used to generate the random number. For cryptography purposes, you should always use SecureRandom instead of Random when you need a random number.

This figure also shows a method named hashAndSaltPassword that you can use to create the salted and hashed password. This method starts by using the getSalt method to get the salt string. Then, it appends the salt string to the password string and passes that string to the hashPassword method shown in the previous figure.

After the two methods, this figure shows a database diagram for a User table that you can use to store the hashed password and the salt. Remember, you need to store the salt string. If you don't, you won't be able to allow the user to log in later because you won't be able to recreate the string that was used to create the hashed password.

The classes used to salt a password

```
java.security.SecureRandom;
java.util.Random;
java.util.Base64;
```

A method for producing a salt value

```
public static String getSalt() {
    Random r = new SecureRandom();
    byte[] saltBytes = new byte[32];
    r.nextBytes(saltBytes);
    return Base64.getEncoder().encodeToString(saltBytes);
}
```

A method for combining the password and salt

```
public static String hashAndSaltPassword(String password)
        throws NoSuchAlgorithmException {
    String salt = getSalt();
    return hashPassword(password + salt);
}
```

A User table with salted passwords

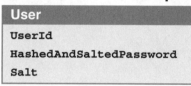

User
UserId
HashedAndSaltedPassword
Salt

Description

- A *salt* is a random string that's appended to a password. To salt a password, you append the salt value to the original password before hashing it.

- A salt prevents rainbow table attacks from working.

- The salt value is only created the first time the password is created. It must be stored in the database so that it can be used later to regenerate the hash.

- The SecureRandom class is a subclass of the Random class that generates random numbers suitable for cryptography purposes.

- You can use the nextBytes method of the SecureRandom class to populate an array with a series of random bytes.

- The Base64 class is only included with Java 8 or newer. If you are not using Java 8, you can use the org.apache.tomcat.util.codec.binary.Base64 class from Tomcat, or the Base64 encoder from Apache Commons Codec (commons.apache.org).

- With Java 8, you can use the getEncoder().encodeToString method of the Base64 class to convert an array of bytes into a string.

- With earlier versions of Java, you can use the encodeBase64String method of Tomcat's Base64 class to convert an array of bytes into a string.

Figure 17-5   How to salt passwords

A utility class for hashing and salting passwords

Figure 17-6 presents a complete utility class named PasswordUtil that you can use for hashing and salting passwords. All of the functionality of the class was covered in the previous figures, but this class includes a main method that you can run to get a better idea of how the class works.

To run this class from within NetBeans, you can right-click on the file in the Projects window and select the Run File command. Or, you can right-click anywhere in its source code editor window and select the Run File command.

When you run this code, it should display output that looks something like this:

```
Hash for 'sesame':
d0c04f4b1951e4aeaaec8223ed2039e542f3aae805a6fa7f6d794e5afff5d272

Random salt:
6v695rTg2864GpVjwE752mSO93GH1ak8U0uRAWdF304=

Salted hash for 'sesame':
1f41a55b2194ee7e064c197c74410fc03fef562ebc5c386cd7198b1b81fb5f45
```

This shows that the hash for "sesame", the random salt that's added to "sesame", and the salted hash for "sesame". Note that the hash and salted hash are the same length. However, they contain different values.

A utility class for hashing and salting passwords

```java
import java.security.MessageDigest;
import java.security.NoSuchAlgorithmException;
import java.security.SecureRandom;
import java.util.Random;
import java.util.Base64;

public class PasswordUtil {
    public static String hashPassword(String password)
            throws NoSuchAlgorithmException {
        MessageDigest md = MessageDigest.getInstance("SHA-256");
        md.reset();
        md.update(password.getBytes());
        byte[] mdArray = md.digest();
        StringBuilder sb = new StringBuilder(mdArray.length * 2);
        for (byte b : mdArray) {
            int v = b & 0xff;
            if (v < 16) {
                sb.append('0');
            }
            sb.append(Integer.toHexString(v));
        }
        return sb.toString();
    }

    public static String getSalt() {
        Random r = new SecureRandom();
        byte[] saltBytes = new byte[32];
        r.nextBytes(saltBytes);
        return Base64.getEncoder().encodeToString(saltBytes);
    }

    public static String hashAndSaltPassword(String password)
            throws NoSuchAlgorithmException {
        String salt = getSalt();
        return hashPassword(password + salt);
    }

    /*  This code tests the functionality of this class.
    */
    public static void main(String[] args) {
        try {
            System.out.println("Hash for 'sesame'        : "
                    + hashPassword("sesame"));
            System.out.println("Random salt              : "
                    + getSalt());
            System.out.println("Salted hash for 'sesame': "
                    + hashAndSaltPassword("sesame"));
        } catch (NoSuchAlgorithmException ex) {
            System.out.println(ex);
        }
    }
}
```

Figure 17-6   A utility class for hashing and salting passwords

How to enforce password strength requirements

Hashing and salting your passwords helps to protect against attackers being able to decipher them if they should gain access to them. But it doesn't stop attackers from guessing weak passwords. In addition to educating your users about the benefits of strong passwords, you can write code to enforce password strength requirements.

The first example in figure 17-7 shows a method named checkPassword-Strength that enforces some password strength requirements. In this case, the method only checks to make sure the password is not empty, is not a series of spaces, and is at least eight characters long. If the password doesn't meet these conditions, this method throws an exception that contains a message that describes why the password isn't strong enough.

A more realistic method would probably enforce stricter password requirements. One way to do that is to use Java's regular expressions API. Regular expressions are outside the scope of this book, but you can learn more about how to use them in Java from several sources online. In addition, you can find pre-written regular expressions from many online sources. These regular expressions can enforce requirements such as minimum length, mandatory special characters, and a mandatory mix of upper and lowercase characters.

The second example shows how to use the checkPasswordStrength method. If the password meets the length requirements, this code prints a message to the output stream that indicates that the password is valid. Otherwise, this code prints the message that's stored in the exception to the output stream. In this case, the code passes a value of "sesame" to the method, which does not meet the length requirement. As a result, this code prints a message to the output stream that indicates that the password is too short.

A more realistic code example would continue processing the password if it met the strength requirements and display the exception message on the web page if it didn't meet the strength requirements. That way, the user would know why his or her password didn't pass the strength check.

A method for enforcing password strength

```
public static void checkPasswordStrength(String password) throws Exception {
    if (password == null || password.trim().isEmpty()) {
        throw new Exception("Password cannot be empty.");
    } else if (password.length() < 8) {
        throw new Exception("Password is too short. Must be at least "
            + "8 characters long.");
    }
}
```

Code that uses this method

```
try {
    checkPasswordStrength("sesame");
    System.out.println("Password is valid.");
} catch (Exception e) {
    System.out.println(e.getMessage());
}
```

Description

- You can start by checking to verify that the password isn't equal to a null value.

- You can use the trim and length methods to verify that the password isn't empty.

- You can use the length method to verify that the password is a minimum number of characters.

- If the password doesn't meet minimum requirements, you can throw an exception that contains a message that describes why the password didn't meet the requirements.

- You can use Java's regular expression API to enforce requirements such as minimum length, mandatory special characters, and a mandatory mix of upper and lowercase characters. To learn more about the regular expression API, you can search the Internet.

Figure 17-7   A method for enforcing password strength requirements

Perspective

Now that you've finished this chapter, you have an additional set of skills you can use to protect your users and your web applications against unauthorized access. But security is a complex topic and there is a lot more to it than we have space to cover in this book.

One important topic this book did not cover is database encryption, which is a good idea if you are storing any sensitive data in your database such as customer credit card numbers, or information that could allow an attacker to steal a user's identity.

Unfortunately, MySQL doesn't provide an easy way to transparently encrypt databases and requires special programming techniques in your application to do so. If you need to encrypt sensitive data, we suggest one of two options.

The first is to use a database that does offer transparent database encryption. Most commercial databases do this, as does the open source database PostgreSQL.

The second option is to encrypt the hard disk the database is stored on. Many operating systems have built in hard disk encryption software. There are also several third party solutions available for this. In addition, some hard disk controllers support encryption at the hardware level. To see if yours does, you can consult the documentation that came with your server, or contact your server provider.

Summary

- *Cross-site scripting (XSS) attacks* allow an attacker to inject Javascript into your page.
- *SQL injection attacks* allow an attacker to run malicious SQL code on your database.
- *Social engineering attacks* are when an attacker attempts to gain unauthorized access to a system by tricking users rather than exploiting technical flaws.
- To prevent social engineering attacks, educate your users about password strength and the dangers of giving out information to unknown persons.
- A *one-way hash algorithm* takes an input string and hashes it to an encoded fixed-length output string. The hash cannot be reversed.
- *Reversible encryption* encrypts data against a key, and the data can later be decrypted when it needs to be read. This type of encryption is useful for tasks such as storing credit card numbers, or securely transmitting documents over a network.
- *Weak passwords* are passwords that an attacker can easily guess or crack.

- *Clear-text passwords*, or *unhashed passwords*, are passwords that are stored in the database or sent over the network without being encrypted.

- In a *dictionary attack*, an attacker attempts to guess passwords by using an automated program and an electronic dictionary.

- In a *rainbow table attack*, and attacker uses a pre-computed database of words and their hash values in an attempt to crack hashed passwords that they have gained access to.

- To hash a string, you use the MessageDigest class.

- A *collision* occurs when two input strings hash to the same value.

- A *salt* is a random string appended to a password. This prevents rainbow table attacks.

- To generate a secure random salt, you can use the SecureRandom class to generate an array of random bytes, and the Base64 class to encode that array to a string value.

Exercise 17-1   Test the PasswordUtil class

1. Open the project named ch17_ex1_password that's in the ex_starts directory.

2. Open the index.jsp page and review its code. Note that this page uses two HTML input tags to get the username and password from the user. In addition, note that this page displays the encrypted value for the password.

3. Open the CheckPasswordServlet class and review its code. Note how it uses the PasswordUtil class to get the values for the encrypted password, the salt value, and the salted and encrypted password.

4. Run the application. When you click on the Login button, note the values for the encrypted password, the salt, and the salted and encrypted password.

5. Click the Login button again. Note that the encrypted password stays the same. However, the salt changes. As a result, the salted and encrypted password changes too.

6. Enter a different password and click the Login button again. This time all three values should change.

18

How to work with HTTP requests and responses

When you write servlets and JSPs, the classes and methods of the servlet API shelter you from having to work directly with HTTP. Sometimes, though, you need to know more about HTTP requests and responses, and you need to use the methods of the servlet API to work with them. So that's what you'll learn in this chapter. Along the way, you'll get a better idea of how HTTP works.

An introduction to HTTP

This topic introduces you to some of the most common headers and status codes that make up the *Hypertext Transfer Protocol* (*HTTP*). This protocol can be used to send a request to a server, and it can be used to return a response from a server.

An HTTP request and response

Figure 18-1 shows the components of a typical HTTP request and a typical HTTP response. As you learn more about these components, you'll get a better idea of how HTTP requests and responses work.

The first line of an HTTP request is known as the *request line*. This line contains the request method, the request URL, and the request protocol. Typically, the request method is GET or POST, but other methods are also supported by HTTP. Similarly, the request protocol is usually HTTP 1.1, but could possibly be HTTP 1.0 or HTTP 1.2.

After the request line, an HTTP request contains the *request headers*. These headers contain information about the client that's making the request. In this figure, the HTTP request contains eight request headers with one header per line, but a request can include more headers than that. Each request header begins with the name of the request header, followed by a colon and a space, followed by the value of the request header.

After the request headers, an HTTP request that uses the POST method may include a blank line followed by the parameters for the request. Unlike a GET request, a POST request doesn't include its parameters in the URL.

The first line of an HTTP response is known as the *status line*. This line specifies the version of HTTP that's being used, a *status code*, and a message that's associated with the status code.

After the status line, an HTTP response contains the *response headers*. These headers contain information about the server and about the response that's being returned to the client. Like request headers, each response header takes one line. In addition, each line begins with the name of the header, followed by a colon and a space, followed by the value of the header.

After the response headers, an HTTP response contains a blank line, followed by the *response entity*, or *response body*. In this figure, the response entity is an HTML document, but it could also be an XML document, plain text, tab-delimited text, an image, a PDF file, a sound file, a video file, and so on.

To learn more about HTTP 1.1, you can search the web for "HTTP 1.1 specification" and view the documentation that's available from www.w3.org. This documentation provides a highly technical description of HTTP 1.1 including a complete list of headers and status codes.

An HTTP request

```
GET http://www.murach.com/email/index.html HTTP/1.1
referer: http://www.murach.com/index.html
connection: keep-alive
user-agent: Mozilla/5.0 (Windows NT 6.1; WOW64) Chrome/33.0.1750.146
host: www.murach.com
accept: text/html,application/xhtml+xml,application/xml;q=0.9,*/*;q=0.8
accept-encoding: gzip, deflate
accept-language: en-US,en;q=0.5
cookie: emailCookie=joel@murach.com; firstNameCookie=Joel
```

An HTTP response

```
HTTP/1.1 200 OK
date: Sat, 17 Mar 2014 10:32:54 GMT
server: Apache/2.2.3 (Unix) PHP/5.2.4
content-type: text/html
content-length: 201
last-modified: Fri, 16 Aug 2013 12:52:09 GMT

<!DOCTYPE html>
<html>
<head>
    <title>Murach's Java Servlets and JSP</title>
</head>
<body>
    <h1>Join our email list</h1>
</body>
</html>
```

Description

- *Hypertext Transfer Protocol* (*HTTP*) is the primary protocol that's used to transfer data between a browser and a server. Three versions of HTTP exist: 1.0, 1.1., and 1.2. Of these, HTTP 1.1 is the most commonly used. Since HTTP 1.1 is a superset of HTTP 1.0, all HTTP 1.0 request headers are also available in HTTP 1.1.

- The first line of an HTTP request is known as the *request line*. This line specifies the request method, the URL of the request, and the version of HTTP.

- After the first line of a request, the browser sends *request headers* that give information about the browser and its request.

- The first line of an HTTP response is known as the *status line*. This line specifies the HTTP version, a *status code*, and a brief description associated with the status code.

- After the first line of a response, the server sends *response headers* that give information about the response. Then, it sends the *response entity*, or *response body*. The body of a response is typically HTML, but it can also be other types of data.

- To learn more about HTTP 1.1, you can search the web for "HTTP 1.1 specification" and view the documentation that's available from www.w3.org.

Figure 18-1   An HTTP request and response

Common MIME types

Figure 18-2 shows some of the most common *Multipurpose Internet Mail Extension* (*MIME*) types that are used by HTTP. You can use them in the accept header of a request or the content-type header of a response.

To specify a MIME type, you can use this format:

```
type/subtype
```

In the past, it was common for experimental and unofficial content types to use an x-prefix. For example, type/x-subtype. However, this ended up causing more problems than it solved. As a result, the practice has been deprecated as of mid-2012 by RFC 6648.

Although the "text/plain" MIME type is the default MIME type for a servlet, the most commonly used MIME type is the "text/html" type. Later in this chapter, you'll learn how to use a few MIME types in HTTP requests and responses.

If you want to learn more about MIME types, you can search the web for "MIME types" and view the documentation that's available from www.iana.org. This documentation provides a highly technical description of MIME types. Or, you can view other websites that provide less technical descriptions of MIME types.

Common MIME types

Type/Subtype	Description
`text/plain`	Plain text document
`text/html`	HTML document
`text/css`	HTML cascading style sheet
`text/xml`	XML document
`text/csv`	CSV (comma-separated values) document
`text/tab-separated-values`	TSV (tab-separated values) document
`image/gif`	GIF image
`image/jpeg`	JPEG image
`image/png`	PNG image
`image/tiff`	TIFF image
`image/x-xbitmap`	Windows bitmap image
`application/atom-xml`	Atom feed
`application/rss-xml`	RSS feed
`application/pdf`	PDF file
`application/postscript`	PostScript file
`application/zip`	ZIP file
`application/gzip`	GZIP file
`application/octet-stream`	Binary data
`application/msword`	Microsoft Word document
`application/vnd.ms-excel`	Microsoft Excel spreadsheet
`audio/x-midi`	MIDI sound file
`audio/mpeg`	MP3 sound file
`audio/vnd.wav`	WAV sound file
`video/mpeg`	MPEG video file
`video/x-flv`	Adobe Flash file

Description

- The *Multipurpose Internet Mail Extension* (*MIME*) types provide standards for the various types of data that can be transferred across the Internet.

- MIME types can be included in the accept header of a request or the content-type header of a response.

- For more information about MIME types, you can search the web for "MIME types" and view the documentation that's available from www.iana.org.

Figure 18-2   MIME types

Common HTTP request headers

Figure 18-3 lists some of the most common HTTP request headers. Today, most web browsers support HTTP 1.1 so you can usually use HTTP 1.1 headers.

Most of the time, a web browser automatically sets these request headers when it makes a request. Then, when the server receives the request, it can check these headers to learn about the browser. In addition, though, you can write servlets that set some of these request headers. For example, chapter 7 shows how to use the servlet API to set the cookie header. And chapter 16 shows how to use the servlet container to automatically set the authorization header.

Common HTTP request headers

Name	Description
accept	Specifies the preferred order of MIME types that the browser can accept. The "*/*" type indicates that the browser can handle any MIME type.
accept-charset	Specifies the character sets that the browser can accept.
accept-encoding	Specifies the types of compression encoding that the browser can accept.
accept-language	Specifies the standard language codes for the languages that the browser prefers. The standard language code for English is "en" or "en-us".
authorization	Identifies the authorization level for the browser. When you use container-managed security as described in chapter 16, the servlet container automatically sets this header.
connection	Indicates the type of connection that's being used by the browser. In HTTP 1.0, a value of "keep-alive" means that the browser can use a persistent connection that allows it to accept multiple files with a single connection. In HTTP 1.1, this type of connection is the default.
cookie	Specifies any cookies that were previously sent by the current server. In chapter 7, you learned how to use the servlet API to work with this header.
host	Specifies the host and port of the machine that originally sent the request. This header is optional in HTTP 1.0 and required in HTTP 1.1.
pragma	A value of "no-cache" indicates to browsers, proxy servers, and gateways that this document should not be cached.
referer	Indicates the URL of the referring web page. The spelling error was made by one of the original authors of HTTP and is now part of the protocol.
user-agent	Indicates the type of browser. Although most browsers identify themselves as "Mozilla", the name of the browser is usually included somewhere in the string.

Figure 18-3   HTTP request headers

Common HTTP status codes

Figure 18-4 summarizes the five categories of status codes. Then, this figure lists some of the most common status codes.

For successful requests, the server typically returns a 200 (OK) status code. However, if the server can't find the requested file, it typically returns the infamous 404 (Not Found) status code. Or, if the server encounters an error while trying to retrieve the file, it may return the equally infamous 500 (Internal Server Error) status code.

Status code summary

Number	Type	Description
100-199	Informational	The request was received and is being processed.
200-299	Success	The request was successful.
300-399	Redirection	Further action must be taken to fulfill the request.
400-499	Client errors	The client has made a request that contains an error.
500-599	Server errors	The server has encountered an error.

Status codes

Number	Name	Description
200	OK	The default status indicating that the response is normal.
301	Moved Permanently	The requested resource has been permanently moved to a new URL.
302	Found	The requested resource resides temporarily under a new URL.
400	Bad Request	The request could not be understood by the server due to bad syntax.
401	Unauthorized	The request requires authentication. The response must include a www-authenticate header. If you use container-managed security as described in chapter 16, the web server automatically returns this status code when appropriate.
403	Forbidden	Access to the requested resource has been denied. This is commonly caused by misconfigured file permissions such that the server does not have permission to access the requested document.
404	Not Found	The server could not find the requested URL.
405	Method Not Allowed	The method specified in the request line is not allowed for the requested URL.
414	Request-URI Too Long	This is typically caused by trying to pass too much data in a GET request. It can usually be resolved by converting the GET request to a POST request.
418	I'm a teapot	The request was denied because the browser attempted to brew coffee using a teapot. Don't believe us? You can read about it in RFC-2324.
500	Internal Server Error	The server encountered an unexpected condition that prevented it from fulfilling the request.

Figure 18-4   HTTP status codes

Common HTTP response headers

Figure 18-5 lists some of the most common HTTP response headers. Most of the time, the web server automatically sets these response headers when it returns the response. However, there are times when you may want to use Java code to set response headers that control the response sent by your web server.

For example, you can use the cache-control header to control how the web browser caches a response. To do that, you can use the cache-control values specified in this figure to turn off caching, to use a private cache, to use a public cache, to specify when a response must be revalidated, or to increase the duration of the cache. You'll see an example of this later on in this chapter.

Common HTTP response headers

Name	Description
cache-control	Controls when and how a browser caches a page. For more information, see figure 18-9 and the list of possible values shown below.
content-disposition	Can be used to specify that the response includes an attached binary file. For an example, see figure 18-9 and 18-11.
content-length	Specifies the length of the body of the response in bytes. This allows the browser to know when it's done reading the entire response and is necessary for the browser to use a persistent, keep-alive connection.
content-type	Specifies the MIME type of the response document. You can use the "maintype/subtype" format shown earlier in this chapter to specify the MIME type.
content-encoding	Specifies the type of encoding that the response uses. Encoding a document with compression such as GZIP can enhance performance. For an example, see figure 18-10.
expires	Specifies the time that the page should no longer be cached.
last-modified	Specifies the time when the document was last modified.
location	Works with status codes in the 300s to specify the new location of the document.
pragma	Turns off caching for older browsers when it is set to a value of "no-cache".
refresh	Specifies the number of seconds before the browser should ask for an updated page.
www-authenticate	Works with the 401 (Unauthorized) status code to specify the authentication type and realm. If you use container-managed security as described in chapter 16, the servlet container automatically sets this header when necessary.

Values for the cache-control header

Name	Description
public	The document can be cached in a public, shared cache.
private	The document can only be cached in a private, single-user cache.
no-cache	The document should never be cached.
no-store	The document should never be cached or stored in a temporary location on the disk.
must-revalidate	The document must be revalidated with the original server (not a proxy server) each time it is requested.
proxy-revalidate	The document must be revalidated on the proxy server but not on the original server.
max-age=x	The document must be revalidated after x seconds for private caches.
s-max-age=x	The document must be revalidated after x seconds for shared caches.

Figure 18-5   HTTP response headers

How to work with the request

This topic shows how to use the methods of the request object to get the data that's contained in an HTTP request.

How to get a request header

You can use the first group of methods in figure 18-6 to get any of the headers in an HTTP request. The getHeader method lets you return the value of any header. The getIntHeader and getDateHeader methods make it easier to work with headers that contain integer and date values. And the getHeaderNames method returns an Enumeration object that contains the names of all of the headers for the request.

You can use the second group of methods to get the request headers more easily. For example, this statement:

```
int contentLength = request.getIntHeader("Content-Length");
```

returns the same value as this statement:

```
int contentLength = request.getContentLength();
```

The first example uses the getHeader method to return a string that contains a list of the browser's preferred languages (based on the user's preferred language). Then, it uses the startsWith method within an if statement to check if the preferred language is Spanish. If it is, the code sets the JSP file to a Spanish version. Otherwise, the code falls back on the default language, which is English in this case.

The second example uses the getHeader method to return a string that identifies the type of browser that made the request. Since older versions of Internet Explorer always included the letters "MSIE" in their user-agent strings, this example uses an indexOf method within an if statement to check if the string contains the letters "MSIE". If so, it calls a method that executes some code that's specific to older versions of Internet Explorer. Otherwise, it calls a method that executes a generic version of the code for any other browser.

Although you may never need to write code that checks the MIME types or the browser type, these examples illustrate general concepts that you can use to check any request header. First, you use the getHeader, getIntHeader, or getDate-Header methods to return a header. Then, you can use an if statement to check the header. For a String object, you can use the indexOf method to check if a substring exists within the string. For int values and Date objects, you can use other comparison operators.

General methods for working with request headers

Method	Description
getHeader(String headerName)	Returns a String value for the specified header.
getIntHeader(String headerName)	Returns an int value for the specified header.
getDateHeader(String headerName)	Returns a Date value for the specified header.
getHeaderNames()	Returns an Enumeration object that contains the names of all headers.

Convenience methods for working with request headers

Method	Description
getContentType()	Returns the MIME type of the body of the request. If the type is not known, this method returns a null value.
getContentLength()	Returns an int value for the number of bytes in the request body that are made available by the input stream. If the length is not known, this method returns -1.
getCookies()	Returns an array of Cookie objects. For information about this method, see chapter 7.
getAuthType()	Returns the authentication type that's being used by the server.
getRemoteUser()	Returns the username of the user making this request, if the user has been authenticated. If the user has not been authenticated, this method returns a null value.

An example that checks the preferred language

```
String language = request.getHeader("accept-language");
if (language.startsWith("es"))
    jsp = "index.spanish.jsp";
else
    jsp = "index.english.jsp";
```

An example that checks the browser type

```
String browser = request.getHeader("user-agent");
if (browser.indexOf("MSIE") > -1)
    doIECode();
else
    doGenericCode();
```

Description

- All of these methods can be called from the request object to return information about the HTTP request.

- For more information about these and other methods and fields of the HttpServletRequest interface, you can refer to the documentation for the Java EE API.

Figure 18-6   How to get a request header

How to display all request headers

Figure 18-7 shows part of a servlet that uses the getHeaderNames method of the request object to return an Enumeration object that contains the names of all of the request headers. After that, it iterates over the enumeration and stores each request header in a hash map, using the header name as the key, and the header value as the value in the map. Then, it sets a request attribute called headers that makes the hash map available from the JSP.

The second part of this figure shows the JSP that displays all of the request headers. If you're developing a web application that needs to check other request headers, you can use this JSP to quickly view the request headers for all of the different browsers that your web application supports. Then, you can write the code that checks the request headers and works with them.

This JSP begins by defining the taglib prefix for the core JSTL tags. Then, it creates a table that contains the request headers. In the first row of the table, the first column is the Name column, and the second column is the Value column.

After the first row of the table, this page uses the forEach JSTL tag to iterate over the hash map that the servlet stored as the headers attribute of the request. As the forEach loop iterates over the hash map, it creates a new row for each item in the map. In the first column, it prints the key from the map, which is the name of the header. In the second column, it prints the value from the map, which is also the value of the header.

The second part of this figure shows the request headers for the Chrome browser. In this case, the accept-language headers shows that the preferred language is U.S. English.

The accept header shows that Chrome accepts several content types, including html and xml. The content types are listed in order of preference. As a result, if the server has both an html and an xml version of the same document, Chrome prefers the html version.

The */* at the end of the accept header is a wildcard that indicates that Chrome accepts any content type, assuming the content is not available in any of the previous preferred formats. In that case, Chrome typically downloads the data and allows the user to choose an application to open it with.

The request headers for other browsers look similar. If you want to see the request headers for other browsers, you can use other browsers to run the sample application for this chapter.

The user-agent header shows that Chrome identifies as Mozilla. Almost all browsers include this in the user-agent header. The reason is because early in the history of the Internet, before there were standards, most browsers strived to be compatible with Netscape's Mozilla browser. As a result, they masqueraded as Mozilla so that web servers that checked the user-agent tag would send them content that might be enhanced for Netscape's Mozilla browser.

The servlet code that gets all request headers

```
Enumeration<String> headerNames = request.getHeaderNames();
Map<String, String> headers = new HashMap<String, String>();
while (headerNames.hasMoreElements()) {
    String headerName = headerNames.nextElement();
    headers.put(headerName, request.getHeader(headerName));
}
request.setAttribute("headers", headers);
```

The JSP code that displays the headers

```
<%@taglib prefix="c" uri="http://java.sun.com/jsp/jstl/core" %>
<h1>Request Headers</h1>
<table>
    <tr>
        <th>Name</th>
        <th>Value</th>
    </tr>
    <c:forEach var="headers" items="${headers}">
    <tr>
        <td><c:out value="${headers.key}"/></td>
        <td><c:out value="${headers.value}"/></td>
    </tr>
    </c:forEach>
</table>
```

All request headers sent by Chrome

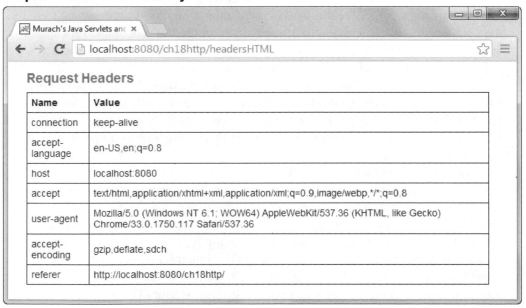

Figure 18-7   How to display all request headers

How to work with the response

Figure 18-8 shows how to use the fields and methods of the response object to set the data that's contained in an HTTP response.

How to set status codes

Most of the time, the web server automatically sets the status code for an HTTP response. However, if you need to set the status code, you can use the setStatus method. To specify the value for this code, you can use either an integer value or one of the fields of the response object. For example, this figure shows two ways to specify the 404 (Not Found) status code.

How to set response headers

Like status codes, the web server usually sets the headers of an HTTP response. However, if you need to set a response header, this figure shows six methods that you can use. To start, you can use the setHeader, setIntHeader, and setDateHeader methods to set all response headers that accept strings, integers, or dates. Here, the setDateHeader accepts a long value that represents the date in milliseconds since January 1, 1970 00:00:00 GMT.

On the other hand, if you're working with commonly used headers, such as the content-type or content-length headers, you can use the setContentType and setContentLength methods. And you can use the addCookie method to add a value to the cookie header as described in chapter 7.

The examples show how to work with response headers. The first statement uses the setContentType method to set the value of the content-type header to the "text/html" MIME type. The second statement uses the setContentLength method to set the content-length header to 403 bytes, although you usually won't need to set this header.

The third statement uses the setHeader method to set the pragma header to "no-cache" to turn off caching for older browsers. The fourth statement uses the setIntHeader method to set the refresh header to 60 seconds. As a result, the browser requests an updated page in 1 minute. Last, the fifth statement uses the setDateHeader to set the expires header so caching for the page expires after 1 hour. To do that, this statement calls the getTime method from a Date object named currentDate to return the current time in milliseconds. Then, it adds 3,600,000 milliseconds to that date (1000 milliseconds times 60 seconds times 60 minutes equals one hour).

The main method for setting the status codes

Method	Description
setStatus(int code)	Sets the status code for this response.

How status codes map to fields of the response object

Code	HttpServletResponse field
200 (OK)	SC_OK
404 (Not Found)	SC_NOT_FOUND
XXX (Xxx Xxx)	SC_XXX_XXX

Examples that set the status code

```
response.setStatus(404);
response.setStatus(response.SC_NOT_FOUND);
```

General methods for setting response headers

Method	Description
setHeader(String name, String value)	Sets a response header with the specified name and value.
setIntHeader(String name, int value)	Sets a response header with the specified name and int value.
setDateHeader(String name, long value)	Sets a response header with the specified name and date value.

Convenience methods for setting response headers

Method	Description
setContentType(String mimeType)	Sets the MIME type of the response being sent to the client in the Content-Type header.
setContentLength(int lengthInBytes)	Sets the length of the content body in the Content-Length header.
addCookie(Cookie cookie)	Adds the specified cookie to the response. For more information about this method, see chapter 7.

Examples that set response headers

```
response.setContentType("text/html");
response.setContentLength(403);
response.setHeader("pragma", "no-cache");
response.setIntHeader("refresh", 60);
response.setDateHeader("expires", currentDate.getTime() + 60 * 60 * 1000);
```

Description

- For more information about these and other methods and fields of the HttpServletResponse interface, you can refer to the documentation for the Java EE API.

Figure 18-8   How to set a response status code or header

Practical HTTP skills

Now that you understand the concepts behind using the servlet API to work with HTTP requests and responses, you're ready to learn some practical skills for working with HTTP.

How to return a spreadsheet

Sometimes, you may want to return data as a spreadsheet so the user can easily open that data with a spreadsheet application such as Microsoft Excel or OpenOffice Calc. To do that, you can use the classes from the Apache POI project to create a workbook. Then, you can use the response object to return that workbook to the client.

For this to work, you need to search the Internet to find the web page for the Apache POI project, download its JAR file, and make that JAR file available to your application. Then, you can create Workbook, Sheet, and Row objects and store your data in these objects.

The code in figure 18-9 starts by creating a Workbook object from the HSSFWorkbook class. This object is designed to work with files that have an .xls extension. Then, this code creates a worksheet within the workbook, creates the first row of the worksheet, and sets a value in the first cell of that row. Next, this code retrieves all of the columns and rows of the User table from a database and stores that data in the cells of the worksheet.

When the code finishes storing the data in the worksheet, the first highlighted statement uses the content-disposition header to specify that the response is an attached file named users.xls. On most systems, the .xls extension is associated with a spreadsheet application such as Microsoft Excel or OpenOffice Calc. As a result, this usually makes it easy for the user to open this file as a spreadsheet.

Finally, the three statements shown in part 2 of this figure get an OutputStream object for the response and use the write method of the Workbook object to return the workbook to the browser.

When you return a workbook to a browser, most browsers provide an easy way for the user to open the workbook with a spreadsheet application. For example, Chrome typically displays a button in its lower left corner that the user can click to open the workbook. However, other browsers may display a dialog box like the one shown in figure 18-10.

How to control caching

The second highlighted statement uses the setHeader method to set the cache-control response header so the document that's returned won't be cached. Otherwise, the server might automatically cache the response. Although it's usually more efficient to allow a document to be cached, preventing caching makes sure that the browser updates the data with every visit.

Import statements for Apache POI classes that work with spreadsheets

```
import org.apache.poi.hssf.usermodel.HSSFWorkbook;
import org.apache.poi.ss.usermodel.Row;
import org.apache.poi.ss.usermodel.Sheet;
import org.apache.poi.ss.usermodel.Workbook;
```

Servlet code that returns a spreadsheet file

```
@Override
public void doGet(HttpServletRequest request,
        HttpServletResponse response)
        throws IOException, ServletException {

    // create the workbook, its worksheet, and its title row
    Workbook workbook = new HSSFWorkbook();
    Sheet sheet = workbook.createSheet("User table");
    Row row = sheet.createRow(0);
    row.createCell(0).setCellValue("The User table");

    try {
        ConnectionPool pool = ConnectionPool.getInstance();
        Connection connection = pool.getConnection();
        Statement statement = connection.createStatement();
        String query = "SELECT * FROM User ORDER BY UserID";
        ResultSet results = statement.executeQuery(query);

        // create the spreadsheet rows
        int i = 2;
        while (results.next()) {
            row = sheet.createRow(i);
            row.createCell(0).setCellValue(results.getInt("UserID"));
            row.createCell(1).setCellValue(results.getString("LastName"));
            row.createCell(2).setCellValue(results.getString("FirstName"));
            row.createCell(3).setCellValue(results.getString("Email"));
            i++;
        }
        results.close();
        statement.close();
        connection.close();
    } catch (SQLException e) {
        this.log(e.toString());
    }

    // set the response headers
    response.setHeader("content-disposition",
            "attachment; filename=users.xls");
    response.setHeader("cache-control", "no-cache");
```

Description

- For this code to work, the application must have access to the JAR file for the Apache POI project. You can download this JAR file from the Apache POI project website. Then, you can add it to a NetBeans project by right-clicking on its Library folder, selecting the Add JAR/Folder item, and using the resulting dialog box to select the JAR file.

- For a file with an .xls extension, you can create an HSSFWorkbook object. Then, you can use the methods of the Workbook, Sheet, and Row classes to create the spreadsheet.

Figure 18-9   An example that returns a spreadsheet (part 1 of 2)

How to compress a response with GZIP

Since most modern browsers support compression, it usually makes sense to compress any large responses that are returned by your web server. Fortunately, most web servers can handle this automatically. For example, if you're using Tomcat as your web server, you can open Tomcat's server.xml file and add a compression attribute to the Connector element to control how Tomcat handles compression. In part 2 of figure 18-9, for instance, the Connector element compresses all responses that contain text data that are returned on Tomcat's 8080 port. Since responses that contain other types of data such as images, sound, or video are usually already compressed, you typically don't get much of a performance gain by compressing these types of responses. As a result, the setting shown in this figure is the setting that's most commonly used.

However, if your web server doesn't automatically handle compression, you can manually encode a response with GZIP compression by checking and modifying the HTTP headers for requests and responses. This can dramatically improve download times for large documents. For example, if the table named User contains a large amount of data, it might make sense to encode the workbook that's returned in the last figure with GZIP compression. To do that, you can add the code shown in the last example.

Here, the first statement uses the getHeader method to return the accept-encoding request header. This request header is a string that contains the types of encoding that the browser supports. Then, the second statement declares an OutputStream object.

In the if block, the if statement tests whether the browser supports GZIP encoding. If it does, this code creates an OutputStream object that uses a GZIPOutputStream object to compress the output stream. This code also uses the setHeader method to set the content-encoding response header to GZIP. That way, the browser knows to use GZIP to decompress the stream before trying to read it.

However, if the browser doesn't support GZIP encoding, the getOutput-Stream method of the response object is used to return a normal OutputStream object. Either way, the OutputStream object is used to return the response to the browser.

Servlet code that returns a spreadsheet file (continued)

```
// get the output stream and send the workbook to the browser
OutputStream out = response.getOutputStream();
workbook.write(out);
out.close();
}
```

How to modify Tomcat's server.xml to automatically handle compression

```
<Connector port="8080" protocol="HTTP/1.1"
           maxThreads="150" connectionTimeout="20000"
           redirectPort="8443" compression="on" />
```

Valid values for the compression attribute of the Connector element

Value	Description
on	Enables compression for text data.
force	Forces compression for all types of data.
int value	Enables compression for text data but specifies a minimum amount of data before the output is compressed.
off	Disables compression.

The import statement for the GZIPOutputStream class

```
import java.util.zip.GZIPOutputStream;
```

How to manually encode a response with GZIP compression

```
String encodingString = request.getHeader("accept-encoding");
OutputStream out;
if (encodingString != null && encodingString.contains("gzip")) {
    out = new GZIPOutputStream(response.getOutputStream());
    response.setHeader("content-encoding", "gzip");
} else {
    out = response.getOutputStream();
}
```

Description

- The getOutputStream method of the response object returns an OutputStream object for a binary output stream.

- The GZIPOutputStream class uses GZIP to compress the data in an OutputStream object.

Figure 18-9   An example that returns a spreadsheet (part 2 of 2)

How to return a binary file as an attachment

Within a web application, you can code an HTML link that points to a downloadable binary file. For example, you can code a link that points to a Portable Document Format (PDF) file. Then, when a user clicks on this link, most browsers use a built-in reader to display the PDF file.

This may be adequate for some applications. However, for other applications you may want to give the user the option to download or open the file. To do that, you can use the content-disposition header to indicate that the file is an attachment with the specified name.

For some browsers, that displays a button. For others, it displays a dialog box like the one shown in figure 18-10. Either way, this gives the user the choice to open or save the file.

The first example shows how to code an HTML link to an MP3 file. For most browsers, clicking a link like this automatically launches an audio player that plays the sound file. If that's not what you want, you can code an HTML link to a servlet that uses the content-disposition header to indicate that the file is an attachment with the specified name as shown in the second example.

The third example shows some code from a servlet that handles the request made by the second example. Within the doGet method, the first three statements get the path and name of the file that's sent as a request parameter. Then, the fourth statement sets the content-type response header to indicate that the response contains generic binary data, and the fifth statement sets the content-disposition header to indicate that the response contains an attached file. This causes the browser to handle the response accordingly.

Once the response headers have been set, this code uses a while loop to read each byte from the specified file. Then, it uses the PrintWriter object to write each byte to the response. Finally, this code closes the input and output streams.

A dialog box that lets you open or save a file

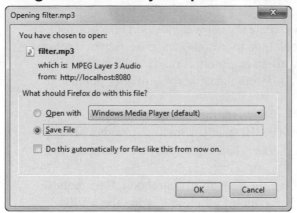

An HTML link to an MP3 sound file

```
<a href="filter.mp3">Joe Rut - Filter</a>
```

An HTML link to the servlet for downloading the file

```
<a href="downloadFile?name=filter.mp3">Joe Rut - Filter</a>
```

The servlet code that identifies the file as an attached binary file

```java
@Override
public void doGet(HttpServletRequest request,
        HttpServletResponse response)
        throws IOException, ServletException {

    ServletContext sc = getServletContext();
    String path = sc.getRealPath("/");
    String name = request.getParameter("name");

    response.setContentType("application/octet-stream");
    response.setHeader("content-disposition",
        "attachment; filename=" + name);

    FileInputStream in = new FileInputStream(path + "/" + name);
    PrintWriter out = response.getWriter();

    int i = in.read();
    while (i != -1) {
        out.write(i);
        i = in.read();
    }
    in.close();
    out.close();
}
```

Description

- When you return a file as an attachment, some browsers display a button that allows you to open or save the file. Other browsers display a File Download dialog box that allows you to open or save the file.

Figure 18-10   How to return a binary file as an attachment

How to create virtual HTML pages

Figure 18-11 shows how you can create virtual web pages. This code uses the last part of the request URL to look up a user in the database. Then, it returns a page specific to that user. However, these pages don't really exist as actual files. Instead, they are created from a JSP template and dynamically populated with data from the database.

The first example shows the URL pattern for the servlet's mapping. As a result, you can request the servlet with a URL that's formatted like the URLs in the second example. Here, the last part of the URL specifies a username that uniquely identifies the user.

The third example begins by calling the getPathInfo method on the request object. This returns any additional URL path information beyond the servlet mapping. However, it does not return any query parameters. As a result, for a URL of "/users/jane_doe", this method returns a value of "/jane_doe".

After making sure the userString variable is not null, this code attempts to look up the user in the database. To start, it calls the substring method on the string with 1 to return only the part of the userString after the first character. In other words, it strips the leading slash that the getPathInfo method returned. Then, it attempts to get a User object by passing the username to the getByUsername method of the UserDB class.

If the user is not null, this code sets an attribute named user to the User object. Then, it forwards to the user.jsp page.

If, on the other hand, the user is null, a user for the specified username doesn't exist. By extension, the requested virtual page doesn't exist. In that case, this code calls the sendError method on the response object to return a 404 error to the browser. To do that, this code sets the status to 404 and includes a message for the browser to display in its 404 error page.

As mentioned earlier in this chapter, you can also call the setStatus method on the HttpServletResponse object to set the response status. However, setting the status does not actually send a response from the server. Because of that, you have to manually forward or redirect the user to an error page just as you would any other page.

The URL pattern for the servlet

```
/users/*
```

Some possible request URLs

```
/users/jane_doe
/users/john_smith
```

The servlet code

```java
@Override
public void doGet(HttpServletRequest request,
        HttpServletResponse response)
        throws ServletException, IOException {

    String userString = request.getPathInfo();
    User user = null;
    if (userString != null) {
        String username = userString.substring(1);  // strip leading slash
        user = UserDB.getByUsername(username);
    }

    if (user != null) {
        request.setAttribute("user", user);
        getServletContext()
            .getRequestDispatcher("/user.jsp")
            .forward(request, response);
    } else {
        response.sendError(404, "The requested user page doesn't exist.");
    }
}
```

Description

- This code creates a virtual path by using the last part of the requested URL as a key to look up a user's page.

- The getPathInfo method of the request object returns the part of the requested URL after the mapping for the servlet.

- The sendError method of the response object sends a 404 status code to the browser along with an error message for the browser to display.

Figure 18-11   How to create virtual web pages

Perspective

Now that you have finished reading this chapter, you should (1) have a better understanding of how HTTP requests and responses work, and (2) be able to use Java to work with HTTP requests and responses. In particular, you should be able to use Java code to check the values in the headers of an HTTP request and also to set the status code and values of the headers of an HTTP response. Most of the time, though, the servlet API and the servlet container shields you from having to work directly with HTTP.

Summary

- An HTTP request consists of a *request line* followed by *request headers*, while an HTTP response consists of a *status line* followed by *response headers* and then by a *response body*. The headers specify the attributes of a request or a response.

- The *Multipurpose Internet Mail Extension* (*MIME*) types provide standards for various types of data that can be transferred across the Internet.

- You can use the get methods of the request object to get the values of request headers, and you can use the set methods of the response object to set the values of response headers.

Exercise 18-1   Work with requests and responses

In this exercise, test and view some code that works with HTTP request and response headers.

Return the request headers in different formats

1. Open the ch18_ex1_http project in the ex_starts folder.

2. Run the application. Then, test the first three links to see how the application can return the request headers in the HTML, XML, and spreadsheet formats. For the spreadsheet format to work, you must have a spreadsheet application on your computer that can open spreadsheet files that use an extension of .xls.

3. Open the index.html page. Note how the first three links are coded.

4. Open the RequestHeadersHTMLServlet class and the headers.jsp file and review the code. Note how it uses the JSP file to return HTML to the browser.

5. Open the RequestHeadersXMLServlet class and review its code. Note how it changes the response type to XML and returns an XML document.

6. Open the RequestHeadersSpreadsheetServlet class and review its code. Note how it stores data in a spreadsheet and how it specifies that data is in an attached file named request_headers.xls.

Return data as a spreadsheet

7. Run the application. Then, test the two links that display the User table as a spreadsheet. For this to work, you must install the murach database on your system as described in the appendices.

8. Open the index.html page. Note how these two links are coded.

9. Open the servlet classes for these links. Note that the only difference between these servlets is the code that adds the GZIP compression.

Return a binary file as an attachment

10. Run the application. Then, test the links that download the MP3 and PDF file. Note how the links that use the servlet work differently than the links that don't.

11. Open the index.html page. Note how the href attributes for the MP3 and PDF files are coded. Then, note that these files are included in the root directory for this application.

12. Open the code for the DownloadFileServlet class. Note how this servlet sets the content-disposition response header.

Test in other browsers

13. Run the application in some other browsers. Then, test all of the links again. Note how some links work differently for different browsers.

19

How to work with listeners

Starting with the servlet 2.3 specification, you can add a listener to a web application. For example, you can create a listener class that contains code that's executed when your web application starts. Or, you can create a listener class that contains code that's executed every time a user starts a new session. In this chapter, you'll learn how to use listeners.

How to use a ServletContextListener

A *listener* is a class that listens for various events that can occur during the lifecycle of a web application and provides methods that are executed when those events occur. For instance, you can use a ServletContextListener to determine when an application is started, and you can use its contextInitialized method to initialize one or more global variables when that event occurs. This lets you initialize the global variables before the first JSP or servlet of an application is requested.

Because this is a common use of a listener, this chapter is going to use a ServletContextListener as its only example. That, however, should give you a good background for using any of the other listeners.

How to code a class for the listener

To code the class for a listener, you must implement one of the listener interfaces that are stored in the javax.servlet and javax.servlet.http packages. In part 1 of figure 19-1, for example, the CartContextListener class implements the ServletContextListener interface that's in the javax.servlet package. In other words, the CartContextListener is a ServletContextListener.

A class that implements a listener interface must override all of the methods of that interface. In this figure, for example, the CartContextListener class overrides the two methods of the ServletContextListener interface: the contextInitialized method and the contextDestroyed method. Both of these methods include a ServletContextEvent object as a parameter.

The contextInitialized method contains the code that's executed right after the application starts. In the method in this figure, the first statement calls the getServletContext method from the event parameter to return the ServletContext object. Note that a listener class doesn't extend the HttpServlet class so it isn't a servlet. As a result, you can't call the getServletContext method of the HttpServlet class directly from the listener class. Instead, you must call this method from the event parameter.

After getting the context object, the rest of the statements in this method initialize global variables and set them as attributes of the ServletContext object. As a result, these attributes are available to all of the JSPs and servlets for the application. Here, the code gets the customer service email address from the application's web.xml file. Then, it gets an int value for the current year. Next, it gets the path for the text file named products.txt that's stored in the WEB-INF directory. Finally, this code uses this path and the ProductsIO class to create an ArrayList of Product objects from the values that are stored in the text file.

In contrast, the contextDestroyed method is used for the code that's executed when the application stops and destroys the ServletContext object. This method typically contains cleanup code that frees any resources such as database connections that are used by the contextInitialized method. In this figure, though, the contextInititalized method doesn't use any resources that need to be cleaned up. As a result, this method doesn't contain any code.

A listener class that implements the ServletContextListener interface

```
package murach.util;

import javax.servlet.*;
import java.util.*;

import murach.business.*;
import murach.data.*;

public class CartContextListener implements ServletContextListener {

    public void contextInitialized(ServletContextEvent event) {

        ServletContext sc = event.getServletContext();

        // initialize the customer service email address
        String custServEmail = sc.getInitParameter("custServEmail");
        sc.setAttribute("custServEmail", custServEmail);

        // initialize the current year
        GregorianCalendar currentDate = new GregorianCalendar();
        int currentYear = currentDate.get(Calendar.YEAR);
        sc.setAttribute("currentYear", currentYear);

        // initialize the path for the products text file
        String productsPath = sc.getRealPath("/WEB-INF/products.txt");
        sc.setAttribute("productsPath", productsPath);

        // initialize the list of products
        ArrayList<Product> products = ProductIO.getProducts(productsPath);
        sc.setAttribute("products", products);
    }

    public void contextDestroyed(ServletContextEvent event) {
        // no cleanup necessary
    }
}
```

Description

- A *listener* is a class that listens for various events that can occur in an application and provides methods that respond to those events when they occur.

- To code the class for a listener, you must implement one of the listener interfaces that are stored in the javax.servlet and javax.servlet.http packages.

- A class that implements a listener interface must override the methods of that interface. For more information about the listener interfaces, see figures 19-2 and 19-3.

Figure 19-1   How to use a ServletContextListener (part 1 of 3)

How to register the listener

After you code the class for a listener, you must register the listener with the web application. To do that, you must add a listener element to the application's web.xml file as shown in part 2 of figure 19-1. Here, the shaded code contains the listener element. Within the listener element, the listener-class element specifies the fully qualified name of the class. In this case, it specifies the CartContextListener class in the murach.util package, which is the class that's shown in part 1 of this figure.

Below the listener element in this figure, you can see the context-param element that defines the context initialization parameter for the customer service email address. This, of course, has nothing to do with the use of listeners, except that this parameter is read by the listener class that's presented in part 1. As you can see, this parameter has a name of custServEmail and a value of "custserv@murach.com".

A web.xml file that includes a listener element

```
<?xml version="1.0" encoding="UTF-8"?>
<web-app version="3.0"
    xmlns="http://java.sun.com/xml/ns/javaee"
    xmlns:xsi="http://www.w3.org/2001/XMLSchema-instance"
    xsi:schemaLocation="http://java.sun.com/xml/ns/javaee
        http://java.sun.com/xml/ns/javaee/web-app_3_0.xsd">

    <servlet>
        <servlet-name>CartServlet</servlet-name>
        <servlet-class>murach.cart.CartServlet</servlet-class>
    </servlet>
    <servlet-mapping>
        <servlet-name>CartServlet</servlet-name>
        <url-pattern>/cart</url-pattern>
    </servlet-mapping>

    <listener>
        <listener-class>murach.util.CartContextListener</listener-class>
    </listener>

    <context-param>
        <param-name>custServEmail</param-name>
        <param-value>custserv@murach.com</param-value>
    </context-param>

    <session-config>
        <session-timeout>30</session-timeout>
    </session-config>
    <welcome-file-list>
        <welcome-file>index.jsp</welcome-file>
    </welcome-file-list>
</web-app>
```

The listener elements

Element	Description
`listener`	Adds a listener to the application.
`listener-class`	Specifies the fully qualified name of a class that implements a listener.

Description

- After you code the class for a listener, you must register the listener with the application by adding a listener element to the application's web.xml file.

Figure 19-1   How to use a ServletContextListener (part 2 of 3)

How to code a JSP that uses the attributes set by the listener

Part 3 of figure 19-1 shows how a JSP within a web application can use the attributes set by the listener. Here, the three shaded portions use EL to get the attributes of the ServletContext object that were set by the listener presented in parts 1 and 2. This code works because EL automatically searches through all scopes, including application scope.

However, if you are worried about possible naming conflicts, you can explicitly specify application scope like this:

`${applicationScope.products}`

That way, you can be sure that this JSP only uses the products attribute that has been set in the ServletContext object. In this case, that attribute contains an ArrayList object that stores all of the Product objects for the application.

A JSP file that uses attributes that have been set by a listener

```jsp
<%@ taglib prefix="c" uri="http://java.sun.com/jsp/jstl/core" %>
<!DOCTYPE html>
<html>
<head>
    <meta charset="utf-8">
    <title>Murach's Java Servlets and JSP</title>
    <link rel="stylesheet" href="styles/main.css" type="text/css"/>
</head>
<body>

    <h1>CD list</h1>
    <table>
        <tr>
            <th>Description</th>
            <th class="right">Price</th>
            <th> </th>
        </tr>
        <c:forEach var="product" items="${products}">
        <tr>
            <td><c:out value='${product.description}' /></td>
            <td class="right">${product.priceCurrencyFormat}</td>
            <td><form action="cart" method="post">
                    <input type="hidden" name="productCode"
                            value="${product.code}">
                    <input type="submit"
                            value="Add To Cart">
                </form></td>
        </tr>
        </c:forEach>
    </table>

    <p>For customer service, please send an email to ${custServEmail}.</p>

    <p>&copy; Copyright ${currentYear} Mike Murach &amp; Associates, Inc.
        All rights reserved.</p>
</body>
</html>
```

Description

- Any of the attributes that are set by the class that implements the ServletContextListener interface are available to the rest of the servlets and JSPs in the application.

Figure 19-1   How to use a ServletContextListener (part 3 of 3)

How to work with other types of listeners

Now that you know how to use a ServletContextListener, you're ready to learn how to work with other types of listeners.

A summary of the listener interfaces

Figure 19-2 summarizes the eight listener interfaces. Of these interfaces, the ServletContext and ServletRequest interfaces are stored in the javax.servlet package, and the HttpSession interfaces are stored in the javax.servlet.http package. If you review the descriptions of these interfaces, you'll see that they let you listen for a variety of events that occur on the ServletContext, HttpSession, and ServletRequest objects. In other words, they let you listen for events that occur at application, session, or request scope.

For example, the HttpSessionListener works like the ServletContextListener. However, it lets you write code that's executed when a new session is created or destroyed. Typically, a session is destroyed when the user hasn't requested a URL from the web application within 30 minutes, but that time is determined by the web.xml file for the application.

As this figure shows, other listeners let you respond to events that occur when an attribute is added to, removed from, or replaced in the ServletContext, session, or request objects. You can also respond to events that occur when an object is bound or unbound from a session or when a session is activated or deactivated. For most web applications, though, the only listener that you're likely to use is the ServletContextListener.

The ServletContext interfaces

Interface	Description
ServletContextListener	Provides methods that are executed when the ServletContext object is initialized and destroyed. This happens when the application is started and stopped.
SerlvetContextAttributeListener	Provides methods that are executed when attributes are added to, removed from, or replaced in the ServletContext object.

The HttpSession interfaces

Interface	Description
HttpSessionListener	Provides methods that are executed when the session object is created and destroyed for a user. This happens every time a new user accesses an application and when the session for a user is destroyed.
HttpSessionAttributeListener	Provides methods that are executed when attributes are added to, removed from, or replaced in the session object.
HttpSessionBindingListener	Provides methods that are executed when an object is bound to or unbound from the session.
HttpSessionActivationListener	Provides methods that are executed when the session is activated or deactivated. This happens when the session is migrating to another JVM.

The ServletRequest interfaces

Interface	Description
ServletRequestListener	Provides methods that are executed when a request object is initialized and destroyed. This happens every time the server receives and processes a request.
ServletRequestAttributeListener	Provides methods that are executed when attributes are added to, removed from, or replaced in the request object.

Description

- The ServletContext and ServletRequest interfaces are stored in the javax.servlet package, and the HttpSession interfaces are stored in the javax.servlet.http package.

Figure 19-2   A summary of the listener interfaces

The methods of the listener interfaces

To round out your understanding of listeners, figure 19-3 presents the methods of the listener interfaces that are summarized in the previous figure. If you study these methods, you'll see that they all include an event object as the sole parameter. Then, you can use the methods that are provided by the event object in your listener methods as described in the next figure.

The ServletContext interfaces
The ServletContextListener interface
contextInitialized(ServletContextEvent e)
contextDestroyed(ServletContextEvent e)

The ServletContextAttributeListener interface
attributeAdded(ServletContextAttributeEvent e)
attributeRemoved(ServletContextAttributeEvent e)
attributeReplaced(ServletContextAttributeEvent e)

The HttpSession interfaces
The HttpSessionListener interface
sessionCreated(HttpSessionEvent e)
sessionDestroyed(HttpSessionEvent e)

The HttpSessionAttributeListener interface
attributeAdded(HttpSessionBindingEvent e)
attributeRemoved(HttpSessionBindingEvent e)
attributeReplaced(HttpSessionBindingEvent e)

The HttpSessionBindingListener interface
valueBound(HttpSessionBindingEvent e)
valueUnbound(HttpSessionBindingEvent e)

The HttpSessionActivationListener interface
sessionDidActivate(HttpSessionEvent e)
sessionWillPassivate(HttpSessionEvent e)

The ServletRequest interfaces
The ServletRequestListener interface
requestInitialized(ServletRequestEvent e)
requestDestroyed(ServletRequestEvent e)

The ServletRequestAttributeListener interface
attributeAdded(ServletRequestAttributeEvent e)
attributeRemoved(ServletRequestAttributeEvent e)
attributeReplaced(ServletRequestAttributeEvent e)

Description
- All of these methods include a parameter for the event that has occurred.
- Since none of these methods return a value, you can use the void keyword for the return type.

Figure 19-3   The methods of the listener interfaces

The methods of the event objects

Figure 19-4 presents the methods of the event objects that are available from the methods of the listener interfaces. For example, if you implement the HttpSessionListener interface, the sessionCreated and sessionDestroyed methods of this interface must include an HttpSessionEvent object as the parameter. Then, you can use the getSession method of the HttpSessionEvent object to return the HttpSession object that raised the event.

Similarly, the ServletContextAttributeEvent object provides getName and getValue methods that return the name and value of the attribute that raised the event. In addition, since the ServletContextAttributeEvent class inherits the ServletContextEvent class, you can also call the getServletContext method from this event object.

The ServletContextEvent class

Method	Description
getServletContext()	Returns the ServletContext object that was initialized or destroyed.

The ServletContextAttributeEvent class

Method	Description
getName()	Returns a string for the name of the attribute that was added to, removed from, or replaced in the ServletContext object.
getValue()	Returns an object for the value of the attribute that was added to, removed from, or replaced in the ServletContext object.

The HttpSessionEvent class

Method	Description
getSession()	Returns the HttpSession object that was changed.

The HttpSessionBindingEvent class

Method	Description
getName()	Returns a string for the name of the attribute that was added to, removed from, or replaced in the HttpSession object.
getValue()	Returns an object for the value of the attribute that was added to, removed from, or replaced in the HttpSession object.

The ServletRequestEvent class

Method	Description
getServletRequest()	Returns the ServletRequest object that was initialized or destroyed.

The ServletRequestAttributeEvent class

Method	Description
getName()	Returns a string for the name of the attribute that was added to, removed from, or replaced in the ServletRequest object.
getValue()	Returns an object for the value of the attribute that was added to, removed from, or replaced in the ServletRequest object.

Description

- The ServletContextAttributeEvent class inherits the ServletContextEvent class. As a result, the getServletContext method is available to this class.

- The HttpSessionBindingEvent class inherits the HttpSessionEvent class. As a result, the getSession method is available to this class.

- The ServletRequestAttributeEvent class inherits the ServletRequestEvent class. As a result, the getServletRequest method is available to this class.

Figure 19-4   The methods of the event objects

Perspective

Now that you've finished this chapter, you should be able to code a ServletContextListener that initializes the global variables for a web application when the application starts. You should also know what events the other listeners can respond to, and with a little experimentation you should be able to figure out how to code one of those listeners if necessary.

Summary

- A *listener* is a class that listens for various events that can occur during the lifecycle of a web application and provides methods that are executed when specific events occur.

- To create a listener, you must code a class that implements one of the listener interfaces, and you must register the listener by adding a listener element to the application's web.xml file.

- All of the methods of a listener interface have an event object as its sole parameter. You can call the methods of this event object in your listener methods.

Exercise 19-1   Work with listeners

Review the application

1. Open the ch19_ex1_cart project in the ex_starts folder.

2. Open the CartContextListener.java file. Note how this class sets four attributes in the ServletContext object.

3. Open the web.xml file. Note how the listener element registers the listener class. Note also how the context-param element stores the context initialization parameter that's read by the listener class.

4. Open the index.jsp and cart.jsp files. Note how these JSPs use attributes of the ServletContext object that were set by the CartContextListener class.

5. Run the application. Note how the two JSPs display the data that was initialized by the CartContextListener class.

Add a listener class

6. Add a class to the murach.util package named CartSessionListener. This class should implement the HttpSessionListener interface. Then, code the declarations for the two methods that are required by the HttpSessionListener interface.

7. In the body of the sessionCreated method, use the getSession method of the event object to get the session object. Use the getServletContext method of the session object to get the ServletContext object. And use the log method of the ServletContext object to print a message to Tomcat's log file that says, "Session created."

8. Modify the web.xml file for the application so it includes a listener element that registers the CartSessionListener class with the web application.

9. Restart Tomcat so it reads the modified web.xml file.

10. Run the application. Then, check the Tomcat log file and note the information that's written to the log file.

11. The "Session created" message should be written each time a new browser window requests a valid URL within the application. To test this, open one or more browser windows and request a URL for any of the JSPs within the application from each window.

20

How to work with filters

Starting with the servlet 2.3 specification, you can add a filter to your web application. For example, you can code a filter class that examines an HTTP request and does some processing based on the values of the HTTP request headers. Sometimes, this processing may include modifying the HTTP response that's returned to the client. Since filters often work closely with HTTP requests and responses, you may want to read chapter 18 before you read this chapter.

An introduction to filters

A *filter* can intercept an HTTP request and execute code before or after the requested servlet or JSP is executed. As a result, filters are ideal for handling *cross-cutting concerns*, which are aspects of an application that cut across different parts of an application

How filters work

The diagram in figure 20-1 shows how filters work. Here, the application uses two filters (Filter1 and Filter2) and two servlets (Servlet1 and Servlet2). In this diagram, Filter1 has been mapped to Servlet1, while Filter1 and Filter2 have been mapped to Servlet2.

When a client requests Servlet1, Filter1 can execute some code before the code for Servlet1 is executed. Then, after the code for Servlet1 is executed, Filter1 can execute more code before the response is returned to the client.

When a client requests Servlet2, both Filter1 and Filter2 can execute some code before the code for Servlet2 is executed. Then, after the code for Servlet2 is executed, Filter2 and Filter1 can execute more code before the response is returned to the client.

Two benefits of filters

One benefit of filters is that they allow you to create modular code that can be applied to different parts of an application. In other words, the requested servlet doesn't need to have any knowledge of the filter. As a result, you should be able to turn a filter on or off without affecting the behavior of the servlet.

Another benefit of filters is that they allow you to create flexible code. This works because you use an application's web.xml file to control when filters are executed. As a result, you can easily apply filters to different parts of an application, and you can easily turn a filter on or off.

When to use filters

As mentioned earlier, filters are ideal for handling cross-cutting concerns. For example, a filter can be used to write data to a log file, handle authentication, or compress a response. In addition, a filter can be used to handle image type conversions, localization, XSL transformations, caching, and so on.

Of course, if your servlet container already provides the type of functionality that you need, it's usually easier and less error-prone to use the built-in functionality. As a result, before you code a custom filter to handle a complex task such as compressing responses, you should check the documentation for your servlet container to see if it already provides this type of functionality. Often, it's just a matter of configuring your servlet container. In chapter 18, for example, you learned how to use Tomcat to automatically compress responses.

How filters work

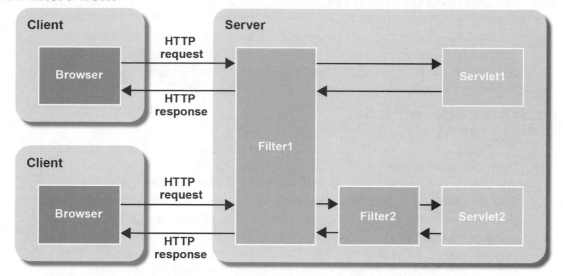

Two benefits of using filters

- **Modular code.** Filters allow you to store code in a single location that can be applied to multiple parts of an application.
- **Flexible code.** You can use the web.xml file to control when filters are executed. This allows you to apply filters to different parts of an application, and it allows you to turn a filter on or off.

Types of tasks that can be performed by filters

- **Logging.** You can use a filter to log the requests and responses of a web application.
- **Authentication.** You can use a filter to only allow authorized users to access certain parts of a web site.
- **Compression.** You can use a filter to compress responses to improve the performance of your web application.

Description

- You can use a *filter* to intercept an HTTP request and do some processing before the requested servlet or JSP is executed. Conversely, you can use a filter to intercept an HTTP response and to do some processing after the requested servlet or JSP is executed but before the HTTP response is returned to the browser.
- Filters are ideal for addressing *cross-cutting concerns*, which are aspects of an application that cut across different parts of an application.
- You can *chain* two or more filters together.
- Filters were introduced with the servlet 2.3 specification.

Figure 20-1   How filters work

How to add a filter

Adding a filter to an application works similarly to adding a servlet to an application. To start, you must code a class for the filter. Then, you add some code to the web.xml file to map the filter to one or more URL patterns.

How to code a filter

Figure 20-2 shows how to code the class for a simple filter that writes some basic information about the request and response to a log file. To start, the package statement stores the class in a package named murach.filters. Then, the three import statements import the packages that are needed to work with a filter. Note that these packages are the same ones that are used to work with a servlet.

After the import statements, the code declares a class named TestFilter1 that implements the Filter interface. This class implements all three methods of the Filter interface: init, doFilter, and destroy. These methods are called when the filter is initialized, executed, and destroyed.

After the declaration for the class, a private instance variable is declared for a FilterConfig object named filterConfig. This object is initialized in the init method. To do that, the init method assigns the filterConfig instance variable to the FilterConfig object that's passed to the init method as an argument.

After the init method, the doFilter method contains the code that's executed by the filter. To start, the first two statements cast the ServletRequest and ServletResponse parameters to HttpServletRequest and HttpServletResponse objects. That way, the doFilter method can call all of the same methods of the request and response objects that are available to servlets. Then, the third statement gets the application's ServletContext object by calling the getServletContext method of the filterConfig instance variable.

After the request, response, and ServletContext objects have been set up, the fourth statement gets the name of the filter from the FilterConfig object, and the fifth statement gets the servlet path from the request object. Then, the sixth statement uses the log method of the ServletContext object to write this data to a log file. And the seventh statement uses the doFilter method of the FilterChain parameter to pass the request and response to the next filter or servlet in the chain. At this point, execution is passed along the chain.

After the servlet is executed, the last statement in the doFilter method is executed. This statement writes the same data to the log file as the sixth statement. However, it appends "after request" to the end of the data to show that this code was executed after the requested servlet was executed but before the response was returned to the client.

The last method in this class is the destroy method, which assigns a null value to the filterConfig instance variable. Although assigning this value isn't necessary, this is generally considered a good programming practice.

As simple as this class is, it illustrates all of the principles that you need for coding a filter, including how to initialize the FilterConfig object and how to get the request, response, and ServletContext objects. In this case, the class just

A class that implements the Filter interface

```
package murach.filters;

import java.io.*;
import javax.servlet.*;
import javax.servlet.http.*;

public class TestFilter1 implements Filter {

    private FilterConfig filterConfig = null;

    @Override
    public void init(FilterConfig filterConfig) {
        this.filterConfig = filterConfig;
    }

    @Override
    public void doFilter(
            ServletRequest request,
            ServletResponse response,
            FilterChain chain) throws IOException, ServletException {

        HttpServletRequest httpRequest = (HttpServletRequest) request;
        HttpServletResponse httpResponse = (HttpServletResponse) response;
        ServletContext sc = filterConfig.getServletContext();

        String filterName = filterConfig.getFilterName();
        String servletPath = "Servlet path: " + httpRequest.getServletPath();

        sc.log(filterName  + " | " + servletPath + " | before request");

        chain.doFilter(httpRequest, httpResponse);

        sc.log(filterName  + " | " + servletPath + " | after request");
    }

    @Override
    public void destroy() {
        filterConfig = null;
    }
}
```

Description

- A filter class must implement the Filter interface that includes the init, doFilter, and destroy methods that are called when the filter is initialized, executed, and destroyed.
- The init method accepts a FilterConfig object as a parameter. You can use this object's getFilterName method to get the name of the filter, and you can use its getServletContext method to get the ServletContext object for the application.
- The doFilter method accepts ServletRequest and ServletResponse objects as parameters. You can cast these objects to the HttpServletRequest and HttpServletResponse objects.
- The doFilter method also accepts a FilterChain object. You can use the doFilter method of this object to forward the request and response to the next filter or servlet in the chain.

Figure 20-2   How to code a filter

logs some data from the FilterConfig object and the request objects, but it could easily vary the processing based on the data that's in the request. If, for example, you want to block requests for unauthorized users, you can check the authorization header of the request to see if the user is authorized. If so, you can call the doFilter method of the FilterChain object to forward the request. If not, you can use a RequestDispatcher object to forward the request to a login page.

How to configure a filter

Part 1 of figure 20-3 shows a web.xml file for an application that configures three filters. Except for the name of the class, all three filters contain the same code as the filter presented in figure 20-2. To start, the three filter elements register the classes named TestFilter1, TestFilter2, and TestFitler3 that are stored in the package named filters. Then, the three filter-mapping elements map the three filters to a URL pattern.

The first filter-mapping element maps TestFilter1 to all URL requests within the current application. To do that, the url-pattern element uses a front slash followed by an asterisk (/*). As a result, this filter is executed for all URLs within the root directory.

The second filter-mapping element also maps TestFilter2 to all URL requests within the current application. However, this element includes two dispatcher elements that indicate that this filter should be executed for (1) requests coming from clients and (2) requests that are forwarded from within the application. By contrast, TestFilter1 is only executed for requests coming from clients.

The third filter-mapping element uses the servlet-name element to map TestFilter3 to all requests for the DownloadServlet. In this web.xml file, this servlet is only mapped to one URL (/download). However, if this servlet was mapped to multiple URLs, TestFilter3 would be mapped to those URLs as well.

This web.xml file shows how easy it is to configure filters. For example, you can easily turn off TestFilter1 by commenting out its servlet-mapping element. Or, you can change the URLs that cause TestFilter2 to be executed by modifying its url-pattern element. Once you do that, you don't have to recompile or modify your filter or servlet classes. As a result, it's easy to experiment with filters. More importantly, it's easy to add or remove features that apply to multiple parts of an application.

A web.xml file that contains three filters

```xml
<?xml version="1.0" encoding="UTF-8"?>
<web-app version="3.0" xmlns="http://java.sun.com/xml/ns/javaee"
    xmlns:xsi="http://www.w3.org/2001/XMLSchema-instance"
    xsi:schemaLocation="http://java.sun.com/xml/ns/javaee
                        http://java.sun.com/xml/ns/javaee/web-app_3_0.xsd">
    <filter>
        <filter-name>TestFilter1</filter-name>
        <filter-class>murach.filters.TestFilter1</filter-class>
    </filter>
    <filter>
        <filter-name>TestFilter2</filter-name>
        <filter-class>murach.filters.TestFilter2</filter-class>
    </filter>
    <filter>
        <filter-name>TestFilter3</filter-name>
        <filter-class>murach.filters.TestFilter3</filter-class>
    </filter>

    <filter-mapping>
        <filter-name>TestFilter1</filter-name>
        <url-pattern>/*</url-pattern>
    </filter-mapping>
    <filter-mapping>
        <filter-name>TestFilter2</filter-name>
        <url-pattern>/*</url-pattern>
        <dispatcher>REQUEST</dispatcher>
        <dispatcher>FORWARD</dispatcher>
    </filter-mapping>
    <filter-mapping>
        <filter-name>TestFilter3</filter-name>
        <servlet-name>DownloadServlet</servlet-name>
    </filter-mapping>

    <servlet>
        <servlet-name>DownloadServlet</servlet-name>
        <servlet-class>murach.download.DownloadServlet</servlet-class>
    </servlet>
    <servlet-mapping>
        <servlet-name>DownloadServlet</servlet-name>
        <url-pattern>/download</url-pattern>
    </servlet-mapping>

    <session-config>
        <session-timeout>30</session-timeout>
    </session-config>
    <welcome-file-list>
        <welcome-file>index.jsp</welcome-file>
    </welcome-file-list>
</web-app>
```

Figure 20-3   How to configure a filter (part 1 of 2)

Part 2 of figure 20-3 begins by summarizing the elements that are used within the web.xml file to map a filter to a URL pattern. If you understand the web.xml file presented in part 1, you shouldn't have much trouble understanding how these elements work. Note, however, that the dispatcher element wasn't introduced until the servlet 2.4 specification. As a result, you can't use this element if you're working with a servlet container that implements the 2.3 specification.

The log data for the first request shows the filters that are executed when the index.jsp file for the application is requested. To start, TestFilter1 is executed, followed by TestFilter2, followed by the servlet for the index.jsp file. Here, it's important to note that the filters are executed in the order that they are specified in the web.xml file. Then, after the servlet for the index.jsp file is executed, TestFilter2 is executed, followed by TestFilter1. Here, it's important to note that the filters are executed in the reverse order.

The log data for the second request shows the filters that are executed when the DownloadServlet that's mapped to the /download URL is requested. To start, all three test filters are executed, just as you would expect. Then, the DownloadServlet forwards the request to the register.jsp file. At this point, since TestFilter2 is the only filter that handles requests that are forwarded from other parts of the application, it is the only filter that's executed. Finally, the servlet for the register.jsp file is executed. After this servlet is executed, TestFilter2 is executed again since it was the last filter to be executed. Then, TestFilter3 is executed, followed by TestFilter2, followed by TestFilter1.

The filter and filter-mapping elements

Element	Description
filter	Adds a filter to the application.
filter-name	Specifies a name for the filter.
filter-class	Specifies the fully qualified name of a class that implements a filter.
filter-mapping	Adds filter-mapping to the application.
url-pattern	Specifies the URLs that cause the filter to be executed.
servlet-name	Specifies a servlet that causes the filter to be executed. The value for this element should match the value of the servlet-name element for the servlet element.
dispatcher	Specifies the types of requests that cause the filter to be executed. Valid values include REQUEST, FORWARD, ERROR, and INCLUDE. REQUEST (the default) executes the filter on requests from the client. FORWARD executes the filter on forwards from within the application. INCLUDE executes the filter when the application uses an include. And ERROR executes the filter when the application uses an error handler. This element was introduced with the servlet 2.4 specification.

The log data when the index.jsp file is requested

```
TestFilter1 | Servlet path: /index.jsp | before request
TestFilter2 | Servlet path: /index.jsp | before request
TestFilter2 | Servlet path: /index.jsp | after request
TestFilter1 | Servlet path: /index.jsp | after request
```

The log data when the servlet that's mapped to /download is requested

```
TestFilter1 | Servlet path: /download | before request
TestFilter2 | Servlet path: /download | before request
TestFilter3 | Servlet path: /download | before request
TestFilter2 | Servlet path: /register.jsp | before request
TestFilter2 | Servlet path: /register.jsp | after request
TestFilter3 | Servlet path: /download | after request
TestFilter2 | Servlet path: /download | after request
TestFilter1 | Servlet path: /download | after request
```

Description

- The request filters are executed in the order that they are declared in the web.xml file.

- The response filters are executed in the reverse order that they are executed for the request.

Figure 20-3   How to configure a filter (part 2 of 2)

Two filter classes

Now that you've learned how to code and configure a simple filter, you're ready to learn how to code filters that do processing on only one side of the request. With request-side processing, the processing is done before the request reaches the target servlet. With response-side processing, the processing is done after the requested servlet has been executed but before the response is returned to the client.

When you code filters that only perform processing on one side of the request, the resulting code can be more modular and give you more flexibility when you configure the filter. However, as you'll see later in this chapter, there are times when a filter must perform both request-side and response-side processing.

How to code a filter that performs request-side processing

Figure 20-4 shows how to code a filter named LogRequestFilter that executes code before the requested servlet is executed. If you study the code for this filter, you'll see that it works similarly to the TestFilter1 presented in figure 20-2. However, there are a few differences.

First, the LogRequestFilter class includes the value of a cookie in the data that it writes to the log file. To do that, this code calls the getCookies method of the HttpServletRequest object to get an array of Cookie objects. Then, it uses the getCookieValue method of the custom CookieUtil class to get the value of the cookie named emailCookie.

Second, this class doesn't do any processing after the requested servlet is executed. In other words, this servlet doesn't do any response-side processing. To do that, all of the code for the doFilter method is coded before the statement that calls the doFilter method of the FilterChain object.

Third, since this class doesn't call any methods from the request object, it doesn't bother to cast the ServletResponse object that it receives as a parameter to the HttpServletResponse object. Instead, it passes the ServletResponse object to the doFilter method of the FilterChain object.

The code for a filter that performs request-side processing

```java
package murach.filters;

import java.io.*;
import javax.servlet.*;
import javax.servlet.http.*;

public class LogRequestFilter implements Filter {

    private FilterConfig filterConfig = null;

    @Override
    public void init(FilterConfig filterConfig) {
        this.filterConfig = filterConfig;
    }

    @Override
    public void doFilter(
            ServletRequest request,
            ServletResponse response,
            FilterChain chain) throws IOException, ServletException {

        HttpServletRequest httpRequest = (HttpServletRequest) request;
        ServletContext sc = filterConfig.getServletContext();

        String logString = filterConfig.getFilterName() + " | ";
        logString += "Servlet path: " + httpRequest.getServletPath() + " | ";

        Cookie[] cookies = httpRequest.getCookies();
        String emailAddress = util.CookieUtil.getCookieValue(
                cookies, "emailCookie");
        logString += "Email cookie: ";
        if (emailAddress.length() != 0)
            logString += emailAddress;
        else
            logString += "Not found";

        sc.log(logString);

        chain.doFilter(httpRequest, response);
    }

    @Override
    public void destroy() {
        filterConfig = null;
    }
}
```

Description

- To code a filter that executes code before the requested servlet is executed, you code all of the code for the filter before you call the doFilter method of the FilterChain parameter.

Figure 20-4   How to code a filter that performs request-side processing

How to code a filter that performs response-side processing

Figure 20-5 shows how to code a filter named LogResponseFilter that executes code after the requested servlet is executed but before the response is returned to the client. If you study the code for this filter, you'll see that it works similarly to the TestFilter1 presented in figure 20-2. However, there are a couple differences.

First, the LogResponseFilter class does all of its processing after the requested servlet is executed. In other words, this servlet doesn't do any request-side processing. To do that, all of the code in the doFilter method is after the statement that calls the doFilter method of the FilterChain object.

Second, this class includes the content type of the response in the log file. To do that, this code calls the getContentType method of the HttpServletResponse object to get the MIME type of the response.

The code for a filter that performs response-side processing

```
package murach.filters;

import java.io.*;
import javax.servlet.*;
import javax.servlet.http.*;

public class LogResponseFilter implements Filter {

    private FilterConfig filterConfig = null;

    @Override
    public void init(FilterConfig filterConfig) {
        this.filterConfig = filterConfig;
    }

    @Override
    public void doFilter(ServletRequest request,
                         ServletResponse response,
                         FilterChain chain)
                         throws IOException, ServletException {

        chain.doFilter(request, response);

        HttpServletRequest httpRequest = (HttpServletRequest) request;
        HttpServletResponse httpResponse = (HttpServletResponse) response;
        ServletContext sc = filterConfig.getServletContext();

        String logString = filterConfig.getFilterName() + " | ";
        logString += "Servlet path: " + httpRequest.getServletPath() + " | ";
        logString += "Content type: " + httpResponse.getContentType();

        sc.log(logString);
    }

    @Override
    public void destroy() {
        filterConfig = null;
    }
}
```

Description

- To code a filter that executes code after the requested servlet is executed but before the response is returned to the client, you code all of the code for the filter after you call the doFilter method of the FilterChain parameter.

Figure 20-5   How to code a filter that performs response-side processing

Other skills for working with filters

Now that you know how to code a filter that performs request-side or response-side processing, you're ready to learn two more skills that are sometimes useful when working with filters. First, you'll learn how to add functionality to a request or response object by creating a custom request or response object. Second, you'll learn how to add initialization parameters to a filter.

How to wrap a request or response

Figure 20-6 begins by summarizing two wrapper classes that you can use to create custom request or response objects. These classes implement a design pattern known as the *wrapper pattern* or the *decorator pattern*.

The HttpServletRequestWrapper class implements the HttpServletRequest interface by providing methods that call the methods of the underlying HttpServletRequest interface. As a result, if you code a class that extends the HttpServletRequestWrapper class, all of the existing methods already work. Then, to add new functionality, you can add a method that doesn't exist in the HttpServletRequest interface. Or, to modify the existing functionality, you can override one of the methods of the HttpServletRequest class.

As you would expect, the HttpServletResponseWrapper class wraps the HttpServletResponse interface just as the HttpServletRequestWrapper class wraps the HttpServletRequest interface. As a result, once you understand how to use one of these classes, you should understand how to use the other. Since the HttpServletRequestWrapper class is more commonly used, this figure shows how to use that class.

If you review the two pages of code in this figure, you'll see that the first page presents the LogResponseCookiesFilter class and the second page presents the ResponseCookiesWrapper class. Since this wrapper class is only used by the LogResponseCookiesFilter class, the wrapper class is nested within the same file as the filter class. Also, since this wrapper class is nested, it can't be declared as public. Instead, it is declared with the default scope.

The LogResponseCookiesFilter class works much like the filters presented earlier in this chapter. However, it uses the ResponseCookiesWrapper class to create a custom response object. This custom response class includes a new method named getCookies that returns all of the Cookie objects that have been stored in the response object. This custom response class also overrides the addCookie method in the underlying response object so it can keep track of the cookies that are added to the response.

Once this filter creates the custom response object, it passes it to the doFilter method of the FilterChain object. That way, any filters or servlets that are called later in the chain use the custom response object instead of the standard response object. As a result, the response-side processing for this filter can call the getCookies method that's available from the custom response object, but isn't available from the standard HttpServletResponse object. Then, this filter can write the cookies that are stored in the response object to the log file.

Two classes for creating custom request and response objects

Class	Description
`HttpServletRequestWrapper`	This class implements the HttpServletRequest interface by providing methods that call the methods of the HttpServletRequest interface.
`HttpServletResponseWrapper`	This class implements the HttpServletResponse interface by providing methods that call the methods of the HttpServletResponse interface.

The code for a filter that uses a custom response object   Page 1

```java
package murach.filters;

import java.io.*;
import java.util.*;
import javax.servlet.*;
import javax.servlet.http.*;

public class LogResponseCookiesFilter implements Filter {

    private FilterConfig filterConfig = null;

    @Override
    public void init(FilterConfig filterConfig) {
        this.filterConfig = filterConfig;
    }

    @Override
    public void doFilter(
            ServletRequest request,
            ServletResponse response,
            FilterChain chain) throws IOException, ServletException {

        HttpServletResponse httpResponse = (HttpServletResponse) response;
        ResponseCookiesWrapper wrappedResponse =
            new ResponseCookiesWrapper(httpResponse);

        chain.doFilter(request, wrappedResponse);

        HttpServletRequest httpRequest = (HttpServletRequest) request;
        ServletContext sc = filterConfig.getServletContext();
        String filterName = filterConfig.getFilterName();
        String servletPath = "Servlet path: " + httpRequest.getServletPath();
        ArrayList<Cookie> cookies = wrappedResponse.getCookies();
        String cookiesString = "";
        for (Cookie c : cookies)
            cookiesString += c.getName() + "=" + c.getValue() + " ";

        sc.log(filterName  + " | " + servletPath + " | cookies: " +
                cookiesString);
    }

    @Override
    public void destroy() {
        filterConfig = null;
    }
```

Figure 20-6   How to wrap a request or response (part 1 of 2)

The ResponseCookiesWrapper class begins by declaring an ArrayList of Cookie objects as an instance variable. Then, the constructor for this subclass uses the super method to pass the standard response object to the super class, which is the wrapper class for the underlying response object. In addition, the constructor initializes the ArrayList of Cookie objects that's used by the custom response object.

After the constructor, this class adds a new method to the custom response object named getCookies. This method contains a single statement that returns the ArrayList of Cookie objects.

After the getCookies method, this class overrides the addCookie method of the HttpServletResponse class. To start, it adds the Cookie object parameter to the instance variable for the ArrayList of Cookie objects. Then, this method calls the getResponse method of the HttpServletResponseWrapper class to get the underlying HttpServletResponse object. Finally, this method calls the addCookie method of the underlying HttpServletResponse object so the Cookie object parameter is added to the underlying response object.

Since the overridden addCookie method passes the Cookie object parameter to the addCookie method of the underlying response object, the addCookie method of the response object works as expected for any components down the chain. In other words, as long as the custom response object implements all the methods of a standard response object, the components that come later in the chain don't know the difference between the standard object and the custom object.

Although this example is simple, you can apply the same principles to create custom request and response objects that perform more complex tasks. If, for example, you want to compress the response that's returned to the client, you can create a custom response object to do that. However, this requires overriding the getOutputStream() and getWriter() methods of the ServletResponse object, which requires a good understanding of working with output streams.

If you want to see an example of this type of filter, Tomcat 6 provides an example within this Tomcat folder:

`webapps\examples\WEB-INF\classes\compressionFilters`

The classes in this folder include a wrapper class for a custom response object and a filter class that uses the custom response object. Of course, before you code a custom filter to compress your application's HTTP responses, you should check to see if your web server or servlet container provides built-in compression.

The code for a filter that uses a custom response object   Page 2

```
class ResponseCookiesWrapper extends HttpServletResponseWrapper {

    private ArrayList<Cookie> cookies = null;

    public ResponseCookiesWrapper(HttpServletResponse response) {
        super(response);
        cookies = new ArrayList<Cookie>();
    }

    // provide a new method for the ResponseWrapper class
    public ArrayList<Cookie> getCookies() {
        return cookies;
    }

    // override the addCookie method of the HttpServletResponse object
    @Override
    public void addCookie(Cookie cookie) {

        // store the cookie in the response wrapper object
        cookies.add(cookie);

        // store the cookie in the original response object
        HttpServletResponse httpResponse =
                (HttpServletResponse) this.getResponse();
        httpResponse.addCookie(cookie);
    }
}
}
```

Description

- The HttpServletRequestWrapper and HttpServletResponseWrapper classes implement a design pattern known as the *wrapper pattern* or the *decorator pattern*.

- The HttpServletRequestWrapper and HttpServletResponseWrapper classes contain methods that call all of the methods of the underlying interface or class. As a result, when you extend these classes, you only need to add new methods or override existing methods.

- When you extend the HttpServletResponseWrapper class, you can use the getResponse method to return the underlying HttpServletResponse object.

Figure 20-6   How to wrap a request or response (part 2 of 2)

How to use an initialization parameter

Figure 20-7 shows how you can supply an initialization parameter for a filter. Since this works much like initialization parameters for servlets, you shouldn't have much trouble understanding how this works.

To start, you add one or more initialization parameters to the web.xml file. In this figure, for example, one initialization parameter with a name of logFile-name and a value of "test_init_params.log" has been added to the filter named TestInitParamsFilter. Then, you can use the getInitParameter method of the FilterConfig object to return the value of the parameter.

A filter element that includes an initialization parameter

```
<filter>
    <filter-name>TestInitParamsFilter</filter-name>
    <filter-class>filters.TestInitParamsFilter</filter-class>
    <init-param>
        <param-name>logFilename</param-name>
        <param-value>test_init_params.log</param-value>
    </init-param>
</filter>
```

The initialization parameter elements

Element	Description
`<init-param>`	Defines a name/value pair for an initialization parameter for a servlet.
`<param-name>`	Defines the name of a parameter.
`<param-value>`	Defines the value of a parameter.

Filter code that reads the initialization parameter

```
String logFilename = filterConfig.getInitParameter("logFilename");
```

Description

- To create an initialization parameter that will be available to a specific filter, you code the param-name and param-value elements within the init-param element. But first, you must identify the filter by coding the filter, filter-name, and filter-class elements.

- You can code multiple init-param elements for a single filter.

- Initialization parameters work similarly for filters and servlets. For more information about initialization parameters, refer to chapter 5.

Figure 20-7 How to use an initialization parameter

How to restrict access by IP address

Usernames and passwords are a good first line of defense for protecting access to your web sites, but sometimes you might want to add an additional level of security. For example, you might want to restrict access to the admin section of your application to only a few IP addresses such as local addresses.

Figure 20-8 shows an example of how you can implement this. Here, the web.xml file maps the SecurityFilter class to the admin pages for the website. In addition, the web.xml file includes an initialization parameter that stores a list of allowed IP addresses.

Within the SecurityFilter class, the first statement creates an instance variable for a FilterConfig object named filterConfig. Then, the second statement creates an instance variable for an array of strings.

The init method calls the getInitParameter method on the filterConfig object to get the list of allowed remote addresses from the filter element. Then, it checks the string. If it isn't null, this code creates an array of strings by using the newline character (\n) to split the string. As a result, you can store a list of allowed IP addresses by placing one per line in the filter's param-value element as shown in part 2 of this figure.

The doFilter method calls the getRemoteAddr method of the HttpServletRequest object to get the IP address of the host that is attempting to connect. Then, it sets the allowed variable to false.

The loop checks each of the IP addresses from the allowedHosts array and trims the leading whitespace before comparing the address to the remote address. If the addresses match, this code sets the allowed variable to true and uses a break statement to end the loop. That's because there's no reason to check the rest of the IP addresses in the list once a match has been found. If the loop ends without finding a match, the allowed variable remains false.

After the loop, the if statement checks the value of the allowed variable. If this variable is true, the filter calls the doFilter method of the FilterChain parameter to handle the request normally. However, if this variable is false, the filter logs some data about the attempt to access the admin features from an unauthorized IP address and sends a 404 error response to the browser. As a result, the filter prevents unauthorized IP addresses from accessing the admin section of the application.

In this case, the code uses a 404 Not Found error instead of a different error as a bit of misdirection. If the code returned a 401 Unauthorized error instead, an attacker would know that there is a resource at the /admin URL, but the server isn't allowing access. However, a 404 error makes it appear as if no resource exists at the URL, which might prevent attackers from bothering with any further attempts to access it.

A filter that restricts access to specified IP addresses

```java
package murach.admin;

import java.io.*;
import javax.servlet.*;
import javax.servlet.http.*;

public class SecurityFilter implements Filter {

    private FilterConfig filterConfig = null;
    private String[] allowedHosts = null;

    @Override
    public void init(FilterConfig filterConfig) throws ServletException {
        this.filterConfig = filterConfig;
        String hostsString = filterConfig.getInitParameter("allowedHosts");
        if (hostsString != null && !hostsString.trim().equals("")) {
            allowedHosts = hostsString.split("\n");
        }
    }

    @Override
    public void doFilter(ServletRequest request, ServletResponse response,
            FilterChain chain) throws IOException, ServletException {

        HttpServletRequest httpRequest = (HttpServletRequest)request;
        HttpServletResponse httpResponse = (HttpServletResponse) response;

        String remoteAddress = httpRequest.getRemoteAddr();
        boolean allowed = false;
        for (String host : allowedHosts) {
            if (host.trim().equals(remoteAddress)) {
                allowed = true;
                break;
            }
        }

        if (allowed) {
            chain.doFilter(request, response);
        } else {
            filterConfig.getServletContext()
                    .log("Attempted admin access from unauthorized IP:" +
                            remoteAddress);
            httpResponse.sendError(404);
            chain.doFilter(request, response);
        }
    }

    @Override
    public void destroy() {
        filterConfig = null;
    }
}
```

Figure 20-8   How to restrict access by IP address (part 1 of 2)

Part 2 of the figure presents the filter and filter-mapping elements that are stored in the web.xml file. The filter element includes an init-param element named allowedHosts that stores the list of allowed IP addresses. The first address is a local address rather than an IP address, and it is what the getRemoteAddr method returns when a connection comes from the same machine that the server is running on.

As a result, if you attempt to connect from the same machine, you should be able to access the servlet normally by using any URL that's within the admin directory. However, if you remove the first line from the param-value element and restart the application, the filter should work differently. In that case, if you use the URL shown in this figure, you should get a 404 Not Found error.

The filter element for the security filter

```
<filter>
    <filter-name>SecurityFilter</filter-name>
    <filter-class>murach.admin.SecurityFilter</filter-class>
    <init-param>
        <param-name>allowedHosts</param-name>
        <param-value>
            0:0:0:0:0:0:0:1
            127.0.0.1
        </param-value>
    </init-param>
</filter>
<filter-mapping>
    <filter-name>SecurityFilter</filter-name>
    <url-pattern>/admin/*</url-pattern>
</filter-mapping>
```

A relative URL that tests the security filter

```
/admin
```

Description

- If the request is from an allowed IP address, the SecurityFilter class processes the request normally. Otherwise, this servlet logs the unauthorized attempt and returns a 404 Not Found error.

- In the web.xml file, the parameter named allowedHosts stores the allowed IP addresses and uses a newline character to separate each address.

- The address of "0:0:0:0:0:0:0:1" is a local address that's returned when the user attempts to access the application from the same machine the server is running on.

Figure 20-8   How to restrict access by IP address (part 2 of 2)

Perspective

Now that you have finished this chapter, you should (1) be able to code and deploy filters, and (2) understand when a filter might be useful. However, before you use a filter to write custom code, you should check to see if this type of functionality is already available to you from your web server or servlet container.

For example, since most web servers (including Apache 2.x) and servlet containers (including Tomcat 4.x and later) provide for compressing responses before they are returned to the client, you don't need to use filters to do that. Instead, you just need to configure your web server or servlet container so it takes advantage of the feature that you want to use. This is easier and less error-prone than coding a filter. For example, chapter 18 shows how to turn on compression for Tomcat.

Summary

- You can use a *filter* to intercept an HTTP request and do some processing before or after the requested servlet or JSP is executed.

- Filters are ideal for addressing *cross-cutting concerns*, which are aspects of an application that cut across different parts of an application.

- You can *chain* two or more filters together.

- To code a filter, you must code a class that implements the Filter interface. In addition, you must map the Filter to a URL pattern by adding a filter element and a filter-mapping element to the application's web.xml file.

- The HttpServletRequestWrapper and HttpServletResponseWrapper classes implement a design pattern known as the *wrapper pattern* or the *decorator pattern*. You can use them to create custom request and response objects.

Exercise 20-1　　Run the Download application

1.　Open the ch20_ex1_download project in the ex_starts folder.

2.　Open the code for the classes named TestFilter1, TestFilter2, and TestFilter3. Then, review this code. Note that the code for these classes is the same.

3.　Open the web.xml file and review it. Note how the TestFilter1, TestFilter2, and TestFilter3 classes are mapped to different URL patterns.

4.　Run the application and click on some of its links. After each click, view the data in the log file. Note when the code for the TestFilter1, TestFilter2, and TestFilter3 classes is executed.

5.　Open and review the code for the LogResponseCookiesFilter class. Note how this class prints information about the cookies that are stored in the response to the log file.

6.　Open the code for the LogRequestFilter class. Then, review this code. Note how this class prints information about the email cookie that's stored in the request to the log file.

7.　Modify the LogRequestFilter class so it prints information about all of the cookies that are stored in the request to the log. To do that, you can use the code in the LogResponseCookiesFilter as a model. In addition, you'll need to use an if statement to make sure that the array of Cookie objects isn't null. Otherwise, a NullPointerException may be thrown when you run the application.

8.　Modify the web.xml file to turn off the three TestFilter classes and to turn on the LogRequestFilter and LogResponseCookiesFilter classes. Then, restart Tomcat.

9.　Run the application and click on some of its links. After each click, view the data in the log file. Make sure to click on the "View all cookies" link and the "Delete all cookies" link. Then, note the cookies that are stored in the response object.

10.　Close your browser and run the application again. Then, after you register for the download, check the log file and note that the email cookie is added to the response object.

21

How to work with JavaServer Faces

You can use JSF (JavaServer Faces) instead of JSP for developing your web pages. Unlike JSP, JSF is a component-based framework, which means that you can develop web applications more like desktop applications, using pre-made user interface components.

Since JSF is a large and complex topic, this book only provides an introduction to it. However, this chapter presents the skills you need to get started with JSF. After that, you should have a good foundation for learning more about JSF.

An introduction to JSF

JSF (*JavaServer Faces*) was designed as a replacement for JSP, which is an older technology. With JSF, you design your web pages using components. This makes designing web pages more like designing desktop applications and introduces powerful new features. For example, JSF allows you to add complex pre-made functionality to your web pages with a single line of JSF code, without having to write any JavaScript.

A summary of JSF versions

JSF is a specification for how view components interact with controller and model components on the server. Several vendors provide implementations of the core JSF specification. Figure 21-1 lists two: (1) the official JSF 2 reference implementation from Oracle (called Mojarra) and (2) Apache MyFaces. These implementations only provide core functionality that replaces standard HTML elements such as form controls.

However, third-party component libraries can greatly extend the power of JSF. This figure lists two of the most popular third-party component libraries: JBoss RichFaces and PrimeFaces. Both of these component libraries provide advanced controls that you can add to your web pages using only a few lines of JSF code. For example, both libraries provide a calendar control that you can add with a single line of code and without having to write any JavaScript event handlers.

Other advanced controls provided by both libraries are auto-complete boxes, drag-and-drop functionality, menus, and editable tables with sortable and resizable columns. These advanced components are beyond the scope of this chapter. However, both RichFaces and PrimeFaces have demos at their websites that show how these components work as well as code examples that show how easy it is to implement them.

How to add a JSF library to a project

To add the core JSF library to a project in NetBeans, you can open the project, right-click on its Libraries folder, select the Add Library item, and use the resulting dialog box to select the library. As of this writing, NetBeans comes with two versions of JSF: JSF 1.2 and JSF 2.2. You should use JSF 2 for all new projects as it is significantly easier to work with than the previous versions of JSF. Also, some of the examples in this chapter may not work with older versions.

The steps you need to follow to add third-party component libraries vary between libraries. As a result, to add a third-party JSF library, you should consult the documentation for the library.

JSF is ...

- A component-based technology that allows you to develop web applications in a way that's similar to how you develop desktop applications.

- Expandable and extensible with complex, JavaScript-driven components that don't require the developer to write the JavaScript.

A summary of JSF providers

- JSF is a specification that's implemented by JSF providers such as Oracle and the Apache Software Foundation.

- Third-party component libraries can add significant functionality to the core JSF components. For example, these libraries can include menus, collapsible panels, calendars, auto-complete boxes, and drag-and-drop functionality.

- Two of the most popular third-party component libraries are JBoss RichFaces and PrimeFaces.

- PrimeFaces is built on top of the popular jQuery library. As a result, it can use jQuery components and themes. However, it shields the developer from having to work directly with jQuery or JavaScript.

Two implementations of the core specification

- Oracle's JSF reference implementation (sometimes called Mojarra)
- Apache MyFaces

Two popular third-party component libraries

- JBoss RichFaces
- PrimeFaces

How to add a JSF library to a project

- In NetBeans, open the project. Then, right-click its Libraries folder, select the Add Library item, and select the JSF 2 library.

- To add a third-party component library, see the documentation that comes with the library.

Figure 21-1   An introduction to JSF

How to use managed beans

A *managed bean*, also known as a *backing bean*, is the server-side model and controller that supports a JSF component.

How to create a managed bean

Figure 21-2 shows a simple managed bean. To declare that a bean is managed, you code a @ManagedBean annotation above the class name. A managed bean is simply a plain old Java object (POJO). The only requirement is that it must have a default constructor.

This class also uses instance variables. In most cases, this is thread safe in JSF since each request or active session has its own copy of the managed bean. There is one exception to this that's shown later in this chapter.

To perform any initialization on the object, you code a method annotated with @PostConstruct. In this figure, for example, the init method creates a new User object and sets the message field.

You might wonder why you couldn't just put this in the constructor instead of use a post construct method. The reason is because the post construct method is guaranteed to run after any dependency injection has been done. The constructor, on the other hand, runs before any dependency injection has been done.

In this case, it doesn't matter, because this class doesn't do any dependency injection. But in a Java EE server, you might want to inject a database access service, for example. In that case, if you attempted to use the database access service in the constructor, you would get a null pointer exception because it hadn't been injected yet. But if you use the database access service in the post construct method, the database service is guaranteed to have been injected already.

Dependency injection is beyond the scope of this book as it is an advanced Java EE topic. For now, you only need to understand that it is always safe to put initialization code inside a post construct method. However, it is not always safe to put initialization code inside the constructor.

When you run this code, you might get a warning that says the faces.ManagedBean annotation has been deprecated and that you should use CDI instead. At the time of this writing, CDI is only supported by Java EE servers, not by Tomcat. As a result, for this chapter, you can ignore the deprecation warning and continue to use the faces annotations.

A class that creates a managed bean

```
package murach.email;

import murach.business.User;

import javax.annotation.PostConstruct;
import javax.faces.bean.ManagedBean;

@ManagedBean
public class EmailList {
    private User user;
    private String message;

    public EmailList() {     // default constructor
    }

    @PostConstruct
    public void init() {
        user = new User();
        message = "Hello!";
    }

    public User getUser() {
        return user;
    }

    public void setUser(User user) {
        this.user = user;
    }

    public String getMessage() {
        return message;
    }
}
```

Description

- To create a *managed bean*, you code the @ManagedBean annotation above the class name.

- Each request for a JSF page that references the managed bean gets its own instance of the bean. As a result, it's thread safe to use instance variables in a managed bean, as this class does.

- As long as the instance variables have get and set methods, they are accessible from in the JSF page as shown later in this chapter.

- To make sure that initialization code is run after all dependency injection is done, code the @PostConstruct annotation above a method that contains the initialization code.

- The class's constructor runs before any dependency injection is done. As a result, it might not be safe to place initialization code inside the constructor when using a managed bean.

Figure 21-2   How to create a managed bean

How to set the scope of a bean

The *scope* of a managed bean determines what part of the application the bean is available to, and when it is available. The highlighted code in figure 21-3 shows how to use an annotation to set the scope of a bean.

A request scoped bean is created when an HTTP request is made and is available for the duration of that request. When the request is complete, the bean goes out of scope and is eligible for garbage collection, freeing up the memory that it uses. This is the default scope if you don't specify a scope. As a result, the @RequestScoped annotation is optional. Also, since a request scoped bean is bound to an individual HTTP request, it is thread-safe to use instance variables in it.

A session scoped bean is bound to a user session. Because of that, it's useful for storing things like the list of items in a shopping cart or a list of user preferences for a site. Basically, if you would store data in a session object when using JSP or servlets, you would store it in a session scoped bean when using JSF.

As with request scoped beans, it's thread-safe to use instance variables in session scoped beans. That's because each user session gets their own copy of the bean. As a result, if user 1 changes the value of the message, user 2 doesn't see that change. This would not be the case if you used instance variables in a servlet.

Session scoped beans can end up consuming a lot of memory, so you should use them sparingly. For example, you should only create them when you need them. In addition, you should avoid creating multiple session beans for each user whenever possible.

Application scoped beans are seen by the entire web application. As a result, they are useful for storing properties that need to be available to all JSF components. For example, you might use an application scoped bean to store a list of sales tax rates.

Because they are seen by the entire application, application scoped beans are not thread-safe. That means you need to make sure that access to any instance variables in an application scoped bean is synchronized. Furthermore, because they are seen by the entire application, you usually don't want to allow data that's entered by users to make any changes to an application scoped bean. Unless, of course, you really do want a change made by a user to be seen by the entire application, and thus by every other user that requests the page.

View scoped beans were added in JSF 2 to address the memory usage concerns with session scoped beans. You can use a view scope when you need a bean to be available for multiple requests to the same view, but not to an entire session. An example of where you might use a view scoped bean is an online form that needs to be submitted in multiple parts. With a view scoped bean, you won't lose the data entered from previous requests, but you don't need to create a session bean that will still exist and use memory even after the user is done with the form.

Code that sets the scope of the bean

```
package murach.email;

import murach.business.User;

import javax.faces.bean.ManagedBean;
import javax.faces.bean.RequestScoped;

@ManagedBean
@RequestScoped
public class EmailList {
    private User user;
    private String message;

    public EmailList() {
    }

    // Additional code
}
```

Managed bean scopes

Scope	Definition
`@RequestScoped`	The bean is created when the user makes a request to the server. After the response is sent, the bean is destroyed and any instance variables are lost. This is the shortest scope. It is also the default scope.
`@SessionScoped`	The bean is available to a single user for the entire session. As a result, this scope can be used to store session data such as a list of shopping cart items.
`@ApplicationScoped`	The bean is available to the entire application. As a result, instance variables in this bean are shared between all sessions and all requests.
`@ViewScoped`	The bean is available through multiple requests as long as the view doesn't change. This is sort of a middle-ground between request scope and session scope.

Description

- You use an annotation above the class name to set the scope of a managed bean.
- Session scoped beans should be used sparingly as they can cause serious performance issues on a busy server with lots of users.
- Application scoped beans are shared by the entire application. As a result, instance variables in these beans are not thread-safe.
- You can use a view scoped bean when you need data to be available for more than one request to the same view, but not for the entire session. This can help avoid the performance problems that session beans can cause.

Figure 21-3   How to set the scope of a bean

How to use standard JSF tags

A JSF 2 page is an XHTML document. This is a major improvement over JSF 1, which used a different XML schema. As a result, in JSF 1, you couldn't include HTML in your JSF page unless you enclosed it inside special tags. With JSF 2, that restriction has been removed.

How to code the head and body tags

Figure 21-4 shows how to code the head and body tags for a JSF page. The first and second lines are the standard xml header and the encoding, followed by the DOCTYPE declaration, describing this as an HTML document that uses XHTML. This line contains a link to the document type definition (DTD) for XHTML. The DTD is used by XML aware text editors for things such as automatic tag completion and syntax checking of documents.

The next line is the opening html tag. Unlike HTML, XHTML allows namespaces. This figure defines two of them.

The first namespace is the set of standard HTML tags. By convention, this is given the h namespace. However, there is nothing magic about the h, and you could give it any namespace you want.

The second namespace is the set of core JSF tags. By convention, this uses the namespace f. This namespace was used instead of c to avoid a namespace collision with JSTL, which already uses the c namespace for the set of core tags.

The rest of the document should look familiar to you. The only difference between this and normal HTML is that you use h:head and h:body instead of the normal HTML head and body tags.

Inside these tags, you can use standard HTML tags. However, these tags need to follow the XHTML syntax, which is stricter than HTML syntax.

First, XHTML is case sensitive, so all tags must be lowercase. Conversely, HTML is not case sensitive, and it's common to see HTML tags in uppercase in older code.

Second, all XHTML tags must be properly closed. As a result, things that are poor style but legal in HTML (such as not closing paragraph tags) are illegal in XHTML. Similarly, empty tags such as the line break tag must include a closing slash.

Third, all tags must be properly nested and elements cannot overlap. For example, in this figure, you must close the italics tag before you close the bold tag. That way, the italics element is nested inside the bold element.

If a tag doesn't follow the stricter XHMTL syntax, it causes an error. However, as long as you write well-formed HTML code, you shouldn't have any problems making the change to XHTML.

Coding the head and body tags

```
<?xml version='1.0' encoding='UTF-8' ?>
<!DOCTYPE html PUBLIC "-//W3C//DTD XHTML 1.0 Transitional//EN"
        "http://www.w3.org/TR/xhtml1/DTD/xhtml1-transitional.dtd">
<html xmlns="http://www.w3.org/1999/xhtml"
      xmlns:h="http://xmlns.jcp.org/jsf/html"
      xmlns:f="http://xmlns.jcp.org/jsf/core">
    <h:head>
        <title>Murach's Java Servlets and JSP</title>
    </h:head>
    <h:body>
        <h1>Hello, world!</h1>
    </h:body>
</html>
```

XHTML syntax rules

- All tags must be lowercase.
- All tags must be closed.
- All tags must be properly nested.

XHTML examples

Causes error	Fixes error
`<TITLE>My Page</TITLE>`	`<title>My Page</title>`
`<p>My paragraph`	`<p>My paragraph</p>`
` `	` `
`<b><i>Bold and italic<b><i>`	`<b><i>Bold and italic<i><b>`

Description

- A JSF 2 page is an XHTML document, as indicated by the DOCTYPE declaration.
- The html tag defines an xml namespace and the set of tags that exist in that namespace.
- By convention, the namespace used for the HTML tags is h.
- By convention, the namespace used for the JSF core tags is f.
- To code the head tag, you use <h:head> instead of <head>.
- To code the body tag, you use <h:body> instead of <body>
- You can use standard HTML tags inside a JSF document as long as they follow the stricter XHTML syntax.

Figure 21-4   How to code the head and body tags

How to display data from a managed bean

Figure 21-5 shows how you display data contained in a managed bean. Here, the first example shows a request scoped managed bean with one string field that contains a message. To allow access to the message, you need to code a getter for its field.

Because this is a request scoped bean, JSF creates the bean the first time you request it in the JSF page. Once the request is finished, it's marked for garbage collection.

To access the value in the JSF page, you supply the class name of the managed bean, starting with a lowercase letter, followed by a dot operator, and the name of the field you want to access. In this figure, the second example displays the value that's stored in the message field.

By default, any embedded HTML tags in the data are escaped. As a result, the second example causes the browser to display "<h1>Hello, world!</h1>" on the JSF page instead of causing the browser to display "Hello, world!" with formatting for the h1 element.

You can nest the path to the field you want to access as deep as necessary. In this figure, the third example accesses the firstName field of the User object that's available from the EmailList class that was presented earlier in this chapter. For this to work, of course, all of the fields must have appropriate get methods. In other words, the EmailList class must have a getUser method that returns a User object, and the User object must have a getFirstName method that returns the first name of the user.

If you don't want the HTML tags escaped, you can code a statement using the outputText tag as shown in the fourth example. Here, the escape attribute prevents JSF from escaping the opening and closing h1 tags. As a result, this statement causes the browser to display "Hello, world!" with formatting for the h1 element.

Using code like the code in the fourth example can make your site vulnerable to a certain type of attack known as a cross-site scripting (XSS) attack. This occurs anytime you aren't sure where the data you want to display came from. In that case, it's possible for an attacker to enter malicious HTML and JavaScript code in a form field that executes later on a user's browser. For more information about XSS attacks, see chapter 17.

To guard against XSS attacks, you should not set the escape attribute to "false" unless you are sure that it's safe for the browser to interpret any HTML or JavaScript that's embedded in the data.

A simple managed bean

```
@ManagedBean
public class MessageBean {
    private String message = "<h1>Hello, world!</h1>";

    public String getMessage() {
        return message;
    }
}
```

How to display the message field of the MessageBean class

```
#{messageBean.message}
```

The output displayed in a browser

```
<h1>Hello, world!</h1>
```

How to display a nested field of the EmailList class

```
#{emailList.user.firstName}
```

How to turn off escaping

```
<h:outputText value="#{messageBean.message}" escape="false"/>
```

The output displayed in a browser

Hello, world!

Description

- To access and display data from a managed bean, you code the pound sign (#) followed by a set of braces ({}). Within the braces, you code the class name of the managed bean, a dot operator, and the field you want to access.

- You can nest fields as deep as necessary.

- The outputText tag is optional in JSF 2 as long as you want the default behavior, which is to escape any embedded HTML. This is the most secure way to display text.

- If you don't want embedded HTML to be escaped, you can use the outputText tag with the escape attribute set to a value of "false". However, this can make your application vulnerable to a cross-site scripting (XSS) attack.

- To guard against XSS attacks, you should never set the escape attribute to "false" when you're displaying data that's entered by a user, unless you are sure the data doesn't contain any malicious HTML or JavaScript code.

Figure 21-5   How to display data from a managed bean

How to code the inputText tag

Of course, displaying data isn't particularly useful if you don't have a way to get data from the user. Fortunately, JSF makes this almost as easy as displaying data.

Figure 21-6 shows how to use the inputText tag to get data from the user. To do this, the first example adds a setMessage method to the MessageBean class. This provides a way to set the message field.

Inside the JSF page, you access this field the same way you access it when displaying the data. First, you provide the name of the class, followed by a period, and then the name of the field you want to set. As with displaying text, you can nest fields as deeply as necessary.

The inputText tag can take several attributes, but this example uses only two. The first is the id attribute. This attribute sets the id of the text box in the DOM, just as it does in HTML. As a result, you can use the id to select this element in CSS or JavaScript.

The second attribute is the value attribute. You can use this attribute to specify the field in the managed bean that corresponds with this text box. If the field in the managed bean already contains a value, this displays the field's value inside the text box.

When the inputText tag is displayed in the browser, it displays the value that's stored in the managed bean. However, the user can edit that value. In this figure, for example, you could edit the message to change it from "Hello, world!" to "Hello, Mike!".

There are several other text components in the core JSF library. This figure lists two. First, you can use the inputSecret tag to create a password box where the text entered by the user isn't displayed. Second, you can use the inputHidden field to create a hidden form field. Both of these components work like the inputText component, so you shouldn't have any trouble using them when you need them.

A managed bean for setting data

```
@ManagedBean
public class MessageBean {
    private String message = "Hello, world!";

    public String getMessage() {
        return message;
    }

    public void setMessage(String message) {
        this.message = message;
    }
}
```

How to set the message field of the MessageBean class

```
<h:form>
    <label class="pad_top">Message:</label>
    <h:inputText id="message" value="#{messageBean.message}"/>
</h:form>
```

The form displayed in a browser

Message:	Hello, world!

A summary of JSF text components

Component	Description
inputText	A standard text box.
inputSecret	A text box for passwords that doesn't show the characters that the user enters.
inputHidden	A hidden text field.

Description

- To get input, you code an inputText tag. Then, you set its value attribute to the corresponding field in the managed bean. For this to work the managed bean must have an appropriate set method.

- The id attribute of the inputText tag work as it does in HTML. You can use it to select this element in CSS or reference it in JavaScript.

- If the field in the managed bean is not null and not empty, the inputText component displays the current value for the field.

- The inputText tag must be coded within a JSF form tag.

Figure 21-6   How to code the inputText tag

How to validate data

When a user enters data, you usually want to validate that data. For example, you might want to make sure the user didn't leave the field blank. Or, you might want to make sure the user entered a numerical value that's within a certain range. Or, you may need to perform other complex forms of custom validation. Figure 21-7 shows two ways to use built-in JSF components to validate data.

The first example makes sure that the user didn't leave the field empty. To do that, this code sets the required attribute of the inputText tag to true. Then, it sets the requiredMessage attribute to the message that's displayed if the validation fails.

To display this message, the first example uses the message tag. This tag takes several attributes. To start, the showSummary attribute determines whether the message set in the requiredMessage attribute should be displayed. Then, the showDetail attribute determines whether the message should display more detailed error information. On a production application, you typically want to set this attribute to false and use the requiredMessage attribute to set a more user-friendly message.

The for attribute of the message tag binds this message to a component using the component's id. In this case, it binds the message component to the input text component that has an id attribute of firstName.

The class attribute of the message tag can be used to set a CSS class for the component that controls the appearance of the text. In this case, it sets the CSS class to a class named error. This applies the styles that are defined for that class in an included stylesheet.

The second example shows how you can bind a validator component to a component. This example binds the validateLongRange component to the inputText component. This makes sure the entered date is between 1900 and 2014. If it isn't, it displays the message that's stored in the validatorMessage attribute of the inputText component.

JSF provides several more validation components, including min and max length validators. In addition, you can write custom validators if there are no built-in validators that do what you need.

The validators presented in this chapter run on the server. In other words, the validation is performed on the server when the form is submitted. If it fails, the form is redisplayed along with the validation error messages. However, some third-party JSF libraries also use JavaScript to perform validation on the client. That way, the validation is performed before the form is submitted to the server. Since this saves round trips to the server, this is usually what you want.

How to require an entry

```
<h:inputText id="firstName" required="true"
             value="#{emailList.user.firstName}"
             requiredMessage="A first name is required"/>
<h:message showSummary="true" showDetail="false"
           for="firstName" class="error" /><br />
```

How to validate a numerical range

```
<h:inputText id="birthYear" required="true"
             value="#{emailList.user.birthYear}"
             requiredMessage="A birth year is required."
             validatorMessage="A valid 4-digit birth year is required">
    <f:validateLongRange minimum="1900" maximum="2014"/>
</h:inputText>
<h:message showSummary="true" showDetail="false"
           for="birthYear" class="error" /><br />
```

Some attributes of the inputText tag

Attribute	Description
required	If true, requires the user to enter a value.
requiredMessage	Specifies the message that's displayed if a required field isn't entered.
validatorMessage	Specifies the validation message that's displayed if the field doesn't pass the validation specified by a validator such as the validateLongRange tag.

Some attributes of the message tag

Attribute	Description
showSummary	If true, displays the text from the bound component's requiredMessage or validatorMessage attribute.
showDetail	If true, shows details such as the component ID that failed validation, and the Java validation failure message.
for	Binds the validator to a component.
class or styleClass	Specify a CSS class that applies styles for the message.

Description

- You can use the inputText tag to require the user to enter a value and to specify the messages that are displayed if the user doesn't enter a valid value.
- You can use the message tag to display validation messages.
- You can use the validateLongRange tag and other built-in validators to perform more complex validations.
- If you can't find a built-in validator to do what you need, you can code custom validators. However, this is beyond the scope of this JSF introduction.
- The validators presented in this chapter perform the validation on the server. However, some third-party JSF libraries use JavaScript to perform the validation on the client too.

Figure 21-7   How to validate data

How to code a form action

Figure 21-8 shows how to code a form action. Here, the first and second examples show how to submit a form to the server for processing, and the third example shows how to redirect to another page.

To submit a form to the server for processing, you add a method to your managed bean that processes the data and then returns a string that indicates the name of the JSF file to display after the processing has completed. In this figure, for example, the addToEmailList method has been added to the EmailList bean.

The addToEmailList method begins by calling a method of the database class to check whether the email address supplied by the user already exists in the database. If so, this code sets the text of the message field to an error message and redisplays the index.xhtml page. This gives the user a chance to enter a different email address. Otherwise, the code calls a method of the database class to insert the user's data into the database and displays the thanks.xhtml page.

In a JSF page, you can call the addToEmailList method by coding a commandButton tag like the one shown in the second example. Here, the action attribute specifies the name of the bean and the name of the method. Then, the value attribute specifies the text that's displayed on the button.

Before the addToEmailList method is called, any validators that were included in the JSF page are run. If any of them fails, the method isn't called. Instead, the user is redirected back to the form and the validator's error message is displayed.

Sometimes, instead of processing data on the server, you might want to redirect a user to a different page. For example, you might want to include a button on a form that allows a user to return to the home page of the site without submitting the form. To do that, you can code a commandButton tag like the one in the third example. Here, the first part of the action attribute specifies the name of the JSF page without the .xhtml extension. Then, the part following the question mark tells JSF that it should redirect to the index page instead of forwarding to it.

An action method in a managed bean

```
public String addToEmailList() {
    if (UserDB.emailExists(user.getEmail())) {
        message = "This email address already exists. " +
                  "Please enter another email address";
        return "index";
    } else {
        UserDB.insert(user);
        return "thanks";
    }
}
```

Code that submits a form and calls an action method

```
<h:commandButton id="submit"
                 action="#{emailList.addToEmailList}"
                 value="Join Now"/>
```

Code that redirects to another page

```
<h:commandButton id="return"
                 action="index?faces-redirect=true"
                 value="Return"/>
```

Some attributes of the commandButton tag

Attribute	Description
action	To submit a form, this attribute specifies the name of the bean and the name of the method that does the processing.
	To redirect to another page, this attribute specifies the name of the JSF file without the .xhtml extension followed by a string that sets the faces-redirect parameter to true.

Description

- A managed bean can contain one or more action methods that perform processing when a form is submitted.

- An action method returns a string that specifies which JSF view should be displayed next. This string includes the name of the JSF file but not the .xhtml extension.

- When the command button is clicked, validators on the page are run before the action method is called. If the validation fails, the user is redirected to the same page to try again.

- You can use a commandButton tag to submit a form or to redirect to another page without submitting the form.

Figure 21-8   How to code a form action

The Email List application

The next four figures present a complete JSF version of the Email List application that has been used throughout this book. All of the concepts and code in this application were covered earlier in this chapter, so you shouldn't have any trouble understanding this application.

The user interface

Figure 21-9 shows the user interface for the JSF version of the Email List application. The first screen shows the validation messages that the application displays if the user clicks the Join Now button without entering any data. This shows how easy JSF makes it to validate data and provide user-friendly messages for invalid data. Then, the second and third screens show the pages that are displayed when the user enters valid data and clicks on the Join Now button.

For all of these pages, the processing is done on the server by a servlet named FacesServlet that's mapped to this URL:

```
/faces/*
```

That's why the browser displays this URL for all three pages.

By default, JSF encodes the session ID in the URL. This works similarly to the JSTL url tag described in chapter 9. Since this can lead to session hijacking, you usually want to add a tracking-mode element to the web.xml file to stop JSF from encoding the session ID in the URL as described in chapter 9. The web.xml for this application includes such a tracking-mode element. That's why the session ID isn't displayed in any of these URLs.

The first page with validation messages

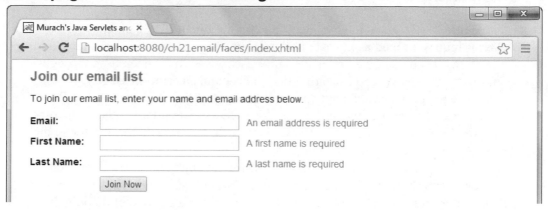

The first page with valid data

The second page

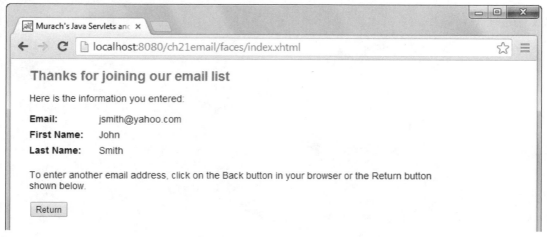

Figure 21-9   The user interface

The EmailList bean

Figure 21-10 shows the managed bean for the Email List application. This class is request scoped as indicated by the annotations above the class name, and it contains two fields. The first is the same User object that's been used throughout this book. The second is a string that can contain an error message.

The code provides a default constructor, which is required for any JavaBean. In this case, the constructor isn't necessary since there aren't any other constructors. However, it's good practice to explicitly include a default constructor so the bean doesn't break if you add another constructor later.

As mentioned in the text, it can be unsafe to do object initialization inside the constructor because dependency injection has not been done yet when the constructor runs. In this case, that wouldn't matter because none of the initialization code calls any injected resources. Nevertheless, this code creates a new User object inside the post construct method instead of in the constructor.

The addToEmailList method is identical to the one you saw earlier in this chapter. First, it checks to see if the user's email address already exists in the database. If so, the code sets the message field to an error message. Then, it returns a string of "index" to send the user back to the index.html page to try again. Otherwise, the code adds the user to the database by calling the insert method of the database class. Then, it returns a string of "thanks" to send the user to the thanks.xhtml page.

The rest of the class provides a get and set method for the user field and it provides a get method for the message field. Since the message field is set by the addToEmailList method, it isn't necessary to provide a set method for it.

The EmailList bean

```
package murach.email;

import murach.business.User;
import murach.data.*;

import javax.annotation.PostConstruct;
import javax.faces.bean.ManagedBean;
import javax.faces.bean.RequestScoped;

@ManagedBean
@RequestScoped
public class EmailList {
    private User user;
    private String message;

    public EmailList() {
    }

    @PostConstruct
    public void init() {
        user = new User();
    }

    public String addToEmailList() {
        if (UserDB.emailExists(user.getEmail())) {
            message = "This email address already exists. " +
                    "Please enter another email address";
            return "index";
        } else {
            UserDB.insert(user);
            return "thanks";
        }
    }

    public User getUser() {
        return user;
    }

    public void setUser(User user) {
        this.user = user;
    }

    public String getMessage() {
        return message;
    }
}
```

Figure 21-10   The EmailList bean

The index.xhtml file

Figure 21-11 shows the code for index.xhtml file. Within this file, the html tag defines a namespace for the JSF tags described in this chapter as well as a namespace for the JSTL tags described in chapter 9.

In the body of this document, this code uses a JSTL if tag to check whether there's a message stored in the EmailList bean. If so, this code displays the message in a p tag. Otherwise, this code doesn't display the p tag.

Within the form tag, this code includes three inputText components that allow the user to enter an email address, first name, and last name. These components use the value attribute to bind their values to the appropriate fields to the User object that's stored in the EmailList bean. In addition, they use the required attribute to make sure the user enters a value. If the user doesn't enter a value, this code uses a corresponding message component to display the validation message that's stored in the requiredMessage attribute.

The bottom of this form includes a commandButton component. This component uses its action attribute to call the addToEmailList method of the EmailList bean. As a result, when the user clicks on the button, the data in the form is submitted to the server and processed by the addToEmailList method.

The rest of this code should be familiar to you as it is just standard HTML. For example, the h1, p, and label tags are used to display a level-1 heading, paragraphs, and labels. Similarly, the id and class attributes are used to identify components so they can work with JavaScript and CSS. For example, all of the components that display validation messages have a class attribute that's set to a value of "error". That way, this application can use an external CSS stylesheet to apply the same formatting to these components.

Although the XHTML in this figure is similar to the HTML presented throughout this book, all of the input and br tags include closing slashes. Since these tags don't require closing to be valid HTML5, they aren't used in the rest of this book. However, these tags must include closing slashes to be valid XHTML. As a result, an error is displayed if these closing slashes aren't included in a JSF page.

The index.xhtml file

```
<?xml version='1.0' encoding='UTF-8' ?>
<!DOCTYPE html PUBLIC "-//W3C//DTD XHTML 1.0 Transitional//EN"
    "http://www.w3.org/TR/xhtml1/DTD/xhtml1-transitional.dtd">
<html xmlns="http://www.w3.org/1999/xhtml"
    xmlns:h="http://xmlns.jcp.org/jsf/html"
    xmlns:c="http://xmlns.jcp.org/jsp/jstl/core">
    <h:head>
        <meta charset="utf-8" />
        <title>Murach's Java Servlets and JSP</title>
        <link rel="stylesheet" href="styles/main.css" type="text/css"/>
    </h:head>
    <h:body>
        <h1>Join our email list</h1>
        <p>To join our email list, enter your name and
           email address below.</p>
        <c:if test="${emailList.message != null}">
           <p class="error">#{emailList.message}</p>
        </c:if>
        <h:form>
            <label class="pad_top">Email:</label>
            <h:inputText id="email" required="true"
                        value="#{emailList.user.email}"
                        requiredMessage="An email address is required"/>
            <h:message showSummary="true" showDetail="false"
                        for="email" class="error" /><br />

            <label class="pad_top">First Name:</label>
            <h:inputText id="firstName" required="true"
                        value="#{emailList.user.firstName}"
                        requiredMessage="A first name is required"/>
            <h:message showSummary="true" showDetail="false"
                        for="firstName" class="error" /><br />

            <label class="pad_top">Last Name:</label>
            <h:inputText id="lastName" required="true"
                        value="#{emailList.user.lastName}"
                        requiredMessage="A last name is required"/>
            <h:message showSummary="true" showDetail="false"
                        for="lastName" class="error" /><br />

            <label> </label>
            <h:commandButton id="submit"
                            action="#{emailList.addToEmailList}"
                            value="Join Now" class="margin_left" />
        </h:form>
    </h:body>
</html>
```

Figure 21-11   The index.xhtml file

The thanks.xhtml file

Figure 21-12 shows the code for the thanks.xhtml file. The EmailList bean sends this page to a user if the user has successfully added his or her email address to the database. The code for this page simply displays a thank you message, followed by the information the user entered on the previous page.

At the bottom of this page, the code includes a form with a commandButton component. This component uses its action attribute to redirect the user to the index.xhtml page. As a result, when the user clicks this button, it doesn't call a method in a managed bean.

Note that you can use a request scoped bean for this application because the entire transaction takes place in one request. First, the form is submitted, which populates the fields in the user object of the EmailList bean. Then, the EmailList bean forwards the user to the thanks.xhtml page. As a result, the User object is still available to the thanks.xhtml page. However, once this page has been sent, the request is complete. As a result, the EmailList bean goes out of scope and is eligible for garbage collection. That means that any future requests to the EmailList bean create a new bean with an empty User object.

The thanks.xhtml file

```
<?xml version='1.0' encoding='UTF-8' ?>
<!DOCTYPE html PUBLIC "-//W3C//DTD XHTML 1.0 Transitional//EN"
    "http://www.w3.org/TR/xhtml1/DTD/xhtml1-transitional.dtd">
<html xmlns="http://www.w3.org/1999/xhtml"
      xmlns:h="http://xmlns.jcp.org/jsf/html">
    <h:head>
        <meta charset="utf-8" />
        <title>Murach's Java Servlets and JSP</title>
        <link rel="stylesheet" href="styles/main.css" type="text/css"/>
    </h:head>
    <h:body>
        <h1>Thanks for joining our email list</h1>

        <p>Here is the information you entered:</p>

        <label>Email:</label>
        <span>#{emailList.user.email}</span><br />
        <label>First Name:</label>
        <span>#{emailList.user.firstName}</span><br />
        <label>Last Name:</label>
        <span>#{emailList.user.lastName}</span><br />

        <p>To enter another email address, click on the Back
        button in your browser or the Return button shown
        below.</p>

        <h:form>
            <h:commandButton id="return"
                             action="index?faces-redirect=true"
                             value="Return"/>
        </h:form>
    </h:body>
</html>
```

Figure 21-12   The thanks.xhtml file

Perspective

This chapter has introduced you to JSF. It has taught you how to code a managed bean, how to display data from the bean on a web page, how to get data from a form and store it in a bean, how to validate that data, and how to use a bean to process it.

Of course, there's much more to learn about JSF. For example, there are many more JSF components than the ones covered in this chapter, including check boxes, radio buttons, tables, and list boxes. Now that you understand how JSF components work, you can learn how to use these and other components by searching the Internet.

With the JSF base components like the ones shown in this chapter, it can be difficult to see how powerful JSF can be. To truly appreciate the potential of JSF, we recommend that you look into some of the third-party component libraries available. This chapter has mentioned two of the most popular ones: JBoss RichFaces and PrimeFaces.

Summary

- *JavaServer Faces* (*JSF*) is a component-based view technology that makes writing a web application similar to writing a desktop application.

- Third-party component libraries can greatly extend the functionality of JSF by providing advanced components.

- JSF uses a *managed bean*, also known as a *backing bean*, to store and retrieve data, call methods in the application, and forward the user to different pages in the application.

- To create a managed bean, you use the @ManagedBean annotation above the class name.

- Managed beans can have four different scopes, as determined by an annotation above the class name: @RequestScoped, @SessionScoped, @ApplicationScoped, and @ViewScoped.

- Instance variables are generally thread-safe in request scoped, session scoped, and view scoped beans. However, they are not thread-safe in application scoped beans.

- You use the @PostConstruct annotation to designate a method that you can use to initialize your bean. This is safer than performing initialization in the constructor.

- To display fields from a managed bean, you code the class name of the managed bean, followed by a path to the field you want to display.

- To code a text box in a form, you use the inputText tag. To make sure the user enters something in the form field, you can set its required attribute to true.

- To display a validation failure message, you can use the message tag.

- To perform more advanced validation, you can use a validator component such as the validateLongRange tag.

- To code a button in a form, you use the commandButton tag. Then, you can perform processing on the server by setting its action attribute to a method of the bean. Or, you can redirect to another web page by setting its action attribute to the name of the page followed by a form-redirect parameter.

Exercise 21-1   Work with JSF

Review the application

1. Open the ch21_ex1_email project in the ex_starts folder.

2. Open the EmailList class. Note how it defines user and message fields. Note also how it defines the addToEmailList method.

3. Open the index.xhtml and thanks.xhtml files. Note how these XHMTL files use the fields and method defined by the EmailList class.

4. Run the application. This may take a while since this application uses JPA to work with the database. As a result, JPA checks the database and creates it if necessary. After it finishes, the XHTML files should display the data that's stored in the EmailList and User beans.

Introduce and fix an XHTML error

5. Open the index.xhtml file. Then, remove the closing slash (/) from one of the br tags.

6. Run the application. This should cause the browser to display an error message that indicates that the br tag needs a closing slash.

7. Fix the error by replacing the closing slash. Then, run the application again. It should run correctly this time.

Add a birthYear field

8. Open the User class. Then, add a birthYear field and its get and set methods.

9. Open the index.xhtml file. Then, add a text box that allows the user to enter a birth year. Use a validateLongRange tag to make sure the user enters a birth year between 1900 and 2014. To do that, you'll need to add the appropriate JSF namespace for that validator component.

10. Open the thanks.xhtml file. Then, add code that displays the birth year.

11. Run the application. This may take a while since JPA needs to modify the structure of the database. After JPA finishes modifying the database, the XHTML files should display the data that's stored in the EmailList and User beans, including the birth year.

Section 5

The Music Store website

One of the best ways to improve your web programming skills is to study websites and applications that have been developed by others. That's why you can download a Music Store website from www.murach.com. And that's why this section presents some of the key components of that website.

In chapter 22, you'll be introduced to this website and to the components that are common to all of its applications. In chapter 23, you'll view the user interface for the applications that let end users listen to sound files and order albums. In addition, you'll view the user interface for the applications that let administrators process orders and prepare reports.

Although the Music Store website isn't a real website, it illustrates the skills that you need for developing a real site. As you study it, you'll see that it requires only the skills that are presented in this book. In other words, this book presents everything you need to know to develop an e-commerce website like this one.

22

An introduction
to the Music Store website

The Music Store website is a website for a fictional record company. This website allows a user to navigate between several web applications. This chapter shows how the Music Store website works, and it describes the common resources that its web applications use.

The website described in this chapter uses JDBC to work with the database. However, the downloadable source code for this book also includes a version of this website that uses JPA instead of JDBC. That's why the end of this chapter describes the similarities and differences between these two approaches.

The user interface

The Music Store application uses JSPs to present the user interface of the application. Although these pages are more complex than the web pages you've seen so far in this book, they don't use any HTML tags that aren't described in chapter 4.

The Home and Catalog pages

Figure 22-1 shows two JSPs of the Music Store application: the Home page and the Catalog page. Both of these pages use the same header and footer, and both use left and right columns. The left column contains four links that let the user navigate through the site, and the right column displays a new release. If, for example, the user clicks on the "Browse Catalog" link in the left column, the site displays the Catalog page in the middle column, but the right column remains the same.

The code for the Home page

Figure 22-2 shows the JSP code for the Home page. This code divides the page into five main parts: the header, the left column, the middle column, the right column, and the footer. To do that, this JSP code uses include files for the header, the left column, the right column, and the footer. Here, the header.jsp file contains all the code for the beginning of each JSP, including the header and top navigation bar. Then, the three JSP files in part 2 of this figure provide the code for the left column, the right column, and the footer. As a result, the code for the Home page only needs to include the code for the middle column of the table.

All of the include files are stored in the includes subdirectory of the root directory. The header.jsp file provides an Admin link that allows you to view the web applications for the administrators of the website. This makes it easy for you to start the admin applications. In addition, this file provides a Delete Cookies link that allows you to delete all cookies that the current browser is sending to this application. This makes it easy for you to test how cookies work with this application. However, these links are included for testing purposes only. As a result, you would remove them after you're done with testing.

Although this code is more complex than the code for most of the JSPs presented in earlier chapters, it's actually simpler than the code for most real-world applications. Nevertheless, it's common for a real-world application to create a three-column layout like the one used by the Music Store site by using aside or div tags with a CSS file as shown in this figure.

The Home page

The Catalog page

Figure 22-1   The Home and Catalog pages

The HTML for the Home page

```
<jsp:include page="/includes/header.jsp" />
<jsp:include page="/includes/column_left_home.jsp" />

<!-- start the middle column -->

<section>
    <h1>Welcome to Fresh Corn Records!</h1>

    <p>Thanks for visiting. Make yourself at home. Feel free to browse
    through our musical catalog. When you do, you can listen to samples from
    the albums on our site, or you can download selected sound files and lis
    ten to them later. We think our catalog contains some great music, and we
    hope you like it as much as we do.</p>

    <p>If you find an album that you like, we hope that you'll use this site
    to order it. Most of the albums we carry aren't available anywhere
    else!</p>
</section>

<!-- end the middle column -->

<jsp:include page="/includes/column_right_news.jsp" />
<jsp:include page="/includes/footer.jsp" />
```

The HTML for the header.jsp file

```
<%@page contentType="text/html" pageEncoding="utf-8"%>
<%@ taglib prefix="c" uri="http://java.sun.com/jsp/jstl/core" %>
<!doctype html>

<html>
<head>
    <meta charset="utf-8">
    <title>Fresh Corn Records</title>
    <link rel="shortcut icon" href="<c:url value='/images/favicon.ico'/>">
    <link rel="stylesheet" href="<c:url value='/styles/main.css'/> ">
    <script src="http://html5shiv.googlecode.com/svn/trunk/html5.js"></script>
</head>

<body>
    <header>
        <img src="<c:url value='/images/logo.jpg'/>"
             alt="Fresh Corn Records Logo" width="58">
        <h1>Fresh Corn Records</h1>
        <h2>Quality Sounds Served Up Fresh!</h2>
    </header>
    <nav id="nav_bar">
        <ul>
            <li><a href="<c:url value='/admin'/>">
                    Admin</a></li>
            <li><a href="<c:url value='/user/deleteCookies'/>">
                    Delete Cookies</a></li>
            <li><a href="<c:url value='/order/showCart'/>">
                    Show Cart</a></li>
        </ul>
    </nav>
```

Figure 22-2   The HTML for the Home page (part 1 of 2)

The code for the column_left_home.jsp file

```
<%@ taglib prefix="c" uri="http://java.sun.com/jsp/jstl/core" %>
<aside id="sidebarA">
    <nav>
      <ul>
          <li><a class="current" href="<c:url value='/' />">
                  Home</a></li>
          <li><a href="<c:url value='/catalog' />">
                  Browse Catalog</a></li>
          <li><a href="<c:url value='/email' />">
                  Join Email List</a></li>
          <li><a href="<c:url value='/customer_service' />">
                  Customer Service</a></li>
      </ul>
    </nav>
</aside>
```

The code for the column_right_news.jsp file

```
<%@ taglib prefix="c" uri="http://java.sun.com/jsp/jstl/core" %>
<aside id="sidebarB">
    <h1>New Release</h1>
    <img src="<c:url value='/images/8601_cover.jpg' />" width="80"
        alt="86 - True Life - Album Cover">
    <h2><a href="catalog/product/8601" class="no_underline">
        86 (the band) - True Life Songs and Pictures
    </a></h2>
    <p class="news_item">A refreshing mix of rock, country, and bluegrass
        that will have you stomping your foot and crying in your beer
        in no time.</p>
</aside>
```

The code for the footer.jsp file

```
<footer>
    <p>&copy; Copyright ${currentYear} Mike Murach &amp; Associates, Inc.
        All rights reserved.</p>
</footer>
</body>
</html>
```

Figure 22-2   The HTML for the Home page (part 2 of 2)

The business layer

The business objects of the Music Store website are stored in the music.business package. All of these business objects follow the rules for coding a JavaBean.

The class diagrams

Figure 22-3 shows the class diagrams for the six business objects of the Music Store web application. These diagrams show that the User class that's used by the Music Store website has more instance variables and methods than the User class that was used earlier in this book. However, the same concepts still apply to this object.

In addition, these class diagrams show that a business object can contain another business object as an instance variable. For example, the Download and Invoice objects can set and get a User object. Similarly, the LineItem object can get and set a Product object. In addition, the Invoice and Cart items can get and set a List object that can contain zero or more LineItem objects. Since the ArrayList class implements the List interface, this allows the Invoice and Cart items to get and set an ArrayList object that can contain zero or more LineItem objects.

The Product class

Figure 22-4 shows the code for the Product class that implements the Product diagram in the last figure. Although this class is one of the simpler classes used by the Music Store website, all of the other classes have the same structure. More specifically, they provide private instance variables, get and set methods for each instance variable, and one zero-argument constructor. In other words, they follow the rules for creating a JavaBean.

In addition, a business class may provide other convenience methods that do some additional work beyond getting and setting instance variables. With the Product class, for example, the getArtistName and getAlbumName methods parse the description instance variable to return useful information. Similarly, the getImageURL and getProductType methods provide more information about the product. Finally, the getPriceCurrencyFormat method applies the currency format to the price instance variable.

If you want to view the code for the other business classes, you can open them in an IDE or a text editor. In fact, due to the highlighting and color-coding that's provided by any text editor that's designed for working with Java, you may find it easier to read these classes when they're opened in a text editor. If not, you can print the code for the classes that you want to review.

The class diagrams for the business objects

User

-firstName : String
-lastName : String
-email : String
-companyName : String
-address1 : String
-address2 : String
-city : String
-state : String
-zip : String
-country : String
-creditCardType: String
-creditCardNumber : String
-creditCardExpirationDate : String

+setFirstName(firstName : String)
+getFirstName() : String
+setLastName(lastName : String)
+getLastName() : String
+setEmail(email : String)
+getEmail() : String
+setCompanyName(company : String)
+getCompanyName() : String
+setAddress1(address1 : String)
+getAddress1() : String
+setAddress2(address2 : String)
+getAddress2() : String
+getAddressHTMLFormat() : String
+setCity(city : String)
+getCity() : String
+setState(state : String)
+getState() : String
+setZip(zip : String)
+getZip() : String
+setCountry(country : String)
+getCountry() : String
+setCreditCardType(cardType : String)
+getCreditCardType() : String
+setCreditCardNumber(cardNo : String)
+setCreditCardNumber() : String
+setCreditCardExpirationDate(date : String)
+getCreditCardExpirationDate() : String

Download

-user : User
-downloadDate : Date
-productCode : String

+setUser(user : User)
+getUser() : User
+setDownloadDate(date : Date)
+getDownloadDate() : Date
+setProductCode(code : String)
+getProductCode() : String

Invoice

-user : User
-lineItems : List<LineItem>
-invoiceDate : Date
-invoiceNumber : int

+setUser(user : User)
+getUser() : User
+setLineItems(items : List<LineItem>)
+getLineItems() : List<LineItem>
+setInvoiceDate(date : Date)
+getInvoiceDateDefaultFormat() : Date
+setInvoiceNumber(num : int)
+getInvoiceNumber() : int
+getInvoiceTotal() : double
+getInvoiceTotalCurrencyFormat() : String

Product

-code : String
-description : String
-price : double

+setCode(code : String)
+getCode() : String
+setDescription(desc : String)
+getDescription() : String
+getArtistName() : String
+getAlbumName() : String
+setPrice(price : double)
+getPrice() : double
+getPriceCurrencyFormat() : String
+getImageURL() : String
+getProductType() : String

Cart

-items : List<LineItem>

+setItems(lineItems : List<LineItem>)
+getItems() : List<LineItem>
+addItem(item : LineItem)
+removeItem(item : LineItem)

LineItem

-item : Product
-quantity : int

+setProduct(product : Product)
+getProduct() : Product
+setQuantity(quantity : int)
+getQuantity() : int
+getTotal() : doubloe
+getTotalCurrencyFormat() : String

Description

- These business classes are stored in the music.business package. These classes are all coded as JavaBeans (see chapter 6).
- Some of these business objects can get and set other business objects.

Figure 22-3   The class diagrams for the business objects

The Product class

```java
package music.business;

import java.text.NumberFormat;
import java.io.Serializable;

public class Product implements Serializable {

    private Long productId;
    private String code;
    private String description;
    private double price;

    public Product() {}

    public void setId(Long productId) {
        this.productId = productId;
    }

    public Long getId() {
        return productId;
    }

    public void setCode(String code) {
        this.code = code;
    }

    public String getCode() {
        return code;
    }

    public void setDescription(String description) {
        this.description = description;
    }

    public String getDescription() {
        return description;
    }

    public String getArtistName() {
        String artistName =
                description.substring(0, description.indexOf(" - "));
        return artistName;
    }

    public String getAlbumName() {
        String albumName =
                description.substring(description.indexOf(" - ") + 3);
        return albumName;
    }
```

Figure 22-4   The Product class (part 1 of 2)

The Product class   Page 2

```
public void setPrice(double price) {
    this.price = price;
}

public double getPrice() {
    return price;
}

public String getPriceCurrencyFormat() {
    NumberFormat currency = NumberFormat.getCurrencyInstance();
    return currency.format(price);
}

public String getImageURL() {
    String imageURL = "/musicStore/images/" + code + "_cover.jpg";
    return imageURL;
}

public String getProductType() {
    return "Audio CD";
}
}
```

Description

- Like all the business classes for this application, the Product class is coded as a JavaBean.

Figure 22-4   The Product class (part 2 of 2)

The controller layer

The controllers of the Music Store website are stored in the music.controllers package. All of these controllers are servlets.

The CatalogController class

Figure 22-5 shows the code for the Catalog controller. This controller handles the requests for browsing the catalog and listening to sound files.

Since this controller implements the doGet and doPost methods, it processes requests that use the HTTP GET and POST methods. However, the doGet method only handles requests for some URLs while the doPost method handles requests for other URLs. For example, the doPost method handles the request that registers users by writing their data to the database. This is common as you often want to use a different HTTP method for different URLs.

Both the doGet and doPost methods start by getting the URI for the request. Then, they use an if/else statement to execute the appropriate code for the URI. To do that, they pass the request and response objects to a helper method that returns a URL for the view.

After the if/else statement, the code gets a RequestDispatcher object for the URL. Then, it uses the forward method to forward the request and response objects to that URL. This displays the appropriate user interface component.

If an HTTP GET request doesn't end with "listen", this code calls the showProduct method and passes the request and response objects to it. This method gets the path for the request, parses it to get the product code, and reads the product for that product code from the database. Then, it sets the product in the session object and returns a URL for the JSP for that corresponds with that product.

If an HTTP GET request ends with "listen", this code calls the listen method and passes the request and response objects to it. This method begins by checking whether a User object exists in the session object. If not, it checks if there is a cookie for that user's email address. If so, it attempts to read that User object from the database. If it can't read that User object from the database, this code returns a URL that displays the JSP for the Register page. Otherwise, it writes the data for the download to the database and returns a URL for a JSP page that lets the user listen to sound files.

If an HTTP POST request ends with "register", this code calls the registerUser method and passes the request and response objects to it. This method begins by getting the user data that's available from the request object parameters. Then, it checks whether the email address already exists in the database. If so, this code reads the User object from the database, stores the data from the request object in the User object, and updates the row in the database. Otherwise, it creates a new User object, sets the data from the request object in the User object, and inserts a new row into the database. Either way, it adds a cookie to the user's browser. Then, it returns a URL for a JSP page that lets the user listen to sound files.

The CatalogController class   **Page 1**

```
package music.controllers;

import java.io.IOException;
import javax.servlet.ServletException;
import javax.servlet.http.*;

import music.business.*;
import music.data.*;
import music.util.CookieUtil;

public class CatalogController extends HttpServlet {

    @Override
    public void doGet(HttpServletRequest request,
            HttpServletResponse response)
            throws ServletException, IOException {

        String requestURI = request.getRequestURI();
        String url;
        if (requestURI.endsWith("/listen")) {
            url = listen(request, response);
        } else {
            url = showProduct(request, response);
        }
        getServletContext()
            .getRequestDispatcher(url)
            .forward(request, response);
    }

    @Override
    public void doPost(HttpServletRequest request,
            HttpServletResponse response)
            throws ServletException, IOException {

        String requestURI = request.getRequestURI();
        String url = "/catalog";
        if (requestURI.endsWith("/register")) {
            url = registerUser(request, response);
        }
        getServletContext()
            .getRequestDispatcher(url)
            .forward(request, response);
    }
```

Figure 22-5   The CatalogController class (part 1 of 3)

The CatalogController class

```java
    private String showProduct(HttpServletRequest request,
            HttpServletResponse response) {
        String productCode = request.getPathInfo();
        if (productCode != null) {
            productCode = productCode.substring(1);
            Product product = ProductDB.selectProduct(productCode);
            HttpSession session = request.getSession();
            session.setAttribute("product", product);
        }
        return "/catalog/" + productCode + "/index.jsp";
    }

    private String listen(HttpServletRequest request,
            HttpServletResponse response) {

        HttpSession session = request.getSession();
        User user = (User) session.getAttribute("user");
        // if the User object doesn't exist, check for the email cookie
        if (user == null) {
            Cookie[] cookies = request.getCookies();
            String emailAddress =
                    CookieUtil.getCookieValue(cookies, "emailCookie");
            // if the email cookie doesn't exist, go to the registration page
            if (emailAddress == null || emailAddress.equals("")) {
                return "/catalog/register.jsp";
            } else {
                user = UserDB.selectUser(emailAddress);

                // if a user for that email isn't in the database,
                // go to the registration page
                if (user == null) {
                        return "/catalog/register.jsp";
                }
                session.setAttribute("user", user);
            }
        }

        Product product = (Product) session.getAttribute("product");

        Download download = new Download();
        download.setUser(user);
        download.setProductCode(product.getCode());
        DownloadDB.insert(download);

        return "/catalog/" + product.getCode() + "/sound.jsp";
    }
```

Figure 22-5   The CatalogController class (part 2 of 3)

The CatalogController class   Page 3

```java
private String registerUser(HttpServletRequest request,
        HttpServletResponse response) {

    HttpSession session = request.getSession();
    String firstName = request.getParameter("firstName");
    String lastName = request.getParameter("lastName");
    String email = request.getParameter("email");

    User user;
    if (UserDB.emailExists(email)) {
        user = UserDB.selectUser(email);
        user.setFirstName(firstName);
        user.setLastName(lastName);
        user.setEmail(email);
        UserDB.update(user);
    } else {
        user = new User();
        user.setFirstName(firstName);
        user.setLastName(lastName);
        user.setEmail(email);
        UserDB.insert(user);
    }

    session.setAttribute("user", user);

    Cookie emailCookie = new Cookie("emailCookie", email);
    emailCookie.setMaxAge(60 * 60 * 24 * 365 * 2);
    emailCookie.setPath("/");
    response.addCookie(emailCookie);

    Product product = (Product) session.getAttribute("product");
    String url = "/catalog/" + product.getCode() + "/sound.jsp";
    return url;
}
}
```

Figure 22-5   The CatalogController class (part 3 of 3)

The structure

This topic shows the overall structure of the Music Store website including the web.xml and context.xml files that are used by the website.

The directory structure

Figure 22-6 shows the directory structure for the files of the Music Store website after it is deployed to a servlet container like Tomcat. If you read chapter 1, you should understand how this directory structure works. Since the Music Store website contains four products, the JSP files for each product are stored in a subdirectory of the catalog directory that corresponds with the product's code. Similarly, the MP3 sound files for each album are stored in a subdirectory of the sound directory that corresponds with the product's code.

The directory structure

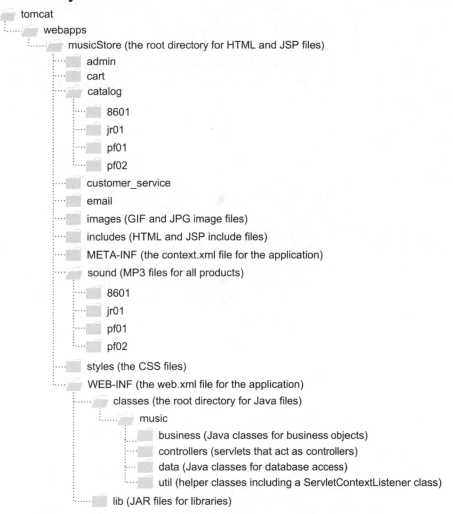

tomcat
    webapps
        musicStore (the root directory for HTML and JSP files)
            admin
            cart
            catalog
                8601
                jr01
                pf01
                pf02
            customer_service
            email
            images (GIF and JPG image files)
            includes (HTML and JSP include files)
            META-INF (the context.xml file for the application)
            sound (MP3 files for all products)
                8601
                jr01
                pf01
                pf02
            styles (the CSS files)
            WEB-INF (the web.xml file for the application)
                classes (the root directory for Java files)
                    music
                        business (Java classes for business objects)
                        controllers (servlets that act as controllers)
                        data (Java classes for database access)
                        util (helper classes including a ServletContextListener class)
                lib (JAR files for libraries)

Description

- The JSP files are stored in the root directory for the application or in one of its subdirectories.
- The context.xml file is stored in the META-INF directory.
- The web.xml file is stored in the WEB-INF directory.
- The Java classes, including servlets, are stored in a subdirectory of the WEB-INF directory that corresponds with the name of the package for the class.
- The JAR files for the class libraries needed by the application can be stored in the WEB-INF\lib directory.

Figure 22-6   The directory structure of the website

The web.xml file

Figure 22-7 shows the web.xml file for the application. If you've read chapters 1-19, you shouldn't have any trouble understanding this web.xml file. However, this shows a realistic web.xml file that provides for a context initialization parameter, servlet mapping, a listener, welcome files, custom error pages, and authentication.

The context.xml file

Figure 22-8 shows the context.xml file for the application. If you've read chapters 12 and 16, you shouldn't have any trouble understanding this file. In short, it configures two DataSource classes that are used by the connection pool. Here, the first DataSource class is for the music database that stores the data for the Music Store web site. The second DataSource class is for the murach database that stores the usernames, passwords, and roles that are used to authorize the administrative users. Finally, it configures the DataSourceRealm that's used to authorize administrative users. This DataSourceRealm uses the second DataSource defined by this context.xml file, the one named murachDB.

The web.xml file

```xml
<?xml version="1.0" encoding="UTF-8"?>
<web-app version="3.1" xmlns="http://xmlns.jcp.org/xml/ns/javaee"
    xmlns:xsi="http://www.w3.org/2001/XMLSchema-instance"
    xsi:schemaLocation="http://xmlns.jcp.org/xml/ns/javaee
                        http://xmlns.jcp.org/xml/ns/javaee/web-app_3_1.xsd">

    <!-- define a context initialization parameter -->
    <context-param>
        <param-name>custServEmail</param-name>
        <param-value>custserv@freshcornrecords.com</param-value>
    </context-param>

    <!-- servlet definitions (alphabetical by complete class name) -->
    <servlet>
        <servlet-name>AdminController</servlet-name>
        <servlet-class>music.controllers.AdminController</servlet-class>
    </servlet>
    <servlet>
        <servlet-name>CatalogController</servlet-name>
        <servlet-class>music.controllers.CatalogController</servlet-class>
    </servlet>
    <servlet>
        <servlet-name>OrderController</servlet-name>
        <servlet-class>music.controllers.OrderController</servlet-class>
    </servlet>
    <servlet>
        <servlet-name>UserController</servlet-name>
        <servlet-class>music.controllers.UserController</servlet-class>
    </servlet>

    <!-- servlet mappings -->
    <servlet-mapping>
        <servlet-name>AdminController</servlet-name>
        <url-pattern>/adminController/*</url-pattern>
    </servlet-mapping>
    <servlet-mapping>
        <servlet-name>CatalogController</servlet-name>
        <url-pattern>/catalog/product/*</url-pattern>
    </servlet-mapping>
    <servlet-mapping>
        <servlet-name>OrderController</servlet-name>
        <url-pattern>/order/*</url-pattern>
    </servlet-mapping>
    <servlet-mapping>
        <servlet-name>UserController</servlet-name>
        <url-pattern>/user/*</url-pattern>
    </servlet-mapping>

    <!-- define a servlet context listener -->
    <listener>
        <listener-class>music.util.MusicStoreContextListener</listener-class>
    </listener>
```

Figure 22-7   The web.xml file (part 1 of 2)

The web.xml file

```xml
        <!-- define the welcome files -->
        <welcome-file-list>
            <welcome-file>index.jsp</welcome-file>
            <welcome-file>index.html</welcome-file>
        </welcome-file-list>

        <!-- Enable the custom error pages -->
        <error-page>
            <error-code>404</error-code>
            <location>/error_404.jsp</location>
        </error-page>
        <error-page>
            <exception-type>java.lang.Throwable</exception-type>
            <location>/error_java.jsp</location>
        </error-page>

        <!-- Define two security roles -->
        <security-role>
            <description>customer service employees</description>
            <role-name>service</role-name>
        </security-role>
        <security-role>
            <description>programmers</description>
            <role-name>programmer</role-name>
        </security-role>

        <security-constraint>
            <!-- Restrict access to the URLs in the admin directory -->
            <web-resource-collection>
                <web-resource-name>Admin</web-resource-name>
                <url-pattern>/admin/*</url-pattern>
            </web-resource-collection>

            <!-- Authorize the service and programmer roles -->
            <auth-constraint>
                <role-name>service</role-name>
                <role-name>programmer</role-name>
            </auth-constraint>
        </security-constraint>

        <!-- Use form-based authentication to provide access -->
        <login-config>
            <auth-method>FORM</auth-method>
            <form-login-config>
                <form-login-page>/login.jsp</form-login-page>
                <form-error-page>/login_error.jsp</form-error-page>
            </form-login-config>
        </login-config>

        <!-- Use cookies (not URL encoding) for session tracking -->
        <session-config>
            <tracking-mode>COOKIE</tracking-mode>
        </session-config>
    </web-app>
```

Figure 22-7   The web.xml file (part 2 of 2)

The context.xml file

```
<?xml version="1.0" encoding="UTF-8"?>
<Context path="/musicStore">

    <!-- the music database that contains the Music Store data -->
    <Resource name="jdbc/musicDB" type="javax.sql.DataSource" auth="Container"
            driverClassName="com.mysql.jdbc.Driver"
            url="jdbc:mysql://localhost:3306/music?autoReconnect=true"
            username="root" password="sesame"
            logAbandoned="true"
            removeAbandoned="true" removeAbandonedTimeout="60"
            maxActive="100" maxIdle="30" maxWait="10000" />

    <!-- the murach database that contains admin usernames and passwords -->
    <Resource name="jdbc/murachDB" type="javax.sql.DataSource" auth="Container"
            driverClassName="com.mysql.jdbc.Driver"
            url="jdbc:mysql://localhost:3306/murach?autoReconnect=true"
            username="root" password="sesame"
            logAbandoned="true"
            removeAbandoned="true" removeAbandonedTimeout="60"
            maxActive="100" maxIdle="30" maxWait="10000" />

    <Realm dataSourceName="jdbc/murachDB" localDataSource="true"
            className="org.apache.catalina.realm.DataSourceRealm"
            userTable="UserPass" userRoleTable="UserRole"
            userNameCol="Username" roleNameCol="Rolename" userCredCol="Password"
            debug="99" />
</Context>
```

Figure 22-8   The context.xml file

The database

The Music Store website uses a MySQL database named music to store the data for the website in its tables.

The database diagram

Figure 22-9 shows the database diagram for the Music Store database. This diagram shows that this database stores most of its data in five tables that correspond to five of the business objects. The asterisk used in this diagram shows that one row in the User table can correspond with zero or more rows in the Download or Invoice table. Similarly, one row in the Invoice table can correspond with one or more rows in the LineItem table. However, a row in the Download table and a row in the LineItem table can have one and only one row in the Product table.

In addition to these five tables, the Music Store website uses two more tables to store usernames, passwords, and roles. The admin section of the website uses these tables to authorize users. As you learned in the previous figure, these tables are stored in the database named murach, not the database named music.

The SQL script for the database

Figure 22-10 shows the SQL script that you can use to create the Music Store database. This script begins by creating a database named music. Then, it creates the first five tables in the database diagram. To do that, it uses five CREATE TABLE statements that identify the column names, data types, primary keys, and so on. Next, this script uses an INSERT INTO statement to insert data into the Product table.

After creating the music database, this script creates a database named murach, and it creates the last two tables in the database diagram. To do that, it uses two CREATE TABLE statements. Then, this script uses two INSERT INTO statements to insert data into the UserPass and UserRole tables. If you want to use your own usernames and passwords for the admin section, you can modify the INSERT INTO statements for the UserPass and UserRole tables before you run this script.

The database diagram

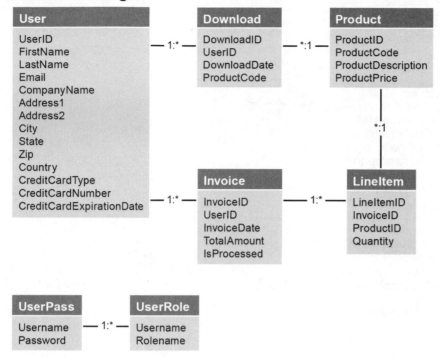

Description

- The User, Download, Product, Invoice, and LineItem tables store the data for the Music Store website. These tables correspond to the business classes of the application.

- The UserPass and UserRole tables store the usernames and passwords for the admin applications.

Figure 22-9   The database diagram

The SQL script for the database

```sql
DROP DATABASE IF EXISTS music;

CREATE DATABASE music;

USE music;

CREATE TABLE User (
    UserID INT NOT NULL AUTO_INCREMENT,
    FirstName VARCHAR(50),
    LastName VARCHAR(50),
    EmailAddress VARCHAR(50),
    CompanyName VARCHAR(50),
    Address1 VARCHAR(50),
    Address2 VARCHAR(50),
    City VARCHAR(50),
    State VARCHAR(50),
    Zip VARCHAR(50),
    Country VARCHAR(50),
    CreditCardType VARCHAR(50),
    CreditCardNumber VARCHAR(50),
    CreditCardExpirationDate VARCHAR(50),

    PRIMARY KEY (UserID)
);

CREATE TABLE Invoice(
    InvoiceID INT NOT NULL AUTO_INCREMENT,
    UserID INT NOT NULL,
    InvoiceDate DATETIME NOT NULL DEFAULT '0000-00-00 00:00:00',
    TotalAmount FLOAT NOT NULL DEFAULT '0',
    IsProcessed enum('y','n') DEFAULT NULL,

    PRIMARY KEY (InvoiceID),
    FOREIGN KEY (UserID) REFERENCES User (UserID)
);

CREATE TABLE LineItem(
    LineItemID INT NOT NULL AUTO_INCREMENT,
    InvoiceID INT NOT NULL DEFAULT '0',
    ProductID INT NOT NULL DEFAULT '0',
    Quantity INT NOT NULL DEFAULT '0',

    PRIMARY KEY (LineItemID),
    FOREIGN KEY (InvoiceID) REFERENCES Invoice (InvoiceID)
);

CREATE TABLE Product(
    ProductID INT NOT NULL AUTO_INCREMENT,
    ProductCode VARCHAR(10) NOT NULL DEFAULT '',
    ProductDescription VARCHAR(100) NOT NULL DEFAULT '',
    ProductPrice DECIMAL(7,2) NOT NULL DEFAULT '0.00',

    PRIMARY KEY (ProductID)
);
```

Figure 22-10   The SQL script for the database (part 1 of 2)

The SQL script for the database   **Page 2**

```
INSERT INTO Product VALUES
    ('1', '8601', '86 (the band) - True Life Songs and Pictures', '14.95'),
    ('2', 'pf01', 'Paddlefoot - The first CD', '12.95'),
    ('3', 'pf02', 'Paddlefoot - The second CD', '14.95'),
    ('4', 'jr01', 'Joe Rut - Genuine Wood Grained Finish', '14.95');

CREATE TABLE Download (
    DownloadID INT NOT NULL AUTO_INCREMENT,
    UserID INT NOT NULL,
    DownloadDate DATETIME NOT NULL,
    ProductCode VARCHAR(10)  NOT NULL,

    PRIMARY KEY (DownloadID),
    FOREIGN KEY (UserID) REFERENCES User (UserID)
);


DROP DATABASE IF EXISTS murach;

CREATE DATABASE murach;

USE murach;

CREATE TABLE UserPass (
  Username varchar(15) NOT NULL PRIMARY KEY,
  Password varchar(15) NOT NULL
);

INSERT INTO UserPass VALUES ('andrea', 'sesame'),
                           ('joel', 'sesame'),
                           ('anne', 'sesame');

CREATE TABLE UserRole (
  Username VARCHAR(15) NOT NULL,
  Rolename VARCHAR(15) NOT NULL,

  PRIMARY KEY (Username, Rolename)
);

INSERT INTO UserRole VALUES ('andrea', 'service'),
                           ('andrea', 'programmer'),
                           ('joel', 'programmer');
```

Description

- This SQL script creates the tables needed by the Music Store application. You can download this SQL script from www.murach.com, and appendix A (PC) or B (Mac) shows how to execute it to create the tables needed by the Music Store application.

Figure 22-10   The SQL script for the database (part 2 of 2)

The data layer

The music.data package stores the data access classes that let the Music Store website access the database. In addition, this package includes a ConnectionPool class and a DBUtil class that are used by the data access classes. For more information about coding these classes, you can refer to chapter 12.

The class diagrams

Figure 22-11 shows the class diagrams for five data access classes. These classes use static methods to read and write business objects to a database. As a result, they don't contain instance variables or constructors.

Most of the methods that read a business object from a database accept a single argument that uniquely identifies the business object. For example, the selectProduct method of the ProductDB class can read a Product object from a database using either a string for the product code or a long value for the product ID.

Most of the methods that write a business object to a database accept the business object as an argument. For example, the insert method of the UserDB class accepts a User object as a parameter.

The ProductDB class

Figure 22-12 shows the code for the ProductDB class. This code implements the ProductDB class diagram. If you read chapter 12, you shouldn't have much trouble understanding this code.

And if you understand this code, you shouldn't have much trouble understanding how the other classes in the data access layer work since they all follow the same pattern. To view the code for the other data access classes, you can open them in an IDE or a text editor. They're all stored in the music.data package.

Class diagrams for the data access classes

ProductDB

+selectProduct(code : String) : Product
+selectProduct(id : long) : Product
+selectProducts() : List<Product>

UserDB

+insert(user : User) : void
+update(user : User) : void
+selectUser(email : String) : User
+emailExists(email : String) : boolean

InvoiceDB

+insert(invoice : Invoice) : void
+update(invoice : Invoice) : void
+selectUnprocessedInvoices() : List<Invoice>

LineItemDB

+insert(invoiceID : long, lineItem : LineItem) : void
+selectLineItems(invoiceID : long) : List<LineItem>

DownloadDB

+insert(download : Download) : void

ReportDB

+getUserEmail() : Workbook
+getDownloadDetail(startDate: String, endDate: String) : Workbook

Description

- These data access classes are stored in the music.data package. You can use them to read business objects from the database and write them to the database.

Figure 22-11   The class diagrams for the data access classes

The ProductDB class

```java
package music.data;

import java.sql.*;
import java.util.*;

import music.business.*;

public class ProductDB {

    public static Product selectProduct(String productCode) {
        ConnectionPool pool = ConnectionPool.getInstance();
        Connection connection = pool.getConnection();
        PreparedStatement ps = null;
        ResultSet rs = null;

        String query = "SELECT * FROM Product "
                + "WHERE ProductCode = ?";
        try {
            ps = connection.prepareStatement(query);
            ps.setString(1, productCode);
            rs = ps.executeQuery();
            if (rs.next()) {
                Product p = new Product();
                p.setId(rs.getLong("ProductID"));
                p.setCode(rs.getString("ProductCode"));
                p.setDescription(rs.getString("ProductDescription"));
                p.setPrice(rs.getDouble("ProductPrice"));
                return p;
            } else {
                return null;
            }
        } catch (SQLException e) {
            System.err.println(e);
            return null;
        } finally {
            DBUtil.closeResultSet(rs);
            DBUtil.closePreparedStatement(ps);
            pool.freeConnection(connection);
        }
    }

    public static Product selectProduct(long productID) {
        ConnectionPool pool = ConnectionPool.getInstance();
        Connection connection = pool.getConnection();
        PreparedStatement ps = null;
        ResultSet rs = null;

        String query = "SELECT * FROM Product "
                + "WHERE ProductID = ?";
        try {
            ps = connection.prepareStatement(query);
            ps.setLong(1, productID);
            rs = ps.executeQuery();
```

Figure 22-12   The ProductDB class (part 1 of 2)

The ProductDB class   **Page 2**

```
            if (rs.next()) {
                Product p = new Product();
                p.setId(rs.getLong("ProductID"));
                p.setCode(rs.getString("ProductCode"));
                p.setDescription(rs.getString("ProductDescription"));
                p.setPrice(rs.getDouble("ProductPrice"));
                return p;
            } else {
                return null;
            }
        } catch (SQLException e) {
            System.err.println(e);
            return null;
        } finally {
            DBUtil.closeResultSet(rs);
            DBUtil.closePreparedStatement(ps);
            pool.freeConnection(connection);
        }
    }

    public static List<Product> selectProducts() {
        ConnectionPool pool = ConnectionPool.getInstance();
        Connection connection = pool.getConnection();
        PreparedStatement ps = null;
        ResultSet rs = null;

        String query = "SELECT * FROM Product";
        try {
            ps = connection.prepareStatement(query);
            rs = ps.executeQuery();
            ArrayList<Product> products = new ArrayList<>();
            while (rs.next()) {
                Product p = new Product();
                p.setCode(rs.getString("ProductCode"));
                p.setDescription(rs.getString("ProductDescription"));
                p.setPrice(rs.getDouble("ProductPrice"));
                products.add(p);
            }
            return products;
        } catch (SQLException e) {
            System.err.println(e);
            return null;
        } finally {
            DBUtil.closeResultSet(rs);
            DBUtil.closePreparedStatement(ps);
            pool.freeConnection(connection);
        }
    }
}
```

Figure 22-12   The ProductDB class (part 2 of 2)

The JPA version compared to the JDBC version

Now that you have been introduced to the JDBC version of the Music Store website, figure 22-13 shows how this version compares to the JPA version. This version of the website is also available from the downloadable code for this book.

The similarities

The user interface is the same for both versions of this website. In other words, both websites use the same HTML and CSS.

The business and controller classes are also the same. However, the business classes for the JPA version include the JPA annotations that map the business objects to the database tables. Also, the controller code that writes data to the database is slightly simpler in the JPA version.

The directory structure, the web.xml file, and the context.xml file are also the same. However, the context.xml file for the JPA version only configures a connection to the database named murach, not the database named music.

The differences

The JPA version includes the JPA libraries. More specifically, the JPA version uses the EclipseLink libraries. Then, it uses the persistence.xml file to configure a connection to a database named music_jpa.

Since JPA automatically generates the database tables based on the annotations in the business objects, the SQL script for the database only needs to create the database, not its tables. Then, when you run the website for the first time, JPA automatically creates the tables. These tables are very similar to the tables described in figure 22-9. However, there are some minor differences. For example, JPA generates a sequence table to keep track of the IDs that it generates for primary key columns. Fortunately, when you use JPA, you can usually ignore the structure of the database since JPA handles that automatically.

For your convenience, the downloadable code for this book includes a SQL script that creates a database named music_jpa for the JPA version of the website. This SQL script also creates the tables and inserts some data into the Product table. That way, JPA doesn't need to check the database and make sure its tables are synchronized with the business objects. This helps the Music Site run more efficiently. However, if you want JPA to check the database, you can modify the persistence.xml file as explained in chapter 13.

As you might expect, the main difference is that the data access classes use JPA, not JDBC. As a result, they are shorter and more flexible. If, for example, you add a field to a business object, JPA can modify the database automatically, and you don't need to update the code for the data access classes. Similarly, the LineItemDB class shown earlier in this chapter isn't necessary when you use JPA since JPA automatically handles reading and writing LineItem objects when you read or write an Invoice object.

The JPA and JDBC versions of the Music Store website

The similarities

- Same HTML and CSS for the user interface.
- Same business classes. However, the JPA version includes annotations that map the business objects to the database tables.
- Same controllers. However, the code that writes data to the database is slightly simpler in the JPA version.
- Same directory structure.
- Same web.xml file.
- Same context.xml file. However, the JPA version doesn't use this file to define a connection for the Music Store database.

The differences

- The JPA version includes the EclipseLink library that implements the JPA specification.
- The JPA version includes a persistence.xml file that defines how JPA connects to the Music Store database.
- JPA automatically generates the tables for the database. As a result, the database for the JPA version has some minor differences.
- The data access classes use JPA. As a result, they are shorter and more flexible.

Description

- This chapter presents a version of the Music Store website that uses JDBC to work with the database.
- The downloadable source code for this book includes JDBC and JPA versions of the Music Store website.
- Both versions of the Music Store website provide the same functionality. However, there are some differences in how they are coded.

Figure 22-13   The JPA version compared to the JDBC version

Perspective

Once you understand the components of the Music Store website that are described in this chapter, you're ready to learn more about the end user and admin applications that are presented in the next chapter. If you had trouble understanding the components in this chapter, though, you may want to review some of the earlier chapters in this book.

To get the most from the Music Store website, you should install it on your computer as described in appendix A (PC) or B (Mac). Then, you can review the figures in any of the chapters in this section as you run the related pages on your computer. If at any time you want to review the code for a component, you can find the component in its directory, open it, and review it.

Exercise note

The exercises for testing and reviewing the Music Store website are at the end of the next chapter.

23

The applications of the website

This chapter presents the user interface of the Music Store website introduced in the previous chapter. First, it presents the user interface for two of the applications for end users of the website. Then, it presents the user interface for administrators of the website.

Although this chapter doesn't present any of the code for this website, the code is available in the download for this book. So, after you read this chapter, you can test the website, review the code in any of its files, and modify that code so it better suits your purposes.

The user interface for end users

To start, this chapter presents the user interface for an application that lets end users download and listen to sound files. Then, it presents the user interface for an application that lets end users order an album.

The Download application

Figure 23-1 shows the web pages for the Download application. The Product page contains a "Listen to Samples" link that the user can click to start the Download application. If the user has already registered, the Download application displays a Sound page that lets the user download MP3 files by clicking links. Otherwise, the Download application displays the Register page. Then, the user must register by entering a name and email address.

The Cart application

Figure 23-2 shows the web pages for the Cart application. To start, the user can display a Cart page by displaying a Product page like the one shown in figure 23-1 and clicking its "Add to Cart" link. This adds an item to the cart and displays the cart. Or, the user can click the "Show Cart" link that's available from the top of every page. This displays the items that are already in the cart.

To change the quantity for an item, the user can enter a new quantity and click the Update button. To remove an item, the user can click the Remove button. To add more items to the cart, the user can click the Continue Shopping button. To proceed to checkout, the user can click the Checkout button.

If the user has a valid cookie and a record for the user exists in the database, the Cart application skips the User page and proceeds directly to the Invoice page. Otherwise, the Cart application displays the User page.

No matter how the user gets to the Invoice page, the user can verify that the order data is correct. If the shipping data isn't correct, the user can click the Edit Address button to display the User page again. Then, the application displays the User page with the current data in its text boxes so the user can modify the current data.

When the user clicks the Continue button from the Invoice page, the application displays the Credit Card page. On this page, the user selects a credit card type, enters a credit card number, and selects an expiration date. To submit the order, the user can click the Submit Order button. This should display the Complete page that informs the user that the order was successful.

Although this Cart application has been simplified for instructional purposes, this application introduces most of the elements of a real e-commerce application.

A Product page

The Register page

Figure 23-1   The Download application (part 1 of 2)

A Sound page

Description

- The Register page is only displayed if the user hasn't already registered with the website. A user can register with the website by using this Register page or by using the Cart application described in the next chapter to make a purchase. Then, the user's browser sends a cookie to the website that indicates that the user has registered.

- To test the Register page, you can click on the "Delete Cookies" link that's displayed at the top of the page to remove cookies from the user's browser. After you do that, you can display the Register page by closing your web browser and running this application again.

Figure 23-1 The Download application (part 2 of 2)

The Cart page

The User page

Figure 23-2   The Cart application (part 1 of 3)

The Invoice page

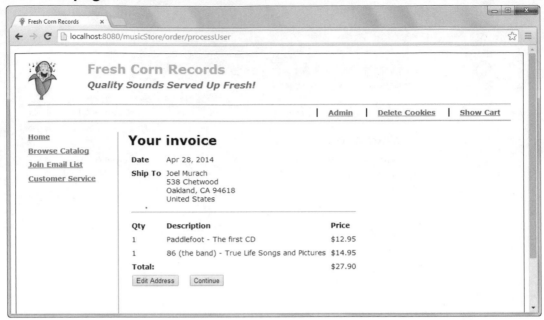

The Credit Card page

Figure 23-2   The Cart application (part 2 of 3)

The Complete page

Figure 23-2   The Cart application (part 3 of 3)

The user interface for administrators

So far, you have seen the user interface for the applications of the Music Store web site that are available to anyone in the world with an Internet connection and a web browser. Now, you'll learn about the applications that are only available to administrators of the website.

The Admin Login page

The web.xml file of the Music Store website uses a security constraint to restrict access to all URLs in the admin directory. As a result, before you can access the admin applications, you must use the login form shown in figure 23-3 to specify a valid username and password.

Like all of the admin pages, the Admin Login page transmits sensitive data. As a result, you should use a secure connection for this page and for all admin pages. However, before you can do that, you need to configure a secure connection as described in chapter 15. Then, you can force all pages in the admin directory to use that secure connection as described in chapter 16. Until then, you can use a regular HTTP connection to test the admin applications as shown in this chapter.

The URL for accessing the admin applications

without a secure connection
`http://localhost:8080/musicStore/admin`

with a secure connection
`https://localhost:8443/musicStore/admin`

The Admin Login page

Description

- The web.xml file for this application uses a security constraint to restrict access to all URLs in the admin directory.

- The security constraint causes an Admin Login page like the one above to be displayed the first time the user requests any page from the admin directory.

- The admin applications should use a secure connection so all data that's passed between the browser and server is encrypted. To learn how to configure and use a secure connection, see chapter 15. Then, you can modify the security constraint in the web.xml file to force a secure connection for these pages as described in chapter 16.

Figure 23-3   The Admin Login page

The Admin Menu page

Figure 23-4 shows the Admin Menu page for the admin applications. The easiest way to display this page is to click the Admin link in the navigation bar that's displayed across the top of all pages. However, you can also enter one of the URLs presented in figure 23-3. From the Admin Menu page, the Process Invoices button leads to the Process Invoices application, and the Display Reports button leads to the Reports application.

The Admin Menu page

Description

- The Admin Menu page lets the user choose between the two main administrative functions: (1) processing invoices and (2) displaying reports.
- You can display the Admin Menu page by clicking on the Admin link in the navigation bar or by entering its URL in your browser.

Figure 23-4   The Admin Menu page

The Process Invoices application

Figure 23-5 presents the web pages of the Process Invoices application. This application allows an admin user to view and process all unprocessed invoices created by the Cart application. From the Invoices page, the user can view a list of unprocessed invoices. Then, to view the details of any unprocessed invoice, the user can click the link for the invoice to display its Invoice page.

If the user determines that the invoice is valid, the user can process the invoice by clicking the Process Invoice button. Then, the application processes the invoice and returns to the Invoices page. However, once the application processes an invoice, it doesn't display it on this page anymore.

The Reports application

Part 1 of figure 23-6 shows the pages of the Reports application. To start, the Reports page displays a list of available reports. If the user selects the first report, the application downloads an .xls file for the report. Then, the browser provides a way for the user to open and view that file. In this figure, for example, the browser shows a button in its lower left corner that the user can click to open and view the report.

If, on the other hand, the user selects the second report, the application displays the Parameters page. This page lets the user enter a start date and end date for the report. Once the user enters those dates and clicks the Continue button, the application downloads an .xls file for the report. Again, this allows the user to open and view the report.

Part 2 of figure 23-6 shows two reports after the user has used Microsoft Excel to open them. However, the user could also use another spreadsheet application such as OpenOffice Calc to open these reports. Either way, this provides a way for the user to view the data, modify it if necessary, save it, and print it. However, if the user only needs to view the report and print a report, a developer could modify this application so it returns the report as an HTML table within a web page.

The Invoices page

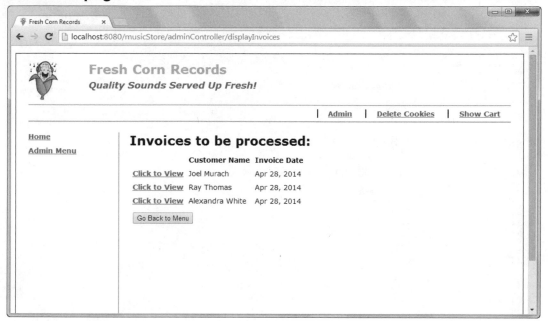

The Invoice page

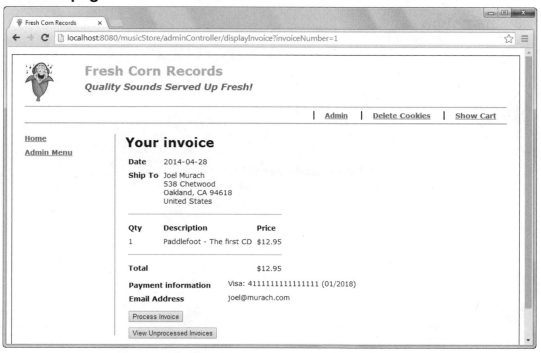

Figure 23-5   The Process Invoices application

The Reports page

The Parameters page

Figure 23-6   The Reports application (part 1 of 2)

The User Email report displayed in a spreadsheet

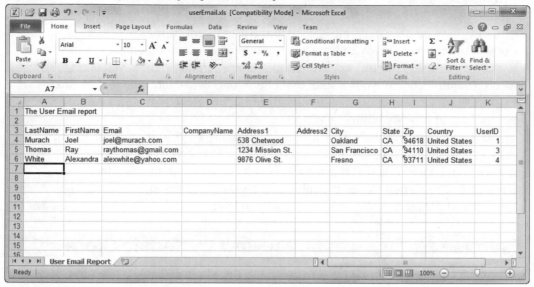

The Downloads report displayed in a spreadsheet

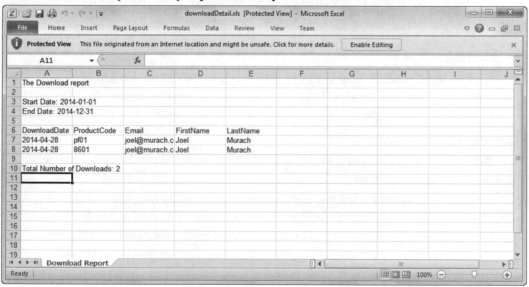

Figure 23-6   The Reports application (part 2 of 2)

Perspective

Now that you have been introduced to the user interface for the Music Store website, you're ready to learn more about this application on your own. To start, you should run this application to see how it works. Then, you can open the source code in your IDE or text editor and review the code that makes it work. At times, you may want to refer to earlier chapters to refresh your memory about how something works.

As you review this website, you should see many ways to improve it. Then, you can try to make some of those improvements. That gives you a chance to modify or enhance someone else's code, which is a common practice in the real-world. This demonstrates the value of a logical directory structure and the use of the MVC pattern. And it's a great way to learn.

Exercise 23-1   Test and review the Music Store site

Test the Download application

1. Open the musicStore project that's in the book_apps directory. Then, run this project. This should display the Home page.

2. Click the Delete Cookies link in the navigation bar, close the browser, and run the project again.

3. View several products and use the Listen to Samples link to download and listen to several sound files. To do that, you should need to register for the first download, but you shouldn't have to register for subsequent downloads.

Test the Cart application

4. Add at least three products to the cart. Then, remove one product and change the quantity for another product to 2.

5. Click the Checkout button and complete the order. To do that, you need to enter user data including a credit card number. Since the data validation for these pages is incomplete, you can enter a fake credit card number. Note that these pages use a regular connection even though they should use a secure connection as described in chapter 15.

6. Completing the order causes the website to attempt to send an email to the customer. However, since the email isn't configured correctly by default, this should display an error message instead that you can view in Tomcat log file.

7. Click the Delete Cookies link in the navigation bar, close the browser, and run the project again.

8. Create another order for another customer.

Test the administrative applications

9. Click the Admin link in the navigation bar to display the Login page. Note that this page uses a regular connection even though it should use a secure connection as described in chapter 15.

10. Log in to the admin section. If you created the database as described in the appendices, you can use a username of "joel" and a password of "sesame".

11. Click the Process Invoices button, view one of the orders that you created earlier in this exercise, and click the Process button to process it.

12. Click the Admin link to return to the Admin Menu page.

13. Click the Display Reports button and view both of the reports. To do that, you can use a spreadsheet application such as Microsoft Excel or OpenOffice Calc to open and view the report.

Review the code

14. Review the JSP files that define the user interface and the CSS file that provides the formatting for these pages. Note how the JSP files for most pages use the include files that are stored in the include directory.

15. Review the business classes in the music.business package. Note how the get methods of these classes correspond with the EL that's used in the JSP files.

16. Review the controller servlets in the music.controllers package. Note how these classes control the flow of the application and work with the classes in the music.business and music.data packages.

17. Open the web.xml file and note how it maps the controller servlets to the URLs within a specified directory. For example, it maps the CatalogController servlet to all URLs under the catalog/product directory. Also, note how it restricts access to files in the admin directory.

18. Review the data access classes in the music.data package. Note that they provide methods for reading and writing the fields of the business objects to the columns in the tables of the database.

19. Open the context.xml file and note how it defines one connection to the music database and another connection to the murach database. Also, note how it defines a DataSourceRealm that uses the murach database.

20. Review the helper classes in the music.util package. Note how these classes set some variables when the application starts and how they make it easier to work with cookies and send email.

21. Use MySQL Workbench to review the structure of the database. For example, expand the User table and view its columns.

Exercise 23-2 Test and review the JPA version

Test the apps

1. Open the musicStoreJPA project that's in the book_apps directory.

2. Follow steps 2 through 13 of exercise 23-1. All of the applications should work the same with both versions of the Music Store website.

Review the code

3. In the Project window, expand the Libraries folder and note that this version of the Music Store application includes the EclipseLink libraries.

4. Open the context.xml file. Note that it defines a connection to the database named murach. Also, note how it defines a DataSourceRealm that uses the murach database.

5. Open the persistence.xml file. Note that it defines a connection to the database named music_jpa. Also, note that it does not automatically generate the database tables. That's because the SQL script that's used to create the databases for this book should have already created the music_jpa database and its tables.

6. Review the data access classes in the music.data package. Note that they provide methods for reading and writing the fields of the business objects to the columns in the tables of the database. If you already did chapter 23-1, note how much easier these classes are to code and maintain than the corresponding JDBC classes.

7. Use MySQL Workbench to review the structure of the database. If you already did chapter 23-1, note the differences between the music and music_jpa databases.

Exercise 23-3 Enhance the site

1. Put yourself in the role of reviewer, and review either the end user or the admin user section of the website. As you review, take notes on what improvements you would recommend.

2. Make the enhancements for one or more of the improvements that you've recommended. This is a great way to learn. If you don't want to modify the project in the book_apps directory, you can make a copy of the project before you begin making improvements.

Appendix A

How to set up your PC for this book

This appendix shows how to install and configure all of the software and source code that you need for running the web applications that are presented in this book. This includes the software for Java, NetBeans, Tomcat, and MySQL that's available for free from the Internet. And it includes the source code for this book that's available for free from www.murach.com.

This appendix is designed for a PC that's running the Windows operating system. For directions on setting up a Mac, please see appendix B.

How to install the source code for this book

Figure A-1 shows how to download and install the source code for this book. This includes the source code for the web applications presented in this book, the starting points for the chapter exercises, and the solutions to the exercises.

When you finish this procedure, the book applications as well as the starting points and solutions for the exercises should be in the directories shown in this figure. Then, you can review the applications presented in this book, and you're ready to do the exercises in this book.

The Murach website

```
www.murach.com
```

The directories for the book applications and exercises

```
C:\murach\servlet_and_jsp\netbeans\book_apps
C:\murach\servlet_and_jsp\netbeans\ex_starts
C:\murach\servlet_and_jsp\netbeans\ex_solutions
```

Procedure

1. Go to www.murach.com.

2. Find the page for *Murach's Java Servlets and JSP (Third Edition)*.

3. Click the "FREE Downloads" tab.

4. Select the "All book files" link, and respond to the resulting pages and dialog boxes. This should download a setup file named jsp3_allfiles.exe onto your hard drive.

5. Use the Windows Explorer to find the setup file on your hard drive.

6. Double-click this file and respond to the dialog boxes that follow. If you accept the defaults, this installs the source code into the directories shown above.

How to use a zip file instead of a self-extracting zip file

- Although we recommend using the self-extracting zip (exe) file to install the downloadable files as described above, some systems won't allow self-extracting zip files to run. In that case, you can download a regular zip file (jsp3_allfiles.zip) from our website. Then, you can extract the files stored in this zip file into the C:\murach directory. If the C:\murach directory doesn't already exist, you should create it.

Description

- You can install the source code for this book by downloading it from murach.com.

Figure A-1   How to install the source code for this book

How to install the JDK

For Java web development, you need to have the *Java Development Kit (JDK)* for *Java SE (Standard Edition)* installed on your computer. If you've already done some Java development, you probably already have the JDK installed on your system. However, you might not have a current version installed.

For this book, we recommend that you install JDK 1.8 or later. To install this version of the JDK, you can use the procedure shown in figure A-2. To start, you download the exe file for the setup program for the most recent version of the JDK from the Java website. Then, you navigate to the directory that holds the JDK, run the setup file, and respond to the resulting dialog boxes.

Since the Java website may change after this book is printed, we've kept the procedure shown in this figure somewhat general. As a result, you may have to do some searching to find the current version of the JDK. In general, you can start by searching the Internet for the download for Java SE. Then, you can find the most current version of the JDK for your operating system.

The download page for Java SE

www.oracle.com/technetwork/java/javase/downloads

Procedure

1. Go to the download page for Java SE. The easiest way to find this page is to search the Internet for "Java SE download".
2. Click on the Download button for the JDK and follow the instructions for your operating system.
3. Save the download file to your hard disk. This file should be an exe file.
4. Double-click on the exe file to run it and respond to the resulting dialog boxes. When you're prompted for the JDK directory, use the default directory.

The default Java SE 8 directory on most Windows systems

C:\Program Files\Java\jdk1.8.0

Description

- For Java web development, you need to install *Java SE* (*Standard Edition*). To do that, you can download and install the *JDK* (*Java Development Kit*).
- For more information about installing the JDK, you can refer to the Oracle website.
- If you already have the JDK for Java SE 8 installed on your computer, you can of course skip this step. However, if you have an earlier release of the JDK installed, we recommend that you upgrade to SE 8.

Figure A-2   How to install the JDK

How to install NetBeans

NetBeans is a software framework for developing *Integrated Development Environments* (*IDEs*). The NetBeans IDE for Java is built on this framework. NetBeans is open-source, available for free from the NetBeans website, and runs on all modern operating systems.

Once you have installed a JDK as described in the previous figure, you're ready to install NetBeans as shown in figure A-3. In summary, once you download the exe file for the NetBeans installation program, you run this installation program and respond to the resulting dialog boxes. As you do, you can also check a box to install a bundled version of the Tomcat server that's configured to work with NetBeans. However, for this book, we recommend that you install a standalone version of Tomcat as described in the next figure. When you finish these dialog boxes, the installation program installs NetBeans and creates a shortcut for starting NetBeans in your Start menu.

Since this works like most Windows installation programs, you shouldn't have any trouble with this procedure. If you encounter any problems, you can view the documentation that's available from the NetBeans website and consult the troubleshooting tips.

The NetBeans website

`www.netbeans.org`

Procedure

1. Go to the NetBeans website.

2. Download the Java EE bundle for NetBeans 8.0. On a Windows system, the exe file should be named something like netbeans-8.0-javaee-windows.exe.

3. Run the install file and respond to the resulting dialog boxes. If you want to install the bundled version of Tomcat, you can check the box that installs the Apache Tomcat server. However, for this book, we recommend installing a standalone version of Tomcat as described in this next figure.

The default installation directory for NetBeans

`C:\Program Files\NetBeans 8.0`

Description

- For information about installing NetBeans, you can refer to the documentation that's available from the NetBeans website.

Figure A-3   How to install NetBeans

How to install Tomcat

As mentioned in the previous figure, NetBeans allows you to install a bundled version of the Tomcat server. However, when you use the bundled version, you can't control the version of Tomcat or the name of the server. As a result, we recommend that you install a standalone version of Tomcat 8.0 as shown in figure A-4. This version of Tomcat supports the 3.1 servlet and 2.3 JSP specifications. And we have tested all of the applications in this book against this version of Tomcat.

Since the Apache Software Foundation is continually updating its website, the procedure in this figure may be out of date by the time you read this. As a result, you may have to do some searching to find the current version of Tomcat. Once you do, you shouldn't have any trouble following the procedure shown in this figure to install Tomcat.

After you've installed Tomcat, its top-level directory is apache-tomcat-8.0.X. This can be referred to as the *Tomcat home directory*. To make it easier to refer to this directory, we recommend that you rename it to tomcat-8.0 as shown in this figure.

The Tomcat website

`http://tomcat.apache.org/`

How to install Tomcat

1. Go to the Tomcat website.
2. Navigate to the Download page for Tomcat 8.X.
3. Navigate to the Binary Distributions heading for the latest stable release. To do that, avoid any headings labeled as alpha or beta releases.
4. Beneath the Core subheading, click on the link for the zip file that's appropriate for your operating system.
5. Save the zip file to your hard disk. By default, this file should be named something like apache-tomcat-8.0.50.zip.
6. Extract the files from the zip file. This should create a directory named apache-tomcat-8.0.X.
7. Move the apache-tomcat-8.0.X directory to your C drive.
8. Rename the apache-tomcat-8.0.X directory to tomcat-8.0.

Our recommended installation directory for Tomcat

`C:\tomcat-8.0`

Description

- The directory that holds the files for Tomcat is known as the *Tomcat home directory*.
- Although it's possible to download the source distribution for Tomcat and build Tomcat from the source code, web developers only need to download and install the binary distribution.

Figure A-4   How to install Tomcat

How to configure a Tomcat server

When you install NetBeans, it can automatically install and configure a bundled version of the Tomcat server. In addition, it usually installs and configures a bundled version of the GlassFish application server, which is a free Java EE server that's based on the open-source project known as GlassFish.

If you don't change the default settings, NetBeans uses one of these servers when you deploy and run your web applications. Although both of these servers are commercial-grade servers that are adequate for developing applications, you typically want to set up your development environment so it uses the same Java EE server as your eventual production environment. If, for example, you know that you are going to deploy your finished web application to a Tomcat server, you should set up NetBeans so it uses this server.

For this book, we recommend that you install the Tomcat 8.0 server as described in the previous figure and configure it as shown in figure A-5. Here, the Tomcat 8.0 server is named Tomcat 8.0. That way, you can be sure that the downloadable applications for this book will work as described in the text.

To add a Tomcat server, you can download and install the Tomcat server that you want to use as described in the previous figure. Then, you add this server to NetBeans. To do that, you start by selecting the Tools→Servers command from the menu system. Then, you can add a new server by clicking on the Add Server button and responding to the dialog boxes shown in part 2 of this figure. After you add the server, you can specify the port that's used by the server. In this figure, for example, the Servers dialog box specifies 8080 as the port for Tomcat, which is usually what you want. However, if port 8080 conflicts with another application, you can use the Servers dialog box to change this port to another port such as 8081.

The Servers dialog box

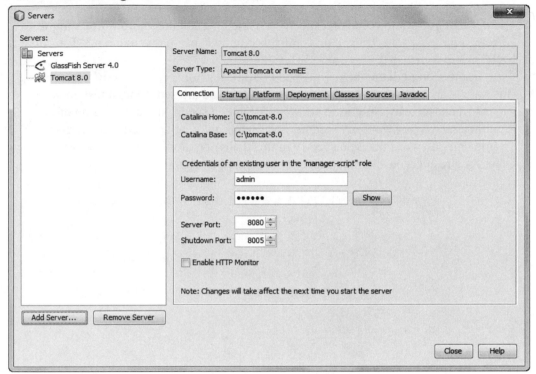

Description

- To view the available servers, select the Tools→Servers command from the menu system.
- The NetBeans installation can install and configure a bundled version of Tomcat. By default this server is named Apache Tomcat, and it runs on port 8084.
- The NetBeans installation typically installs and configures a bundled version of the Glassfish application server.
- All of the projects in this book were designed to work with a Tomcat 8.0 server named Tomcat 8.0. As a result, we recommend that you configure NetBeans so it has a Tomcat 8.0 server named Tomcat 8.0.
- To change the settings for a server, select the server in the Servers pane and use the other tabs to modify the settings for that server.
- To add another server, click on the Add Server button and respond to the dialog boxes shown in part 2 of this figure.
- After you add a server, you can specify the port that's used by the server. For example, you can use the Servers dialog box to change the port for Tomcat to 8080, which is the default port for Tomcat.
- To remove a server, select the server in the Servers pane and click the Remove button.

Figure A-5   How to configure a Tomcat server (part 1 of 2)

When you click on the Add Server button in the Servers dialog box, the first dialog box in part 2 of figure A-5 is displayed. Then, you select the type of server that you want to add and specify a name for it. In this figure, for example, I selected the Apache Tomcat or TomEE server and specified a name of "Tomcat 8.0".

In the second dialog box, you specify Tomcat's home folder along with the username and password for the manager role. If you are setting up a test environment where security isn't an issue, we recommend specifying a username of "admin" and a password of "sesame." NetBeans automatically adds the username and password that you specify in this dialog box to the tomcat-users.xml file. As a result, you shouldn't need to manually edit this file.

The first Add Server Instance dialog box

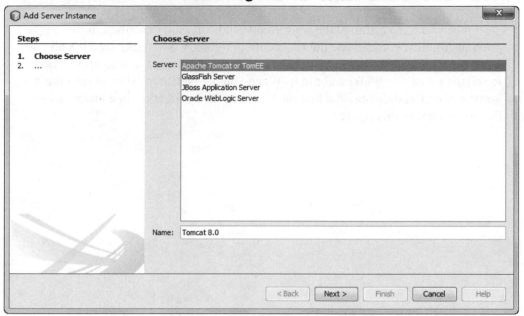

The second Add Server Instance dialog box

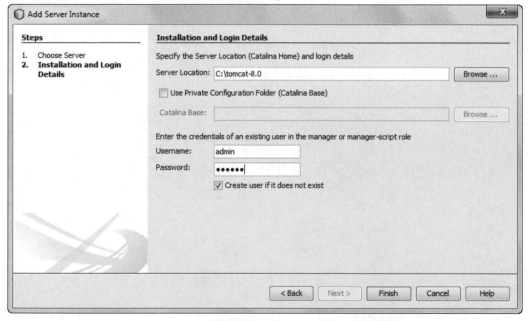

Our recommended username and password for the manager role

```
Username: admin
Password: sesame
```

Figure A-5   How to configure a Tomcat server (part 2 of 2)

How to test NetBeans and Tomcat

Once you have installed the source code and software described in the previous figures, you can use the procedure in figure A-6 to make sure it's all working correctly. To do that, you can start NetBeans, open the web application for chapter 2 of this book, and run it. When you do, NetBeans should start the Tomcat server and display the first page of the web application in a browser like the one shown in this figure.

NetBeans after running the app for chapter 2 on the Tomcat server

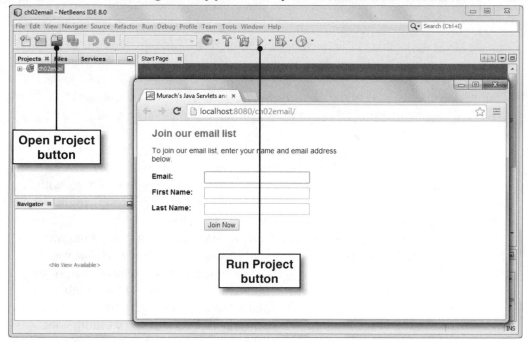

Procedure

1. Start NetBeans.

2. Click the Open Project button ( ) and open this project:
   `C:\murach\servlet_and_jsp\netbeans\book_apps\ch02email`

3. Press F6 or click the Run Project button ( ) to compile and run the project. If NetBeans displays the first page of this web application in a browser, NetBeans and Tomcat are configured correctly on your system.

Description

- You can test NetBeans and Tomcat to make sure they're configured correctly on your system by running the web application from chapter 2.

Figure A-6   How to test NetBeans and Tomcat

How to install MySQL

Figure A-7 shows how to install all of the software that you'll need to work with a MySQL database. This includes the MySQL Community Server and MySQL Workbench. Both of these software products are available for free from the MySQL website. We tested the procedure in this figure against MySQL Community Server 5.5 and MySQL Workbench 6.0. However, you should be able to use similar procedures to install earlier and later versions of these products.

MySQL Community Server is a database server that's free and easy to use. Since it's designed to run on most modern computers, it's ideal for developers who want to install it on their own computer so they can learn how to work with a MySQL database. That's why this book assumes that you have installed the Community Server on your computer as shown in this figure.

When you install MySQL on your computer, you need to specify a password for the root user. When you do, *make sure to remember the password that you enter.* If security isn't a concern for you as you're learning, *we recommend using "sesame" as the password.* That way, the password will be easy to remember.

MySQL Workbench is a free graphical tool that makes it easy to work with MySQL databases. Since MySQL Workbench is an ideal tool for working with MySQL, it is bundled with the Community Server in one convenient installation package. However, if you want to install MySQL Workbench separately, you can do that too. For example, if you want to install the latest version of MySQL Workbench, you can do that by searching the Internet for "MySQL Workbench". Then, you can follow the links to the download for the latest version.

If you want to install a different version of MySQL, or if you want to install MySQL on a different operating system, you can follow the instructions that are available from the MySQL website to do that. When you install MySQL on most systems, the MySQL database server starts every time you start your computer, which is usually what you want. If it isn't, you can use the Server Administration part of MySQL Workbench to change this behavior.

The URL for the MySQL Installer

`http://dev.mysql.com/downloads/installer/`

Procedure

1. Find the download page for the MySQL Installer for Windows. This page is currently available at the URL shown above. If necessary, you can search the Internet for "MySQL Installer for Windows".

2. Follow the instructions provided on that web page to download the installer file to your hard drive.

3. Find the installer file on your hard drive and run it.

4. Respond to the resulting dialog boxes. You can accept most of the default options, but you should specify a password for the root user. *Make sure to remember the password that you enter.* If security isn't a concern for you as you're learning, *we recommend using "sesame" as the password.*

5. To make sure that the database has been installed correctly, start MySQL Workbench when the installation is finished. Then, use the password you entered in the previous step to log in to the database server as the root user.

The default installation directory for MySQL 5.5

`C:\Program Files\MySQL\MySQL Server 5.5`

Recommended username and password

Username: root
Password: sesame

Notes

- You can also install MySQL Server and MySQL Workbench separately. For more information about that, you can visit the Downloads page of the MySQL website.

- To make it easy to start MySQL Workbench, you may want to pin the program to your taskbar or add a shortcut to your desktop.

Figure A-7   How to install MySQL

How to create the databases for this book

If a web application uses a database, you must create the database before the web application can work correctly. The web applications in this book only use the four databases shown in this figure. They are named murach, murach_jpa, music, and music_jpa. The easiest way to create these databases is to use MySQL Workbench to run the SQL script that's stored in the create_databases.sql file as shown in figure A-8. This script should be in the directory shown in this figure if you installed the source code for this book as described earlier in this chapter.

To determine if the SQL script ran successfully, you can review the results in the Output window. In this figure, for example, the Output window shows as a series of statements that have executed successfully. In addition, the Object Browser window shows that all four databases have been created.

However, if the script encounters problems, MySQL Workbench displays one or more errors in the Output window. Then, you can read these errors to figure out why the script isn't executing correctly.

Before you can run the create_databases.sql script, the database server must be running. By default the database server is automatically started when you start your computer, so this usually isn't a problem. However, if it isn't running on your system, you can use the Server Administration tab of MySQL Workbench to start it.

How to restore the databases for this book

As you work with the applications that are presented in this book, you may make changes to the databases or tables that you didn't intend to make. In that case, you may want to restore the databases to their original state so your results match the results shown in this book. To do that, you can run the create_databases.sql file again. This drops the databases described in this figure and recreates them.

The directory that contains the create_databases.sql file

```
C:\murach\servlet_and_jsp\db
```

MySQL Workbench after executing the create_databases.sql file

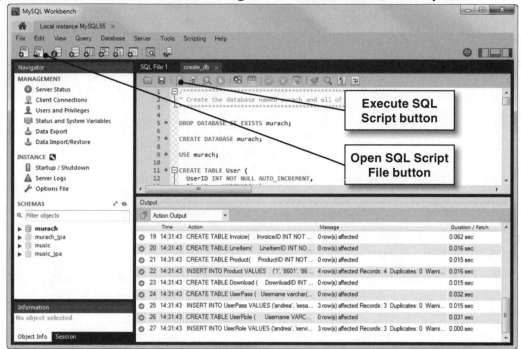

How to create the databases

1. Start MySQL Workbench.

2. Connect as the root user to an instance of MySQL that's running on the local-host computer. To do that, double-click on the stored connection named "Local instance" and enter the password for the root user if prompted.

3. Open the script file by clicking the Open SQL Script File button (🗒) in the SQL Editor toolbar. Then, use the resulting dialog box to locate and open the create_databases.sql file. When you do, MySQL Workbench displays this script in a code editor tab.

4. Execute the script by clicking the Execute SQL Script button (⚡)in the code editor toolbar. When you do, the Output window displays messages that indicate whether the script executed successfully.

How to restore the databases

*   Run the create_databases.sql script again to drop the databases and recreate them.

Description

*   For the create_databases.sql file to run, the database server must be running. By default, the database server is automatically started when your start your computer. If it isn't running, you can use the Server Administration tab of MySQL Workbench to start it.

Figure A-8   How to create and restore the databases for this book

Appendix B

How to set up your Mac for this book

This appendix shows how to install and configure all of the software and source code that you need for running the web applications that are presented in this book. This includes the software for Java, NetBeans, Tomcat, and MySQL that's available for free from the Internet. And it includes the source code for this book that's available for free from www.murach.com.

How to install the source code for this book

Figure B-1 shows how to download and install the source code for this book. This includes the source code for the web applications presented in this book, the starting points for the chapter exercises, and the solutions to the exercises.

When you finish this procedure, the book applications as well as the starting points and solutions for the exercises should be in the directories shown in this figure. Then, you can review the applications presented in this book, and you're ready to do the exercises in this book.

The Murach web site

```
www.murach.com
```

The directories for the book applications and exercises

```
/murach/servlet_and_jsp/netbeans/book_apps
/murach/servlet_and_jsp/netbeans/ex_starts
/murach/servlet_and_jsp/netbeans/ex_solutions
```

Procedure

1. Go to www.murach.com.

2. Find the page for *Murach's Java Servlets and JSP (Third Edition)*.

3. Click the "FREE Downloads" tab.

4. Select the "All Book Files" link for the regular zip file, and respond to the resulting pages and dialog boxes. This will download a file named jsp3_allfiles.zip onto your hard drive.

5. Use Finder to browse to this file and double-click on it to unzip it. This creates the servlet_and_jsp directory and its subdirectories.

6. Use Finder to create the murach directory directly on the Mac hard drive.

7. Use Finder to move the servlet_and_jsp directory into the murach directory.

A note about right-clicking

- This book often instructs you to right-click, because that's common on PCs. On a Mac, right-clicking is not enabled by default. Instead, you can use the Ctrl-click instead of the right-click. Or, if you prefer, you can enable right-clicking by editing the system preferences for your mouse.

Description

- You can install the source code for this book by downloading it from murach.com.

Figure B-1   How to install the source code for this book

How to install the JDK

For Java web development, you need to have the *Java Development Kit* (*JDK*) for *Java SE* (*Standard Edition*) installed on your computer. If you've already done some Java development, you probably already have the JDK installed on your system. However, you might not have a current version installed.

For this book, we recommend installing JDK 8 or later. To install this version of the JDK, you can use the procedure shown in figure B-2. To start, you download the dmg file for the setup program for the most recent version of the JDK from the Java web site. Then, you run this installation program and respond to the resulting dialog boxes.

Since the Java web site may change after this book is printed, we've kept the procedure shown in this figure somewhat general. As a result, you may have to do some searching to find the current version of the JDK. In general, you can start by searching the Internet for the download for Java SE. Then, you can find the most current version of the JDK for your operating system.

The download page for the JDK

`www.oracle.com/technetwork/java/javase/downloads`

Procedure

1. Go to the download page for Java SE. The easiest way to find this page is to search the Internet for "Java SE download".

2. Click on the Download button for the Java Platform (JDK) 8 or higher and follow the instructions for your operating system.

3. Save the download file to your hard disk. This file should be a dmg file named something like jdk-8-macosx-x64.dmg.

4. Double-click on the dmg file to run it and respond to the resulting dialog boxes. You will need your administrator password.

Description

- For Java web development, you need to install *Java SE* (*Standard Edition*). To do that, you can download and install the *JDK* (*Java Development Kit*).

- For more information about installing the JDK, you can refer to the Oracle web site.

- If you already have the JDK for Java SE 8 installed on your computer, you can of course skip this step. However, if you have an earlier release of the JDK installed, we recommend that you upgrade to SE 8.

Figure B-2   How to install the JDK

How to install NetBeans

NetBeans is a software framework for developing *Integrated Development Environments* (*IDEs*). The NetBeans IDE for Java is built on this framework. NetBeans is open-source, available for free from the NetBeans web site, and runs on all modern operating systems.

Once you have installed the JDK as described in the previous figure, you're ready to install NetBeans as shown in figure B-3. In summary, once you download the dmg file for the NetBeans installation program, you run this installation program and respond to the resulting dialog boxes. When you finish these dialog boxes, the installation program installs NetBeans in your Applications folder.

Since this works like most Mac installation programs, you shouldn't have any trouble with this procedure. If you encounter any problems, you can view the documentation that's available from the NetBeans web site and consult the troubleshooting tips.

The NetBeans web site

`www.netbeans.org`

Procedure

1. Go to the NetBeans web site.
2. Download the Java EE bundle for NetBeans 8. Its .dmg file should be named something like netbeans-8.0-javaee-macosx.dmg.
3. Run the standard installation file and respond to the resulting dialog boxes.

The default installation directory for NetBeans

`/Applications/NetBeans`

Description

*   For information about installing NetBeans, you can refer to the documentation that's available from the NetBeans web site.

Figure B-3   How to install NetBeans

How to install Tomcat

Although NetBeans comes with a bundled version of the Tomcat server, we recommend that you install a standalone version of Tomcat 8.0 as shown in figure B-4. This version of Tomcat supports the 3.1 servlet and 2.3 JSP specifications. We have tested all of the applications in this book against this version of Tomcat.

Since the Apache Software Foundation is continually updating its web site, the procedure in this figure may be out of date by the time you read this. As a result, you may have to do some searching to find the current version of Tomcat. Once you do, you shouldn't have any trouble following the procedure shown in this figure to install Tomcat.

After you've installed Tomcat, its top-level directory is apache-tomcat-8.0.5. This can be referred to as the *Tomcat home directory*. To make it easier to refer to this directory, we recommend that you rename it to tomcat-8.0 as shown in this figure.

The Tomcat web site

`http://tomcat.apache.org/`

How to install Tomcat

1. Go to the Tomcat web site.

2. Navigate to the Download page for Tomcat 8.X.

3. Navigate to the Binary Distributions heading for the latest stable release. To do that, avoid any headings labeled as alpha or beta releases.

4. Beneath the Core subheading, click on the link for the tar.gz file that's appropriate for your operating system.

5. Save the tar.gz file to your hard disk. By default, this file should be named something like apache-tomcat-8.0.5.tar.gz.

6. Extract the files from the tar.gz file. To do that, use Finder to navigate to this file and double-click on it. This should create a directory named something like apache-tomcat-8.0.5.

7. Move the apache-tomcat-8.0.5 directory to your Applications folder. You may need your administrator password for this.

8. Rename the apache-tomcat-8.0.5 folder to tomcat-8.0. You may need your administrator password for this.

Our recommended installation directory for Tomcat

`/Applications/tomcat-8.0`

Description

- The directory that holds the files for Tomcat is known as the *Tomcat home directory*.

- Although it's possible to download the source distribution for Tomcat and build Tomcat from the source code, web developers only need to download and install the binary distribution.

Figure B-4   How to install Tomcat

How to configure a Tomcat server

When you install NetBeans, it can automatically install and configure a bundled version of the Tomcat server. In addition, it usually installs and configures a bundled version of the GlassFish application server, which is a free Java EE server that's based on the open-source project known as GlassFish.

If you don't change the default settings, NetBeans uses one of these servers when you deploy and run your web applications. Although both of these servers are commercial-grade servers that are adequate for developing applications, you typically want to set up your development environment so it uses the same Java EE server as your eventual production environment. If, for example, you know that you are going to deploy your finished web application to a Tomcat server, you should set up NetBeans so it uses this server.

For this book, we recommend that you install the Tomcat 8.0 server as described in the previous figure and configure it as shown in figure B-5. Here, the Tomcat 8.0 server is named Tomcat 8.0. That way, you can be sure that the downloadable applications for this book will work as described in the text.

To add a Tomcat server to NetBeans, select the Tools→Servers command from the menu system. Then, click on the Add Server button and responding to the dialog boxes shown in this figure.

When you click on the Add Server button in the Servers dialog box, the first dialog box is displayed. In this dialog box, select the Apache Tomcat or TomEE option and specify a name of "Tomcat 8.0".

In the second dialog box, you specify Tomcat's home folder along with the username and password for the manager role. If you are setting up a test environment where security isn't an issue, we recommend specifying a username of "admin" and a password of "sesame." NetBeans automatically adds the username and password that you specify in this dialog box to the tomcat-users.xml file. As a result, you shouldn't need to manually edit this file.

The first Add Server Instance dialog box

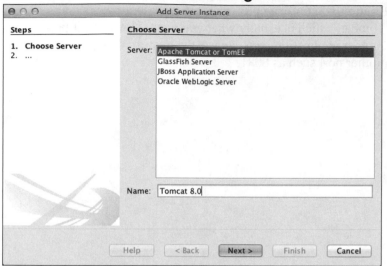

The second Add Server Instance dialog box

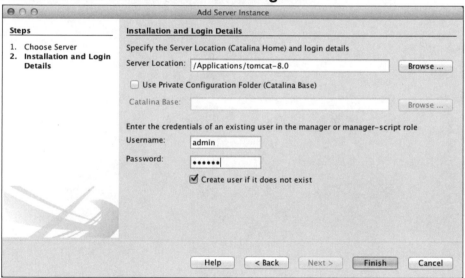

Procedure

1. Start NetBeans.

2. Select the Tools→Servers command from the menu system.

3. Click on the Add Server button.

4. In the "Choose Server" section, select the "Apache Tomcat or TomEE" server. Then, name the server Tomcat 8.0.

5. In the "Installation and Login Details" section, set the server location to "/Applications/ tomcat-8.0". Then, specify a username and password. We recommend a username of "admin" and a password of "sesame".

Figure B-5   How to configure a Tomcat server (part 1 of 2)

After you add the server, you can specify the port that's used by the server. In the second part of figure B-5, for example, the Servers dialog box specifies 8080 as the port for Tomcat, which is usually what you want. However, if port 8080 conflicts with another application, you can use the Servers dialog box to change this port to another port such as 8081.

The Servers dialog box

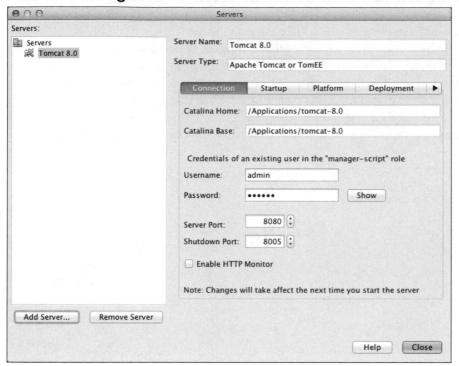

Description

- All of the projects in this book are designed to work with a Tomcat 8.0 server named Tomcat 8.0. As a result, we recommend that you configure NetBeans so it has a Tomcat 8.0 server named Tomcat 8.0.

- To change the settings for a server, select the server in the Servers pane and use the other tabs to modify the settings for that server.

- To add another server, click on the Add Server button and respond to the dialog boxes shown in part 1 of this figure.

- After you add a server, you can specify the port that's used by the server. For example, you can use the Servers dialog box to change the port for Tomcat to 8080, which is the default port for Tomcat.

- To remove a server, select the server in the Servers pane and click the Remove button.

Figure B-5   How to configure a Tomcat server (part 2 of 2)

How to test NetBeans and Tomcat

Once you have installed the source code and software described in the previous figures, you can use the procedure in figure B-6 to make sure it's all working correctly. To do that, you can start NetBeans, open the web application for chapter 2 of this book, and run it. When you do, NetBeans should start the Tomcat server and display the first page of the web application in a browser like the one shown in this figure.

When you attempt to start the Tomcat server, you may get an error that says, "Deployment error: Starting of Tomcat failed, check whether the catalina.sh and related scripts are executable." If so, you can correct this problem by following the second procedure in this figure.

NetBeans after running the app for chapter 2 on the Tomcat server

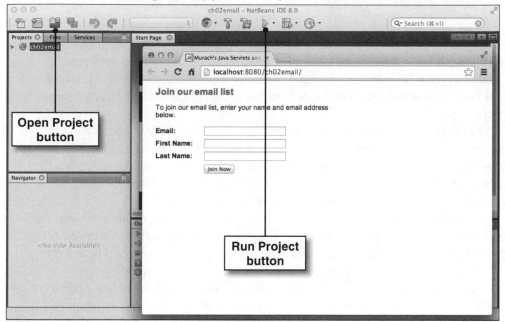

How to test NetBeans and Tomcat

1. Start NetBeans.
2. Click the Open Project button (⊞)and open this project:
   ```
   /murach/servlet_and_jsp/netbeans/book_apps/ch02email
   ```
3. Press F6 or click the Run Project button (▷) to compile and run the project. If NetBeans displays the first page of this web application in a browser, NetBeans and Tomcat are configured correctly on your system.

How to make the catalina.sh script executable

1. Start the Terminal application.
2. Change the directory to Tomcat's bin directory like this:
   ```
   cd /Applications/tomcat-8.0/bin
   ```
3. Change the mode of the script files like this:
   ```
   chmod 755 *.sh
   ```

Description

- You can test NetBeans and Tomcat to make sure they're configured correctly on your system by running the web application from chapter 2.

Figure B-6   How to test NetBeans and Tomcat

How to install the MySQL Community Server

The next two figures show how to install the MySQL Community Server and MySQL Workbench. Both of these software products are available for free from the MySQL web site. The procedures for installing these products were tested against MySQL Community Server 5.5 and MySQL Workbench 6.0. However, you should be able to use similar procedures to install earlier and later versions of these products.

MySQL Community Server is a database server that's free and easy to use. Since it's designed to run on most modern computers, it's ideal for developers who want to install it on their own computer so they can learn how to work with a MySQL database. That's why this book assumes that you have installed the Community Server on your computer as shown in figure B-7.

In addition to the server itself, the download for MySQL Community Server includes the MySQL preference pane. You can use the MySQL preference pane shown in this figure to start and stop the server and to control whether the MySQL server starts automatically when you start your computer.

All of the SQL statements presented in this book have been tested against the MySQL Community Server 5.5. As a result, you can use the statements presented in this book to work with this version of the database. Since MySQL is backwards compatible, these statements should also work with future versions of MySQL. In addition, most statements presented in this book work with earlier versions of MySQL.

The URL for the MySQL Installer

`http://dev.mysql.com/downloads/mysql/`

Procedure

1. Find the download page for the MySQL Installer for Mac OS X. This page is currently available at the URL shown above. If necessary, you can search the Internet for "MySQL Installer for Mac".

2. Follow the instructions provided on that web page to download the installer file to your hard drive.

3. Find the installer file on your hard drive and run it.

4. Respond to the resulting dialog boxes.

5. Double-click the MySQL.prefPane file and respond to the resulting dialog box to install the MySQL preference pane.

6. Make sure MySQL has been installed correctly by going to System Preferences under the Apple menu and double-clicking on MySQL icon. If the MySQL preference pane indicates that the server is running or if you can start the server, MySQL is installed correctly.

The MySQL preference pane

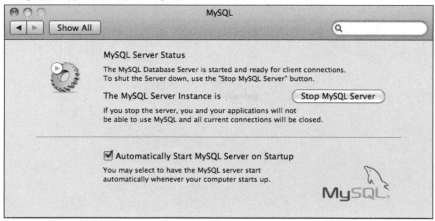

Notes

- You can use the MySQL preference pane to start and stop MySQL and to control whether MySQL starts automatically when you start your computer.

Figure B-7   How to install MySQL

How to install MySQL Workbench

MySQL Workbench is a free graphical tool that makes it easier to work with MySQL databases. To install MySQL Workbench, you can use the procedure in figure B-8.

After you install MySQL Workbench, you should test it to be sure that you can connect to the MySQL server. If a connection isn't created automatically, you can create one from the Home tab of MySQL Workbench as described in this figure. Then, you can double-click on the connection to connect to the server.

All of the skills for working with MySQL Workbench that are presented in this book were tested against version 6.0. As a result, if you're using this version of MySQL Workbench, these skills should work exactly as described. However, MySQL Workbench is being actively developed and is changing quickly. As a result, if you're using a later version of MySQL Workbench, these skills may not work exactly as described, but they should work similarly.

The URL for the MySQL Workbench Installer

`http://dev.mysql.com/downloads/tools/workbench/`

Procedure

1. Find the download page for the MySQL Workbench Installer for Mac OS X. This page is currently available at the URL shown above. If necessary, you can search the Internet for "MySQL Workbench Installer for Mac".

2. Follow the instructions provided on that web page to download the dmg file to your hard drive.

3. Drag the MySQL Workbench icon to your Applications folder.

4. To make sure that the database has been installed correctly, start MySQL Workbench.

The default installation directory for MySQL Workbench

`Applications/MySQLWorkbench`

Notes

*   To make it easy to start MySQL Workbench, you may want to add an alias to your desktop.

Figure B-8   How to install MySQL Workbench

How to create the databases for this book

If a web application uses a database, you must create the database before the web application can work correctly. The web applications in this book only use the four databases shown in this figure. They are named murach, murach_jpa, music, and music_jpa. The easiest way to create these databases is to use MySQL Workbench to run the SQL script that's stored in the create_databases.sql file as shown in figure B-9. This script should be in the directory shown in this figure if you installed the source code for this book as described earlier in this chapter.

To determine if the SQL script ran successfully, you can review the results in the Output window. In this figure, for example, the Output window shows as a series of statements that have executed successfully. In addition, the Object Browser window shows that all four databases have been created.

However, if the script encounters problems, MySQL Workbench displays one or more errors in the Output window. Then, you can read these errors to figure out why the script isn't executing correctly.

Before you can run the create_databases.sql script, the database server must be running. By default the database server is automatically started when you start your computer, so this usually isn't a problem. However, if it isn't running on your system, you can use the Server Administration tab of MySQL Workbench to start it.

How to restore the databases for this book

As you work with the applications that are presented in this book, you may make changes to the databases or tables that you didn't intend to make. In that case, you may want to restore the databases to their original state so your results match the results shown in this book. To do that, you can run the create_databases.sql file again. This drops the databases described in this figure and recreates them.

The directory that contains the create_databases.sql file

```
/murach/servlet_and_jsp/db
```

MySQL Workbench after executing the create_databases.sql file

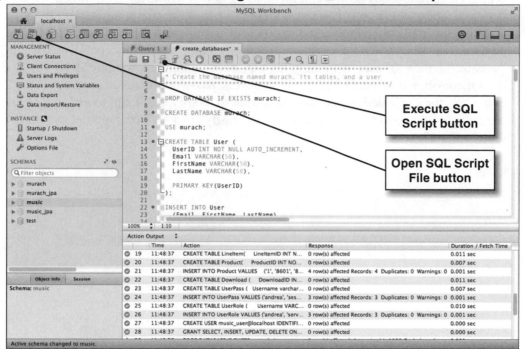

How to create the databases

1. Start MySQL Workbench.

2. Connect as the root user to an instance of MySQL that's running on the localhost computer. To do that, double-click on the stored connection named "Local instance" and enter the password for the root user if prompted.

3. Open the script file by clicking the Open SQL Script File button ( ) in the SQL Editor toolbar. Then, use the resulting dialog box to locate and open the create_databases.sql file. When you do, MySQL Workbench displays this script in a code editor tab.

4. Execute the script by clicking the Execute SQL Script button ( ) in the code editor toolbar. When you do, the Output window displays messages that indicate whether the script executed successfully.

How to restore the databases

- Run the create_databases.sql script again to drop the databases and recreate them.

Description

- For the create_databases.sql file to run, the database server must be running. By default, the database server is automatically started when your start your computer. If it isn't running, you can use the Server Administration tab of MySQL Workbench to start it.

Figure B-9   How to create and restore the databases for this book

How to update the password for the root user

When you install the Community Server on your computer, the root user is created automatically so you can log in to the server. However, a password isn't assigned to this user by default. In other words, the server is not secure. In addition, the applications presented in this book assume that the root user has a password of "sesame". As a result, we recommend that you assign a password of "sesame" to the root user by running the SQL script described in figure B-10.

Of course, a password of "sesame" is a weak password that isn't secure either. So, for a production system, you'd want to modify this script to assign a secure password to the root user that can't be easily cracked. For more details, see chapter 17.

The directory that contains the update_root_password.sql file

```
/murach/servlet_and_jsp/db
```

Procedure

1. Start MySQL Workbench.

2. Connect as the root user to an instance of MySQL that's running on the local-host computer. To do that, double-click on the stored connection named "Local instance" and enter the password for the root user if prompted.

3. Open the update_root_password.sql file by clicking the Open SQL Script File button in the SQL Editor toolbar and navigating to the /murach/servlet_and_jsp/db directory.

4. Click the Execute SQL Script button. This should update the root password to "sesame".

Description

- By default, the root user doesn't have a password. This is not secure. In addition, the applications in this book assume that the root user has a password of "sesame".

- For the applications presented in this book, you can get your system to work correctly by running a script like the one shown in this figure to change the password for the root user to "sesame".

- For a production system, you can modify the script shown in this figure to make the password for the root user more secure.

Figure B-10   How to update the password for the root user

Index

Books for Java programmers

Murach's Beginning Java with Eclipse	$57.50
Murach's Beginning Java with NetBeans	57.50
Murach's Android Programming (2nd Ed.)	57.50
Murach's Java Programming (4th Ed.)	57.50
Murach's Java Servlets and JSP (3rd Ed.)	57.50

Books for .NET developers

Murach's ASP.NET 4.5 Web Programming w/ C# 2012	$57.50
Murach's C# 2015	54.50

Books for web developers

Murach's HTML5 and CSS3 (3rd Ed.)	$54.50
Murach's Dreamweaver CC	54.50
Murach's JavaScript (2nd Ed.)	54.50
Murach's jQuery (2nd Ed.)	54.50
Murach's PHP and MySQL (2nd Ed.)	54.50

Books for database programmers

Murach's SQL Server 2012 for Developers	$54.50
Murach's MySQL (2nd Ed.)	54.50
Murach's Oracle SQL and PL/SQL (2nd Ed.)	54.50

*Prices and availability are subject to change. Please visit our web site or call for current information.

If you need to refresh your Java skills...

Murach's Java Programming will deliver the core skills you need for Java web programming and Android programming. Great to have on hand whenever you need to learn a new Java skill or brush up on an old one.

The software for this book

- Java SE 8 (JDK 1.8).
- Tomcat 8.0 (servlet 3.1/JSP 2.3).
- NetBeans IDE 8.0.
- MySQL 5.5.
- MySQL Workbench 6.0.
- You can download this software for free and install it as described in appendix A (PC) or appendix B (Mac).

The downloadable source code for this book

- Complete source code for the applications presented in this book so you can view, compile, and run the code for the applications as you read each chapter.
- Source code for the starting points of the exercises presented at the end of each chapter so you can get more practice in less time.
- Source code for the solutions to the exercises so you can check your solutions.
- All source code is compatible with the NetBeans IDE.

How to download the source code for this book

- Go to murach.com.
- Go to the page for *Murach's Java Servlets and JSP (3rd Edition)*.
- Follow the instructions there to download the file that contains the source code for this book. For Windows, download the self-extracting zip file. For Mac, download the regular zip file.
- Double-click the downloaded file and respond to the resulting dialog boxes.
- For more details, see appendix A (PC) or appendix B (Mac).

How to use another IDE with this book

- Although we recommend using NetBeans with this book, you can use another IDE such as Eclipse if you prefer. To do that, you will need to figure out how to import the source code for this book into your IDE so you can compile and run the sample applications and complete the exercises. In addition, you will need to learn how to use your IDE to perform the tasks presented in chapter 3.

www.murach.com